INTERNATIONAL COMMERCIAL TAX

Inspired by a postgraduate course the authors have jointly taught at the University of Cambridge since 2001, Peter Harris and David Oliver use their divergent backgrounds (academia and tax practice) to build a conceptual framework that not only makes the tax treatment of complex commercial transactions understandable and accessible, but also challenges the current orthodoxy of international tax norms.

Designed specifically for postgraduate students and junior practitioners, it challenges the reader to think about tax issues conceptually and holistically, while illustrating the structure with practical examples. Senior tax practitioners and academics will also find it useful as a means of refreshing their understanding of the basics and the conceptual framework will challenge them to think more deeply about tax issues.

Peter Harris is a Reader at the Law Faculty of the University of Cambridge. Until his recent retirement, David Oliver was an international tax partner at the London office of PricewaterhouseCoopers and joint editor of the *British Tax Review*.

CAMBRIDGE TAX LAW SERIES

Tax law is a growing area of interest, as it is included as a subdivision in many areas of study and is a key consideration in business needs throughout the world. Books in the Cambridge Tax Law series expose and shed light on the theories underpinning taxation systems, so that the questions to be asked when addressing an issue become clear. Written by leading scholars and illustrated by case law and legislation, they form an important resource for information on tax law while avoiding the minutiae of day-to-day detail addressed by practitioner books.

The books will be of interest for those studying law, business, economics, accounting and finance courses in the UK, but also in mainland Europe, USA and ex-Commonwealth countries with a similar taxation system to the UK.

Series Editor

Professor John Tiley, Queens' College, Director of the Centre for Tax Law.

Well known internationally in both academic and practitioner circles, Professor Tiley brings to the series his wealth of experience in tax law study, practice and writing. He was made a CBE in 2003 for services to tax law.

INTERNATIONAL COMMERCIAL TAX

PETER HARRIS AND DAVID OLIVER

CAMBRIDGE UNIVERSITY PRESS
Cambridge, New York, Melbourne, Madrid, Cape Town, Singapore,
São Paulo, Delhi, Dubai, Tokyo

Cambridge University Press
The Edinburgh Building, Cambridge CB2 8RU, UK

Published in the United States of America by Cambridge University Press, New York

www.cambridge.org
Information on this title: www.cambridge.org/9780521853118

First published 2010

Printed in the United Kingdom at the University Press, Cambridge

A catalogue record for this publication is available from the British Library

Library of Congress Cataloguing in Publication data
Harris, Peter, 1964–
International commercial tax / Peter Harris, David Oliver.
p. cm. – (Cambridge tax law series)
Includes bibliographical references and index.
ISBN 978-0-521-85311-8
1. International business enterprises–Taxation–Law and legislation. 2. Income tax–Foreign income. 3. Double taxation. 4. International business enterprises–Taxation–Law and legislation–Great Britain. 5. Income tax–Great Britain–Foreign income. 6. Double taxation–Great Britain. I. Oliver, David (J. David B.) II. Title. III. Series.
K4542.H375 2010
343.04–dc22
2010011234

ISBN 978-0-521-85311-8 Hardback

CONTENTS

PREFACE

The authors found inspiration for this book in a postgraduate course they have jointly taught at the Law Faculty of the University of Cambridge since 2001. The authors have divergent backgrounds, one heavily focused in academia with the outlet of drafting tax laws for an international organisation, the other for twenty-five years a tax partner in an international firm of chartered accountants with the outlet of editorship of the UK's leading tax journal. This divergence gives rise to a synergy from which each author has benefited greatly.

The book is designed for postgraduate students and junior practitioners. It is more than an introduction to the subject. It challenges the reader to think about tax issues conceptually and holistically, while illustrating the structure with practical examples. More senior tax practitioners and academics may also find it useful as a means of refreshing their understanding of the basics and the conceptual framework may challenge them to think more deeply about tax issues than they currently do.

Consistent with the purpose of this book, the authors are firmly of the view that any future edition should not exceed 500 printed pages of text and will do their utmost to ensure that that limit is never exceeded.

The law in this book is stated as at 20 March 2010. The agreed contributions of the authors to this book are 75 per cent Peter Harris and 25 per cent David Oliver.

Peter Harris and David Oliver
Cambridge
March 2010

ABBREVIATIONS

ACT	Advance corporation tax
CTA 2009	Corporation Tax Act 2009 (UK)
CTA 2010	Corporation Tax Act 2010 (UK)
ECJ	Court of Justice of the European Union
EFTA	European Free Trade Association
EU	European Union
EU Law	Law of the European Union
FEU Treaty	Treaty on the Functioning of the European Union
HMRC	Her Majesty's Revenue Commissioners
ICTA 1988	Income and Corporation Taxes Act 1988 (UK)
ITA 2007	Income Tax Act 2007 (UK)
ITTOIA 2005	Income Tax (Trading and Other Income) Act 2005
OECD	Organisation for Economic Co-operation and Development
OECD Model	Organisation for Economic Co-operation and Development's Model Convention on Income and Capital
PE	Permanent establishment
TCGA 1992	Taxation of Chargeable Gains Act 1992 (UK)
TIOPA 2010	Taxation (International and Other Provisions) Act 2010 (UK)
UN	United Nations
UN Model	United Nations Model Double Taxation Convention between the Developed and Developing Countries
UK	United Kingdom
US	United States

TABLE OF CASES

Case Name	Reference (chapter number in bold followed by footnote number)
Australia	
FCT *v* Lamesa Holdings BV (1997) 36 ATR 589 (FFC)	***3:*** 9, 233, 239
Haque *v* Haque (No 2) (1965) 114 CLR 98 (HC)	***3:*** 12, 238
Thiel *v* FCT (1990) 171 CLR 338 (HC)	***3:*** 34
Undershaft (No. 1) Limited *v* FCT [2009] FCA 41 (FC)	***3:*** 1, 236
Canada	
Crown Forest Industries Ltd *v* Canada [1995] 2 SCR 802 (SC)	***1:*** 59; ***2:*** 58
GlaxoSmithKline Inc *v* The Queen [2008] TCC 324 (TC)	***3:*** 284
Knights of Columbus *v* The Queen [2008] TCC 307 (TC)	***1:*** 27; ***3:*** 57, 68, 73
MIL (Investments) SA *v* The Queen [2006] TCC 460 (TC)	***1:*** 72
Prévost Car Inc *v* The Queen [2008] TCC 231 (TC), [2009] FCA 57 (FCA)	***1:*** 72; ***5:*** 80
R *v* Dudney [2000] FCJ No 230 (FCA)	***3:*** 51, 258
Sunbeam Corp (Canada) Ltd *v* Minister of National Revenue [1963] SCR 45 (SC)	***3:*** 57
European Free Trade Association	
Case E-7/07 Seabrokers AS *v* Staten v/Skattedirektoratet (2008) 10 ITLR 805 (EFTAC)	***4:*** 121, 148
EU	
Case 26/62 NV Algemene Transport- en Expeditie Onderneming van Gend & Loos *v* Netherlands Inland Revenue Administration [1963] ECR 3 (ECJ)	***1:*** 77; ***2:*** 76, 138

Case Name	**Reference (chapter number in bold followed by footnote number)**
Case C-141/99 Algemene Maatshappij voor Investering en Dienstverlening NV *v* Belgische Staat [2000] ECR I-11619 (ECJ)	***4:*** 142
Case C-294/99 Athinaiki Zithopiia AE *v* Elliniko Dimosio (Greek State) [2001] ECR I-6797 (ECJ)	***3:*** 199
Case C-324/00 Lankhorst-Hohorst GmbH *v* Finanzamt Steinfurt [2002] ECR 2002 I-11779 (ECJ)	***3:*** 298
Case C-58/01 Oce Van der Grinten NV *v* IRC [2003] ECR I-9809 (ECJ)	***3:*** 206; ***5:*** 90
Case C-168/01 Bosal Holding BV *v* Staatssecretaris van Financiën [2003] ECR I-9409 (ECJ)	***1:*** 78; ***2:*** 81; ***3:*** 201; ***4:*** 112, 129; ***5:*** 68, 95
Case C-234/01 Gerritse *v* Finanzamt Neukölln-Nord [2003] ECR I-5933 (ECJ)	***3:*** 26, 260
Case C-422/01 Forsakringsaktiebolaget Skandia *v* Riksskatteverket [2003] ECR I-6817 (ECJ)	***3:*** 264
Case C-9/02 Hughes de Lasteyrie du Saillant [2004] ECR I-2409 (ECJ)	***6:*** 107
Case C-315/02 Lenz *v* Finanzlandesdirektion für Tirol [2004] ECR I-7063 (ECJ)	***4:*** 54
Case C-319/02 Manninen [2004] ECR I-7477 (ECJ)	***2:*** 155; ***4:*** 53
Case C-219/03 Commission *v* Spain [2004] ECR 0 (ECJ)	***4:*** 16, 23
Case C-242/03 Minestre des Finances *v* Weidert and Paulus [2004] ECR I-7379 (ECJ)	***4:*** 111
Case C-253/03 CLT-UFA SA *v* Finanzamt Köln-West [2006] ECR I-1831 (ECJ)	***3:*** 162
Case C-376/03 D *v* Inspecteur van de Belastingdient [2005] ECR I-5821 (ECJ)	***2:*** 166; ***5:*** 403
Case C-446/03 Marks & Spencer *v* Halsey [2005] ECR I-10837 (ECJ)	***1:*** 76; ***2:*** 146, 152, 167; ***4:*** 150; ***6:*** 3, 47
Case C-150/04 European Commission *v* Denmark [2007] ECR I-1163 (ECJ)	***3:*** 265
Case C-196/04 Cadbury Schweppes [2006] ECR I-7995 (AG), [2006] ECR I-7995 (ECJ)	***1:*** 81; ***2:*** 149, 152, 153; ***4:*** 94; ***5:*** 106; ***6:*** 3

Case Name	Reference (chapter number in bold followed by footnote number)
Case C-379/05 Amurta S.G.P.S. *v* Inspecteur van de Belastingdienst [2007] ECR I-9569 (ECJ)	***3:*** 211
Case C-194/06 Staats van Financiën *v* Orange European Smallcap Fund NV [2008] ECR I-3747 (ECJ)	***4:*** 27; ***5:*** 96
Case C-248/06 European Commission *v* Spain [2008] ECR I-47 (ECJ)	***3:*** 267
Case C-284/06 Finanzamt Hamburg-Am Tierpark *v* Burda GmbH [2008] ECR I-4571 (ECJ)	***3:*** 203; ***5:*** 95
Case C-293/06 Deutsche Shell *v* Finanzamt für Grossunternehmen in Hamburg [2008] ECR I-1129 (ECJ)	***2:*** 147, 151; ***4:*** 117
Case C-414/06 Lidl Belgium GmbH & Co KG *v* Finanzamt Heilbronn [2008] ECR I-3601 (ECJ)	***4:*** 130, 169
Cases C-428/06; 429/06; 430/06; 431/06; 432/06; 433/06 and 434/06 Unión General de Trabajadores de La Rioja et. al [2008] ECR I-6747 (ECJ)	***2:*** 172
Case C-443/06 Hollmann *v* Fazenda Pública [2007] ECR I-8491 (ECJ)	***3:*** 241
Case C-48/07 Belgium *v* Les Vergers du Vieux Tauves [2008] ECR 00 (ECJ)	***3:*** 197
Case C-105/07 NV Lammers & Van Cleeff *v* Belgische Staat [2008] ECR I-173 (ECJ)	***3:*** 302
Case C-138/07 Belgium *v* NV Cobelfret [2009] ECR 00 (ECJ)	***4:*** 146
Case C-157/07 Finanzamt für Körperschaften III in Berlin *v* Krankenheim Ruhesitz am Wannsee-Seniorenheimstatt GmbH [2008] ECR I-8061 (ECJ)	***4:*** 135
Case C-282/07 Belgian State *v* Truck Center SA [2008] ECR 00 (ECJ)	***3:*** 224
Case C-285/07 AT *v* Finanzamt Stuttgart-Körperschaften [2008] ECR 00 (ECJ)	***6:*** 76
Case C-303/07 Aberdeen Property Fininvest Alpha [2009] ECR 00 (ECJ)	***3:*** 210
Case C-418/07 Société Papillon *v* Ministère du budget, des comptes publics et de la function publique [2008] ECR I-8947 (ECJ)	***4:*** 175

Case Name	Reference (chapter number in bold followed by footnote number)
Clark (Inspector of Taxes) *v* Oceanic Contractors Inc [1983] 2 AC 130 (HL)	***2:*** 5
De Beers Consolidated Mines *v* Howe [1906] AC 455 (HL)	***2:*** 38, 41
Deutsche Morgan Grenfell Group Plc *v* IRC [2006] UKHL 49 (HL)	***3:*** 171
Dreyfus *v* CIR (1929) 14 TC 560 (CA)	***2:*** 15, 18
DSG Retail Ltd *v* RCC [2009] UKFTT TC00001 (TC)	***3:*** 284; ***4:*** 64
Fleming *v* London Produce Co Ltd (1968) 44 TC 582 (Ch)	***3:*** 76
Fothergill *v* Monarch Airlines Ltd [1981] AC 251 (HL)	***1:*** 56, 64, 68
Garland *v* Archer-Shee [1931] AC 212 (HL)	***2:*** 24
George Wimpey International Ltd *v* Rolfe [1989] STC 609 (Ch)	***4:*** 6
Government of India *v* Taylor [1955] AC 491 (HL)	***7:*** 27
Hill Samuel Investments Ltd *v* RCC [2009] UKSPC SPC00738 (SC)	***4:*** 15
Re Hoyles, Row *v* Jagg [1911] 1 Ch 179 (CA)	***3:*** 9, 12
Indofood International Finance Ltd *v* JP Morgan Chase Bank NA [2006] EWCA Civ 158 (CA)	***2:*** 69; ***5:*** 75
IRC *v* Burrell [1924] 2 KB 52 (CA)	***5:*** 30
IRC *v* Commerzbank (1990) 63 TC 218 (Ch)	***1:*** 56; ***7:*** 16
IRC *v* Mangin [1971] AC 739 (HL)	***1:*** 51
Laerstate BV *v* HMRC [2009] UKFTT 209 (TC)	***2:*** 47
Legal & General Assurance Society Ltd *v* RCC [2006] EWHC 1770 (Ch)	***4:*** 103
Leigh *v* IRC [1928] 1 KB 73 (KB)	***3:*** 218
McGuckian *v* IRC [1997] STC 908 (HL)	***1:*** 53
Marks & Spencer plc *v* Halsey [2007] EWCA Civ 117 (CA); [2009] UKFTT TC00005 (TC)	***4:*** 159, 161
Memec plc *v* IRC [1998] STC 754 (CA)	***1:*** 56; ***2:*** 24; ***3:*** 308; ***5:*** 5, 37
Murray *v* ICI Ltd [1967] Ch 1038 (CA)	***3:*** 322
Muscat *v* Cable & Wireless plc [2006] EWCA Civ 220 (CA)	***3:*** 248
NEC Semi-Conductors Ltd *v* IRC [2003] EWHC 2813 (Ch); [2006] EWCA Civ 25 (CA) (for further appeal to HL see Boake Allen)	***3:*** 157, 159

Case Name	Reference (chapter number in bold followed by footnote number)
United States	
Compania de Tabacos *v* Collector of Internal Revenue (1927) 275 US 87 (SC)	***1:*** 2
Morrissey *v* Commissioner (1935) 296 US 344 (SC)	***2:*** 11
National Westminster Bank plc *v* United States (2005) 69 Fed Cl 128 (CFC); (2008) 512 F 3d 1347 (FCA)	***3:*** 43, 95, 101, 124, 138
Square D Company *v* Commissioner (2006) 438 F 3d 739 (FCA)	***3:*** 261
Whitney *v* Robertson (1888) 124 US 190 (SC)	***1:*** 29

TABLE OF STATUTES

Statute Name	Page Reference
Afghanistan	
Income Tax Law (2005)	
Art. 20	125
Australia	
Income Tax Assessment Act 1936	
s. 47	365
International Tax Agreements Act 1953	374
Fringe Benefits Tax Act 1986	217
Income Tax Assessment Act 1997	
s. 4–1	72
s. 4–15	72
s. 6–1	72
s. 6–5	373
s. 25–85	363
s. 701–1	51
Canada	
Constitution Act, 1867	
s. 92	14
Cyprus	
Income Tax Law of 2002	
s. 2	60
Germany	
Corporate Tax Law (Körperschaftsteuergesetz)	
s. 8	248
Income Tax Law (Einkommensteuergesetz)	
s. 2	72
s. 4h	254
s. 49	76

Statute Name	Page Reference
Prussian income tax law of 1891	
s. 2	136
India	
Income-tax Act, 1961	
s. 115O	185
Finance Act, 2009	
s. 2	170
Malaysia	
Income Tax Act, 1967	
s. 8	60
Mexico	
Income Tax Law (Impuesto sobre la Renta)	
Art. 10	72
Nepal	
Income Tax Act, 2058	
s. 67	77
The Netherlands	
Corporate Income Tax Act (Wet op de vennootschapsbelasting 1969)	
Art. 15	51
Singapore	
Income Tax Act.	
s. 2	60
South Africa	
Income Tax Act, 1962	
s. 64B	185
Tanzania	
Income Tax Act, 2004	
s. 68	77
Trinidad	
Corporation Tax Act	
s. 2	60
United Kingdom	
Constitution Act, 1867	
s. 92	14

Statute Name	Page Reference
s. 150	235
s. 153	255, 346
s. 155	434
s. 157	234
ss. 191–194	255
ss. 218–230	241
s. 220	460
s. 232	352
ss. 236–242	352, 367
s. 243	352
s. 250	368
ss. 260–353	255, 318
United States	
Internal Revenue Code	
s. 1	285
s. 61	72
s. 163	254
s. 861	78
s. 881	395
s. 884	190
s. 902	289–90
s. 904	274
s. 7701	49–50

TABLE OF TREATIES

Treaty Name	Page Reference
Australia/UK (2003)	
Art. 6	124
Art. 10	248
Art. 21	373
Bangladesh/UK (1979)	
Art. 22	280
Botswana/UK (2005)	
Art. 13	206
Art. 23	280
Canada/US (1980)	32
Art. 5	141, 150
China/India (1994)	
Art. 12	206
China/UK (2005)	
Art. 13	206
Convention on Mutual Administrative Assistance in Tax Matters (1988)	455–6, 466
Arts 11–16	466
EU Arbitration Convention (1990) 90/436/EEC	462–3
Art. 1	463
Art. 3	463
Art. 4	463
Art. 5	463
Art. 6	463
Art. 7	463–4
Arts. 9–13	464

Treaty Name	Page Reference
EU Treaty	
Art. 3	80
France/UK (1968)	
Art. 5	125
FEU Treaty	
Art. 8	96
Art. 18	96–97
Art. 20	68–9
Art. 21	69
Art. 26	80, 96
Art. 45	81, 100, 219
Art. 49	81–2, 151–2, 176–80, 194, 197, 384
Art. 52	100
Art. 54	69, 82, 384–5, 406–7
Art. 56	82–3, 152, 222, 225–26
Art. 57	83, 222
Art. 62	62
Art. 63	83–5, 101–2, 129, 194, 296
Art. 64	296
Art. 65	9, 101–2, 294
Art. 101	96
Art. 107	110–11
Art. 110	9
Art. 111	9
Art. 112	9, 14
Art. 113	9, 14
Art. 115	26
Arts 251–281	39
Art. 258	41
Art. 267	41, 282
Recovery of Claims Directive (1976) 76/308/EEC	466
Exchange of Information Directive (1977) 77/779/EEC	457
Mergers Directive (1990) 90/434/EEC(consolidated as 2009/133/EC)	27, 152
Art. 1	85, 432, 437, 439, 442, 445, 447

INTERNATIONAL COMMERCIAL TAX

PETER HARRIS AND DAVID OLIVER

Introduction

Tax law is a dynamic area where politics, law, economics, commerce and accountancy intersect. It is renowned for its complexity and intricacy; typically the income tax law (or general tax code if applicable) is the longest law that a country has. At least in Britain, this has been the case for centuries.[1] Tax law in practice is never pure from a conceptual or theoretical perspective. It is a fascinating mix of history, compromise and political rhetoric. Unlike other areas of law, where academic literature strives to uncover controversial and challenging issues, tax law is rife with *fat and juicy* issues. The challenge in the tax law field is securing agreement on any particular issue. Any change to a tax law almost inevitably involves winners and losers and so all tax reform is controversial.[2] Added to this, the most important modern taxes are broad based and touch nearly every dealing, every interaction of life. Tax law is, therefore, necessarily a reflection of life. In this era of globalisation, the information age and the never-ending search for greater efficiency, our lives have become increasingly complex. So has tax law.

While any tax law book must struggle with these types of issues, an international tax law book takes on further dimensions. The international extension involves dealings taking place across international borders. As such, the participants in the dealing face not one but two systems of tax law. In addition, the participants face the interaction between the two systems, often in the form of tax treaties, and sometimes, such as within the European Union, a supra-national level of law. Finally, by its very nature a cross-border dealing is often (likely) undertaken by sophisticated market players such as multinationals and so the dealing is complex of itself. These extra dimensions make the study and analysis of international tax law much like the proverbial

[1] See Harris (2006, p. 58) referring to the length of English direct tax laws dating to the sixteenth century.

[2] Hence the adage that *an old tax is a good tax*.

onion. Care must be taken in dissecting each of the different layers if a full appreciation of the overall position is to be attained.

The primary purpose of this book is to act as a guide, a mind map in dissecting international tax law issues. It seeks to do so by investigating and analysing the different systems of income tax rules that interact and sometimes clash in the context of international commercial transactions. It identifies the circumstances in which two or more sets of income tax laws may clash, explains why clashes arise and sets out options for resolving clashes. The book takes account of both theoretical and practical considerations in evaluating whether to resolve any clash, if so, how any clash should be resolved and how clashes are resolved in practice (whether by agreement between governments or by the actions of taxpayers).

The book adopts a detailed conceptual structure that is intended to promote lateral thinking. It draws on particular bodies of legal rules as well as practical examples to illustrate the structure and demonstrate how international tax law *works* in practice. The main body of legal rules that attempts to resolve the clash of two or more income tax systems is bilateral double tax treaties based on the Organisation for Economic Co-operation and Development's Model Convention on Income and Capital (the OECD Model).[3] In recent years, European Union Law (EU Law) has become increasingly important in resolving international tax issues within the European Union (the EU).[4] The influence of this body of law has been recognised outside the EU, because the EU is viewed, to some extent, as an accelerated version of where globalisation is leading. So EU Law applicable to direct taxation is also considered, where relevant, both because of its independent importance and as a point of comparison with the OECD Model, highlighting consistencies and peculiarities of each body of law.

The OECD Model does not comprehensively regulate many important international tax issues and has not been adopted by countries on a uniform basis. So a further purpose of this book is to analyse the limitations inherent in the OECD Model and identify how tax treaties diverge from the Model in practice. Interaction between tax treaties and EU Law is another theme of this book. The book also seeks to highlight and analyse how the limitations of tax treaties and their divergence simultaneously give rise to potential double taxation as well as international

[3] OECD (1992–).

[4] European Union Law is that based on or under the Treaty on European Union and the Treaty on the Functioning of the European Union (FEU Treaty), both of which came into effect on 1 December 2009, following ratification of the Lisbon Treaty. These treaties amend and consolidate treaties dating back to the 1950s.

tax planning opportunities. Double tax treaties (and EU Law) overlay domestic tax law, which also fills any gaps in them. This book considers the interaction and integration between domestic tax law and double tax treaties (and EU Law). Where domestic tax law is relevant, reference is made to United Kingdom (UK) tax law as illustrative. If UK tax law is not illustrative, then the tax laws of other countries may be referred to.

As will be seen from the above, there are a number of limitations inherent in the scope of this book. First, it is limited to a consideration of income tax.[5] Second, it does not seek to cover all international income tax issues. Rather, it focuses on those issues arising out of commercial transactions. Further, it does not purport to be comprehensive in its reference to legal provisions, treaties, case law or academic literature. Many works provide a detailed consideration of the various levels of law referred to in this book.[6] The focus is on the OECD Model, using EU Law as a point of comparison. So other model tax treaties, such as that of the United Nations (UN) or the United States (US), are not referred to unless they provide a unique illustration of a particular point.[7] In all these matters, the focus is on illustrating and analysing how international tax law works in practice while providing sufficient references to facilitate more detailed research into particular issues.

The book comprises seven chapters. It begins by setting the scene with a number of important preliminary matters. Chapter 1 discusses relevant fundamentals of an income tax. It does not discuss all the fundamentals of income taxation, but rather focuses on those that are particularly important when projected into an international setting. As this introduction has already demonstrated, there are a number of important sources of international tax law. Chapter 1 proceeds to identify the relevant sources and consider how they interrelate. These sources are quite different in their nature and form. The approach to interpretation of them may be different

[5] Some countries, such as the UK, limit a reference to 'income tax' to the taxation of income of individuals, or entities other than corporations, the tax on corporate profits being referred to as 'corporation tax'. This book uses the term 'income tax' to include any tax on corporate profits.

[6] For example, as regards the OECD Model, see Baker (2001–); as regards the application of EU Law to direct taxation, see Terra and Wattel (2008); and as regards UK income and corporation tax, see Tiley (2008).

[7] Regarding the UN Model, see United Nations (2001). Regarding the US Model, see United States (2006). van Raad (2009) is a useful publication that contains these Models, as well as the OECD Model and Commentary, various OECD papers and drafts, other important international material, relevant FEU Treaty provisions and EU Directives together with relevant direct tax decisions of the European Court of Justice.

depending on the source and the forum doing the interpreting. The general approach to interpretation of material is the final matter considered in Chapter 1.

Chapter 2 looks at the big picture, the justification or jurisdiction to tax in an international setting. It identifies separately the importance of the person and their activities within the concept of economic allegiance and how, in the context of an income tax, the concepts of residence and source are used as proxies. The chapter proceeds to discuss the situation of divided allegiance (primarily where source and residence are in different countries) and the problem of double taxation that arises. This discussion takes account of broad principles that underlie and limit cross-border taxation, including non-discrimination, inter-nation equity, source-country entitlement and reciprocity of withholding tax rates. Comparable principles that underpin EU Law are also considered. The principles are only outlined at this stage; they are used in detail throughout the book in practical examples.

Chapter 2 is critical for the purposes of this book because it develops the *Base Case* upon which much of the remainder of the book is structured. The *Base Case* is illustrated in Figure 1. It considers the simple scenario in which a person (Allan) in one country (Country A) rents a property in that country that is owned by another person (Beth) in a second country (Country B). Allan pays rent to Beth, i.e. a cross-border payment.

Focusing on this simple scenario facilitates a breakdown of the primary types of issues faced in international taxation. As mentioned, international tax at the least involves the application and interaction of two tax systems. In the *Base Case*, these are the tax systems of Country A and Country B. The tax system of Country A (the source state) is considered in Chapter 3 and the tax system of Country B (the residence state) is considered in Chapter 4. These chapters are the central basis of the book. Both have a similar format in that they consider the tax treatment of Beth, i.e. the person receiving the rent, and subsequently proceed to consider the tax treatment of expenses, i.e. the treatment of Allan in Country A with respect to paying the rent and that of Beth in Country B with respect to any expenses incurred in Country B in deriving the income. In this context, each chapter considers the relevant rules in tax treaties, EU Law and, where relevant, underlying domestic law. Within this primary structure, the content of the two chapters is very different.

Chapter 3 proceeds to consider source-country taxation of our income recipient, i.e. Beth. The structure broadly follows that of the OECD Model and so is schedular in nature, dealing with different types of income

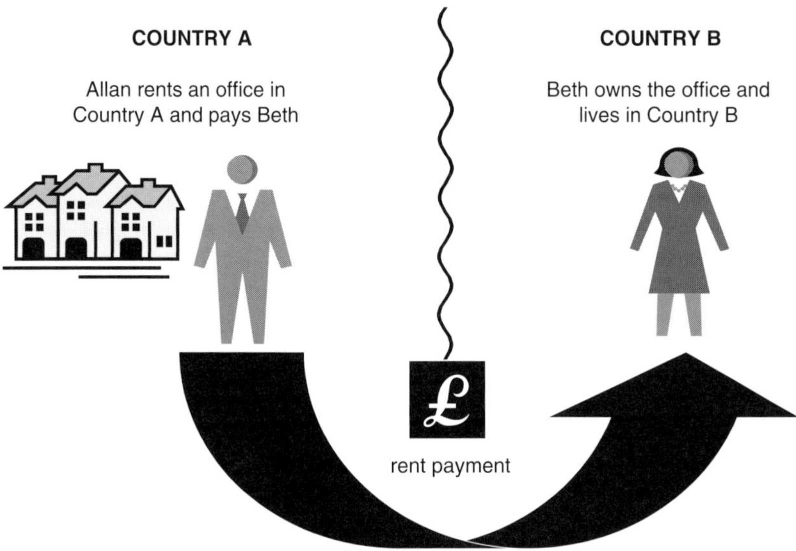

separately. While structured around the OECD Model, at the end of the consideration of each type of income there is a consideration of how source-country taxation may be affected where the country is a member of the EU, i.e. an evaluation of how EU Law might alter the treatment by the source country. EU Law is considered in a similar manner throughout the book. Chapter 3 proceeds to consider the treatment of the payer by the source state. This is primarily a consideration of any rules that may affect the deductibility of the payment by the payer (Allan) in the source country. The chapter then reflects on some income tax fundamentals (identified at the start of Chapter 2) that have a substantial impact on source-country taxation. Within this context the discussion considers the difficult issues of transfer pricing and thin capitalisation.

Chapter 4 switches to the residence or home state of the income recipient, i.e. Country B. It presumes taxation of the recipient (Beth) by the source state (Country A) in accordance with the rules and considerations outlined in Chapter 3. It begins by looking at the likely response of the residence state under its tax law to taxation by the source state, i.e. it outlines methods of foreign tax relief. These are primarily the exemption and foreign tax credit methods and each gives rise to problems in calculating foreign income, essentially an issue of deductibility of expenses. The chapter then turns to consider particular problems that arise where the income is derived through a corporation in the source state. These include the risk of economic double taxation and methods to relieve it as well as potential deferral of residence-state (Country B) taxation and the use of controlled foreign corporation rules to prevent any deferral.

Chapter 4 then dissects the difficult issue of expenses incurred in deriving foreign-source income. This initially involves the allocation of expenses between domestic income and foreign income but it proceeds to consider the situation where the expenses give rise to losses. The use of losses in a cross-border scenario is particularly problematic because of the lack of treaty rules regulating the scenario. At this point the comparison with EU Law is particularly instructive because EU Law has much greater scope for regulating the situation. The chapter ends with a consideration of the use of losses by international groups of corporations.

As mentioned, tax treaties do not regulate all income tax issues arising in a cross-border scenario. Chapters 3 and 4 consider the rules that do exist. By contrast, Chapter 5 focuses on the limited scope of tax treaties, i.e. issues treaties do not cover. It begins by continuing the focus on the simple bilateral situation, i.e. the *Base Case*. It returns to some of the income tax fundamentals outlined in Chapter 2 and considers what happens if there is disagreement between the two countries about some of these fundamentals. The consequence of disagreement is potential double taxation or potential non-taxation, but in this increasingly integrated world, the potential is that a given cross-border dealing is not simply bilateral but will involve three or more countries. Issues arising in this sort of scenario are the focus of the second part of Chapter 5. In practice, the issues are highly complex, but it is hoped that the foundations set by the preceding chapters will enable readers with even little tax experience to grapple with the conceptual issues and secure a basic understanding of the practical rules.

As mentioned, Chapter 2 identifies separately the importance of the person and their activities in founding taxing rights. Chapters 3, 4 and 5 presume the location of the person and their activities is constant. By contrast, Chapter 6 considers the consequences where there is an establishment or relocation of the elements giving rise to the fundamental right to tax. It discusses a number of issues that keep international tax practitioners busy (and make them a lot of money). The chapter begins by considering changes in the activity that produces income. In particular, it considers the tax treatment in both the host (source) and home (residence) countries when a foreign business (activity) is established. It then similarly considers situations where an existing foreign business is terminated, is transferred and where the form of a foreign business is changed (e.g. from a branch into a subsidiary). The chapter then turns to consider changes in the location of the person, i.e. the tax consequences of commencing or ceasing residence.

Chapters 3 to 6 consider the primary rules that regulate international taxation. Of course, those rules must be administered. In large part the domestic tax law of the countries concerned will regulate this administration. This is not a book about tax administration. However, there are a number of tax administration issues that are peculiar to the cross-border integration (clash) of tax systems and these are reflected in tax treaties. Chapter 7 considers three of these. The first involves the power of the tax administrations concerned to exchange information about a cross-border dealing or, indeed, specifically collect information for the other tax administration. The second involves how to resolve issues where the tax administrations of the countries concerned do not agree on what is the appropriate treatment of a particular cross-border dealing. Here the discussion considers the mutual agreement procedure and arbitration. The final issue involves the power of one tax administration to assist the other in collecting its taxes.

1

Fundamentals and sources of international tax law

The purpose of this chapter is to outline background material that is important in later discussions. It is structured under three headings. The first considers some tax fundamentals that identify the nature of income tax and its basic attributes. As mentioned in the introduction, the purpose of this heading is to identify a number of income tax fundamentals that are important when projected into an international setting. The second heading proceeds to identify the sources of law that will be referred to and analysed in the remainder of this book. The focus is primarily on three sources of law – domestic law, tax treaties and EU Law – although residually a number of others are mentioned. The heading considers how these sources take effect in domestic law and how they interact with each other. The last heading considers the approach to interpretation of the sources by relevant courts. Here the focus is on the approach to interpreting treaties, which may be substantially different from that used for interpretation of domestic legislation. Also of particular importance is the jurisprudence of the European Court of Justice, the central court appointed to interpret EU Law.

1.1 Tax fundamentals[1]

A responsible government is one that is elected to represent its community members. It is a basic premise of the relationship between community members that they will share the burden of funding their common government. Taxes are the way in which those community members are, at least initially, obliged to share that burden. More particularly, taxes are a compulsory contribution levied by government to raise funds to be spent for public purposes (public services), including the support of the government. At some level, if there were no taxes there would be no

[1] For a more detailed consideration of tax and particularly income tax fundamentals, see Harris (1996, pp. 1–37).

government. In the words of the famous American judge Oliver Wendell Holmes, '[t]axes are what we pay for civilized society'.[2] The result is an economic or financial relationship between community members and their government.

However, not all government levies are taxes. It can be particularly important to distinguish taxes from other levies where the word 'tax' is referred to in a constitutional document, as it is, for example, a number of times in the FEU Treaty.[3] Taxes are often distinguished from a governmental charge for services. With a charge for services there will be an identifiable service provided for the payment. There is a big difference between a road toll paid to use a new road and paying tax for the general defence of the country. Further, the charge must vary in some respect to the service received and not according to some general notion of ability to pay. There must be some connection between the cost of the service to be provided by the government and the amount of revenue to be raised (but a reasonable profit is okay). A UK example of a charge for services is the television licence, which funds the British Broadcasting Corporation (BBC).[4]

Having identified what a tax is, wealth is an important concept in identifying the main types of taxes that governments rely on. Perhaps the reason for this importance is that taxes are payable from wealth, inevitably in money, although this was not always the case.[5] The fact that tax is payable in money, local currency, causes problems which impact on tax design. These will be returned to shortly. Governments often impose taxation by reference to the stages of wealth: creation, holding, transfer and consumption (destruction). The major example of a tax on the creation of wealth is the income tax. Taxes on the holding of wealth were once common in Europe but have been in decline for a number of years. The major example of a tax on the holding of wealth in

[2] *Compania de Tabacos* v *Collector of Internal Revenue* (1927) 275 US 87 (SC) at p. 100.

[3] The word 'tax' is used in the FEU Treaty in, among other provisions, Art. 65(1), which is one of the provisions dealing with acceptable limitations on the free movement of capital and Part three Title VII Chapter 2 (Arts. 110–113), which deals with tax provisions.

[4] For an example of a licence fee held to be a tax and therefore invalid without sanction of Parliament, see *AG* v *Wilts United Dairies* [1922] All ER 845 (HL). Generally regarding the difference between a tax and a charge for services, see Tiley (2008, p. 4).

[5] Historically, contributions to support government might have been made by the provision of labour (often called 'statute labour'), an English example of which is the knight's fee. Particularly in colonial times, taxes might have been paid in local produce, such as corn, tobacco or even alcohol. Generally see Harris (2006), especially at pp. 16, 84, 144 and 478.

the UK is now the local land rate. Taxes on the transfer of wealth include stamp duties and inheritance tax. The value added tax (goods and services tax in some countries) is often viewed as the major example of a tax on consumption, although its name might suggest that it is a tax on the creation of wealth.[6]

Taxes on the stages of wealth each have a relationship one with the others. This is important because it assists in understanding that there are many issues common to all of the major taxes imposed by a certain country. In particular, a tax on the creation of wealth, such as the income tax, is related to each of the other stages of wealth. Wealth once created may be used in only one of two ways, saving or consumption. Saving results in the holding of wealth and often wealth held itself creates further wealth, e.g. in the form of rent. Taxes on wealth held and on the return on wealth held often produce similar results. If all wealth created is consumed, an income tax and a consumption tax will produce the same result. Many income taxes in practice provide concessionary treatment of some forms of saving (particularly in the context of saving for retirement) and so blur the line between an income tax and a consumption tax.

An income tax is also related to taxes on the transfer of wealth. This is because the transfer of wealth is a realisation event upon which the income tax is typically based.[7] The income tax does not seek to tax all creations of wealth but typically only those that have been 'realised'. Realisation is a particularly slippery but important concept in income taxation. While there is no perfect definition of what realisation involves, it is clear that it has its origins in the history of accounting.[8] For present purposes, it is enough to suggest a realisation involves an exchange with another person and the exchange will typically involve a payment.[9] Therefore, a realisation-based income tax taxes creations of wealth accruing to a person only when and if they are transformed by a payment by another person. In this way, payments become the building blocks of the income tax base. Payments received count positively towards the calculation of income

[6] Whether a value added tax is a tax on the creation or consumption of wealth depends on the timeliness with which excess input tax credits are refunded and how consumption is defined (purchase by end user or actual destruction of wealth).

[7] This relationship is especially clear in the context of a tax on capital gains. The UK seeks to integrate, to some extent, capital gains on death and the imposition of inheritance tax, for example see TCGA 1992 s. 260.

[8] See the discussion in Harris (2006, pp. 135, 393–4 and 401).

[9] Adam Smith once noted: 'The goods of the merchant yield him no revenue or profit till he sells them for money, and the money yields him as little till it is again exchanged for goods' (1776, book II chapter I p. 133).

(profits) and payments made may (depending on the circumstances) count negatively.

'Payment' is not meant in the narrow sense of a cash transfer but rather in the broad sense of any manner in which one person may bestow value (capable of monetary quantification) on another person. The ways in which value may be bestowed are limited. The most obvious type of payment is the transfer of an asset, including a transfer of cash. The other manners in which value may be bestowed have caused (and still cause) headaches for the income tax. Value may be bestowed by reducing a liability of a person, such as in the case of a forgiveness of debt. Value may be bestowed by creating an asset in another person, i.e. where the person creating the asset never becomes the owner of the asset created. Often such a payment will look like a transfer and so this case will be essentially a question of legal form.[10] Finally, value may be bestowed by granting the use of an asset or by the provision of services.

Some types of payment involve an adjustment of existing assets. This is the case with payments involving the transfer of an asset or reduction of a liability. This can also be the case with a payment involving the creation of an asset, such as where other assets are incorporated into the asset created or the creation of the asset simultaneously involves the creation of a liability. However, payments involving the use of an asset or the provision of services do not involve such an adjustment. In a sense, they involve pure or direct creations of wealth. The receipt of any of the five types of payment will be taken into account positively in determining a person's income. However, when it comes to claiming deductions for payments made, it is only those payments that involve the transfer of an asset or the incurring of a liability that are taken into account in reducing income.

All payments, whether accounted for positively or negatively, display certain fundamental features. These features of a payment are critical in understanding the difficulties of income tax in both a domestic and an international setting. For purposes of administering the income tax law, a payment must be *allocated*. It must be considered made by one person and received by another person. Second, a payment must be *quantified*. Unless a payment is denominated in local currency, i.e. the currency in which the

[10] Two examples of a payment by creation are the granting of a lease and the issue of shares by a corporation. The lessor does not own the lease before its creation and the company does not own its shares before they are issued. This demonstrates that the classic creation-type payment is where one person grants rights against themselves in another person. Other forms are possible, such as the creation of a building on another's land (the building being a fixture and so only ever being part of the land).

tax calculation is made, then the value bestowed by the payment must be converted or quantified in an amount of local currency. Wealth creation is potentially a continuous activity but income tax is periodic. Income tax is charged on income derived during a year. As a result, payments made and payments received that are to be taken into account in determining a person's tax liability must be allocated to one period (year) or another. Therefore, third, the tax law must determine the *timing* of a payment.

Finally, the tax consequences of making or receiving some types of payment are different from making or receiving other types of payment. This means that the *character* of a payment is important. Is the payment rent, interest, dividends, royalties, wages, service fees, capital or revenue and what is the geographical location of the payment? Under the tax laws of many countries, the characterisation issue is taken further and taxpayers are required to calculate their income separately for different types of income or activities. This is referred to as a *schedular* system and is usually contrasted with a *global* system under which there is, in theory, one calculation of income.[11] The UK income tax law is, and always has been, a schedular system.[12]

All of these features can be seen in the *Base Case* (Figure 1 on p. 5). The payment is *allocated* as made by Allan and received by Beth. The payment must be *quantified* for a number of purposes. Under the income tax law of Country A, it must be quantified in Country A currency for purposes of determining Beth's income and for purposes of determining any deduction claimable by Allan. It must be quantified in Country B currency for the purposes of determining Beth's income under Country B's income tax law. The *timing* of the payment of rent must also be determined for the purposes of Country A's income tax law and for that of Country B. When must Beth bring the rent into account: monthly or weekly as the rent accrues, when she sends a bill, when she receives a cheque or when payment is credited to her bank account? Finally, the payment from Allan to Beth has been *characterised* as rent for the use of immovable property.

Taxes on the stages of wealth are not the only types of taxes, but they are the major types. There may be taxes on certain activities, e.g. business licences or polluting, and a head or poll tax is also a possibility. Each year

[11] Regarding the difference between a schedular and a global system, see Burns and Krever (1998).

[12] The description of a tax system as 'schedular' derives from the historic structure of the UK tax law, which literally broke the income tax charge into schedules, see below at 2.1.2.1. Regarding the origins of the UK schedular system, see Harris (2006), particularly at p. 403.

the OECD publishes a table that breaks down the types of taxes levied by member states.[13] These figures show that on average OECD members take more than one third of all gross domestic produce in taxes, the EU average being nearly four percentage points higher and the US being ten points lower.[14] The figures also show a breakdown between the different types of taxes used. The value added tax (goods and services tax) is the single largest revenue raiser, weighing in at an average of nearly one third of all tax levied. However, if personal income tax and corporate income tax are added together, the income tax raises more revenue than the value added tax. This is particularly so in the US where taxes on goods and services are twelve percentage points lower than in the EU. If social security contributions, which are like a tax on wage income, are added to the income tax, the income tax approximates 60 per cent of all tax levied, with 30 percent to the value added tax and the remaining 10 per cent to other taxes. These figures explain why this book focuses on the income tax.

Finally, it is useful to mention a few other ways in which taxes are typically classified. A tax may be adjusted according to the personal circumstances of the taxpayer, in which case it is referred to as a *personal* tax. Other taxes are referred to as *in rem* taxes, taxes on things or activities. The income tax is typically classified as a *personal* tax. This classification becomes unclear once income tax is imposed on non-residents, where the tax is not adjusted according to personal circumstances. A value added tax is an *in rem* tax, the supply being the subject of the tax.

Taxes are also classified as either *direct* or *indirect*. A direct tax is paid by the person *intended* to bear the burden of the tax whereas an indirect tax is *intended* to be passed on in prices. Emphasis is placed on government *intention* because, in an economy in which the government does not set prices, it cannot know who precisely bears the burden of any tax. Further, the distinction between a direct and an indirect tax is often blurred. In principle, the income tax is a direct tax, but in the case of, for example, wage withholding, the tax is paid by the employer and reduces the amount received by the employee. Is this

[13] For example, see OECD (2008d, pp. 58–9).

[14] These figures are premised on a levy being classified as a 'tax' (see above). A good example of the importance of this classification is that Australia shows on the table as collecting no social security contributions. This is because retirement savings in Australia are funded through compulsory contributions (that look and feel very much like social security contributions) to *private* superannuation funds. The government heavily regulates these funds and the average person may struggle to see a great deal of difference between this system and one involving social security contributions.

sufficiently different from the collection of value added tax from the retailer to justify the different label? Again, the distinction can be particularly important where a constitutional document refers to 'direct' or 'indirect' taxes.[15]

In the UK, as in much of Europe, the distinction between direct and indirect taxation is more of historical significance than current importance. In feudal times, the king had a right to impose certain levies (hence the word 'customs'). By contrast, direct taxation (aides, grants or subsidies) could in large part be levied only with the consent of the people. This was one of the reasons why the English Parliament was first called. As a result, a new law was required for every grant of direct taxation. This practice continues currently with direct taxation typically re-imposed each year by the annual Finance Act. By contrast, indirect taxes are perpetual, with one base law imposing a continual charge. This distinction between direct and indirect taxation was reflected in the separation of the tax administration into the Board of Inland Revenue and Her Majesty's Commissioners for the Customs and Excise. It was not until 2005 that these separate branches were amalgamated into Her Majesty's Revenue Commissioners (HMRC).[16]

1.2 Sources of international tax law and their interrelationship

The discussion now moves from the general consideration of income tax fundamentals to the sources of international tax law.

1.2.1 Domestic law

The *charge to tax* is inevitably found in the domestic law of each state. As mentioned, in the UK the charge to direct taxation is typically found in the annual Finance Act, which also sets the rates at which tax is charged. Separately, there are a number of integrated laws setting out how that charge is calculated. Historically, the UK system was relatively straightforward, with all persons being subject to income tax and a single law

[15] The FEU Treaty Art. 112 generally prohibits 'indirect taxation' of exports and imports within the EU. Article 113 provides a procedure for the harmonisation of 'indirect taxation'. The Canadian constitution also incorporates a reference to 'direct taxation' in allocating taxing rights to the provincial governments, see the Constitution Act, 1867 (UK/Canada) s. 92 item 2.

[16] Generally regarding the historic distinction between direct and indirect taxes, see Harris (2006, pp. 30–1) and the references cited therein.

governing the calculation. Leaving aside Profits Tax and it predecessors, things became slightly more complex with the introduction of corporation tax in 1965, which largely replaced the income tax charge on corporations. Corporation and income tax were merged into a single law in 1970, although there was a separate law governing capital gains, which also dated from 1965, and a separate tax administration law, dating from the 1870s. The tax law rewrite that began in the 1990s substantially complicated this situation by fragmenting the single law. The income tax is now divided between three laws plus the capital gains tax law and a separate law for capital allowances (depreciation).[17] Similarly, the corporation tax is divided between the old single law dating from 1988 and three new laws dating from 2009 and 2010.[18]

The situation is less complicated in most other countries, but there are common features with the UK. Some countries still impose just income tax, i.e. on both individuals and corporations, but it is also common to have a separate corporation tax. Most countries, including the US, have a single law, although others, including Germany, have a separate law for corporation tax. A number of common law countries follow the UK tradition of imposing the tax by a separate law. This is the case with Australia, although in Australia's case the charging law is perpetual.

Domestic law is the background over which other sources of international tax law are overlaid. If a matter is not regulated by these other sources, or if there are no other sources, then domestic law applies. This means that the domestic law specifies when and in what manner a domestic charge arises with respect to a cross-border dealing. In particular, it identifies relevant factors that bring a transaction or dealing within the charge to tax, often called 'connecting factors'. The most common of these in international income taxation are source and residence and these are further considered below at 2.1. Domestic law also specifies any special considerations in calculating the charge to tax on a cross-border dealing. In particular, domestic law specifies how the domestic charge is to

[17] Income Tax (Earnings and Pensions) Act 2003, Income Tax (Trading and Other Income) Act 2005 (ITTOIA 2005), Income Tax Act 2007, Taxation of Chargeable Gains Act 1992 (TCGA 1992) and the Capital Allowances Act 2001, respectively.

[18] Income and Corporation Taxes Act 1988 (ICTA 1988), Corporation Tax Act 2009 (CTA 2009), Corporation Tax Act 2010 (CTA 2010) and Taxation (International and Other Provisions) Act 2010 (TIOPA 2010). There are some important provisions in ICTA 1988 that are not rewritten by these Bills, most notably the controlled foreign corporation rules.

interact with any charge imposed by a foreign country. The most common form of interaction is some form of foreign tax relief and this is further considered below at 2.2.

Before leaving domestic law, it is important to note that in some jurisdictions the constitution may have a direct impact on the application of tax laws. The constitution may refer to taxation directly (as mentioned above). However, even where there is no direct reference to tax, general constitutional principles may affect the imposition of taxation. This is particularly the case where the constitution refers to certain fundamental rights of citizens such as equality or fairness. There is a wide difference between a country like Germany or Spain, where constitutional principles (and the constitutional court) can have a substantial impact on the application of tax law, and a country like the UK, where there is virtually no day-to-day impact.

1.2.2 Tax treaties

What are they and where did they come from?

The domestic direct tax laws of countries involve the unilateral exercise of sovereignty, and so they do not coordinate/integrate very easily. This was particularly the case when the income tax became increasingly common in the second half of the nineteenth century. These early laws were very different in nature and countries began concluding tax treaties in order to better coordinate their laws, removing potential double taxation of cross-border dealings and so freeing up international trade. These treaties were concluded on a bilateral basis in order to provide for specific integration between two tax systems. The first bilateral double tax treaty dealing with direct taxation was that between Prussia and Austria–Hungary in 1899, although it was apparently based on the German Imperial Double Taxation Law of 1870, which sought to relieve double taxation between German states. Importantly, both of these sources incorporated an essentially schedular approach in allocating the right to tax some types of income to one country and other types of income to the other. A handful of further bilateral tax treaties of a similar nature was concluded in central Europe before the First World War.[19]

After the First World War, a few further bilateral tax treaties were concluded and in the mid to late 1920s the League of Nations sought to facilitate the further conclusion of such treaties by issuing a number of model treaties. These models were largely based on existing treaty practice and

[19] See Harris (1996, pp. 288–93).

so incorporated a schedular approach, which had become deeper in the sense that more types of income were specified. The League of Nations models were not particularly popular and only twenty bilateral tax treaties had been concluded by the outbreak of the Second World War. The League produced two further Models during the War. After the War, the UN did not initially take up the League's role with respect to model tax treaties, despite the matter being on the agenda. Rather, in the mid-1950s, in the context of closer economic integration within Europe, the Organisation for European Economic Co-operation (OEEC) took upon itself the task of producing a model treaty for use between its members. By this time there were fifty-six bilateral tax treaties.[20]

The OEEC became the OECD in 1961 and issued a first model tax treaty in 1963. Like the League of Nations models before it, the 1963 OECD Model was essentially based on existing treaty practice and incorporated a schedular approach. Also like the League of Nations models, the OECD Model incorporated Commentaries on its various articles. However, the Commentaries of the League of Nations models were prepared by the Secretariat of the League and so did not reflect an agreed interpretation of the models. By contrast, the OECD Fiscal Committee (now the Committee on Fiscal Affairs) was largely made up of tax officials of member states. OECD Commentaries were drafted by this Committee, and so with the agreement of OECD member states (subject to any reservations made). Over the ensuing decade and a half, the OECD Model proved a moderate success and by 1977 there were 179 bilateral double tax treaties between OECD member states. A revised model was produced in 1977.

The OECD Model represents the position of developed countries. By the late 1970s it was felt that something should be done to facilitate the conclusion of tax treaties between developing countries and between developed and developing countries. The result was the 1980 UN Model, which largely followed the OECD Model, with some important exceptions that will be explored in this book. In 1992, the OECD moved to a continuous (loose-leaf) Model, which is updated with amendments every few years. By the mid-1990s, there were more than 1,000 tax treaties worldwide. The UN produced an updated model treaty in 2001, this time with Commentaries, which is still largely consistent with the OECD Model. There are currently in excess of 2,500 double tax treaties worldwide.[21]

[20] See Harris (1996, pp. 297–312).

[21] See Harris (1996, pp. 311–12) and, generally, Vann (2008). This is not to suggest that there will be a complete worldwide double tax treaty network any time soon. Drevet

This background to tax treaties is important for a number of reasons. First, it explains that tax treaties are, subject to limited exceptions, bilateral in nature. These are ordinary treaties concluded in the ordinary way and take effect according to the laws of the contracting states.[22] They draw their status from domestic law, a point that will be returned to shortly. Tax treaties are essentially a bilateral agreement as to how two states agree to divide taxation of cross-border dealings between them. The bilateral nature of treaties means that they do not work so well in situations involving three or more countries, a point that will be returned to in Chapter 5.

Second, the principal purpose of tax treaties has been to provide for relief from double taxation as between the two states. Hence, they are typically termed 'double tax treaties', 'double taxation conventions' or 'double taxation agreements'. Increasingly in recent years, there has been additional focus on the supplementary purpose of preventing fiscal evasion.[23] This will be returned to in Chapter 7. The principal beneficiaries of relief from double taxation are taxpayers and treaties foresee and intend that many of the provisions that they contain will be transposed into taxpayer rights. A peculiar feature of tax treaties is that these taxpayer rights are mixed up in and derived from the very nature of tax treaties as an agreement between two states as to how to divide the tax base between them. That is, treaties allocate taxing rights between the two states and taxpayers derive their rights from this allocation. As will be discussed shortly, the origins of taxpayer rights under EU Law are very different.

Third, the bilateral tax treaty network is extremely rigid and limits the ability of countries to engage in domestic tax reform. Many countries have upwards of 50 treaties, some upwards of 100.[24] If a country wishes to change its law in a way inconsistent with treaties, it is not possible to

and Thuronyi (2009) note that there are 18,336 possible income tax treaties between UN members and at the current rate of concluding treaties it will take a further 150 years to complete the network.

22 For example, see OECD Model Arts. 30 (Entry into Force), referring to exchange of instruments of ratification, and 31 (Termination), providing for termination by notice through diplomatic channels.

23 These purposes are mentioned under the Title of the OECD Model and in the Introduction to the OECD Commentaries para. 16. As an example, the 2001 UK/US treaty is described as being 'for the avoidance of double taxation and the prevention of fiscal evasion with respect to taxes on income and capital gains'. The OECD Model also deals with taxes on capital but, as discussed in the introduction, this book considers only income tax.

24 The UK has more than 120 tax 'arrangements' (see footnote 30 below), but not all of these are with states recognised by the UN. For a list of UN countries and numbers of treaties concluded, see Drevet and Thuronyi (2009).

renegotiate all the treaties on a timely basis and it is commercially impossible to terminate them.[25] Further, the fact that there are so many treaties, whether in total or on a country basis, means that they have been concluded over a substantially extended time, decades. This protracted period of conclusion, coupled with the nature of treaties as a negotiation, means that there are substantial and irreconcilable differences between treaties worldwide and even treaties concluded by particular countries. The tax treaty network is consistent in its inconsistency and this has major impact when it comes to tax planning and treaty abuse, discussed in Chapter 5. Further, the inflexibility makes amendment of model treaties difficult. Any amendment to the model could take decades to be reflected in practice. This is one reason why there is a temptation and practice of making substantive amendments by changing the agreed meaning of existing provisions through amendments to the OECD Commentaries.

Fourth, tax treaties still incorporate a schedular system, a reflection of the fact that their basic structure has not changed since the beginning. This is an important point for countries whose domestic law does not adopt a schedular approach or whose domestic law adopts a schedular approach that is not consistent with that used in tax treaties. Therefore, the way in which different types of income are dealt with in a treaty may simply not match up with how they are dealt with in domestic law. In the case of the UK, there is surprising consistency between the schedular approach used in domestic law and that used in tax treaties, though it is not a perfect match. This is further discussed in Chapter 2.

Fifth, and perhaps most importantly, model tax treaties are reactionary, customary and, at their worst, an historical accident. In their origin they were based on existing domestic tax laws and treaty practice and that practice still largely dictates the direction in which they develop.[26] One of the biggest mistakes made by students of international tax is to believe that tax treaties are planned and have some sort of conceptual structure based on principle. This is simply not the case. Tax treaties and model treaties are built on political compromise. They are comparatively short, their language is often difficult (and explained only by historic precedent) and, as Chapter 5 will demonstrate, they are far from comprehensive. Tax treaties simply do not deal with all tax issues that arise from international

[25] This is not to suggest that countries do not terminate treaties, they just do not terminate them all at once. For a recent example in which Denmark terminated its treaties with France and Spain, see Malgari (2008).

[26] Avery Jones et al. (2006) trace the origins of concepts and expressions used in the OECD Model.

dealings. They deal only with those matters on which agreement can be reached and, in many cases, the language is left unclear in order to promote flexibility. As one Canadian judge put it:

> Treaties ... are not beacons of clarity. Maybe this is the risk of dozens of negotiators of several languages negotiating the OECD Model, and then two countries trying to adopt that model to their circumstances – we end up with a camel rather than a horse.[27]

Despite these limitations, the gradual osmosis of model treaties has produced a number of principles (or at least a number of principles have developed based on the rules in model tax treaties).

How tax treaties take effect in domestic law

An important question in relation to tax treaties as a source of law and their interrelationship with other sources is how the treaties take effect in domestic law. As mentioned, it is the intention of tax treaties that taxpayers should be granted certain rights. However, a treaty is an agreement between the two contracting states. So how does a person (the taxpayer) that is not a party to the treaty derive rights from it? This depends on the position that each state takes in relation to the status of the treaties as instruments of international law. A distinction is to be drawn between those states that follow the *monist* view that national law and international law are part of a single system and those states that follow the *dualist* view that they are separate systems.

In a *monist* state, international laws and agreements prevail over national law. No further action is therefore necessary in order to grant rights to taxpayers. Taxpayers can directly rely on the treaty provisions once the treaty has been completed and the treaty provisions prevail over the domestic law. In some states, the national constitution (Argentina, France, Italy, Netherlands) or decisions of the Supreme Court (Belgium) ensure that the monist view is adopted.[28] Nevertheless, provisions in the constitution, including constitutional amendments after the conclusion of a tax treaty, will almost invariably override the treaty. Countries like the US, where treaties rank equally with domestic law, face more difficulties. Here a later domestic law has priority over a treaty, despite the treaty having direct effect.[29]

[27] *Knights of Columbus* v *The Queen* (2008) TCC 307 (TC) at para. 82 per Miller J.

[28] For an article regarding the monist approach in Italy, see Arginelli and Innamorato (2008).

[29] *Whitney* v *Robertson* (1888) 124 US 190 (SC) at 194.

In *dualist* systems, tax treaties become part of national law only by specific incorporation or transformation into domestic law. Australia and the UK are states that take the dualist view, although they implement tax treaties into domestic law through different mechanisms. Australia gives effect to its tax treaties by enacting the treaty as a statute in its domestic law. The UK has an umbrella provision in its domestic law enabling tax treaties to take effect in the national law. TIOPA 2010 provides:

> s. 2(1) If Her Majesty by Order in Council declares-
> (a) that arrangements ... have been made in relation to any territory outside the United Kingdom with a view to affording relief from double taxation in relation to taxes within subsection (3), and
> (b) that it is expedient that those arrangements should have effect, those arrangements have effect.
>
> (3) The taxes are ... income tax ... corporation tax ... capital gains tax ... and ... any taxes imposed by the law of the territory that are of a similar character.
>
> s. 6(2) Double taxation arrangements have effect in relation to income tax and corporation tax so far as the arrangements provide-
> (a) for relief from income tax or from corporation tax,
> (b) for taxing income of non-UK resident persons that arises from sources in the United Kingdom,
> (c) for taxing chargeable gains accruing to non-UK resident persons on the disposal of assets in the United Kingdom,
> (d) for determining the income or chargeable gains to be attributed to non-UK resident persons,
> (e) for determining the income or chargeable gains to be attributed to agencies, branches or establishments in the United Kingdom of non-UK resident persons,
> (f) for determining the income or chargeable gains to be attributed to UK resident persons who have special relationships with non-UK resident persons ...[30]

Therefore, under the UK approach the arrangements specified in the Order in Council (the treaty provisions are attached to the Order as a schedule) take effect in accordance with s. 6.

[30] Note the reference to 'arrangements' rather than 'treaties'. Historically, this enabled the UK to conclude agreements with colonies that, at the time, were not independent states. Note also that there is no reference to 'government' of the 'territory'. This facilitates agreements with authorities that, for political reasons, the UK may not wish to recognise as a government, such as in the case of Taiwan (Chinese Taipei).

The difference between the monist and dualist approach may be important in the interrelationship between the treaty and domestic law and on the procedural implementation of treaty provisions. Either approach may potentially give rise to *treaty override* or *treaty underride*. Treaty override occurs where a state gives effect to a treaty but subsequently enacts a domestic law that is inconsistent with the treaty. This may occur, for example, where the domestic law is enacted to close a perceived tax avoidance problem. The interaction between tax treaties and domestic anti-abuse provisions is a complex area that is beyond the scope of this study.[31] It is a contentious area, where interpretation of the treaty is critical, a topic turned to shortly. In a monist state, treaty override is possible only if domestic law is at least the equivalent of treaty law. This is the case in the US, where, as mentioned, a domestic law that postdates a treaty may override the treaty. In a number of monist states treaty law is higher than domestic law, akin to constitutional law.

In a dualist country, treaty override is possible because the treaty takes effect only through domestic law and so a subsequent domestic law may alter the situation. The UK position on treaty override is well illustrated by *Woodend (KV Ceylon) Rubber & Tea Co* v *Ceylon CIR*, heard by the Privy Council as an appeal from Ceylon, as it then was.[32] Following substantial tax reforms in the late 1950s (spearheaded by Nicholas Kaldor), Ceylon introduced an additional tax on the profits of Ceylon branches of non-resident companies, in this case a UK company. The additional tax was triggered by remittances of profits to head office by those branches. The UK/Ceylon treaty prohibited Ceylon from taxing Ceylonese branches of UK companies other, higher or more burdensome than the taxation to which Ceylonese enterprises are or may be subjected in respect of like profits.[33] A British company claimed that additional tax imposed on its Ceylonese branch breached this provision. The Privy Council concluded:

> In the end [the question] is whether the Ceylon legislature must have intended the expression "non-resident company" in section 53C(1) of the 1959 Act to apply to all non-resident companies or to be exclusive of those to whom the 1950 agreement applied. In reaching a decision their Lordships have in mind that, as already stated, the 1959 Act was a statute of very comprehensive character introducing a number of radical changes in the taxation laws of Ceylon. It is unlikely that in the course of

[31] See Arnold (2004).

[32] [1971] AC 321 (HL).

[33] A similar provision is found in OECD Model Art. 24(3), which is discussed below at 3.1.3.4.

> preparing such a measure agreements such as the 1950 agreement would have been completely overlooked: and it may well be that the legislature considered that the provisions of the 1959 Act if given their full literal meaning would not be repugnant to the 1950 Act – as indeed the Supreme Court have held in this case.
>
> Such a view would of course have bearing on the legislature's intention. But leaving aside all speculation on this point, their Lordships are unable to find in the 1959 Act or in the circumstances which bear upon the present problem any evidence sufficient to justify the conclusion that while section 53C uses the general expression "non-resident company" it must nevertheless be construed as embodying the very important exclusion of those non-resident companies who were within the scope of the 1950 agreement. It seems to them that the general words must receive their full meaning.[34]

This was broadly the approach taken by the UK courts in the more recent case of *Padmore* v *IRC (No 2)*,[35] where the court had to construe statutory provisions specifically overriding, with prospective effect, the decision of the courts in an earlier treaty case.[36]

In contrast to treaty override, treaty underride occurs where a state never gives full effect to the tax treaty in its domestic law. This is possible only in the case of dualist states. Consider TIOPA 2010 s. 6 (above). It provides that treaties are to take effect only 'in so far as' they provide for certain things. Anything in a tax treaty that is not covered by the list is not implemented into domestic law and may result in treaty underride. One example will illustrate the problem. In *R* v *IRC ex parte Commerzbank*[37] a UK branch of a German bank claimed interest (repayment supplement) on a repayment of overpaid tax. Under domestic law, the interest was available only to residents. The taxpayer claimed that, under the non-discrimination provision in the Germany/UK treaty, taxation was not to be less favourably levied on the taxpayer in the UK than the taxation levied on enterprises of that other territory carrying on the same activities.[38] The court rejected this argument 'because the repayment supplement, although connected with the levy of taxation, does not affect the amount of that levy and cannot be brought within the language of [s. 6]'.[39]

[34] [1971] AC 321 at 334–5.

[35] [2001] STC 280 (Ch).

[36] The earlier case was *Padmore* v *IRC* (1989) 62 TC 352 (CA).

[37] (1991) 68 TC 252 (QBD).

[38] This provision was similar to that in question in the *Woodend* case, see footnote 32 above.

[39] (1991) 68 TC 252 (QBD) at 260. Note that *Boake Allen Ltd & Ors* v *RCC* [2007] UKHL 25 (HL), discussed below at 3.1.3.4, and *Sun Life Assurance Co of Canada* v *Pearson* (1984) 59 TC 250 (CA), discussed below at 5.2.1.1, also involved treaty underride.

If a state effectively engages in treaty override or treaty underride the taxpayer has no legal grounds for complaint. The taxpayer is not a party to the treaty. However, the other contracting state may complain and in an extreme case may use the breach as grounds for terminating the treaty. In particular, the state in breach cannot use its own domestic law as a defence against the breach. Article 27 of the Vienna Convention on the Law of Treaties provides: 'A party may not invoke the provisions of its internal law as a justification for its failure to perform a treaty.'[40]

As mentioned, tax treaties are concluded in the same manner as other treaties. This can cause problems where a partner to a treaty is a federal state as the federal constitution may limit the federal government's power to conclude treaties that bind the state, provincial or local governments. In such a case, taxes imposed by lower tier governments may not be included in the taxes covered by a treaty.[41] When the 1975 UK/US treaty was originally negotiated, it contained provisions to limit the power of the state of California to make pricing adjustments on a formulary basis.[42] This version of the treaty failed to gain the requisite majority in the US Senate Foreign Relations Committee because a minority considered that this provision was an interference with state rights and the provision had to be renegotiated. The current UK/US treaty, like previous treaties, does not include state and local taxes within the taxes covered.

Another issue regarding the application of treaties is the question of what happens when a state breaks up into a number of smaller territories. This caused particular problems with the break up of Czechoslovakia, Yugoslavia and the Soviet Union. Of course, the reverse can happen, such as with the unification of East and West Germany. Does a tax treaty concluded by an original state automatically continue in force binding the successors post separation or unification? For an answer one must turn to the rules of public international law on state succession, something that is beyond the scope of this book.

Can a treaty create or increase tax?

As mentioned, the OECD Model, and tax treaties generally, operate to relieve double taxation by allocating taxing rights between the two states

[40] A treaty partner may be alerted to a treaty override by reason of a provision such as OECD Model Art. 2(4), which requires contracting states to 'notify each other of any significant changes that have been made in their taxation laws'.

[41] OECD Model Art. 2(3) envisages a list of taxes covered by a treaty. These are usually specified by reference to the law upon which they are based.

[42] The power to make pricing adjustments under tax treaties is discussed below at 3.3.1.

and, where double taxation still results, a treaty typically provides a method for relieving that residual double taxation. Taxing rights granted by a treaty are usually permissive. Taking Article 11(1) of the OECD Model as an example, it provides that 'Interest arising in a Contracting State and paid to a resident of the other Contracting State *may* be taxed in that other State'.[43] Such wording does not appear to mandate a charge to tax where none would arise under domestic law.

The field in which the issue may be said to arise more acutely is with respect to the pricing (quantification) of dealings between related persons. Article 9 of the OECD Model authorises an adjustment if the pricing is not at arm's length. Article 9 is discussed in more detail at 3.3.1. The present issue is whether the provisions of Article 9 can authorise an increase in tax if such an increase is not supported by domestic law, i.e. absent a treaty, domestic law does not authorise an adjustment. There are differing views on this point. The better view appears to be that, irrespective of the interpretation put on the treaty provisions, the answer depends on how the treaty is incorporated into domestic law. In a monist state, there could be such an increase irrespective of a basis in domestic law, as the treaty is automatically given legal effect. This would result in discrimination against taxpayers from treaty partners and so may raise constitutional issues.[44] In a dualist state, it will depend on the supporting domestic law. Using the UK as an example, TIOPA 2010 s. 2 provides no apparent authority for a treaty to charge tax or to increase a liability. Effective transfer pricing adjustments under UK tax treaties, therefore, depend on application of the underlying domestic transfer pricing rules.[45]

1.2.3 EU Law

FEU Treaty

As mentioned in the introduction, EU Law is that based on or under the EU and FEU Treaties. Being treaty based law, EU Law is, at least initially, integrated into domestic law in the same manner as other treaties

[43] Emphasis added.

[44] See Arginelli and Innamorato (2008) discussing the Italian position.

[45] But see TIOPA 2010 s. 6(2) and Oliver (1998). Controversially, the Australian Tax Office takes the contrary view. This might be particularly important if the treaty transfer pricing adjustment justifies recharacterisation of an amount where such recharacterisation is not available under domestic law. See Australian Tax Office (2009), 'Decision Impact Statement: *Roche Products Pty Ltd* v *Commissioner of Taxation*', 23 January 2009, available at http://law.ato.gov.au/atolaw, accessed 4 March 2010.

including tax treaties. So, the UK, being a dualist country, has introduced EU Law into UK law through a dedicated statute, the European Communities Act 1972. In particular, s. 2(1) of this Act provides:

> All such rights, powers, liabilities, obligations and restrictions from time to time created or arising by or under the Treaties, and all such remedies and procedures from time to time provided for by or under the Treaties, as in accordance with the Treaties are without further enactment to be given legal effect or used in the United Kingdom shall be recognised and available in law, and be enforced, allowed and followed accordingly...

Without labouring the point, the scope for treaty underride seems minimal, especially when compared with section 788(3) of ICTA 1988 (discussed above).

The treaties referred to include those pre-dating the UK's accession, which established the European Coal and Steel Community (1951), the European Atomic Energy Community (1957) and the European Economic Community (1957). These Communities had separate institutions until they were merged in 1967 and the treaties became know as the European Communities Treaties. The Treaty of Maastricht (1992) is also included. It established the European Union with these European Communities, renamed the European Community, as one of three pillars. In late 2009, the Lisbon Treaty abolished the pillar system. This book considers only matters originating from the European Economic Community.

As will be discussed shortly, EU Law is to be applied according to the judgments of the European Court of Justice. Interpretation of EU Law by this court is critically important. In particular, the Court has decided that the provisions of the EU Treaties may be relied on directly by EU nationals (direct effect) irrespective of the legal traditions of Member States. The result is effectively, as far as the European Court of Justice is concerned, a monist view of the UK's obligations under the FEU Treaty.

Directives

Article 115 of the FEU Treaty provides:

> [T]he Council shall, acting unanimously in accordance with a special legislative procedure and after consulting the European Parliament and the Economic and Social Committee, issue directives for the approximation of such laws, regulations or administrative provisions of the Member States as directly affect the establishment or functioning of the internal market.

Article 94 provides for secondary EU Law in the form of directives. The mechanism by which directives can be issued is important because it is restrictive. The reference to the 'Council' is a reference to the Council of the European Union, the principal decision-making institution within the EU. Historically, the Council is a more powerful legislative body than the European Parliament. The Council is composed of 27 national ministers, one from each of the member states. The exact membership of the Council depends on the topic under discussion. In the context of tax matters it is made up of the member state finance ministers. The important point is that a directive cannot be issued on income tax matters without the unanimous agreement of the finance ministers of each member state.

Only four directives have been issued to date with respect to direct taxation. These are the Parent-Subsidiary Directive (1990), the Mergers Directive (1990), the Interest and Royalties Directive (2003) and the Savings Directive (2003).[46] These directives have a rather narrow scope and are primarily concerned with companies. They will be discussed further at appropriate points in the course of this book. These directives take effect through the FEU Treaty and, as discussed below, have been interpreted by the European Court of Justice to also have direct effect. This means that a person can simultaneously claim rights under the FEU Treaty and a directive. This is further mentioned below at 1.3.3.

1.2.4 Other sources

A number of other sources of international law may be relevant in a tax context. These are not further discussed in this book but a brief word regarding the most important is appropriate.

GATT and the WTO

As a rule, there is a sharp divide between the imposition of tariffs on trading transactions in goods and services and the taxation of income and profits. Tariffs and the like are indirect taxes and regarded as a main subject of the provisions of the General Agreement on Tariffs and Trade (the GATT). By contrast, direct taxation is not so clearly targeted by the GATT.[47] It may fall within the ambit of the GATT if a direct tax concession constitutes a 'subsidy'. The potential for such concessions to fall within the GATT was increased with the introduction of the

[46] Council Directives 90/435/EEC, 90/434/EEC (consolidated as 2009/133/EC), 2003/49/EC and 2003/48/EC, respectively.

[47] In particular, GATT Art. III does refer to 'taxes' on products but the assumption has largely been that this must be a reference to indirect taxation to the exclusion of direct taxation.

Subsidies Code included in the 1994 version of the GATT. Annex I to this Code includes a specific reference to '[t]he full or partial exemption, remission, or deferral specifically related to exports of direct taxes... paid or payable by industrial or commercial enterprises'. The US famously fell foul of the prohibition on export subsidies with respect to its concessionary corporation tax treatment of Domestic International Sales Corporations (DISCs). The Foreign Sales Corporations regime, which replaced the DISC regime, suffered a similar fate, as did the Extraterritorial Income Exclusion, which replaced the Foreign Sales Corporation regime.[48]

European Convention on Human Rights

The European Convention on Human Rights (1950) is yet another treaty obligation that may affect direct taxation, and not just with respect to cross-border dealings. The UK ratified this convention in 1951 but did not implement it into domestic law (in the usual dualist manner) until enactment of the Human Rights Act 1998. The scope for application of this treaty to cross-border commercial dealings seems rather limited. A number of treaty articles may have taxation implications including Article 1 of the First Protocol (protection of property), Article 6 (right to a fair trial) and Article 14 (prohibition of discrimination). Of some relevance to individuals may be Article 8 (right to respect for private and family life) and Article 9 (freedom of thought, conscience and religion). Consistency of interpretation of the treaty, as between states, is assisted by the jurisdiction of the European Court of Human Rights, which sits in Strasbourg, and by reference in proceedings before national courts to the jurisprudence of that court. The Convention rights seem to have a broad application, applying to all natural and legal persons within a state, regardless of nationality or residence.[49]

1.3 Approaches to interpretation of material

As mentioned, the nature of the various sources of international tax law varies substantially and it is not surprising that courts adopt different approaches when interpreting them. Interpretation may vary depending

[48] Generally, see Lang et al. (2005), McDaniel (2004) and Schön (2004). The US Model Tax Treaty Art. 1(3) seeks the agreement of treaty partners that questions of interpretation or application of the treaty are to be determined exclusively under the terms of the treaty and excludes certain provisions of the General Agreement on Trade in Services.

[49] Regarding the application of this convention in taxation matters, see Baker (2008) and Baker (2000).

on the forum (court) or just the source of law. It is useful to consider the courts' approach to interpretation with respect to each of the main categories of international tax law identified at 1.2. This serves as a useful background when various court decisions on that material are discussed later in this book.

1.3.1 Domestic law

Each country has its own domestic rules of interpretation and construction of domestic tax statutes. In most countries, these principles are similar if not the same as those applied to other statutes. In a similar fashion, where constitutional provisions may affect tax matters, the usual approach to constitutional interpretation will be adopted, which may be very different from the approach to interpreting general statutes. As a general point, common law jurisdictions (outside the US) are renowned for adopting a more formal interpretation of tax statutes than civil law jurisdictions, although in recent decades the common law approach has been more purposive.[50]

In the context of UK tax law, UK courts apply ordinary rules of statutory interpretation, even if they once construed tax law strictly as being penal in nature. Therefore, courts first give words used in a tax law their ordinary meaning. Second, courts do not read into or imply into a tax law something that is not expressed in its language. Third, a tax law is construed with the object of giving effect to the intention of the legislature. Fourth, 'the history of an enactment and the reasons which led to its being passed may be used as an aid to its construction'.[51] Particularly with respect to the last principle, courts may consult official records of Parliamentary debates (Hansard).[52] Citing *McGuckian* v *IRC*,[53] Tiley notes that in recent years UK courts have interpreted the words of a tax law 'in a purposive way but in their context'.[54]

The UK approach to interpreting tax law may take account of special considerations in one particular area. This is with respect to statutory provisions that provide relief from international double taxation. One reason for taking a slightly different approach in this case may be the objective

[50] Generally, see heading 6 of each of the country entries in Part One of Ault and Arnold (2004).

[51] *IRC* v *Mangin* [1971] AC 739 (HL) at 746 per Lord Donovan.

[52] *Pepper* v *Hart* [1993] AC 593 (HL).

[53] [1997] STC 908 (HL).

[54] Tiley (2010, p. 158). Also, see Gordon (2004).

of such provisions in trying to marry up two different tax systems. As Wilberforce J put it in *Brooke, Bond & Co Ltd* v *Butter*:

> I would start with the observation that this Schedule [giving unilateral relief] must necessarily be drafted in a somewhat general way because it is designed to apply to a great multitude of cases where tax had been paid under foreign systems; which foreign systems may involve fiscal demands and methods of assessment widely different from those known in this country, and which perhaps would not fit into our conception at all. No doubt it is because of that that somewhat general language is used.[55]

Outside of this sort of consideration, there is no reason to suppose that UK courts would adopt a different approach to interpreting the domestic international tax law rules than the purely domestic rules.

1.3.2 Treaty interpretation

Like the interpretation of domestic law, interpretation of a tax treaty is a matter for the domestic courts of the country in which the issue is raised. However, the rules of interpretation are broader than the rules for domestic law because, while the treaty provisions have been incorporated into domestic law, so as to take effect, what is being interpreted is a treaty and not domestic law. The UK approach to treaty interpretation was summarised by Mummery J in *IRC* v *Commerzbank*.[56] It involves the following:

> (1) Look first for a clear meaning of the words used in the relevant article of the convention… A strictly literal approach to interpretation is not appropriate in construing legislation which gives effect to or incorporates an international treaty… If the provisions of a particular article are ambiguous, it may be possible to resolve that ambiguity by giving a purposive construction to the convention, looking at it as a whole.
>
> (2) The process of interpretation should take account of the fact that – 'The language of an international convention has not been chosen by an English parliamentary draftsman. It is neither couched in the conventional English legislative idiom nor designed to be

[55] (1962) 40 TC 342 (Ch) at 353.

[56] (1990) 63 TC 218 (Ch) at 235–6. The passage referred to is a summary of the approach laid down by the House of Lords in *Fothergill* v *Monarch Airlines Ltd* [1981] AC 251 (HL) and was approved by the Court of Appeal in *Memec plc* v *IRC* [1998] STC 754 (CA) at 766; see *Smallwood* v *RCC* (2008) 10 ITLR 574 (SC) at para. 94.

construed exclusively by English judges…' '[A convention] should be interpreted… on broad principles of general acceptance.'

(3) Among those principles is the general principle of international law, now embodied in Article 31(1) of the Vienna Convention on the Law of Treaties.

(4) If the adoption of this approach to the article leaves the meaning… unclear or ambiguous or leads to a result which is manifestly absurd or unreasonable recourse may be had to 'supplementary means of interpretation'. Article 32 of the Vienna Convention.

(5) Subsequent commentaries on a convention or treaty have persuasive value only, depending on the cogency of their reasoning. Similarly, decisions of foreign courts on the interpretation of a convention or treaty text depend for their authority on the reputation and status of the court in question.

(6) Aids to the interpretation of a treaty such as travaux préparatoires, international case law and the writings of jurists are not a substitute for study of the terms of the convention. Their use is discretionary, not mandatory, depending, for example, on the relevance of such material and the weight to be attached to it.

This subheading continues to consider, in particular, the relevant provisions of the Vienna Convention, the OECD Commentaries and the possible resolution of questions of interpretation by agreement by the competent authorities of a tax treaty.

Vienna Convention

The provisions of Articles 31 and 32 of the Vienna Convention on the Law of Treaties are relevant when interpreting a tax treaty. The extent to which these provisions might be followed by states that have not yet ratified the Convention is debatable.[57] On one view, the Convention is simply declaratory of customary international law and so its ratification should not make a difference.[58]

Article 31 of the Vienna Convention provides:

1. A treaty shall be interpreted in good faith in accordance with the ordinary meaning to be given to the terms of the treaty in their context and in the light of its object and purpose.
2. The context for the purpose of the interpretation of a treaty shall comprise, in addition to the text, including its preamble and annexes:

[57] The US has signed but not yet ratified the Vienna Convention.

[58] Note, however, Article 26 (*Pacta sunt servanda*) and Article 27 (*Internal law and observance of treaties*).

a. any agreement relating to the treaty which was made between all the parties in connexion with conclusion of the treaty;
b. any instrument which was made between the parties in connexion with the conclusion of the treaty and accepted by the other parties as an instrument related to the treaty.

3. There shall be taken into account, together with the context:
   a. Subsequent agreement between the parties regarding the application of the treaty or the application of its provisions;
   b. Any subsequent practice in the application of the treaty which establishes the agreement of the parties regarding its interpretation;
   c. Any relevant rules of international law applicable in relations between the parties.
4. A special meaning shall be given to a term if it is established that the parties so intended.

Article 32 of the Vienna Convention provides:

> Recourse may be had to supplementary means of interpretation, including the preparatory work of the treaty and the circumstances of its conclusion, in order to confirm the meaning resulting from the application of article 31, or to determine the meaning when the interpretation according to article 31:
>
> a. leaves the meaning ambiguous or obscure; or
> b. leads to a result which is manifestly absurd or unreasonable.

Because of Article 31, it is clear that reference can be made to any exchange of notes between the parties, such exchange being part of the context to which Article 31(2) refers. An exchange of notes is common in tax treaty practice and the commercial tax treaty databases usually file any such exchange with the primary text of a treaty. For example, an exchange of notes dated 24 July 2001 took place with respect to the 2001 UK/US treaty.

By contrast, a US Treasury Department Technical Explanation of the treaty seeking to explain the treaty provisions, or UK guidance notes published in the UK HMRC Tax Bulletin, are not part of the context. They are unilateral actions. Exceptionally, in the *Crown Forest* case,[59] the Supreme Court of Canada referred to the US Treasury Department Technical Explanation of the 1980 Canada/US treaty. However, in the context of that treaty, the Canadian authorities had participated in negotiations on the preparation of the Explanation and had publicly expressed their

[59] *Crown Forest Industries Ltd* v *Canada* [1995] 2 SCR 802 (SC).

agreement. In those circumstances, the Explanation could be said to be part of the context.[60]

While the object and purpose of a double tax treaty is primarily to relieve double taxation, some writers have raised the question whether it is consistent with that object and purpose if the result of applying the treaty is that there is no taxation in either state, so that there is, as they would describe it, double non-taxation.[61] This position may arise where one state (say, the residence state) does not, for its own reasons, tax a particular item of income but the other state (the source state) does tax it.[62] Suppose that there is a treaty between two states under which the source state gives up its taxing rights to the income in question. As a result, there is no taxation at all. The robust answer to this proposition is that if contracting states do not like this result then they should take steps to word their treaty to ensure that it does not arise (e.g. by inserting a 'subject to tax' condition). Moreover, there are many cases (e.g. cases involving pension funds and charities) where as a matter of policy a residence state does not tax income.

In relation to the interpretation of tax treaties, Article 3(2) of the OECD Model is particularly important. It provides that:

> As regards the application of the Convention at any time by a Contracting State, any term not defined therein shall, unless the context otherwise requires, have the meaning which it has at that time under the law of that State for the purposes of the taxes to which the Convention applies, any meaning under the applicable tax laws of that State prevailing over a meaning given to the term under other laws of that State.

Therefore, unless the context otherwise requires, terms used in the treaty and not otherwise defined are to be given their domestic law meaning in the state applying the treaty and are to be given an ambulatory meaning (i.e. one that adjusts with time) rather than a static meaning.

An example of a problem arising in this area is the meaning of 'beneficial owner', which is used in Articles 10, 11 and 12 of the OECD Model and is discussed further below at 5.2.3.2. Is this term intended to have a treaty meaning or a domestic law meaning? In common law states, beneficial owner is a well-known term in relation to equitable interests while it is unrecognised as such in civil law states. Did the treaty negotiators

[60] It seems the same is true of the 2007 protocol to the Canada/US tax treaty, see Fuller (2008).

[61] Generally, see Lang (2004).

[62] A residence state that does not tax capital gains is an example, see *Smallwood* v *RCC* [2009] EWHC 777 (Ch).

intend the term to have a special meaning as referred to in Article 31(4) of the Vienna Convention? Where would evidence of that intention be found? Consider also the meaning of 'income from land' in Article 6 of the OECD Model. Is this expression to be given its domestic meaning? Some states in their domestic law define the receipt of a premium on the grant of a short lease as giving rise to income over the term of the lease. Is such a premium taxable as income from land under a treaty following the OECD Model? Similar questions are raised throughout this book with respect to other terms used in the OECD Model.

OECD Commentaries

As mentioned at 1.2.2, an Introductory Commentary and a Commentary to each article accompanies the OECD Model. The OECD Commentaries are peculiar in that they seek to explain the operation of the various articles of the OECD Model. They are not a commentary on the provisions of any particular treaty. Therefore, what if any is the role of the OECD Commentaries when interpreting real treaty provisions that reflect the wording of the OECD Model? There seems to be a consensus that the OECD Commentaries may be referred to, but less agreement as to the ground on which they may be referred to or *which* Commentaries (in time) may be referred to.

The OECD Commentaries do not fall within Article 31(2) of the Vienna Convention as the text, a preamble or an annexe. With respect to provisions based on the OECD Model, are the Commentaries an agreement made by the parties with respect to the conclusion of a tax treaty? Such an approach might exclude treaties concluded by non-OECD member states even if they are based on the OECD Model. The OECD has opened the Commentaries for comment by a number of non-member states in an outreach programme that seeks to draw their acquiescence to the provisions of the Model.[63] To say that the Commentaries are in connection with the conclusion of a particular treaty may be somewhat stretching the wording of the Vienna Convention. Article 31(3) of the Vienna Convention does not seem very apt to take in the OECD Commentaries.

Article 32 of the Vienna Convention is more promising for supporting use of the OECD Commentaries in interpreting provisions of an actual treaty. 'Supplementary means of interpretation' is a broader expression.

[63] The OECD recently stated that there are '60 countries setting out their positions on the model – 30 member countries and 30 non-member countries…' Non-member country positions are now included in the Model and Commentaries. See Weiner (2008).

It includes, but is not limited to, the preparatory work of the treaty, the *travaux préparatoires*, and the circumstances of its conclusion. In the UK case of *Sun Life Assurance Co of Canada*, Vinelott J observed:

> The 1980 Treaty is based upon a Draft Convention drawn up by the Fiscal Committee of the OECD following the recommendation of the Council of the OECD calling upon Governments of member countries when revising or concluding bilateral double taxation treaties to conform to a Draft Convention prepared by the Fiscal Committee. The Draft Model Convention when agreed was embodied in a report by the Fiscal Committee which contains a commentary on each article of the Convention. I think I should refer to two passages in the report which explain the way in which the commentary came to be written and its purpose:
>
> 26. As these Commentaries have been drafted and agreed upon by the experts appointed to the Committee on Fiscal Affairs by the Governments of Member countries, they are of special importance in the development of international fiscal law. Although the Commentaries are not designed to be annexed in any manner to the conventions to be signed by Member countries, which alone constitute legally binding international instruments, they can nevertheless be of great assistance in the application of the conventions and, in particular, in the settlement of any disputes.
> 27. Observations on the Commentaries have sometimes been inserted at the request of some Member countries who were unable to concur in the interpretation given in the Commentary on the Article concerned. These observations thus do not express any disagreement with the text of the Convention, but furnish a useful indication of the way in which those countries will apply the provisions of the Article in question.
>
> It is common ground that in the light of the decision of the House of Lords in *Fothergill* v *Monarch Airlines Ltd* [1981] AC 251 the Commentaries can and indeed must be referred to as a guide to the interpretation of the Treaty.[64]

So that's clear then, or is it? In *Fothergill v Monarch Airlines Ltd*, what the court was considering was the meaning of the Warsaw Convention on international carriage by air (as amended by the Hague Protocol of 1955) and incorporated into UK law by the Carriage by Air Act 1932 and by the Carriage by Air Act 1961 (which replaced the 1932 Act). In doing so, the court considered the circumstances in which it might refer to the *travaux préparatoires*. Lord Wilberforce considered that *travaux préparatoires* might be referred to if two conditions were met. First, the material

[64] *Sun Life Assurance Co of Canada* v *Pearson* [1984] STC 461 at 510–11.

involved must be public and accessible. Second, the *travaux préparatoires* must clearly and indisputably point to a definite legislative intention.

However, the OECD Model is not itself a treaty, it is a model. If an argument were to be made that the Commentaries are *travaux préparatoires*, it would have to run along the following lines. In negotiating the terms of a bilateral treaty, both parties are taken, where the treaty wording follows the OECD Model, to have had the Model in mind in settling the wording and thereby to have had in mind the Commentaries to the Model as well.[65] The Recommendation of the OECD Council concerning the Model recommends the governments of member countries 'when concluding new bilateral conventions or revising existing bilateral conventions to conform to the Model Tax Convention as interpreted by the Commentaries thereon'.[66] In that sense, the Model and the Commentaries form part of the *travaux préparatoires* and both meet Lord Wilberforce's test for admissibility, assuming that to be the relevant test. This argument would hold good as between member countries; it is not so clear in the case of non-member countries, although some have been consulted as part of the OECD outreach programme.[67] This is not to say that, for example, the Technical Explanation of the US Model Income Tax Treaty could be admitted on the same basis. It is a unilateral statement of position.

If this argument is sustainable then it fills what would otherwise be a gap. In negotiating a bilateral tax treaty each party will no doubt keep records of what has been agreed and their own understanding of the effect. These records, however, will not be disclosed to the other party because of the nature of the negotiation nor would the party concerned be willing to disclose them in litigation, contending that by contrast with the negotiation of a multilateral convention such as the Warsaw Convention, they are not true *travaux préparatoires*.[68]

[65] *Smallwood* v *RCC* (2008) 10 ITLR 574 (SC) at para. 98.

[66] The recommendation is reproduced in van Raad (2009, p. 3).

[67] In *Smallwood* v *RCC* (2008) 10 ITLR 574 (SC) at para. 98 the Special Commissioners noted that 'the negotiators on both sides could be expected to have the commentary in front of them and can be expected to have intended that the meaning in the commentary should be applied in interpreting the treaty when it contains the identical wording. This is as much true of the United Kingdom which is a member of the OECD as it is of Mauritius, which is not. The difference is that the United Kingdom had the opportunity of stating that it disagreed with any part of the commentary by making an observation, while Mauritius did not, although the commentary does now contain observations by a number of non-OECD member countries, but not including Mauritius.'

[68] Note the point made by Lord Fraser in *Monarch Airlines* in relation to the minutes of the states at the Hague conference that 'we should decline to give effect to the alleged

Finally, in relation to *travaux préparatoires*, records prepared by contracting states in negotiation of a treaty may well be of a type that the authorities wish to influence interpretation of the treaty. If these records remain private, they would not be regarded as *travaux préparatoires*. Such records, or at least some of them, may well find their way into an exchange of notes in order to ensure that they do influence interpretation of the treaty.[69]

Which Commentary?

If the Commentaries may be referred to, *which* Commentaries may be referred to? Is it only the Commentaries in existence at the time when the bilateral treaty is concluded or may a reference include later Commentaries concluded after the conclusion of the treaty but before its application in a particular case?[70] Three points might be made in this respect. First, which Commentaries may be referred to perhaps depends on the nature of the issue: if a change to the Commentary clears up an obvious nonsense then maybe the later Commentary should be used since the earlier treaty wording was obviously wrong or unintended. Second, if the Commentary is favourable to the taxpayer then the taxpayer may choose to hold the tax administration to the position taken in the Model.[71] Third, if it comes to litigation and the taxpayer's position would be less favourable, the taxpayer may contend that neither the *travaux préparatoires* nor the supplementary means of interpretation include materials arising after the conclusion of the agreement.[72]

agreement or to take judicial notice of it, because it has not been sufficiently published to persons whose rights would be affected by it, such as Mr. Fothergill…' [1981] AC 251 (HL) at 287.

69 It seems likely that this may have happened with respect to the Exchange of Notes on the 2001 UK/US Treaty mentioned above.

70 The OECD Introductory Commentary considers this issue at paras. 33–36.1.

71 This would be on the basis that the contracting state has bound itself to that interpretation by agreeing to the later Commentary. Question whether, from a legal perspective, an estoppel would bind the contracting state in such a case.

72 In *Smallwood* v *RCC* (2008) 10 ITLR 574 (SC) at para. 99 the Special Commissioners noted that: 'The relevance of commentaries adopted later than the treaty is more problematic because the parties cannot have intended the new commentary to apply at the time of making the treaty. However, to ignore them means that one would be shutting one's eyes to advances in international tax thinking, such as how to apply the treaty to payments for software that had not been considered when the treaty was made. The safer option is to read the later commentary and then decide in the light of its content what weight should be given to it.' Contrast the approach of the Canadian Federal Court of Appeal in *MIL (Investments) SA* v *The Queen* [2006] TCC 460 (TC) at para. 86, which refused to refer to the OECD Commentaries prepared after the ratification of the Canada-Luxembourg treaty, and the same court reaching a different view in *Prévost Car Inc.* v *The Queen* [2009] FCA 57 (FCA) at para. 9. Generally, see Kandev and Wiener (2009).

The issue is important because of the difficulty of giving early effect to a change in the text of the OECD Model. A change in the text, unless it is simply clarifying, takes effect only once incorporated into existing or new treaties. As mentioned at 1.2.1, this will take time to achieve. If the Commentary is amended and it is permissible to refer to the most recent Commentary then changes in the position under existing treaties can be effected immediately. Hence, in recent updates, there has been a tendency to amend the Commentary rather than the text. Of course, the same issues arise for states that are not members of the OECD if, indeed, the Commentaries may be referred to in the first place (see above).

Dispute resolution

There are two avenues for the resolution of interpretation issues under bilateral tax treaties. One is recourse to the domestic courts of the country concerned. The courts will apply treaty rules of interpretation in interpreting the treaty. The other avenue is recourse to the mutual agreement procedure in Article 25 of the OECD Model. This procedure is further discussed below at 7.2, but it typically involves agreement between the tax administrations of the contracting states. In particular, Article 25(3) provides:

> The competent authorities of the Contracting States shall endeavour to resolve by mutual agreement any difficulties or doubts arising as to the interpretation or application of the Convention.

Any such agreement is another source of law that might be relied on when interpreting tax treaties.

Use of the domestic courts and the mutual agreement procedure are not necessarily mutually exclusive, but a tax administration may be reluctant to take up a taxpayer's case with the other tax administration if the taxpayer is, at the same time, pursuing the matter through the domestic courts. Equally, a taxpayer is not required to exhaust other remedies first before pursuing the mutual agreement procedure. Again, these are matters pursued further below at 7.2.

1.3.3 Jurisprudence of the ECJ

As mentioned at 1.2.3, EU Law is to be applied according to the judgments of the European Court of Justice (the ECJ). The establishment of the ECJ, whose decisions are binding on member states of the EU, blurs the distinction between the EU and a standard federal state. The difference with the bilateral tax treaty network is dramatic. The ECJ not only binds Member

States, but also ensures, in the large part, a uniform interpretation of the FEU Treaty. Both these aspects are lacking in the bilateral tax treaty network. For reasons that will be discussed shortly, treaty override and treaty underride are not aspects of EU Law. The ECJ behaves very much like a central constitutional court of a federal state. Most such courts attract power to themselves over protracted periods, often called centralisation. Like other such courts, the ECJ has gone through periods of stagnation, rapid growth and even retraction with respect to centralisation.[73]

The ECJ was set up in 1952 to ensure enforcement of EU Law. The court has jurisdiction over EU Law. It is made up of twenty-seven Judges and eight Advocates General. The Judges and Advocates General are appointed by common accord of the governments of the member states and hold office for a renewable term of six years. Each member state of the EU has the power to nominate one Judge, so their number coincides most of the time with the number of member states.[74] The Advocates General assist the ECJ by presenting, with impartiality and independence, an 'opinion' in the cases assigned to them. They can question the parties involved and give their opinion on a legal solution to the case before the Judges deliberate and deliver their judgment. The opinion given does not have to be followed by the Judges. One Advocate General is nominated as of right by each of France, Germany, Italy, Spain and the UK. The other three positions rotate in alphabetical order between the 20 smaller member states.[75]

As mentioned at 1.2.3, the UK has implemented the FEU Treaty through the European Communities Act 1972. The importance of the ECJ is conferred by s. 3(1) of this Act, which provides:

> For the purposes of all legal proceedings any question as to the meaning or effect of any of the Treaties, or as to the validity, meaning or effect of any EU instrument, shall be treated as a question of law (and, if not referred to the European Court, be for determination as such in accordance with the principles laid down by and any relevant [decision of the ECJ or any court attached thereto]).

As a result, in matters of EU Law the decisions of the ECJ are paramount and bind not only UK courts but arguably the UK legislature.

The ECJ has the primary tasks of interpreting EU Law and ensuring its uniform application throughout the EU. The ECJ has placed great

[73] There is an increasing recognition of this link between the ECJ and central federal state courts, particularly in the US. For example, see Mason (2008) and Avi-Yonah (2007).

[74] See FEU Treaty Part six, Title I, Chapter 1, Section 5 (Arts. 251–81), which regulates the ECJ.

[75] From 2010, the ECJ may request an additional three Advocates General.

emphasis on the so-called *teleological* approach, that is, giving priority to the objective of a provision rather than the actual words used. As a result, ECJ decisions are often shorter and easier to read than the decisions of UK courts, although, as will be demonstrated throughout this book, not necessarily easier to interpret. Further, unlike UK courts, the ECJ only issues one decision per case, i.e. there are no dissenting judgments. So the more controversial cases, where the Judges may be struggling to reach agreement on common reasoning, are precisely the cases where a judgment may be less than instructive.

The ECJ has acknowledged and confirmed a number of general principles inherent in the EU legal order. The most fundamental of these are the *supremacy* and *direct effect* of EU Law. The principle of supremacy ensures that EU Law has primacy over conflicting national law. In this regard, the ECJ has consistently noted that:

> according to settled case-law, although direct taxation falls within their competence, Member States must none the less exercise that competence consistently with Community law.[76]

The principle of direct effect means that individuals can invoke their Community rights directly before national courts. As mentioned above at 1.2.3, as far as the ECJ is concerned, the result is a monist approach to domestic implementation of EU Law. The ECJ recognised at an early stage that the combined impact of the principles of supremacy and direct effect is that member states have limited their sovereignty by concluding the EU Treaties.[77]

As mentioned above at 1.2.3, the ECJ has also decided that directives have direct effect. This means that persons may simultaneously claim rights under the FEU Treaty as well as under a directive. If a directive permits taxation by a member state, the taxpayer may nevertheless argue that the taxation is contrary to fundamental rights granted by the FEU Treaty.

> [T]he possibility offered by Article 4(2) of the directive to refuse the deduction of costs incurred by parent companies in connection with holdings in the capital of their subsidiaries… may be exercised only in compliance with the fundamental provisions of the Treaty, in this case Article [49] thereof.[78]

[76] Case C-446/03 *Marks and Spencer* v *Halsey* [2005] ECR I-10837 (ECJ) at para. 29.

[77] Case 26/62 *NV Algemene Transport- en Expeditie Onderneming van Gend and Loos* v *Netherlands Inland Revenue Administration* [1963] ECR 3 (ECJ).

[78] Case C-168/01 *Bosal Holding BV* v *Staatssecretaris van Financiën* [2003] ECR I-9409 (ECJ) at paras. 25–6.

Under Article 258 of the FEU Treaty, the ECJ has jurisdiction to hear a complaint by the European Commission that a member state has not complied with its obligations under the FEU Treaty. A minority of direct tax cases have been brought under this procedure, although these do include what is recognised as the first direct tax case to be decided by the ECJ.[79] The most common jurisdiction exercised by the ECJ in direct tax matters is that set out in Article 267 of the FEU Treaty. Under this provision, the ECJ has power to hear complaints by referral from national courts by way of an application for a preliminary ruling on the interpretation of the FEU Treaty as well as directives. The competent tribunal or court of the member state concerned makes the application or 'reference' to the ECJ.

When faced with an EU Law issue, a national court first determines whether it believes the interpretation of EU Law is clear (*acte claire*) or whether the court should seek the guidance of the ECJ. If the latter, then the issue is put by the national court to the ECJ by way of a question or questions to be answered by the ECJ. A reference to the ECJ is not an *appeal* as such because it does not finally decide the case. Rather, it is in the nature of an interlocutory proceeding. Written and oral submissions are made, not only by the parties to the dispute (the national government and the taxpayer), but also in many cases by the governments of other member states.

Following the written and oral submissions but before the Judges begin their deliberations the reference may be assigned to an Advocate General. The Advocate General prepares an opinion, setting out the relevant facts and law and suggesting a decision. This opinion is usually, but not always, followed by the Judges who may add additional reasoning or who may, at least impliedly, not adopt certain reasoning expressed by the Advocate General. As mentioned, the decision of the Judges is reached by consensus, which means that there are no dissenting judgments and the reasoning may be brief. Having received the answer from the ECJ, it is for the national court to determine the matter as appropriate, bearing in mind the answer received, and the manner in which the judgment is to be implemented.

This form of procedure means that much turns on the wording of the question put to the ECJ. Moreover, the answer inevitably relates only to the questions asked without any guidance as to what the position would be in analogous cases or as to what might be analogous

[79] Case 270/83 *Commission* v *French Republic* [1986] ECR 273 (ECJ) ('avoir fiscal').

cases. The results are rather hit and miss, decisions relying purely on the cases referred to the ECJ. There has been no systematic approach to the detection and testing of possible breaches of EU Law in the direct tax laws of the member states, although the Commission has taken a more active role in recent years. As will be noted throughout this book, case law is lacking in many important areas where EU Law may apply to direct taxation.

When the ECJ has made a decision, there is often the further issue of courts interpreting domestic law in accordance with the decision. In the *Vodafone 2* case,[80] Morritt C was faced with interpreting UK tax law in light of the ECJ decision in *Cadbury Schweppes*.[81] In doing so, he adopted principles set out by counsel for the UK tax administration:

> [T]he obligation on the English courts to construe domestic legislation consistently with Community law obligations is both broad and far-reaching. In particular:
>
> (a) It is not constrained by conventional rules of construction...
> (b) It does not require ambiguity in the legislative language...
> (c) It is not an exercise in semantics or linguistics...
> (d) It permits departure from the strict and literal application of the words which the legislature has elected to use...
> (e) It permits the implication of words necessary to comply with Community law obligations...
> (f) The precise form of the words to be implied does not matter...[82]

This case is further discussed below at 4.1.2.2. On the facts, the Court of Appeal was willing to interpret words into UK tax law that the Judge at first instance thought would be an unjustified exercise of legislative power.

[80] *Vodafone 2* v *RCC* [2009] EWCA Civ 446 (CA).
[81] Case C-196/04 *Cadbury Schweppes* [2006] ECR I-7995 (ECJ).
[82] *Vodafone 2* v *RCC* [2009] EWCA Civ 446 (CA) at para. 37.

2

The jurisdiction to tax

The basic obligation of community members to fund their government was noted at 1.1. It was also noted that the fundamental justification for a government levying taxes on their community members is the services provided by the government to community members. This is inherent in the concept of responsible government. However, each community is only one member of a larger community, the community of nations. As members of various communities are mobile and may receive services from governments other than their own, the issue arises as to who are the persons from which a particular government may appropriately extract taxes. In other words, on whom does the obligation to fund a particular government fall? This issue is traditionally analysed according to the doctrine of *economic allegiance*.

The doctrine of *economic allegiance* suggests that those who benefit from government services are obliged to fund the government.[1] Put another way, a particular government has no justification, no jurisdiction to tax unless there is an appropriate connecting factor, i.e. a recognised basis of economic allegiance. This chapter is structured under two primary headings. The first heading considers which forms of economic allegiance are recognised in international tax law as grounding a jurisdiction to impose income tax. This consideration highlights that a person may simultaneously owe economic allegiance to more than one state, i.e. divided allegiance. This raises the potential for a double or multiple imposition of income tax and questions as to whether double taxation is appropriate and, if not, how any relief should be organised. Divided allegiance is considered under the second primary heading.

2.1 Forms of economic allegiance

The concept of economic allegiance, with its inherent regulation of taxing rights, sits uneasily with the idea of national sovereignty. Whether there

[1] For a more detailed consideration of the doctrine of economic allegiance, see Harris (1996, pp. 276–7) and the references cited therein.

is any limitation on a state's taxing power with respect to international or foreign dealings will be determined by domestic constitutional law, customary international law, administrative considerations and, of course, any treaty limitations. Customary international law is particularly vague in this area, but it is, perhaps, appropriate to suggest that it requires some sort of connecting factor, some link to a state in order for that state to have a recognisable jurisdiction to tax. This may be little more than a reflection of the fact that, if there is no connecting factor, a state will find it near impossible to enforce its tax outside its territorial limits. Many states, including the UK, are reluctant to enforce the tax laws of other states.[2] It is useful to take a UK example to demonstrate the difficulties in pinning down the concept of economic allegiance and reducing it to appropriate connecting factors.

Agassi v *Robinson* involved the famous tennis player Andre Agassi.[3] Agassi was not and never had been resident or domiciled in the UK but he did come to play tennis tournaments in the UK (including Wimbledon). Agassi owned and controlled a company, which was neither incorporated nor resident in the UK. The business of Agassi's company included entering into contracts with manufacturers of sports clothing and equipment. Agassi would sponsor or advertise the manufacturers' products in return for payments made to his company. This type of contract had been entered into with Nike and Head; neither was incorporated, resident nor carried on a business in the UK. Agassi played tournaments in the UK in the 1998/99 tax year. In the same year, his company received payments from Nike and Head. The payments were not received in the UK. These payments were made between foreign companies, outside the UK.

The UK tax administration argued that the payments had a prescribed connection with Agassi's activities in the UK and that Nike and Head should have deducted UK tax from the payments made to Agassi's company and remitted it to the UK tax administration. Agassi argued that Parliament could not have intended to subject foreign individuals and companies with no residence or trading presence in the UK to such UK tax obligations.[4] The tax administration argued that if Agassi was right it would mean that foreign entertainers and sportsmen, who earned money from commercial sponsorship contracts connected with their professional

[2] This is reflected in the move to extend tax treaties to provide for mutual assistance in the collection of taxes, further discussed below at 7.3.

[3] [2006] UKHL 23 (HL).

[4] The relevant provision was ICTA 1988 s. 555(2); now see ITA 2007 s. 966.

activities in the UK, could avoid liability to UK tax on that money. They could do this simply by ensuring that the payment was made to a foreign company with no trading presence or assets in the UK.

While the UK courts agreed that the law to be applied was settled, applying that law to the facts proved divisive. The Special Commissioners and the Judge at first instance found in favour of the tax administration, the Court of Appeal found in favour of the taxpayer, while the House of Lords in a split decision found in favour of the tax administration. In the course of his judgment, Lord Scott noted:

> Counsel for Mr Agassi relies very heavily on well-known authorities such as *Re Sawers, ex p Blain* (1879) 12 Ch D 522 and, more recently, *Clark (Inspector of Taxes)* v *Oceanic Contractors Inc.* [1983] 2 AC 130. In *Ex p Blain* James LJ referred (at 526) to the:
>
> > broad, general, universal principle that English legislation, unless the contrary is expressly enacted or so plainly implied as to make it the duty of an English Court to give effect to an English statute, is applicable only to English subjects or to foreigners who by coming into this country, whether for a long or a short time, have made themselves during that time subject to English jurisdiction...
>
> And in the *Oceanic Contractors* case, Lord Scarman, having cited the above passage with approval repeated ([1983] 2 AC 130 at 145) the same principle. But Lord Scarman noted also that 'the principle is a rule of construction only' and that 'British tax liability has never been exclusively limited to British subjects and foreigners resident within the jurisdiction'. And Lord Wilberforce ([1983] 2 AC 130 at 152) referred to the 'territorial principle' as being 'really a rule of construction of statutes expressed in general terms'. The question to be asked, said Lord Wilberforce, is '[w]ho... is within the legislative grasp, or intendment, of the statute under consideration?'[5]

The result is that there are customary limits on the right to tax, even if only rooted in practical considerations. Custom requires some factor connecting the subject of taxation to the taxing jurisdiction. In the context of an income tax, what factors might be relevant? To explore these

[5] [2006] UKHL 23 (HL) at para. 16. In *Clark* v *Oceanic Contractors Inc.*, Lord Scarman noted that 'Parliament recognises the almost universally accepted principle that fiscal legislation is not enforceable outside the limits of the territorial sovereignty of the kingdom. Fiscal legislation is no doubt drafted in the knowledge that it is the practice of nations not to enforce the fiscal legislation of other nations. But, in the absence of any clear indications to the contrary it does not necessarily follow that Parliament has in its fiscal legislation intended any limitation other than that imposed by such unenforceability.' [1983] 2 AC 130 (HL) at 145.

factors, it is best to return to some fundamentals outlined at 1.1. At that point, a distinction was made between a *personal* tax and an *in rem* tax. The first focuses on the person and, in particular, personal circumstances. The second focuses on an activity or thing. When stepping into an international setting, it is not surprising that a personal tax requires some connection between the person and the taxing jurisdiction and an *in rem* tax requires some connection between the activity or thing and the taxing jurisdiction.

So, which is an income tax, a personal tax or an *in rem* tax? The *composite tax* principle recognises that, in an international setting, an income tax is both.[6] The UK income tax has always recognised this, as did its predecessors dating back to 1515 and earlier.[7] The income tax often focuses on the activity or thing from which the income is derived and at the same time the person deriving the income. Since progressive taxation became popular more than a century ago, the focus of the income tax has been on the person but the *in rem* element remains important in an international setting. In terms of economic allegiance, if a person who derives income or an activity or thing that generates income is within or sufficiently connected with a particular state that state is entitled to a contribution towards public services. This heading proceeds to consider each of these forms of economic allegiance in turn.

2.1.1 The person

Most states seek to exercise jurisdiction to impose income tax based on a sufficient connection between a person deriving income and that state. What sort of connection with the person is sufficient for this purpose? There are a number of possible connecting factors based on the person, some borrowed from other areas of law. These include presence, residence or domicile within the jurisdiction as well as citizenship or nationality of the state concerned. Some of these possible connections are more substantial than others and some are more formal. When assessing the

[6] For further on the composite tax principle, see Harris (1996, pp. 447–50).

[7] Regarding source and residence in the UK's first modern income tax of 1799, see Harris (2006, pp. 413–18). The direct tax law of 1515 is the first that clearly and expressly taxed movables of persons resident in England and movables situated in England of those not resident. The law of 1489 expressly taxed land on the basis of situs and movables on the basis of residence. In a non-legislative form, taxation on the alternate basis of inhabiting or situs of property dates back to at least the fourteenth century. See Harris (2006, pp. 44, 55 and 58–9) and the references cited therein.

appropriateness of a connecting factor perhaps it is useful to recall that taxes, including the income tax, are general contributions towards government and the primary justification for demanding a contribution is the services government provides. So any substantial imposition of tax should be supported by the potential to receive substantial government services.

Residence is generally accepted as an appropriate connection justifying the imposition of income tax. It is not too fleeting, as mere presence may be, and is not too formal, as citizenship may be. A person may be present in a particular state but not receive any substantial government services. The same may be argued with respect to citizenship, where the person is not living within the state of citizenship. Nevertheless, some countries, including the US and Mexico, do use citizenship as a connecting factor in their domestic income tax law. Domicile can also be rather formalistic, although precisely what it means and how it is tested varies from country to country. The UK uses domicile as a connecting factor for limited purposes.[8] This book proceeds to focus on residence as the accepted connecting factor founding economic allegiance based on the person but it will note presence and nationality as relevant at various points.

While residence is the primary connecting factor founding economic allegiance based on the person, a preliminary question is what does 'person' even mean? This is important not only in relation to the charge to tax under domestic law but also in relation to the application of tax treaties. In particular, Article 1 of the OECD Model states:

> This Convention shall apply to persons who are residents of one or both of the Contracting States.

This provision highlights the two issues with which this subheading is concerned. The first is identifying who or what is considered a person for the purposes of international tax law. The second is when is a person sufficiently connected with a particular state such that the person is considered a resident of that state. As Article 1 demonstrates, these issues are critically important under tax treaties, but, in this respect, tax treaties essentially reflect the relevance of these issues in domestic law. The following discussion considers the issues of who is a person and when a person is resident from both domestic law and tax treaty perspectives.

[8] Persons that are resident but not domiciled in the UK (under UK law there is a substantial difference between the two) receive a special treatment as regards their foreign source income. See Tiley (2008, pp. 1137–45). Non-domiciliaries are not further considered in this book.

As EU Law is not concerned with the imposition of tax, these issues are not so clearly reflected in EU Law. Nevertheless, there are analogous issues. These issues involve what sort of entities may potentially rely on rights granted by EU Law and what sort of factors connecting such entities to the EU are sufficient to entitle an entity to the rights provided by EU Law. These EU Law issues are also considered under this subheading.

2.1.1.1 Who is a person: the tax subject

A person may be a natural person (an individual) or a legal person (an artificial person). An individual is a person (a *natural* person) and this will be recognised under the tax laws of all states and for the purposes of tax treaties. But what is the position with various forms of organisation or entity such as companies, partnerships, clubs or trusts? Are these organisations or entities regarded as possessing separate legal personality for general law purposes and, if so, is that separate personality recognised for tax purposes? If they do not possess separate personality at general law, are they nevertheless recognised as a person for tax law purposes, i.e. recognised as a tax subject?

An organisation that is not recognised as a person (whether for general law or tax law purposes) is said to be *transparent*, i.e. the law *looks through* it to see who are the persons that stand behind it and so, for example, who are to be charged to tax. In the case of a partnership, is the partnership regarded as a person in its own right and taxed on its income? Alternatively, is the partnership regarded as transparent and, instead, the partners taxed on their respective shares of the income derived through the partnership? The issue of identifying which organisations and entities are considered 'persons' is often referred to as an issue of 'entity characterisation' or 'entity classification'.

Domestic characterisation of entities Domestic tax law will specify which entities are considered persons for its purposes, i.e. identify who are tax subjects. In this context, domestic tax law must deal with two issues. The first is characterisation of entities organised under domestic law and the second is characterisation of entities organised under foreign law. The latter may be taxed in their own right, where there is a sufficient connecting factor with the taxing state, but even where they are not, the characterisation of foreign entities can be important in determining the tax treatment of a domestic entity, e.g. in working out what type of income has been derived by a domestic entity.

Generally, the domestic law under which domestic entities or other forms of association are established will provide whether they are to be regarded as having separate personality and what is the effect of that separate personality. Domestic tax law usually respects the characterisation given by the general domestic law but this is not always the case and the exceptions can be important in practice. Tax law can vary from general law in this respect in two ways. First, the domestic tax law may treat some entities that do not have legal personality at general law as nevertheless a person for tax law purposes. Alternatively, an entity that has legal personality at general law may nevertheless be treated as transparent for tax law purposes.

UK tax law provides examples of both these approaches. Section 1121 of CTA 2010 provides that:

> 'company' … means any body corporate or unincorporated association, but does not include a partnership, a local authority or a local authority association.[9]

A 'body corporate' is an entity that has a separate legal personality. So, by definition, an 'unincorporated association' does not have a legal personality but is nevertheless treated as a company for tax purposes and so a person.[10] Partnerships are excluded from this definition and would not otherwise be regarded as a person for tax purposes. However, partnerships set up under the Limited Liability Partnerships Act 2000 (UK) are granted many of the characteristics of a company, including, under section 1, separate personality. Section 1258 of CTA 2009, however, provides that a partnership 'is not to be regarded for corporation tax purposes as an entity separate and distinct from the partners'. The effect is that a limited liability partnership is regarded as transparent for tax purposes despite its separate legal personality under the Limited Liability Partnerships Act 2000.

The UK is not peculiar in this disjuncture between the characterisation of entities under tax law and that under general law. Under section 7701(a)

[9] A similar definition is used in ITA 2007 s. 992.

[10] The position is slightly more complex than this as the Interpretation Act 1978 Sch. 1 defines 'person' to include a 'body of persons'. The latter term is defined in CTA 2010 s. 1119 and ITA 2007 s. 989 to mean 'any body politic, corporate or collegiate and any company, fraternity, fellowship and society of persons whether corporate or not corporate'. This definition of 'body of persons' is based on the coverage of entities and organisations under the direct tax of England predating the introduction of the modern income tax in 1799. Its origins can be seen in the direct tax law of 1489, which referred to both 'fraternity' and whether 'incorporate or not incorporate'. See Harris (2006, pp. 59 and 412). See also Avery Jones (1991).

(3) of the US Internal Revenue Code, 'corporation' is defined to include 'associations, joint-stock companies, and insurance companies'. Being an *includes* definition, the term 'corporation' encompasses anything that is 'incorporated' under US law. The definition extends the ordinary meaning of this term by the specific inclusions and so the definition anticipates that things other than corporations might be considered corporations for tax purposes. In *Morrissey* v *Commissioner* the US Supreme Court suggested that an organisation will be treated as an association if the corporate characteristics are such that the organisation more nearly resembles a corporation than a partnership or trust.[11] Relevant corporate characteristics include such things as association (more than one person), objective to carry on business and divide the gains therefrom, continuity of life, centralisation of management, limited liability, free transferability of interests and holding title to property as an entity.[12]

In the result, the US adopts a substance approach to what is an 'association' for the purposes of being a corporation under the tax law. So, depending on their characteristics, limited partnerships and some trusts may have found themselves being taxed as corporations. The substance approach was problematic in itself, but the US states added to the problems by enacting Limited Liability Company statutes. These laws played on the federal list, trying to grant organisations as many corporate attributes as possible without resulting in classification as a corporation for US federal tax purposes. From the start of 1997, the US tax administration gave up on this approach and adopted an elective regime know as the 'check-the-box' regime. Under this regime many business entities may elect whether to be treated as a corporation or transparent for tax purposes.[13]

Divergence may also arise in the domestic tax law characterisation of corporate groups. Under corporate law, each member of a corporate group is a separate person, although corporate law may *pierce the corporate veil* of subsidiaries for various purposes and consolidated accounts will be required. In the majority of countries, domestic tax law follows suit and generally views subsidiaries as tax subjects separate from their parent corporation. In principle, this separate entity approach recognises transactions

[11] (1935) 296 US 344 (SC). In this case, a trust created to develop certain real estate was treated as a corporation for tax purposes.

[12] These factors were used by the US tax administration in the former regulation on section 7701.

[13] See Title 26 Code of Federal Regulations (US) § 301.7701–1 and following. The election is not available for businesses incorporated under state laws, insurance companies, banks and state owned corporations. The election is made by filing Form 8832.

between members of a corporate group and gives rise to the problem of transfer pricing, discussed in an international context at 3.3.1. However, there are exceptions to the separate entity approach for corporate groups in domestic tax laws. In particular, some countries consolidate the identity of subsidiaries into their parent corporation and only the parent (representing the whole group) is considered a tax subject for various domestic tax law purposes.[14]

As mentioned, domestic tax law needs to characterise not only domestic entities but also those organised under foreign laws. The immediate problem with foreign entities is that these are entities unknown to domestic law. Some countries recognise legal status granted by a foreign country, but in other countries, particularly common law countries, that is not the case. As expressed in one UK case:

> The position of a foreign company of any sort in this country is really anomalous. A foreign company is not recognised as a legal entity; there is no definition of or status given to a foreign company. It is only by the comity of nations that we recognise that there are such things as companies which have an entity analogous to the incorporated company as we know it over here.[15]

So what status is to be given to a foreign entity? How should it be characterised for domestic tax purposes? The approach adopted by the UK courts, which is somewhat similar to the approach adopted in a number of other countries, is a two stage process:

(i) Ask what characteristics are given to the entity by the foreign corporate or commercial law. The treatment under the foreign *tax* law is generally irrelevant in this process. Therefore, in classifying a US entity for UK tax purposes it is irrelevant what election the entity has made in the US as to how it is to be treated for US tax purposes, whether as transparent or not.[16]

[14] There are various approaches to consolidation for tax purposes, which recognise to varying extents the separate identity of group members. Australia and the Netherlands are two countries that adopt relatively pure versions of consolidation, which essentially collapses the identity of subsidiaries into that of their parent corporations. See Income Tax Assessment Act 1997 (Australia) s. 701–1 and Corporate Income Tax Act (*Wet op de vennootschapsbelasting* 1969) (Netherlands) Art. 15(1).

[15] Lord Hanworth in *Ryall v Du Bois* (1933) 18 TC 431 (CA) at 440. Also, see Lord Hanworth in *Dreyfus* v *CIR* (1929) 14 TC 560 (CA) at 575–6.

[16] Tax laws are changing, if somewhat slowly. A number of circumstances are noted in Chapter 5 where the domestic tax law treatment does depend on how an entity is characterised under a foreign *tax* law.

(ii) Given those characteristics, ask whether the entity is one that would be regarded as transparent or as a separate entity under the general law of the UK. Is it more like a partnership (transparent) or a corporation (separate personality)?

A particular difficulty in the UK in making an appropriate comparison is that the UK really has only three forms in which business may be conducted. These are the individual (sole trader), the partnership (transparent) and the company (separate personality).[17] In civil law countries, there tends to be a much wider range of choice.

A leading UK case on characterisation illustrates the approach. In *Dreyfus* v *CIR*,[18] a French *société en nom collectif*, Louis Dreyfus et Compagnie, was carrying on business in the UK through a branch. The question for the court was whether it was to be regarded as a separate entity for UK tax purposes, so that it was itself taxable on the profits arising, or whether it was to be treated as transparent. The court considered carefully and quoted from the various features attributed to the *société* in the facts as found by the Special Commissioners:

> 'A *société en nom collectif* owes its existence not to the combination of the parties but to a written document which must be (i) deposited with the Registrar of the Commercial Court and with the Civil Court and (ii) published in a paper of legal publications.' Now as we are proceeding to investigate the question whether or not the result of the execution of this deed was to constitute a partnership according to English law, it is perhaps material to note that in Lord Lindley's book on Partnership: 'Partnership, though often called a contract, is a relation resulting from a contract.' Now we are told that this '*société*' owes its existence not to the combination of the parties at all but to a written document, and it is there and there only that you will find what is the nature of the embodiment of these persons. I read on [from the Special Commissioners' findings as to French law]: 'When these formalities have been complied with the *société* becomes a legal person as from the date of the deed, distinct from the individuals of which it is composed… The ownership of the assets of the *société* is in the *société* alone and not in the individuals who compose it. The debts of the *société* are its own debts and not the debts of the members. Only the managing associés (*gérants*) can bind the *société*.'[19]

[17] Unlike many other common law jurisdictions, such as Australia, New Zealand, South Africa and the US, the trading trust is relatively unknown in the UK.

[18] (1929) 14 TC 560 (CA).

[19] (1929) 14 TC 560 (CA) at 573–4 per Lord Hanworth.

Lord Hanworth then noted that an 'inventory' must be made at the end of each year and the net profits distributed. The evidence was that the associés meet to examine the balance sheet and profit and loss account for the year and the *société* then makes various resolutions and a distribution of the profit is taken at the instance of the *société*. Lord Hanworth concluded that the associés were 'associates' of the entity 'but they were not partners inter se'.[20]

The current view of the UK tax administration is that the case was wrongly decided and that a French *société en nom collectif* is comparable to a partnership.[21] Indeed, it is similar to a partnership formed in the UK under Scots law, which has separate personality and can hold assets in its own name. Perhaps the real question is not simply whether there is separate personality but rather, where there is separate personality, what is the *effect* of that separate personality? The UK tax administration's view seems to be that if fuller evidence had been presented in *Dreyfus* concerning the position on the distribution of the profits to the members the *société* would have been found to be a partnership and transparent.[22] Perhaps this misses the point and the real question is: 'To whom do the profits belong?' It is possible for an organisation to be considered a person for tax purposes and nevertheless for profits to be allocated as derived by its owners. That is, there are two issues, one of classification of the entity and the other of allocation of the income.

As mentioned, the characterisation of a foreign entity can also be important where a resident person receives (and there is no dispute that the recipient is a 'person') income from an entity formed under the law of another state. This characterisation of the foreign entity may determine the character of the income in the hands of the recipient and the location of the source from which that income is received. This point is illustrated by the UK case of *Ryall* v *Du Bois*.[23] A UK resident corporation was the beneficial owner of

[20] *Ibid* at 575.

[21] The HMRC *International Manual* para. 180030 lists foreign entities that the tax administration considers are transparent or 'opaque' (a separate tax subject) for UK tax purposes. The French *société en nom collectif* is listed as transparent. See www.hmrc.gov.uk/manuals/intmanual/INTM180020.htm, accessed 5 March 2010.

[22] This is consistent with the finding in *Von Hellfeld* v *E Rechnitzer and Mayer Fréres and Co* [1914] 1 Ch 748 (CA). This was a conflicts of law case where the court set a writ aside on the ground that the plaintiff had failed to demonstrate to the satisfaction of the court that a French *société en nom collectif* had the attributes of a corporate entity. It seems this case was not cited in *Dreyfus*. Also, see *Oxnard Financing SA* v *Rahn* [1998] 1 WLR 1465 (CA) and the case note in Kent (1999).

[23] (1933) 18 TC 431 (CA).

all the capital of a German *Gesellschaft mit beschränkter Haftung* (GmbH, as it is usually abbreviated). The issue for the court was what was the nature of this interest held in the GmbH. Was it in the nature of a share in a corporation or was it a direct participation in the profits of the GmbH? If the former, income from the interest would be akin to dividends, if the latter it would be of the nature of business profits derived by the GmbH. The answer was important because under domestic law at that time income arising from 'stocks, shares or rents in any place out of the United Kingdom' was taxed on a different basis to profits arising from a foreign trade. The Court of Appeal refused to reverse the decision of the Judge at first instance, who decided that what was received was 'income from stocks and shares'.[24]

Finally, in relation to foreign entity classification, it is useful to again turn to US experience. The US approach to the classification of domestic entities was discussed above. The same approach was also adopted for the classification of foreign entities but with increased importance as no foreign entity fell within the ordinary meaning of the term 'corporation', that term being reserved for entities organised under US law. This means that many foreign entities may elect (check-the-box) whether to be treated as transparent or a corporation for US tax purposes. An increasing number of foreign entities are being placed on the 'per se' list, resulting in their classification as a corporation without a choice. These are typically foreign entities of a type that may be listed on the local stock exchange and so include the UK public company as well as the German stock corporation (*Aktiengesellschaft*) and the European Company (*Societas Europaea*).[25]

Meaning of 'person' in the OECD Model Article 1 of the OECD Model initially limits application of a tax treaty to resident 'persons'. The Model goes on to frame its own definition of 'person'. Article 3(1) provides:

> a. the term 'person' includes an individual, a company and any other body of persons;
> b. the term 'company' means any body corporate or any entity that is treated as a body corporate for tax purposes.

[24] Two cases that similarly involved the classification of interests in foreign entities in order to determine the character of income received by a resident are *Garland* v *Archer-Shee* [1931] AC 212 (HL) (a New York trust) and *Memec plc* v *CIR* [1998] STC 754 (CA) (a German silent partnership).

[25] See Title 26 Code of Federal Regulations (US) § 301.7701–2(b). In mid-2009, President Obama proposed substantially tightening up the circumstances in which a foreign entity is treated as transparent under the check-the-box regime.

As discussed above at 1.3.2, when interpreting a term, Article 3(2) requires reference back to the law of the state applying the treaty, unless the term is defined in the treaty or the context otherwise requires.

The central issues arising under these definitions of 'person' and 'company' may be explored by considering the position of a partnership under the OECD Model.[26] The UK case of *Padmore* provides an illustration.[27] A UK resident was a partner in a Jersey partnership. The partnership conducted no business in the UK. The double tax relief order (equivalent of a treaty) between Jersey and the UK dated from 1952 and had similarities with the OECD Model, but the two were still substantially different. In particular, the order provided that a Jersey enterprise was not to be taxed in the UK unless it had a permanent establishment in the UK.[28] The taxpayer argued that the partnership was a 'person' as defined in the order and so the UK could not tax the UK partners on their share of the partnership profits. The UK tax administration pointed out the anomaly this would create. If the taxpayer's contention was upheld, the UK could tax a UK individual carrying on business in Jersey as a sole proprietor, it could also tax the dividends of a Jersey corporation distributed to a UK resident but it would never have a right to tax a UK partner in a Jersey partnership.

The case largely turned on the definition of the word 'person' in the 1952 order and whether it included the Jersey partnership. Like the OECD Model, the definition included 'any body of persons' but with the additional words 'corporate or not corporate'. The phrase 'body of persons' is not defined in the OECD Model and so, unless the context otherwise requires, it will take its meaning under the law of the state applying the treaty, i.e. by reason of Article 3(2). This is what the UK tax administration argued and, by reference to domestic law, it suggested that a partnership was not a 'body of persons'.[29] While that may be the correct position with respect to wording based on the OECD Model, unfortunately for the UK tax administration the definition of 'person' in the 1952 order included 'any body of persons, corporate or not corporate'. The words 'corporate or not corporate' are used in the UK domestic law definition of 'body of persons'. This was reason for

[26] The OECD Commentary to Article 1 paras. 2–6.7 tries to address some of these issues in the context of the application of the Model to partnerships classified differently by different states. This will be returned to in Chapter 5.

[27] *Padmore* v *IRC* (1989) 62 TC 352.

[28] OECD Model Art. 7 is to similar effect, discussed further below at 3.1.3.3.

[29] See the definition in CTA 2010 s. 1119, reproduced in footnote 10 above. The argument seems to be that a partnership is not edjustim generis with the other entities and organisations referred to. Generally, see Avery Jones (1991).

the court to reflect and ultimately come to the conclusion that the phrase 'body of persons' in the 1952 order should not take a technical meaning from UK domestic law but should be given its ordinary meaning in the context of the 1952 order. In the result, the Jersey partnership was a 'body of persons' and so a 'person' referred to in the order. The court proceeded to hold that the partnership was resident in Jersey and the UK could not tax the UK partners on their share of profits from the partnership.

Padmore is instructive on a number of levels despite the fact that the wording of the treaty in question did not precisely follow the OECD Model. First, it demonstrates the importance of the term 'person', a fundamental in applying tax treaties. Second, it illustrates the care that must be taken when interpreting the wording of a tax treaty and, in particular, the importance of Article 3(2) of the OECD Model.[30] Third, it illustrates the care that must be taken when drafting tax treaties, particularly when altering the wording of the Model. Finally, 'body of persons' is a well-known phrase in UK tax law; a *term of art*, but that phrase is virtually unknown in most other countries. How would a court interpret it where the OECD wording was followed, without additions like those in *Padmore*? Would a court accept the UK internal meaning or would it nevertheless give the phrase a treaty meaning, as in *Padmore*? Giving the term a technical UK meaning would likely result in the term being applied differently in each of the two contracting states, if the phrase does not have the same technical meaning in the other state. Giving the phrase a special treaty meaning may not give effect to the intention of the contracting states, at least the UK. Is it possible that the phrase could be interpreted and intended to have a domestic meaning in the UK but nevertheless have a treaty meaning in the other contracting state?[31]

Another type of organisation raising interesting issues as to classification under tax treaties are US limited liability companies (LLCs). As mentioned, these organisations are not expressed to be corporate but are granted many corporate characteristics by US state legislatures. They will not be a 'company' within the definition of that term in Article 3(1) of the OECD Model unless they are characterised as such by domestic law. So, for example, this is likely to be the case in the UK, given the definition of 'company' in ICTA 1988 discussed above, but will not be the case in the

[30] Tax treaty interpretation was discussed above at 1.3.2.

[31] Avery Jones et al. (2006, p. 699) suggest '[t]he internal tax law meaning, which for example does not include a partnership, is almost certainly not intended to be incorporated into treaties, a case of the context otherwise requiring'.

US if an LLC makes an election under the check-the-box regime to be taxed on a transparent basis. Nevertheless, an LLC is likely to be a 'person' under Article 3(1) as a 'body of persons'.[32] Even the technical UK meaning of this phrase should cover an LLC.

Finally, it is useful to say a few words about corporate groups. It was noted above that the domestic law of a number of countries identifies corporate groups as tax subjects rather than each of the group members. That is not the approach taken in tax treaties, which invariably recognise each member of a corporate group as a separate 'person'.[33] In particular, the OECD Model defines 'person' to include a 'company' and a 'company' to mean a 'body corporate'. In the vast majority of cases, a subsidiary is a body corporate and so a 'person' for tax treaty purposes, as will be its parent, but could the group be a 'body of persons' and so a person of itself? A special treaty meaning seems to open this possibility.

2.1.1.2 Residence as a connecting factor

Once the tax subject, the 'person', is identified, the next issue is whether that person has the appropriate degree of economic allegiance to justify taxation. As mentioned, the focus here is on the customary form of economic allegiance of the person recognised in international tax law, that of residence. It is essentially a question of domestic law whether a person is resident in a particular state. Tax treaties respect this classification, but with important qualifications. In either case, because income tax is typically imposed for periods of one year, there is the further question as to whether a person can be resident for part of a year or whether they can be resident only for full years. This latter issue is explored briefly below at 6.2.1.

Domestic law Different countries adopt different tests for determining whether a person is resident in their jurisdiction. Necessarily, these tests differ depending on the nature of the person and, in particular, whether the person is a natural person (an individual) or an artificial person such as a corporation. With respect to individuals, most tests focus on the maintenance of a dwelling or abode in the particular country.[34] However,

32 This may not be the case, e.g. where the LLC is owned and run by a single person. The HMRC *International Manual* para. 180030 lists a US LLC as 'opaque'. See www.hmrc.gov.uk/manuals/intmanual/INTM180020.htm, accessed 5 March 2010.

33 See Sasseville (2008) and Vann (2006, p. 363). This is reinforced by OECD Model Art. 5(7), discussed below at 3.1.3.3.

34 The original approach in English direct tax law was to ask whether a person was an 'inhabitant' of the realm. The 'inhabitant' test is seen as early as the fourteenth century.

other factors usually include family and social ties, income-producing activities, bank accounts, citizenship, domicile, right to stay (e.g. visa status) and a prolonged physical presence in a country. A common test in the latter respect is the 183-day (half year) test. The approach is usually to consider the facts and circumstances of a particular individual and weigh up on balance whether there is sufficient connection with the state to find the individual is resident there.

Determining the residence of an individual can be a complex matter and often depends on the facts of the situation. Most often, this has little to do with cross-border commercial transactions, which are the focus of this book, and so little time will be spent on this issue. With respect to UK domestic law, it is suffice to note that there is no statutory definition of 'residence' and the matter is largely determined according to case law with some statutory qualifications. The case law largely takes into consideration the types of issues referred to in the last paragraph when weighing up whether on balance an individual is resident in the UK.[35] A 183-day test is part of the statutory qualifications under which an individual that is in the UK for some temporary purpose and has not resided in the UK for 183 days or more in a tax year may not be considered a resident for specified purposes.[36]

The facts and circumstances test usually applied to individuals does not work well when applied to artificial persons. Artificial persons are legal fictions and do not have personal, family or social attributes. At some level, determining where, say, a corporation 'resides' is a nonsense and its relevance is probably explained only by history. Early direct tax laws focused on individuals when they spoke of 'inhabiting' or 'residing' and these laws predate the existence of the modern corporation by hundreds of years. When a corporation was referred to, it would be in the sense of one granted its legal personality by the state in question and the residence of corporations would not have been envisaged.[37]

The graduated poll tax of 1379 is the first to expressly use the word 'resident' although for many years the word 'inhabitant' and 'resident' were used interchangeably. See Harris (2006, pp. 43, 45 and 67–8).

35 Generally regarding the residence of individuals under UK law, see Tiley (2008, pp. 1097–103).

36 ITA 2007 s. 831. The origins of the 183-day test in the UK are old. The first modern income tax of 1799 treated persons temporarily in Great Britain as not resident. The amending act of 1800 introduced a rule that a person was deemed resident after a presence of six months. See Harris (2006, pp. 416 and 421).

37 For example, see the reference to 'corporation ... within England' in the direct tax of 1553 referred to in Harris (2006, pp. 67–8).

As the registered company became common during the second part of the nineteenth century, courts were asked to apply the general wording of the tax law to these companies, including the concept of residence. In the first UK reported tax case on corporate residence in 1876, Baron Huddleston stated:

> [t]he use of the word 'residence' is founded upon the habits of a natural man, and is therefore inapplicable to the artificial and legal person whom we call a corporation. But for the purpose of giving effect to the words of the legislature an artificial residence must be assigned to this artificial person, and one formed on the analogy of natural persons.[38]

Two main tests have developed in this struggle to determine the residence of artificial persons under domestic tax laws. Most countries now use a combination of both tests. These countries include Australia, Austria, Belgium, Denmark, France, Germany, Ireland, Italy, Luxembourg, the Netherlands, Portugal, Spain and the UK.

The first test for corporate residence focuses on the state under whose law the artificial person is organised or from which it gains its status. In the context of corporations, this is usually the state of incorporation, registered office or, in civil law jurisdictions, statutory seat. This is a simple, formal test and once a corporation is formed under the law of a particular state, it is not open to manipulation.[39] A number of countries, including Finland, Greece, Sweden and the US, use this test as the sole determinant of the residence of a corporation.

The alternate test for corporate residence is based on the place of management or principal office. Most often, the focus is on where high-level management decisions are made. This can be a difficult test to apply, particularly so in this era of electronic means of communication, and it may not be clear where such management decisions are made or they may be made in a number of places simultaneously. High-level management decisions are particularly mobile and so this test is open to manipulation. This is the traditional case law based approach in the UK and, as a result, is

[38] *Calcutta Jute Mills* v *Nicholson* (1876) 1 ExD 428 (Ex) at 432. Also see Lord Lorburn in *De Beers Consolidated Mines* v *Howe* [1906] AC 455 (HL) at 458.

[39] Case C-212/97 *Centros Ltd* v *Erhvervs- og Selskabsstyrelsen* [1999] ECR I-1459 (ECJ) and the cases that follow it hold that a corporation may be incorporated in one member state and carry on its business wholly in another solely for the purpose of avoiding the incorporation requirements of the other member state. The proposed 14th Company Law Directive would extend this to facilitate a corporation moving its place of incorporation or statutory seat from one member state to another member state. See European Parliament (2009).

often used in British Commonwealth countries. Historically, this was the only test used in most of these countries, but most now apply a combined test, though some countries continue to apply the sole traditional test.[40]

Until 1988, UK tax law did not specify any test for the residence of a corporation and the matter was left to case law. In 1906 in the *De Beers* case, the UK House of Lords finally rejected the argument that a corporation was resident in the country where it was incorporated or registered. Lord Loreburn stated:

> An individual may be of foreign nationality, and yet reside in the United Kingdom. So may a company. Otherwise it might have its chief seat of management and its centre of trading in England under the protection of English law, and yet escape the appropriate taxation by the simple expedient of being registered abroad and distributing its dividends abroad... [A] company resides for purposes of income tax where its real business is carried on... I regard that as the true rule, and the real business is carried on where the central management and control actually abides.[41]

The 'central management and control' test has been consistently applied in cases since *De Beers* and is commonly used in common law countries based on the UK tradition.

The central management and control test focuses on the highest level of decision making of the business of a corporation. Thus, in *New Zealand Shipping Co Ltd* v *Thew*, a New Zealand company with two boards of directors (one in the UK and one in New Zealand) was found to be resident in the UK because the New Zealand board was subject to the powers of the UK board.[42] The place where a corporation's board of directors meets is not always determinative of the central management and control of the corporation. This may be the case where a subsidiary follows the orders of the board of its parent corporation. Thus, in *Unit Construction Co Ltd* v *Bullock*, the East African subsidiaries of a UK parent corporation were held to be resident in the UK.[43]

[40] For example, Cyprus, Malaysia, Singapore and Trinidad are such countries: Income Tax Law of 2002 (Cyprus) s. 2, Income Tax Act, 1967 (Malaysia) s. 8, Income Tax Act (Singapore) s. 2 and Corporation Tax Act (Trinidad) s. 2.

[41] *De Beers Consolidated Mines* v *Howe* [1906] AC 455 (HL) at 458. It was part of the argument in the *De Beers* case that a foreign corporation (having no legal existence in the UK) could not be resident in the UK, if it was resident anywhere it was the place of its incorporation.

[42] (1922) 8 TC 208 (HL).

[43] [1960] AC 351 (HL).

Therefore, in the case of overseas subsidiaries of UK parent corporations, it is important to secure for the board of the subsidiary a level of independence from the board of the UK parent.[44] But what level of independence is sufficient? In *Untelrab Ltd* v *McGregor*, the test was whether the board of the subsidiary would refuse to carry out any proposal that was improper or unreasonable.[45] In *Wood* v *Holden*, Chadwick LJ in the Court of Appeal stated that:

> In seeking to determine where 'central management and control' of a company incorporated outside the United Kingdom lies, it is essential to recognise the distinction between cases where management and control of the company is exercised through its own constitutional organs (the board of directors or the general meeting) and cases where the functions of those constitutional organs are 'usurped' – in the sense that management and control is exercised independently of, or without regard to, those constitutional organs. And, in cases which fall within the former class, it is essential to recognise the distinction (in concept, at least) between the role of an 'outsider' in proposing, advising and influencing the decisions which the constitutional organs take in fulfilling their functions and the role of an outsider who dictates the decisions which are to be taken. In that context an 'outsider' is a person who is not, himself, a participant in the formal process (a board meeting or a general meeting) through which the relevant constitutional organ fulfils its function.[46]

Wood v *Holden* involved the issue of whether a Dutch corporation was resident in the UK. The corporation was a 'special purpose vehicle' in the sense that it had been set up (acquired) for a limited purpose. Special purpose vehicles are common in international transactions. The court made it clear that when dealing with special purpose vehicles, the acts of central management and control may involve very little, in this case just the purchase and sale of some shares. Another common feature of the case was that the Dutch directors acted in accordance with the instructions of tax advisers, who in this case were based in the UK. Chadwick LJ continued by quoting from Parke J at first instance:

> If directors of an overseas company sign documents mindlessly, without even thinking what the documents are, I accept that it would be difficult to say that the national jurisdiction in which the directors do that is the jurisdiction of residence of the company. But if they apply their minds to

[44] See the approach in HMRC's Statement of Practice SP1/90.

[45] (1996) STC (SCD) 1 (SC).

[46] [2006] EWCA Civ 26 (CA) at para. 27.

> whether or not to sign the documents, the authorities… indicate that it is a very different matter.[47]

In applying this UK case law test, it is important to remember the purpose for which it is being applied. The central management and control test

> is essentially a one-country test; the purpose is not to decide where residence is situated, but whether or not it is situated in the United Kingdom… There is nothing impossible in finding [central management and control] in two countries, in spite of the word 'central'.[48]

The UK relied solely on this case law test until 1988. In that year the case law test was supplemented with an incorporation test.[49] The exception to the incorporation test is where a UK incorporated company is treated as resident in another state for the purposes of a tax treaty, a point that will be returned to shortly.[50]

'Residence' under the OECD Model As has been noted, residence is critically important as a requirement for access to a tax treaty.[51] The OECD Model contains only two lengthy definitions, one of which is of 'resident' in Article 4.[52] Article 4(1) provides:

> the term 'resident of a Contracting State' means any person who, under the laws of that State, is liable to tax therein by reason of his domicile, residence, place of management or any other criterion of a similar nature… This term, however, does not include any person who is liable to tax in that State in respect only of income from sources in that State.

Therefore, Article 4(1) is primarily a reference to the domestic law definition of resident, and this causes few problems.[53] However, it raises a number of residual issues.

[47] [2006] EWCA Civ 26 (CA) at para. 36. In *Laerstate BV* v *HMRC* [2009] UKFTT 209 (TC), the First Tier Tribunal held that a sole Dutch director did not meet this test. The corporation in question was resident in the UK, where its controller was viewed as making relevant decisions.

[48] *Smallwood* v *RCC* (2008) 10 ITLR 574 (SC) at para. 111. The case goes on to cite relevant authority and notes, at para. 115, the peculiar decision in *Wood* v *Holden* [2006] EWCA Civ 26 (CA) at para. 40 that a company was resident in the Netherlands under the central management and control test, rather than just not resident in the UK.

[49] CTA 2009 s. 14.

[50] CTA 2009 s. 18.

[51] OECD Model Art. 1.

[52] The other is of 'permanent establishment' in OECD Model Art. 5, which is considered at 3.1.3.3.

[53] One issue that has been raised is whether there is a conceptual difference between treaty residence and domestic law residence. In *Smallwood* v *RCC* (2008) 10 ITLR 574 (SC) at

A first issue is what is meant by the phrase 'liable to tax'. It is generally accepted that this does not require an actual payment of tax. Therefore, a person that does not pay tax in a given year because of losses is nevertheless liable to tax. Further, subject to what is discussed below, it seems that a person that is exempt from tax on some of its income only is nevertheless 'liable to tax... by reason', etc.[54] More difficult is the case of persons that are recognised as such for tax purposes but are generally exempt based on social policy, such as charities and pension funds. The OECD Commentary suggests that countries are split in their approach to this issue, some accepting that the entities are nevertheless subject to tax and entitled to treaty benefits and others requiring that they be expressly mentioned in a treaty.[55]

The Commentary to Article 4 of the OECD Model suggests that where a partnership is treated as transparent for tax purposes, it is the partners rather than the partnership that is 'liable to tax' and so the partnership is not entitled to treaty benefits.[56] It may be presumed that a similar approach should be adopted with respect to other transparent entities, e.g. a US LLC that has elected for transparent treatment. A particular problem may arise with respect to corporate groups. If a country adopts a pure consolidation regime, the tax identity of a subsidiary is lost in the parent corporation. As discussed above at 2.1.1.1, the subsidiary will nevertheless be a 'person' for the purposes of tax treaties but will the subsidiary be a 'resident'? Is it 'liable to tax'? If not, it is not entitled to benefit from a treaty. This point is discussed further at 5.1.1.

paras. 88–102, the Special Commissioners pointed out that the treaty definition of 'resident' in OECD Model Art. 4(1) is premised on 'liability to tax' based on residence, etc. whereas often the domestic law gives rise to a charge to tax because of residence. The suggestion was that this may result in a person being considered a resident for treaty purposes before they are resident for domestic law purposes, such as where the beginning of residence during a year makes the person liable to tax for the whole of the year. In such a case, the person may be a treaty resident for the whole year but only resident for domestic law purposes for part of the year (though chargeable for the whole year). Mann J in the High Court rejected this approach. He considered, at least in the context of OECD Model Art. 13(5) (discussed below at 3.1.5), that an OECD based treaty envisaged only one residence country at any particular time. See [2009] EWHC 777 (Ch) at para. 36. These issues are touched on further below at 6.2.

54 But see OECD Commentary on Art. 4 para. 8.2 regarding 'conduit companies', discussed further below at 5.2.3.2.

55 OECD Commentary on Art. 4 paras. 8.5 and 8.6.

56 OECD Commentary on Art. 4 para. 8.7. Note that the 'liable to tax' requirement was absent from the definition of 'resident' in the order in issue in the *Padmore* case, discussed above at footnote 27. So, rather bizarrely, the partnership was entitled to the benefits of the order despite not being liable to tax in Jersey.

A second issue with Article 4(1) of the OECD Model is the effect of the reference to 'place of management'. For example, many countries, including the UK, tax non-residents if they conduct business within the state through a permanent establishment and 'permanent establishment' is often defined in domestic law to include a place of management.[57] Does this mean that a foreign company that has a place of management in the UK and is liable to tax by reason thereof is a resident of the UK and so may claim the benefits of UK tax treaties? Effectively, this was the argument run in the Canadian *Crown Forest* case.[58] In that case, a Bermuda company whose sole office and place of business was in the US, sought the benefit of the Canada/US tax treaty. In holding that the Bermuda company was not a US resident for the purposes of the treaty the Supreme Court of Canada, rather questionably, distinguished between the company's liability to tax in the US based on conducting trade or business in the US (and having income therefrom) and having a place of management in the US. The latter was a 'factual proposition which merely informs domestic tax liability' rather than constituting a 'residency criterion' under the treaty.

> [T]he only way for Norsk to benefit from residency status under the Convention is if source taxation on a business effectively connected with the contracting party constitutes a criterion similar to the other enumerated criteria in Article IV (residence, place of management, place of incorporation, domicile). It is not similar, since all of the other criteria constitute grounds for taxation on world-wide income, not just source income.[59]

The reasoning in the *Crown Forest* case is particularly questionable where a state exempts the profits of a foreign permanent establishment of a person that is resident under domestic law. This is often the case in European countries such as France and the Netherlands. For example, suppose a French bank has a UK branch and the UK branch receives income from Russia. Assume that the OECD Model applies between all countries. Can the French bank claim the benefit of the UK/Russia treaty, the France/Russia treaty or neither? One might try to argue that the residence of a person should be fragmented between states and treaty entitlement granted accordingly. However, this approach seems to be denied by the second sentence of Article 4(1), which perhaps exacerbates the problem.[60]

[57] CTA 1988 s. 19 and CTA 2010 ss. 1141–53, respectively.

[58] *Crown Forest Industries Ltd* v *Canada* [1995] 2 SCR 802 (SC).

[59] [1995] 2 SCR 802 (SC) at para. 68.

[60] OECD Commentary on Art. 4 para 8.3 notes the difficulties with the second sentence and territorial systems, without clarifying how this may be addressed.

Permanent establishments and treaty entitlement will be returned to below at 5.2.3.1.

A person (natural or artificial) may be simultaneously resident under the domestic laws of two states. This is because most countries adopt more than one test of residence and, in any case, different countries adopt different tests. However, it would be wrong to assume that a person *must* be a resident of at least one country. Take for example a corporation registered in Singapore that is centrally managed and controlled from the US. The company is not resident in Singapore, which adopts a management test only, and is not resident in the US, which adopts the place of incorporation test only, so the company may not be resident anywhere. This is not common and not necessarily a good thing as a person that is not resident anywhere will not have access to any country's tax treaty network.

The problem is, rather, with persons that are dual residents. Article 4(1) of the OECD Model initially preserves the possibility of dual residence by referring to domestic law. However, when application of domestic law results in a person being considered a resident of both contracting states, Article 4(2) and (3) contain *tiebreaker* rules. These rules are not tests of residence in themselves as they apply only if, according to the domestic laws of the contracting states, there is dual residence. Further, tiebreakers usually only determine residence for the purposes of the tax treaty in question.[61] For example, a corporation that is resident in both France and the UK might be treated as being resident only in France under the France/UK tax treaty. Does this mean that the corporation is not a resident of the UK for the purposes of other UK tax treaties? Might the corporation have access to the tax treaty networks of both France and the UK? The UK has a special domestic law rule, which provides that in such a case the corporation resident in France under the France/UK tax treaty is not treated as a UK resident for domestic law purposes.[62] The OECD Commentary was adjusted in 2008 to deal with dual resident corporations.[63] Dual resident corporations are further considered at 5.2.2.

Article 4(2) of the OECD Model contains a tiebreaker where an individual is resident in both contracting states. The test is cascading in that there is a series of progressive tests to determine the residence of the individual for the purposes of a treaty. The tiebreaker first focuses on where the individual has a permanent home: if that does not resolve the issue

[61] This should be the position in a dualist state but the position of a monist state may be different.

[62] CTA 2009 s. 18.

[63] OECD Commentary on Art. 4 para. 8.2.

then the test turns sequentially to the location of the individual's vital interests, habitual abode and nationality. If none of these tests resolves the issue then the competent authorities of the contracting states may settle the issue by mutual agreement. As mentioned, this book does not focus on the residence of individuals.

Article 4(3) of the OECD Model contains a tiebreaker where an artificial person is resident in both contracting states. It states:

> Where by reason of the provisions of paragraph 1 a person other than an individual is a resident of both Contracting States, then it shall be deemed to be a resident only of the State in which its place of effective management is situated.

This is the rule that applies to determine, for the purposes of the treaty, the residence of an otherwise dual resident corporation, the focus of the following discussion, but it applies to other artificial persons such as trusts and partnerships where they qualify as a 'person' (see above).

The main issue under Article 4(3) of the OECD Model is the meaning to be given to 'place of effective management'.[64] Does it have a special meaning,[65] a particular treaty meaning or is it to be interpreted according to domestic law under Article 3(2)? The Commentary to Article 4(3) might suggest a special treaty meaning but it is so qualified that this is not clear. The UK Special Commissioners have suggested that the word 'effective' be understood in the sense of 'real' and in doing so appear to favour a special treaty meaning.[66]

The 'place of effective management' test has regard to the substance of where responsibility lies for actual day-to-day operations. This is:

> the place where the key management and commercial decisions that are necessary for the conduct of the entity's business as a whole are in substance made.[67]

Commonly, the place of effective management is where the head office, in the sense of the central directing source of the entity, is located. In 2008, the OECD Commentary deleted a controversial reference to the place of effective management ordinarily being where 'the most senior person or group of persons (for example, a board of directors) makes it decisions'.[68] As with

[64] Regarding the origins and uncertainty surrounding this phrase, see Avery Jones (2005) and Avery Jones (2009).

[65] See Article 31(4) of the Vienna Convention, discussed above at 1.3.2.

[66] *Smallwood* v *RCC* (2008) 10 ITLR 574 (SC) at para. 112, using the French version of the OECD Model as an interpretation aid.

[67] OECD Commentary on Article 4 para. 24.

[68] OECD Commentary on Article 4 para. 24 (pre-2008 amendment).

domestic law tests of residence, in certain fact patterns there is a risk that the place of effective management of a subsidiary is with its parent.[69]

The UK tax administration previously identified effective management with central management and control, i.e. the case-based test under domestic law (see above).[70] However, the two tests have different purposes and scope of operation. First, as noted above, the better view is that in particular circumstances a corporation may be centrally managed and controlled in more than one place. By contrast, the OECD is of the opinion that a corporation can have only one place of effective management.[71] Further, the UK tax administration now accepts that the two tests do not necessarily coincide, the domestic test being more concerned with where strategic decisions are made and the treaty test rather focusing on where the top-level decisions are formulated.[72] The place of effective management of a corporation is likely to be the place where the managing director, finance director, sales director and the like are located. The corporation's records and senior administrative staff are likely to be situated there. With the 'effective management' test, there is less focus on where the directors actually meet.[73]

Note again that the tiebreaker operates only as between the two contracting states and even in this limited context may not solve a dual corporate residence issue. It will solve any type of dual residence issue provided the place of effective management is in one of the contracting states;[74] but this may not be the case. The place of effective management might be in a third country. For example, suppose a corporation is

69 See the discussion of Morritt C in *Indofood International Finance Ltd* v *JP Morgan Chase Bank NA* [2006] EWCA Civ 158 (CA) at para. 57 dealing with the setting up of a special purpose subsidiary in the Netherlands to issue loan notes guaranteed by an Indonesian parent. This case is further discussed at 5.2.3.2.

70 See *Smallwood* v *RCC* (2008) 10 ITLR 574 (SC) at paras. 119–22.

71 OECD Commentary on Article 4 para. 24. The purpose of 'effective management' as a tiebreaker would be defeated if it were in more than one place at a time.

72 However, in *Wood* v *Holden* [2006] EWCA Civ 26 (CA) at para. 6 Chadwick LJ stated that it was not clear to him that the effective management test 'differs in substance' from the central management and control test and 'if the two tests are not, in substance, the same, I find it very difficult to see how, in the circumstances ... they could lead to different answers'.

73 In Statement of Practice 1/90, the UK tax administration give as an example a company run by foreign executives but where the decisions of foreign executives are subject to approval by UK based non-executive directors. In such a case, it is possible that the corporation is effectively managed overseas but the central management and control is with the UK directors. A non-executive director is merely an officeholder and does not have a contract of service (employment) with the corporation. Further, see Oliver (2001) and Owen (2003).

74 The purpose of the place of effective management test 'is to resolve residence under domestic law in both states, caused for whatever reason, which could include incorporation in one state and management in the other, or different meanings of management

centrally managed and controlled from the UK, incorporated in France but is effectively managed in Belgium. Would the tiebreaker in the UK/France tax treaty work in such a situation? It seems unlikely. Further, it is conceivable that in this era of increased electronic communication a corporation may have no 'place' of effective management, e.g. in the case of a corporation that has four director/managers located in four different countries making equal contribution to management.

Note also that the tiebreaker in the OECD Model may not always be acceptable to states. The US is an example. As mentioned, its domestic law only has a place of incorporation test and so the US refuses to incorporate the place of effective management as a tiebreaker in its treaties. Therefore, it is not safe to presume that this is a universal tiebreaker and attention must be paid to the provisions of particular treaties. In 2008, the OECD Commentary added an alternative Article 4(3), which leaves the competent authorities to decide where a dual resident corporation is resident for the purposes of a treaty.[75]

2.1.1.3 Beneficiaries of EU Law

In accordance with the doctrine of economic allegiance, domestic tax law typically imposes tax based on source and residence. The latter of these 'connecting' factors is picked up in order to identify who are entitled to the benefits of tax treaties, i.e. only 'resident persons' are so entitled. By contrast, EU Law is not concerned with the imposition of tax and residence is not used as a connecting factor to identify who may benefit from EU Law. But, of course, EU Law must identify who is entitled to rely on that law. As noted at 1.3.3, an initial point is that the ECJ's principle of direct effect means that EU nationals can invoke EU Law, but what is the legal basis for this?

Early case law suggests that the FEU Treaty can have direct effect only as regards nationals of member states.[76] This is now reflected in Part 2 of the FEU Treaty, which provides for EU citizenship. Under Article 20(1) EU citizenship is determined by reference to the nationality of a member

applied in each state, or divided management'. *Smallwood* v *RCC* (2008) 10 ITLR 574 (SC) at para. 112.

[75] OECD Commentary on Article 4 para. 24.1.

[76] Case 26/62 *NV Algemene Transport- en Expeditie Onderneming van Gend & Loos* v *Netherlands Inland Revenue Administration* [1963] ECR 3 (ECJ). This case concerned the European Economic Community Treaty (1957). In particular, the ECJ noted that 'the nationals of the states brought together in the Community are called upon to cooperate in the functioning of this Community through the intermediary of the European Parliament and the Economic and Social Committee'.

state. In a fashion that is broadly consistent with the early case law, Article 20(2) provides:

> Citizens of the Union shall enjoy the rights and be subject to the duties provided for in the Treaties.

This might suggest that, as a minimum, nationals of member states are entitled to benefit from EU Law but the European Commission appears to interpret the EU citizenship provisions narrowly.[77] This raises two issues that are parallel to those considered above in the context of domestic tax law and tax treaties; first, which entities may qualify to be nationals and, second, what is the relevant connecting factor to qualify as a national.

Leaving aside the position of individuals, which is comparatively straightforward, can an artificial entity be regarded as a national and thereby secure the benefits of the FEU Treaty? For example, does a corporation have a nationality or is nationality something peculiar to individuals? While some EU and even international law texts are not clear on the issue, it is presumed the answer is yes.[78] So far as the connecting factor is concerned, the better view is that in common law jurisdictions a corporation is a national of its state of incorporation whereas in civil law jurisdictions it will be the place of its statutory seat.

What of entities that do not have a legal personality – can they be considered nationals? There must be a substantial risk that they cannot and so will not be entitled to invoke EU Law directly unless they are expressly granted rights.[79] This is despite the fact that, as discussed above, many countries' tax laws treat as persons (tax subjects) entities that have no legal personality at general law and such 'tax persons' will be entitled to tax

[77] The Treaty of Maastricht (1992) (establishing the European Union) inserted EC Treaty Arts. 17–22, which all appear under Part 2 of the FEU Treaty. The 'Citizenship of the Union' webpage on the official *Europa* website lists the rights of EU citizens, which do not specifically include any rights under Title IV of Part 3. Part 3 includes the four fundamental freedoms (outlined below at 2.2.1) upon which further discussion of the FEU Treaty focuses. The clear suggestion is that the fundamental freedoms are not premised on grounds of EU citizenship. It seems the European Commission feels that the fundamental freedoms themselves must be looked to in order to determine who is entitled to their benefit. See http://europa.eu/legislation_summaries/justice_freedom_security/citizenship_of_the_union/index_En.htm accessed 5 March 2010.

[78] FEU Treaty Art. 21 says that every citizen of the EU 'shall have the right to move and reside freely' and the 4th recital of the European Company Statute (Council Regulation (EC) No. 2157/2001) makes specific reference to Art. 21 in the context of European Companies.

[79] An example is FEU Treaty Art. 54, which expressly grants partnerships the right to freedom of establishment.

treaty benefits.[80] This is also relevant in the context of corporate groups. It seems clear that each member of a corporate group may invoke EU Law, i.e. like tax treaties, EU Law adopts a separate entity approach.[81] This seems to be the case even if, for domestic tax purposes, the identity of a subsidiary is collapsed into that of its parent, i.e. consolidation is adopted. The difficulties caused by this separate entity approach are discussed at a number of points throughout this book. Whether nationals of non-EU countries can invoke the FEU Treaty and, if so, in what circumstances is further explored below at 2.1.2.3.

These issues are largely overcome in the context of EU Directives, although other problems are created. For example, the Parent-Subsidiary Directive (1990) in Article 2(1) identifies the types of entities that are covered by the Directive and requires that they be resident in a member state and that they be subject to one of the specified member state direct taxes 'without the possibility of an option or of being exempt'. A similar provision is found in Article 3 of the Mergers Directive (1990) and Article 3 of the Interest and Royalties Directive (2003). Importantly, this list approach effectively excludes entities that do not have separate legal personality under the general law of the state where they are established, e.g. partnerships and unincorporated associations. Further, new forms of entity are excluded until the list is updated.

Each of these Directives defines a 'company of a Member State' and then proceeds to incorporate the three requirements (form, residence and subject to tax) without apparently appreciating that these requirements may be present in multiple jurisdictions. For example, a company may be formed under UK law, resident in France but pay only German corporate tax. The Directives do not specify whether such a company is a company of the UK, France, Germany, just two of them or all three of them. That is, in contrast to Article 4(3) of the OECD Model, the Directives do not contain a reconciliation rule that specifies which member state the company belongs to. Allowing a company to belong simultaneously to more than one member state may have unintended consequences that are beyond the scope of this book. If a company can belong to only one member state,

[80] The position under the FEU Treaty can be contrasted with the OECD Model, which does have a definition of 'national' in Art. 3(1)(g). This definition expressly includes 'any legal person, partnership or association deriving its status as such from the laws in force in that Contracting State'. This definition is further discussed in the context of the non-discrimination rule in Art. 24(1) below at 2.2.1.

[81] A good example of the ECJ adopting this approach is Case C-168/01 *Bosal Holding BV* v *Staatssecretaris van Financiën* [2003] ECR I-9409 (ECJ), discussed below at 4.2.1.

while attributing the company to the state of formation is consistent with the scope of the fundamental freedoms, the better view seems to be that it should belong to the state of residence. The matter is not without doubt.

The Savings Directive (2003) is targeted at payment of interest to individuals by 'paying agents', defined in Article 4(1) in terms of an 'economic operator' (undefined term).

2.1.2 *The activities*

Taxation may also be based on economic allegiance arising from activities taking place within a particular jurisdiction. In the context of an income tax, these are activities giving rise to or producing income, referred to as the 'source' of income. This immediately raises the schizophrenic nature of the concept of source as used in tax parlance. In one sense, 'source' is used to mean the activity from which the income arises. In a second sense, 'source' is used to mean the geographical location of that activity. In the UK, 'source' typically takes the former meaning and, as a result, reference is often made to the 'location of the source' or 'from where the income arises'. Care must be taken to identify the context in which the word 'source' is used and so which of the meanings the word should take.

Taxation based on source produces a similar array of issues as arise in the context of taxation based on residence. Just as the tax subject is the 'person' in the context of a residence based tax, the activity is the tax subject in the context of a source based tax. As noted at 1.1, this is the difference between a personal and an *in rem* tax. Further, just as residence is the connecting factor used as a proxy for economic allegiance in the context of a residence based tax, locating, assigning or sourcing the activity in a particular jurisdiction is the connecting factor used as a proxy for economic allegiance in the context of a source based tax. As with subheading 2.1.1, this subheading first considers how activities subject to tax based on source may be characterised from both a domestic law and a tax treaty perspective. It then considers the basis on which those activities are assigned to particular jurisdictions under domestic law and tax treaties. Finally, it considers analogous issues under EU Law.

2.1.2.1 Characterising income producing activities

Domestic characterisation At 1.1, it was suggested that payments are the fundamental building blocks of the income tax base and, amongst other fundamental features, payments will have a particular character. However, not all payments made or received by a person are relevant or taken into account for income tax purposes. In a broad sense, only payments that are incurred or derived in the course of or in connection with an earning activity are taken into account. The usual distinction is between acts or activities of a personal character and those where there is some intention or prospect of producing income (creating wealth). It is in this context that the personal needs of individuals (like food, clothing, shelter, education and leisure) become important and if payments are associated with such needs, they are not normally taken into account for income tax purposes. Artificial persons, such as corporations, do not have such needs and, as a result, some countries' tax laws take the view that all payments made or received by a corporation are associated with income earning activities.

As mentioned at 1.1, an income tax is targeted at creations of wealth, but what are the fundamental ways in which or activities by which wealth is created? At an essential level, wealth may be created by the provision of labour, the use of assets or a combination of both. Few domestic tax laws expressly use this basic characterisation of income earning activities but, nevertheless, this basic structure underlies all income tax laws. As noted at 1.1, the domestic tax laws of some countries adopt a global approach in that all payments with a sufficient nexus to an income earning activity are lumped together to produce a single income calculation. For example, the Australian and Mexican income tax laws are commonly viewed as global systems.[82]

The vast majority of income tax laws do expressly categorise the activities that give rise to tax, and where the income is calculated separately for each activity the result is a schedular approach.[83] These will broadly coincide with the fundamental categories outlined above but inevitably involve further subcategorisation. For example, the provision of labour may be subcategorised into employment (provision of service) or independent contracting (provision of services). Use of assets may be subcategorised in many ways including use of immovable property, use of movable property, use of tangible property and use of intangible property. Tax laws may be more specific, referring to things such as the holding of debt claims, shares, intellectual property, houses, ships, etc. The combined provision of labour and use of assets is typically identified as business

[82] See Income Tax Assessment Act 1997 (Australia) ss. 4–1, 4–15 and 6–1 and Income Tax Law (*Impuesto sobre la Renta*) (Mexico) Art. 10.

[83] The UK schedular system is discussed briefly below. For two further examples where income producing activities subject to tax are specified, see the German Income Tax Law (*Einkommensteuergesetz*) s. 2 and the US Internal Revenue Code s. 61.

but business may be subcategorised into things like agricultural business, banking business, insurance business, construction business, etc. Income from the use of assets is broadly referred to as 'passive income' and that from the provision of labour or business is broadly referred to as 'active income', 'active' denoting the human involvement.

As noted at 1.1, the UK income tax has always been schedular and it is useful to outline the main categories of income producing activities that are targeted by the UK tax law. In their origins, these date back to the introduction of the modern income tax in 1799, particularly as modified in 1803.[84] Classically, these were:

Land (Schedule A)
Trade (Schedule D Case I)
Profession or vocation (Schedule D Case II)
Movable property (Schedule D Case III)
Employment (Schedule E)
Distributions from UK resident corporations(Schedule F)
Residual category (Schedule D Case VI)
Disposal of Capital Assets (TCGA 1992)

After an initial century of stability, these categories have proved quite fluid over the last century.[85]

Any country that adopts a schedular system (and every country schedularises its income tax to some extent) requires at least two steps in the calculation of income that, at least theoretically, are not required under a pure global system. The first is to identify the scope of an activity of a person and whether it is within one of the categories or schedules referred to in the tax law.[86] Characterisation of activities is a question of degree rather than absolutes and so every country faces difficult issues in appropriately characterising an activity; one of the main difficulties is always distinguishing employment from independent contracting. Further,

[84] See Harris (2006, pp. 392–402, 408–18, 429–31).

[85] In the current confused state of the UK income tax (see 1.2.1), these categorises still have some relevance. For individuals, they are now found in Income Tax (Earnings and Pensions) Act 2003 (employment), ITTOIA 2005 Part 2 (trade, profession and vocation), Part 3 (land), Part 4 (debt claims, shares) and Part 5 (intangible property, other income) and TCGA 1992 (capital gains). For corporations, they are now found in CTA 2009 Part 3 (trading), Part 4 (land), Parts 5 and 6 (debt claims), Parts 8 and 9 (intangible property), Part 9A (shares), Part 10 (other income) and TCGA 1992 (capital gains).

[86] For example, as regards the UK, see Tiley (2008) Chapter 13 regarding the scope of employment and Chapter 19 regarding the scope of trade.

often there is overlapping characterisation, such as rent from land derived in the context of a business. Domestic tax laws often incorporate reconciliation rules to deal with such overlaps.[87]

The second additional step under a schedular system is to identify payments made or received by a person as connected to or arising out of that activity, i.e. determine that a payment has a sufficient nexus with the activity. These steps are in addition to identification of the fundamental features (mentioned at 1.1) of each payment to be taken into consideration. Again, this is a question of degree and not absolutes and it may not be clear whether a particular payment should be allocated to one activity or another, i.e. it may have a dual nexus. In such a case, the domestic tax law will either allocate the whole of the payment to one activity (which may be a non-earning activity) or apportion the payment between activities, a necessarily more complex process.[88]

OECD Model characterisation Like UK domestic tax law, the OECD Model adopts a schedular approach when it comes to source based taxation. As the Model was historically based on treaty practice, and that treaty practice on integrating tax laws, particularly within central Europe, it is not surprising that a schedular approach was adopted. It is also not surprising that the types of classifications used are at least broadly consistent with the approach adopted in the domestic laws of many European countries, including the UK.[89] But it would be a mistake to think that the income activity categories used in the OECD Model are consistent with those used in any particular country's domestic tax law – they are not. However, with the force of globalisation and the importance and inflexibility of the bilateral tax treaty network based on the OECD Model, there are signs that countries amend their domestic tax laws in a fashion to create broad consistency with the OECD Model.[90]

[87] For example, see CTA 2009 ss. 201, 287, 288, 464, 465, 906, 982 and ITTOIA 2005 s. 2.

[88] For example, see Tiley (2008, pp. 431–9) regarding dual purpose expenditure.

[89] During the nineteenth century and at the height of the British Empire, the UK income tax was viewed as the only example of a successful income tax. Therefore, it was influential in the development of income tax in many regions including Prussia, Italy, the United States and, of course, former colonies and possessions of the UK (including India). Generally see Harris (forthcoming).

[90] Two UK examples of this are the incorporation of the *permanent establishment* concept into domestic tax law in 2003 and the incorporation of OECD style *transfer pricing* rules in 1998. See CTA 2009 ss. 19–33, TIOPA 2010 ss. 146–217 and CTA 2010 ss. 1141–53.

The activities categorised by the OECD Model that will be discussed in this book are-

Article 6 Immovable Property
Article 7 Business
Article 10 Shares and Similar Rights
Article 11 Debt Claims
Article 12 Intellectual Property
Article 13 Alienation of Property
Article 15 Employment
Article 21 Residual

Each of these provisions is discussed in turn at 3.1. As mentioned, there is broad consistency between the OECD categories and the UK's schedular domestic tax law; Article 6 aligning with Schedule A, Article 7 with Schedule D Case I and Case II,[91] Article 10 with Schedule F, Articles 11 and 12 with Schedule D Case III, Article 13 with TCGA 1992, Article 15 with Schedule E and Article 21 with Schedule D Case VI. While there is broad consistency, the activities identified under UK domestic tax law and those under the OECD Model are not the same, they are different tests and so raise potential mismatches. The potential for such disjuncture is far greater under global systems (e.g. Australia's system) but in these cases the tax returns that taxpayers are required to file often schedularise the tax system in any case.

Any disjuncture is unlikely to have much practical implication, particularly when most countries, including the UK, have a residual income category. It will be the domestic classification that must be used when a taxpayer is completing a tax return. So, for example, if the treaty concept of 'business' is broader than the UK domestic law concept of 'trade', any income generated by a business that is outside the scope of a trade would still be covered by Article 7 of a treaty but may fall into the residual category of Schedule D Case VI when filing a tax return. Further, it is clear that Articles 11 and 12 of the OECD Model were, historically, subsumed within Schedule D Case III of UK domestic law, and so there is not perfect alignment in this case.[92] The scope of activities used in the OECD

[91] OECD Model Art. 14 was deleted in 2000 but it continues to exist in the UN Model and many tax treaties. It dealt with Independent Services, which broadly aligns with Schedule D Case II of UK domestic tax law. Independent services are now encompassed within the concept of business and so are regulated by OECD Model Art. 7. This is further discussed below at 3.1.3.

[92] OECD Model Art. 10 is now covered by ITTOIA 2005 Part 4 and CTA 2009 Parts 5 and 6. Art. 11 is now covered by ITTOIA 2005 Part 5 and CTA 2009 Parts 8 and 9.

model, and so their associated definitions, are further considered at 3.1. Unless the context otherwise requires, there is no further consideration of their alignment with domestic tax law classifications, e.g. under the UK schedular system.

2.1.2.2 Locating the activity

Domestic law The income tax laws of all countries contain rules that assign taxable activities to their jurisdiction, i.e. source rules. Some countries' laws are organised sufficiently to locate all these rules in one convenient place. Perhaps it is not surprising that Germany is one such country.[93] It is perhaps equally unsurprising that the UK is not one of those countries, but the UK has plenty of company in this respect.[94] The source rules (or connecting factors) in the UK tax law were traditionally imbedded in the charging provision of each Schedule. It is useful to align these rules with the categories of activity subject to tax noted above.

Schedule A refers to profits from 'land in the United Kingdom'.[95] Schedule D Case I and II (covering trade, profession, vocation) refers to 'carried on... in the United Kingdom'.[96] Traditionally, Schedule D also referred to 'any property whatever in the United Kingdom'.[97] ITTOIA 2005 changed this traditional categorisation of income from movable property. With respect to savings and investment income, section 368 of ITTOIA 2005 refers only to the income arising 'from a source in the United Kingdom', rather than the location of the property giving rise to the income. The same section also refers, somewhat inelegantly, to 'a comparable connection to the United Kingdom' for 'any income which does not have a source'. For the residual category of income, section 577 of ITTOIA 2005 is to similar effect.

The tax on employment income (former Schedule E) is charged on 'earnings in respect of duties performed in the United Kingdom'.[98] For income tax purposes, the Schedule F rules are now subsumed within the general source rules for savings and investment income and so simply

[93] See the German Income Tax Law (*Einkommensteuergesetz*) s. 49.

[94] Much of the company is former UK colonies whose income tax laws were influenced by the UK.

[95] ITTOIA 2005 s. 264 and CTA 2009 s. 205.

[96] ITTOIA 2005 s. 6(2).

[97] ICTA 1988 s. 18. The reference to property within the UK was particularly old, dating back to the direct taxes of the early sixteenth century; see Harris (2006, pp. 58–9).

[98] Income Tax (Earnings and Pensions) Act 2003 s. 27.

refer to income arising 'from a source in the United Kingdom'.[99] Question whether a dividend of a UK resident corporation could ever have a foreign source. Capital gains are essentially only charged on a residency basis, although there is an exception for assets held by a UK branch or agency of a non-resident and for gains realised by temporary non-residents if and when the person subsequently becomes a resident once again.[100]

Unfortunately, this is not the end of the story when locating the source of income. As explained at 1.1, and again at 2.1.2.1, payments are the building blocks of the income tax base. However, only payments that are sufficiently connected with an earning activity are recognised for tax purposes. So far, what has been considered is the identification of the activity for tax (and treaty) purposes, at 2.1.2.1, and how, for domestic law purposes, a relevant activity may be allocated to a particular jurisdiction. But an earning activity may be conducted either simultaneously or consecutively in more than one jurisdiction. Take the example of a business conducted across borders, or a mobile employee or independent contractor that provides services in more than one jurisdiction. In such a case, a domestic tax law must not allocate payments made and received only to the earning activity (business, profession or employment), but also allocate those payments geographically to the part of the activity being conducted in a particular jurisdiction. That is, for income tax purposes, it is often not sufficient to allocate net income to particular jurisdictions but it is also necessary to allocate particular payments (that make up net income) to particular jurisdictions or parts of activities.

It is possible to start by identifying the geographical source of all payments made or received that are sufficiently connected with a particular jurisdiction. The net income from a particular jurisdiction would be the difference between the payments made and the payments received that have been sourced in that jurisdiction. Very few countries adopt such an approach.[101] More countries, indeed most, source payments received, which in many countries constitute 'income' on a gross conception of that term. This is particularly the case with passive income, where countries

[99] ITTOIA 2005 s. 368. Under section 20 of ICTA 1988 the simple rule was to charge dividends of UK companies although, theoretically, it might have been possible for shares in a foreign company to be sited in the UK and dividends therefrom sourced in the UK for 'other' income (Schedule D Case VI) purposes. Before Schedule F was enacted in 1965, all dividends sourced in the UK fell under Schedule D Case VI.

[100] TCGA 1992 ss. 2, 10 and 10A.

[101] Two examples are Income Tax Act, 2058 (Nepal) s. 67 and Income Tax Act, 2004 (Tanzania) s. 68.

often tax non-residents on gross payments received from their jurisdiction without deductions. In such a case the tax is most often collected by means of requiring the payer to withhold (or deduct) the tax from the payment and remit it to the tax administration. Gross rent is typically sourced where the property is situated, gross royalties may be sourced at the place of use of the intangible property or the place of legal protection (if this is different) and interest and dividends are commonly sourced where the payer is resident. In the latter case the source is sometimes the location of the debt, shares or the source of the profits from which dividends are paid.[102] Source rules are often extended to interest and royalties paid by permanent establishments within the jurisdiction.[103]

In the UK, receipts from business sales generally fall within the charge to tax if the contract of sale was made in the UK. There are important exceptions to this general rule.[104] There are no express rules for sourcing expenses that may be deducted in calculating UK business profits. Rent from land situated in the UK is subject to a 20 per cent withholding tax.[105] This is not a final withholding tax, deductions may be claimed and the withholding tax credited against any net tax liability. Subject to important exceptions, the UK imposes a 20 per cent withholding tax on interest 'arising' in the UK, including if paid to a non-resident.[106] Similarly, royalties and certain other annual payments that 'arise' in the UK may be subject to a 20% withholding.[107] In these cases, if a non-resident (who has no UK representative) receives the payment, the withholding tax is a final tax.[108] UK source dividends are not subject to domestic withholding tax and non-residents are not chargeable with respect thereto (unless they have a UK representative).[109]

One final quirk involves the UK treatment of non-resident corporations. They are charged to *corporation tax* only with respect to trading

[102] For example, US Internal Revenue Code s. 861(a)(2)(B) treats as having a US source certain dividends paid by a foreign corporation that has US source profits. Generally, see Avery Jones et al. (2006, pp. 744–5).

[103] Generally, see Ault and Arnold (2010, pp. 510–15). For a good discussion of the conceptual difficulties in designing source rules, see OECD (2003).

[104] The distinction is usually made between trading *within* the UK and trading *with* the UK. Generally, see Tiley (2008, pp. 1159–61) and the references cited therein.

[105] ITA 2007 s. 971 making provision for the issue of regulations.

[106] ITA 2007 s. 874.

[107] ITA 2007 ss. 899 and 900. Contrast the charge to withholding tax on non-patent royalties, which simply refers to a payment that is 'charged' to tax, ITA 2007 s. 906.

[108] ITA 2007 ss. 811 and 815.

[109] ITA 2007 ss. 811 and 815.

income arising through a UK permanent establishment and income or chargeable gains from property or rights used or held by such a permanent establishment.[110] With respect to such income and gains, they are not subject to *income tax*, which generally does not apply to corporations in a domestic UK context. However, non-resident corporations may be subject to *income tax* with respect to other income, e.g. rent, interest and royalties not arising through a UK permanent establishment.[111] As explained in the last paragraph, any such liability is likely to be collected by withholding tax.

Assignment of taxing rights under the OECD Model The OECD Model does not contain explicit source rules. Rather, it talks about particular countries having taxing rights. Many of these translate into effective source rules because they permit taxation based on the location of factors other than residence. Consistent with the schedular approach outlined above at 2.1.2.1, these differ depending on the type of activity in question. In broad outline, the main source country taxing rights are with respect to the following:

Article 6 Income from immovable property in the country
Article 7 Profits derived through a permanent establishment situated in the country
Article 10 Dividends paid by a resident corporation
Article 11 Interest paid by a resident or incurred by a permanent establishment situated in the country
Article 13 Gains from the alienation of immovable property or property forming part of a permanent establishment situated in the country
Article 15 Remuneration from employment exercised in the country

Otherwise, the OECD Model generally allocates taxing rights to the country of residence.[112]

The OECD Model 'source' rules are similar but not the same as those in domestic law. Most often, domestic source rules have a broader scope than OECD Model taxing rights. In this case, the OECD Model has a restricting effect and reference can simply be made to the applicable tax treaty to determine the appropriate taxation of a non-resident. However, in some circumstances the domestic law source rule may be narrower than that

[110] CTA 2009 s. 19.
[111] CTA 2009 s. 3.
[112] Particularly, see OECD Model Art. 21.

in a tax treaty (based on the OECD Model) or there may be no domestic charge to tax on a particular type of income that the treaty permits be taxed by the source state. In such as case, the treaty is only permissive and will not ground a charge to tax (see 1.2.2). Take, for example, a country like New Zealand or Singapore that does not impose tax on capital gains. Even though a treaty permits such taxation, a non-resident will not be subject to tax on a New Zealand or Singapore capital gain that is not grounded in a domestic charge to tax.

The OECD Model 'source' rules are not taken further at this stage. They form the core of the discussion in Chapter 3.

2.1.2.3 Activities covered by EU Law

As noted above, EU Law is not directly concerned with taxing rights. Nevertheless, EU Law regulates only certain activities and these provide an analogy to the issues discussed with respect to domestic law and tax treaties at 2.1.2.1 and 2.1.2.2. In the usual way, this regulation may be found directly under the FEU Treaty or under Directives. The key activities that are regulated by the sources of EU Law that are relevant for tax purposes are outlined in the following discussion.[113] As with domestic law and tax treaties, there are two primary issues for consideration. The first is identifying the type of activity that is regulated. The second is identifying any jurisdictional nexus required to bring the activity within the regulation of EU Law.

Fundamental freedoms A fundamental purpose of EU Law is to establish 'an internal market' by, amongst other things, ensuring, as between member states, 'the free movement of goods, persons, services and capital'.[114] These 'fundamental freedoms' are particularly important as regards the scope of application of EU Law in direct tax matters. Title II of Part three of the FEU Treaty deals with the free movement of goods but it is essentially relevant only in indirect tax matters. The same is true of Chapter 2 of Title VII, which contains a number of 'tax provisions'.

The core freedoms that are relevant in direct tax matters are those outlined in Title IV of Part three of the FEU Treaty, which is entitled 'Free

[113] As mentioned in the introduction, no attempt is made to comprehensively deal with the general EU Law issues that are relevant in the context of direct taxation. Rather, only an outline is provided. For a general study on EU Law, see Barnard (2007), and for a specialised text on EU direct tax law, see Terra and Wattel (2008).

[114] EU Treaty Art. 3 and FEU Treaty Art. 26(2).

movement of persons, services and capital'. Title IV is broken into four chapters, each of which contains a core freedom. Despite elaborating on only three of the four fundamental freedoms, these core freedoms are also commonly referred to as 'fundamental freedoms' or 'personal freedoms'. These core freedoms seek to regulate certain activities and, as a result, may regulate taxation rules that apply to these activities. There is a substantial correlation between the types of activities regulated by the fundamental freedoms and categories of activities schedularised under the OECD Model and domestic tax laws. This is, perhaps, not surprising as one seeks to regulate economic activities while the others deal with the taxation of them. The following briefly outlines each of the relevant freedoms.

Article 45 of the FEU Treaty provides:

> 1. Freedom of movement for workers shall be secured within the Union.
> 2. Such freedom of movement shall entail the abolition of any discrimination based on nationality between workers of the Member States as regards employment, remuneration and other conditions of work and employment.

This freedom is primarily concerned with employment and, from a direct tax perspective, is most often in issue with respect to the tax treatment of frontier workers, i.e. persons living in one EU member state who have their employment in another. Obviously, this scenario is more likely when land borders are involved and, as a result, the UK has had little involvement in ECJ case law based on this Article. The correlation with Schedule E (employment income) of the UK tax law and Article 15 of the OECD Model is clear.

The jurisdictional nexus required to bring employment within the regulation of EU Law involves two aspects. As paragraph 3 of Article 45 of the FEU Treaty makes clear, the freedom involves presence within a member state for the purposes of employment and so, at least implicitly, the exercise of employment within a particular jurisdiction. This is consistent with UK tax law and the OECD Model as regards employment. The second aspect requires the employee be a 'national' of a member state. This is an attribute of the person employed as opposed to the employment, and is consistent with the general jurisdictional connection with respect to the person used in EU Law as discussed above at 2.1.1.3.

Article 49 of the FEU Treaty provides:

> [R]estrictions on the freedom of establishment of nationals of a Member State in the territory of another Member State shall be prohibited. Such

> prohibition shall also apply to restrictions on the setting-up of agencies, branches or subsidiaries …
>
> Freedom of establishment shall include the right to take up and pursue activities as self-employed persons and to set up and manage undertakings, in particular companies or firms… under the conditions laid down for its own nationals by the law of the country where such establishment is effected…

While it may not at first seem obvious, this freedom is primarily concerned with business, irrespective of the form in which it is conducted. This derives from the reference to 'self-employed persons' and the managing of 'undertakings', which clearly encompasses the concept of 'enterprise' as used in the OECD Model (as to which see 2.1.2.1). Once again, there is correlation between activities covered by this freedom and those in Schedule D Cases I and II of the UK tax law (trade, profession and vocation) and Article 7 of the OECD Model (enterprise or business).

As regards jurisdictional nexus required to bring a business or undertaking within the regulation of EU Law, this is again similar to that in Article 7 of the OECD Model and requires an 'establishment' within the jurisdiction. The definition of 'permanent establishment' in Article 5 of the OECD Model is discussed below at 3.1.3.3. At the end of that discussion, there is a brief comparison with the concept of 'establishment' under EU Law. It is clear that the EU Law concept of 'establishment' is broader than the OECD Model concept of 'permanent establishment'.

As with the free movement of workers, Article 49 of the FEU Treaty incorporates a second personal jurisdictional nexus, requiring the establishment be of a 'national' of a member state, which is again consistent with the general jurisdictional connection with respect to the person used in EU Law discussed above at 2.1.1.3. However, Article 54 extends the personal jurisdictional nexus by making Article 49 available to:

> Companies or firms formed in accordance with the law of a Member State and having their registered office, central administration or principal place of business within the Union …

The reference to 'central administration or principal place of business' is a test much in the spirit of the management style test of corporate residence for tax purposes as reflected in the 'place of effective management' tiebreaker used in Article 4(3) of the OECD Model, discussed above at 2.1.1.2.

Article 56 of the FEU Treaty provides:

> [R]estrictions on freedom to provide services within the Union shall be prohibited in respect of nationals of Member States who are established in a Member State other than that of the person for whom the services are intended.

Article 57 makes clear that the scope of this freedom is additional or supplemental to the other fundamental freedoms. In particular, it provides a definition of services for the purposes of the freedom that requires the services be provided 'for remuneration'. It goes on to give examples of the services covered, which include activities of an industrial or commercial character, of craftsmen and of the professions. As regards the activities covered, there is clearly a substantial overlap with the freedom of establishment and both may apply to business activities. Finally, Article 57 provides:

> [T]he person providing a service may, in order to do so, temporarily pursue his activity in the Member State where the service is provided, under the same conditions as are imposed by that State on its own nationals.

As regards jurisdictional nexus required to bring the provision of services within the regulation of EU Law, this is unlike the OECD Model and, perhaps, has more in common with some countries' domestic source rules. Article 56 of the FEU Treaty focuses on the location of the beneficiary of the services whereas Article 57 focuses on 'where the service is provided'. Historically, these will coincide but, as will be discussed further in Chapter 3, in this electronic age this is not necessarily the case. The jurisdictional connection seems analogous to the rule the UK would typically use for locating the source of professional income.[115] Again, note the additional personal jurisdictional nexus requiring the person providing the services to be a national of a member state.

Article 63 of the FEU Treaty provides:

> 1. [A]ll restrictions on the movement of capital between Member States and between Member States and third countries shall be prohibited.
> 2. [A]ll restrictions on payments between Member States and between Member States and third countries shall be prohibited.

The precise distinction between 'movements of capital' and 'payments' is beyond the scope of this work but the freedom clearly covers the provision of capital and the return thereon. The scope of the freedom, therefore,

[115] 'The source of income is situated at the place where the profession or vocation is exercised or carried on.' *Bennett* v *Marshall* [1938] 1 KB 591 (CA) at 613 per Romer LJ.

clearly covers the types of matters regulated by Articles 10 (dividends), 11(interest), 12 (royalties) and 13 (capital gains) of the OECD Model.

The jurisdictional nexus required to bring the provision of capital and return thereon within the regulation of EU Law is, on the face of Article 63 of the FEU Treaty, extremely broad. It appears that as long as the movement or payment originates or is received in a Member State the freedom has potential application. This is substantially broader than the OECD Model connecting factors for capital income (e.g. residence of the payer for dividends and interest) and even than for domestic law. UK tax law requires more than a simple payment of income from the UK before the source of the income will be considered located in the UK.

Another particularly important feature of free movement of capital is that it does not incorporate the additional personal jurisdictional nexus requiring the person owning the capital or receiving the payment to be a national of a member state. Article 63 of the FEU Treaty has its origins in Article 67 of the European Economic Community Treaty (1957) (see above at 1.2.3). This provision referred to 'restrictions on the movement of capital belonging to persons resident in Member States and any discrimination based on the nationality or on the place of residence of the parties or on the place where such capital is invested'. At least the 'nationality' qualification reflected some consistency with the other fundamental freedoms. Nevertheless, the ECJ decided that this provision did not have direct effect,[116] placing it in stark contrast with the other fundamental freedoms. The Treaty of Maastricht (1992) reformulated the freedom without the qualifications and the ECJ has decided that the new version does have direct effect.[117]

To date, the ECJ has applied Article 63 of the FEU Treaty in the same way to movements of capital between member states and third countries as it does to movements of capital between member states.[118] However, justifications as a defence for a restriction may involve different considerations where a third country is involved. It is apparent that EU nationals can rely on Article 63 with respect to movements of capital involving third countries. Less clearly, it also seems that the ECJ will entertain claims by third country nationals to invoke the free movement of capital. That is, the ECJ seems to recognise at least the right to free movement of capital in

[116] Case 203/80 *Casati* [1981] ECR 2595 (ECJ).

[117] Cases C-358 and 416/93 *Bordessa* [1995] ECR I-361 (ECJ) and Cases C-163, 165 and 250/94 *Sanz de Lera* [1995] ECR I-4821 (ECJ).

[118] Case C-101/05 *Skatteverket* v *A* [2007] ECR I-11531 (ECJ) at paras. 26–7.

a national of a country that is not even a party to the EC Treaty.[119] A number of important cases are pending that involve third country pension funds seeking the benefit of the free movement of capital.[120]

The overall structure of the fundamental freedoms is surprisingly consistent with the fundamental activities from which income may be derived set out above at 2.1.2.1. The free movement of workers and, to some extent, the freedom to provide services are targeted at the provision of labour. The free movement of capital is targeted at the provision of capital. The freedom of establishment and, to some extent, the freedom to provide services are targeted at the combined provision of capital and labour, i.e. business. In the result, the fundamental freedoms have potential application to most income earning activities.

Directives As mentioned at 1.2.3, the EU directives on direct taxation are rather narrowly focused. The activities covered by the Parent-Subsidiary Directive (1990) are set out in Article 1 of the Directive. Broadly, these are 'distributions of profits' by a subsidiary of one member state to a parent company of another member state. This means that the scope of the Directive overlaps with Article 10 of tax treaties, indeed a number of the provisions of the Directive were inspired by Article 10 of the OECD Model. This is further discussed below at 3.1.4.1. The jurisdictional nexus for the application of the Directive is that the distribution must be received by a company 'of' a member state and distributed by a company 'of' a member state. The latter aspect is consistent with Article 10 of the OECD Model. As regards a company being 'of' a member state, this is the personal jurisdictional connection and was outlined above at 2.1.1.3.

As for the Mergers Directive (1990), its scope is also outlined in Article 1 of the Directive. It applies to:

> mergers, divisions, partial divisions, transfers of assets and exchanges of shares in which companies from two or more Member States are involved

It also applies to the transfer of the registered office of European companies established under the European Company Statute.[121] The activities covered by this Directive do not correspond with any provision of the OECD Model. Further, from a UK tax law perspective, while the issues

[119] In Case C-452/04 *Fidium Finanz AG* v *Bundesanstalt für Finanzdienstleistungsaufsicht* [2006] ECR I-9521 (ECJ) the ECJ entertained such a claim by a Swiss corporation.

[120] Generally, see O'Brien (2008).

[121] See footnote 78 above.

that arise will often fall under TCGA 1992 (capital gains), some of the activities covered by the Mergers Directive are dealt with under other provisions and schedules of the tax law. As regards a company being 'from' a member state, this is the personal jurisdictional connection, is similar to that in the Parent-Subsidiary Directive (1990) and was outlined above at 2.1.1.3. The Mergers Directive is further considered in Chapter 6.

Article 1 of the Interest and Royalties Directive (2003) outlines the scope of the Directive. Broadly, it applies to '[i]nterest or royalty payments arising in a Member State...provided that the beneficial owner... is a company of another Member State...' Interest or royalties 'arise' in a member state if paid by a company 'of' a member state. This makes the scope of the Directive broadly similar to that of Articles 11 and 12 of the OECD Model and these OECD provisions inspired a number of the provisions of the Directive. However, similar to the OECD provisions, there is no direct correlation with the schedules of UK tax law. A company 'of' a member state is the personal jurisdictional connection and, as outlined above at 2.1.1.3, is similar to that in the Parent-Subsidiary and Mergers Directives.

The Savings Directive (2003) is not structured in the same manner as the other direct tax directives. Article 1 of the Savings Directive outlines its aim as enabling

> interest payments made in one Member State to beneficial owners who are individuals resident... in another Member State to be made subject to effective taxation in accordance with the laws of the latter Member State.

Again, as regards activity covered, there is potentially substantial overlap with Article 11 of the OECD Model (interest), though not the Interest and Royalties Directive. A limited number of concepts used in the Savings Directive seem to have been inspired by the OECD Model, particularly the concept of beneficial ownership, discussed further below at 5.2.3.2. As mentioned above at 2.1.1.3, the Savings Directive is targeted at payment of interest to individuals by paying agents 'established' in a member state. Therefore, the jurisdictional nexus is similar to but not the same as under the OECD Model.

2.2 Divided allegiance: the problem of double taxation

From the discussion at 2.1, it is clear that a person may owe economic allegiance to more than one country at the same time. In the context of the income tax, this is classically where the activity giving rise to the income is located in one country (the source country) and the person deriving the income is resident in another country (the residence country). As the source country may impose its *in rem* tax on the income generating activity and the residence country may impose its personal tax on the person deriving the income, the result may be double taxation. Double taxation may also arise as a result of two countries claiming the source of the income is in their jurisdiction or by two countries claiming the person is resident in their jurisdiction.[122] These less common forms of double taxation are considered below at 5.2.

The rest of this chapter is concerned with what, if anything, should be done about this double taxation. The heading proceeds by seeking to uncover the principles that might guide, or have been suggested should guide, the resolution of the double taxation problem. This is a particularly slippery area and the discussion ranges broadly. The discussion begins by identifying the tripartite relationship that arises in a double taxation situation. This enables the discussion to proceed to consider principles that may have relevant application to each of the three relationships. This discussion begins with the relationships between the taxpayer, on the one hand, and the source and residence countries, on the other. These relationships may be affected by economic considerations, a particularly important aspect of international and domestic taxation. After an overview of the economic considerations, the discussion moves into the legal framework to consider the principles (as opposed to rules), if any, which underlie or are incorporated in the OECD Model and compares that to the situation under EU Law.

The focus is then upon the interstate relationship and the comparative tax takes of the source and residence countries. The discussion grabbles with the fuzzy concept of inter-nation equity and then moves to consider two principles that emerge from the OECD Model. Next on the list is harmful tax competition, which involves the deliberate attempt by one country through its tax system to distort the amount of economic activity attracted from international commerce to the detriment of other countries. The position taken by the OECD is compared to that taken within the EU. The latter involves competition within the EU and so affects the allocation of taxing rights between member states, an issue on which the discussion of principles finishes.

[122] The double taxation may also be broader, such as where a country taxes on a basis other than the conventional source and residence bases. An example is where a country taxes based on domicile or nationality.

The last subheading of this chapter presumes that something should be done to restrict double taxation of cross-border income. It considers the options or methods for relieving double taxation and allocating taxing rights between countries. As with the principles that precede it, this discussion is important because these principles and methods will be discussed, analysed and applied throughout the remainder of the book to particular situations. It is only in this chapter that an attempt is made at sketching the big picture.

2.2.1 Principles

Tripartite relationship

Consider the *Base Case* (Figure 1 on p. 5). On the facts, Country A may tax Beth's rental income based on the source of the income. Country B may tax Beth with respect to the rental income based on her residence in the country. The result is that Beth has a relationship, in the form of taxation, with both Country A and Country B. In addition, there is the third relationship between Country A and Country B, which involves the comparative amount of taxation that each collects with respect to Beth's income. Each cross-border transaction giving rise to income involves a similar tripartite relationship, at the least.[123]

Various principles may be relevant in governing each of these three primary relationships. The standard principles that govern the levy of taxes, i.e. the state/taxpayer relationship, are equity (fairness), efficiency and simplicity and each of these may have some relevance to the taxpayer's relationship with the source and residence countries.[124] As mentioned, when it comes to the interstate relationship, the relevant principles are more slippery. The problem for the taxpayer is that the taxpayer is in some ways the *meat in the sandwich*, especially when a treaty is involved. Governments wish to divide the tax take from international transactions between themselves but in doing so get the taxpayer messed up in their relationship. In the result, the interstate relationship causes substantial problems with the standard principles directly applicable to taxpayers, but first consideration will be given to the standard principles without considering this complicating factor.

[123] See Harris (1996, pp. 281–2).

[124] For example, see OECD (2003). Generally regarding these principles, see Harris (1996, pp. 6–16) and the references cited therein.

Economic considerations

The principle of efficiency involves economic considerations and, as mentioned, is particularly influential in current tax policy. What efficiency requires of a tax depends on the market to which it is applied. If the market contains imperfections, often called market failure, the tax should seek to correct those failures. In other cases, an efficient tax is considered one that does not influence a market allocation of resources. In a functioning market, a market allocation of resources causes resources to be attracted to where they are most productive and so produce maximum overall production to the benefit of the general populace. Presuming such a market, it is then possible to speak of a *neutral* tax, one that does not distort a market allocation of resources.

Stepping into an international environment raises big questions as to what is meant by a market or allocation that is not to be distorted. Here, for a number of decades, there have been three competing versions of neutrality: national neutrality, capital export neutrality and capital import neutrality.[125] How neutrality is applied to international transactions depends on whether you take a national or international perspective. *National neutrality* seeks to maximise the total return to a country from international transactions, whether in the form of tax collected by the country or return received by a resident. Typically, it is only referred to in the context of residence countries, which compare pre-tax domestic returns with foreign returns net of foreign taxes.[126] In the result, national neutrality supports double taxation of cross-border income. The result would be discrimination against cross-border investment.

Proponents of globalisation suggest that the only way to maximise the well-being of all on a worldwide basis is by removing any discrimination so that capital can flow to where it is most productive.[127] As the name suggests, this involves a global approach and is concerned with allocating resources efficiently between all nations and not just maximising the resources of one nation. Even if it is agreed that the global approach is appropriate, there is little consensus on how tax systems should be coordinated to ensure this type of efficiency. Traditionally, this involves the competing notions of capital export and capital import neutrality.

[125] Generally regarding these principles, see Harris (1996, pp. 318–20) and the references cited therein.

[126] Bizarrely, if national neutrality were applied to a source country it might suggest a prohibition on foreign investment (100 per cent tax on foreigners).

[127] Otherwise, the allocation of resources will result in dead-weight costs.

Capital export neutrality requires that taxation does not distort the decision of a person to invest in one of a range of countries. This is considered met in an income tax context when residents pay the same amount of income tax on their income regardless of the location of the activity that gives rise to the income. By contrast, *capital import neutrality* requires investors in a particular market pay the same amount of income tax regardless of the location of the owner of the investment. Two general points can be made regarding these competing notions of neutrality. First, these principles are not concerned with which country gets the tax, only with distorting the economic activity of market players. Second, each focuses on one of the recognised grounds of economic allegiance and so the personal and the *in rem* features of the income tax. Capital export neutrality is centred on the person and capital import neutrality on the activity that gives rise to the income and so capital export neutrality is often viewed as particularly relevant for residence countries and capital import neutrality for source countries.

This is not the place to provide a critique of capital export and capital import neutrality but a few basic points are appropriate. In practice, no country's income tax adheres to capital export neutrality because no residence country is willing to refund excess taxes levied by a source country where the source country's tax is higher than what it might have been in the residence country. Further, it is questionable logic to suggest that all income producing activities in different countries should be taxed at the same rate because those activities will be subject to very different environments and qualify for different government services. Two persons with the same residence may owe very different economic allegiances precisely because their income is not derived from the same place.

Capital import neutrality is equally open to serious criticisms. It is premised on the basis of a market and historically a market has been identified with a nation state, but globalisation is breaking this down and it is not clear where one market ends and another begins. For example, what does this mean in the context of the EU? Do each of the member states constitute a market for capital import neutrality purposes or is it the common EU market that is important. Indeed, the concept of globalisation envisages a global market. It is often argued that capital import neutrality also facilitates harmful tax competition between states, discussed below, which may be viewed as a particular form of market failure.

These traditional notions of international tax neutrality have been challenged or at least discredited by newer notions of neutrality. In particular,

Desai and Hines have suggested that in maximising production, what matters is capital ownership.

> If the productivity of capital depends on the identities of its owners (and there is considerable reason to think that it does), then the efficient allocation of capital is one that maximizes output given the stocks of capital in each country. It follows that tax systems promote efficiency if they encourage the most productive ownership of assets within the set of feasible investors.[128]

From this position, they develop the concepts of capital ownership neutrality and national ownership neutrality. The former requires that 'tax rules not distort ownership patterns, which is equivalent to ownership of an asset residing with the potential buyer who has the highest reservation price in the absence of tax differences'. The latter suggests that, because 'outbound foreign investment need not be accompanied by reduced domestic investment', 'countries should want to exempt foreign income from taxation'.[129] As with their predecessors, while these notions of neutrality seem straightforward to state, what they mean for the practical development of legal rules is less clear. In that context, both the old and newer notions of neutrality will be cross-referenced at various points in this book.

Cross-border restrictions

The discussion now moves from these economic considerations, which seek to guide tax policy with respect to the promotion of efficiency, to the more concrete legal rules of the current international tax order. In particular, as noted at 2.1.2.2, the OECD Model and so tax treaties incorporate provisions that limit countries' taxing rights and by doing so impact on the state/taxpayer relationships. The rest of this book is particularly concerned with rules that formulate those limitations. However, at this point it is useful to consider the extent to which the OECD Model incorporates any principles that underlie the relationship between the source and residence countries, on the one hand, and the taxpayer, on the other. The position under the OECD Model is then contrasted with that under EU Law.

OECD Model Tax treaties based on the OECD Model are agreements between states as to how they allocate tax rights on cross-border

128 Desai and Hines (2003, p. 24).
129 Desai and Hines (2004, p. 26).

transactions between them. As will be discussed shortly, there are a number of principles that may be viewed as underlying the OECD Model but the majority of these pertain directly to the interstate relationship rather than the relationship between the taxpayer and the contracting states. In this sense, tax treaties based on the OECD Model are not like domestic law and do not appear to have been drafted with the standard principles that govern the levy of taxes (equity (fairness), efficiency and simplicity) directly in mind. This is particularly clear in a dualist state (see 1.2.2) where a tax treaty will take effect only to the extent it is implemented in domestic law. Further, tax treaties do not clearly incorporate the types of fundamental principles that are often apparent in constitutions, such as equality, fairness and ability to pay. In this context, there is a stark contrast with EU Law, which does contain fundamental principles (such as those discussed at 2.1.2.3) that are intended for the direct benefit of persons that are not a direct party to the EU Treaties.

The exception is the non-discrimination provision in Article 24 of the OECD Model. A quick perusal of the OECD Model identifies the peculiar nature of Article 24. The other rules in the Model are comparatively mechanical in dividing up the tax base or more procedural, such as the rules discussed in Chapter 7.[130] The other rules are essentially to the effect of 'you get this and I get that' with the primary object of removing international double taxation. A principle of non-discrimination is fundamentally different and is more concerned with equity, i.e. taxpayers shall be treated fairly. The non-discrimination provision is akin to the type of principle that might be used in a constitutional context. There are no other principles of this nature on the face of the OECD Model. Note, in particular, that while tax treaties are clearly designed to remove barriers to cross-border investment, there is no provision express or implied to the effect that the purpose of tax treaties is to create an efficient allocation of resources between the contracting states. Again, EU Law is in stark contrast.

The non-discrimination principle in Article 24 of the OECD Model is particularly weak. Indeed, it is not so much a principle as (like the rest of the OECD Model) a series of rules. It has been suggested that Article 24:

[130] It is true that the mutual agreement procedure in OECD Model Art. 25 grants certain rights to taxpayers to present a case to their competent authority but the essence of the provision is to provide the competent authorities of the contracting states a mechanism to resolve disagreements. The provision would lose little effect if the right of the taxpayer was not mentioned as the taxpayer would likely be entitled to make such a presentation under domestic law in any case.

> has two main objectives. The first… is to prevent discrimination of any kind by one state in taxing *nationals* of the treaty partner state… The second is to prevent discrimination by one state in relation to *residents* of the other state in three cases, all relating to business income.[131]

The second set of rules is of significant importance and each of the three rules is discussed further in Chapter 3. However, it will be noted that these rules apply only as regards discrimination of 'residents' of the other state. By their very nature, this means that these rules can apply only to actions of the source state, leaving the residence state free of such limitations.

This leaves Article 24(1) of the OECD Model, which states in part:

> Nationals of a Contracting State shall not be subjected in the other Contracting State to any taxation or any requirement connected therewith, which is other or more burdensome than the taxation and connected requirements to which nationals of that other State in the same circumstances, in particular with respect to residence, are or may be subjected.

As an initial point, it will be noted that Article 24(1) applies to 'any taxation' and so is not limited in scope to taxes listed in Article 2 to which the primary provisions of the treaty apply. Article 24(6) confirms this. The usual approach in applying Article 24(1) is as follows:

(i) Identify a national of one contracting state that is taxed by the second contracting state
(ii) Identify a hypothetical national of the second contracting state that is 'in the same circumstances' as the national of the first state
(iii) Determine whether the taxation (or connected requirements) imposed by the second state on the national of the first state is 'other or more burdensome' than the treatment by the second state of its own hypothetical national

'National' is defined in Article 3(1)(g) of the OECD Model. The nationality of individuals is straightforward but that of artificial entities requires further discussion. Irrespective of whether a corporation can have a nationality under international law, the OECD Model treats a corporation as a national of the country from which it derives its status and so Article 24(1) may apply to a corporation.

As to the second factor in applying Article 24(1) of the OECD Model, the words 'in particular with respect to residence' are important, although the OECD Commentary notes that a difference of residence would mean

[131] Avery Jones et al. (1991, p. 359).

taxpayers are not 'in the same circumstances' in any case.[132] The result is that a country may discriminate based on residence but not nationality. Consider the *Base Case* (Figure 1 on p. 5). Presume that Beth is a national of Country B (the residence state) and that Country A (the source state) decided to tax Beth at 40 per cent with respect to the rental income when the highest rate that might be suffered by a resident of Country A was 30 per cent. Would this obvious discrimination breach Article 24(1)? It seems that would depend on how a Country A national who is, like Beth, resident in Country B would be treated by Country A when deriving a similar income. If the hypothetical Country A national who is resident in Country B would also be taxed at 40 per cent, and so suffer discrimination, there would be no breach of Article 24(1).[133] A clear application of Article 24(1) would be where Beth was resident in Country A but Country A still sought to tax her at 40% when resident nationals were only chargeable up to 30 per cent.

As noted, an artificial entity is treated as a national of the country from which it derives its status. This is also a test of residence in the domestic laws of many countries; see above at 2.1.1.2. For a country that uses only this test of residence, e.g. the US with respect to corporations, it seems there is no scope for applying OECD Model Art. 24(1) as artificial nationals of the other contracting state will always be in different circumstances to local artificial nationals, especially with respect to residence. For dual resident persons (corporations or individuals), a question is whether the reference to the word 'residence' in Article 24(1) derives its meaning from application of Article 4(3), i.e. the tiebreaker (discussed above at 2.1.1.2). The better view is that it does and, in any case, the application of the

132 OECD Commentary to Article 24 para. 3. In *R* v *IRC ex parte Commerzbank* (1991) 68 TC 252 (QBD) (also discussed above at 1.2.2), a German bank (incorporated in Germany and not resident in the UK) had a UK branch. It claimed discrimination under the equivalent of Art. 24(1) in the Germany/UK treaty because it was not entitled to interest on a UK tax repayment while a UK resident corporation would have been so entitled. The court held (equating nationality with incorporation) that the correct comparison was between a corporation incorporated in Germany and not resident in the UK and a corporation incorporated in the UK and not resident in the UK, i.e. same circumstances with respect to residence. At this time there was no incorporation test for corporate residence in UK domestic law.

133 Why OECD Model Art. 24(1) is limited in this way is not particularly clear. Perhaps one explanation is that some countries have non-discrimination entrenched in their constitutions and constitutions typically grant rights to nationals (citizens). In such a case, would our hypothetical Country A national who is resident in Country B be able to claim taxation at 30 per cent based on constitutional grounds? If so, would Beth be able to invoke Article 24(1) as a result?

tiebreaker is likely to mean that two persons resident in a particular country under domestic law where one is not considered resident for tax treaty purposes are not 'in the same circumstances'.[134]

There are other situations in which a foreigner cannot put itself 'in the same circumstances' as a national. In particular, the OECD notes the position of domestic public bodies or services, which are integral parts of the state and so inherently not comparable with foreign organisations. It takes the same view with respect to private charitable institutions, which are often exempt from taxation and whose domestic immunity is justified by the benefits derived by the state and its nationals.[135]

When two persons have appropriately been identified as comparable, the third issue is whether the taxation (or connected requirements) imposed by the second state on the national of the first state is 'other or more burdensome' than the treatment by the second state of its own hypothetical national. The OECD suggests that this means that the same form must be used 'as regards both the basis of charge and method of assessment, the rate must be the same' and other formalities are not to be more onerous for foreigners.[136] So, to continue the example from the penultimate paragraph, assuming Beth to be in the same circumstances as a Country A national, she must not only be taxed at the same rate (or rates) but on the same basis, e.g. offered the same deductions and subjected to the same collection procedure including any withholding. The negative phrasing of Article 24(1) of the OECD Model means that a country is permitted to treat foreign nationals *more favourably* than its own nationals.[137] This can be contrasted with the position under the FEU Treaty state aid rules, discussed below.

EU Law As regards fundamental principles, the state/taxpayer relationship under EU Law is in stark contrast to that under tax treaties. The FEU Treaty does contain fundamental principles, such as the freedoms discussed above at 2.1.2.3. Further, one of the reasons why these principles are given direct effect is because of the cooperation between nationals of member states that the FEU Treaty calls for.[138] Despite difficulties in

[134] OECD Commentary to Article 24 paras. 17, 24 and 25.

[135] OECD Commentary to Article 24 paras. 10–12.

[136] OECD Commentary to Article 24 para. 15.

[137] OECD Commentary to Article 24 para. 14.

[138] See the quote from the ECJ in Case 26/62 *NV Algemene Transport- en Expeditie Onderneming van Gend and Loos* v *Netherlands Inland Revenue Administration* [1963] ECR 3 (ECJ) above in footnote 76.

securing a 'constitution' for the EU, the ECJ thinks and behaves like a constitutional court when interpreting the fundamental principles incorporated in the FEU Treaty. This is also clear in its observation that member states limited their sovereignty by entering into the EU Treaties (see above at 1.3.3).

The FEU Treaty, at least indirectly, incorporates the standard principles of equity and efficiency. The latter is clear in the requirement that the 'internal market shall comprise an area without internal frontiers in which the free movement of goods, persons, services and capital is ensured' and the prohibition of practices that 'have as their object or effect the prevention, restriction or distortion of competition within the internal market'; Articles 26(2) and 101(1), respectively. The European Commission has had reason to reflect on the differences between EU Law and international tax law based on the bilateral tax treaty network.

> The difference between these two approaches results from the difference between the principal objectives of the relevant Community law provisions and international law, respectively. While the four freedoms provisions aim at removing the borders between Member States, in as much as possible, for intra-Community economic activities, the very starting point of international tax law is the existence of these borders.[139]

As regards equity, the FEU Treaty has as one of its stated aims the elimination of inequalities within the activities covered by the treaty.[140] Article 18 supports this aim:

> Within the scope of application of the Treaties, and without prejudice to any special provisions contained therein, any discrimination on grounds of nationality shall be prohibited.

It is not clear that this provision will be given direct effect but, in any case, its application is residual:

> [T]he general prohibition of all discrimination on grounds of nationality laid down by art 6 [now 18] of the EC Treaty applies independently only to situations governed by Community law for which the treaty lays down no specific non-discrimination rules.[141]

[139] European Commission (2001, p. 309).

[140] FEU Treaty Art. 8.

[141] Cases C-397/98 and 410/98 *Metallgesellschaft Ltd* v *IRC and AG; Hoechst AG* v *IRC and AG* [2001] ECR I-1727 (ECJ) at para. 38

The point appears to be that, at least in tax matters, discriminatory behaviour will usually be found to breach one of the four freedoms in Title IV of Part three of the FEU Treaty (discussed above at 2.1.2.3), leaving little if any scope for the application of Article 18.[142] Using discrimination as the test for breach of the four freedoms is now somewhat outdated but it is, perhaps, correct to suggest that discrimination is still the touchstone for breach of these freedoms.

Discrimination is the fundamental basis upon which the ECJ has found member states' direct tax measures to breach the four freedoms. So, at least in a broad sense, there is a commonality of principle here between tax treaties based on the OECD Model and EU Law, both incorporating an underlying principle of non-discrimination. So what does the concept of discrimination involve?

> It is also settled law that discrimination can arise only through the application of different rules to comparable situations or the application of the same rule to different situations.[143]

It is implicit that the concept of discrimination involves comparing the factual situation in question with a hypothetical situation. Identifying an appropriate hypothetical situation can be problematic and the difficulty for both tax treaties and EU Law is determining when situations are comparable and when they are different. Identifying an appropriate hypothetical comparator will be a continuing theme of this book as it seeks to apply the principles of non-discrimination to various situations.

A similarity between the non-discrimination concepts in Article 24(1) of the OECD Model and Article 18 of the FEU Treaty is that both are based on nationality. However, as discussed, the OECD specifically identifies residence as a factor sufficient to distinguish the circumstances between nationals. The FEU Treaty includes no such qualification and the direct tax case law of the ECJ suggests, to the contrary, that a difference of residence of itself is not a sufficient distinguishing factor. For example, in the *Schumacker* case, the ECJ noted:

> 26. The court has consistently held that the rules regarding equal treatment forbid not only overt discrimination by reason of nationality

[142] Kingston (2007, p. 1328) notes that the 'ECJ initially interpreted Articles [45, 49 and 56] as amounting to specific applications of the general Article [18] prohibition of – direct and indirect – discrimination on grounds of nationality'.

[143] Case C-279/93 *Finanzamt Koln-Altstadt* v *Schumacker* [1995] ECR I-225 (ECJ) at para. 30.

but also all covert forms of discrimination which, by the application of other criteria of differentiation, lead in fact to the same result…

27. It is true that the rules at issue in the main proceedings apply irrespective of the nationality of the taxpayer concerned.
28. However, national rules of that kind, under which a distinction is drawn on the basis of residence in that non-residents are denied certain benefits which are, conversely, granted to persons residing within national territory, are liable to operate mainly to the detriment of nationals of other member states. Non-residents are in the majority of cases foreigners.
29. In those circumstances, tax benefits granted only to residents of a member state may constitute indirect discrimination by reason of nationality.[144]

As income tax laws are typically based on residence rather than nationality, most direct tax cases that come before the ECJ are based on covert or indirect breaches of the freedoms. Nevertheless, the ECJ in *Schumacker* went on to note that 'the situations of residents and of non-residents are not, as a rule, comparable' because international norms, including the OECD Model, presume that it is the residence country's responsibility to adjust taxation to the personal circumstances of the taxpayer. This is, of course, consistent with the residence based tax as a personal tax. Nevertheless, on the facts of the case, the court held that residents and non-residents are comparable where the 'major part' of the person's taxable income is derived in the state of source.[145]

From the mid-1990s, the ECJ began to accept that proving discrimination was not necessary in order to show a breach of the fundamental freedoms and this broader approach flowed into direct tax cases. Further, like the OECD Model non-discrimination provision, early direct tax cases before the ECJ focused on the host or source country, i.e. the place where the activity was situated. This also changed. The current position is clear from the following passage:

[144] Case C-279/93 *Finanzamt Koln-Altstadt* v *Schumacker* [1995] ECR I-225 (ECJ). The OECD Commentary on Art. 24 para. 1 now specifically suggests that Art. 24 'should not be unduly extended to cover so-called "indirect" discrimination based on nationality'. The difference between the approach in OECD Model Art. 24(1) and that in EU Law is starkly illustrated by the ECJ leg of the *Commerzbank* litigation. Despite constituting no breach of Article 24(1) (see above at footnote 132), the refusal by the UK to pay a non-resident interest on overpaid tax, when such was available to a resident, did constitute a breach of the freedom of establishment under EU Law. See Case C-330/91 *R* v *IRC, ex parte Commerzbank AG* [1993] ECR I-4017 (ECJ) particularly at para. 15.

[145] Case C-279/93 *Finanzamt Koln-Altstadt* v *Schumacker* [1995] ECR I-225 (ECJ) at paras. 31–6.

> Even though, according to their wording, the provisions concerning freedom of establishment are directed to ensuring that foreign nationals and companies are treated in the host Member State in the same way as nationals of that State, they also prohibit the Member State of origin from hindering the establishment in another Member State of one of its nationals or of a company incorporated under its legislation.[146]

This expanded approach to the freedom of establishment was applied by the ECJ in *Deutsche Shell*, a direct tax case where it was not possible to show discrimination but where the facts nevertheless gave rise to a prohibited obstacle.[147] The case involved a German corporation that injected capital into an Italian permanent establishment (before the introduction of the Euro). The corporation suffered an exchange loss on repatriation of the capital due to a fall in the Italian currency. Italy could not account for this loss as the profits and capital of the establishment were calculated in its currency. The same could be said of a German establishment with German capital. There was no apparent comparator such as to ground an allegation of discrimination. Nevertheless, the ECJ noted:

> 28 According to settled case-law, all measures which prohibit, impede or render less attractive the exercise of that freedom must be regarded as obstacles.
>
> 30 The tax system concerned in the main proceedings increases the economic risks incurred by a company established in one Member State wishing to set up a body in another Member State where the currency used is different from that of the State of origin. In such a situation, not only does the principal establishment face the normal risks associated with setting up such a body, but it must also face an additional risk of a fiscal nature where it provides start-up capital for it.
>
> 31 Because it exercised its freedom of establishment Deutsche Shell suffered financial loss which was not taken into account either by the national tax authorities for the purposes of calculating the basis of assessment for corporation tax in Germany or with respect to the assessment for tax of its permanent establishment in Italy.
>
> 32 It must be held that the tax system at issue in the main proceedings constitutes an obstacle to the freedom of establishment.

Tax measures that prima facie breach the fundamental freedoms may be acceptable if they are sufficiently justified. The process of justification is subtly different depending on whether overt or covert discrimination is

[146] Case C-446/03 *Marks and Spencer* v *Halsey* [2005] ECR I-10837 (ECJ) at para. 31.

[147] Case C-293/06 *Deutsche Shell* v *Finanzamt für Grossunternehmen in Hamburg* [2008] ECR I-1129 (ECJ).

involved, but as most direct tax issues involve covert discrimination that is the present focus.[148] The ECJ takes a three-step approach to justification:

1 Does the discriminatory measure pursue a legitimate objective compatible with the FEU Treaty?
2 Are the national rules appropriate to attain that objective?
3 Do the rules go no further than what is necessary for that purpose, i.e. is there proportionality?[149]

The ECJ has been quite restrictive in the grounds it accepts for justifying discrimination.[150] The following, amongst others, are not acceptable grounds:

- The need, in the absence of harmonisation, to take account of differences between national tax rules
- The fact that the non-resident could have avoided the discrimination, e.g. by setting up a subsidiary instead of a branch
- Economic aims or protection of the revenue
- The absence of reciprocity
- Administrative difficulties including discretionary or equitable procedures to ensure appropriate fiscal treatment

Historically, the most common ground raised for justification of discriminatory taxation was coherence of the tax system.[151] Of more importance is the three-pronged approach to justification accepted in the *Marks & Spencer* case. The facts concerned a refusal to grant a parent company, in one member state, tax relief for losses incurred by a subsidiary in another member state. The case is considered in more detail at 4.2.4. The ECJ accepted that the following might justify the discrimination identified on the facts:

[148] Regarding the difference in approach, see Kingston (2007, pp. 1328–9). In effect, overt discrimination can be justified only on grounds of express FEU Treaty derogations such as those in Arts. 45(3), 52 and 62. Van Thiel (2008, p. 279) states that '[t]he starting assumption is that the justifications that are explicitly provided for by the [FEU] Treaty are of no use in the tax area'.

[149] For an early non-tax case, see Case C-19/92 *Kraus* v *Land Baden-Wurtemburg* [1993] ECR I-1663 (ECJ). This approach is still clear under the broader approach to the freedoms as, for example, in Case C-196/04 *Cadbury Schweppes* [2006] ECR I-7995 (ECJ).

[150] Generally, see van Thiel (2008).

[151] The argument was successfully raised in Case C-204/90 *Bachmann* v *Belgian State* [1992] ECR I-249 (ECJ). For a recent consideration of the scope of this ground, see Case C-293/06 *Deutsche Shell* v *Finanzamt für Grossunternehmen in Hamburg* [2008] ECR I-1129 (ECJ) at paras. 37–40.

1 Symmetry, profits and losses must be treated similarly in the same tax system (regarding jurisdiction) to protect a balanced allocation of taxing rights
2 Possibility of losses being taken into account twice
3 Risk of tax avoidance

An issue is whether each of these can independently comprise a justification for discrimination. It is clear that the risk of tax avoidance can of itself justify discrimination (provided the measure is appropriately targeted and proportionate).[152] Here the test is whether the restrictive legislation has the specific objective of preventing

> conduct involving the creation of wholly artificial arrangements which do not reflect economic reality, with a view to escaping the tax normally due on the profits generated by activities carried out on national territory.[153]

The second point for justification in the *Marks & Spencer* case seems to be largely an example of the risk of tax avoidance. The greater issue is the first point, i.e. the extent to which the balance of taxing rights created by tax treaties may be used as a justification for discriminatory treatment. This will be further investigated throughout the book but, as a preliminary matter, it is clear that discrimination permitted by the terms of a tax treaty is not automatically justified by the allocation of taxing rights under the treaty.[154]

To this point, the focus has been on the approach to the free movement of workers, the freedom of establishment and the freedom to provide services. There was a question as to whether the ECJ would adopt the same approach with respect to the free movement of capital. The width of Article 63 of the FEU Treaty was noted above at 2.1.2.3. This width is limited by Article 65, which provides in part:

> 1. The provisions of Article 63 shall be without prejudice to the right of Member States… to apply the relevant provisions of their tax law which distinguish between taxpayers who are not in the same situation with regard to their place of residence or with regard to the place where their capital is invested…

[152] Case C-196/04 *Cadbury Schweppes* [2006] ECR I-7995 (ECJ) is an example. See van Thiel (2008, pp. 282–7) regarding anti-avoidance as a justification for restrictive practices.
[153] Case C-196/04 *Cadbury Schweppes* [2006] ECR I-7995 (ECJ) at para. 55.
[154] For example, see Case C-170/05 *Denkavit Internationaal BV and Denkavit France SARL* v *Ministre de l'Économie, des Finances et de l'Industrie* [2006] ECR I-11949 (ECJ) at para. 53 and generally see O'Brien (2008, pp. 649–51).

> 3. The measures and procedures referred to in paragraphs 1... shall not constitute a means of arbitrary discrimination or a disguised restriction on the free movement of capital and payments ...

The reference to 'residence' in Article 65(1) seems to reflect the use of that term in Article 24(1) of the OECD Model, discussed above. The issue is how the limitation in Article 65(1) of the FEU Treaty should be read in light of paragraph 3 of that article. What difference, if any, is there between discrimination and 'arbitrary' discrimination or between a restriction and a 'disguised' restriction. Perhaps the ECJ has not yet given a final word on these distinctions, but in *Manninen* it noted:

> Article [65](1)(a) of the Treaty, which, as a derogation from the fundamental principle of the free movement of capital, must be interpreted strictly... The derogation in Article [65](1)(a) [FEU] is itself limited by Article [65](3) [FEU]... A distinction must therefore be made between unequal treatment which is permitted under Article [65](1)(a) [FEU] and arbitrary discrimination which is prohibited by Article [65](3)... [T]he difference in treatment must concern situations which are not objectively comparable or be justified by overriding reasons in the general interest, such as the need to safeguard the cohesion of the tax system... In order to be justified, moreover, the difference in treatment between different categories of dividends must not go beyond what is necessary in order to attain the objective of the legislation.[155]

In effect, the ECJ appears to have read down the limitation in Article 65(1) of the FEU Treaty to the point where it is not clear that it has any greater effect than the circumstances in which discrimination may be justified in the context of the other freedoms. Considering the recent growth in cases concerning the free movement of capital, this is important.

As noted above at 2.1.2.3, the free movement of capital can apply in third country situations. While the situation is still evolving, it seems arguable that justifications for a restriction on the movement of capital with third countries may be broader than those available for movements within member states. In particular, the ECJ has identified mutual assistance in tax matters as potentially important in this regard. The Exchange of Information Directive (discussed below at 7.1.3) applies only within the EU. Its lack of applicability outside the EU may mean that

[155] Case C-319/02 *Manninen* [2004] ECR I-7477 (ECJ) at paras 28–9. Van Thiel (2008, p. 279) notes that 'even the explicit tax justifications in the Maastricht Treaty articles on the free movement of capital have given no extra room for Member States to apply discriminatory anti-avoidance measures.'

> a Member State will be able to demonstrate that a restriction on the movement of capital to or from third countries is justified for a particular reason in circumstances where that reason would not constitute a valid justification for a restriction on capital movements between Member States.[156]

By analogy, it seems that exchange of information measures that do apply between member states and third countries (discussed below at 7.1.1 and 7.1.2) may also be important in determining available justifications.[157]

Interstate relationship

Inter-nation equity Starting with a model in which most countries tax on both a residence and source basis, the elimination of international double taxation requires some sort of sacrifice or limitation on taxing rights of the residence country, the source country or both. It is often suggested that how this elimination should be achieved is a matter of inter-nation equity, i.e. a fair allocation of taxing rights between source and residence countries.[158] The starting point of inter-nation equity is the principle of source country entitlement. This principle suggests that the source country is entitled to some priority regarding taxation of cross-border income. This is evident in the general practice of residence countries providing relief from international double taxation. Historically, this principle may have been founded on the administrative fact that the country where the income arises has first access to the income for tax purposes, the residence country often having to wait for repatriation. Irrespective of its origins, the source country entitlement principle is generally accepted.[159]

The source country's right to tax is not without limitation. First, it may be limited by practical constraints. Capital importing countries find it difficult to tax highly mobile income, i.e. income where the geographical source is easily moved. Any attempt to tax such income may result in capital flight, i.e. the capital may move to another country that does not tax that type of income. The residence country may be in a superior position to tax highly mobile income, as historically persons have not been as mobile as income. While this is probably still true, globalisation has

[156] Case C-101/05 *Skatteverket* v *A* [2007] ECR I-11531 (ECJ) at para. 37. For a case in which this argument did not succeed, see Case C-521/07 *European Commission* v *Netherlands* [2009] ECR 00 (ECJ).

[157] Generally, see O'Brien (2008, pp. 662–5).

[158] The concept of inter-nation is attributable to the Musgraves in the early 1970s. For a more recent reconsideration of the inter-nation equity principle, see Brooks (2008).

[159] Generally, see Harris (1996, pp. 313–15) and the references cited therein.

increased the mobility of persons and income and countries are increasingly relying on stable factors such as land and employees. High wage/high tax countries have even found that their employee tax base can disappear offshore with devastating local effects.

Further, tax treaties commonly limit source country taxing rights, indeed that is one of their primary effects. If that is the effect of tax treaties, then why do countries enter into them? If capital and income flows between two countries are relatively proportionate, then limiting source country taxing rights has little impact on the overall tax take of the treaty partners. This perhaps explains why the worldwide tax treaty network was initially focused in the developed world. If the capital and income flows between two countries are disproportionate, then limiting source country taxing rights affects the capital importing country to a greater extent than it affects the capital exporting country. Why then should such a capital importing country conclude a tax treaty with a capital exporting country? Tax treaties are about more than just limiting source country taxing rights. They also guarantee that the residence country will provide foreign tax relief, although it is true that most countries do this unilaterally in any case. Further, for some developing countries the conclusion of tax treaties is a sign of legitimacy. It is recognition of the country's place in the international community and fosters confidence in potential investors. A tax treaty also provides for communication between tax authorities with the potential to resolve disputes involving double taxation, discussed below in Chapter 7.

In large part, tax treaties based on the OECD Model allocate the primary right to tax particular types of income to either the source country or the residence country. In this context, the treaty will usually say nothing about the rate at which a country may tax and so the usual domestic rates apply. However, in two instances the source country's right to tax a particular type of income is limited to a specific rate of the gross amount of the income. This is the case for dividends and interest.[160] This taxation, which is usually collected by way of withholding tax, is underlined by the principle of reciprocity of withholding tax rates. This means that a country negotiating a tax treaty expects to have the right to impose tax on dividends and interest at the same rate as the other contracting state. The rate is the same for dividends and interest flowing in either direction between the two states. This principle is so ingrained in tax treaties that countries will reserve reciprocal rights to impose a tax at the same rate on

[160] Under the UN Model this is also the case for royalties.

these types of income even if they do not and never have taxed that type of income of non-residents. For example, under many of its treaties the UK still reserves the right to apply a dividend withholding tax, even though for the vast majority of its history it has not imposed one.

Harmful tax competition The previous discussion assumed that source countries actually wish to levy substantial tax from international transactions. However, as mentioned, some types of income are highly mobile and attempts to tax it may result in capital flight, but to where will the capital fly? The most likely scenario is that it will fly to a low tax jurisdiction. Countries have been long aware of the magnetic attraction of low taxation to highly mobile capital. Accordingly, a country in need of capital may seek to attract that capital by intentionally targeting mobile capital with preferential tax rules in order to secure a disproportionate allocation of capital. When this distorting behaviour is intentional it is often referred to as 'harmful tax competition'. The risk posed by harmful tax competition is that countries will continually attempt to undercut their competitors' tax rates with the result that governments are under-funded and the services they provide are negatively affected.

At its worse, harmful tax competition involves the design of a tax system in order to assist taxpayers in avoiding taxation imposed by other countries. If it is important to ensure the removal of double taxation of international transactions, it seems equally important to ensure that income from such transactions is appropriately taxed. The variation of tax rates between countries exposes the basic essence of tax planning. For example, corporate tax rates vary dramatically between countries. Even within the EU this can range from between 10 and 40 per cent. In this context, basic tax planning involves locating deductions in high tax countries (to ensure no income is subject to high tax) and locating income receipts in low tax countries. This basic strategy increases a multinational's after tax profits without changing the nature of what it does. Harmful tax competition means that resources do not flow to where they are most productive, with a resultant loss in efficiency.

In 1996, the OECD began a project to coordinate a response to harmful tax competition, with a major report being released in 1998.[161] In many ways, this project paralleled a similar project within the EU, which will be considered shortly. The report noted that harmful tax measures are

[161] OECD (1998). Both Luxembourg and Switzerland abstained from the report.

often targeted at highly mobile factors such as financial and other services activities. The report listed key factors in identifying a harmful tax regime. These include no or a low effective tax rate, making a regime available only to non-residents or other international players (so called 'ring-fencing'), a lack of transparency as to who is entitled to a regime and the benefits available as well as a refusal or resistance for exchanging information at the tax administration level. By June 2000, the OECD had proceeded to list 47 preferential tax regimes of member countries and 35 countries as tax havens. It engaged with these countries in seeking commitments. The project became highly political, especially following a change of government in the US, and the project became identified as essentially an issue of transparency and exchange of information.

By April 2002, the OECD had secured commitments to transparency and effective exchange of information from some 31 jurisdictions and considered these cooperative jurisdictions. Those countries that did not make such commitments were identified as uncooperative tax havens. In 2002 these were Andorra, Liechtenstein, Liberia, Monaco, the Marshall Islands, Nauru and Vanuatu. Pressure continued and in 2003 Vanuatu was removed from the list, as was Nauru later that year. In 2007, both Liberia and the Marshall Islands were removed from the list, leaving Andorra, Liechtenstein and Monaco as uncooperative tax havens. The remaining three jurisdictions were removed in 2009 and the OECD's attention has moved to focus on a grey list of countries that do not comply with the commitments that have been made.[162]

The main difficulty faced by the harmful tax competition project was not so much the importance of the issue but rather the alleged hypocrisy of the group of countries driving it. The OECD project seemed targeted at non-member countries, pressuring them into exchange of information when countries within the OECD refused to engage in effective exchange of information with respect to certain issues.[163] This was particularly a problem when the draft EU Savings Directive became essentially focused on exchange of information and some countries, namely Switzerland and Luxembourg, were given long transition periods before being required to relax their financial privacy laws.[164]

[162] Generally, regarding the OECD's work on countering international tax evasion, see OECD (2009).

[163] Switzerland, Luxembourg, Austria, Belgium and even the US have been mentioned in this regard. For example, see Scott (2004).

[164] During the transition period, Switzerland and Luxembourg impose substantial withholding taxes on payments of interest falling within the Savings Directive.

Some commentators are not concerned by tax competition, arguing that it encourages governments to behave efficiently in providing public services. The risk, however, is that tax competition will mean that governments are encouraged to provide only those services that assist in producing income and not, for example, those that serve a redistribution function. The *doom and gloom* forecasters predict that even the most socialist of countries will give in to market forces with the risk of social unrest. In its 1998 report the OECD outlined a number of methods by which countries could counteract harmful tax competition including controlled foreign corporation rules, effective transfer pricing rules, greater exchange of information and the limitation of treaty benefits. It also outlined topics for further study including restrictions on deduction for payments to tax havens, withholding taxes on such payments, broader residence rules and thin capitalisation rules. Each of these mechanisms will be considered in the remainder of this book.

Events in 2008 and 2009 gave new impetus to the OECD harmful tax competition project. These are recounted below at 7.1. In particular, there has been a flurry of activity on the exchange of information front, but there has also been renewed attention on the type of counteracting measures mentioned in the last paragraph to be used against countries that do not meet the OECD prescribed standards. It is also clear that a system for monitoring compliance with these standards is being formalised.[165]

The OECD harmful tax competition project focuses on competition between source countries as to the location of capital. In that context, it was often pointed out that countries adopting a capital import neutrality philosophy are particularly prone to this sort of competition. As discussed above, capital import neutrality suggests that the total tax levied on international transactions should be based on the tax rate in the source country. Proponents of capital export neutrality, taxation at the residence country rate, could suggest that their philosophy was not prone to this sort of competition and with effective exchange of information and current taxation residence countries could neutralise harmful tax competition. This is true, but simply places greater pressure on residence as the dominant connecting factor. As mentioned, recently it is becoming clear that an increasing number of taxpayers *are* willing to move their residence for tax purposes. This will be returned to at 6.2.

[165] For a recent restatement by Finance Ministers from 19 countries at a conference held in Berlin in June 2009, see Finance Ministers (2009).

EU Law considerations Unlike tax treaties, the FEU Treaty is not directly concerned with allocating rights to direct taxation between member states. As noted above, subject to a weak concept of non-discrimination, the rights of taxpayers under double tax treaties stem directly from the manner in which the contracting states have allocated taxing rights between themselves. This is simply not true of the FEU Treaty. Here the fundamental freedoms read with a general provision on non-discrimination give taxpayers the protection of a holistic non-discrimination principle. At least historically, in applying the provisions of the FEU Treaty the ECJ has not been concerned with which country gets tax with respect to cross-border transactions. Rather, the focus has been on the state/taxpayer relationship and whether a country has engaged in discriminatory or restrictive practices regarding the taxpayer.

This fundamental distinction between tax treaties and the FEU Treaty was at the heart of the disquiet with ECJ centralist jurisprudence in direct tax matters when it was at its height in the period from 2000 to mid-2005. Accusations were made that the ECJ was destroying member states' direct tax systems and that it did not understand the nature of the tax treaty network. Of course, this was not the problem. Member states were used to taxpayers deriving their rights only from the manner in which they had allocated taxing rights under tax treaties. In short, they were used to discriminatory practices inherent in or permitted by tax treaties. The ECJ, by contrast, was looking at the fundamental rights in the FEU Treaty, the application of which pays no respect for any allocation of taxing rights agreed at the state level.

While there is a certain academic attraction to a pure approach to non-discrimination in direct tax matters, politically the member states were not ready for it. And winning cases was not always good news for taxpayers, who often found that a member state losing a case would simply bring their offending international restriction onshore, i.e. also apply it to domestic transactions and thereby cure the discrimination. The *D* case in the middle of 2005[166] marked a watershed for ECJ centralist jurisprudence and a number of cases since then have recognised the need to preserve 'a balanced allocation of the power to impose taxes between Member States'.[167] In the *Thin Cap* case the ECJ endorsed the arm's length principle of tax treaties,[168] which, as will be discussed at 3.3.1.4, is the primary

[166] Case C-376/03 *D* v *Inspecteur van de Belastingdient* [2005] ECR I-5821 (ECJ).

[167] Case C-446/03 *Marks and Spencer* v *Halsey* [2005] ECR I-10837 (ECJ) at para. 46.

[168] Case C-524/04 *Test Claimants in the Thin Cap Group Litigation* [2007] ECR 00 (ECJ).

method that protects the allocation of taxing rights under tax treaties. Therefore, with this developing jurisprudence, the ECJ has recognised that the manner in which member states have allocated taxing rights between themselves is relevant in justifying discriminatory or restrictive practices. As discussed above, the precise manner in which this is relevant is not yet clear.

In contrast with the FEU Treaty, the directives dealing with direct taxation do involve a direct allocation of taxing rights between member states. In this sense, they are comparable with tax treaties and, as noted at 2.1.2.3, the Parent-Subsidiary Directive and the Interest and Royalties Directive contain provisions derived from tax treaties. Like with tax treaties, taxpayers are caught up in the allocation involved in these directives and hence that allocation may affect taxpayer behaviour. The primary aim of the directives is the elimination of withholding taxes on cross-border distributions of passive income between members of corporate groups. These withholding taxes are particularly distorting with respect to cross-border investment largely because they are levied on a gross basis and do not permit a deduction for what are sometimes substantial expenses. This difficulty will be returned to below at 4.2.

Of particular interest to the present discussion is the manner in which these directives affect the allocation of taxing rights between member states and the effect that this may have on the behaviour of taxpayers. The Parent-Subsidiary Directive will typically result in pure benefit to the taxpayer. It prohibits the taxation of dividends by the source state but usually the tax forgone is not then levied by the residence state, which is obliged to provide underlying foreign tax relief (as to which see below at 4.1.2.1). The Directive preserves the source state right to levy its corporate tax, the primary source country tax. As a result, the Parent-Subsidiary Directive does little to address the problem of harmful tax competition between source countries and, in some situations, may make it more acute.

The Interest and Royalties Directive is of a very different nature. It is true that it removes the distorting effect of non-deductible expenses but it also results in a fundamental shift of taxing rights from source to residence countries. Source countries are prohibited from taxing interest and royalties and yet, in usual circumstances, they will be required to grant a deduction to the payer of the interest or royalties. The result is a flow of pure untaxed funds from the source country in the anticipation that it will be taxed in the residence country of the recipient. The result, in fundamental contrast to the Parent-Subsidiary Directive, is tax competition, not between the location of the activity giving rise to the income, but where an artificial person is considered resident. As discussed above at 2.1.1.2, corporate residence is a difficult concept and is often easily manipulated.

In some ways, the inconsistency in approach between these two important directives leaves the tax systems of member states exposed. They leave the corporate profits tax in the country where an activity is located open to tax competition and so underscore an incentive to locate corporate profits in low tax jurisdictions. If this is not possible, a corporate group may refinance and seek to erode the corporate tax base where an activity is located with inter-group interest and royalty payments. The group can then manipulate the taxation of these payments by locating the residence of the recipient corporation in a low tax jurisdiction. In the usual way, it is left to anti-abuse rules to protect the potential negative consequences of these poorly thought through policy decisions.

As pre-empted above, the EU Code of Conduct, issued in 1997, paralleled the OECD project on harmful tax competition for Business Taxation.[169] This was in many ways a predecessor to the OECD Harmful Tax Competition Report of 1998. In 1998, the EU Council set up a group (the 'Primarolo Group') to assess tax measures that may fall within the Code. The group reported in 1999 and identified 66 target regimes. Like the OECD project, the EU Code of Conduct takes the form of a non-binding arrangement. However, unlike the OECD project, the EU code is to some extent supported by EU Law. The Code noted that the regimes covered by it may breach the EU state aid rules and these are the primary source of sanction in this regard. In particular, Article 107(1) of the FEU Treaty provides:

> Save as otherwise provided in the Treaties, any aid granted by a Member State... which distorts or threatens to distort competition by favouring certain undertakings or the production of certain goods shall, insofar as it affects trade between Member States, be incompatible with the internal market.

Unlike the fundamental freedoms (discussed above at 2.1.2.3), Article 107(1) does not have direct effect.[170] Nevertheless, it is important to understand how this provision balances those freedoms. The latter are targeted at member states' discrimination against nationals of other states conducting activities in their jurisdiction or their own nationals conducting activities in the jurisdictions of other member states. They are targeted at restricting cross-border activity. By contrast, the state aid rules are targeted at member states engaging in conduct that will increase cross-

[169] European Union (1997).

[170] Case C-74/76 *Ianelli and Volpi SpA* v *Meroni* [1977] ECR 557 (ECJ).

border activity in an excessive, distorting manner. Member states must navigate their tax systems in the safe waters between these two extremes.

The state aid rules provide yet another fundamental distinction between tax treaties and EU Law. Tax treaties contain nothing akin to the state aid rules. The only rules that have some affect in this area on a worldwide basis are the WTO rules, see above at 1.2.4 and the references cited there. When interpreting Article 107 of the FEU treaty in the context of direct tax rules, a distinction is made between low general tax rates and more targeted concessions.

> [A] low general corporate tax rate in one Member State will not be regarded as a State aid, while selective tax breaks clearly focused on certain companies (like for instance firms in underdeveloped regions) would indeed need to be assessed following the Treaty provisions on State aid.
>
> This distinction between general and specific measures is thus a very important one. Let me take an Irish example, the special 10 % rate of corporation tax for manufacturing. This measure is specific to one sector of the economy. Accordingly, the Commission had to take action under the State aid rules and in 1998 agreed with the Irish Government the conditions for phasing out the manufacturing rate. In contrast, Ireland's general reduction of corporation tax to 12.5 % is a general measure outside the scope of the State aid rules and the Commission's control.[171]

There is a substantial and developing case law of the ECJ regarding state aid and direct taxation. Most of this is concerned with specific concessions (e.g. for banks, underdeveloped areas, research and development) but does not raise tax treaty issues unless implemented in a discriminatory fashion. Accordingly, like the WTO rules, the FEU Treaty state aid rules are not further discussed in this book.[172]

2.2.2 *Methods for relief*

This subheading considers the options or methods for relieving international double taxation and allocating taxing rights between countries.

[171] Monti (2003, paras. 21–2).

[172] For example, see Sheppard (2006) regarding ECJ case law developments in 2005. The European Commission has been particularly active in ensuring accession states' tax laws comply with the state aid rules, e.g. see Gnaedinger (2003). Particular problems arise where the tax rates are different across economically independent regions of a state and there is a growing jurisprudence on the level of independence required to justify such tax rate differentials, e.g. see Cases C-428/06; 429/06; 430/06; 431/06; 432/06; 433/06 and 434/06 *Unión General de Trabajadores de La Rioja* et al. [2008] ECR I-674 (ECJ).

As with the principles discussed at 2.2.1, there are two levels of relationships to be considered in this discussion. Double taxation is primarily an affliction of the taxpayer and so the subheading first considers the methods available for relieving the taxpayer of double taxation. The focus here is on a particular taxpayer with respect to particular income. The manner in which a taxpayer is relieved of international double taxation affects or contributes to the allocation of taxing rights between countries, but that allocation is a much broader issue than relief with respect to one taxpayer with one item of income. The methods of allocating taxing rights between countries take effect at the interstate level and overlay the methods of double tax relief provided to taxpayers. This chapter ends with a consideration of the methods of allocation.

Double tax relief[173]

The present discussion presumes that double taxation arises from the simultaneous exercise of the right to tax by both the country where the source of the income is located and the country where the person deriving the income is resident. As noted above, there are other situations giving rise to international double taxation (see below at 5.2) but this is the most common. The options available for relieving this common type of international double taxation are a simple function of the mechanics giving rise to the double taxation. The double taxation arises due to the application by two countries of their tax equation to the same income of the same person, as in Figure 2.

These two tax equations provide six points of possible relief, three with respect to the source country's tax equation and three with respect to the residence country's tax equation.

In accordance with the source country entitlement principle, the focus is usually on relief provided by residence countries. The residence country may provide relief from international double taxation by exempting foreign income of residents, referred to as the *exemption method*. Moving to the second element of the residence country tax equation, relief may be provided by reducing the tax rate applicable to foreign income of residents, referred to as the *foreign income differentiation method*. Under this method, foreign income is still included in the taxpayer's taxable income for the purposes of progressive taxation. Where the tax rate is reduced to nil, this method is similar to the exemption method. However, because the foreign income is still included in taxable income, it may affect the

[173] Generally, see Harris (1996, pp. 282–3) and the references cited therein.

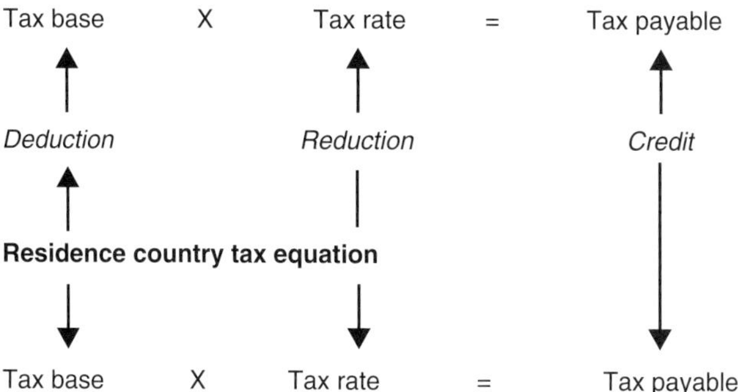

tax rate applicable to other income, e.g. domestic source income, so the foreign income differentiation method may produce *exemption with progression*. Finally, with respect to residence country relief, the country might grant a credit directly deductible against tax payable with respect to foreign income. Almost invariably, the credit is calculated by reference to the tax paid or payable in the source country, referred to as the *foreign tax credit method*.

Each of these methods will be discussed in more detail at 4.1.1, but it is appropriate to make some general comments at this stage. It is often suggested that the exemption method is consistent with capital import neutrality and the foreign tax credit method with capital export neutrality (see above at 2.2.1). This is true in some situations but in nearly as many cases will not be true. A cynic might suggest that capital import neutrality and capital export neutrality are terms invented to describe the basic economic operation of the exemption and credit methods, respectively. Unfortunately, the manner in which they are implemented in practice means that the exemption method and the foreign tax credit method do not produce consistent results.

For example, when passive income is involved, the exemption method is almost invariably replaced with the foreign tax credit method, and this is often the case when harmful tax competition is an issue. The foreign tax credit method produces overall taxation at the residence country's tax rate only where the source country's tax is lower than or equal to that in the residence country. Where it is higher, the credit method behaves like the exemption method, as it often does where a corporation is used to trap income before it reaches the beneficiary. The borderline between the exemption method and the foreign tax credit method can be blurred and complex. This will be returned to at 4.1.1.

Despite the source country entitlement principle, source countries often provide relief from international double taxation, particularly in the context of tax treaties. Residence country relief tends to be residual (like its taxing rights) but source country relief is typically targeted at particular circumstances. In principle, the methods that are available to source countries for relieving international double taxation match those available to residence countries and so may impact on one of the three elements of the source country's tax equation. The source country may exempt the income of non-residents. For example, this is often the case with some types of interest, royalties, capital gains and business income not derived through a permanent establishment.

The source country may also relieve international double taxation by reducing the tax rate applicable to non-residents. This is often the case with rent, dividends, interest and royalties, which may be taxed at a reduced rate but on a gross basis, i.e. without deductions. Almost never does a source country provide relief by reference to tax collected by a residence country. Source country relief from international double taxation will be discussed in further detail in Chapter 3 as part of the consideration of the general taxing rights of source countries.

Interstate relationship[174]

The options for allocating income taxing rights at the interstate level depend on the form of relationship between the source and residence countries. This relationship may take the form of a tax treaty or there may be no such direct relationship, in which case the relationship will be governed by international norms, i.e. custom. Where there is no direct relationship, a country will act unilaterally in providing relief from international double taxation, referred to as *unilateral relief*. Unilateral relief is not dependent on reciprocity of the other country and is particularly important from a residence country perspective because residence countries often provide broader relief from double taxation unilaterally than they do under tax treaties. The same is not generally true of source countries, which tend to exercise greater taxing rights unilaterally than they do under tax treaties. By contrast, the interstate relationship may be

[174] Generally, see Harris (1996, pp. 283–6) and the references cited therein.

formalised by treaty. A background to tax treaties was provided above at 1.2.2.

Irrespective of the form of the interstate relationship, source and residence countries may adopt a number of options in allocating tax rights between them. The simplest approach adopts only one of the six methods of double tax relief discussed above. In such a case, only the source country or only the residence country relieves double taxation with respect to income flowing in one direction between them. Most likely, the other country would provide relief for income flowing in the other direction. However, things are never that simple and countries inevitably adopt a combination of the six methods for relieving double taxation with respect to income flowing between them. A combination of the six primary methods may involve at least three approaches.

The first such approach applies a combination of methods of relief from international double taxation to a particular item of income. Therefore, for example, the source country may provide partial relief from double taxation through one method and the residence country the remainder through another. This is referred to as the *itemised division of tax method* and is commonly used in the context of passive income subject to limited gross taxation by source countries. Second, double taxation may be relieved by adopting different methods depending on the type of income in question, referred to as the *allocation according to type of income method*. Accordingly, the source country may provide relief with respect to some types of income using a particular method and the residence country provide residual relief or relief with respect to other types of income using a different method. In addition, one country may use one method of relief for one type of income and use a different method of relief for another type of income.

Third, the allocation of taxing rights and method of double tax relief may be made according to the type of or characteristics of taxpayers, e.g. corporations, individuals, partnerships, governmental organisations, students, academics, family commitments, etc. In this case, the residence country may provide relief with respect to some types of taxpayer, or different methods of relief depending on the type of taxpayer, and the source country provide relief with respect to other types of taxpayer. This is referred to as the *allocation according to type of taxpayer method*.

In all these instances, the interstate relationship is determined by each country's relationship with taxpayers deriving cross-border income. Here, with respect to each item of cross-border income of each taxpayer there is truly a tripartite relationship. However, source and residence countries may agree to free their relationship from their relationships with taxpayers. A further method of allocating taxing rights between source and residence countries is the *interstate payments method*. This involves the countries concerned selecting a method of relieving double taxation, which may differ as between type of income or taxpayer, etc. That will initially determine the tax collection by the countries but they may then decide to share the overall tax take according to some other criteria. This will almost invariably require one country to make payments to another in order to adjust the initial allocation of tax to the primary manner in which the countries have agreed to share tax.

Within the context of this framework of options, the OECD Model looks particularly complex. It simultaneously adopts all three of the itemised division of tax, allocation according to type of income and allocation according to type of taxpayer methods of allocating taxing rights between source and residence countries. Further, it simultaneously adopts more than one method of relief from double taxation for source countries and more than one method for residence countries. It seems the only option the OECD Model does not adopt is the interstate payments method. This underlines the point made earlier that it is a fundamental feature of the OECD Model that taxpayers derive their rights directly from the manner in which countries have agreed to allocate taxing rights between them.

The position with respect to EU Law is less prescribed. Article 293 of the EC Treaty used to impose on member states an obligation to negotiate with a view to eliminating double taxation within the EU. The ECJ held that Article 293 was too broad to have direct effect and so taxpayers could not rely on it in litigation. Further, in the absence of harmonisation of direct taxation, member states are, in principle, free to define the criteria for allocating taxing powers between themselves with the view to eliminating double taxation.[175] This reinforces the point made earlier, that while the ECJ has a lot to say about the appropriate treatment of taxpayers, it is not concerned with which country benefits from any tax collected. Considering its ineffectiveness, Article 293 was deleted by the Lisbon Treaty in late 2009.

The EU direct tax directives are more prescriptive as regards the allocation of taxing rights. The Parent-Subsidiary Directive protects the right of source countries to impose their corporation tax on cross-border income and obliges residence countries to provide relief (although

[175] Case C-336/96 *Gilly* v *Directeur des Services Fiscaux du Bas-Rhin* [1998] ECR I-2793 (ECJ).

source countries are denied the right to tax dividends). This allocation only applies with respect to corporate groups, demonstrating the allocation according to type of taxpayer method. Similarly, the Interest and Royalties Directive only applies to corporate groups. However, reversing the position under the Parent-Subsidiary Directive, the Interest and Royalties Directive removes source country taxing rights to the benefit of residence countries. The difficulties and distortions resulting from this contradiction were mentioned above at 2.2.1.

Finally, the Savings Directive provides a rare example of the inter-state payments method of allocating taxing rights between states. Under Article 12, during the transitional period, any state levying a withholding tax on interest payments covered by the Directive is obliged to transfer 75 per cent of the tax collected to the beneficiary's country of residence. In return, under Article 14 the residence state is obliged to provide double tax relief in the form of a foreign tax credit for the withholding tax. A peculiar feature of this double tax relief is that the residence country is obliged to refund any excess credits, a point that will be returned to at 4.1.1.

3

Source country taxation

Chapter 2 has laid the foundations and principles upon which the rest of this book is built. As mentioned in the introduction, the discussion now proceeds to consider the tax treatment in the country in which the income arises, the country in which the source of the income is located. In the context of the *Base Case*, Figure 1 on page 5, this is Country A, the country where the office building is located with respect to which the rent is paid. There are two persons involved in the *Base Case*, the payer, Allan, and the recipient, Beth, and the treatment of each by Country A must be considered. It is not always the case that there are tax consequences for the payer in the country where the income is sourced but in international commercial transactions, this is most common and is, therefore, the basis upon which the following discussion proceeds.

Dealing with the income recipient first, i.e. Beth, the tax treatment by the source country, i.e. Country A, typically depends on the type of income derived and whether or not a tax treaty applies. As discussed at 2.1.2.1, both UK domestic law and tax treaties incorporate a schedular approach to taxation based on source. The discussion under the first heading of this chapter considers taxation of the income recipient by the source country. It proceeds in accordance with the schedular approach adopted by the OECD Model, rather than that adopted under UK domestic law. The type of income received by Beth in the *Base Case* is income from immovable property and that is one type of income considered. However, the discussion also considers the treatment by the source country on the basis that what Beth receives is, alternatively, various other types of income.

The second heading of the chapter proceeds to consider the tax treatment of the payer, i.e. Allan, by the source country, i.e. Country A. As mentioned in the introduction, this primarily involves a consideration of any rules that may affect the deductibility of the payment for Allan. It is in this context that the non-discrimination principles in the OECD Model and the FEU Treaty are of particular importance and the rather stark difference between the approaches emerges. The discussion under the final heading of this chapter returns to some of the income tax fundamentals identified at the start of Chapter 1. In particular, the discussion selects a number of issues where the fundamental features of a payment have a substantial impact on source country taxing rights. The discussion does not attempt to be comprehensive but, rather, illustrative of the problems flowing from quantification and characterisation of cross-border payments.

3.1 The recipient/schedular approach

The discussion under this heading is primarily concerned with two issues: (i) locating the source of income, and (ii) the tax treatment by the source country of that income in the hands of non-residents. The discussion incorporates other important considerations. In particular, the *Base Case* focus is on a particular payment received by a non-resident as income. However, the non-resident may have incurred expenses in deriving that income, e.g. in the context of the *Base Case*, Beth may have incurred interest expense with respect to funds borrowed in acquiring the offices from which the rent is derived. The discussion under this head also considers the extent to which a source country accounts for expenses in determining the tax liability of the income recipient.

The methods of relief from international double taxation were identified above at 2.2.2. As noted there, it is often the case that the source country does provide substantial and important relief from double taxation. In the context of tax treaties, this is achieved by limiting source country taxing rights, whether by excluding the possibility of taxation, reducing the rate at which tax may be imposed or imposing a non-discrimination restriction. The extent to which source countries provide such relief with respect to particular types of income, i.e. the extent to which source country taxing rights are limited, is noted throughout the following discussion.

The following discussion adopts the schedular approach in the OECD Model identified above at 2.1.2.1. Not only is this the approach adopted throughout the bilateral tax treaty network which regulates the vast majority of cross-border transactions, but the domestic source rules adopted by countries are often vague, imprecise and vary substantially, making them inferior for purposes of analysis. Nevertheless, while treaties usually override domestic source rules, domestic source rules remain important. The majority of countries take the view that a charge to tax must be based on domestic law, i.e. a treaty cannot create a charge to tax. So, if a domestic source rule is narrower than taxing rights granted by a treaty, the source country's right to tax is limited by the domestic rule. Within this limited context, the following discussion also considers domestic source rules.

The following discussion proceeds by first considering the last schedule of activity in the OECD Model, i.e. 'other income' in Article 21. This is the residual category of income and it is appropriate to consider it first. It is standard analysis to consider whether income from a particular category falls within the scope of activities in the articles preceding Article 21. If the analysis suggests that the income does not fall within those preceding articles then it is appropriate to consider at that point whether Article 21 applies. That is, Article 21 is supplementary or ancillary to each of the other schedules and should be considered simultaneously with them. Looking at Article 21 first facilitates this consideration.

After considering Article 21, the discussion proceeds to consider, in order of their appearance in the OECD Model, the other major provisions dealing with source country taxing rights. So, the discussion considers income from land (Article 6), income from business (Articles 7 and 9), dividends, interest and royalties (Articles 10, 11 and 12), capital gains (Article 13), and income from independent and dependent services (former Article 14 and Article 15). While individuals are not the focus of this book, it is appropriate to consider Articles 14 and 15 because they have a substantial impact on employers even where the employer is a corporation. The consideration of these articles focuses on that impact.

At a number of points, the discussion considers the tax treatment in the source country of a source country resident corporation that is controlled by non-residents, i.e. a source country subsidiary. The presumption for the purposes of this chapter is that such a subsidiary derives income only from the source country. Nevertheless, the taxation of such a subsidiary is not concerned solely with source based taxation. As the subsidiary is resident in the source country, it also concerns the taxation of a *resident* of the source country. In this context, it may help readers to think of the source state as the *host* state and the country of the non-resident controller of the subsidiary as the *home* state. The host/home state distinction is often used interchangeably with the source/residence state distinction but, in the context of subsidiaries, it can have this important difference in meaning.

One reason for dealing with subsidiaries in this chapter (rather than Chapter 4) is that the OECD Model deals with subsidiaries as part of its schedular approach. This is most obvious in the context of the related business profit articles, Articles 7 and 9. The former regulates business income derived by a non-resident person directly in the source country whereas the latter regulates business income derived through a subsidiary resident in the source country that is owned by a non-resident. Another reason for dealing with subsidiaries in this chapter is that this is what happens in the real world. When considering whether to conduct business or other activities in a source/host country, one of the most important initial decisions that an investor must make is whether to conduct those activities directly or through a source country subsidiary.

3.1.1 Other income

Article 21 of the OECD Model provides the default or residual rule that allocates taxing rights to the residence state:

> 1. Items of income of a resident of a Contracting State, wherever arising, not dealt with in the foregoing Articles of this Convention shall be taxable only in that State.

Paragraph 2 of Article 21 provides an exception and excludes the application of paragraph 1 if the 'right or property in respect of which the income is paid is effectively connected' with a permanent establishment in the other contracting state. In this case, Article 7 applies, discussed below at 3.1.3.

Article 21 is not as broad as it might appear at first glance and it raises a number of issues. The first is that it refers to 'income', raising the question as to whether this term is to take a special treaty meaning or whether it will take its meaning from domestic law (see above at 1.3.2). For example, in the UK and many other common law jurisdictions the word 'income' has a technical meaning that excludes capital gains. Many older treaties concluded by such countries did not include a capital gains article (Article 13, discussed below) because those countries did not tax capital gains. When such countries began to tax capital gains, the issue arose as to whether capital gains were caught by the other income article. Some countries like Australia took the view that they were not, which meant that the treaties in question did not cover at least some types of capital gains, leaving the country where the capital gain arose free to tax them.[1] There are similar

[1] For example, Australian Tax Office Ruling TR 2001/12 and Avery Jones et al. (2006, p. 403). Vogel (1997, p. 826) seems to suggest that the other income article can cover capital gains. See the Australian Federal Court in *Undershaft (No. 1) Limited* v *FCT* [2009] FCA 41 (FC) (which caused the withdrawal of TR 2001/12 in 2009), discussed below at 3.1.5. However, even in civil law countries, there is an argument that the word 'income' as used in OECD Model Art. 21 does not include capital gains. Art. 21(2) suggests that the 'income' must be paid 'in respect of' a 'right or property'. Arguably, a capital gain is not paid in respect of property but, rather, in respect of its disposal. A different issue

problems with notional income such as income attributed under controlled foreign corporation rules, discussed below at 4.1.2.2.

The word 'income' is also used in an undefined manner in the article on income from immovable property and the interpretation of 'income' is discussed further in that context below. Irrespective of any limitations inherent in the word 'income', Article 21 of the OECD Model is commonly applied to a number of types of income including alimony, income from sophisticated financial instruments and income arising in third countries, presuming these are not effectively connected with a permanent establishment.

Another important issue regarding the scope of Article 21 of the OECD Model is the meaning of the words 'not dealt with in the foregoing Articles'. When is income 'dealt with' by a prior article? Is it enough that the heading of the Article deals with the matter, e.g. 'business profits' or 'dividends', or is income only dealt with if the source country is granted a specific taxing right? In many cases, whichever approach is taken, the result is to deny source country taxation. This is because if a specific article does not grant source country taxing rights neither will the other income article.[2] The situation changes dramatically when the other income article in the UN Model is considered.

In practice, many tax treaties do not include an article dealing with other income and a substantial number of OECD members and non-members have reserved the right to tax income arising in their jurisdiction.[3] The result is that income not specifically covered by an article may be taxed by the source state, although questions arise as to whether the residence country is obliged to provide foreign tax relief in such a case. Article 21 of the UN Model begins by broadly following the OECD approach. However, it includes a paragraph 3 that overrides paragraphs 1 and 2 and provides:

> [I]tems of income of a resident of a Contracting State not dealt with in the foregoing articles of this Convention and arising in the other Contracting State may also be taxed in that other State.[4]

is whether OECD Model Art. 7 covers capital gains made by a business so as to exclude source country taxation where there is no PE. This is considered further below at 3.1.5.

2 There remains the possibility that income may not be dealt with by any article in the OECD Model including the other income article, in which case the treaty does not regulate taxing rights. Essentially, this seems to be the argument with respect to attributable income, such as under a controlled foreign corporation regime, discussed further below at 4.1.2.2.

3 OECD Commentary to Article 21 paras. 13–17 and the Positions of Non-Member Countries.

4 Note that Article 21(3) of the UN Model does not limit the rate at which the source country can tax (other than as might be provided by Article 24(1), discussed above at 2.2.1).

Here, as with the situation in treaties that do not include an other income article, it can be critical to determine when income is 'dealt with' by an earlier article. If income is 'dealt with' there may be no source country taxing right but if it is not then Article 21(3) will provide that right. This is largely a question of scope of the earlier articles and so will be discussed further at various points in the context of those articles.

3.1.2 *Income from immovable property*

Article 6 of the OECD Model grants full, though not exclusive, taxing rights to the source state with respect to income from immovable property situated therein. Because of the indivisible connection between a state and land situated within its borders, local land has historically been a major subject of taxation.[5] Like movables, even individuals change residence and citizenship, but land has a fixed location, an important point in a world of increasing mobility. Two major issues that arise in the context of Article 6 are what counts as 'immovable property' and what counts as 'income' therefrom.

Immovable property

Article 6(2) of the OECD Model contains a definition of 'immovable property'. The term primarily takes its meaning from the law of the state in which the property is situated. This apparently simple rule is not without difficulties. First, many countries do not use the term 'immovable property' in their tax laws. Second, even if they do, there must be some inherent limit on what could be included within such a definition. It would be inappropriate that a source state could include all matter of things in a domestic tax law definition of 'immovable property' and thereby secure full taxing rights. At a minimum, there must be 'property' and the better view is that what is included must also be capable of fairly falling within the term 'immovable'.[6] These points are illustrated by reference to UK law.

The UK, like many common law countries, does not use the term 'immovable property' in its domestic tax law but, rather, uses the term

[5] Harris (2006) generally covers the history of the taxation of land in England. See also Daunton (2008) and the references cited therein, which also covers the history of the taxation of land in India and New Zealand.

[6] Note, however, OECD Model Art. 6(2) expressly excludes 'ships, boats and aircraft'. Does the exclusion of these express items mean that a country may otherwise define

'land', primarily for Schedule A purposes.[7] In this context, 'land' will take its meaning from Schedule 1 of the Interpretation Act 1978 to include 'buildings and other structures, land covered with water, and any estate, interest, easement, servitude or right in or over land'.[8] But can this definition of 'land' be used for the purposes of Article 6 of a tax treaty? UK rules on the conflict of laws recognise the concept of 'immovable property'. For example, under English law it includes all estates, interests and charges in or over English land.[9] This may be more appropriate for the purposes of Article 6, but, as demonstrated below, is both narrower and broader than the concept of 'land' used in UK tax law.

What may fairly be included in a domestic definition of 'immovable property'? Section 266 of ITTOIA 2005 provides that:

> a right to use a caravan or houseboat at only one location is treated as a right deriving from an estate or interest in land.

Profits from such a right are chargeable as 'income from land'. Assume a non-resident owns a houseboat moored at a particular location in the UK and leases it out. Could the UK tax the rent under the equivalent of Article 6 of the OECD Model? Is it conceivable that property such as caravans and houseboats, which are specifically designed to be movable, could really be encompassed by the term 'immovable property' in a tax treaty?

Similar problems arise where land is held indirectly through an artificial entity such as a corporation. Can shares held in a land holding company constitute 'immovable property'? In UK legal terminology, such

'immoveable property' as it likes? With reference to Articles 26 and 31(1) of the Vienna Convention on the Law of Treaties (see above at 1.3.2), Arnold (2006, p. 8) notes that 'the only limitation on the use of the domestic law meaning is a limitation based on a country's obligation to carry out its treaties in good faith… combined with the requirement that treaties be interpreted in good faith'.

7 For example, see CTA 2009 s. 205 and ITTOIA 2005 s. 266. Regarding Schedule A, see above at 2.1.2.1. Also, see Avery Jones et al. (2006, p. 733) noting that 'immoveable property' is used in civil law.

8 For capital gains tax purposes, 'land' takes the meaning in TCGA 1992 s. 288(1).

9 *Re Hoyles, Row* v *Jagg* [1911] 1 Ch 179 (CA) at 183 and 186. Also see Avery Jones et al. (2006, p. 733). UK law also knows the distinction between 'real' and 'personal' property, the former being such as historically descended to the heir-at-law. Again, while 'real property' essentially encompasses interests in land, it can include other property such as a title of honour. In some of its treaties, the UK replaces the reference to 'immoveable property' with a reference to 'real property', e.g. UK/US (2001) Art. 6 and Australia/UK (2003) Art. 6. In *FCT* v *Lamesa Holdings BV* (1997) 36 ATR 589 (FFC) at 596–7 the Full Federal Court of Australia questions whether this replacement is appropriate or helpful.

shares are personal property and do not constitute an interest in the land itself. To say that such shares cannot be immovable property opens a simple route to avoiding taxation under Article 6 of the OECD Model. If it were accepted that such shares could be immovable property (and the better view is that they cannot),[10] then the result might be that dividends paid by such a company fall within Article 6 and Article 10 simultaneously.[11] Land holding companies also cause problems in the context of capital gains. These are discussed further below at 3.1.5.

By contrast, if the English conflict of laws meaning is given to 'immovable property' in Article 6 of the OECD Model, it seems this would include mortgages secured on land.[12] A consequence would be that interest paid on a mortgage secured on English land would be covered by Article 6, despite the definition of 'interest' in Article 11(3) specifically covering interest paid on a debt claim 'secured by mortgage'. The OECD Commentary on Article 6 suggests the issue is 'settled by Article 11'.[13] The issue is important, because source state taxation of interest on a mortgage is limited under Article 11, whereas Article 6 gives a full right of taxation. Despite the inclinations of the OECD, there is a strong argument that mortgage interest can fall within Article 6. If it does, it is an example of income falling within Article 6 that is not taxed as income from land under UK tax law,[14] demonstrating the point made at 2.1.2.1 that despite the similarity between the schedular approach under the OECD Model and that under UK law there are cases in which the schedules do not align.

A second example of such a mismatch in classification is provided by the second part of the definition of 'immovable property' in Article 6(2). It extends the meaning of the term, irrespective of the domestic law definition. For example, the UK excludes income from farming, forestry and

[10] At least in the context of UK law, this doubt seems to be confirmed by the France/UK treaty (1968) Art. 5(2)(b). This provision specifically includes shares in land holding companies within the definition of 'immoveable property'.

[11] This is a live issue in Afghanistan, where the definition of 'immoveable property' in Income Tax Law (Official Gazette No. 867, 26 November 2005) Art. 20 includes shares in a foreign company holding Afghan land.

[12] *Re Hoyles, Row* v *Jagg* [1911] 1 Ch 179 (CA). This is not necessarily the case in other common law jurisdictions, e.g. see *Haque* v *Haque (No 2)* (1965) 114 CLR 98 (HC) (although note the strong dissent of Barwick CJ).

[13] OECD Commentary on Art. 6 para. 2. OECD Commentary on Art. 11 para. 18 provides: 'It is recognised… that mortgage interest comes within the category of income from movable capital… even though certain countries assimilate it to income from immoveable property.'

[14] Historically, interest was charged under Schedule D Case III, now CTA 2009 s. 295 (triggering the loan relationship rules for corporations) and ITTOIA 2005 s. 369.

mining from the scope of Schedule A. Rather, this income falls within the scope of Schedule D Case I.[15] Nevertheless, the UK reserves its right to tax a non-resident under Schedule D Case I with respect to such income by reason of Article 6.[16]

Income from immovable property

Once 'immovable property' has been identified, application of Article 6 of the OECD Model depends on there being 'income from' that property. Paragraph 1 expressly includes within the scope of the article 'income from agriculture and forestry'. As with Article 21 (discussed above), this raises the question of what is meant by 'income'. Two features of the term 'income' require further discussion. The first is whether 'income' includes capital gains. The second is whether 'income', in the context of Article 6, is a gross or net concept.

Rent paid for the lease of land is the clearest example of income covered by Article 6 of the OECD Model, but what of an inducement to enter into a lease, i.e. an upfront payment by the lessee (or the lessor), a premium? In UK tax law, a premium paid by a tenant is capital and not income in nature.[17] There are specific rules in the tax law that treat such premiums on leases of less than 50 years as rent and so taxable as income.[18] So, if a tenant of UK land pays a lease premium to a non-resident landlord and a tax treaty is applicable, may the UK tax the premium as income from land? This depends on interpretation of the word 'income' where it appears in Article 6. As discussed at 1.3.2, as an undefined term, the word 'income' takes its meaning from UK tax law unless the 'context' of the treaty otherwise requires.

The very existence in a treaty of an article dealing with capital gains (Article 13 of the OECD Model), particularly one that expressly deals with capital gains on the alienation of immovable property, suggests that 'income' in Article 6 of the OECD Model does not have a special treaty meaning.[19] In this case, the term should take its meaning from UK tax

[15] CTA 2009 ss. 36–9 and 208 and ITTOIA 2005 ss. 9–12 and 267.

[16] The Mauritius/UK treaty (1981) is an exception. It excludes income from an agricultural or forestry enterprise from the scope of Art. 6, deferring to Art. 7.

[17] *O'Connor* v *Hume* [1954] 2 All ER 301 (CA).

[18] CTA 2009 s. 217 and ITTOIA 2005 s. 277, although these provisions carefully do not treat the premium as income but rather the landlord is treated as receiving the premium from a transaction entered into 'for generating income from land'. The UK tax law continues to contain analogous rules dealing with premiums where work is required, payments for the surrender of a lease and leases granted at an undervalue.

[19] Arnold (2006, p. 9).

law, but which UK meaning should it take, the general meaning of the word 'income', and so excluding capital gains, or a statutorily extended meaning, and so including premiums? While not without doubt, the better view seems to be the latter as, consistent with Article 3(2) of the OECD Model, that is the meaning under 'the applicable tax law' of the UK.[20]

Often such a detailed analysis will not be required, because if the source country is not granted taxing rights under the equivalent of Article 6 of the OECD Model, it will be granted taxing rights under Article 13 (capital gains). Unfortunately, Article 13 refers to gains from the 'alienation' of immovable property and it is not clear that the granting of a premium on a lease is such an alienation. Difficulties in interpreting the word 'alienation' are returned to below at 3.1.5. If neither Article 6 nor Article 13 apply to lease premiums then could Article 21 (other income) apply? This is open to the same doubt as the application of Article 6 because a lease premium is capital and not income in nature. It is presumed (again not without doubt) that the word 'income' in Article 21 should be interpreted in a fashion that is consistent with its interpretation in Article 6. If the lease premium is not covered by Articles 6, 13 or 21 then it is not covered by the treaty with the result that the UK may tax it without treaty limitation.

The second issue with respect to use of the word 'income' in Article 6 of the OECD Model is whether it is used in a gross or net sense. For example, assume that a non-resident borrows money in order to acquire UK land, which the non-resident leases to another person. How much may the UK tax under Article 6, the full amount of the rent received or the rent received less financing costs? Again, this will depend on whether the word 'income' has a special treaty meaning or derives its meaning from domestic law. Presuming the latter, the UK interprets 'income' according to the flow concept as opposed to the gain concept.[21] The result is a right to tax on a gross basis.[22]

[20] Additionally, as mentioned in footnote 18, UK tax law does not expressly deem lease premiums to be 'income'. Rather, the relevant provisions treat the premium as a receipt from a transaction to generate income from land.

[21] Lord MacNaghten famously stated that income tax 'is a tax on what "comes in" – on actual receipts'. *Tennant* v *Smith* [1892] AC 150 (HL) at 163.

[22] If the word 'income' has a special treaty meaning, there seems to be a strong argument that a net concept is anticipated. Here it might be argued that the OECD Model and Commentaries use the terms 'income', 'profits' and 'gains' interchangeably and so as the last two are net concepts, 'income' should be interpreted in this fashion. This is supported by amendments made to the OECD Commentary on Art. 5 in 2008 with the insertion in para. 42.23 of an optional services PE provision. That provision incorporates a new

There are two qualifications to this right to tax on a gross basis. The first was mentioned above at 1.2.2, that a treaty does not, of itself, create or increase a charge to tax. Therefore, if there is a right to be taxed on a net basis under domestic tax law, the taxpayer may claim to be taxed on this basis despite a right to tax on a gross basis in a treaty.[23] Secondly, issues of discrimination arise where a non-resident is taxed on a gross basis but residents may claim deductions. Article 24 of the OECD Model, which deals with non-discrimination, was discussed above at 2.2.1. For reasons discussed at that point, the nationality non-discrimination provision in Article 24(1) is unlikely to have any application to the taxation of land on a gross basis.

Of greater interest is Article 24(3) of the OECD Model dealing with permanent establishments of non-resident enterprises. This is discussed in more detail below at 3.1.3.4 in the context of Articles 5 and 7. However, Article 6(4) applies Article 6 to income from immovable property of an enterprise, giving effective priority to Article 6 over Article 7. Article 7 deals with 'profits' of an enterprise, a concept that is definitely a net concept. The priority given to Article 6 may result, with a country like the UK, in a right to tax income from land of a non-resident enterprise on a gross basis even where the enterprise has a permanent establishment in the UK. This right would be qualified by Article 24(3), which is not limited in its scope to Article 7 and so may apply to taxation under Article 6 as well.[24] If a domestic enterprise were taxed on a net basis with respect to income from land, the same right must be granted to a non-resident enterprise with a permanent establishment in the country. This rather limited and disjointed approach to non-discrimination may be contrasted with that under EU Law, a point to which the discussion now briefly turns.

EU Law

It was noted that the non-discrimination provisions in Article 24 of the OECD Model have limited application in the context of the taxation of income from land owned by a non-resident. Any meaningful application is limited to businesses (enterprises) where the non-resident has a

concept of 'gross revenues' rather than the word 'income'. In countries adopting the *flow* concept of income, 'income' means 'gross revenues'.

[23] As mentioned above at 2.1.2.2, while the UK imposes a withholding tax on gross rent received by a non-resident from UK land, this is not a final tax and a non-resident may file a tax return and claim any allowable deductions and credit for the withholding tax imposed.

[24] See Arnold (2006, p. 13) and the references cited therein.

permanent establishment in the source state. EU Law non-discrimination principles have broader potential to apply in the context of income from land. In particular, where there is no permanent presence of the non-resident in the source state (and so the freedom of establishment does not apply) the free movement of capital may nevertheless have application.

A case in point is *Stauffer*.[25] In this case, an Italian non-profit organisation held commercial premises in Germany and was taxed on the rental income from the premises. A similar German non-profit organisation would not have been taxed. The ECJ noted that the mere passive holding of property, without active management, did not involve an exercise of the freedom of establishment. Nevertheless, the ownership and administration of the premises by the Italian organisation triggered the free movement of capital principle, i.e. Article 63 of the FEU Treaty. For the purposes of applying this Article, the ECJ compared the Italian organisation to a German non-profit organisation and found that, by comparison, the German tax law presented an obstacle to the free movement of capital by the Italian organisation. The ECJ went on to find that the breach of the free movement of capital was not justified.

By analogy, it seems that taxation of a non-resident in receipt of income from land on a gross basis when a resident would be taxed on a net basis would also breach the free movement of capital (presuming this results in greater taxation of the non-resident).[26]

3.1.3 *Business profits*

One of the most important, and controversial, provisions in the OECD Model is Article 7, entitled 'Business Profits'. After more than a decade of review, the OECD released an important report on Article 7 in 2008.[27] At the same time, it revised the Commentary on Article 7 and released a discussion draft on a new version of the Article and Commentary.[28] These amendments are slated for 2010 but even should that timetable be met, the vast majority of treaties contain the existing version of Article 7, which is the focus of the following discussion. Any major amendments slated for 2010 are noted.

[25] Case C-386/04 *Centro Di Musicologia Walter Stauffer* v *Finanzamt Munchen Fur Korperschaften* [2006] ECR I-8203 (ECJ).

[26] This is consistent with the decisions in Case C-234/01 *Gerritse* v *Finanzamt Neukölln-Nord* [2003] ECR I-5933 (ECJ) and Case C-290/04 *FKP Scorpio Konzertproduktionen GmbH* v *Finanzamt Hamburg-Eimsbüttel* [2006] ECR I-9461 (ECJ).

[27] OECD (2008a).

[28] OECD (2008b).

Currently, Article 7(1) provides:

> The profits of an enterprise of a Contracting State shall be taxable only in that State unless the enterprise carries on business in the other Contracting State through a permanent establishment situated therein. If the enterprise carries on business as aforesaid, the profits of the enterprise may be taxed in the other State but only so much of them as is attributable to that permanent establishment.[29]

Fundamentally, Article 7(1) of the OECD Model may be divided into an exclusive right of taxation (up to 'taxable only in that State') and a shared right of taxation (the remainder of the provision).[30] A pre-condition to the application of this provision is the existence of 'an enterprise of a Contracting State'. As will be discussed shortly, a source country subsidiary of a non-resident constitutes 'an enterprise of' the source country whereas direct activities of the non-resident in the source country will not. Accordingly, as far as source/host country taxation is concerned, the first part of Article 7(1) (exclusive taxation) applies to subsidiaries whereas the second part (shared taxation) applies to direct activities of non-residents. Each of these aspects of Article 7(1) is considered in turn.

Where a source/host country is granted taxing rights by Article 7(1) of the OECD Model (either exclusive or shared), that right to tax is, as in the case of income from land, a full right to tax. However, unlike in the case of income from land, taxation of business profits under Article 7 is limited by specific non-discrimination rules in Article 24. Article 24(5) regulates discrimination of source country subsidiaries whereas Article 24(3) regulates discrimination of direct business activities of non-residents in the source/host country. This subheading concludes with a consideration of these limitations on source/host country taxation.

3.1.3.1 Enterprise of a contracting state

The concept of a 'resident' of a state under Article 4 of the OECD Model was discussed above at 2.1.1.2, but Article 7(1) uses the term 'enterprise' of

[29] The expression 'business profits' is not defined nor, indeed, used anywhere in the text of the OECD Model, which refers only to 'profits of an enterprise'. The reason for this is discussed below at 3.1.3.1.

[30] The exclusive right of taxation uses the same words ('shall be taxable only') as the exclusive rights of taxation given to residence countries in OECD Model Arts 12(1) (royalties), 13(5) (capital gains), 15(1) (employment income) and 21(1) (other income). However, the exclusive right of taxation in Art. 7(1) is subject to Art. 7(7), discussed below at 3.3.3.

a state.[31] This critical phrase is defined in Article 3(1), together with two supplementary definitions. 'Enterprise of a Contracting State' is defined in terms of 'an enterprise carried on by a resident of a Contracting State'. The first supplementary definition is of the term 'enterprise', which 'applies to the carrying on of any business'. Therefore, 'enterprise of a Contracting State' is synonymous with a business carried on by a resident. The second supplementary definition results from the deletion of Article 14 (independent personal services) in 2000. In that year, the definition of 'business' was inserted to cover 'the performance of professional services and of other activities of an independent character'. Article 14 and, in particular, income from services is discussed further below at 3.1.6.2.

It will be noted that each of the definitions of 'enterprise of a Contracting State' and 'enterprise' as well as Article 7 of the OECD Model itself refer to 'carrying on' and either expressly or implicitly what is carried on is a 'business'. The OECD provides little guidance as to what amounts to 'carrying on a business'. This raises two issues. The first is whether an activity should be characterised as business in nature. Subject to the extension for professional services, the OECD note that 'business' should take its meaning from domestic law.[32] The tax laws of most countries deal with what constitutes 'business' although sometimes another term is used. For example, the UK uses the concept of 'trade' and there is much case law on whether or not an activity is sufficient to amount to a trade.[33] Many businesses do not involve 'trading' but the UK interprets 'trade' broadly and, while 'trade' under domestic law is likely to be narrower than 'business' under a treaty, this difference seems unlikely to result in any significant disjuncture.[34]

The second issue is whether an isolated transaction of a business character can constitute 'carrying on' business and so whether Article 7 can apply to such a transaction. The issue is well demonstrated by the Australian case of *Thiel* v *FCT*.[35] In this case, the taxpayer was a Swiss

[31] Avery Jones et al. (2006, p. 701) note that the term 'enterprise' is a civil law concept and not often used in domestic tax laws of common law jurisdictions.

[32] OECD Commentary on Article 3 para. 10.2.

[33] For example, see Tiley (2008, Chapter 19).

[34] '[S]ince the internal tax law category of "trade" is narrower than business, in particular excluding investment activities, there is little doubt that anything that is a trade will be a business (and consequently an enterprise).' Avery Jones et al. (2006, p. 704). The UK does use the term 'business' (undefined) in the context of the Schedule A charge with respect to income from land, CTA 2009 Part 4 Chap. 2 (ss. 203–8) and ITTOIA 2005 Part 3 Chap. 2 (ss. 263–7).

[35] (1990) 171 CLR 338 (HC).

resident who held an interest in trust property that was exchanged for shares in a company that was listed on the Australian Stock Exchange. Once the shares were listed, the taxpayer began selling the shares at a gain. The Australian tax administration sought to tax him with respect to the gain. The taxpayer argued that the gains were profits of an enterprise and as he did not have a permanent establishment in Australia, Australia had no right to tax due to Article 7 of the Australia/Switzerland tax treaty. The Australian tax administration retorted that the taxpayer was not 'carrying on' an enterprise and therefore Article 7 did not preclude Australian taxation.

The High Court of Australia noted that the term 'enterprise' did not have a settled meaning in Australian law and so could only be interpreted in the context of the treaty, i.e. Article 3(2) was of no use.[36] In that context, an enterprise may be comprised of one or more transactions provided they were entered into for business or commercial purposes, i.e. a single transaction of a business nature may constitute an enterprise.[37] Further, the expression 'carrying on' implied no element of repetition or system and was, rather, no more than a 'linking expression'. The majority used the heading of Article 7 to support this position, noting that 'the heading "Business Profits", supports the notion that one or more transactions entered into for business or commercial purposes is an enterprise for the purposes of the Agreement'.[38]

Once a 'business' has been identified, 'enterprise of a Contracting State' refers to the carrying on of that business 'by a resident of' that state. It is clear that a single person may conduct one or more businesses and so the activities of a single person resident in a particular state may constitute one or more enterprises of that state. Further, a business of a person resident in a particular state will constitute an enterprise of *that* state even if none of the activities of that business occurs within the state, i.e. the business is wholly carried on overseas. Therefore, where a resident of one state conducts business activities directly in the source state, the business

[36] Contrast the OECD Commentary on Art. 3 para. 4, which suggests that the term 'enterprise' has 'always been interpreted according to the provisions of the domestic laws of the Contracting States'.

[37] Despite the suggestion in the OECD Commentary noted in the previous footnote, the Australian majority judgment in the High Court used the Commentary on Art. 3 para. 4 to support the proposition that a single activity may of itself constitute an enterprise. (1990) 171 CLR 338 at p. 344.

[38] (1990) 171 CLR 338 at p. 345. Further regarding this case, see Avery Jones et al. (2006, pp. 703–4).

will nevertheless be an enterprise of the residence state, *not* an enterprise of the source state, even if the business is wholly conducted within the source state.

A single person may have more than one enterprise (business) but can more than one person carry on a single enterprise (business)? This happens in practice and partnerships are the clearest example. It can also happen in the context of corporate groups where the activities of individual members may be viewed as contributing to a *group business*. The separate entity approach to related parties under the OECD Model was noted above at 2.1.1.1. Each partner and each member of a corporate group constitute a separate 'person' and may be a 'resident' of a state for the purposes of the Model. The definition of 'enterprise of a Contracting State' refers to a business carried on by *a* resident. The implication is that more than one resident of a particular state cannot constitute a single enterprise of that state.[39] Rather, the business is split and each piece considered a separate enterprise of that state carried on by each resident.

This has important implications for corporate groups. Even if a corporate group is considered to conduct a single business, each member of the corporate group (each corporation) is independently an enterprise of the state of which it is resident. Therefore, where a parent corporation resident in a home state establishes a subsidiary in a source/host state,[40] the parent corporation will be considered an enterprise of the home state and the subsidiary is independently an enterprise of the source/host state. By contrast, if the parent corporation decided to conduct its activities in the source/host state directly (rather than through a subsidiary), it would not have created an independent enterprise of the source/host state.

3.1.3.2 Subsidiaries: exclusive taxation

A subsidiary corporation established in a source country by a treaty partner resident is an enterprise of the source country. Accordingly, assuming

[39] Even if a partnership or corporate group could collectively constitute a 'person' under OECD Model Art. 3(1)(a) (e.g. as a 'body of persons' or 'treated as a body corporate for tax purposes'), partnerships and corporate groups are typically not 'liable to tax' (i.e. they are transparent) and so cannot be a resident under Art. 4. If they were 'liable to tax', the situation might be different. For example, if a corporate group is subject to taxation as such, say under a consolidation regime, it seems possible for the group to constitute a single enterprise of a particular state. Further consideration of this difficult issue is beyond the scope of this book.

[40] Most commonly, this happens when the parent corporation subscribes for shares in a new corporation created and registered under the corporate law of the source/host state.

all the activities of the subsidiary are conducted in the source country, the source country has the exclusive right to tax the business profits of the subsidiary under the first part of Article 7(1) of the OECD Model. Indeed, as the source state is both the source and residence country in this case, it might seem that this should be clear without Article 7(1) and that the treaty should have no scope for application. However, the holding of the parent corporation in the subsidiary raises the potential application of the non-discrimination rule in Article 24(5) to taxation by the source country, discussed below at 3.1.3.4. Further, Article 7(1) may be of relevance in determining the scope of controlled foreign corporation rules in the treaty partner state, discussed below at 4.1.2.2.

Article 7(1) of the OECD Model provides exclusive source country taxing rights only with respect to 'profits' of an enterprise, i.e. in the present case, profits of a business carried on by the subsidiary. This raises the question of what is meant by 'profits' in this context.[41] The context does not seem to require that this term has a special treaty meaning and so it seems that Article 3(2) will apply to attribute a domestic tax law meaning to this term. As the present case involves a subsidiary, Article 9(1) will qualify this interpretation. Article 9(1) is entitled 'Associated Enterprises' and applies where 'an enterprise of a Contracting State participates directly or indirectly in the management, control or capital of an enterprise of the other Contracting State'. For the reasons discussed at 3.1.3.1, the subsidiary is an enterprise of the source/host state and its parent corporation is a separate enterprise of the home state. Accordingly, as the parent corporation will have a participation of the relevant type in the subsidiary, Article 9(1) applies. Article 9(1) also applies to two enterprises where a third person or persons have a relevant participation in each. The issue of who are associates is further considered below at 3.3.1.1.

Where it applies, Article 9(1) of the OECD Model goes on to provide that if

> conditions are made or imposed between the two enterprises in their commercial or financial relations which differ from those which would be made between independent enterprises, then any profits which would, but for those conditions, have accrued to one of the enterprises, but, by reason of those conditions, have not so accrued, may be included in the profits of that enterprise and taxed accordingly.

[41] The concept of 'profits' is discussed in OECD (2008a, paras. 59–79), but apparently only for purposes of determining shared taxing rights (i.e. taxation of permanent establishments) and not for purposes of determining exclusive taxing rights.

This provision authorises what are commonly referred to as 'transfer pricing' adjustments and incorporates what is commonly referred to as the 'independent enterprise approach'.

There are a number of qualifications and limitations inherent in Article 9(1). It applies only to 'relations' between associated enterprises and so does not authorise adjustments to any relations that are with non-associated parties. The words 'conditions' and 'relations' are words of wide import and might apply to any activity of a person with another person. However, the relations must be in the context of two 'enterprises' and so in the context of two businesses. This raises serious questions as to whether Article 9(1) of the OECD Model can apply outside the context of a business, discussed further below at 3.3.1. Within the context of businesses, the reference to 'commercial or financial' relations seems sufficiently broad to cover all types of business relations.

Even where the subject matter of a business relation falls within Article 9(1) of the OECD Model, that provision permits an adjustment only where the relations are not what would have occurred between 'independent enterprises'. Presuming conditions in such relations are not of a type that would have been made between independent enterprises, Article 9(1) authorises an adjustment to include only profits that 'but for those conditions' would have accrued to the enterprise. This authorises an adjustment to an 'arm's length amount'. How an arm's length amount should be determined is discussed below at 3.3.1.2.

Note, however, that Article 9(1) of the OECD Model is premised on 'conditions' made with respect to 'relations'. The authorised adjustment is an amount of profits that 'by reason of those conditions' have not accrued. This raises the question as to whether Article 9(1) authorises a challenge of the very nature of the commercial or financial relations between associated enterprises or only conditions based on those relations. For example, if a subsidiary sells goods to a parent, may a tax authority use Article 9(1) to challenge whether there is a sale or not or may it challenge only the conditions of sale that affect profits, such as the price? This is particularly important in the context of the financing of a subsidiary and the question as to whether or not a tax authority may challenge whether a financing relation is debt or equity (a loan or share capital) or only the rate of return on such a financing, e.g. the rate of interest. This is discussed further at 3.3.2.2.

3.1.3.3 Permanent establishments: shared taxation

The second part of Article 7(1) of the OECD Model authorises taxation of business profits by the state in which a permanent establishment is situated. This is a shared right of taxation, as the residence state is not precluded from taxation. Two particular issues arise in the context of this right to share taxation. The first involves interpretation of the phrase 'permanent establishment'. Second, the state of the permanent establishment may tax only the amount of the enterprise's profits 'attributable' to the permanent establishment. Each of these issues is considered in turn.

Permanent establishment threshold In Article 5, the OECD Model contains a definition of 'permanent establishment' (hereafter PE). This is a complex provision containing a number of exceptions and qualifications. The definition is of primary importance to the application of Article 7 (business profits) but it has importance in other respects. In particular, the term is used in the dividends, interest, royalties, capital gains and other income articles (Articles, 10, 11, 12, 13 and 21) to grant full taxing rights to the PE state where these types of income are effectively connected with a PE. In addition, the concept plays an important role in granting source country taxing rights with respect to employment income (Article 15) and one of the specific non-discrimination rules (Article 24(3)) is devoted to PEs. Each of these will be discussed in their place, but the concept of PE is discussed here.

Article 5 of the OECD Model requires a non-resident to have a sufficient direct presence in a state before there can be said to be a PE situated there and so the taxing rights that flow from that concept under Article 7. The concept of permanent establishment appears to be German in origin[42] and seems to be based on the rationale that without such a presence it would be difficult, if not impossible, to apply a direct tax law to the business income of a non-resident. Article 5 recognises two forms of presence, physical presence through the concept of a fixed place of business, and personal presence through individuals acting on behalf of the enterprise. The article incorporates express limitations to both of these forms as well as some express inclusions with respect to the former. The exclusions are particularly important. They mean that a source country will not have taxing rights with respect to certain business activities conducted by a non-resident directly within its borders whereas it would have taxing rights if the non-resident conducted those activities through a source country subsidiary.

[42] In particular, the Prussian income tax law of 1891 s. 2(b) incorporated the concept of an 'industrial or trade establishment'. Regarding this provision and its influence on the early development of tax treaties, see Avery Jones et al. (2006, pp. 722–3) and Harris (1996, pp. 290–3).

Physical presence The following discussion considers when a physical presence may amount to a PE under Article 5 of the OECD Model. This involves first a consideration of the general test in Article 5(1) and the illustrative list in Article 5(2). The discussion proceeds to briefly consider the special rule for building sites in Article 5(3) and then the express exclusions from the definition incorporated in Article 5(4).

General test The general test of PE is set out in Article 5(1) of the OECD Model, which provides:

> For the purposes of this Convention, the term 'permanent establishment' means a fixed place of business through which the business of an enterprise is wholly or partly carried on.

The concept of 'enterprise' was discussed above at 3.1.3.1. At that point, it was noted that the OECD provides little in the way of guidance as to what amounts to 'carrying on a business' and this is largely left to domestic law. However, in most countries it is clear that the mere passive holding of an investment will not constitute carrying on a business and so will not amount to a PE. This is especially important when dealing with immovable property activities (and so Article 6), as immovable property always constitutes a 'fixed place'.

Leaving aside whether an activity is of a business character and of sufficient scale to constitute 'carrying on business', the definition of PE in Article 5(1) of the OECD Model proves difficult in at least two other respects. Immovable property always constitutes a 'fixed place' and it seems possible for more than one location to constitute a single PE.[43] But how general can a location be and still constitute 'a fixed place' of business, i.e. how 'fixed' does a location have to be? The second difficulty is when may a person be said to be carrying on their business 'through' a fixed place. A few examples will illustrate these two issues, which are often intertwined.

Take, for example, a salesperson that sells biscuits from a van. Assume that the person commonly crosses the border into Country A and stops at a number of usual locations where the person has regular customers. Does the salesperson have a 'fixed place' of business in Country A? Can the truck constitute a fixed place or only the locations where the truck

[43] In *National Westminster Bank plc* v *United States* (2005) 69 Fed Cl 128 (CFC) a US court treated six branch locations of a UK bank in the US as a single PE. This can be important for the purposes of offsetting losses.

stops? Does it matter how often the person stops at particular locations or is the relevant issue how often the person crosses into Country A? Can the fixed place be a general region of Country A in which the salesperson is moving about? The point of this example is to demonstrate that often the existence of a PE is a question of degree and not absolutes on which different countries may take different positions.

The OECD Commentary on Article 5(1) contains a number of examples dealing with these issues that do not necessarily make clear or coherent distinctions. What they do is provide some useful general guidance. For example, the Commentary notes that the PE concept requires a degree of permanency. While this need not be measured in a temporal sense:

> experience has shown that permanent establishments normally have not been considered to exist in situations where a business had been carried on in a country through a place of business that was maintained for less than six months.[44]

As regards carrying on business 'through' the fixed place, the OECD notes that the word 'through' should be given a wide meaning 'so as to apply to any situation where business activities are carried on at a particular location that is at the disposal of the enterprise for that purpose'.[45] Usually, this involves personnel of the enterprise conducting the business of the enterprise at the location. However, the OECD notes that business can also be carried on by automated equipment. In particular, the Commentary contains an example involving the use and maintenance of vending machines.[46]

Electronic commerce is another area involving automated equipment. The PE concept has received much criticism for being based on nineteenth century methods of doing business and not easily adapted to twenty-first century methods of doing business. In particular, websites allow customers to place orders, make payments and download goods in ways that were not contemplated when the PE concept was devised. Many source countries feel that their traditional source tax base is being eroded by the increasing ability of foreign entrepreneurs to gain substantial access to their markets without creating a PE and, in particular, without creating a fixed base. To take but one example, foreign financial institutions increasingly have the ability to access markets and conduct general business such as banking without creating a physical presence in the form of a branch.

[44] OECD Commentary on Art. 5 para. 6.
[45] OECD Commentary on Art. 5 para. 4.6.
[46] OECD Commentary on Art. 5 para. 10.

The OECD looked into the impact of electronic commerce on the PE concept and concluded, in its usual way, that no adjustment to the Model was necessary and an addition to the Commentary would suffice. In particular, the OECD is of the view that a mere website is not sufficient to constitute a PE for the purposes of Article 5(1) of the OECD Model. A website is merely a combination of software and electronic data that does not, in itself, involve any tangible property. As such, it cannot constitute a place of business.[47]

By contrast, the OECD accepts that the server on which the website is stored may constitute a PE. A server is tangible equipment that has a physical location and, as noted with the vending machine example, automated equipment may constitute a PE. If the enterprise carrying on business through a website also owns (or leases) and operates the server on which the website is stored and used, the server could constitute a PE of the enterprise if the other requirements of Article 5 of the OECD Model are met. In particular, in order to constitute a fixed place of business, a server must be located at a certain place for a sufficient period to be viewed as fixed. In addition, the location of the server is often irrelevant to customers and the business of the enterprise and consequently it is sometimes doubted whether the business of the enterprise is carried on 'through' the server.[48]

The issue of whether a business is being 'carried on' at what is obviously a fixed place becomes particularly difficult when a person is conducting work at a client's premises. The OECD notes that a person need not have legal title to occupy a particular location in order to carry on business there. It is sufficient that the person has 'a certain amount of space at its disposal which is used for business activities'.[49] The OECD Commentary contains a number of examples in this respect, which again are not particularly enlightening.[50] What is clear is that importance is placed on the amount of time spent at the client's premises and account should be taken of what the person is doing there. It is useful to use a controversial Canadian case to illustrate the difficulties.

In *R* v *Dudney*,[51] the taxpayer was a US resident who was contracted to provide computer services and training for a client. In accordance with the

[47] OECD Commentary on Art. 5 para. 42.2.

[48] OECD Commentary on Art. 5 paras. 42.3–42.6. At para. 45.5 the UK has entered a reservation that it is of the view that 'a server used by an e-tailer' cannot constitute a PE.

[49] OECD Commentary on Art. 5 para. 4.1.

[50] OECD Commentary on Art. 5 paras. 4.2–4.5.

[51] [2000] FCJ No 230 (FCA).

contract, he provided the services at the client's premises in Canada for approximately 300 days in one year and 40 days in the following year. The taxpayer was provided with office space, which changed from time to time and was sometimes shared. He was permitted to enter the client's premises only during normal business hours and to use the client's telephone only on the client's business. The issue was whether the taxpayer was subject to Canadian tax and this depended on whether he had a 'fixed base' for the purposes of the independent services article of the Canada/US treaty.[52]

With reference to the Commentary on former Article 14 (independent services) of the OECD Model, the Canadian Court of Appeal noted that the concept of 'fixed base' was founded on similar principles to that of PE and in turn considered the Commentary on Article 5(1). The court held that the taxpayer did not have a fixed base for the operation of his own business at the client's premises. The court emphasised that he was entitled to use the premises only during normal working hours in working for the client. He was not entitled to any degree of control over the premises and they were not objectively identifiable to another party as his place of business. In particular, the court said that the taxpayer did not necessarily have a fixed place of business wherever he was providing services. Further, the long duration of his contract was not relevant to the question of whether he had a place of business in Canada but only to the question of whether, if he had such a place of business, it was permanent.

As noted, the *Dudney* case is controversial.[53] It is often asked, 'if Dudney was not conducting his business at the premises in Canada, then what was he doing there?' The Canadian court appears to have drawn a distinction between a 'fixed place of business' and a place at which business might be 'carried on'. Indeed, this is a distinction inherent in the wording of Article 5(1) of the OECD Model. The OECD seeks to blur this distinction in a way that was clearly not acceptable to the Canadian court, which quoted the following passage from the Commentary:

> The term 'place of business' covers any premises, facilities or installations used for carrying on the business of the enterprise whether or not they are used exclusively for that purpose.[54]

[52] It is generally accepted that the concept of 'fixed base' in former OECD Model Art. 14 is the same as 'fixed place' as used in Art. 5(1).

[53] There are a number of decisions by continental European courts that may be viewed as conflicting with *Dudney*. Two Norwegian cases are discussed in *Dudney* itself. This book retains a focus on the UK and so common law jurisdictions. However, in this regard see Baker (2001–, para. 5B.09) and the references cited therein.

[54] OECD Commentary on Art. 5 para. 4.

In this passage, the OECD seems to equate a 'place of business' with a place where business is carried on. If this were the correct interpretation of Article 5(1), then it would not be necessary to refer to a 'fixed place of business' through which business is carried on; it would have been sufficient to simply refer to a 'fixed place' through which business is carried on.[55] That is, if there is no distinction then there is no need to refer to 'business' twice in Article 5(1).[56]

As noted above, at the least, the OECD accepts that the premises must be 'at the disposal' of the enterprise for the purposes of carrying on business. This can have an impact on the classic case of a travelling salesperson employed by an enterprise. Such a person may regularly stay at a particular hotel when on business in a particular country and then travel daily to the offices of customers of the enterprise. A question arises as to whether the hotel room where the salesperson stays may constitute a PE of the enterprise. While this will depend on the facts of each case, usually the hotel room will not constitute a PE. This is because usually, the hotel room is not at the disposal of the enterprise for the purposes of conducting business. Rather, it is at the disposal of the salesperson in a personal capacity.

The Canadian *Knights of Columbus* case (discussed below) demonstrates this in the context of insurance agents.[57] Canadian commission-based agents generally worked out of home offices and visited the homes of prospective applicants in soliciting insurance applications for a US insurer. Miller J held that the home offices were not at the disposal of the US insurer whose products the agents promoted and so the home offices could not constitute a PE of the US insurer. Miller J suggested that the home offices might be at the disposal of the US insurer if the insurer:

> paid for all expenses in connection with the premises, required that the agents have that home office and stipulate what it must contain, and

[55] Interestingly, the Canada/US (1980) treaty was amended to incorporate a 'services PE' provision, in Art. 5(9), along the lines of that used in the UN Model, discussed below. It has been suggested that Canada wanted this provision in order to deal with the *Dudney* case. See Arnold (2008).

[56] See Avery Jones et al. (2006, p. 705), suggesting that the French version of Article 5(1) is clearer and translate it as 'a fixed place of business through which the enterprise carries on all or part of its activities'. As this translation still uses the concept of 'fixed place of business', it does not resolve the issue in the *Dudney* case.

[57] *Knights of Columbus* v *The Queen* [2008] TCC 307 (TC). For an analogous Canadian case dealing with provincial allocation of source, see *Sunbeam Corp (Canada) Ltd* v *Minister of National Revenue* [1963] SCR 45 (SC).

> further required that clients were to be met at the home office and in fact [the insurer's] members were met there.[58]

Payment to the agents of an expense commission (unrelated to expenses) was not sufficient to create this right of disposal.

Article 5(2) of the OECD Model contains an inclusive list of things that are PEs. It seems that this list is meant to be illustrative only. The Commentary suggests that this list should be interpreted 'in such a way that such places of business constitute permanent establishments only if they meet the requirements of paragraph 1'.[59] Again, if this were the case then one might expect to find in Article 5(2) the words 'subject to paragraph 1'. It is clear that some countries use Article 5(2) to include things that could not fall within Article 5(1).[60]

Building sites In the 1963 OECD Model, building sites were originally listed in Article 5(2). In 1977, they were moved to a dedicated provision in Article 5(3), which provides:

> A building site or construction or installation project constitutes a permanent establishment only if it lasts more than twelve months.

The wording suggests that for a building site to constitute a PE, even if it lasts longer than twelve months, it must nevertheless meet the general test in Article 5(1). This can be contrasted with the position under the UN Model where a building site *is* treated as a PE if it lasts longer than *six* months. In addition, the UN Model covers assembly projects and supervisory activities in connection with the building site, etc.

The express temporal feature of Article 5(3) of the OECD Model is particularly problematic. If source country tax is to be avoided, it provides an incentive to ensure that building sites, etc. do not last the requisite period, e.g. by dividing what might otherwise be a single contract up into shorter contracts with various members of the same group of corporations. And it may be wondered why a particular activity should be taxed when the same activity would not be taxed if it were done in exactly the same way only faster, especially if only slightly faster. This *bright line* rule puts pressure on interpretation of terms used in the provision such as 'building site'.[61] It also raises issues of when a building site or project starts to exist

[58] *Knights of Columbus* v *The Queen* [2008] TCC 307 (TC) at para. 78.

[59] OECD Commentary on Art. 5 para. 12.

[60] For example, see India/UK (1993) Art. 5(2)(k) under which the provision of certain services may constitute a PE.

[61] The OECD Commentary on Art. 5 para. 17 seeks to define these terms, at least by inclusion. This is reflective of the common practice of the OECD of inserting definitions in the Commentary rather than the Model.

and when it finishes and when a series of activities are to be considered a single building site or project. While, from an academic perspective, this is not a particularly riveting area, its sensitivity, particularly for developing countries, is demonstrated by the shorter temporal limit and the extension of subject matter in the UN Model.[62]

Express exclusions Paragraphs 1 to 3 of Article 5 of the OECD Model are subject to paragraph 4. This provides that certain activities are not to constitute a PE even if there would be a PE under the earlier paragraphs of the Article. These exclusions can be particularly important but are often difficult to apply in practice. The first two exceptions exclude the mere storage, display or delivery of stock. It is assumed the word 'or' is conjunctive and so premises may be used for all of these purposes simultaneously and yet fall within the exception. In this case, a distribution centre, i.e. a centre that is used for storage and delivery, falls within the exception. Similarly, the maintenance of stock for processing by another enterprise is excluded, as is maintenance of a fixed place of business for purchasing goods or collecting information. An example of the latter is a press agency of a newspaper that collects information for relay and publication in the jurisdiction of its head office.

The residual category is maintaining a fixed place of business for any other activity of a preparatory or auxiliary character. The OECD Commentary gives as examples a fixed place of business used solely for advertising, supplying information, conducting scientific research or servicing a patent or know-how contract. The proviso is that an activity is not preparatory or auxiliary if its 'general purpose is one which is identical to the general purpose of the whole enterprise'.[63] In addition, a PE does not exist where there is a combination of activities mentioned in the previous categories provided the overall activity is still preparatory or auxiliary. Even if use of the word 'or' were interpreted in an exclusive sense, this combination category permits, e.g. the combining of storage, display and delivery of stock, provided the overall activity is preparatory or auxiliary.

[62] For example, in the Indian case of *CIT* v *Visakhapatnam Port Trust* (1983) 144 ITR 146 (HCAP), a German company supplied machinery to an Indian customer. The Indian customer employed a local contractor to carry out the installation. The German company supplied an electrician and an engineer to supervise the installation. The Indian court held there was no PE, the German company was not involved in a construction or installation project and the supervision of the project did not constitute a PE. Contrast OECD Commentary on Art. 5 para. 18, which suggests that '[o]n-site planning and supervision of the erection of a building are covered by paragraph 3'. The UN Model expressly covers supervision.

[63] OECD Commentary on Art. 5 paras. 23 and 24.

Each of the categories is expressly limited to use or maintenance of facilities, stock or a fixed place of business 'solely' for the purpose specified. Any other activities may *infect* the exclusion and bring all of the activities within the PE. Where such a risk is present, it is common to locate any possibly infecting activities at a different place, perhaps in a different member of a group of corporations. In addition, the use or maintenance must be 'solely' for the enterprise. Each member of a corporate group will typically constitute a separate enterprise and so an exclusion does not apply if, e.g. in addition to its own stock, an enterprise maintains goods for other members of a corporate group to which it belongs.

Personal presence Article 5 of the OECD Model also contemplates the creation of a PE through a personal presence, i.e. without the creation of a fixed place of business. Such a 'deemed' PE may arise through the presence of a dependent agent in a particular jurisdiction. However, it will not arise if an agent is sufficiently independent of the person they are acting for. These matters are dealt with in Article 5(5) and (6) and are discussed below. Many countries take the view that these rules do not grant source countries sufficient taxing rights and so have extended the circumstances in which the provision of services in a jurisdiction might amount to a PE. This is reflected in Article 5(3)(b) of the UN Model, which is also briefly considered. Finally, the discussion considers the clarifying rule in Article 5(7) of the OECD Model that deals with group companies.

Agency permanent establishment Article 5(5) of the OECD Model provides that where a person

> is acting on behalf of an enterprise and has, and habitually exercises, in a Contracting State an authority to conclude contracts in the name of the enterprise, that enterprise shall be deemed to have a permanent establishment in that State in respect of any activities which that person undertakes for the enterprise.

There are two qualifications to the application of Article 5(5), which are not reproduced above. First, no PE is created where the person is an independent agent, discussed below.[64] Second, no PE is created where the person's activities are akin to those mentioned in Article 5(4), discussed above. Those qualifications aside, the critical issue for Article 5(5) is assessing when a person has 'an authority to conclude contracts' for the enterprise.

[64] For a historical assessment of Article 5(5) and (6) and the difficulties they pose, see Vann (2006).

A person who is authorised to act on behalf of another is an *agent* of the other person, the other being referred to as the *principal*. Article 5(5) avoids use of the word 'agent', but if this is not implicit in the phrase 'acting on behalf of an enterprise' then it is in the reference to 'an authority to conclude contracts in the name of the enterprise'.[65] The classic example of an agent of an enterprise is an employee of the enterprise and because an employee is dependent on the employer the exception in Article 5(6) will not apply. So, in many cases, the issue under Article 5(5) is whether the presence of an employee within a jurisdiction creates a PE there for the employer. Of course, an agent may be neither an employee nor independent of the employer, discussed below, and so create a PE of their principal if appropriately authorised.

Article 5(5) does not specify the type of contracts for which authority must be granted and so it does not seem to make a difference whether the authority is to purchase stationery, to sell stock or to borrow money. There is, however, the limitation provided by the reference to Article 5(4). So, for example, if the employee/agent has authority only to advertise or acquire stationery, a deemed PE may not be created if these activities are of a preliminary or auxiliary nature. Note that these exceptions to the creation of a PE may be used in conjunction, e.g. where an employee with power to conclude contracts is posted at a fixed place of business but activities are preliminary or auxiliary in nature.

A simple plan to prevent the creation of a PE under Article 5(5) is to ensure that the agent does not have authority to conclude contracts. This is particularly straightforward in this age of electronic communication and has resulted in what are often referred to as 'echo' systems. An echo system involves the agent negotiating all the relevant terms of an agreement with a client and relaying them to head office for formal conclusion of any agreement. The OECD notes this as a potential problem and suggests that if the head office as a matter of course approves all such contracts as negotiated the agent may be viewed as having concluded the contract.[66] This, in turn, has induced a practice to ensure that the terms negotiated by an agent are, on a regular basis, rejected or adjusted by the head office.

[65] Vann (2006, p. 363) notes the argument that agency is used 'in a strict legal sense' and how this gives greater scope to the rule in OECD Model Art. 5(7) 'that associated enterprises do not, merely by reason of the association, become PEs of each other'.

[66] Note, by contrast, the controversial decision of the Italian Supreme Court of Cassation in *Ministry of Finance (Tax Office)* v *Philip Morris GmbH* (2002) 4 ITLR 903 (SCC). In this case, the court suggested that the mere presence of an agent at negotiations of a contract might amount to an authority to conclude contracts.

It is not sufficient that an agent has authority to enter into contracts, the person must also 'habitually exercise' such authority. At the least, this implies repetition but how much repetition is not clear and the OECD says '[i]t is not possible to lay down a precise frequency test'.[67] Further, it raises the issue as to whether the first exercise of a power to conclude contracts can ever be habitual. The better view seems to be that some pattern must be established before a PE can be created. This pattern must have occurred in the subject country. So, it seems a first exercise of the power to conclude contracts in a new jurisdiction does not create a PE in that jurisdiction even if the person has habitually exercised the power elsewhere.

A Canadian case will demonstrate some of the above-mentioned points. In *Knights of Columbus*,[68] a US insurance company sold insurance products to Canadians with the assistance of commission-based Canadian sales agents. The agents would solicit insurance applications from Canadians and submit them to the US insurer for consideration. The approval rate was around 90 per cent. The agents could provide a limited form of temporary insurance while the application for permanent coverage was under consideration. The Canadian government argued that the Canadian sales agents constituted an agency PE based on the routine approval of applications and the provision of temporary insurance.[69] Miller J held that the 90 per cent approval rate was not 'routine approval' and the screening process involved more than 'legalistic formality'.[70] Further, the temporary insurance contracts were subject to successful approval of permanent insurance and held not to be a separate contract. With respect to the temporary insurance, the agent did not conclude the contract; it was 'simply the messenger'.[71]

So far, the discussion has presumed the existence of a clear authority bestowed on the employee/agent, i.e. express authority. However, authority may be subtler. An agent may have 'implied' authority. This happens where an agent concludes contracts in the name of the principal without express authority to do so. If the principal acquiesces in such conduct and acts in a way that is consistent with being bound by these contracts, the agent may be viewed as having implied actual authority to conclude the contracts on behalf of the principal. Similarly, implied actual authority

[67] OECD Commentary on Art. 5 para. 33.

[68] *Knights of Columbus* v *The Queen* [2008] TCC 307 (TC).

[69] The further argument that the agents' home offices were fixed places of business of the US insurer was discussed above.

[70] *Knights of Columbus* v *The Queen* [2008] TCC 307 (TC) at paras. 56–7.

[71] *Knights of Columbus* v *The Queen* [2008] TCC 307 (TC) para. 64.

may result from 'usual' authority. Thus, if a person is appointed managing director, it will be assumed or implied that, without express restriction, that person has all the powers typically bestowed on a managing director, including the power to conclude contracts. In all these cases, the authority is actual and the conduct of the agent may found a PE of the principal.

More problematic is the situation where the agent has no actual authority, express or implied, but only apparent or ostensible authority. This may occur, for example, where a person appointed to a particular position, say managing director, *appears* to have authority to conclude a particular contract but the principal has expressly prohibited the director from concluding such a contract.[72] In any suit by the other party to the apparent contract, the principal may be *estopped* from denying that the managing director had authority. While in such a case the principal is effectively bound by the contract, it is not true to suggest the employee/agent had authority. By very definition, apparent authority is not real or actual authority, it gives rise only to an estoppel. It is suggested that, while activity based on implied actual authority may form the basis of a PE, that based on apparent authority cannot. While Article 5(5) of the OECD Model does refer to 'an authority', apparent authority is not really authority at all. Further, it would seem inappropriate for actions that have not been authorised by an enterprise to give rise to a PE of the enterprise.

The UN Model addresses the concern of many developing countries that limitation of the agency PE to agents with an authority to conclude contracts is too restrictive. It extends the deemed PE through an addition to Article 5(5). A deemed PE may be created not only by an agent with authority to conclude contracts but also by an agent that 'habitually maintains… a stock of goods or merchandise from which he regularly delivers goods or merchandise on behalf of the enterprise'. In this case, there is no exception for activities of a preparatory or auxiliary character or that otherwise fall within Article 5(4). The result is that warehousing functions may be caught if performed by a dependent agent.

The UN Model further extends the agency PE concept with a provision dedicated to insurance enterprises. Article 5(6) deems a PE if an insurance enterprise collects premiums or insures risks in a state through a dependent agent (other than with respect to reinsurance). The UN Model also precludes the independent agent exception to a deemed PE (see below)

[72] Apparent authority can arise through other types of representations, such as where a person has represented that another has authority to act on their behalf, when they do not, even if the other person is not appointed to any formal position.

where the agent's activities are wholly or almost wholly devoted to the enterprise and the relations with the enterprise are not at arm's length. In *Knights of Columbus*, Miller J drew as an inference from the lack of an insurance clause along UN Model lines (that did exist in other US and Canadian treaties) that the countries intended that 'extensive insurance business activities could take place in the other country without tax liability'.[73]

Independent agent exception An agency PE will not be created under Article 5(5) of the OECD Model because of the actions of an independent agent of the type mentioned in Article 5(6). Article 5(6) specifically mentions brokers and general commission agents as well as 'any other agent of an independent status'. The OECD suggests that the agent needs both legal and economic independence. Legal independence depends on the extent and type of obligations that the person owes to the enterprise. If the agent's commercial activities for the enterprise are subject to detailed instructions or comprehensive control by the enterprise, the agent will not be regarded as legally independent of the enterprise. Economic independence focuses on the extent of entrepreneurial risks borne by the agent.[74]

> All the facts and circumstances must be taken into account to determine whether the agent's activities constitute an autonomous business conducted by him in which he bears risk and receives reward through the use of his entrepreneurial skills and knowledge.[75]

A UK case that raised the issue of the independence of an agent is *Fleming* v *London Produce Co Ltd*.[76] This case involved a UK subsidiary selling meat in the London meat market on behalf of its South Africa parent. Megarry J was dealing with UK legislation that taxed the principal through their agent unless the agent was a 'broker', which was defined to include a 'general commission agent'.[77] He noted that

> the word 'general' in the phrase 'general commission agent' itself must have some import; and in the context I think the most likely sense is that of a commission agent who holds himself out as being ready to work for clients generally, and who does not in substance confine his activities to

[73] *Knights of Columbus* v *The Queen* [2008] TCC 307 (TC) at para. 83.

[74] OECD Commentary on Art. 5 paras. 37–8.

[75] OECD Commentary on Art. 5 para. 38.6.

[76] (1968) 44 TC 582 (Ch).

[77] Megarry J traces the UK origins of the rule, which are the origin of the OECD rule, see Avery Jones et al. (2006, p. 728).

> one principal, or an insignificant number of principals... If that view is right, then in my judgment the only possible conclusion... is that L.P. were neither brokers nor general commission agents. They did many acts not characteristic of brokers; and they were sadly lacking in generality of custom... L.P. was little more than the English end of Kaiapoi's business, doing all that had to be done for them, and far more than is truly broker-like. I do not think it is within either the letter or the spirit of the section that a non-resident should be able to escape taxation by virtue of the proviso if in substance what is done is that he carries on business within the United Kingdom through the medium of an agent who is virtually a sole agent, running the entire business for him and merely sending him remittances on request.[78]

This passage well articulates the general requirement for Article 5(6) of the OECD Model and the OECD accepts the relevance of 'the number of principals represented by the agent'.[79]

An additional requirement in Article 5(6) of the OECD Model is that to fall within the exception the independent agent must be acting 'in the ordinary course of their business'. The OECD suggests that this is an objective test, measured by reference to 'activities customarily carried out within the agent's trade as a broker [etc.]... rather than the other business activities carried out by that agent'.[80] This can be particularly useful for an agent that is new to a particular business as whether a particular action is within the agent's 'ordinary course of business' is tested by reference to activities customary to that type of business and not the agent's subjective business. A classic example of the type of agent falling within Article 5(6) is an insurance broker that sells insurance for a number of foreign insurance companies. Such insurance companies often have neither a fixed place of business nor a deemed PE, due to the independent nature of the brokers used (regarding the UN Model extension see discussion above with respect to agency PEs).

Services PE The above discussion has identified a number of sensitive areas where tax planning may ensure that substantial penetration is made into a market and yet no taxable presence, i.e. PE, is created. This is especially so with respect to the provision of services. The UN Model seeks to address this issue through an extension to Article 5(3). As already mentioned, this provision is different from the OECD Model in that it expressly provides that a building site, etc. *does* create a PE if the requisite

[78] (1968) 44 TC 582 (Ch) at 596–7.
[79] OECD Commentary on Art. 5 para. 38.6.
[80] OECD Commentary on Art. 5 para. 38.8.

temporal period is met. Further, Article 5(3) of the UN Model is extended to incorporate a test for what is commonly referred to as a 'services PE'. Article 5(3)(b) provides that a PE is created by:

> The furnishing of services, including consultancy services, by an enterprise through employees or other personnel engaged by the enterprise for such purpose, but only if activities of that nature continue (for the same or a connected project) within a Contracting State for a period or periods aggregating more than six months within any twelve-month period.

This is a popular provision, particular among developing countries, but also features in many treaties between developed and developing countries, and more recently in treaties between developed countries.

This popularity and the increasing importance of services in the global economy prompted the OECD in 2008 to make changes to the Commentary on Article 5, which now incorporates a draft services PE provision.[81] This provision is substantially longer and more complex than the UN provision but in essence follows its format. The OECD provision creates a 'deemed' PE and, like deemed agency PEs (but unlike the UN Model provision), it is subject to Article 5(4) of the OECD Model. An apparent limit on both the UN and OECD provisions is that they still require presence in the source state when providing the services.[82] This can be contrasted with the technical services provision sometimes inserted in the royalties article, discussed below at 3.1.4.3 and 3.1.6.

Position of associated corporations The final provision of Article 5 of the OECD Model states:

> The fact that a company which is a resident of a Contracting State controls or is controlled by a company which is a resident of the other Contracting

[81] OECD Commentary on Art. 5 para. 42.23. Arnold (2008) notes that the Canada/US treaty (1980) Art. 5(9), inserted by a 2007 protocol, is based on an earlier draft of the OECD provision.

[82] Arnold (2008) notes: 'The question arises whether services can be performed in a country when the service provider is not present in that country. Such situations are likely to be rare in practice, although they may arise more frequently with technological advances. The important point is that the rule operates on the basis of where the services are performed, not where the services are consumed or used.' He is speaking about the provision in the Canada/US (1980) treaty, which, like the OECD provision, uses the word 'provide' rather than 'furnish', which is used in the UN Model. OECD Commentary on Art. 5 para. 42.18 states that 'all Member States agree that a State should not have source taxation rights on income derived from the provision of services performed by a non-resident outside that State'.

> State, or which carries on business in that other State (whether through a permanent establishment or otherwise), shall not of itself constitute either company a permanent establishment of the other.[83]

At one level, the rationale for this provision may be questioned when it appears to state the obvious. However, Vann convincingly draws a connection between this provision and the agency PE provision in Article 5(5). He notes the argument that

> a subsidiary would be an agency PE of its parent (and presumably a fixed place of business PE, assuming the subsidiary has a fixed place of business) if its activities were economically integrated with those of its parent. The subsidiary would be part of the same firm as the parent because it is not independent.[84]

This is consistent with the argument noted above at 3.1.3.1, that an integrated group of companies might be viewed as conducting a single business and so a single 'enterprise', even if that enterprise cannot be 'of a Contracting State'. There is a certain resonance between this argument and the position of subsidiaries under EU Law, discussed below.

Vann goes on to note how Article 5(7) of the OECD Model reinforces the 'separate legal personality of associated corporations as a fundamental precept of international taxation', a point noted above at 2.1.1.1.[85] Of course, this does not mean that one corporation cannot be a dependent agent of an associated corporation if the requirements of Article 5(5) and (6) are met.[86] However, as discussed above, a formal legal relationship of agency is required for this to happen, which may be avoided in a corporate group context in order to ensure no agency PE is created.[87]

EU Law Above at 2.1.2.3, an analogy was drawn between the concept of PE in Article 5 of the OECD Model and that of 'establishment' in Article 49 of the FEU Treaty. While the basic idea underlying these concepts is similar, in the usual way, it is clear that the EU Law concept is substantially broader. Article 49 of the FEU Treaty focuses on the legal form of

[83] Note this is the only provision in OECD Model Art. 5 (or Art. 7) that refers to 'company', as opposed to 'enterprise'. Regarding the definition of 'company' in Art. 3(1)(b), see above at 2.1.1.1.

[84] Vann (2006, p. 361).

[85] Vann (2006, p. 363).

[86] OECD Commentary on Article 5 para. 41.

[87] '[S]o long as a subsidiary is not an agent in the legal sense of a parent company, its lack of legal and economic independence from the parent company, which will usually be the case, will not make it a PE.' Vann (2006, p. 363).

the establishment ('agencies, branches or subsidiaries') with a general reference to activities pursued. It does not incorporate the limitations in Article 5 of the OECD Model. There is no requirement that the establishment be constituted by 'a fixed place of business'. There is no exception for certain activities (e.g. those of a 'preparatory or auxiliary character'). In the context of agencies, there is no limitation to agents with the 'authority to conclude contracts' and no exclusion for independent agents.

Perhaps the greatest difference between the OECD Model and EU Law in this regard is with respect to subsidiaries. The OECD Model says that a subsidiary is not of itself a PE of its parent corporation. By contrast, Article 49 of the FEU Treaty covers the establishment of a subsidiary in one member state by a parent corporation of another member state. The subsidiary *is* an establishment of the parent. This means that when it comes to a consideration of discrimination (discussed below at 3.1.3.4) the FEU Treaty only needs one rule to deal with both PEs and subsidiaries (the freedom of establishment), whereas the OECD Model uses two (not quite consistent) provisions (Article 24(3) and (5)).

It was noted above how the OECD concept of a PE may be extended, e.g. under the UN Model, to include the provision of certain services. In this respect, the PE concept in tax treaties may be broader than that of 'establishment' in Article 49 of the FEU Treaty. Article 49 is supplemented with Article 56 of the FEU Treaty, the freedom to provide services. The concept of 'services' used in Article 56 is substantially broader than any services PE concept used in tax treaties.

Despite these differences between the OECD Model and the FEU Treaty, the tax treaty PE concept is used in the EU directives on direct taxation, although not uniformly. Article 2(2) of the Parent-Subsidiary Directive (1990) defines PE in the following terms:

> [A] fixed place of business situated in a Member State through which the business of a company of another Member State is wholly or partly carried on in so far as the profits of that place of business are subject to tax in the Member State in which it is situated by virtue of the relevant bilateral tax treaty.

This is clearly based on Article 5(1) of the OECD Model and the limiting words (after 'in so far as') appear to allow limitations of the type in Article 5(3) and (4). It is not possible for an agency or services PE to fall within the Directive. The definition in Article 3(c) of the Interest and Royalties Directive (2003) is the same but without the limiting words. By contrast, the Mergers Directive (1990) uses the PE concept but it is not defined. The

PE concept is not used in the Savings Directive (2003), but this Directive does use the concept of 'place' or 'Member State of establishment'.

Attribution of profits: separate enterprise approach Having identified that an 'enterprise' carries on business through a PE in a state, the second sentence of Article 7(1) of the OECD Model permits the state to tax the 'profits' of the enterprise that are 'attributable' to the PE. The OECD suggests that Article 7(2) is 'part of the context' of the second sentence of Article 7(1) and 'that sentence should not be interpreted in a way that could contradict paragraph 2'.[88] Article 7(2) provides:

> where an enterprise of a Contracting State carries on business in the other Contracting State through a permanent establishment situated therein, there shall in each Contracting State be attributed to that permanent establishment the profits which it might be expected to make if it were a distinct and separate enterprise engaged in the same or similar activities under the same or similar conditions and dealing wholly independently with the enterprise of which it is a permanent establishment.

Thus, the profits attributable to a PE are to be calculated according to a 'separate enterprise' approach.[89]

Historically, it has been doubted whether any country in practice attempts to determine the income of a PE in strict accordance with the separate enterprise approach.[90] Any other approach necessarily involves some sort of formulary apportionment. The right to use a formulary apportionment in attributing profits to a PE is reserved by Article 7(4) of the OECD Model, but subject to a 'result' in accordance with the separate enterprise approach.[91] A formulary apportionment approach would take the profits (or elements making up the profits) of the enterprise and apportion them between the PE and the rest of the enterprise according to a formula. The formula may involve comparative turnover but there are other methods involving measured mixes of assets, staff and sales.[92] A usual consequence

[88] OECD Commentary Art. 7 para. 11. Amendments to the second sentence of OECD Model Art. 7(1) are slated for 2010 to remove any potential conflict with Art. 7(2). See OECD (2008b, para. 1).

[89] There is no *de minimis* rule in OECD Model Art. 7. If there is a PE then the profits attributable to that PE, however small, may be taxed by the PE state. Instead, the definition of PE is left to act as a form of *de minimis* limitation in that it excludes certain activities (discussed above at 3.1.3.3) to which, in practice, little profit could be attributed.

[90] Arnold and McIntyre (2002, pp. 27 and 124).

[91] It is proposed to delete OECD Model Art. 7(4) in 2010, see OECD (2008b, para. 1).

[92] Formulary apportionment, including that prescribed by OECD Model Art. 7(4), is further considered at 3.3.1.3.

of a formulary apportionment is that if the overall enterprise has a profit the PE will have a profit and, if a loss, the PE will have a loss, i.e. it is not possible for the enterprise to have a loss and the PE a profit or vice versa. The OECD is firmly of the view that this limitation does not apply when using the separate enterprise approach in Article 7(2) of the OECD Model.[93]

The OECD suggests that in the majority of cases, the 'profit properly attributable' to a PE can be determined from the trading accounts of the PE, which are the appropriate starting point.[94] The process is then to check whether Article 7(2) of the OECD Model requires any adjustment to these figures. Adjustments should not 'construct hypothetical profits figures', they should 'start with the real facts of the situation as they appear from the business records of the permanent establishment'.[95] Rather, adjustment should be made in accordance with a two-step approach.[96]

The first step involves identifying the activities carried on through the PE and thereby the transactions and dealings to be attributed to it. The second step involves the quantification of those dealings for tax purposes. Where the dealings are with outsiders independent of the PE, the quantification will be according to the terms of the dealing. If, however, the dealings are with the owner of the PE or an associate of that owner, transfer pricing rules will affect quantification of the dealing.[97] Once the dealings attributable to a PE are identified and quantified the profit calculation

[93] '[T]he directive of paragraph 2 may result in profits being attributed to a permanent establishment even though the enterprise as a whole has never made profits; conversely, that directive may result in no profits being attributed to a permanent establishment even though the enterprise as a whole has made profits.' OECD Commentary on Art. 7 para. 11. Taken in isolation, one would be forgiven for thinking that OECD Model Art. 7(1) is inconsistent with the separate enterprise approach and rather prescribes a formulary apportionment; 'the profits of the enterprise... attributable to that permanent establishment' may be taxed in the PE state. This apparent inconsistency will be remedied by amendments slated for 2010, see OECD (2008b, para. 1).

[94] Vann (2003, pp. 157–67) notes that this accounts based approach is generally consistent with a civil law approach to taxation, which places heavier emphasis on the correlation between accounts and taxable profits. By contrast, he suggests that common law jurisdictions have historically placed greater emphasis on allocation methods of attributing profits to overseas activities and that any perceived inconsistency within the provisions of OECD Model Art. 7 is attributable to the differences between these accounts and allocation based approaches. As discussed below, from 2010 the accounts based system will be the only OECD recognised approach.

[95] OECD Commentary on Art. 7 para. 16. In *National Westminster Bank plc* v *United States* (2008) 512 F 3d 1347 (FCA), the US Federal Court of Appeals insisted that branch accounts be relied on in determining the profits of a US branch of a UK bank.

[96] OECD Commentary on Art. 7 para. 18.

[97] Transfer pricing rules applying to transactions between associates are considered below at 3.3.1.

proceeds in the usual way. The calculation of the profits is determined according to the domestic tax rules of the PE state based on the attributed dealings (but subject to the rest of the treaty).

The present discussion focuses on the first step in the adjustment process under Article 7(2) of the OECD Model. This involves two aspects. The first is identifying the activities carried on through the PE. The second involves identifying (and constructing) from these activities the transactions and dealings attributable to the PE, which are used as the basis for calculating the profit attributable to the PE. Each of these aspects of the first step is considered in turn. As noted above at 2.1.2.1, in 2003 the UK largely adopted Article 7 into its domestic law.[98]

Delineating activities Article 7(2) of the OECD Model treats the deemed separate enterprise as 'engaged in the same or similar activities under the same or similar conditions' as the *activities*[99] 'carried on through' the PE. In identifying these activities, the OECD specifies that a 'functional and factual analysis' should be undertaken. Apparently, this involves identifying:

> the economically significant activities and responsibilities undertaken through the permanent establishment... in the context of the activities and responsibilities undertaken by the enterprise as a whole.[100]

Profits may be attributed to a PE only when they result 'from activities carried on by the enterprise through that permanent establishment'.[101]

The specifics involved in this identification process are different depending on whether a fixed place of business, agency or services PE is involved.

[98] CTA 2009 ss. 19–33.

[99] For the purposes of consistency, the French text, which uses the word 'activities', is preferred here rather than the English text reference to 'business'. See Avery Jones et al. (2006, p. 705).

[100] OECD Commentary on Art. 7 para. 18. Vann (2006, pp. 377–8) notes that '[i]n the case of separate companies the dividing lines between the various enterprises in a group is clear at least in concept because they are legally separate and can enter into legally valid transactions with each other. In the case of a PE the dividing lines are unclear and the functional analysis performs the additional task of delineating the parts of a single enterprise which are to be treated as a separate enterprise under Article 7(2) of the OECD Model for attributing profits to the PE'.

[101] OECD Commentary on Art. 7 para. 24. The wording of OECD Model Art. 7(2) was important in *National Westminster Bank plc* v *United States* (2008) 512 F 3d 1347 (FCA). This case involved a US branch of a UK bank. The US government argued that the independent enterprise comparator should be considered a separate corporation with the result that the hypothetical corporation would need its own regulatory capital for US

With respect to a place of business PE, the OECD uses a building site to demonstrate the types of activities that are not carried on through a PE and should not be attributed to it. If other parts of the enterprise supply goods in connection with the site, profits from that supply:

> do not result from the activities carried on through the permanent establishment and are not attributable to it. Similarly, profits resulting from the provision of services (such as planning, designing, drawing blueprints, or rendering technical advice) by the parts of the enterprise operating outside the State where the permanent establishment is located do not result from the activities carried on through the permanent establishment and are not attributable to it.[102]

A fixed place of business PE often involves direct activities of the enterprise but may involve the enterprise acting through third parties, i.e. agents. By definition, an agency PE always involves acting through third parties and so always involves at least two tax subjects, the PE and the agent. Here, the functional analysis must delineate between activities that the agent performs on their own account and those performed by the agent on behalf of the enterprise. Only assets and risks with respect to the latter (and capital necessary to support them) are attributed to the PE for profit calculation purposes.[103]

In the context of a services PE, it seems clear that the activities to be attributed to the PE are those that cause it to be a PE, i.e. the services. Where an individual carries on an enterprise, it may be that individual who provides the services. However, in a typical case an agent will perform the services, usually an employee. The services constituting a services PE are likely to generate fee income. The OECD suggests that it is inappropriate to tax that fee income on a gross basis; this is inconsistent with the 'profit' concept in Article 7 of the OECD Model. '[D]irect or indirect expenses incurred for the purpose of performing these services…' must be deductible in calculating the profits attributable to a services PE.[104] Therefore, activities generating these expenses must also be allocated to the services PE.

banking regulation purposes. This would affect the amount of interest deductible by the branch. The US Federal Court of Appeals held that it was inappropriate to presume that the hypothetical comparator was a separate corporation as such a corporation would not be operating under the 'same or similar conditions' as a branch (which could rely on the regulatory capital of the UK bank).

102 OECD Commentary on Art. 7 para. 25.

103 OECD Commentary on Art. 7 para. 26.

104 OECD Commentary on Art. 5 para. 42.47.

The rationale for requiring a PE in a state before the business profits of a non-resident are taxable is apparently that until this point is reached the non-resident cannot be properly 'regarded as participating in the economic life' of the state sufficient to justify taxing rights. On this basis, it might be assumed that when a PE is created the state of location has a justification in taxing profits from all business activity in that state. Some states do this by virtue of a *force of attraction* rule. Under such a rule, any activities in a state from generating business profits are *attracted* to a PE situated therein and may result in taxable profits of the PE, even if the activities are not carried on 'through' the PE.[105] The OECD rejects this practice as inconsistent with the Model and unconvincingly seeks to justify this position on grounds of interference with 'ordinary commercial activities'.[106]

In the result, the PE concept in the OECD Model is more than a *de minimis* limitation in taxing business profits. It is also a substantive limitation. A source state may tax profits only from business activities carried on *through* a PE and not tax profits from business activities carried on *in* its jurisdiction once a PE is established. An important consequence of this substantive limitation is that it places pressure on the correct allocation of activities to a PE. Many types of activity, by their very nature, are difficult (if not impossible) to allocate to a fixed place, an agent or specific services. Further, as enterprises often have control over the activities carried on through their PEs, the substantive limitation in Article 7 is something that can be planned around.

By contrast, Article 7(1) of the UN Model contains a limited force of attraction rule. A PE state may tax not just the profits attributable to the PE. It may also tax profits attributable to sales in the PE state of 'goods or merchandise of the same or a similar kind as those sold through' the PE as well as 'other business activities carried on' in the PE state 'of the same or similar kind as those effected through' the PE. For source states, this can be a particularly useful extension as it prevents an enterprise from seeking to avoid taxation by segregating profitable activities away from a PE. In doing so, it also removes some of the importance in identifying the activities that are properly attributable to a PE. Once a PE has been identified, then profits from *all* activities in the state of the type carried on

105 A number of countries adopt at least a limited force of attraction rule, including the US. See Ault and Arnold (2010, pp. 498–502).

106 OECD Commentary on Art. 7 para. 9. See also Commentaries on Art. 10 para. 31, Art. 11 para. 24, Art. 12 para. 20 and Art. 13 para. 27.

through the PE become taxable. Unfortunately, there are practical problems associated with this provision.[107]

Calculating PE profits Once activities carried on through a PE have been identified, these activities are used to identify the dealings or transactions that are relevant in determining the profits attributable to the PE. These dealings or transactions will give rise to actual or notional 'payments' (in the broad sense, see above at 1.1) made and received that are attributed to the PE. These payments will be quantified in accordance with the second step (outlined above and possibly involving transfer pricing rules) and the net result, determined in accordance with the domestic tax law of the PE state, will be the profits attributable to the PE.

The OECD suggests that the activities carried on through a PE may give rise to three sorts of dealings.[108] The first involves *real transactions* with independent persons, e.g. sales made through the PE to independent third parties. These transactions, once identified with the PE, give rise to little difficulty. The legal basis of the transaction will be accepted for tax purposes, as will the price paid under the transaction. The second also involves *real transactions* with associated persons. Here, as a rule, the legal basis of the transaction will also be accepted for tax purposes.[109] However, this is not necessarily true of the price paid under the transaction, which may be adjusted by transfer pricing rules (i.e. under the second step mentioned above), discussed below at 3.3.1. The third type of dealing mentioned by the OECD involves *dealings* between the PE and other parts of the enterprise (or its owner). On the basis that people cannot deal with themself, these are necessarily fictitious *dealings*. Fictitious *transactions* (and payments) need

[107] Not least of these problems is that UN Model Art. 7(2) does not apply to the extensions and so there is no guidance on how a PE state should calculate the profits attributable to these similar activities. Arguably, the PE state may tax the full profit attributable to these similar activities, and not what might be a substantially smaller amount calculated under the separate enterprise approach. Nevertheless, there may be positive outcomes to this lack of clarity, e.g. non-residents may ensure that all their similar activities in a state are carried on through a PE there (an incentive not incorporated in the OECD Model).

[108] OECD Commentary on Art. 7 para. 17. Para. 17 refers to transactions between the enterprise and 'independent enterprises' and between the enterprise and 'associated enterprises'. As a single person may simultaneously conduct two or more enterprises, this is confusing. A *transaction* can be conducted only between different 'persons' (and not two enterprises of the same person) and so the text refers to 'persons'.

[109] OECD (1995–2000, para. 1.36). This is not always the case, particularly with respect to excessive debt financing. See below at 3.3.2.2.

to be constructed from these fictitious dealings purely for tax purposes. This is the meaning of the separate enterprise approach.

Real transactions As discussed above at 1.1, payments are the building blocks of the income tax. Further, as discussed at 2.1.2.2, most countries source or locate business receipts for domestic tax law purposes. In this context, the attribution of activities, transactions and payments to a PE is important. Real payments received under real transactions attributable to activities carried on through a PE will have real tax consequences. However, the domestic tax laws of many countries, like the UK, do not have express rules for sourcing expenses that may be deducted in calculating business profits. Rather, the domestic tax law, express or implied, typically has a general test that payments made are deductible if they constitute 'proper business expenses', or if they are incurred 'in the production of income' or 'wholly and exclusively' for business purposes.[110] Accounting principles of deductibility often perform an important role in applying such a general test.

Rather than seeking to identify payments made in the context of the activity carried on through a PE, Article 7(3) of the OECD Model contains a general deductibility test. It provides:

> In determining the profits of a permanent establishment, there shall be allowed as deductions expenses which are incurred for the purposes of the permanent establishment, including executive and general administrative expenses so incurred, whether in the State in which the permanent establishment is situated or elsewhere.

In other words, in order to be deductible, expenses need not be incurred as part of the activity carried on through a PE, it is enough that they are 'incurred for the purposes' of the PE. This can be contrasted with payments received, which are accounted for in a PE profit calculation only if they result from activities carried on through the PE. Of course, Article 7(3) does not authorise the deduction of expenses that are not incurred for the purposes of the PE, even if they are incurred in carrying on activities through the PE.[111]

Article 7(3) of the OECD Model causes a certain amount of disquiet among source states. It is often suggested that it is inconsistent with the separate

[110] In the context of income from a trade, the UK uses the 'wholly and exclusively' test, CTA 2009 s. 54 and ITTOIA 2005 s. 34(a).

[111] Although domestic tax law may authorise such a deduction.

enterprise approach in Article 7(2).[112] The OECD retorts that Article 7(3) simply provides guidance on how to apply the separate entity approach in Article 7(2).[113] Since 2008, its argument progresses to suggest that, contrary to its wording, Article 7(3) does not authorise a deduction of the expenses mentioned for tax purposes; that is a matter for domestic tax law determined in light of the non-discrimination rule in Article 24 (3) (discussed below at 3.1.3.4). Rather, Article 7(3) merely 'attributes' expenses to the PE for the purposes of determining its profits.[114] It is presumed this means attributing the activity involved in, say, a head office making a payment to the PE so that the activity falls within the prescription of Article 7(2).

One could be forgiven for struggling with a fictitious allocation of expense activity to a PE in light of the OECD's dogma that a PE's profits must be calculated according to a 'functional and factual analysis' of the 'activities and responsibilities undertaken *through* the permanent establishment'.[115] However, it seems that the OECD's position is wrong, or at least misleading. Following the OECD approach, Article 7(3) of the OECD Model is not a *tax law* rule authorising a deduction.[116] Rather, it

[112] Article 7(3) authorises the deduction of expenses that might have been incurred, not by the PE but by other parts of the enterprise such as the head office. If the PE and the head office are truly treated as separate taxpayers, why should the PE be entitled to deduct such an expense? Most all countries' tax laws prevent one person deducting an expense incurred by another person.

[113] OECD Commentary on Art. 7 para. 29. Perhaps reinforcing the 'guidance' nature of OECD Model Art. 7(3), OECD Commentary on Art. 7 para. 51 appears to suggest that Art. 7(3) can be ignored where 'adequate accounts' are not available or where it is not 'reasonably practicable' to adopt these records, as might be the case for insurance enterprises. In these cases, it may be 'necessary… to estimate the arm's length profits based on other methods'.

[114] OECD Commentary on Art. 7 para. 30.

[115] OECD Commentary on Art. 7 para. 18. Emphasis added.

[116] So OECD Model Art. 7(3) is unlike the domestic tax law rules (referred to above) that it replicates. Avery Jones et al. (2006, pp. 738–9) discuss the origins of Art. 7(3). They suggest the provision was inserted to prevent some countries, including the UK, denying expenses incurred both on behalf of the PE and the head office (dual purpose expenditure) or incurred outside the jurisdiction. If that is its only intention, the provision as drafted is too broad. That intention would be sufficiently achieved by stating that 'a deduction shall not be denied merely by reason that'. A negative formulation of this type already exists in the context of Art. 7(5). As it stands, the express wording of Art. 7(3) is mandatory, 'there shall be allowed as deductions'. The express wording of the provision seems incapable of being limited to the intention identified by Avery Jones et al. In any case, the intention identified by Avery Jones et al. suggests Art. 7(3) *is* a *tax law* rule (preventing the denial of a deduction under the tax law of the PE state), contrary to the current OECD Commentary. OECD (2008a, para. 290) accepts the Avery Jones et al. position. The OECD position is more problematic in the context of the UK provision that directly implements it, i.e. CTA 2009 s. 29.

is a rule for determining the amount of profits (more like accounting than tax law profits) that *may* be taxed by a PE state under Article 7(1). However, even in this more limited role, Article 7(3) must indirectly limit the amount of profits that can be taxed by the PE state. Assume that £100 is derived through a PE. Assume that the head office incurs expenses of £20, which are properly for the purposes of the PE and fall within Article 7(3). The combined effect of Article 7(2) and (3) is that the profits attributable to the PE are £80 (100 – 20) and that is the amount that may be taxed under Article 7(1). This is the limit even if domestic tax law of the PE state denies deduction of the £20 expense in a non-discriminatory fashion.

Some expenses may be incurred, e.g. by the head office of the enterprise, both for the purposes of the head office and for the purposes of the PE, i.e. dual-purpose expenditure. This is particularly the case for central administration expenses and similar costs such as those relating to the training of employees. The domestic laws of some countries, like the UK, deny a deduction for dual-purpose expenditure.[117] Other countries are reluctant to accept such expenses on the basis that they are primarily headquarters expenses. These situations are not expressly dealt with by Article 7(3), which does not incorporate an apportionment rule. Nevertheless, the OECD suggests that apportionment of such dual-purpose expenses is appropriate under Article 7(3) although no preferred method of apportionment is specified.[118]

It has generally been accepted that, where it applies, Article 7(3) of the OECD Model requires a direct allocation of expenses to a PE, i.e. the deduction of expenses incurred 'for the purposes of' the PE. In this respect, particular problems are caused by the allocation of interest on debt. The concern of PE states is that a PE may be excessively funded with debt and the direct allocation of interest thereon to the PE may substantially erode the PE tax base. In addition, such directly attributable debt might exceed what an 'independent enterprise' could have borrowed. This has caused the OECD to accept a limitation on the amount of interest that can be attributed to a PE based on the concept of 'free capital' of the PE.[119]

[117] See Tiley (2008, pp. 431–9).

[118] OECD Commentary on Art. 7 para. 27 suggesting apportionment based on turnover or gross profits as possible. Most countries use a direct allocation method of expenses (i.e. an allocation made on the relative usage of such services, generally attributed on a time charged basis). A few countries, such as Switzerland, also apply an indirect or formula basis (i.e. where costs are shared between head office and branch on the basis of key factors such as sales, salaries or net assets). The US has comparatively detailed rules allocating deductions; see Ault and Arnold (2010, p. 503).

[119] OECD Commentary on Art. 7 para. 45.

As this is essentially a question of excessive debt financing, it is discussed further below at 3.3.2.2 in the context of excessive debt financing between associated enterprises.

In light of these problems with Article 7(3) of the OECD Model, the OECD proposes to delete it in 2010 and simply rely on Article 7(2). Article 7(2) does not specify any particular approach to deductions and so these will essentially be regulated by the non-discrimination rule in Article 24(3), discussed below at 3.1.3.4.[120] Article 7(3) will remain part of treaty practice for decades to come.[121]

Intra-enterprise dealings Article 7(3) of the OECD Model deals with *real transactions* of the type mentioned above, i.e. actual transactions between the enterprise and independent or associated persons. However, the separate enterprise approach means that a PE can deal with the rest of the enterprise. The OECD suggests that in identifying dealings attributable to the PE reliance on the accounting records of the PE should be extended to 'agreements between the head office and its permanent establishments'. In particular it notes:

> to the extent that the trading accounts of the head office and the permanent establishments are both prepared symmetrically on the basis of such agreements and that those agreements reflect the functions performed by the different parts of the enterprise, these trading accounts could be accepted by tax authorities.[122]

These intra-enterprise agreements or dealings may be of two types. The first involves straightforward dealings between the PE and, say, head office, i.e. are not triggered by *real transactions* with other persons. These typically involve the reallocation of assets and funds between parts of the enterprise.

Second, an intra-enterprise dealing might be triggered by a *real transaction* between the enterprise and a third party. This *real transaction* may be directly attributed to the activities carried on through the PE with no further consequences. However, it may also be considered that the rest of the enterprise, e.g. the head office, acts as some sort of intermediary in the *real transaction*, creating a secondary dealing between the head office and the PE. In this second case, there are two dealings for tax purposes as opposed to the one *real transaction*. This type of case typically

[120] OECD (2008b, paras. 1, 27 and 29).

[121] It will be interesting to see whether and when the UK deletes its equivalent of OECD Model Art. 7(3) in CTA 2009 s. 29.

[122] OECD Commentary on Art. 7 para. 19.

arises in the context of the application of Article 7(3) of the OECD Model, where, say, the head office incurs expenses for the purposes of the PE. The issue is whether the head office should charge some mark-up for the intermediation.

Intra-enterprise dealings of the first type may be of many types. They often involve the transfer of tangible assets or funds from, say, the head office to the PE or vice versa or the use by the PE of intangible property owned by the enterprise. Such a transfer may also involve the provision of services or any other type of 'payment' (in the broad sense discussed above at 1.1). How should such transfers be characterised? In the context of the transfer or use of assets or funds, there are at least three possible characterisations.

The transfer may be characterised as a mere right of use. So, where a tangible asset is transferred from, say, the head office to a PE, or vice versa, the dealing would be characterised as a lease. In this case, the separate enterprise approach suggests the PE be treated as paying a notional rent to the head office for the use of the asset. The same would be true of a transfer of funds, e.g. from the bank account of the head office to the PE's bank account. This could be characterised as a use of funds and so a loan, in which case the PE might be treated as paying a notional interest to the head office for the use of the funds. Again, assume the PE has the right to use intellectual property owned by the enterprise, the PE might be treated as paying a notional royalty to the head office for that use. In their domestic tax laws, most countries, including the UK, do not recognise such notional payments.[123]

Such a refusal was at the heart of the dispute in the US *Natwest* case.[124] A UK bank carried on business in the US through branches. The branch accounts recorded a notional interest charge credited by the branches to the UK head office for the use of funds loaned by the head office. Instead of recognising this charge as reducing the branch profits, the US tax administration sought to apportion interest paid by the UK bank among its various parts including the US branches. The US Federal Court of Appeals confirmed that this was contrary to the separate entity approach incorporated in the UK/US tax treaty under the equivalent of Article 7(2) of the OECD Model. The court confirmed that intra-enterprise dealings that are

[123] Ault and Arnold (2010, p. 503) note that none of the jurisdictions they cover 'in their domestic rules recognize "self-charged" expenses for payments or transfers made between the branch and the head office. Thus, internally computed "interest" or "royalty" charges do not affect the income of the branch or head office. Only expenses that are actually paid or accrued to third parties support deductions, determined on either a "direct" or a formulary basis.'

[124] *National Westminster Bank plc* v *United States* (2008) 512 F 3d 1347 (FCA).

accurately reflected in a branch's accounts could not be ignored, but could be adjusted to an arm's length amount.

Alternately, the transfer or use of an asset might be viewed as a sale of the underlying asset by, say, the head office to the PE.[125] In this case, the separate enterprise approach suggests the transfer is a realisation event and the head office might be taxable on any hidden gains in the asset (market value above cost).[126] Intangible property, such as intellectual property, causes particular problems in this respect. Can a PE ever be considered to own intellectual property?[127] While some countries may accept that a PE can hold intellectual property, particularly where it created it or where the intellectual property was purchased for the purposes of the PE from a third party,[128] few countries accept that ownership of intellectual property created by an enterprise can be transferred from one part of the enterprise to another.

A transfer of funds is also problematic. If this is not characterised as a loan, how should it be characterised, as a gift or contribution to capital? The latter are not dealings that would take place between independent enterprises. Indeed, the third manner in which to characterise a transfer or use of assets or funds is to suggest that independent persons would not engage in such a transfer and so the transfer should not be recognised at all.

Intra-enterprise dealings of the second type involve a *real transaction*, which may be directly attributed to the PE as discussed above. However, where this *real transaction* is facilitated by, say, the head office, the issue is whether the facilitation should be treated as a secondary dealing under which the head office charges the PE a mark-up.[129] Take the simple example of where the head office borrows funds from a bank and transfers them

[125] OECD (2008a, para. 104) suggests that there is 'broad consensus among the OECD member countries for applying use as the basis for attributing economic ownership of tangible assets in the absence of circumstances in a particular case that warrant a different view'.

[126] Some countries, including the UK, do not adopt this approach. The tax consequences of transferring assets to PEs are further considered below at 6.1.1.

[127] With respect to intangible rights, OECD Commentary on Art. 7 para. 34 provides that '[s]ince there is only one legal entity it is not possible to allocate legal ownership to any particular part of the enterprise and in practical terms it will often be difficult to allocate the costs of creation of intangible rights to one part of the enterprise.'

[128] With respect to internally developed trade intangibles, OECD (2008a, para. 122) notes that 'the key factor is whether the PE undertakes the active decision-making with regard to the taking on and active management of the risks related to the creation of the new intangible'.

[129] This can also happen in the reverse, where a PE facilitates the provision of assets or labour for the head office.

for use by the PE. The interest should be deductible by the PE (assuming the requirements of Article 7(3) of the OECD Model are met), but should the head office be entitled to a mark-up for its facilitation? The same issue arises in other cases, particularly where services, including technical support, are provided by, say, a head office to a PE.

The OECD suggests a common approach to characterisation of both types of intra-enterprise dealings. Characterisation depends on the nature of the dealing in the context of the ordinary business of the enterprise:

> The question must be whether the internal transfer of property and services, be it temporary or final, is of the same kind as those which the enterprise, in the normal course of its business, would have charged to a third party at an arm's length price, i.e. by normally including in the sale price an appropriate profit.[130]

So if the transfer is of trading stock, i.e. assets sold in the ordinary course of the enterprise, then this will typically be treated as a sale (assuming this is consistent with the treatment in the enterprise's accounts). Apparently, this treatment applies whether or not what is transferred to the PE is finished or unfinished trading stock. The transfer of other types of tangible assets will have a different consequence. For example, the transfer to a PE of machinery that constitutes a fixed rather than circulating asset of the enterprise should not be treated as a sale. Rather, the use of the machinery by the PE will give rise to a claim for depreciation in the PE state.[131]

Article 7(5) of the OECD Model supports this approach to classification. It prescribes that no profits shall be attributed to a PE merely due to the PE purchasing goods for the enterprise. The Commentary suggests that this provision is targeted at the situation where a PE 'carries on purchasing for its head office'.[132] It is presumed that in such a case the PE does not purchase the goods as trading stock for the activities carried on through the PE, if it did there should be a deemed sale to the head office as described in the last paragraph. In this case, Article 7(5) is consistent with the no mark-up rule, i.e. if the purchase is not in the ordinary course of the activities carried on through the PE then no secondary dealing based on the PE's intermediation for the head office should be recognised.

With respect to the use by a PE of intangible rights of the enterprise, the OECD suggests that a PE cannot claim a deduction for virtual royalties.[133]

[130] OECD Commentary on Art. 7 para. 31.
[131] OECD Commentary on Art. 7 para. 33.
[132] OECD Commentary on Art. 7 para. 57.
[133] To similar effect see CTA 2009 s. 31.

It is presumed that, similarly, there is no deemed sale of intangible rights between a PE and the rest of the enterprise so that in the context of intangible property no intra-enterprise dealing is to be recognised at all. Rather, the OECD suggests that the PE may claim a portion of expenses incurred, e.g. by head office, with respect to the development and maintenance of the intellectual property.[134]

The OECD notes that the intra-enterprise provision of services raises particular difficulties. Assume that a head office temporarily sends one of its employees to provide services for a PE. Because the employee acts on behalf of the enterprise, this involves the provision of services by the head office to the PE. The question to be answered is whether the nature of the services performed for the PE is of a type that the head office might provide to an independent third party. If the enterprise provides, say, computer services to third parties and that is what the head office employee does for the PE, then an intra-enterprise dealing should be recognised. 'In such a case, it will usually be appropriate to charge a service at the same rate as is charged to the outside customer.'[135]

There is also the situation in which the services are not provided outside the enterprise but, rather, the ordinary activities of, say, the head office or a PE is to provide such services to other parts of the enterprise. The OECD accepts that this is also a case in which a dealing between the different parts of the enterprise should be recognised, including a profit margin. Another situation is where 'the provision of services is merely part of the general management activity of the company taken as a whole'. In such a case, an intra-enterprise dealing should not be recognised and the cost of providing the services 'should be allocated on an actual cost basis to the various parts of the enterprise... without any mark-up to represent profit'. An example is where, say, a head office sends an employee to perform specialised staff training for a PE, and the enterprise never provides this sort of service to an independent third party. A more controversial example is the general supervisory management of, say, the board of directors of a corporation.[136]

With respect to the intra-enterprise provision of funds, the general position of the OECD is that no intra-enterprise dealing should be recognised. Usually, such a provision will not be in the ordinary course of business of an

[134] '[I]t would be appropriate to allocate between the various parts of the enterprise the actual costs of the creation or acquisition of such intangible rights, as well as the costs subsequently incurred with respect to these intangible rights, without any mark-up for profit or royalty.' OECD Commentary on Art. 7 para. 34.

[135] OECD Commentary on Art. 7 para. 35.

[136] OECD Commentary on Art. 7 paras. 36–8.

enterprise.[137] The exception is the special case of banks and financial institutions, where the provision of funds is in the ordinary course of business and such an intra-enterprise dealing may be recognised.[138] Consistently, where, say, the head office acts as an intermediary, borrowing funds and forwarding them to a PE, no secondary intra-enterprise dealing is to be recognised, i.e. no mark-up is to be made for the intermediation. In such a case, any interest and other expenses associated with the loan (such as loan fees) would be attributed to the PE. As noted above, the limitation of allocation of excessive interest on *real* debt financing is further discussed below at 3.3.2.2.

This area is the primary focus of the changes that the OECD wishes to make in 2010. It intends to delete Article 7(3), (4) and (5) and amend Article 7(1) so that sole reliance is placed on the separate entity approach in Article 7(2).[139] In doing so, it will remove the current approach of limiting the circumstances in which a mark-up can be charged for facilitation and rather rely on the functional and factual analysis approach to determine whether a mark-up is appropriate in a particular case. In this sense, in an effort to create greater uniformity between the approaches of countries, the move is towards increasing subjectivity and the compliance costs associated therewith.

There is some confusion as to whether the recognition of a dealing between a PE and the rest of the enterprise under Article 7 of the OECD Model might carry with it wider implications for other Articles. The potential for recognition of intra-enterprise dealings in the form of notional interest or royalty payments will be even greater under the amendments proposed for 2010. Might such notional payments be subject to withholding tax under other provisions of the OECD Model, such as Articles 11 and 12 (discussed below at 3.1.4.2 and 3.1.4.3, respectively)? Most countries do not recognise such notional payments for other purposes. Amendment of Article 7(2) of the OECD Model will make it clear that the separate enterprise approach is limited in its application to Article 7 and Article 23 (double tax relief).[140]

137 OECD Commentary on Art. 7 paras. 41–2. In particular, the OECD notes that 'the ban on deductions for internal debts and receivables should continue to apply generally'. CTA 2009 s. 32 generally prohibits a PE deducting notional interest payments to other parts of the enterprise.

138 The attribution of profits to PEs is particularly important for banks, which, for regulatory purposes, more commonly conduct their overseas operations through PEs than other types of business vehicle. This special treatment recognised by the OECD Commentary was in issue in the US case of *National Westminster Bank plc* v *United States* (2008) 512 F 3d 1347 (FCA).

139 OECD (2008b, para. 1).

140 OECD (2008b, paras. 1 and 25) and see OECD (2008a, para. 238).

3.1.3.4 Discrimination in taxation of business profits

Once a source country PE or subsidiary has been established and its profits identified, then Article 7 of the OECD Model gives the source country a *full* right to tax those profits. As noted above at 3.1.3, a limit on that taxing right is provided by Article 24(3) and (5), which are two of the three non-discrimination rules applicable to residents of the other contracting state (see above at 2.2.1). The first of these rules applies to PEs and the second to subsidiaries, recognising the point made at 3.1.3.3 that a subsidiary does not of itself constitute a PE of the parent corporation. By contrast, the concept of 'establishment' under the FEU Treaty encompasses both the establishment of a PE as well as a subsidiary and so the freedom of establishment prohibits discrimination against both PEs and subsidiaries. The OECD Model provisions are considered and then the EC freedom of establishment is compared.

OECD Model

Permanent establishments

Article 24(3) of the OECD Model provides:

> The taxation on a permanent establishment which an enterprise of a Contracting State has in the other Contracting State shall not be less favourably levied in that other State than the taxation levied on enterprises of that other State carrying on the same activities.

Like the other provisions in Article 24, Article 24(3) applies to all forms of source country taxation and not just those listed in Article 2; Article 24(6). There are a number of problems associated with Article 24(3). First, its wording is different from that used in Article 24(1) (discussed above at 2.2.1) and (5) (discussed below). In particular, those other provisions refer not just to 'taxation' but also 'any requirement connected therewith'. In *UBS Ag* v *RCC*, Arden LJ drew from this the following conclusion with respect to the equivalent of Article 24(3):

> The presence of the words 'any requirement connected therewith' in other parts of the articles is an indication that the expression 'the taxation' does not cover all aspects of liability to tax. It may therefore be limited to provisions which impose the tax, as distinct from collateral obligations of the taxpayer, such as the obligation to file a return. This approach is supported by the meaning of the word 'levied' which on its ordinary meaning means 'raised'. If that is so, art [24(3)] has a more limited field of operation than say art [24(1)].[141]

[141] [2007] EWCA Civ 119 (CA) at para. 72. According to Arden LJ at para. 80, the conclusion is that 'the taxation' does not cover the refund of a tax credit attached to a dividend. The judge at first instance and Moses LJ took the opposite view.

Second, Article 24(3) of the OECD Model does not specify which activities are being referred to; the activities of the overall enterprise or just the activities carried on through the PE. Inevitably, it is the latter. On this basis, what must be compared is taxation of the activities carried on through a PE in, say, Country A with the taxation of an enterprise of a resident of Country A carrying on the same activities as the PE. Article 24(3) does not specify whether these are the only activities that the hypothetical enterprise is considered to be carrying on, but inevitably this seems to be the case.[142]

All the activities conducted by a PE involve interactions with third parties and other parts of the enterprise of which the PE is part. How these activities translate into transactions and dealings that are recognised in calculating the PE's attributable profits was discussed above at 3.1.3.3. It seems inevitable that only those transactions and dealings should be attributed to the hypothetical enterprise under Article 24(3) of the OECD Model. This excludes any intra-enterprise transfers or provisions that are not recognised in accordance with the rules of Article 7. With respect to these transactions and dealings, Article 24(3) does not specify what should be the relationship between the hypothetical enterprise and the third parties involved in these transactions and dealings. Of course, in the factual situation of the PE, these transactions and dealings may have been with independent third parties or with associated enterprises or other parts of the enterprise.

The OECD suggests that Article 24(3) of the Model is restricted to a comparison of rules directed at taxation of the activities carried on by a PE, rather than the taxation of the PE as the independent enterprise prescribed by Article 7(2).[143] It seems that for this purpose it is to be assumed that the hypothetical enterprise is to be considered independent and isolated.[144] All the transactions and dealings to be recognised are assumed to be with independent parties. Article 24(3):

142 In *UBS Ag* v *RCC* [2007] EWCA Civ 119 (CA) at para. 77, the Court of Appeal was dealing with a tax credit granted with respect to dividends received that a resident corporation could use against tax on its own distributions. A PE was not granted such a tax credit and it had no tax liability with respect to its own distributions. Arden LJ noted that the comparison which must be made for the purposes of the equivalent of OECD Model Art. 24(3) 'is with the specific activity which the permanent establishment is carrying on and on which it is being taxed, and no other. Accordingly, no relevant comparison falls to be made with a UK enterprise which itself makes distributions'.

143 The latter approach is clearly open on the wording of OECD Model Art. 24(3).

144 For example, OECD Commentary on Art. 24(3) para. 58 confirms that a source country can tax the profits of a PE even if a loss at the head office means the enterprise has an overall loss.

> does not extend to rules that take account of the relationship between an enterprise and other enterprises (e.g. rules that allow consolidation, transfer of losses or tax-free transfers of property between companies under common ownership) since the latter rules do not focus on the taxation of an enterprise's own business activities similar to those of the permanent establishment but, instead, on the taxation of a resident enterprise as part of a group of associated enterprises.[145]

For example, the UK permits losses to be transferred from one resident corporation to another resident corporation, if both are members of the same 75 per cent owned group of corporations. The OECD approach means that Article 24(3) does not require the extension of this rule to allow a transfer of losses from a UK resident corporation to a UK PE of a non-resident corporation even if both corporations are in the same 75 per cent group.[146]

A straightforward example of the application of Article 24(3) of the OECD Model involves a country taxing the profits of PEs of non-resident corporations situated there at a higher rate than resident corporations. Some countries use this higher rate as a substitute for the fact that they do not tax remittances of PEs whereas they do tax dividends remitted by local subsidiaries of non-resident corporations.[147] This disparity between PEs and subsidiaries is discussed further below at 3.1.4.1. The OECD is clearly of the view that a simple increase in tax rate applicable to PEs by comparison with resident corporations is a breach of Article 24(3).[148]

Another example of the potential application of Article 24(3) of the OECD Model involves the application of progressive tax rates. In the UK, for example, the lower corporate tax rate facilitated by section 18 of CTA 2010 is limited to resident corporations. The UK tax administration accepts that this lower rate must be extended to UK PEs of non-resident corporations where they are covered by an Article 24(3) provision in a treaty. However, in determining the amount of relief available, the UK will take into account the entire profits of the enterprise of the

[145] OECD Commentary on Art. 24 para. 41. In a somewhat inconsistent fashion, the OECD suggests this approach is not to deny application of the arm's length standard under Articles 7(2) and 9(1) to a PE's dealings and transactions with other parts of the enterprise and with associated enterprises. OECD Commentary on Art. 24 para. 42. This is discussed further below at 3.3.1.2.

[146] The transfer is permitted by CTA 2010 s. 99. This rule was extended to UK PEs of non-resident corporations by reason of the decision of the ECJ in Case C-264/96 *ICI Plc* v *Colmer* [1998] ECR I-4695 (ECJ), discussed below.

[147] This was the approach in Germany before 2000, discussed below. It is still current practice in India, see Finance Act, 2009 (India) s. 2.

[148] OECD Commentary on Art. 24 para. 60.

non-resident corporation (and its associates).[149] This approach is authorised by the OECD,[150] and so constitutes an exception to the principle that the hypothetical enterprise in Article 24(3) is independent and isolated. Similar fragmentation issues can arise where there are different times at which tax has to be paid (instalment system) depending on the size of a corporation or its income.

Other examples of the application and scope of Article 24(3) of the OECD Model will be returned to at various points in this book, in particular at 3.1.4.1 (receipt of dividends by PE), 3.3.1.2 (transfer pricing rules applied to PE) and 5.2.1.1 (availability of foreign tax relief for PE).[151]

Subsidiaries Article 24(5) of the OECD Model provides:

> Enterprises of a Contracting State, the capital of which is wholly or partly owned or controlled, directly or indirectly, by one or more residents of the other Contracting State, shall not be subjected in the first-mentioned State to any taxation or any requirement connected therewith which is other or more burdensome than the taxation and connected requirements to which other similar enterprises of the first-mentioned State are or may be subjected.

As with Article 24(1) and (3), Article 24(5) applies to all forms of taxation and not just those listed in Article 2. Further, it seems Article 24(5) may apply to non-controlling shareholdings, but its most common application is in the context of subsidiaries, the focus of the following discussion. Despite serving similar purposes, Article 24(3) and (5) are substantially different in their drafting. First, the 'other or more burdensome test' is the same as in Article 24(1) and contrasts with the 'not less favourable' test in Article 24(3).[152]

Another difference between Article 24(3) and 24(5) of the OECD Model is that in the former the comparator is 'enterprises of [the source state] carrying on the same activities' whereas in the latter it is 'similar enterprises of the [source state]'. As noted above, the OECD interprets the

[149] See Tiley (2008, p. 851).

[150] OECD Commentary on Art. 24 para. 56.

[151] Two cases involving the equivalent of OECD Model Art. 24(3) are *Woodend (KV Ceylon) Rubber and Tea Co* v *Ceylon CIR* [1971] AC 321 (HL) and *R* v *IRC ex parte Commerzbank* (1993) 68 TC 252 (QBD). Both were discussed above at 1.2.2.

[152] Avery Jones et al. (1991, p. 425) suggest that these phrases mean the same, 'in the sense of the quantum of the tax'. In *UBS Ag* v *RCC* [2007] EWCA Civ 119 (CA) at para. 25 Moses LJ described the contrast in language between OECD Model Art. 24(3) and (5) as defying 'sensible explanation'.

reference to 'activities' in Article 24(3) to restrict its scope. That restriction is not possible in Article 24(5), where it is clear that it is the taxation of the 'enterprise' that is relevant. However, in amendments made to the Commentary in 2008, the OECD uses very similar wording in the Commentary on Article 24(5) as it does in the Commentary on Article 24(3) (reproduced above) despite the very different wording of the two provisions.

The OECD points out that Article 24(5) of the OECD Model prevents discrimination of a resident subsidiary, not discrimination of a non-resident parent. This point will be returned to in the context of the taxation of dividends at 3.1.4.1. The OECD suggests that:

> it follows that [Article 24(5)] cannot be interpreted to extend the benefits of rules that take account of the relationship between a resident enterprise and other resident enterprises (e.g. rules that allow consolidation, transfer of losses or tax-free transfer of property between companies under common ownership).[153]

Consistent with the interpretation of the non-discrimination provision for PEs, it might be suggested that the hypothetical comparator for a source state subsidiary of a non-resident parent corporation is with an isolated independent corporation of the source state.[154] This would mean that two source country subsidiaries (even if one is the parent of the other) that are owned by non-residents need not be given the same form of inter-corporate reliefs as are granted to locally owned related corporations.

The Commentary does not distinguish between two importantly different scenarios. The first is the relationship between the source state subsidiary and its non-resident parent corporation. The second is the relationship between the source state subsidiary and other source state subsidiaries of a common non-resident parent. The Commentary on Article 24(5) of the OECD Model does not incorporate any examples with respect to the second scenario and parts of the Commentary may be viewed as suggesting that Article 24(5) does not extend to this case. This is further explored in the context of the UK *Boake Allen* case, which appears to

[153] OECD Commentary on Art. 24 para. 77. Further like the Commentary on OECD Model Art. 24(3), in a somewhat inconsistent fashion, the Commentary continues at para. 79 to suggest that this approach is not to deny application of the arm's length standard in Article 9(1) to transactions between the source state subsidiary and related parties. This will be considered further below at 3.3.1.

[154] OECD Commentary on Art. 24 para. 78 suggests – 'paragraph 5 is aimed at ensuring that all resident companies are treated equally regardless of who owns or controls their capital'.

have buoyed the OECD in its 2008 efforts to restrict the scope of Article 24(5).[155]

Boake Allen involved the UK's former advance corporation tax system of corporate taxation, abolished in 1999. Every time a UK resident corporation distributed a dividend it had to pay a corporate distributions tax calculated as a fraction of the amount of the distribution, typically 25 per cent. A corporation that received a dividend that had suffered advance corporation tax (or ACT) could redistribute that dividend without further ACT. If a distribution was made between two resident corporations within a 51 per cent controlled group, the corporations could elect that no ACT would be payable, called a 'group income election'. This would mean, however, that the recipient corporation would have to pay ACT when it redistributed the dividend, unless a further election to defer ACT was available.

In the *Metallgesellschaft* and *Hoechst* cases (discussed below) the ECJ held that it was contrary to the freedom of establishment under EU Law to limit the group income election to resident corporations.[156] The election must also be available when a UK subsidiary distributed a dividend to an EU parent corporation. In *Boake Allen*, one of the issues was whether the equivalent of Article 24(5) of the OECD Model meant that the group income election must also be extended to distributions from a UK subsidiary to a non-EU parent corporation. Park J at first instance noted that there were at least four possible meanings that might be given to 'similar enterprises' in Article 24(5). Each of these meanings presumed the comparator was also a subsidiary and so had a parent corporation, the different meanings involving the residence of the parent in different countries. The meaning Park J preferred was to compare the UK subsidiary of a non-resident parent with a UK subsidiary of a UK parent.[157]

Park J expressly rejected the view that under Article 24(5) of the OECD Model the subsidiary should be compared with an independent corporation that did not have a parent corporation, i.e. which was not part of a corporate group.[158] In the result, Park J held that Article 24(5)

[155] *Boake Allen Ltd and Ors* v *Revenue & Customs Commissioners* [2007] UKHL 25 (HL).

[156] Cases C-397/98 and 410/98 *Metallgesellschaft Ltd* v *IRC and AG; Hoechst AG* v *IRC and AG* [2001] ECR I-1727 (ECJ).

[157] *NEC Semi-Conductors Ltd* v *IRC* [2003] EWHC 2813 (Ch) at para. 27. The change of case name to *Boake Allen* occurred in the House of Lords. Before this case, the UK tax administration maintained that the comparator was a third country resident parent corporation.

[158] '[I]t is necessary to assume that, if the actual company is a subsidiary of another company, then so is the hypothetical comparator company'. [2003] EWHC 2813 (Ch) at para. 28.

should be interpreted to extend the group income election to the UK subsidiaries in question but that the provision had not been properly incorporated into domestic law, i.e. treaty underride (see above at 1.2.2), and so the taxpayer lost. Before the Court of Appeal, the tax administration more clearly pressed that the comparator under Article 24(5) is a UK corporation owned perhaps by UK residents but not by a UK parent. Nevertheless, all members of the Court of Appeal adopted the reasoning of Park J and used as a comparator a UK subsidiary of a UK parent corporation.[159]

In the House of Lords, the judgment on the interpretation of Article 24(5) of the OECD Model was given by Lord Hoffman, with whom the other members of the House agreed. Unfortunately, Lord Hoffman did not interpret the express wording of Article 24(5), but rather preferred to rely on the Commentary on Article 24(1):

> [16] The question, as it seems to me, is whether s 247 discriminates against a United Kingdom company *on the ground that* its capital is 'wholly or partly owned or controlled, directly or indirectly' by residents of the United States, or Japan, or some other foreign state. In relation to art 24(1) of the OECD model convention, which prohibits discrimination between residents on grounds of nationality, the commentary says that the 'underlying question' is whether two residents are being treated differently 'solely by reason of having a different nationality'. It does not repeat this observation in relation to art 24(5), but the principle must be the same. Does s 247 discriminate on the grounds that the capital of the subsidiary is controlled by a non-resident company?
>
> [17] In my opinion it plainly does not. For example, if a United States parent were to interpose a United Kingdom resident holding company between itself and its United Kingdom-resident subsidiary, the control would remain in the United States but there would be no objection to an election by the United Kingdom subsidiary and its immediate, United Kingdom-resident parent. On the other hand, an individual United States shareholder and the company he controls in the United Kingdom could not elect, but the reason is not because the company is subject to United States control. An individual United Kingdom shareholder and his company could not elect either, for the same reason that a non-resident company cannot elect. It is because an individual is not liable to corporation tax. An election is a joint decision by two entities paying and receiving dividends that one rather than the other will be liable for ACT. This is not a concept which can meaningfully be applied when one of the entities is not liable for ACT at all.

[159] *NEC Semi-Conductors Ltd* v *IRC* [2006] EWCA Civ 25 (CA) especially at para. 41 per Lloyd LJ.

Lord Hoffman seems to have rewritten the test in Article 24(5). Rather than asking whether the non-resident controlled corporation is subject to more burdensome taxation than a 'similar enterprise' of the subject country, the test seems to be whether the non-resident controlled corporation is discriminated against on the ground of its non-resident control.

Lord Hoffman's test seems different from that suggested by the OECD. In May 2007, just before the House of Lords' decision, a working group of the OECD suggested that the 'right comparator' for the purposes of Article 24(5) of the OECD Model is 'a domestic enterprise owned by residents'.[160] Note this comparator is not necessarily a subsidiary controlled by a domestic parent. As noted above, by 2008 and after the House of Lords decision, the OECD suggests that Article 24(5) of the OECD Model 'cannot be interpreted to extend the benefits of rules that take account of the relationship between a resident enterprise and other resident enterprises'. The suggestion still seems to be that Article 24(5) would not necessarily require the group income election be available to a UK subsidiary of a UK holding corporation that was in turn controlled by a non-resident parent corporation.

By contrast, this case of two UK corporations controlled by a non-resident corporation would meet Lord Hoffman's test if denial of the election was based solely on indirect foreign control of the UK subsidiary. That such a denial might breach Article 24(5) of the OECD Model seems implicit in the extended example given by Lord Hoffman (in paragraph 17 reproduced above). If this is true, then, while Lord Hoffman did not express an opinion on the nature of the comparator under Article 24(5) of the OECD Model, it seems it must be with a UK subsidiary of a UK controlled UK parent. This would be broadly consistent with the approach in the courts below. However, unlike the courts below, Lord Hoffman introduced the additional limitation that the provision is breached only where the more burdensome taxation is by reason of foreign ownership and not some other reason.

As mentioned, the Commentary contains no examples involving the application of Article 24(5) of the OECD Model to dealings between two domestic subsidiaries of a non-resident parent corporation. Further, there is no express view as to whether the comparator may be a domestic subsidiary of a domestic owned domestic parent corporation. By contrast, the Commentary now expressly incorporates Lord Hoffman's additional test that 'the paragraph prevents the discrimination of a resident enterprise

[160] OECD (2007b, para. 88).

that is solely based on who owns or controls the capital of that enterprise'. It also incorporates an example similar to the issue in the *Boake Allen* case, effectively agreeing with the decision of the House of Lords.[161]

If *Boake Allen* is viewed as permitting application of Article 24(5) of the OECD Model to dealings between two domestic subsidiaries of a non-resident parent corporation then that provision could apply to other benefits available to group corporations such as the transfer of losses and the transfer of capital assets at book value. More difficult is the question as to whether Article 24(5) of the OECD Model can ever apply to the first scenario mentioned above, i.e. extend domestic reliefs available to corporate groups to dealings between a domestic subsidiary and its non-resident parent corporation. Much was made by Lord Hoffman in *Boake Allen* of the fact that a group income election required the joint election of both the subsidiary and its parent corporation as to who would be liable for ACT. But what of a case where a joint election is not required, but nevertheless a tax benefit is granted because of the existence of a corporate group?

An example of such a provision is section 171 of TCGA 1992. It permits the transfer of assets at book value (i.e. without the realisation of a gain) between two resident members of the same 75 per cent owned corporate group. No election, joint or otherwise, is required or permitted. The provision is just as much about preventing the realisation of losses on the transfer of assets between group members as it is about providing relief from taxation. This provision is not available with respect to the transfer of an asset from a UK subsidiary to a non-resident parent corporation. Clearly this can result in taxation of the UK subsidiary that is 'other or more burdensome' than a UK subsidiary making a transfer to a UK parent. However, using Lord Hoffman's additional requirement, it may be argued that the denial of the relief is not because of the control of the UK subsidiary by the non-resident but because the asset is, for the future, going beyond the reach of the UK tax jurisdiction.

EU Law As explained at 3.1.3.3, both a PE and a subsidiary may constitute an exercise of the right of freedom of establishment under Article 49 of the FEU Treaty. So while the OECD Model contains two relevant provisions dealing with non-discrimination, one for PEs and one for subsidiaries, the FEU Treaty contains one. In the usual way, the notion of non-discrimination inherent in the freedom of establishment under the FEU Treaty is broader in application than that in Article 24(3) and (5) of

[161] OECD Commentary on Art. 24 paras. 78 and 79.

the OECD Model; at least in the way the OECD interprets the latter. The OECD seeks to limit the application of Article 24(3) to *taxation* of the *activities* of a PE and Article 24(5) to different tax treatment *solely based* on foreign ownership or control of a source state enterprise.

By contrast, Article 49 of the FEU Treaty extends to the right to 'pursue activities... and to set up and manage undertakings... under conditions laid down for' nationals of the host state. So, unlike the OECD interpretation of Article 24(3) and (5), Article 49 of the FEU Treaty can extend to conditions based on the relationship between the establishment and associated enterprises. Further, the ECJ has interpreted Article 49 to require equal treatment of PEs and subsidiaries, at least so far as source/host country taxation is concerned, i.e. PEs and subsidiaries of non-residents are comparable. This is not true under the OECD Model, perhaps because it incorporates a separate provision for PEs and subsidiaries whereas the FEU Treaty has one combined provision. Further, Article 49 of the FEU Treaty can extend to any form of discrimination and so can apply to discriminatory treatment of subsidiaries triggered by something other than purely foreign ownership. Each of these features is illustrated by ECJ case law.

Before 2000, Germany taxed the retained profits of resident corporations at a higher rate than distributed profits. PEs of non-resident corporations were typically taxed at a rate somewhere between these two rates. In 1994, these rates were 45 per cent, 30 per cent and 42 per cent respectively. In *CLT-UFA*,[162] the taxpayer complained that the non-availability for PEs of the lower rate for distributed profits was contrary to the freedom of establishment under EU Law.[163] The ECJ agreed, finding that the freedom involved the right to choose the appropriate legal form in which to pursue activities in another member state. A person exercising their freedom to establish in the form of a branch (PE) is entitled to pursue their activities 'under the same conditions as those which apply to subsidiaries'.[164] The ECJ noted that the German rules for determining taxable income did not draw a distinction between branches (PEs) and subsidiaries. This made the German tax situation of branches and subsidiaries 'objectively' comparable and so a difference in tax treatment of branches could not be justified.[165]

162 Case C-253/03 *CLT-UFA SA* v *Finanzamt Köln-West* [2006] ECR I-1831 (ECJ).

163 Earlier in Case C-311/97 *Royal Bank of Scotland plc* v *Elliniko Dimosio (Greek State)* [1999] ECR I-2651 (ECJ), the ECJ held as contrary to the freedom of establishment the taxation of a PE's profits at a higher rate than that applied to residents.

164 Case C-253/03 *CLT-UFA SA* v *Finanzamt Köln-West* [2006] ECR I-1831 (ECJ) at para. 15.

165 Case C-253/03 *CLT-UFA SA* v *Finanzamt Köln-West* [2006] ECR I-1831 (ECJ) at paras. 29–30.

There are two features of this decision worthy of note. As under Article 24(3) of the OECD Model, the application of Article 49 of the FEU Treaty to PEs requires the identification of an appropriate comparator. However, unlike the OECD approach, the ECJ *did* take into account the relationship between the PE and the rest of the enterprise and analogise that relationship to the comparator. Where the OECD suggests limiting the application of Article 24(3) by comparison to a hypothetical enterprise that is independent and isolated, under EU Law the comparator was a hypothetical subsidiary, i.e. an associated entity. Therefore, irrespective of the specifics of Article 7 of the OECD Model, it seems that under EU Law the determination of profits of PEs should be the same as that for subsidiaries including with respect to the deductibility of expenses.[166] Another example will further illustrate this point.

Originally the UK loss transfer provisions mentioned above were limited to transfers between UK resident corporations. After 1999, the UK extended the loss transfer rules to permit a loss to be transferred between UK corporations and UK PEs of non-UK corporations provided the requisite holding requirements are met. This change was caused by the decision of the ECJ in *ICI*.[167] While this case did not involve a PE, it made clear that differential tax treatment based on a subsidiary's 'seat' breached Article 49 of the FEU Treaty and, therefore, applied to the relationship between the establishment and an associated corporation.

The *Metallgesellschaft* and *Hoechst* cases have already been mentioned above.[168] They involved the same ACT rules as were in issue in the *Boake Allen* case.[169] However, in the *Metallgesellschaft* and *Hoechst* cases the ECJ was interpreting Article 49 of the FEU Treaty whereas in *Boake Allen* the House of Lords was interpreting Article 24(5) of the OECD Model (the Article 24(5) argument was not pursued in the *Metallgesellschaft* and *Hoechst* cases). In contrast to the *Boake Allen* case, the ECJ found that the inability of a UK subsidiary with an EU parent corporation to make a group income election was a restriction on the freedom of establishment of the parent corporation. This was the case even though the subsidiary could later use the ACT paid to reduce its own UK corporation tax liability, i.e. the imposition of ACT was typically just a cash flow disadvantage.

[166] European Commission (2001, p. 361).

[167] Case C-264/96 *ICI Plc* v *Colmer* [1998] ECR I-4695 (ECJ).

[168] Cases C-397/98 and 410/98 *Metallgesellschaft Ltd* v *IRC and AG; Hoechst AG* v *IRC and AG* [2001] ECR I-1727 (ECJ).

[169] *Boake Allen Ltd and Ors* v *Revenue & Customs Commissioners* [2007] UKHL 25 (HL).

The UK tax administration pointed out that if the UK subsidiary of an EU parent corporation did not pay ACT then the group would not pay ACT at all, whereas a UK parent would pay ACT when it redistributed the subsidiary's dividends. The ECJ reinforced that loss of revenue could not be used to justify the discriminatory cash flow advantage of UK corporate groups.

> [T]he difference in the tax treatment of parent companies depending on whether or not they are resident cannot justify denial of a tax advantage to subsidiaries, resident in the United Kingdom, of parent companies having their seat in another Member State where that advantage is available to subsidiaries, resident in the United Kingdom, of parent companies also resident in the United Kingdom, since all those subsidiaries are liable to [mainstream corporation tax] on their profits irrespective of the place of residence of their parent companies.[170]

Note how the ECJ compared a UK subsidiary with an EU parent with a UK subsidiary with a UK parent, i.e. it considered the relationship between the subsidiary and another enterprise (its parent corporation). Further, note how the ECJ was considering UK taxation of the subsidiary as a separate person entitled to claim rights under the FEU Treaty and not the corporate group as a whole.

In *Boake Allen*, Lord Hoffman sought to distinguish this approach of the ECJ when interpreting Article 24(5) of the OECD Model.

> [20] … [T]he prohibition on discrimination implied in art [49 FEU] has an altogether different purpose from the prohibition on discrimination in [tax treaties]. Freedom of establishment under art [49 FEU] is the freedom of the resident of a member state to establish itself in another member state. In the case of parent and subsidiary, it is the freedom of the parent to establish a subsidiary.
> [21] Discrimination against the group as a whole is thus a restriction on the parent's freedom of establishment. If a group with a United Kingdom parent has a cash flow advantage which a group with a parent in another member state does not enjoy, that is a restriction on the latter's freedom of establishment.
> [22] A [tax treaty], on the other hand, does not give a company or individual resident in one country a right of establishment in the other. As the commentary on the OECD model says, the equality it ensures is only that any enterprise it owns in the other country will not be subject to taxation which discriminates on the ground of its foreign control. In my opinion,

[170] Cases C-397/98 and 410/98 *Metallgesellschaft Ltd* v *IRC and AG; Hoechst AG* v *IRC and AG* [2001] ECR I-1727 (ECJ) at para. 60.

> the denial of the right of election was not on the ground of the company's foreign control but on the ground that s 247 cannot be applied to a case in which the parent company is not liable to ACT.

Whether this reasoning is considered compelling or not, it is clear that Article 49 of the FEU Treaty is substantially broader in scope than Article 24(5) of the OECD Model as interpreted by the House of Lords.

In the *Metallgesellschaft* and *Hoechst* cases, the ECJ left it to the UK courts to work out the practical consequences of its decision. Various claims then proceeded through the UK courts under a group litigation order. A large part of the dispute in these claims concerned the retrospective nature of refunds of ACT claimed by UK subsidiaries of EU parent corporations because of the inability to make group income elections. In *Deutsche Morgan Grenfell* the House of Lords decided that a claim for refund based on restitution was not statute barred.[171] *Pirelli Cable* concerned the interaction of the refund claim with certain tax treaties under which non-resident parent corporations were granted refunds of dividend tax credits supported by the payment of ACT. The House of Lords decided that a subsidiary could not claim a refund of ACT if the parent corporation claimed a refund of dividend tax credits.[172] A detailed consideration of these cases is beyond the scope of this book.[173]

3.1.4 Dividends, interest and royalties

This subheading considers a source country's right to tax dividends (Article 10), interest (Article 11) and royalties (Article 12) under the OECD Model. These provisions were drafted by the predecessor of the OECD at the same time and share many common features and a common format. They involve classic forms of *passive* income and the taxing rights granted to source states may be contrasted with those granted to source states with respect to income from immovable property and, in particular, business profits. With respect to dividends, interest and royalties, source country taxing rights are either eliminated or limited to a specific rate of gross payments. The following discussion considers source country taxation of each in turn, first in the context of the OECD Model and then in the context of EU Law. The definitions of 'dividends', 'interest' and

[171] *Deutsche Morgan Grenfell Group Plc* v *IRC* [2006] UKHL 49 (HL).

[172] *Pirelli Cable Holding Nv and Ors* v *Inland Revenue Commissioners* [2006] UKHL 4 (HL). On remittal to the High Court and further appeal to the Court of Appeal, see [2008] EWCA Civ 70 (CA).

[173] See Virgo (2008).

'royalties' in these articles and the boundary (or lack thereof) between them are considered at 3.3.2.1.

3.1.4.1 Dividends

OECD Model[174]

Scope of Article 10 Article 10(1) of the OECD Model provides:

> Dividends paid by a company which is a resident of a Contracting State to a resident of the other Contracting State may be taxed in that other State.

The purpose of this provision is to state the general principle that dividends are taxable in the country where the shareholder is resident. However, the provision also incorporates limits on the general scope of Article 10. Article 10 applies to dividends 'paid'. While not defined in the Model, the OECD provides in the Commentary that a payment is 'the fulfilment of the obligation to put funds at the disposal of the shareholder in the manner required by contract or custom'.[175] One question is whether the article limits the taxation of 'dividends' before they are 'paid' (prospective dividends). This could be relevant, for example, to the application of controlled foreign corporation rules by residence countries, discussed below at 4.1.2.2.[176]

Further, Article 10 of the OECD Model covers only dividends paid by a corporation resident in one state to a resident of the other state. Thus, Article 10(1) incorporates an implicit source rule for the purposes of tax treaties. Dividends are sourced where the corporation paying the dividend is resident. This is a particularly fragile source rule, especially where the treaty in question contains a tiebreaker rule of the type in Article 4(3) (discussed above at 2.1.1.2). A change in effective management of a corporation can change its residence and so the source of dividends, even for dividends paid out of profits derived before the change. This can be contrasted with a rule that sources dividends where the profits from which the dividends are derived are sourced, see above at 2.1.2.2. The scope of Article 10 of the OECD Model is limited by its implicit source rule. It applies only to dividends distributed by corporations resident in one of the two contracting states. The consequences of this are further discussed below in the context of dividends and PEs.

174 Regarding the origins of OECD Model Art. 10, see Harris (2000).

175 OECD Commentary on Art. 10 para. 7.

176 Article 21 (other income) could not apply to dividends before they are paid as 'dividends' are 'dealt with' in OECD Model Art. 10. See above at 3.1.1.

Limited source country taxation A limited right to tax dividends in the source state (state of residence of the paying corporation) is granted by Article 10(2) of the OECD Model. The limitation is different depending on whether the shareholder is a *portfolio* investor in the distributing corporation. *Non-portfolio* investment is typically limited to that of a parent corporation in its subsidiary corporations. This is also considered a form of *direct* investment. However, there is no comprehensive definition or distinction for these two types of investment; only technical rules that seek to identify a level of control or influence. This book will consider a number of such technical rules, the first of which is discussed below in the context of Article 10(2).

Portfolio investors Article 10(2)(b) of the OECD Model incorporates a residual rule that the source state may tax dividends distributed by resident corporations at a rate not exceeding '15 per cent of the gross amount of the dividends'. Under their domestic laws, many countries levy withholding tax on dividends distributed by resident corporations to non-residents. The effect of Article 10(2)(b) is to reduce the domestic rates of withholding tax that would otherwise apply. In actual treaties, the rate limitation varies dramatically. Indeed, countries hold such widely disparate views on source taxation of dividends that the UN Model simply leaves the rate blank and so for negotiation between contracting states. Despite this variation from treaty to treaty, within a particular treaty the rate limitation is usually the same for both countries, i.e. dividends flowing from state to state in either direction. As explained at 2.2.1, this reflects the principle of reciprocity of withholding tax rates.

Often, the limitation on dividend tax rates in treaties is higher than the 15 per cent in the OECD Model, but more often, it is lower. There are two reasons for this. First, the tax entitlement is on the gross amount of dividends, i.e. without deduction of expenses in deriving dividends. Where those expenses are substantial, the tax authorised by the OECD Model can be a substantial impediment to cross-border investment. This problem is similarly acute with other forms of withholding tax such as those imposed on interest and royalties. Residence countries are typically in a better position than source countries for granting relief for expenses in deriving dividends (and do so, although the UK is an exception in that to a large extent it taxes dividends received by individuals on a gross basis). Therefore, reducing dividend taxation by source countries below the OECD 15 per cent rate reduces the cross-border investment impediment.

Second, the OECD Model presumes what is commonly referred to as a classical corporate tax system. A classical system is a corporate tax system under which corporate profits are taxed and dividends distributed from those profits are taxed without relief for one tax against the other, i.e. economic double taxation.[177] Tax treaties do not interfere with a country's right to tax resident corporations (presuming the corporation derives domestic source income).[178] Further, tax treaties based on the OECD Model then preserve the source country's right to tax distributions by resident corporations. The problem is that most countries do not have a full classical system and so provide at least some relief from the economic double taxation of corporate income. This is a second reason why source state taxation of dividends is often reduced below the OECD 15 per cent rate.

A country can provide dividend relief (i.e. relief from the classical system at the point dividends are distributed) in at least six ways.[179] The UK provides this relief through a combination of two methods; by granting shareholders reduced tax rates with respect to their dividend income and by providing them with a dividend tax credit.[180] Generally, non-residents are not entitled to the dividend tax credit when they receive dividends from UK corporations. This is quite common, e.g. both Australia and New Zealand grant their residents dividend tax credits but do not extend them to non-residents.[181] However, as a rule, the UK does not tax non-residents with respect to the receipt of dividends from UK resident corporations.

The granting of dividend tax credits (or any other form of dividend relief) to resident shareholders in resident corporations but denying such a credit to non-resident shareholders in such corporations constitutes discrimination, at least at some level. However, the non-discrimination principle in Article 24 of the OECD Model is too narrow to deal with this situation. The nationality clause in Article 24(1) (discussed above at 2.2.1) is usually inapplicable because source countries inevitably deny the dividend tax credits to their own non-resident nationals. Article 24(3) (discussed above at 3.1.3.4) applies to PEs and dividends received by non-residents through a source country PE are further considered below. Article 24(5) (also discussed above at 3.1.3.4) requires further consideration.

177 Generally regarding the classical system, see Harris (1996, pp. 60–1).

178 This is expressly preserved in the resuming words of OECD Model Art. 10(2).

179 See Harris (1996, pp. 56–72).

180 ITA 2007 ss. 8 and 13 and ITTOIA 2005 ss. 397 and 398.

181 While somewhat dated, the discussion in Harris (1996, pp. 349–81) is still generally accurate.

Article 24(5) of the OECD Model prevents discrimination of a resident corporation on grounds of non-resident ownership. It does not prevent discriminatory taxation of dividends distributed to non-residents unless that taxation pertains to the resident corporation. So, despite the obvious discrimination:

> withholding tax obligations that are imposed on a resident company with respect to dividends paid to non-resident shareholders but not with respect to dividends paid to resident shareholders cannot be considered to violate paragraph 5.[182]

By contrast, some forms of dividend relief operate to grant tax relief to the distributing corporation, such as a dividend deduction system or a system that applies a lower corporate tax rate to distributed profits than retained profits (split rate system). Article 24(5) would be breached if the deduction or lower rate were denied just because the distribution was to a non-resident shareholder. This anomaly under Article 24(5), i.e. that it protects against discrimination under corporate level dividend relief systems but not shareholder level dividend relief systems, has played an important role in the steady extinction of corporate level dividend relief systems.

Despite the ability to discriminate under shareholder level dividend relief, from the 1970s to the 1990s a treaty practice grew whereby some countries (primarily France and the UK) extended dividend tax credits to non-residents under treaty. With the disintegration of most European imputation (dividend tax credit) systems due to decisions of the ECJ (discussed below), this treaty practice is largely of historical relevance only.[183] This practice has been the subject of a number of important ECJ decisions, which will be further discussed at relevant points.

The OECD fixation on whether taxation involves the shareholder or the distributing corporation extends to the source country taxation of dividends that is limited by Article 10(2) of the OECD Model. That provision limits shareholder taxation of dividends only and Article 10(2) expressly does 'not affect the taxation of the company in respect of the profits out of which the dividends are paid'. Many countries have viewed these words as entitling them to tax dividends in the hands of the paying corporation without any limit under Article 10(2). This was clear under the UK's former ACT system, discussed above at 3.1.3.4. Under this system the UK would charge the distributing corporation with ACT,

[182] OECD Commentary on Art. 24 para. 78.

[183] This treaty practice is described in Harris (1996, pp. 368–76).

typically at the rate of 25 per cent of the amount distributed, which the UK considered was not limited by treaty. India and South Africa currently impose a corporate distributions tax,[184] and both countries take the view that it is not limited by treaty. The High Court of South Africa confirmed this in 2008.[185]

By contrast, a number of countries, including the UK (see above at 2.1.2.2), Australia and Singapore, effectively do not tax dividends distributed by resident corporations to non-residents. Nevertheless, treaties concluded by these countries contain positive rates in the dividend article of their tax treaties. Despite this right to tax such dividends under the treaty, the fact is that under their domestic laws these countries do not tax such dividends. This is an example of the principle discussed above at 1.2.2; a treaty does not create a charge to tax where one does not otherwise exist.

Direct investors In contrast with the treatment of portfolio investors, Article 10(2)(a) of the OECD Model provides that source country taxation of dividends shall not exceed…

> 5 per cent of the gross amount of the dividends if the beneficial owner is a company… which holds directly at least 25 per cent of the capital of the company paying the dividends.

This provision provides greater relief from source country taxation of dividends. Its primary purpose is to mitigate the cascading of tax as dividends are distributed between corporations. Even classical countries typically provide relief from economic double taxation of inter-corporate dividends, e.g. the UK exempts such dividends distributed by UK resident corporations.[186] Of course, the OECD Model does not provide full relief from this form of economic double taxation, and the 5 per cent rate does provide scope for the cascading of tax on dividends distributed up a corporate chain. It is for this reason that many treaties reduce this rate even further, often to zero. In particular, from 2001 the US, historically a classical country, opened itself to negotiating in its tax treaties a zero rate dividend withholding tax on certain non-portfolio dividends distributed by US subsidiaries. Other countries, including the UK, have more generally been open to zero rate withholding taxes.

[184] Income-tax Act, 1961 (India) s. 115O and Income Tax Act, 1962 (South Africa) s. 64B. The South African tax is to be converted into a conventional dividend withholding tax.

[185] *Volkswagen of South Africa (Pty) Ltd* v *Commissioner* (2008) 11 ITLR 770 (HC).

[186] CTA 2009 ss. 931B and 931D.

The OECD Model requires that the recipient corporation hold at least '25 per cent of the capital' of the distributing corporation. This is quite conservative in two respects and this requirement is often varied in tax treaties. A holding of 25 per cent is quite high and many countries are willing to reduce this substantially, e.g. UK treaties often reduce it to 10 per cent. Second, under the OECD Model the holding must be direct. For example, assume A Co holds 80 per cent of B Co and that C Co is held as to 20 per cent by each of A Co and B Co. A Co will not qualify for the reduced rate on dividends distributed to it by C Co. While directly and indirectly it holds 36 per cent of C Co (20 per cent + 80 per cent of 20 per cent), directly it holds only 20 per cent. Again, many treaties, including some of the UK's, count indirect as well as direct holdings. Another respect in which actual tax treaties vary from this test of direct investment in the OECD Model is with respect to the reference to 'capital'. Often this is replaced by a test based, e.g. on 'voting power'.

As mentioned above, some countries impose a corporate distributions tax and the imposition of this tax is not limited by treaty. Just as the taxation of dividends in the hands of corporate shareholders may have a cascading effect, the imposition of corporate distributions tax in the hands of the distributing corporation may have a cascading effect. Accordingly, corporate distributions tax is often excluded for the redistribution of dividends that have already suffered the tax. This was the case under the former UK ACT system and is the case under the current Indian corporate distributions tax. More difficult is the case where there is an exception for even the initial application of the tax for distributions between corporate groups. The group income election from ACT was discussed above at 3.1.3.4 as was the decision in the *Boake Allen* case that denying this election for distributions by UK subsidiaries to non-resident parents did not breach Article 24(5) of the OECD Model.

Dividends and PEs Article 10(4) and (5) of the OECD Model are two provisions that essentially deal with dividends and PEs. In some senses they deal with opposite scenarios; Article 10(4) dealing with dividends received by PEs while Article 10(5) covers the taxation of remittances or distributions out of profits derived through a PE.

Article 10(4) of the OECD Model deals with the situation in which dividends received by a non-resident from a resident corporation are 'effectively connected' with a PE that the non-resident has in the source state, i.e. the state of the corporation's residence. Such dividends are simultaneously business profits of the PE and dividends, a classic example of dual characterisation. Article 10(4) is essentially a reconciliation rule that says that in such a case the dividends are to be taxed in accordance with Article 7 and not Article 10, i.e. the dividends are to be taxed as business profits of the PE. A provision similar to Article 10(4) is found in Article 11 (Interest) and Article 12 (Royalties). These are discussed further below at 3.3.3, with other reconciliation rules in the OECD Model.

At this point, it is useful to consider a particular feature regarding the taxation dividends received by PEs. Article 10 of the OECD Model authorises a limited tax on the gross amount of dividends without any protection against discrimination under Article 24. Article 7, by contrast, authorises full taxation of dividends but after the allowance of expenses and with the protection against discrimination provided by Article 24(3).[187] As mentioned, many countries provide dividend relief to alleviate the economic double taxation of corporate income. A particular question is whether the non-discrimination rule in Article 24(3) means that dividends received through a PE must be granted the same form of dividend relief as is granted to residents in receipt of dividends. This is an important question because, if dividend relief is granted, often the source country taxation of dividends will be less if received through a PE than if received directly. That is, granting dividend relief to PEs may provide an incentive to hold shares as part of the activities carried on by a PE.

The OECD in the Commentary notes divergent views of member states as to whether Article 24(3) of the OECD Model requires the extension of dividend relief to PEs. It does not state an opinion as to the application of Article 24(3) in this situation but merely invites states to clarify their position in treaties, including by applying the taxation authorised by Article 10(2) to dividends received by PEs.[188] The better position seems to be that Article 24(3) does require the extension of dividend relief where that is generally available. For example, a country that generally exempts dividends paid between two resident corporations should, when faced with Article 24(3), extend the exemption to dividends paid by a resident corporation to a PE of a corporation resident in a treaty partner. The argument is less strong if the domestic relief is available only where the recipient corporation requires a minimum holding in the distributing corporation, e.g. as with the participation exemption in the Netherlands. Such a case raises

[187] OECD Commentary on Art. 24 para. 65 confirms that a source country withholding tax imposed on receipts of non-residents only, including receipts derived through a PE, breaches OECD Model Art. 24(3). PEs 'must be treated as resident enterprises and hence in respect of such income be subjected to tax on profits solely'.

[188] OECD Commentary on Art. 24 paras. 48–54.

the question as to whether the requisite holding should be attributed to the hypothetical comparator under Article 24(3). As discussed above at 3.1.3.4, the OECD is of the opinion that Article 24(3) 'does not extend to rules that take account of the relationship between an enterprise and other enterprises'.[189]

A UK case in point is *UBS Ag* v *RCC*.[190] In this case, UBS had a UK PE in receipt of dividends from UK corporations. The dividends carried with them a tax credit even though the dividends were not subject to corporation tax in the hands of a resident corporate shareholder. A resident corporation could set the credit against ACT liability levied on its own distributions (see above at 3.1.3.4). As an alternative, the credit might reduce losses and be refunded. Like resident corporations, PEs were not subject to corporation tax on the receipt of dividends from UK corporations but they were denied the tax credit granted to such a corporation. Not making distributions themselves, PEs were not subject to ACT. UBS, however, claimed to set the credits against its losses and wanted a refund based on the equivalent of Article 24(3) of the OECD Model.

As with a number of other UK cases, *UBS* raises the issue of whether the UK had properly implemented the equivalent of Article 24(3) of the OECD Model into domestic law, i.e. the *treaty underride* issue discussed above at 1.2.2. That aside, the judge at first instance and Moses LJ in the Court of Appeal took the view that denying a refund of the tax credit could constitute a breach of Article 24(3).[191] As mentioned at 3.1.3.4, Arden LJ took the view that refund of the tax credit did not constitute 'taxation' within Article 24(3) and so the provision did not apply. While exemption from corporation tax with respect to receipt of the dividends by UBS's UK PE was not in issue, the reasoning of all the judges is consistent with a need to extend that general exemption to UK PEs for the purposes of Article 24(3).

The potential of favourable treatment of dividends received through a PE instead of directly arises because repatriations of profits by a PE to its head office are not subject to dividend taxation under Article 10 of the OECD Model. This is not just an issue with respect to dividends received by PEs. Any income derived through a PE may be repatriated from the

[189] OECD Commentary on Art. 24 para. 41.

[190] [2007] EWCA Civ 119 (CA).

[191] However, both Moses LJ and Arden LJ in the Court of Appeal took the view that because Article 10 of the relevant treaty granted dividend tax credits to certain non-residents (not including PEs), the more general provision in the equivalent of OECD Model Art. 24(3) should not be interpreted to grant that right to PEs.

source state without further taxation. This can be contrasted with the situation where the foreign enterprise sets up its presence in the source state in the form of a subsidiary. The repatriation of profits from the subsidiary will be subject to dividend taxation under Article 10. In short, the OECD Model creates a bias in favour of setting up direct investments in the form of PEs rather than subsidiaries.

There are two ways of addressing this distortion. The first involves eliminating source state taxation of dividends paid by a subsidiary to its parent corporation. As noted above, a number of treaties provide such an exemption. The second method involves increasing the taxation of PEs so as to equalise their taxation with the situation of subsidiaries. There are at least three ways of imposing extra source taxation of PE profits in order to equalise the treatment with subsidiaries. A simple method is to increase the rate of tax applied to a PE's profits. As noted above at 3.1.3.4, the OECD agrees that this simple mechanism breaches Article 24(3) of the OECD Model.[192]

The second and third methods of imposing extra source taxation of PEs involve the taxation of remittances of PEs to head office and the taxation of dividends distributed out of PE profits by the non-resident corporation holding the PE. Article 10(5) of the OECD Model prohibits both of these methods. The first part of this provision prohibits a country from taxing the dividends of a treaty-partner resident corporation just because those dividends are distributed from profits derived from that country. Note that this provision extends the scope of Article 10. The Article applies not just to dividends distributed by a corporation resident in a treaty state to a resident of the other state but also to dividends distributed by a corporation resident in one state to a resident of *that* state.

By contrast, Article 10 of the OECD Model does not cover dividends distributed by a corporation resident in a third country. Assume that a corporation resident in Country C derives income from Country A and distributes it to a shareholder in Country B. Assume that the domestic tax law of Country A would tax the dividend as having a source there. This dividend is not covered by an OECD style Article 10 in the Country A and Country B treaty because the distributing corporation is resident in neither Country A nor Country B. This does not mean that the Country A/Country B treaty does not limit Country A's taxing rights. As the distribution is not 'dealt with' by Article 10, Article 21 (other income) of the treaty may apply; see above at 3.1.1. The effect of that provision is that only

[192] OECD Commentary on Art. 24 para. 60.

Country B can tax the distribution (residence country) and Country A's taxing right is effectively excluded.

The second part of Article 10(5) of the OECD Model prohibits the taxation of a treaty partner resident corporation's 'undistributed profits'. This provision is intended to prevent what is referred to as a branch profits tax. A number of countries, including the US, impose a tax on remittances of branches to their foreign head office at the same rate as the tax imposed on distributions by resident subsidiaries to non-resident parent corporations.[193] Because a PE or branch is not a separate legal person, a branch profits tax is a tax on the undistributed profits of a non-resident corporation.

Countries that impose a branch profits tax often expressly preserve the right to impose that tax in their treaties, e.g. the US and Canada. In particular, Article 10(8) of the US Model Income Tax Treaty provides:

> A corporation that is a resident of one of the States and that has a permanent establishment in the other State… may be subject in that State to a tax in addition to the tax allowable under the other provisions of this Convention. Such tax, however, may be imposed on only the portion of the business profits of the corporation attributable to the permanent establishment… that… represents the dividend equivalent amount of such profits.[194]

The rate of this addition tax is not to exceed the rate applicable to non-portfolio dividends. Despite a number of recent treaties where the US negotiated a zero rate of source tax on dividends distributed by certain US subsidiaries, the branch profits tax was not suppressed.[195]

EU Law The taxation of dividends is an area in which there have been major developments in EU Law. It is one of the few areas with a dedicated directive. It is also an area with a substantial number of decisions of the ECJ, both with respect to the directive as well as the application of the fundamental freedoms in the FEU Treaty.

Parent-Subsidiary Directive The reasons for a lower rate of source country taxation of dividends paid by subsidiaries to their parent corporations under Article 10 of the OECD Model was discussed above. The EU thought that any taxation of dividends on direct shareholdings is a major barrier to achieving an internal market and the Parent-Subsidiary Directive (1990) was the result.

[193] The US branch profits tax is imposed by Internal Revenue Code s. 884(a).
[194] United States (2006).
[195] For example, UK/US Treaty (2001) Art. 10(7).

It applies to 'distributions of profits received by companies' of one member state 'from their subsidiaries' of another member state.[196] In 2003, the Directive was extended to dividends received by EU PEs of EU companies. As mentioned at 2.1.1.3, there is a list of companies covered by the Directive in the annex to it, which was extended in 2003. In particular, European Companies incorporated under EU legislation (Societas Europaea) are now included.

Article 3 of the Directive defines a parent company in terms of having 'a minimum holding of 10% in the capital of a company of another Member State…' This percentage was steadily reduced from a height of 25 per cent but has now reached its minimum. The reduction was agreed to because of the need that this holding be direct, i.e. indirect holdings (discussed above) do not count towards the 10 per cent.[197]

For present purposes, the critical provision is in Article 5 of the Directive:

> Profits which a subsidiary distributes to its parent company shall be exempt from withholding tax.

The purpose of this provision is to eliminate source country taxation of dividends between parent and subsidiary corporations. Unlike Article 10 of the OECD Model, which just refers to dividends being 'taxed' by contracting states, the Parent-Subsidiary Directive strangely refers to 'withholding tax'. This phrase is defined in exclusive terms in Article 7 of the Directive. An 'advance payment or prepayment (précompte) of corporation tax' is not a withholding tax. It seems clear that this exclusion was intended to facilitate the levy of *advance corporation tax* and *equalisation taxes* imposed under European imputation systems at the time the Directive was passed.[198]

The meaning of 'withholding tax' was subject to interpretation by the ECJ in the *Athinaiki* case in 2001.[199] This case concerned a Greek rule under which income of corporations that was exempt from tax when derived was included in the corporate tax base and taxed on distribution.

[196] Parent-Subsidiary Directive (1990) Art. 1.

[197] In Case C-48/07 *Belgium* v *Les Vergers du Vieux Tauves* [2008] ECR 00 (ECJ), the ECJ held that, due to the clear wording of the capital requirement, the Directive cannot be applied to a situation in which the shares are held under a usufruct. The ECJ noted, however, that the fundamental freedoms might apply in a usufruct scenario. It seems likely that the ECJ would adopt a similar approach if the recipient were the beneficiary of shares held by a trustee. It seems a trustee recipient, as legal owner, could qualify as a parent; see at para. 34.

[198] Regarding these taxes, see Harris (1996, pp. 158–69).

[199] Case C-294/99 *Athinaiki Zithopiia AE* v *Elliniko Dimosio (Greek State)* [2001] ECR I-6797 (ECJ).

The imposition was similar to an equalisation tax. It was not like a typical withholding tax, in the sense of a tax deducted from a payment. Rather, the previously exempted profits were simply included in the corporate tax base on distribution along with other income derived. The ECJ took a substance approach, holding that the Greek imposition was a 'withholding tax' for the purposes of the Parent-Subsidiary Directive simply because it was payable in the event of the distribution of profits.[200]

In *Athinaiki*, the ECJ did not seem to care whether the tax was formally imposed on the subsidiary's profits or was in fact a tax on the parent corporation's receipt of dividends. One can have sympathy with this approach, as the effect of the tax is the same in either case. However, as mentioned above at 2.1.1.3, this is inconsistent with the ECJ's typical approach of drawing a strict distinction between the taxation of parent corporations and that of subsidiaries.[201] Subsequent decisions of the ECJ made subtle additions to the approach in *Athinaiki*. In the *FII* case, the ECJ adopted a three-step test in identifying a withholding tax:

> [A]ny tax on income received in the State in which dividends are distributed is a withholding tax on distributed profits where [i] the chargeable event for the tax is the payment of dividends or of any other income from shares, [ii] the taxable amount is the income from those shares and [iii] the taxable person is the holder of the shares.[202]

Surprisingly, the ECJ cited *Athinaiki* as authority for this approach, but the additional requirement (iii) raised the question as to whether the decision in *Athinaiki* is good law.

This question was put to rest in the *Burda* case.[203] This case involved an imposition of equalisation tax under the former German imputation system. The ECJ found that the equalisation tax was a tax on the subsidiary, not a tax on the shareholding parent corporation. Accordingly, the third requirement was not met and so the equalisation tax was not a withholding tax. The ECJ specifically rejected an argument that, following the *Athinaiki* ruling, the third requirement was not necessary. In doing so, the

[200] Case C-294/99 *Athinaiki Zithopiia AE* v *Elliniko Dimosio (Greek State)* [2001] ECR I-6797 (ECJ) at para. 33.

[201] 'Unlike operating branches or establishments, parent companies and their subsidiaries are distinct legal persons, each being subject to a tax liability of its own.' Case C-168/01 *Bosal Holding BV* v *Staatssecretaris van Financiën* [2003] ECR I-9409 (ECJ) at para. 32.

[202] Case C-446/04 *Test Claimants in the FII Group Litigation* [2006] ECR I-11753 (ECJ) at para. 108.

[203] Case C-284/06 *Finanzamt Hamburg-Am Tierpark* v *Burda GmbH* [2008] ECR I-4571 (ECJ).

ECJ also rejected the Commission's argument that adopting such a formal approach would compromise the effectiveness of the Directive, i.e. make it easy to avoid.[204] This decision is of significance in the context of tax competition within Europe. It appears to authorise a tax system such as that in Estonia in which corporate profits are taxed (to the subsidiary) only upon distribution, i.e. there is no taxation of retained profits.[205]

As mentioned above, between the 1970s and 1990s a treaty practice grew under which some countries, including the UK and France, granted dividend tax credits available under their imputation systems to treaty partner residents. The practice here was to pay *lip service* to the provisions of Article 10 of the OECD Model. Dividend tax credits would be extended to treaty partner residents but the grossed-up dividend (dividend plus tax credits) would be subjected to a notional withholding tax at OECD rates. The tax was *notional*, because the credits granted exceeded the tax (the excess credits being refunded to the treaty partner shareholder) and even if they did not, there was no domestic mechanism for imposing or collecting the tax (at least in the case of the UK).

In the *Oce* case, a Dutch corporation argued that this notional tax under the Netherlands/UK tax treaty was a withholding tax prohibited by the Parent-Subsidiary Directive.[206] The ECJ held that the tax was a prohibited withholding tax to the extent it was 'imposed on the dividends paid'. The part of the tax calculated by reference to the tax credit (the gross-up) was not such a withholding tax. However, the ECJ found that even the prohibited part of the tax was permitted because the overall treatment of the Dutch parent by the UK (an effective refund of part of the corporation tax imposed on the UK subsidiary) fell within the special rule in Article 7(2) of the Directive. This provision permits special arrangements (such as tax treaties) 'designed to eliminate or lessen economic double taxation of dividends, in particular provisions relating to the payment of tax credits to the recipients of dividends'.

Fundamental freedoms The Parent-Subsidiary Directive (1990) is limited in scope to non-portfolio shareholdings (direct investments), but, even where it does apply, it is clear that the fundamental freedoms may simultaneously have application, see above at 1.3.3. Indeed, at some level the Directive, like other directives, is only of limited application.

[204] Case C-284/06 *Finanzamt Hamburg-Am Tierpark* v *Burda GmbH* [2008] ECR I-4571 (ECJ) at paras. 56–64.

[205] See Klauson (2008).

[206] Case C-58/01 *Oce Van der Grinten NV* v *IRC* [2003] ECR I-9809 (ECJ).

Taxation that is permitted by the Directive may nevertheless be struck down by the fundamental freedoms. Further, the scope of the fundamental freedoms is substantially greater in its application to the taxation of dividends than the Directive, e.g. they potentially apply to portfolio shareholders. The only substantive scope for the application of the Directive is where it goes beyond what is required to remove discrimination and other restrictions. Viewed from this perspective, while the fundamental freedoms are essentially about individual rights and not about which state collects taxes (allocation of tax), the directives on direct tax are much more akin to tax treaties. They are substantially about the allocation of taxing rights between states. A few ECJ cases will demonstrate these points.

The two freedoms that are in issue in ECJ cases concerning source state taxation of dividends are the freedom of establishment and the free movement of capital, i.e. Articles 49 and 63 of the FEU Treaty. In the context of portfolio shareholders, only Article 63 can have application, whereas in the case of non-portfolio shareholders, read literally it seems that both Articles could apply.[207] Reconciliation where more than one freedom may apply is further considered at 3.3.3. For present purposes, it is sufficient to note that, within the EU, the ECJ's approach to each freedom is similar.

A leading ECJ case concerning freedom of establishment and source state taxation of dividends is *Denkavit*.[208] The facts of this case predate the introduction of the Parent-Subsidiary Directive and so provide an interesting example of how the freedom of establishment may produce a result that is similar to that under the Directive. A French subsidiary distributed a dividend to its Dutch parent corporation. In accordance with the France/Netherlands tax treaty (and the OECD Model), France imposed a 5 per cent withholding tax on the dividend. France did not impose such withholding tax on distributions between French subsidiaries and their parent corporations and so the Dutch parent argued that the imposition of the withholding tax was contrary to the freedom of establishment.

[207] As a qualification, an individual with a controlling shareholding in a corporation may be considered to exercise their right to freedom of establishment under FEU Treaty Art. 49. This can be contrasted with the usual approach, as evidenced in the OECD Model and the Parent-Subsidiary Directive, that an individual is always a portfolio rather than a non-portfolio shareholder.

[208] Case C-170/05 *Denkavit International BV, Denkavit France SARL* v *Ministre de l'Economie, des Finances et de l'Industrie* [2006] ECR I-11949 (ECJ).

The ECJ agreed, finding that there was a restriction and that it could not be justified. In particular, the ECJ held that despite the usual lack of comparability between residents and non-residents (see above at 2.2.1):

> as soon as a Member State... imposes a charge to tax on the income, not only of resident shareholders, but also of non-resident shareholders, from [domestic] dividends... the situation of those non-resident shareholders becomes comparable to that of resident shareholders.[209]

Under the terms of the France/Netherlands tax treaty there was an obligation on the Netherlands to credit the French tax against Dutch taxation (foreign tax credits are discussed below at 4.1.1). The French suggested that this cured or justified the discrimination. In rejecting this argument, the ECJ looked beyond the terms of the treaty and into Dutch domestic tax law noting that the French dividend was exempt in the hands of the Dutch parent corporation with the result that there was no tax liability to set the credit against. Accordingly, even if in form the treaty overcame the restriction, this did not occur in fact.[210]

The ECJ came to a similar conclusion with respect to the free movement of capital in the *Amurta* case.[211] This case concerned Dutch dividend withholding tax on dividends paid with respect to a 14 per cent Portuguese shareholding in a Dutch corporation. The shareholder argued that if it were a Dutch recipient corporation the dividend withholding tax would not have been imposed. Again, the issue was raised of the creditability of the withholding tax in the state of the shareholder (Portugal) as a method of neutralising the discrimination. The ECJ held that the discriminating country (the Netherlands) could not rely on unilateral measures in the state of the shareholder to cure its breach (e.g. a unilateral foreign tax credit). However, a tax treaty might cure the discrimination if the domestic court decided to consider it and it had that effect on the facts.[212]

[209] Case C-170/05 *Denkavit International BV, Denkavit France SARL* v *Ministre de l'Economie, des Finances et de l'Industrie* [2006] ECR I-11949 (ECJ) at para. 35.

[210] Case C-170/05 *Denkavit International BV, Denkavit France SARL* v *Ministre de l'Economie, des Finances et de l'Industrie* [2006] ECR I-11949 (ECJ) at paras. 46 and 47. For a similar case where the Parent-Subsidiary Directive (1990) did not apply but the freedom of establishment was in issue, see Case C-303/07 *Aberdeen Property Fininvest Alpha* [2009] ECR 00 (ECJ). In this case, the recipient was not an entity of a type covered by the Directive; indeed, it was an open-ended investment company exempt in its home jurisdiction of Luxembourg.

[211] Case C-379/05 *Amurta S.G.P.S.* v *Inspecteur van de Belastingdienst* [2007] ECR I-9569 (ECJ).

[212] Case C-379/05 *Amurta S.G.P.S.* v *Inspecteur van de Belastingdienst* [2007] ECR I-9569 (ECJ) at paras. 78–83.

As mentioned above, some countries (including the UK) grant residents dividend tax credits when they receive dividends or provide some other form of dividend relief (such as exemption or reduced rates). An issue is whether granting such credits or relief to residents but denying the credits or relief to non-residents is contrary to the fundamental freedoms. This issue was considered in the *ACT* case.[213] In that case, the UK High Court asked the ECJ whether it was contrary to the freedom of establishment or the free movement of capital for the UK to grant tax credits to UK individual shareholders but not to grant equivalent credits to non-resident parent corporations of UK subsidiaries. The ECJ handed down its decision two days before the *Denkavit* case and its reasoning was consistent with that case.

As mentioned above at 2.1.2.2, in effect, the UK does not tax outbound dividends. On this basis, the ECJ reasoned that the country of the recipient shareholder is in a better position than the United Kingdom to prevent economic double taxation and adjust the tax liability according to the shareholder's 'ability to pay'. The ECJ also noted that, in granting a tax credit to final UK shareholders, the UK's position is not comparable to that of a member state in which distributed profits are derived but the final shareholders are not resident. Accordingly, so long as the UK does not tax them, the UK is not obliged by the fundamental freedoms to grant dividend tax credits to non-resident shareholders.[214]

Finally, there is the issue of dividends and PEs. It was noted above at 3.1.3.4 that the OECD is not clear as to whether Article 24(3) of the OECD Model requires a state to grant to PEs situated there any dividend relief available to resident corporations. However, such dividend relief must be granted under EU Law because, as also discussed at 3.1.3.4, a PE is comparable with a resident subsidiary. In *Avoir Fiscal*,[215] the first substantive ECJ decision on direct taxation, a French branch of an Italian insurance company received dividends from French corporations. French dividends carried a dividend tax credit (*avoir fiscal*). Resident corporations could claim a refund of excess credits but this was denied to non-resident corporations. The ECJ held this was contrary to the freedom of establishment. The restriction could not be justified by other advantages

[213] Case C-374/04 *Test Claimants in Class IV of the ACT Group Litigation* v *CIR* [2006] ECR I-11673 (ECJ).

[214] Case C-374/04 *Test Claimants in Class IV of the ACT Group Litigation* v *CIR* [2006] ECR I-11673 (ECJ) at paras. 60–74.

[215] Case 270/83 *Commission* v *French Republic* [1986] ECR 273 (ECJ) ('avoir fiscal').

available to the Italian corporation, e.g. lack of French taxation. Further, the fact that the company could have established a subsidiary to gain the refund was not relevant as this would interfere with the Italian corporation's freedom to trade in a vehicle of its own choice, whether branch or subsidiary.

A further issue is whether branch profits taxes are contrary to EU Law. It seems clear that they are because branches and subsidiaries are comparable; at least as far as source country taxation is concerned. If branch profits taxes are a tax on the branch, then the *CLT-UFA* case (discussed above at 3.1.3.4) suggests they are contrary to the freedom of establishment. This should also be the case if, which seems unlikely, remittances of branches are analogised to dividends. In such a case, the head office may claim that the taxation of a remittance is comparable to the taxation of dividends from a subsidiary. As dividends from a subsidiary are exempt due to the Parent-Subsidiary Directive, it would be contrary to the freedom of establishment to tax remittances of branches.

In all these matters of taxation triggered by distributions, a striking feature is the potential width and uniformity of Article 49 of the FEU Treaty, particularly when compared with Articles 10 and 24 of the OECD Model. In the context of subsidiaries, Article 49 may apply whether taxation is in the form of a dividend tax on the parent corporation or corporate distributions tax on the subsidiary. The limit in Article 10(2) applies to the former, but in this case, there is no protection against discrimination under Article 24(5). The limit in Article 10(2) does not apply to the latter and Article 24(5) provides no protection to its imposition or, according to *Boake Allen*, group exceptions to it.

ECJ case law suggests that source country subsidiaries and PEs will often be comparable for the purposes of Article 49 of the FEU Treaty. Accordingly, PEs in receipt of source state dividends must be granted any dividend relief available for distributions between source state corporations. The position under Article 24(3) of the OECD Model is unclear. Further, Article 49 prohibits the higher taxation of PEs with respect to retained *or* distributed profits compared to that of subsidiaries. Article 24(3) prevents the higher taxation of PE profits and Article 10(5) the taxation of distributions of PEs or the taxation of distributions of the owner of the PE out of PE profits. The latter would be prohibited by the Parent-Subsidiary Directive (1990) and, inevitably, by Article 49.

3.1.4.2 Interest

OECD Model

Scope of Article 11 The general format of Article 11 of the OECD Model, dealing with the taxation of interest, generally follows that of Article 10. Article 11 begins by stating that interest 'arising' in a state and 'paid' to a treaty partner resident may be taxed in the residence state. Here the scope of the provision and the concept of 'payment' raise greater issues than under Article 10.[216] This is because many countries, including the UK, tax at least some forms of interest as it accrues rather than on payment.[217] Taxing non-residents on interest on an accrual basis can be problematic and historically this has been done on payment by means of withholding tax from the payment.[218] This can cause a mismatch if the payer may claim a deduction for the interest on an accrual basis.

Under UK domestic tax law the word 'arising' has both timing and location of source of income implications. In Article 11(1) of the OECD Model, 'arising' is used in the latter sense. The first sentence of Article 11(5) deems interest to 'arise' in a state when the payer is resident there. Here there is a direct analogy with the implicit source rule in Article 10, which also focuses on residence of the paying corporation. However, Article 11(5) has a special source rule for interest 'borne' by a PE, which extends the scope of the article. This is further discussed below.

Limited source country taxation As with Article 10(2), Article 11(2) of the OECD Model incorporates a limited source country right to tax. The state in which interest arises may tax the interest at a rate not exceeding 10 per cent of the gross amount of the interest. As with Article 10, the UN Model leaves the rate blank and so for negotiation between states. Further, note that the taxation is also on a gross basis, so no deductions.

As with Article 10, under Article 11(2) the source country 'may' tax and so if there is no domestic charge to tax there will be no source taxation of interest. This is often the case with interest paid by financial institutions

[216] OECD Commentary on Art. 11 para. 5 confirms that 'paid' has the same meaning as in OECD Model Art. 10.

[217] In the UK, for corporations this occurs under the loan relationship rules, which are triggered by CTA 2009 s. 295.

[218] The UK still uses this approach. This is because interest received by non-residents otherwise than through a UK PE, if subject to tax, is subject to income tax, not corporation tax. Under income tax, interest is chargeable on an 'arising' basis, see above at 2.1.2.2. This is interpreted to require receipt. As Rowlatt J famously stated, 'for income tax purposes "receivability" without receipt is nothing'. *Leigh* v *IRC* [1928] 1 KB 73 (KB) at 77.

but some countries, like the Netherlands, do not tax interest paid directly to non-residents at all. Further, many tax treaties provide for an exemption of source country taxation of interest, including many UK treaties.[219] Further, even developing countries sometimes exempt interest paid to certain non-residents and in other cases a limit to a 10 per cent withholding tax is common. The importance of such limited source state taxation should not be underestimated in international taxation. Not only is interest taxed very lightly by many source states but much of the interest will be deductible to the payer, discussed further below at 3.2. Often, the result is a flow of pure untaxed funds from the source state. This can be contrasted with dividends, which, as discussed above at 3.1.4.1, are often subject to economic double taxation by source states. This makes characterising a payment as dividends or interest critical, which is further discussed at 3.3.2.

So why do source states tax interest so lightly? The non-taxation of non-residents with respect to domestic source interest goes back a long way, especially interest on government debt.[220] The problem is that the taxation of interest is often 'shifted' to the borrower. If a state attempts to tax interest paid to non-residents, the non-residents demand a higher rate of interest to compensate. This higher rate may have an undesirable inflationary effect, which countries seek to avoid by exempting interest paid to non-residents. The problem is that, in principle, the shifting occurs only with respect to *marginal* investors, i.e. those that would, in the face of taxation, invest elsewhere. Often, interest exemptions are poorly targeted and so exempt more than just marginal investors. The exemption or low taxation of interest causes much tax planning which seeks to secure this beneficial treatment. Again, this is discussed further at 3.3.2.

Article 11(4) and (6) contain exceptions to the application of the limit in Article 11(2). Article 11(4) is considered shortly. Article 11(6) provides that if interest is paid between related parties, any amount that is more than that which would be paid between independent parties (i.e. more than the arm's length amount) may be taxed by the source state under its usual domestic rules. This provision is further considered below at 3.3.2.

[219] US Model Income Tax Treaty Art. 11 generally exempts interest from source state taxation, subject to certain exceptions, see United States (2006). A similar effect is achieved under the EC Interest and Royalties Directive (2003), discussed further below.

[220] The 1803 UK income tax expressly exempted non-residents with respect to interest received on government debt. There are earlier precedents, such as in 1667 when the King's debts were specifically excluded from direct taxation. See Harris (2006, pp. 139 and 430).

Interest and PEs Article 11(4) of the OECD Model contains a rule similar to that in Article 10(4). If interest arising in a state is 'effectively connected' with a PE of a non-resident situated there, the source state is to apply Article 7, i.e. full taxation. As discussed in the context of dividends, this is not necessarily a bad thing, 10 per cent of the gross amount of interest can be substantially more than full taxation of interest less expenses, i.e. net interest.

Article 11(5) of the OECD Model determines where interest is deemed to arise, and so largely determines the scope of the Article. The first sentence of Article 11(5) was considered above. The second sentence is supplementary. It provides that where interest is borne by a PE situated in a state, that interest is deemed to arise in the PE state and that state may tax it in accordance with Article 11(2). So just as Article 10(5) extends the application of that Article to dividends paid by a corporation resident in one state to a resident of *that* state, Article 11(5) extends the application of that article to interest paid between two residents. However, while the purpose of Article 10(5) is to prohibit taxation, for example, by a PE state of dividends distributed from PE profits, the purpose of Article 11(5) is to permit taxation by a PE state of interest borne by the PE.

There are other substantial differences in the way that Articles 10(5) and 11(5) extend the scope of their respective Articles. As noted at 3.1.4.1, Article 10(5) does not extend the scope of that Article to dividends paid by corporations that are residents of neither contracting state. By contrast, the PE source rule in Article 11(5) applies irrespective of whether the PE is owned by a resident of the other contracting state or a resident of a third state. Assume, for example, that a resident of Country C has a PE in Country A and that PE pays interest to a resident of Country B. Under an OECD style Country A/Country B tax treaty, the interest is regulated by Article 11 and Country A's taxing right is limited, despite the fact that the interest is paid by a person that is not resident in either contracting state. Accordingly, the potential scope of application of Article 21 (other income) is less in the context of interest than it is in the context of dividends.

Article 11(5) of the OECD Model contains a dual sourcing rule, the first sentence contains one test for sourcing interest and the second sentence another. An issue is what is the relationship between these two rules, which might both have potential application in a purely bilateral situation. For example, assume a resident of Country B has a PE in Country A, which pays interest to a resident of Country A. Taken in isolation, each sentence of Article 11(5) may apply, the first to source the interest in Country B and the second to source the interest in Country A. If the first sentence applies, then Country B may tax the interest under Article 11(2). If the second sentence applies, then Article 11 is not applicable because interest arising in one state is not paid to a resident of the other state, i.e. the source of the interest and residence of the recipient are in the same country. The better view is that the second sentence qualifies the first sentence and so in this example Country B has no right to tax.[221] Such a qualification to prevent the dual source of interest cannot apply in situations involving three or more countries. This is considered below at 5.2.1.2.

EU Law

Directives There are two EU directives that potentially apply to the taxation of cross-border interest. The first is the Savings Directive (2003), which involves effective exchange of information with respect to interest received by an individual resident in one member state from a paying agent in another member state. As noted above at 2.2.2, as a transitional measure the Directive contains certain rules regarding the imposition of source country withholding tax on such interest payments. These are beyond the scope of this book. The exchange of information aspect of this Directive is briefly considered below at 7.1.3.

The second directive is the Interest and Royalties Directive (2003). The purpose of this Directive is to exempt certain inter-EU interest and royalty payments from source country tax. As mentioned above at 2.1.2.3, there are similarities between the drafting used in this Directive and that used in Articles 11 and 12 of the OECD Model. Like Article 11 of the OECD Model, Article 1(2) of the Directive contains a dual sourcing rule:

> A payment made by a company of a Member State or by a permanent establishment situated in another Member State shall be deemed to arise in that Member State.

Article 1(6) expressly deals with the potential dual source of interest by providing that where a PE is considered the payer of interest 'no other part of the company shall be treated as the payer…' Article 1(3) of the Directive provides that a PE is considered to make a payment only insofar as the

[221] Question whether OECD Model Art. 21 could apply to this example (is the interest 'dealt with' by Art. 11?). If the interest is 'dealt with' by Art. 11, then it may be argued that it does not specifically limit Country B's right to tax and so Country B may tax. This view is discounted as inconsistent with the purpose of Art. 11. On this basis, whether Art. 21 applies is largely academic because under Art. 21 Country A would also be the only country with a right to tax.

payment is a deductible expense in the state of the PE, a rule that is not incorporated in Article 11 of the OECD Model.

Importantly, the exemption in Article 1 of the Directive is limited to payments by a company of one EU member state to a company of another EU member state, including where paid or received through an EU PE. Further, the two companies must be 'associated'. 'Associated' is defined in Article 3(b) and covers payments between a parent company and a subsidiary in which it directly holds 25 per cent of the capital. Similarly, the payment can be between two 25 per cent subsidiaries of a common parent. This 25 per cent test is similar to the original test in the Parent-Subsidiary Directive (1990). However, while the holding requirement in that Directive has been reduced to 10 per cent, there is no proposal to introduce a similar reduction in the Interest and Royalties Directive.

The importance of the Interest and Royalties Directive (2003) from a tax planning perspective should not be underestimated. It effectively eliminates source country taxation, both at the level of the payer (through a deduction that is typically available) and the payee (where the Directive provides the exemption). Further, it specifically applies in the context of corporate groups. This provides an incentive to locate group members in receipt of interest and royalties in low tax EU countries and, therefore, puts pressure on anti-abuse rules such as controlled foreign corporation measures, discussed further at 4.1.2.2. In this context, it is not surprising that the Directive preserves the right for source states to impose various forms of anti-abuse rules.[222] Further, under a 2003 proposal, the exemption would apply only if the recipient 'is effectively subject to tax on the interest or royalty payment' in the residence state.[223]

Fundamental freedoms As mentioned above, even a 10 per cent source based tax on interest can be high because it is based on the gross amount of interest without allowance for expenses. Difficulties caused by lack of deductions have inspired a number of countries to conclude tax treaties denying source state taxation of interest and similar concerns seem to have inspired the Interest and Royalties Directive (2003). However, there

[222] For example, under Interest and Royalties Directive (2003) Art. 4(1), interest on profit sharing debentures, convertible notes and long-term debt (50 years or more) may be excluded from the exemption. Art. 4(2) is a provision similar to OECD Model Art. 11(6) and so excludes the Directive applying to non-arm's length interest. Art. 5 contains a general power to deny the benefits of the Directive in the case of evasion, avoidance, fraud or abuse.

[223] See van Raad (2009, p. 1931).

remain many situations in which cross-border interest payments within the EU are subject to gross based taxation in the source state. The result can be substantially greater taxation of cross-border interest than domestic interest and this raises the issue of discrimination prohibited by the fundamental freedoms. This is a general issue for all types of non-resident income subject to final withholding tax.

The *Truck Centre* case illustrates the issue well.[224] A Belgian corporation paid interest to its 48 per cent Luxembourg parent corporation. The payment was made before the Interest and Royalties Directive (2003) and so was subject to a 15 per cent Belgian withholding tax under the Belgium/Luxembourg tax treaty. No withholding tax was payable on interest payments between two Belgian corporations, but the recipient would be taxed by assessment. So this was a classic case of gross versus net taxation. The Belgian corporation refused to withhold tax on the basis that it was contrary to the fundamental freedoms.

The ECJ found that the situation was correctly assessed by reference to the freedom of establishment. It held that due to the different jurisdictions to tax, interest payments between two Belgian corporations were 'not objectively comparable' to cross-border payments of the type in question.[225] In particular, a resident recipient remained subject to Belgian corporation tax whereas a non-resident recipient did not. In any case, the ECJ found that:

> the difference in treatment resulting from the tax legislation at issue in the main proceedings does not necessarily procure an advantage for resident recipient companies because, firstly… those companies are obliged to make advance payments of corporation tax and, secondly, the amount of withholding tax deducted from the interest paid to a non-resident company is significantly lower than the corporation tax charged on the income of resident companies which receive interest.[226]

Accordingly, the Belgian rules did not breach the freedom of establishment.

At first blush, the case seems at odds with decisions of the ECJ in the dividend tax area, such as *Denkavit*, *Amurta* and *ACT*, discussed above at 3.1.4.1. However, in the first two of these cases, the dividends received by the comparable resident parent corporation would have been exempt from tax, making any withholding tax on dividends to non-resident parents an

224 Case C-282/07 *Belgian State* v *Truck Center SA* [2008] ECR 00 (ECJ).

225 Case C-282/07 *Belgian State* v *Truck Center SA* [2008] ECR 00 (ECJ) at para. 41.

226 Case C-282/07 *Belgian State* v *Truck Center SA* [2008] ECR 00 (ECJ) at para. 49.

obvious discrimination. The *ACT* case is distinguishable because, in substance, the UK did not tax the dividends paid to non-residents at all. In *Truck Centre*, Belgium, like most other countries, would have taxed the resident comparator on the receipt of interest.

The *Truck Centre* case does not resolve all issues in this area. One critical question it did not answer was what if deductions meant that the higher rate of tax imposed by assessment would actually have been less than that imposed by withholding? The ECJ has recognised in a number of cases the right of a non-resident to claim deductions in determining source country taxation. The cases have occurred most frequently in the context of the movement of workers and the freedom to provide services but there have also been cases dealing with the freedom of establishment. However, outside the exemption in the Interest and Royalties Directive, the most likely freedom to be involved in the context of interest withholding tax is the free movement of capital. Here the case law is more limited.[227]

One case of relevance is *Bouanich*.[228] This case involved a French resident who disposed of shares in a Swedish corporation through a share buy-back. In accordance with the terms of the France/Sweden tax treaty, Bouanich was taxed by Sweden at 15 per cent of the sale proceeds, i.e. on a gross basis. Swedish residents had the option of being taxed at 30 per cent on the net amount, i.e. after deducting acquisition costs and other expenses. The ECJ found that Bouanich could be compared with a Swedish resident and so whether free movement of capital had been breached depended on whether, on the facts, the 15 per cent tax on the gross amount was greater than the 30 per cent tax on the net amount. Again, it is to be noted that the ECJ takes account of tax treaties in determining whether there is a restriction.

Currently, it is not clear whether this reasoning will apply to expenses incurred in deriving interest or royalties. Here the connection between the income and expenses is not as close as it is in the case of sale proceeds and acquisition costs where assets are sold. However, there remains a sound argument that expenses should be available to reduce source country taxation to no more than it would have been had the non-resident been a resident. This would be achieved, e.g. by permitting non-residents to file a tax return and claim expenses. A slightly different but equally important issue is whether exempt institutions such as pension funds and non-profit

[227] Generally, see O'Shea (2007).

[228] Case C-265/04 *Bouanich* v *Skatteverket* [2006] ECR I-923 (ECJ).

organisations should be exempt from source country taxation of interest (and other forms of capital income) based on the free movement of capital if they would be exempt if organised under the law of the source state. This issue is beyond the scope of this book.[229]

3.1.4.3 Royalties

OECD Model Article 12 of the OECD Model, dealing with royalties, is somewhat more straightforward than the related Articles 10 and 11 because it eliminates source taxation of royalties altogether.[230] Article 12(1) provides:

> Royalties arising in a Contracting State and beneficially owned by a resident of the other Contracting State shall be taxable only in that other State.

Despite using similar terminology as in Article 11, Article 12 does not incorporate a rule that determines where royalties arise. One possible explanation is that a source rule is unnecessary because Article 12 is broadly consistent with Article 21 (other income), granting exclusive right to tax to the residence state.[231]

Many treaties, including between developed countries, do not follow the exemption in Article 12 of the OECD Model but, rather, permit source taxation of royalties on a gross basis. In particular, Article 12 of the UN Model incorporates both a source state right to tax royalties and a source rule. The right to tax follows that in Articles 10 and 11 and so is limited to a rate applied to the gross amount of royalties. Consistent with those Articles in the UN Model, the rate of taxation by the source state is left blank, i.e. left for negotiation between states. The source rule in Article 12(5) of the UN Model follows that used in the OECD Model for interest,

[229] In this regard, see Gutmann, Austry and Le Roux (2009).

[230] Regarding the origins of OECD Model Art. 12 and why it incorporates a source country exemption, see Vann (2008).

[231] This discounts the type of argument noted above in footnote 221 that royalties that are not mentioned in OECD Model Art. 12(1) are nevertheless 'dealt with' by Art. 12 and if taxation is not expressly prohibited by that provision then it may be imposed. For example, suppose a country taxes some royalties that, on a fair interpretation of the word, do not arise there, such as might happen with royalties unconnected with a state but for the fact that they are calculated by reference to a royalty sourced there, i.e. a reflective royalty with a deemed source. If such a royalty is 'dealt with' by Art. 12, then neither Art. 12(1) nor Art. 21 specifically regulate it and it might be argued that the state is not prohibited from taxing that royalty. Similarly, where a resident of one state with a PE in the other state pays a royalty to a resident of the PE state through the PE, it might be argued that taxation by the first state is not prohibited. As mentioned above in footnote 221, these arguments are discounted on the basis that they are inconsistent with the purpose of Art. 12.

i.e. residence of payer or borne by a PE situated there, and so the discussion above at 3.1.4.2 is relevant.

Two other rules in Article 12 of the OECD Model follow those in Article 11. The first is Article 12(3), which preserves full source state taxation of royalties effectively connected with a PE situated there, but on a net basis under Article 7. The second is Article 12(4), which follows Article 11(6) and preserves source state taxation of the non-arm's length amount of any royalties paid between parties with a special relationship.

The problem of source country taxation of services was considered above at 3.1.3.3 in the context of the taxation of PEs. At that point, there was discussion of the services PE provision in the UN Model and in the Commentary of the OECD Model. It was noted that a services PE may be created only where the services are physically provided in the source state. Where a services PE is created it grants the source country a *full* right to tax but on a *net* basis, i.e. after deduction of appropriate expenses. For some countries, even a services PE provision does not grant sufficient taxing rights. So, a number of treaties grant source countries the right to tax 'technical services fees' by withholding tax whether in replacement of or in addition to the right to tax a services PE. Often this right is inserted in the royalties article and so taxation of technical services fees is at the same rate as for royalties, although many treaties contain a separate provision. The source rule is typically like interest and royalties, i.e. where the payer is resident.[232]

EU Law For present purposes, EU Law raises no further issues with respect to royalties than those discussed above at 3.1.4.2 in the context of interest. Therefore, the Interest and Royalties Directive (2003) is important in exempting inter-EU royalties paid between associated EU companies. Further, there is a question as to whether the free movement of capital requires a source state that taxes non-residents in receipt of royalties on a gross basis to permit taxation at domestic rates on a net basis (i.e. deduction of expenses), at least where that would produce less taxation.

[232] For example, see the Botswana/UK Treaty (2005) Art. 13 (separate article), China/UK Treaty (1984) Art. 13 (separate article), India/UK Treaty (1993) Art. 13 (with royalties) and Pakistan/UK Treaty (1986) Art. 13 (separate article). A combined provision for royalties and services is a particular feature of Indian tax treaty practice, e.g. China/India Treaty (1994) Art. 12, India/Russia Treaty (1988) Art. 12 and India/US Treaty (1989) Art. 12.

3.1.5 *Capital gains*

OECD Model Article 13 of the OECD Model deals with capital gains. The first three paragraphs of this Article are in some ways reconciliation rules but they do not direct that another article of the Model will apply. Rather, they incorporate rules that are consistent with earlier articles of the Model. For example, Article 13(1) provides that 'gains' from 'the alienation of immovable property referred to in Article 6' may be taxed in the country in which the property is situated. Similarly, Article 13(2) provides that gains from the alienation of 'movable property forming part of the business property of a permanent establishment' may be taxed by the PE state. Article 13(3) deals with shipping and aircraft and so corresponds to Article 8, which is not considered in this book.

Article 13 applies to 'alienations' of property, a term that is not defined in the OECD Model. Literally, the term suggests a loss of ownership and perhaps requires a transfer of ownership. The OECD suggests the word covers

> 'sale or exchange of property and also… a partial alienation, the expropriation, the transfer to a company in exchange for stock, the sale of a right, the gift and even the passing of property on death.'[233]

Capital gains taxation imposed by many countries is broader than might be suggested by the word 'alienation' even as extended by the passage cited. For example, in the UK it covers the destruction or expiry of property and even capital payments received with respect to property.[234] It is difficult to see how such matters, particularly the latter, fall within the concept of 'alienation' of property, especially if that term has a special treaty meaning. If the term has a domestic law meaning, it is equally difficult to equate the term 'alienation' to that of 'disposal', which has a technical and extended meaning under TCGA 1992.

The receipt of a premium on the grant of a lease, discussed above at 3.1.2, is an example of the problems that may arise at the interface of Articles 6, 13 and 21 of the OECD Model. If the sorts of items mentioned in the last paragraph do not fall within Article 13, then it is difficult to see how they fall within Article 21 (other income), discussed above at 3.1.1, unless

[233] OECD Commentary on Art. 13 para. 5. To similar effect, see the Australian decision of *FCT* v *Lamesa Holdings BV* (1997) 36 ATR 589 at 596 (FFC).

[234] TCGA 1992 ss. 22 and 24. Some countries, mainly civil law countries, tax revaluations of business assets but issues of 'alienation' under OECD Model Art. 13 are unlikely to arise because, as discussed below, they will tax such revaluations under Art. 7 not Art. 13.

the word 'income' as used in that article is interpreted to include capital payments. As discussed at 3.1.2, the use of the word 'income' in Article 6 and the very existence of Article 13(1) tell against that approach. It may be that such items are simply not covered by tax treaties. In any case, few countries would attempt to tax such items on a source only basis under their domestic law. As mentioned at 2.1.2.2, the UK does not tax capital gains of non-residents.

Each paragraph of Article 13 of the OECD Model refers to 'gains' but there is no prescription as to how 'gains' should be calculated. This seems to be a matter appropriately left to domestic law,[235] with one possible qualification. The OECD Model uses different concepts under different articles to determine what may be taxed. In the articles considered by this book, these include 'income' (Articles 6 and 21), 'profits' (Article 7), 'payments' (Articles 10, 11 and 12) and 'gains' (Article 13). Inevitably, these terms are not intended to mean the same thing. 'Payments' are necessarily gross amounts and the issue as to whether 'income' is net or gross was discussed above at 3.1.1 and 3.1.2. 'Profits' seems inherently net in concept, i.e. after deductions, and Article 7(3) (discussed above at 3.1.3.3) reinforces this. Similarly, 'gains' seems inherently net in concept. Accordingly, it seems that Article 13 would not permit a charge, for example, on gross proceeds from the sale of property.

Article 24 of the OECD Model (non-discrimination) has no independent provision dealing with capital gains. As noted above at 3.1.2, there is no express limitation against discrimination with respect to the taxation of income from immovable property and the same is true of capital gains from immovable property. However, Article 24(3) (discussed above at 3.1.3.4) is sufficiently broad to cover capital gains derived through a PE and so this constitutes a difference between a source country's right to tax capital gains from immovable property (other than as part of a PE) and its right to tax capital gains derived through a PE. The *Hollmann* case (discussed below) is an example of discrimination in the taxation of non-residents disposing of immovable property that is prohibited by EU Law but that does not clearly breach the OECD Model.

Article 13(2) of the OECD Model requires further specific comment. Some countries, especially civil law jurisdictions, tax capital gains arising in the context of a business as business profits, i.e. in the same manner as

[235] The calculation of gains varies substantially from country to country. For example, the UK still uses indexation in calculating the capital gains of corporations, TCGA 1992 ss. 53 and 54.

profits or gains arising in the ordinary course of a business. Accordingly, they apply Article 7 to business capital gains, despite the overlapping application of Article 13(2). In *Undershaft (No. 1)*, the Australian Federal Court was faced with the 1967 Australia/UK tax treaty, which did not contain a capital gains tax article.[236] The court held that the equivalent of Article 7 covered capital gains made in the context of a business. This meant that Australia had no right to tax the gain made on the disposal of shares in an Australian company by a treaty partner enterprise as that enterprise had no PE in Australia.

Another issue involves the meaning of the word 'movable property' in Article 13(2) of the OECD Model. 'Immovable property', as used in Article 13(1), takes its meaning from Article 6(2), discussed above at 3.1.2,[237] but the term 'movable property' is not defined in the OECD Model. The Commentary provides the following definition:

> The term 'movable property' means all property other than immovable property… It includes also incorporeal property, such as goodwill, licences, etc.

Under English conflict of laws rules, 'movable property' may be either tangible movables (choses in possession) or intangible movables (choses in action). The problem in identifying intangibles as 'movable' was noted by a Chief Justice of the Australian High Court:

> Physical objects not attached to land… are movables, as must be every proprietary interest in them. But rights, or choses in action, have no physical quality which can really be described as movable or immovable. They are concepts: physical mobility is not a quality of the conceptual. But choses in action must be fitted into a scheme of things which requires that they be classified as either movable or immovable.[238]

Indeed, it is difficult to see how intangibles could constitute movable property in the UK (as suggested by the OECD) unless the conflict of laws rules are used to determine the concepts of movable and immovable property.

[236] *Undershaft (No. 1) Limited* v *FCT* [2009] FCA 41 (FC).

[237] If, in England, 'immovable property' takes its meaning from the rules on conflict of laws, this means that a mortgage debt secured on English land falls within OECD Model Art. 13(1) and so the UK may tax any gains on the disposal of such a security.

[238] *Haque* v *Haque (No 2)* (1965) 114 CLR 98 (HC) at 107 per Barwick CJ. Barwick continued to note that English law sites choses in action and that '[t]hese "locations" spring in part from historical considerations and in part from convenience… The location of each such chose in action is capable of change and, therefore, is in a sense mobile'.

Article 13(5) of the OECD Model contains the residual rule that other gains from the alienation of property are taxable only in the residence country. A problem with this rule is that it excludes source country taxation even where the residence country does not tax. This rule is particularly important with respect to the sale of investments such as shares, debentures and intellectual property and other income producing movable property. Source countries have a right to tax dividends, interest and often royalties (see discussion above at 3.1.4) but do not have a right to tax gains on the disposal of the underlying property (other than as part of a PE). This makes little sense from a policy perspective. So, instead of distributing dividends to a non-resident shareholder, source country taxation may be avoided by leaving the corporation inflated with profits and selling the shares. Similar results may be achieved with deferred interest debentures although these cases may raise anti-abuse issues where the purchaser is resident in the source country (dividend and bond stripping).

Article 13(5) of the OECD Model may provide a way of avoiding source country taxation under other articles, e.g. Articles 6 and 7. Gains on the disposal of land held directly by a non-resident are subject to source country tax, Article 13(1). However, if the land is held through a corporation and the shares are sold, that is not subject to source country tax, see discussion above at 3.1.2. Similarly, gains on the disposal of a PE owned by a non-resident are subject to source country tax, Article 13(2). However, if the non-resident sets up a source country presence in the form of a subsidiary, sale of shares in the subsidiary is not subject to source country tax. The UN Model deals with both these issues. The OECD Model deals only with the former (from 2003).

Article 13(4) of the OECD Model is inspired by the same provision of the UN Model. A source country may tax gains on the disposal of shares if the shares derive more than 50 per cent of their value from immovable property in that country. The UN test is slightly different in that it does not focus on the value of the shares but on property held 'directly or indirectly' by the subject corporation. Both provisions appear to avoid the problem in the Australian *Lamesa Holdings* case.[239] In that case, the provision in the Australia/Netherlands tax treaty referred only to the corporation whose shares were sold holding land. Therefore, the provision did not preserve source country taxation with respect to shares in a corporation where further corporations were interposed between that corporation and the Australian land.

[239] *FCT* v *Lamesa Holdings BV* (1997) 36 ATR 589 (FFC).

Article 13(5) of the UN Model provides an additional source country taxing right. Gains on the disposal of a substantial participation in a resident corporation are taxable by the state of corporate residence. In the usual UN fashion, the level of shareholding required to trigger the taxing right is not specified and left for negotiation. This provision does seem open to the problem in the Australian *Lamesa Holdings* case and so may be avoided by holding the subsidiary's shares through a holding company resident in another country and selling the shares in the holding company rather than the subsidiary.

EU Law Capital gains raise no further issues under EU Law than those already discussed. In particular, it seems clear that both the freedom of establishment and the free movement of capital may apply to gains on the disposal of assets. In particular, the freedom of establishment prohibits discrimination both with respect to taxation of a subsidiary as well as taxation of disposal of shares in a subsidiary. This creates a level of parity with non-discrimination in the taxation of a PE and the sale of the PE, in contrast with the OECD approach where source country taxation is preserved for the taxation of PEs, the sale of PEs, the taxation of subsidiaries but not the sale of shares in subsidiaries.

Further, the *Bouanich* case (discussed above at 3.1.4.2),[240] suggests that free movement of capital requires non-discrimination between residents and non-residents in the taxation of gains on the disposal of assets. Tax payable is what must be compared, including the effects of deductions as well as tax rate. This approach is also clear from the *Hollmann* case.[241] In this case, Portugal taxed a German resident on a capital gain on disposal of immovable property at the flat rate of 25 per cent. Residents were taxable at progressive rates up to 42 per cent but only on half the gain. In the result, non-residents were subject to greater taxation than even the highest taxed residents. In these circumstances, the ECJ found the taxation of residents and non-residents comparable and the discrimination unjustified. The same approach applies with respect to the freedom of establishment.

3.1.6 *Income from employment and independent personal services*

The domestic tax laws of every country use, at some level, the distinction between an employee and an independent contractor, i.e. the distinction

[240] Case C-265/04 *Bouanich* v *Skatteverket* [2006] ECR I-923 (ECJ).
[241] Case C-443/06 *Hollmann* v *Fazenda Pública* [2007] ECR I-8491 (ECJ).

between a contract of service and a contract for services. In the UK, they are subject to different schedules (see above at 2.1.2.1) and, therefore, different calculation rules and rules regarding the timing and collection of tax. In particular, independent contractors generally have greater scope for the deduction of expenses and pay tax by instalments, whereas employees typically suffer tax deducted from wage payments, i.e. withholding tax. Further, there can be major differences between the treatment of employees and independent contractors for the purposes of social security contributions.

In a world of increasing globalisation with high mobility of factors of production, employees are viewed as less mobile than many other factors. This has meant a gradual but obvious increase in reliance on employee taxation.[242] Further, greater global competition has forced increased flexibility in the workplace with greater use of outsourcing. The result is that many workers have been presented with the prospect of working as independent contractors (or had it forced on them). This has meant an increase in tax planning by both workers and service users in how work arrangements are conducted. As governments react and seek to protect one of their most reliant sources of tax, particularly the wage withholding tax, the result has put increased pressure and importance on the employee/independent contractor distinction.[243]

As noted in the introduction, this book focuses on tax issues arising out of international commercial transactions. In particular, the focus is on the taxation of business, especially corporations, rather than individuals. Accordingly, the following discussion of the taxation of personal services is particularly brief. It recognises the importance of workers for international business but focuses on them from a business perspective. It does not engage in a detailed consideration of the employee/independent contractor distinction but does consider the rules that govern taxing rights with respect to each in an international setting.

3.1.6.1 Employment

OECD Model Article 15 of the OECD Model deals with income from employment. Article 15(1) provides for source country taxation of

[242] For much of the twentieth century, earned income was taxed at lower rates than income from capital. This was referred to as 'differentiation'. From the 1990s, and tracking increased globalisation, there is a reverse trend whereby capital income is taxed more lightly than wage income.

[243] In the UK, this is referred to as the 'IR 35' debate after a notorious Budget press release of 1999. Generally, see Tiley (2008, pp. 226–9) and the references cited therein.

employment income, i.e. taxation by the country in which the employment is exercised. Article 15(2) (a particularly poor example of legal drafting) qualifies this source country taxing right. Broadly (and trying to remove the double negatives), a source country may tax under Article 15 in any of the following three cases:

(i) An employer resident in the source state pays the remuneration
(ii) A non-resident employer pays the remuneration but it is 'borne' by a source state PE
(iii) A non-resident employer pays the remuneration *and* the employee is present in the source state for at least 183 days (half a year) during a 12 month period

Article 15 raises a number of issues including the type of activity covered, i.e. 'employment' and who is the employer, the type of payments covered, i.e. 'salaries, wages and other similar remuneration', the inherent source rule, i.e. employment 'exercised in' a state, and issues arising from the special qualifications for non-resident employers.

Employment The term 'employment' is used in Article 15(1) and (2) but only Article 15(2) refers to 'employer'. Both refer to income 'derived' by a person 'in respect of employment', but do not use the term 'employee'. Article 15(2) additionally refers to 'the recipient', which is presumed to be the same person as that deriving the income. None of these terms is defined in the OECD Model and, as usual, an initial question is whether any or all has a special treaty meaning, and if so what is their relationship, or whether Article 3(2) (discussed above at 1.3.2) applies to give these terms a domestic law meaning. The OECD Commentary is particularly unhelpful in this respect. It does discuss the term 'employer' as used in Article 15(2) and, perhaps, suggests a special treaty meaning (discussed below). The Commentary does not discuss the general concept of 'employment' and it is presumed (tentatively) that it has a domestic law meaning. While most domestic laws use the terms 'employer' and 'employment' in a complementary sense, the possibility that the OECD Model uses them in a disjunctive sense is considered below.

Whether a relationship gives rise to 'employment' is a question of degree not absolutes. The sorts of factors often taken into account include:

- *How the work is done:* Independent contractors are told what is required but not how to do it. Employees are subject to instructions as to not only what they are to do but also how they are to do it.

- *Whose materials and equipment are used:* Independent contractors use their own equipment to perform the task and purchase the materials to complete the task. Employees are provided with equipment and materials.
- *Timing of Work:* Independent contractors are told by when a job must be completed but within this timeframe set their own hours. Employees are told when to work. These are typically set hours that are similar for other employees. The typical employee works full time.
- *Who Does the Work:* Independent contractors may hire third parties to perform the work. Employees have no power to delegate.
- *Exclusivity:* Independent contractors work for more than one client and often many. Employees typically have just one job.
- *Training:* Independent contractors arrange and pay for their own training. Employers arrange and pay for the training of employees.
- *What is Paid For:* Independent contractors are paid to produce a result or otherwise for hours worked. Employees are paid to attend for a set time, typically by the week or month.
- *Continuing Relationship:* Independent contractors have a limited relationship with the contractor, typically determined by the scope of the task. Employees have a continuing relationship with their employer.
- *Calculation of Remuneration:* Independent contractors take risk and derive varying returns. Typically, their expenses are not reimbursed and they have an opportunity for profit or loss. Employees have their proper business expenses reimbursed, their remuneration is a flat amount for time worked and there is no opportunity for additional profit or loss.

The UK approach is broadly consistent.[244] Typically, no particular factor is determinative. In the vast majority of cases, it is obvious whether a person is an employee or not. However, tax administrations often raise concerns with high paid executives who argue that they are not employees.

Business and workers often try to avoid employee status by engaging the worker through their own corporation (often called a 'services corporation'). The structure involves the worker being employed by their own corporation and then the corporation hiring out the services of the worker to the relevant business. In the flimsiest of cases, such a worker may still be an employee of the business, even under industrial law. In other cases, some countries, including the UK, have enacted specific tax rules to tax

[244] See Tiley (2008, pp. 222–6) and the references cited therein.

the service fees received by the corporation as though it were wage income of the worker. Under the UK rules, the services corporation is treated as making a payment to the worker 'which is to be treated as earnings from an employment'.[245] Importantly, the worker is not deemed an employee of the business (recipient of the services) nor the business an employer and this may have an impact in applying Article 15 of the OECD Model.

For example, assume that a non-resident individual provides services to a UK business in the UK. The services are not provided directly to the business but are provided through a non-resident services corporation owned by the individual. The business pays a services fee to the services corporation. The UK rules might treat this fee as paid by the services corporation to the individual as wages. It would not treat the relationship with the UK business as employment (which it might have done). Accordingly, Article 15(1) of the OECD Model could not apply to the service fee paid by the UK business. However, the individual has exercised their employment with the services corporation in the UK and so this falls within Article 15(1) and, prima facie, the UK has a right to tax.

A problem is that from a domestic law perspective the 'employer' is still the services corporation, i.e. a non-resident.[246] This can be important because, as noted above, source country taxation is more limited where a non-resident employer is involved. In particular, source country taxation may be excluded where the worker is not present in the source country for 183 days in a year. The OECD notes this problem in the context of Article 15(2) and suggests that the term 'employer' (with no mention of the concept of 'employment') 'should be interpreted in the context' of this provision. The Commentary proceeds to give a definition of 'employer':

> it is understood that the employer is the person having rights on the work produced and bearing the relative responsibility and risk... In this context, substance should prevail over form, i.e. each case should be examined to see whether the functions of employer were exercised by the user.

The Commentary then gives a list of 'circumstances' for establishing 'that the real employer is the user of the labour (and not the foreign intermediary)'.[247] These circumstances replicate the types of consideration outlined above in order to determine whether there is an employment

[245] Income Tax (Earnings and Pensions) Act 2003 s. 50(1).

[246] For example, Income Tax (Earnings and Pensions) Act 2003 s. 56(2) applies the tax law as if 'the worker were employed by the intermediary'.

[247] OECD Commentary on Art. 15 para. 8.

relationship but, as noted, the Commentary does not purport to be providing a definition of 'employment' and does not refer to Article 15(1).

This situation is unsatisfactory and, as noted above, leads to the possibility that 'employment' has a domestic law meaning but 'employer' has a special treaty meaning. In the example provided, the UK would ground its source country taxing right under Article 15(1) of the OECD Model on the employment by the intermediary. However, when it comes to a consideration of whether that taxing right is prohibited by Article 15(2), the service user (UK business) may be considered the 'employer' based on a special treaty interpretation, even if, as in the UK, the intermediary is specifically deemed to be the employer. One way to deal with any inconsistency is to read the Commentary (the special treaty meaning of 'employer') in a way that is consistent with domestic law, i.e. accept that domestic law already takes a substance approach to identifying employment[248] and that the Commentary requires no more. Under this approach, if domestic law already identifies the intermediary as the employer that will also be true for the purposes of Article 15(2) of the OECD Model.

Another common example raising issues in identifying the employer for the purposes of Article 15(2) of the OECD Model is with respect to employees sent by a parent corporation resident in Country B to provide services for a subsidiary resident in Country A. If the employee stays for less than 183 days, the parent will argue that, because it is the employer, Country A has no right to tax the employment income under Article 15. Further, any service fee paid by the subsidiary is not taxable in Country A because the parent corporation is not resident there.

There are two risks for the parent corporation in this example. The first is that the subsidiary is considered, 'in substance', the employer and so Country A has the right to tax the employment income irrespective of how short the employee's presence in that country is. Second, the employee may create a PE of the parent corporation in Country A. Here the existence of a services PE provision in the relevant treaty may be particularly important (see the discussion above at 3.1.3.2).[249] This may mean that not only is the service fee paid by the subsidiary taxable in Country A (as forming part of the profits of the PE) but also the employment income

[248] The UK may be viewed as doing so, e.g. see the decision of the Court of Appeal in *Muscat v Cable & Wireless plc* [2006] EWCA Civ 220 (CA).

[249] Because of OECD Model Art. 7(5), the subsidiary is unlikely to constitute a PE of the parent corporation.

can be taxed by Country A (as it is 'borne' by that PE). The latter is likely to be deductible in calculating the former.

Salaries, etc. Article 15 of the OECD Model encompasses 'salaries, wages and other similar remuneration derived... in respect of an employment'. The OECD notes that this phrase is 'generally understood... to include benefits in kind received in respect of an employment'.[250] Article 15 merely preserves a source country's taxing right. It does not specify the manner of taxation. Some countries tax fringe benefits in the hands of the employer through a special tax, e.g. fringe benefits tax in Australia.[251] Other countries deny the employer a deduction for certain types of benefits provided to employees. The latter approach only indirectly taxes employment income and is subject to the special non-discrimination rule in Article 24(4), discussed below at 3.2.

Intermediaries again raise issues in the identification of income subject to Article 15 of the OECD Model. As noted above, where an individual provides services to third parties through a services corporation, UK domestic tax law may treat the corporation as making a payment of employment income to the individual based on service fees received by the corporation. So if a service fee of, say, £100 is received by the corporation from a third party, anything up to £95 of this fee may be treated as paid as employment income by the corporation to the individual, irrespective of whether the corporation ever pays that sum to the individual. Is this deemed income covered by Article 15, is it 'derived' in respect of the employment? Article 15(2) also refers to the 'recipient' of the income.

It is difficult to see how this type of deemed income could be considered to fall within Article 15 of the OECD Model without considering that there is an employment with the third party and the service fee is paid in respect of that employment. Assume that 'employment' as used in Article 15 has a domestic law meaning and that under UK law the employment continues to be with the intermediary corporation. The individual is considered to exercise that employment in the UK and so the UK has taxing rights. Further, assume that a treaty meaning is given to 'employer' in Article 15(2) and that the third party is treated as the employer so that the UK retains its taxing right even if the individual is in the UK for less than 183 days. This will not help with taxation under Article 15(1); it is still limited to 'salaries, wages and other similar remuneration' from the

[250] OECD Commentary on Art. 15 para 2.1.
[251] Imposed by the Fringe Benefits Tax Act 1986 (Australia).

employment with the intermediary corporation. If the deemed income does not fall within this phrase, it is not taxable by the UK.

This potential disjuncture will not occur if the treaty meaning given to 'employer' in Article 15(2) of the OECD Model applies more broadly and results in the individual having 'employment' with the third party for the purposes of Article 15(1). In this case, the service fee will clearly be 'salaries, wages or other similar remuneration' from this employment and so taxable in the UK. The potential inconsistency that would otherwise arise demonstrates the importance of interpreting 'employment' where used in Article 15 and 'employer' where used in Article 15(2) according to the same set of rules, whether they be domestic law or a special treaty meaning.

Exercised in The implicit source rule in Article 15(1) of the OECD Model is the state in which the employment is exercised. The OECD confirms that this is

> the place where the employee is physically present when performing the activities... One consequence of this would be that a resident of a Contracting State who derived remuneration, in respect of an employment, from sources in the other State could not be taxed in that other State in respect of that remuneration merely because the results of this work were exploited in that other State.[252]

This well represents the type of tax base being lost by source countries due to electronic means of communication. An employee may be resident in Country B and provide services electronically for use in Country A and because the employee is not physically present in Country A the employment income cannot be taxed by Country A, even if the employer is resident there. At the time the OECD Model was developing, the employee would have had little choice but to go to Country A to provide the services. Further, Country A may be prohibited from denying a deduction to the employer for the employment income due to Article 24(4), discussed below at 3.2.

Non-resident employers The more limited source country taxation of employment income in the case of non-resident employers in Article 15(2) of the OECD Model has been mentioned above, as has interpretation of the word 'employer' in this context. Source country taxation will

[252] OECD Commentary on Art. 15 para. 1.

be preserved if the employment income is 'borne' by a PE situated there. The OECD suggests consideration should be given to whether the remuneration 'could give rise to a deduction' by the PE, not whether a deduction is actually claimed.[253] If employment income incurred by a non-resident employer is not borne by a source state PE, then source country taxation of employment income will be preserved only if the 'recipient' (presumed to be the employee) is present there for 183 days in a twelve-month period. Note it is days of presence that are counted, not days in exercising the employment.[254]

EU Law As noted above at 2.1.2.3, Article 45 of the FEU Treaty deals with the free movement of workers. It involves the abolition of discrimination of workers of member states based on nationality. At 2.2.1, it was noted that the freedoms also provide protection against indirect discrimination and so often cover discrimination against non-residents if they are comparable to residents. The focus of this freedom is on employees and so there is a correlation with Article 15 of the OECD Model.[255] However, the Model contains no specific protection against discrimination of employees. The only provision of some relevance is Article 24(1), but as discussed above at 2.2.1, it is based on nationality and non-residents are considered non-comparable with residents.

As noted above at 2.2.1, the *Schumacker* case decided that residents and non-residents are comparable if a non-resident derives the 'major part' of their income from the source state.[256] There is substantial case law of the ECJ on the free movement of workers in the FEU Treaty. This case law is of particular relevance to countries with substantial land borders within Europe where it is possible to live in one state and work in another (where the major part of a person's income is derived) without becoming resident in the source state. To a country with sea borders, like the UK, this is of less relevance. Further, much of the case law involves the application of

[253] OECD Commentary on Art. 15 para. 7.1.

[254] OECD Commentary on Art. 15 para. 5.

[255] With respect to FEU Treaty Art. 45, the ECJ has held that '[a]ny person who pursues activities which are real and genuine, to the exclusion of activities on such a small scale as to be regarded as purely marginal and ancillary, must be regarded as a "worker". The essential feature of an employment relationship is, according to that case law, that for a certain period of time a person performs services for and under the direction of another person in return for which he receives remuneration'. Case C-10/05 *Mattern* v *Ministre du Travail et de l'Emploi* [2006] ECR I-3145 (ECJ) at para. 18 and see the case law cited there.

[256] Case C-279/93 *Finanzamt Koln-Altstadt* v *Schumacker* [1995] ECR I-225 (ECJ).

progressive rates and personal allowances and the treatment of pension contributions. These are of limited direct relevance in a consideration of international commercial taxation. This book does not consider Article 45 of the FEU Treaty further.[257]

3.1.6.2 Independent personal services

OECD Model The difficulty in determining whether a person is an employee or an independent contractor was mentioned above. Before 2000, the OECD Model, in Article 14, contained a provision dedicated to independent personal services, a version of which continues in the UN Model. Since 2000, the business profits article (Article 7) of the OECD Model covers a person providing independent services. In particular, 'activities of an independent character' are covered by the definition of 'business' in Article 3(1)(h); see above at 3.1.3.1.[258] This means that Article 15 covers employees and Article 7 independent contractors. A problem is that these articles contain very different source rules and so, at the margin, there may be tax planning as to whether a person providing services is an employee or independent contractor in order to eliminate source country taxation.

Assume that an individual from a residence country needs to be physically present in a source country to provide services for a second party resident in the source country. That person may wish to avoid an employment relationship with the second party as the source state may tax the individual's remuneration for any time spent providing the services in the source state; see above at 3.1.6.1. By contrast, if the individual provides the services as an independent contractor, the source state may tax the services fee only if the individual creates a PE in the source state. This will typically require the individual to create a 'fixed place of business' in the source state, which can be problematic where only services are provided (see above at 3.1.3.2). Even where the tax treaty in question contains a services PE article, that article will typically require that the services be provided for at least six months. In this example, the appropriate tax treatment simply involves the application of Article 15 or Article 7.

[257] Generally regarding the free movement of workers and direct taxation, see European Parliament (2008a, paras. 31–52).

[258] As noted at that point, a business must be 'carried on' at a fixed place for a PE to be established. This is not an express requirement of OECD Model former Art. 14. Question whether this could (or should) make a difference as to the application of Art. 7 compared to former Art. 14, e.g. on the facts of *R* v *Dudney* [2000] FCJ No 230 (FCA).

If the treaty contains the equivalent of Article 14 of the UN Model, the analysis is similar to that where the treaty contains an OECD style services PE article. Under the UN Model, the definition of PE has not been extended to specifically cover the provision of independent services. Rather, Article 14 gives the source state a right to tax if *either* the individual has a fixed base in the source state *or* the individual is present there for 183 days. Former Article 14 in the OECD Model contained the fixed base test only. In the result, since the OECD introduced the possibility of a services PE provision in 2008, the OECD position has moved to a point similar to that in the UN Model, although these points are now achieved through different articles (OECD Article 7 and UN Article 14).

The issues, while essentially the same, become more complex where an employer that is not resident in the source country already employs the individual. Few problems occur where the individual, the services recipient and the non-resident employer are all independent of each other. Here source country taxation of the service fee paid by the services recipient to the non-resident employer will depend on Article 7 of the OECD Model and so on the creation of a PE. Again, a services PE provision in the treaty may be relevant.[259] As for the employee, Article 15 (as limited by Article 15(2)) will determine source country taxation of the employment income. Here it will be taxable if the non-resident employer has created a PE and the wages are 'borne' by that PE. Otherwise, the employment will be taxable only if the individual is present in the source country for 183 days.

As noted above at 3.1.6.1, cases where the individual is related to the non-resident employer or the non-resident employer is related to the services recipient are more concerning for source countries. At that point, an example of the former was given where the service provider intentionally creates an employment with a non-resident employer (e.g. through use of an interposed non-resident services corporation) in an effort to prevent employment with the source country services recipient. In addition to the issues mentioned in the last paragraph, this case raised issues of whether, in substance, the services recipient is to be considered the employer for the purposes of Article 15 of the OECD Model. The case of a non-resident parent providing services to a source country subsidiary is an example where the employer and the services recipient are related. This case essentially

[259] Article 14 of the UN Model is unlikely to apply in this scenario. It applies where an individual provides the services directly and not where an employee of, say, a non-resident corporation provides the services. This is one reason why the UN Model has a PE services provision *in addition to* Article 14. See UN Commentary on Art. 14 para. 9.

raises the same issues and, in particular, whether the subsidiary might be considered the employer.

EU Law One of the fundamental freedoms in the FEU Treaty is dedicated to services. The scope of this freedom was discussed above at 2.1.2.3 and, in particular, two points are worth focusing on in contrast to source country taxing rights under the OECD Model. First, Article 56 of the FEU Treaty covers not only the physical provision of services in another member state but also where the 'person for whom the services are intended' is a national of another member state. Second, Article 57 permits the services provider to 'temporarily pursue his activity in the State where the service is provided'.

These provisions are unlikely to be invoked very often in cases involving treaties based on the OECD Model. This is because of the limited right to tax services under the OECD Model. If a source country does not tax services provided by non-residents then it cannot be accused of discrimination or restricting this freedom. Of course, the source country might have taxing rights where a PE is created or an employee works in the source state but these cases will often involve the freedom of establishment and the free movement of workers rather than the freedom to provide services (see below at 3.3.3). There may be exceptions in particular treaties creating greater source country taxing rights over services and Articles 16 and 17 of the OECD Model create such a right in respect of directors' fees and income of artistes and sportspersons, but these are not considered by this study.

Where a source country has the right to tax and the freedom to provide services is invoked, the primary issue is the deductibility of expenses in deriving services income. The ECJ has shown a tendency to accept that residents and non-residents are comparable as regards the deduction of expenses in providing services. So even where a treaty permits a source state to impose a flat withholding tax on service fees, the freedom to provide services is likely to entitle the non-resident to deduct expenses that have a 'direct connection to the activity pursued'.[260] As noted above at 3.1.4.2 with respect to *Bouanich*, it is only where the gross taxation (which may be at a lower rate) is more than the net taxation of a resident (which may be at a higher rate) that the freedom is breached.

[260] Case C-345/04 *Centro Equestre da Leziria Grande Lda* v *Bundesamt fur Finanzen* (*Centro Equestre*) [2007] ECR I-1425 (ECJ) at para. 23. Also see Case C-234/01 *Gerritse* v *Finanzamt Neukölln-Nord* [2003] ECR I-5933 (ECJ). Both cases involved the taxation of artistic performances.

The freedom to provide services is more likely to be in issue where the source state seeks to indirectly tax services by denying the recipient of the services a deduction for the service fee. This is considered below at 3.2.

3.2 The payer/deductions

OECD Model

The *Base Case* (Figure 1 on p. 5) outlines the basic issues with which this book is concerned. In the context of those issues, heading 3.1 has considered source state taxation of the income recipient, i.e. the taxation of Beth by Country A. The discussion now turns briefly to consider the tax treatment of Allan by Country A. In particular, if Allan pays the rent to Beth in the course of an income earning activity he will seek to deduct the expense. In most countries, this will be available and so the present discussion is concerned with denying Allan a deduction purely because the payment is made to a non-resident, i.e. it is concerned with discrimination based on residence of the recipient.

Denying a deduction for payments to non-residents is an indirect method of taxing the income of non-residents and so if there were no restrictions in this regard it would give source countries an easy method of avoiding the limitation of source country taxing rights considered above at 3.1. Article 24(4) of the OECD Model provides:

> Except where the provisions of paragraph 1 of Article 9, paragraph 6 of Article 11, or paragraph 4 of Article 12, apply, interest, royalties and other disbursements paid by an enterprise of a Contracting State to a resident of the other Contracting State shall, for the purpose of determining the taxable profits of such enterprise, be deductible under the same conditions as if they had been paid to a resident of the first-mentioned State.

For example, assume a scenario in which an individual resident in Country B provides services that are used in Country A and paid for by a Country A resident. The OECD Model grants Country A no right to tax such services and Article 24(4) prevents Country A doing this indirectly by denying its resident a deduction for payment of the service fee.

There are a number of interesting features of Article 24(4) of the OECD Model. First, it applies only to 'payments' made by 'an enterprise' of a state. The 'payment' requirement raises the issue of whether the provision has any application before payment. The US Internal Revenue Service has argued that it can deny a deduction for interest accrued but not paid to a non-resident even though a deduction would be available at the point of accrual where a resident debtor is involved.[261] This is because Article 24(4) is not engaged until the point of payment. This seems a particularly formalistic argument and echoes the issue discussed above at 3.1.4 as to whether Articles 10, 11 or 12 prohibit any withholding tax until there is a payment.

'Enterprise' of a state was discussed above at 3.1.3.1 and raises the issue of whether Article 24(4) of the OECD Model can apply outside the context of a business. Further issues arise when Article 24(4) is compared with the other non-discrimination rules based on residence, i.e. Articles 24(3) and (5). As discussed above at 3.1.3.4, the OECD seeks some consistency in the application of Article 24(3) and (5) despite their difference in wording. In common, however, and unlike Article 24(4), neither Article 24(3) nor (5) is subject to Articles 9, 11(6) or 12(4). This raises particular concerns if there is any potential overlap between Article 24(4), on the one hand, and Article 24(3) and (5), on the other. This is further considered in the context of transfer pricing (below at 3.3.1) and thin capitalisation (below at 3.3.2.2), but it is useful to make a few general comments at this point.

Article 24(5) prevents discriminatory taxation of a resident based on foreign ownership. Article 24(4) prevents discriminatory tax treatment based on the non-residence of the recipient of a payment. These provisions might overlap. For example, suppose a source state denies a resident subsidiary of a non-resident parent corporation a deduction for royalties paid to non-residents (whether related or unrelated). Further, assume the deduction would be available if residents controlled the subsidiary or if the royalties were paid to a resident. In the *Boake Allen* case, Lord Hoffmann said that Article 24(5) was triggered where the different tax treatment was 'solely by reason of' foreign ownership (see above at 3.1.3.4). By analogy, it may be presumed discrimination under Article 24(4) must be 'solely by reason of' the residence of the recipient.

In the present example, the discrimination is not *solely* on the grounds of foreign ownership or *solely* on the grounds of residence of the recipient. It seems inconceivable that neither provision should apply, so which provision should dominate? Before 2008, the OECD Commentary suggested that Article 24(5) of the OECD Model should 'take second place' to Article 24(4).[262] In 2008, the Commentary changed to suggest that, like Article 24(4), Article 24(5) must be read in its 'context' and so as permitting

[261] United States Internal Revenue Service (2009). The US rule was upheld in *Square D Company* v *Commissioner* (2006) 438 F 3d 739 (FCA), but in the context of OECD Model Art. 24(5) not Art. 24(4).

[262] Former OECD Commentary on Art. 24 para. 58.

adjustments under Articles 9(1) and 11(6).[263] The situation is far from satisfactory – particularly as it seeks to read a limitation into Article 24(5) that is express in Article 24(4), the provision that immediately precedes it.

While there is potential overlap between Article 24(4) and (5) of the OECD Model, there is no such potential with respect to Article 24(3) and (4). Because it requires the payer to be an 'enterprise' of the source state (and so a person resident in the source state), Article 24(4) cannot apply with respect to expenses incurred by a source state PE (which is not a person of itself). So how should discrimination against a PE as regards deduction of expenses be prevented? Clearly Article 24(3) has some scope for application. If the activities of an independent source state enterprise would give rise to a deduction for a payment then Article 24(3) suggests a similar deduction should be available to a source state PE.

Further, there is an interesting parallel between Article 24(4) of the OECD Model and the PE deduction provision in Article 7(3), discussed above at 3.1.3.3. While both concern available deductions and, in this respect, serve a similar purpose, their wording and so the scope of each is substantially different. Indeed, the confused relationship between Article 24(4) and (5) is reflected in a reverse confused relationship between Article 7(3) and Article 24(3). Can Article 7(3) apply to permit a deduction even if there is no discrimination under Article 24(3)? Similar to the approach with respect to Article 24(5), the OECD suggests reading down the broader provision, i.e. Article 7(3), so that it does not mandate deductions but rather prevents denying them on the basis of whether they serve a dual purpose or they are made outside the source country (see above at 3.1.3.4). As mentioned at 3.1.3.3, the OECD proposes to delete Article 7(3) from the Model in 2010.

EU Law

When it comes to the deduction of expenses paid to non-residents, the relationship between Articles 7(3) and 24(3), (4) and (5) of the OECD Model is somewhat confused. Consistent with the discussion above at 3.1.3.4, the situation is less confusing under EU Law, though still requires careful analysis. Generally, if a resident incurs an expense in favour of a resident of another EU member state the freedom to provide services is likely to be in issue, i.e. Article 56 of the FEU Treaty. As noted above at 3.1.6.2, this freedom includes the situation in which the

[263] OECD Commentary on Art. 24 para. 79.

beneficiary of the services is in the source state and the service provider is in another state, even if the services are not physically provided in the source state.

It is clear that the freedom to provide services applies not only to direct discrimination in the form of taxation of the services provider but also to indirect discrimination in the form of the denial of a deduction for the service fee paid by the beneficiary of the services. For example, in *Skandia* the corporation paid premiums for an employee's pension to affiliated insurance companies in other EU member states.[264] It was denied an immediate deduction for the payment, which would have been available if the premium was paid to a Swedish insurance company. The ECJ held this breached the freedom of the EU insurance companies to provide services in Sweden.

In the similar case of *European Commission* v *Denmark*,[265] a Danish rule granted deduction for payments made under a pension or life insurance contract only if the recipient was a Danish fund. The ECJ held this violated not only the freedom to provide services but also the free movement of workers and the freedom of establishment (though not the free movement of capital), depending on the facts of each case. In particular, the ECJ noted that nationals of a member state might be deterred from establishing themselves in another member state if that state denied a deduction for payments to non-residents.[266] Interestingly, this reasoning need not involve discrimination of the national exercising their right of establishment (see above at 2.2.1).

This reasoning can be applied to source state subsidiaries of non-resident parent corporations. More importantly, it can also be applied to a source state PE, which, as noted at 3.1.3.4, is generally comparable to a subsidiary. This takes care of a difficulty that might otherwise arise in the context of the freedom to provide services. Article 56 of the FEU Treaty seems to require that the establishment providing the services be situated in a different state from the nationality of the beneficiary of the services. So, it does not easily apply where the beneficiary of the services is a PE, situated in one member state, of a national of another member state and the service provider has the same nationality as the beneficiary.

[264] Case C-422/01 *Forsakringsaktiebolaget Skandia* v *Riksskatteverket* [2003] ECR I-6817 (ECJ).

[265] Case C-150/04 *European Commission* v *Denmark* [2007] ECR I-1163 (ECJ).

[266] Case C-150/04 *European Commission* v *Denmark* [2007] ECR I-1163 (ECJ) at para. 44.

EU case law in this area also reveals an inherent limitation in Article 24(4) of the OECD Model. It expressly applies only to 'deductions' for various expenses. Rather than granting deductions, some countries grant tax credits in respect of expenditure incurred. This is particularly the case with respect to research and development (R&D) costs. The availability of such credits is often limited to payments by or to resident persons. It is not clear how such discrimination would breach Article 24(4), though in an appropriate case it may breach Article 24(3) or (5). By contrast, *Commission* v *Spain* is a case in which the ECJ held that discriminatory provision of R&D credits breached both the freedom of establishment and the freedom to provide services.[267]

3.3 Quantification and characterisation issues

Above at 1.1, payments were identified as the building blocks of the income tax base. At that point, four fundamental features of a payment were identified that are particularly important in an international setting. The purpose of this heading is to discuss some of the more important issues for source countries that arise from the *quantification* and *characterisation* features of a payment. The first is the thorny issue of quantifying the price of transactions between associated persons, i.e. persons that are related. Related party dealings are a problem for all income taxes, but, in an international setting, related parties may price dealings in a way that erodes a source country's tax base, i.e. that underquantifies the amount of income derived in a source country.

The second and third subheadings focus on characterisation issues. The second subheading is concerned with the inherent fungibility (substitutability) of different types of income and, particularly, focuses on the dividing line drawn in the OECD Model in the definitions of 'dividends', 'interest' and 'royalties'. In this case, the choice is with a payment being one *or* another but in other cases a particular payment or item of income may be simultaneously characterised in more than one manner. As the OECD Model (and EU Law) has different rules that depend on type of income or activity, the question in these dual characterisation cases is under which of two or more applicable rules may a source state claim taxing rights, i.e. the final subheading deals with characterisation reconciliation rules.

[267] Case C-248/06 *European Commission* v *Spain* [2008] ECR I-47 (ECJ).

3.3.1 *Quantification: transfer pricing between associates*

Some transactions do not involve cash payments, such as where an employee provides labour in return for fringe benefits. These types of transaction cause particular difficulty for income taxes, as what is in effect a barter transaction must be quantified for tax purposes. Most transactions, however, involve the provision of goods or services in return for a cash payment. Domestically, these transactions are simple to quantify as the cash payment is the appropriate measure. Difficulties arise even with cash transactions where the parties do not behave in an economically independent fashion, particularly if they are part of a single economic unit. The classic example of a single economic unit that is made up of different persons is the family, but a corporate group is in many senses comparable.

The members of a group may behave in a way as to manipulate which member of the group derives income. If all members of the group are taxed in the same manner, or as a group, then there is little or no incentive to manipulate which group member derives income. But in most countries this is not the case, particularly for families in the face of progressive taxation. Every tax law must decide how to treat associated or related persons and dealings between them for tax purposes. There is a spectrum of options. At one extreme, each member of the group is separately recognised and dealings between them are priced as though they were independent of each other. At the other extreme, the group is identified as a single taxpayer. Between these extremes, there are varying degrees of recognition of the separate nature of group members and yet not treating them as fully independent of other members of the group, e.g. where a transaction between group members is recognised for tax purposes but cannot give rise to a gain or a loss.

The situation becomes more difficult in an international setting. Here even cash transactions may have to be quantified for tax purpose if they are denominated in a foreign currency. Further, because tax rates vary across countries, manipulation of in which country income is derived always results in a tax benefit. This risk of manipulation becomes particularly acute in the context of multinational groups of corporations. Multinationals are made up of numerous member corporations conducting business in various countries and yet all these members are part of the same economic unit, i.e. the multinational. For such a group, it will pay to derive income in low tax countries and locate deductions in high tax countries.

This potential for cross-border manipulation raises a fundamental issue of income taxation. In a cross-border setting, what should an income tax seek to tax? At 1.1, it was noted that an income tax is fundamentally a tax on wealth created. With respect to taxation based on residence, the tax is on all creations of wealth allocated to a taxpayer irrespective of where the creation occurs. With taxation based on source of income, it seems logical that the tax should be fundamentally based on wealth created in a particular jurisdiction irrespective of to whom that wealth is allocated. To use another, yet dangerous analogy, under an income tax a source country should seek to tax all value added within its jurisdiction. This is consistent with the fundamental nature of the income tax. The question then becomes one of how best to measure wealth created in a particular country or allocate wealth created to it.

The most obvious method of providing this measure of value added within a particular jurisdiction is to leave it to market forces. If goods or services are provided cross border between independent parties the pricing of the transaction will naturally take account of the value added in the jurisdiction from which the provision occurs. In practice, the situation can become complex, not least because of the difficulty of determining the country from which a provision is made, i.e. the geographical source, but in theory, this seems possible. If this is acceptable then it suggests that, when the parties to a cross-border transaction are related, their transactions should be priced as though they were independent. In that way, the value added in a particular jurisdiction may be largely quantified and there is consistency in the measurement of the tax base between competitors in the same market.[268]

While as a general principle it is true to suggest that arm's length pricing of transactions between related parties focuses on value added in a particular jurisdiction, it does not get at all value added by related parties. One of the main reasons for creating multinationals is the additional value that comes from the creation of large conglomerates, i.e. firm specific benefits, economies of scale. As Vann points out, arm's length pricing of individual transactions does not allocate profits attributable to this additional value added between the countries where a multinational does its business.[269] Rather, it

[268] This is the OECD's primary justification for use of the arm's length principle, see OECD (1995–2000, para. 1.7).

[269] Vann (2003, p. 141) notes that '[i]f transactions at market prices do not account for all the value added by a firm, there are at least two strategies to deal with the matter within a regime based on adjusting prices and not transactions. The additional value can be left as a residual that effectively belongs to the chosen company that holds the rights and its jurisdiction, or the value can be spread over the firm on some express or implied transactional basis'.

seems the residual falls to be taxed by the country in which members of the multinational are resident. This gives large scope for tax planning.[270]

The problem with using a separate and independent entity approach is that to do this accurately involves the specific quantification of every transaction between related parties by reference to market value pricing. The process can be exceptionally complex. The alternative is to adopt a more arbitrary approach and involves, to varying extents, failing to recognise the members of a group as separate entities. At the extreme, an economic group is considered a single taxpayer and the group income is apportioned between jurisdictions based on some sort of formula involving the location of factors of production, i.e. factors that typically produce income.

The OECD Model has a number of rules that address manipulation of the tax base and still more qualifications scattered throughout the Commentary dealing with treaty abuse. The discussion under this subheading is primarily concerned with the rules in Articles 7(2) and 9(1) of the Model. It begins with a general consideration of the types of economic relationship between separate persons recognised under the Model, i.e. who are associated or related persons. It continues to consider the dominant approach underlying the Model, which involves the separate and independent entity approach. As noted at 2.1.1.1, the OECD Model treats members of an economic group separately. This subheading considers the special rules that prescribe that transactions between such members must be quantified on the presumption that they act independently of each other. This is the arm's length pricing criteria. The discussion then briefly considers the limited (and waning) recognition of formulary apportionment under the OECD Model. Finally, the situation under the OECD Model is compared with that under EU Law.

3.3.1.1 Identifying associates

The OECD Model incorporates a number of provisions where the relationship between two persons is important. Many of these are of a different nature and use different concepts. These rules may be grouped into three broad categories. The first covers provisions where the tax status or treatment of a person depends on their relationship with another person. So, for example, whether or not a person has a PE may depend on whether the

[270] Some features of the OECD Transfer Pricing Guidelines might be viewed as directed towards allocating this additional value added, but a detailed consideration of these is beyond the scope of this study. See Vann (2003, pp. 145–6, 168) and OECD (1995–2000, paras. 3.2–3.57, 6.1–8.43, Annex 2).

person is acting through a dependent or independent agent, Article 5(5) and (6) (see above at 3.1.3.3). There is a loose connection here with former Article 14 and Article 15, which before 2000 were entitled 'independent persons services' and 'dependent personal services' (now 'income from employment'), respectively. Employment is largely a question of the relationship with the person engaging the services. An employee cannot be an independent agent for the purposes of Article 5(6) but even an independent contractor may be insufficiently independent to qualify. So, the concept of independence is used in a somewhat different sense depending on its context.

Two provisions that are particularly relevant to the tax status and treatment of corporations are Articles 5(7) and 24(5) of the OECD Model. The former provision (see above at 3.1.3.3) prevents, without more, a subsidiary creating a PE of a parent corporation and vice versa. It expressly refers to 'companies' and 'control' or being 'controlled'. The non-discrimination rule in Article 24(5) was discussed above at 3.1.3.4. It simultaneously refers to 'enterprises' and 'capital of' them, and so while it clearly covers corporations it is not clear what other types of persons conducting an enterprise are covered. The capital must be 'owned or controlled' by the second person. So, while Article 5(7) refers to control of the company, Article 24(5) refers to ownership or control of capital in an enterprise and partial ownership or control is sufficient.

There are three provisions where the relationship between two persons may affect the rate of tax that may be charged by the source country. The first is the lower tax rate for non-portfolio dividends in Article 10(2) of the OECD Model, discussed above at 3.1.4.1. Like Article 5(7), it refers to 'companies' but like Article 24(5) it refers to 'capital' in the distributing company, this time with the specification of at least a 25 per cent direct holding. Further, whereas Article 24(5) refers to capital 'owned or controlled', Article 10(2) simply refers to 'holding' capital. The other two provisions are Article 11(6) and Article 12(4), which are similar. These provisions deal with excessive interest and royalty payments arising from a 'special relationship' between the payer and the payee. The former is discussed further below at 3.3.2.2. The excessive amount may be taxed under the domestic law of the source state without the rate limitations in Articles 11 and 12.

The taxation preserved by Articles 11(6) and 12(4) of the OECD Model also falls into the third category of situation where the relationship between two persons is relevant, that of profit calculation. The right that these provisions preserve is that 'the payments shall remain taxable according to' domestic law. The OECD is clearly of the opinion that this may be direct taxation, e.g. through withholding tax, or indirect taxation, e.g. through re-characterisation and denying the payer a deduction for the interest or royalties.[271] There are two further provisions where the relationship between two persons may affect profit calculation, Articles 7(2) and 9(1). These provisions are related although Article 7(2) deals only with a fictitious relationship between a PE and the rest of the enterprise on the presumption that they are separate enterprises (see above at 3.1.3.3).

The primary focus of the rest of this subheading is Article 9(1) of the OECD Model. The above discussion provides a useful context in which to analyse some of the features of Article 9(1). It provides-

> Where
> a) an enterprise of a Contracting State participates directly or indirectly in the management, control or capital of an enterprise of the other Contracting State, or
> b) the same persons participate directly or indirectly in the management, control or capital of an enterprise of a Contracting State and an enterprise of the other Contracting State,
>
> and in either case conditions are made or imposed between the two enterprises in their commercial or financial relations which differ from those which would be made between independent enterprises, then any profits which would, but for those conditions, have accrued to one of the enterprises, but, by reason of those conditions, have not so accrued, may be included in the profits of that enterprise and taxed accordingly.

Unlike Articles 11(6) and 12(4), which simply preserve the application of domestic tax law, Article 9(1) authorises an increase in profits that may or may not be supported by domestic tax law. If domestic law does not support Article 9(1), the risk is that it will be viewed as an ineffective attempt to create a charge to tax by treaty (see above at 1.2.2).[272] Most countries, including the UK, support Article 9(1) with a domestic law right to adjust prices between related parties for tax purposes.[273]

[271] OECD Commentary on Art. 11 para. 35.

[272] This was a reason for the domestic introduction of transfer pricing rules in the UK in the Finance Act 1951, shortly after the UK began developing a tax treaty network. See Harris and Oliver (2008, p. 256).

[273] The UK rules are in TIOPA 2010 Part 4 (ss. 146–217) and incorporate features from OECD Model Art. 9 as well as the OECD Transfer Pricing Guidelines, discussed below at 3.3.1.2.

In many countries, this domestic law right to adjust prices does not extend to transactions between two resident enterprises, i.e. the transfer pricing rules have international application only.[274] The OECD is of the opinion that such unbalanced application of transfer pricing rules does not contravene Article 24(5). That provision applies only where the discrimination is due to the ownership and control of capital in a subsidiary and, apparently, that test is not met where the transfer pricing rules apply generally to cross-border transactions between associates. In such a case, the application of the rules to associates is too broad to constitute a breach of Article 24(5).[275]

Article 9(1) authorises adjustment by way of attribution of additional profits directly or the disallowance of expenses, often called a primary adjustment. Further, like Articles 11(6) and 12(4), the OECD considers that Article 9(1) authorises re-characterisation of the adjusted amount, often called a 'secondary adjustment'. For example, suppose that a subsidiary transfers goods to its parent corporation but the parent pays less than the market value of the goods. In such a case, there has been a value transfer from the subsidiary to the parent amounting to the difference between the value of the goods and the price paid. The tax laws of some countries involve a secondary adjustment characterising this shortfall as a dividend distributed by the subsidiary to the parent corporation. If the value is transferred from the parent to the subsidiary, it may be characterised as a loan or capital contribution. This happens only to a limited extent under UK tax law.[276]

Like Article 24(4) and (5), Article 9(1) of the OECD Model refers only to 'enterprises' and therefore raises the question as to whether it can have any application outside the context of a business. In particular, question whether Article 9(1) can apply to income from land (Article 6) or income from employment (Article 15), the better view seems to be it cannot unless, in the former case, a business is involved. This is reinforced by the reference to 'commercial or financial relations' in Article 9(1) and the existence of Articles 11(6) and 12(4), which, with respect to the passive holding of loans or intellectual property, can protect source country taxation in a

[274] This is not the case with the UK transfer pricing rules, which, like most European countries, also apply domestically.

[275] OECD Commentary on Art. 24 para. 79. The OECD continues that in any case Art. 24(5) of the Model must be read in 'context' and so adjustments under Art. 9(1) 'could not be considered to violate the provisions of paragraph 5'.

[276] For example, excessive interest may be characterised as a distribution by CTA 2010 s. 1000(1)E.

similar manner as Article 9(1).[277] It will be noted that the non-discrimination rule for deductible payments in Article 24(4) (discussed above at 3.2) is specifically subject to each of Articles 9(1), 11(6) and 12(4).

Further, Article 9(1) of the OECD Model refers to 'participating' and this contrasts with Article 5(7) 'control', Article 10(2) 'holding' and Article 24(5) 'owning or controlling'. What must be participated in under Article 9(1) is 'management, control or capital' of an enterprise and this contrasts with Article 5(7) 'company', Article 10(2) 'capital' and Article 24(5) 'capital'. In this respect, the potential scope of Article 9(1) seems substantially greater than these other provisions and consistency seems to have played little role in drafting these four provisions.[278] One potential limitation is that Article 9(1) does not easily apply to related individuals, its terminology being more apt for artificial entities. To apply to individuals, there must be two businesses conducted by two individuals and one individual in the context of their business must 'participate' in the business of the other individual.

Article 9(1) of the OECD Model compares conditions imposed between the related enterprises with those that would have occurred between 'independent' enterprises. Indeed, the type of relationship required between the enterprises to trigger Article 9(1) is so loosely defined that lack of 'independence' seems the dominant test. 'Independence' plays an important role in other provisions of the OECD Model. It is the test used in determining whether an agent can create a PE of their principal under Article 5(5) and (6). It is also used in the definition of 'business' in Article 3(1) due to the deletion of Article 14, which also used the term in apparent contra distinction to employment where 'control by the employer is an important feature'.[279] Article 7(2) also uses the concept. For purposes of determining profits attributable to a PE, it treats a PE not only as a hypothetical separate enterprise (see above at 3.1.3.3) but also on the assumption that its dealings with the rest of the enterprise are conducted 'independently'.

It is a matter for debate whether 'independence' is to be interpreted consistently in each of these four provisions. However, it is clear that the OECD believe that it is used consistently in Articles 7(2) and 9(1)

277 This is also supported by the possible extension of OECD Model Art. 21 mentioned in the Commentary on Art. 21 para. 7.

278 UK domestic implementation of this OECD Model Art. 9(1) requirement is more specific and based on a statutory definition of 'control' of a body corporate or partnership: see TIOPA 2010 s. 157.

279 Avery Jones et al. (2006, p. 756).

of the OECD Model. They suggest that what is required is a comparison with arm's length pricing, i.e. market value of goods and services. While Article 7(2) refers to 'dealings' and Article 9(1) to 'conditions in commercial and financial relations', this difference in terminology is a consequence of the fact that, in legal terms, a PE cannot *transact* with the enterprise of which it is a part but, apparently, it can 'deal' with it.[280] The same approach to transfer pricing should be used under both Articles 7(2) and 9(1).

3.3.1.2 Independent enterprise approach

The independent enterprise approach to profit determination in the OECD Model applies both to transactions between associated enterprises and recognised dealings between PEs and the enterprise of which they are a part. In accordance with this approach, transactions between associates should be priced at an arm's length amount for tax purposes. Arm's length pricing is not an exact science and often there is a range of such prices. In 1979, the OECD published guidelines for transfer pricing methodologies that should be used in arriving at an arm's length price for the purposes of the OECD Model. An important revision of these guidelines was published in 1995, which is revised periodically.[281]

Vann outlines the general approach under the guidelines as follows:

> The guidelines and the modern transfer-pricing analysis begin with a functional analysis to identify the functions undertaken by various entities in the relevant corporate group in the light of the assets used and risks assumed by each of them. The pricing of transactions is subsequently undertaken based on this analysis which is designed to identify the value drivers as a means of allocating profits among the members of the group.[282]

Transfer pricing is a highly specialised field, in which economists play no small part. There are few purely legal issues that arise (other than whether arm's length pricing of individual transactions is appropriate) and negotiation and documentation is an important feature of transfer pricing in practice. The following discussion is a brief overview of the main features including some of the special issues that arise for PEs.

[280] UK domestic implementation uses the word 'transaction', which is defined broadly in TIOPA 2010 s. 150.

[281] OECD (1995–2000). Regarding the background to the OECD Transfer Pricing Guidelines, see Vann (2004, pp. 135–9).

[282] Vann (2006, p. 377).

Arm's length pricing The OECD Transfer Pricing Guidelines authorise various methods for establishing an arm's length price. These are usually divided into three 'traditional transaction methods' and two acceptable 'other methods'. One pricing methodology may be more appropriate in certain types of transactions. Further, the relative availability of appropriate data or documentation may make some methodologies more reliable in determining an arm's length price. In the case of each method, the key issue is comparability. The Guidelines outline five comparability factors; characteristics of the property or services, functional analysis, contractual terms, economic circumstances and business strategies.[283]

Generally, the preferred approach is the 'comparable uncontrolled price' method or 'CUP'.[284] An arm's length price is established by reference to sales of similar products made between unrelated persons in similar circumstances. An internal CUP compares the related party price with that charged or paid by the enterprise in transactions with unrelated parties. For example, if a manufacturer of mobile phones sells those phones to a subsidiary in another country the transfer price may be set by reference to the price charged for those phones by the parent corporation to an independent third party. An external CUP compares the price charged between related parties with the price paid between wholly unrelated parties for a similar product. In this case the price charged by the parent corporation to the subsidiary would be determined by reference to the price charged for a similar phone by a competitor in a similar market.

A problem with the CUP method is that many transactions that initially appear comparable can be distinguished. The sort of factors that are relevant include market size and market share, packaging, time of sale (e.g. same season), turnover rate, unique features, geographical market distinctions and comparative bargaining power. In *DSG Retail Ltd* v *RCC* [2009] UKFTT TC00001 (TC), the latter made finding a CUP difficult. An additional factor is the extent of marketing and packaging assistance provided to the related party. Transactions are not comparable where the goods and services are so special that there is no external market for them

283 OECD (1995–2000, paras. 1.19–1.35).

284 This preference was upheld in the Canadian case of *GlaxoSmithKline Inc.* v *The Queen* [2008] TCC 324 (TC). In that case, the court held that the price paid to a related party by a Canadian distributor for the active pharmaceutical ingredient in ulcer medication should, for tax purposes, be compared to third-party manufacturers' sales of a generic version of the medication in Canada (i.e. an external CUP). It rejected use of the resale price method or use of the TNM method (see below) as a reasonableness check on the price paid for the ingredient.

and they are not offered for sale to third parties. This is often the case with semi-finished products or technology transfers. Another point of distinction arises when the transfer occurs at a different stage of production or distribution or due to differences in volume or after sales services, e.g. manufacturers' guarantees.

Where a CUP is not readily available, it may be appropriate to use one of the other traditional methods. The resale price method involves establishing an arm's length price by subtracting an appropriate mark-up from the price at which the goods are ultimately sold to unrelated parties. The mark-up should represent the re-seller's costs and some profit. This method is most appropriate when apportioning consulting or marketing charges. A difficulty with this method is ascertaining an appropriate mark-up, especially where the related re-seller adds value to the product. The mark-up percentage should be that of a typical distributor engaging in similar activities. It is also difficult to use this method if significant time passes between when the re-seller purchases the goods from the related party and when it resells them to an independent party. With the resale price method the comparison of the product is not as critical as comparing the mark-up of an independent sales agent if the re-seller's functions, terms and risks are comparable. A feature of this method is that the distributor always makes a profit, i.e. for tax purposes, entrepreneurial risk is allocated to the manufacturer/supplier.

The other traditional pricing method recognised by the OECD is the cost plus method. This establishes an arm's length price using the manufacturing and other costs of the related seller as the starting point. An appropriate percentage of profit is added to these costs. This method is often appropriate when determining the arm's length price of semi-finished products sold between related parties (especially where a valuable brand name is attached by the purchaser) or for the provision of services. A difficulty with this method is determining an appropriate margin and cost base on which to add a mark-up. Under this method, the manufacturer always makes a profit, i.e. for tax purposes, entrepreneurial risk is allocated to the purchaser of the goods. Further, this method depresses the incentive of the producer to save costs, i.e. the higher the costs the higher the profit.

When none of the traditional methods yields a satisfactory result, the OECD approves two other methods. It proposes to give these equal status with the traditional methods; selection will depend solely on the most appropriate method in the circumstances. One other method is the Transactional Net Margin Method, or 'TNM', which is based on the Comparable Profits Method, or 'CPM'.[285] These methods involve the comparison of an enterprise's profitability with that of a similar business enterprise. It evaluates whether the amount charged in a controlled transaction is arm's length based on objective measures of profitability derived from business activities under similar circumstances.[286] The idea is to establish an arm's length range of profits on a set of transactions. If the taxpayer's reported profits are within the range, then its transfer prices are accepted for tax purposes. If the profits are not within the range, a tax administration can adjust the profits, typically to the midpoint of the range.

As with other methods that rely on external market benchmarks, the greater the degree of comparability between the controlled and uncontrolled parties, the more reliable the results derived from the application of TNM/CPM. The degree of comparability depends on features such as relevant lines of business, the product or service market, the asset composition employed, the size and scope of operations and the stage in a business or product cycle. The degree of functional comparability required to obtain a reliable result under TNM/CPM is generally less than that required under the re-sale price or cost plus methods, and thus, product similarity is not as crucial. Under TNM/CPM, adjustments should be made to comparables to account for differences in business characteristics such as economic conditions, risks, product lifecycle and similar.

The second 'other' method recognised by the OECD is the profit split method. Under this method, the worldwide profits of a multinational are allocated among its members in proportion to their contribution by reference to functions performed, risks assumed and resources employed. The OECD suggests that this method may be useful in the absence of comparables. It notes that this method is particularly appropriate in circumstances where 'independent enterprises might decide to set up a form of partnership and agree to a form of profits split'.[287] The division may be of the total profits or a residual profit that remains after the division of profits that can be allocated under other methods. This method is not based on individual transactions. A difficulty is how to determine an appropriate profit

[285] The difference between the two is that with TNM the OECD seeks to maintain a transaction focus even though, like CPM, it is concerned with a comparison of net margins. There is some scepticism about whether TNM maintains a transaction focus.

[286] These profit level indicators are financial ratios that measure the relationships among profits, costs and resources, e.g. profits to capital, profits to gross sales, profits to operating expenses.

[287] OECD (1995–2000, para. 3.5).

split. The OECD identifies comparing the way profits are split between uncontrolled persons that are engaged in comparable activities as one possible approach. A difficulty is that such information is often confidential and so inaccessible to the taxpayer, although it may be in the hands of tax administrations through contact with other taxpayers.

Problem areas: services and intellectual property Each particular transaction between members of a multinational group must be analysed to determine the most appropriate approach to transfer pricing for them. Often it will be possible to identify a comparable where the sale or use of tangible goods are involved or in financing transactions, such as where money is loaned, although even these have their problems. Two particularly difficult areas that are singled out for special consideration in the OECD Transfer Pricing Guidelines are the provision of intangible property and the provision of services. If the intangible or services are sold in the ordinary course of business, few problems arise. The difficulties occur where the intangible or services is something that is not provided to third parties and, by its nature, that possibility would not be considered.

The problem with pricing the sale or use of intangible property is that it is often unique and so there is an absence of comparables. For tax administrations, there is a temptation to use hindsight based on profits generated by the user of intangible property to determine what should have been a market price. The US has been notorious in adjusting the value of royalties charged periodically based on profits derived from use of intellectual property. This may occur irrespective of whether the royalties were fixed at a time when facts to support profitability were not available. A similar approach has been applied to sales of intellectual property, especially where unrelated parties would not have engaged in such a sale, to value the sale price as the present value of profits subsequently generated from use of the property. The OECD cautiously endorses this approach.[288]

With services, the difficulties often revolve around management or administrative services and stewardship or shareholder services. Often, management and administrative services are not comparable to services performed by an independent service provider. In such a case, the cost plus method is often appropriate. In most countries, stewardship expenses may not be allocated to the related party to which the expense pertains. The valuation of a service requires an understanding of the function of each entity and its role in the group. Relevant factors include

[288] OECD (1995–2000, paras. 6.33–6.35).

the identification of the type of service supplied, whether any benefit has been conferred and an evaluation of an appropriate charge.

The OECD Transfer Pricing Guidelines proceed to consider cost contribution arrangements, which are most commonly used with respect to research and development, the mining industry and group management services. These arrangements are a method of group members sharing costs and benefits of a particular activity. In order to be recognised for tax purposes, the arrangement will be in the form of a legally binding contract and should be limited to parties that may benefit from the activity in question. Parties to the agreement should bear costs in proportion to expected benefits and the keeping of records in this regard is crucial. The importance of these arrangements should not be underestimated. One author has commented that 'cost sharing is probably the key element in current transfer pricing law because it is the principal way in which profits from intangibles get shifted from the United States to low-tax jurisdictions'.[289]

Administrative matters In general, it is in the taxpayer's interest to maintain adequate documentation to justify particular pricing policies. Whether available documentation is adequate is a question of interpretation. Documentation is of greater reliability if it is contemporaneous. In recent years, countries have raised the hurdle with respect to the requirements of transfer pricing documentation. In 2005, in an effort to promote greater uniformity in these requirements within the EU, the EU approved a code of conduct on transfer pricing that standardises the documents that companies must provide for cross-border transactions.[290] This code requires members of a corporate group with cross-border intra-group transactions to file two different sets of transfer pricing documentation. The first contains general information about the corporation's type of business activity, its cross-border transactions, and its transfer pricing policy and is available to all relevant member states. The second set is country specific and details transactions taking place in a member state, contractual terms and information about the corporation's transfer pricing methods.

Recognising that transfer pricing is often a question of negotiation, many countries permit their tax administrations to enter into binding advance pricing agreements (or APAs) with taxpayers. These agreements

[289] Avi-Yonah (2009).

[290] See van Raad (2009, pp. 2363–8).

set a pre-determined level of pricing for transactions between related parties of a multinational group. Their purpose is to create greater certainty for multinationals in planning their tax obligations. Unilateral APAs are quite common but bilateral agreements less so. A US academic has suggested that 'about half of the approximately 350 multinational companies enter into APAs'.[291] The UK made legislative provision for APAs in 1999.[292] For bilateral APAs, the UK relies on the existence of a mutual agreement article in the relevant double tax treaty. The mutual agreement article is further discussed below at 7.2.1.

Special PE issues Independent pricing is also a critical feature in the application of Article 7(2) of the OECD Model. The main difference is that whereas Article 9(1) generally applies to transactions between *real* entities, Article 7(2) applies to PEs as a *deemed* entity. So in the case of Article 7(2) there are two fictions, the PE as an entity and independent pricing; in Article 9(1) there is only one. The main problem for Article 7(2) is identifying dealings to which arm's length pricing can attach. This was discussed above at 3.1.3.3. Once those dealings have been identified and characterised, the application of arm's length pricing is similar to that under Article 9(1) and here, once again, the OECD Transfer Pricing Guidelines are relevant.

In its present form, it might be questioned why independent pricing is required under Article 7(2) of the OECD Model in addition to that prescribed by Article 9(1). Might Article 7(2) simply deal with the separate entity aspect leaving Article 9(1) to prescribe the independent pricing? No doubt, this would be possible. At present, Article 9(1) requires one associated enterprise to be 'of a Contracting State' and the other 'of the other Contracting State'. As discussed above at 3.1.3.1, this requires each enterprise to be held by a person resident in each state, and so Article 9(1) cannot apply to two enterprises of the same person.[293] Further, as discussed above at 3.1.3.3, in deeming a PE to be a separate enterprise, Article 7(2) does not prescribe that the PE is an enterprise 'of' a particular state. So, Article 9(1) cannot apply directly to a PE. Rather, in transactions between a PE and associated enterprises of the enterprise that holds the PE, Article 9(1) can affect the profit calculation only through first applying Article 9(1) between the associated enterprises and then applying Article 7(2) to the result.

[291] Avi-Yonah (2009).

[292] Now TIOPA 2010 Part 5 (ss. 218–30).

[293] A person may have more than one enterprise, see Avery Jones et al. (2006, p. 702).

If the PE were deemed by Article 7(2) of the OECD Model to be an enterprise of the country in which it is located, then Article 9(1) could apply both to transactions between the PE and associated enterprise of the enterprise that holds the PE and, possibly, to dealing between the PE and the rest of its enterprise. The problem with such an approach is that, as an enterprise of the country in which it is located, the PE would be deemed a resident of that country, at least indirectly. This would raise confusion as to whether the PE could access the treaty network of that country, further discussed below at 5.2.3.1. Of course, the PE could be deemed an enterprise of the country in which it is located just for the purposes of Articles 7 and 9. At present, the OECD is of the view that a PE is deemed a separate person only for the purposes of Article 7.

3.3.1.3 Formulary apportionment

An inability to determine precise prices according to the arm's length principle and the high compliance costs of attempting to do so have led over the years to many suggestions that international taxation should move to a method of formulary apportionment. Advocates are often from federal countries that apply formulary apportionment in allocating the tax base for state or provincial income tax purposes.[294] Despite these suggestions, the OECD remains wed to the arm's length principle. Indeed, the OECD is moving away from formulary apportionment in the one area in which it is authorised.

Article 7(4) of the OECD Model preserves the right of a country to apply customary methods of apportionment to the total profits of an enterprise in determining the profits attributable to a PE. This has often been done by applying a formula and has been commonly applied to insurance companies. The OECD accepts that using Article 7(4) results in the override of attribution based on separate accounting prepared by a PE. However, use of this method is qualified not only by the need that it be 'customary' but also by the requirement that it gives an allocation that 'can fairly be said to be in accordance with the principles contained in the Article'.[295] Accordingly, the formulary apportionment is supposed to be consistent with the arm's length principle, something that the OECD now accepts is not possible.[296] This inconsistency is recognised by Article 7(6), which is meant to restrict alternating from year to year between methods of

[294] For example, see Avi-Yonah and Clausing (2007).

[295] OECD Commentary on Art. 7 para. 52.

[296] OECD (2008a, para. 296).

attribution. Like Article 7(3) and (5) (discussed above at 3.1.3.3), Article 7(4) and (6) are to be deleted from the Model in 2010. They will remain a feature of tax treaties for years to come.

3.3.1.4 EU Law

EU Law interfaces with transfer pricing rules in three areas. First, the EU Joint Transfer Pricing Forum specialises in dispute avoidance and resolution procedures between EU member states with respect to transfer pricing. This Forum has issued proposed guidelines on advance pricing agreements.[297] It also oversees a special dispute resolution procedure, which is briefly considered at 7.2.2. Second, there is a question as to the extent to which discriminatory treatment that prima facie breaches one of the fundamental freedoms can be justified by reference to the arm's length principle. Third, the European Commission is currently developing a proposal for an EU consolidated tax base for group corporations that involves adoption of formulary apportionment as a means of allocating the tax base between member states. The latter two are briefly considered in turn.

Fundamental freedoms As noted above at 3.3.1.1, some countries apply their transfer pricing rules only to international transactions between associates. The same is true of thin capitalisation rules, which, as discussed below at 3.3.2.2, are related to transfer pricing rules. This was the situation with respect to both Germany's and the UK's thin capitalisation rules. In its landmark decision in *Lankhorst-Hohorst* in 2002, the ECJ decided that this unbalanced approach under the German rules breached the freedom of establishment as it constituted a restriction on EU corporations establishing German subsidiaries.[298] The Germans sought to justify their rules on various grounds including anti-avoidance and the 'internationally recognised arm's length principle'. The ECJ rejected these arguments, pointing out that the rules were not limited to 'wholly artificial arrangements'. In hindsight, it appears that the argument based on the arm's length principle was not sufficiently linked to that of tax avoidance.

This case represented a substantial divergence between EU Law and the OECD Model. As noted above at 3.3.1.1, the OECD is of the opinion that the application of Article 9(1) is not limited by the non-discrimination rule in Article 24(5) and Article 24(4) is expressly subject to Article 9(1).

[297] European Commission (2007a).

[298] Case C-324/00 *Lankhorst-Hohorst GmbH* v *Finanzamt Steinfurt* [2002] ECR 2002 I-11779 (ECJ).

Due to the decision in *Lankhorst-Hohorst*, Germany amended its thin capitalisation rules to apply domestically as well as internationally. The UK responded by substantially restricting the scope of its thin capitalisation rules and applying its transfer pricing rules domestically as well as internationally.[299] The pre-2004 UK thin capitalisation rules came before the ECJ in the *Thin Cap Group Litigation* case.[300]

In the *Thin Cap Group Litigation* case, the ECJ again decided that the limited application of thin capitalisation rules to just international transactions was a restriction on the freedom of establishment. However, the UK argued that these rules were needed to protect against tax avoidance and limiting them by reference to the arm's length principle was proportionate. The ECJ accepted this approach. In particular, application of the arm's length principle was a proportionate method providing objective and verifiable elements in determining whether a transaction was purely artificial. The qualification was that the taxpayer be given an opportunity 'to provide evidence of any commercial justification that there may have been for' the transaction.[301] The ECJ followed the *Thin Cap* case in *NV Lammers and Van Cleeff* to strike down a Belgian provision that reclassified interest paid to a non-resident as a dividend (and so denied a deduction) according to a specified formula. The provision breached the freedom of establishment because 'it cannot be ruled out that that reclassification will also apply to interest paid on loans granted on an arm's length basis'.[302] *Société de Gestion* involved a more traditional transfer pricing issue in which the approach in *Thin Cap* was followed.[303]

Despite this apparent win for the UK, it is unlikely that the UK will move back to applying its transfer pricing rules to purely international transactions. In an international setting, most countries would view as unacceptable that transfer pricing rules could be negated by taxpayers producing a commercial justification for not using an arm's length price. By contrast, applying transfer pricing rules to both domestic and international transactions seems to cure any restriction on the freedom of establishment and so means that such rules do not require justification.

[299] The changes in the UK occurred in the Finance Act 2004.

[300] Case C-524/04 *Test Claimants in the Thin Cap Group Litigation* [2007] ECR 00 (ECJ).

[301] Case C-524/04 *Test Claimants in the Thin Cap Group Litigation* [2007] ECR 00 (ECJ) at para. 82. In *Test Claimants in the Thin Cap Group Litigation GLO* [2009] EWHC 2908 (Ch) the English High Court found that the taxpayer was not granted such an opportunity.

[302] Case C-105/07 *NV Lammers and Van Cleeff* v *Belgische Staat* [2008] ECR I-173 (ECJ) at para. 33.

[303] Case C-311/08 *Société de Gestion Industrielle SA (SGI)* v *Belgium* [2010] ECR 0 (ECJ).

Common consolidated corporate tax base Surveys show that there is a high cost for EU corporate groups in complying with up to 26 different corporate tax systems.[304] This, together with the subjective nature of transfer pricing rules, represents an obstacle to the integration of the internal market. In 2001, the European Commission expressed the view that substantial efficiency gains may be made by permitting EU groups to use a single corporate tax base.[305] Further, if this tax base were consolidated, the need for transfer pricing rules for inter-EU transactions would be eliminated.[306] In 2004, the Council of Ministers established a working group to develop the Commission's proposal for a 'common consolidated corporate tax base' (CCCTB).

A detailed consideration of the Commission's proposal for a CCCTB is beyond the scope of this work, but a few of its more fundamental features are in point. First, the profits of a 75 per cent commonly owned EU corporate group would be calculated according to EU prescribed rules. These profits would be calculated ignoring transactions (including dividends and capital gains) between group members. Non-EU income would be exempt, but there would be controlled foreign corporation rules and a switchover clause for non-EU PEs (see below at 4.1.2.2). The EC's favoured approach is to apportion the EU tax base between member states based on a formulary apportionment involving a mixture of payroll, employee compensation, physical property and sales measured on a destination basis. Member states would then apply their own corporate tax rates to the part of the profits they have been allocated. So, tax rate competition is a feature of the Commission's proposal.

In an effort to secure support for this proposal, use of the CCCTB would not be prescribed but would be on an elective basis, both for member states and corporate groups. The election would apply for five years. Despite being in advanced stages of development, there is still a substantial risk that this proposal will not be implemented. A directive is proposed for implementation of the CCCTB and, as mentioned above at 1.2.3, this means the consent of every member state is required. If it were implemented, it would represent a substantial departure from the arm's length principle. At the time of writing, the Commission's proposal has been put on hold.[307]

304 For example, see European Commission (2004).

305 European Commission (2001).

306 They would still be required for transactions with associates resident in third countries.

307 See Parillo (2009) and the references cited therewith.

3.3.2 *Characterisation: focus on dividends, interest and royalties*

The point has been made that some types of payments are inherently fungible (substitutable). Three such types of payments are dividends, interest and royalties. Source country taxation of these payments was considered above at 3.1.4. At that point, it was noted that Articles 10, 11 and 12 of the OECD Model, the provisions dealing with this taxation, have a number of common features. One common feature (not considered above at 3.1.4) is that each of the Articles contains a definition of their subject matter, i.e. 'dividends', 'interest' and 'royalties', respectively. The boundaries between these definitions are important in tax planning because the source country has very different taxing rights depending on which type of payment is in issue. So, as noted above at 3.1.4, a source country not only has the right to tax dividends at a 5/15 per cent rate but it also has the right to tax the corporate profits from which the dividends are distributed. By contrast, a source country may tax interest at 10 per cent but the interest is often deductible to the payer. At the extreme is royalties, which a source country is not entitled to tax and which may still be deductible to the payer.

The following discussion first considers and compares the definitions in Articles 10, 11 and 12 of the OECD Model. It then turns to compare EU Law. The FEU treaty does not focus on these terms and so does not contain definitions of them. However, Articles 10, 11 and 12 were influential in drafting the Parent-Subsidiary Directive (1990) and the Interest and Royalties Directive (2003). The discussion compares any relevant definitions in these directives, but even where one of these definitions seems to clearly characterise a payment, payments remain substitutable. This is particularly a problem with excessive debt financing. Multinational corporations have an incentive to fund their subsidiaries with debt (loan capital) as the return on debt is most often subject to substantially less source country taxation than the return on equity (share capital). This is the problem of *thin capitalisation*, which is considered after the OECD Model definitions.

3.3.2.1 Defining the boundaries

As mentioned, Articles 10, 11 and 12 of the OECD Model contain a definition of 'dividends', 'interest' and 'royalties', respectively. Each is a *means* definition and so the focus is on the wording of the definition rather than the ordinary meaning of these terms. Further, while the definition of 'dividends' leaves some scope for the domestic law definition of the term, the definitions of 'interest' and 'royalties' do not refer to domestic law. While not without doubt, these definitions appear to be mutually exclusive. A payment cannot be simultaneously characterised as both dividends and interest, dividends and royalties or interest and royalties. Finally, each definition is expressly limited to use of the term in the Article in which it is defined. So, for example, the definition of 'interest' and 'royalties' in Articles 11 and 12 cannot be used for the purposes of interpreting their use in Article 24(4).[308] Each definition is considered in turn.

Dividends Article 10(3) of the OECD Model defines the term 'dividends' as follows:

> The term 'dividends' as used in this Article means income from shares... or other rights, not being debt-claims, participating in profits, as well as income from other corporate rights which is subjected to the same taxation treatment as income from shares by the laws of the State of which the company making the distribution is a resident.[309]

This is a particularly poor definition and shows its age. It is not well suited to the modern world in which the types of interests held in corporations have become more diverse, synthetic and complex. As a result, often this definition is not followed in tax treaties. 'Dividends' is dominantly defined as 'income from shares', but 'shares' is not defined. The clear presumption is that 'shares' are to be distinguished from 'debt-claims' and this seems to lean towards a commercial or formal classification of corporate financing into share capital and loan capital. Further, the definition appears to distinguish between 'rights... participating in profits' and 'other corporate rights'.

A particular difficulty with this definition is whether debt claims (particularly those that do not participate in profits) may fall within the concept of 'other corporate rights', i.e. whether the second 'other' excludes both rights participating in profits and *any* debt claim or just the former. This is not clear. On the one hand, it might be that 'corporate rights' must be akin to shares and so encompass not just the right to participate in profits but also other typical shareholder rights, in particular the right to share in a surplus on winding up. On this view, even interest paid on debt claims participating in profits could be dividends if the claim also gives a right to share in a surplus on winding up. However, this is a very civil law

[308] In *Memec Plc* v *IRC* [1998] STC 754 (CA), the Court of Appeal refused to interpret the word 'dividend' where appearing in an Article dealing with underlying foreign tax relief (as to which see below at 4.1.2.1) consistently with the definition of that term in the dividend article.

[309] Generally regarding difficulties with this definition, see Avery Jones, Baker, De Broe et al. (2009).

view.[310] It also seems rather formalistic, making it easy to avoid dividend treatment, and contrary to the express wording of the provision.

On the other hand, there are reasons for suggesting that income from debt claims generally cannot fall within the definition. First, it would be bizarre if income on debt claims participating in profits could not constitute dividends (even if domestic law treats it in this manner) even though interest on plain debt could (if domestic law treated it as dividends).[311] Second, as will be discussed shortly, the definition of 'interest' in Article 11(3) of the OECD Model includes 'income from debt-claims of every kind'. If income from debt claims can fall within the definition of 'dividends', it might be expected that there would be an exclusion in Article 11(3) for income falling within the definition of 'dividends'.[312]

It is instructive to consider the interrelationship between the OECD Model definition of 'dividend' and the UK domestic tax law definition of 'distribution' (even though UK treaties do not follow either definition precisely). The UK defines 'distribution' in section 1000 of CTA 2010. In particular, this provision may re-characterise interest paid on various debt claims as a distribution, including interest 'beyond a reasonable commercial return' and interest paid on profit-sharing debentures, convertible notes, debt claims linked to shares (stapled securities) and certain long-term debt claims between associated corporations. There are important exceptions to these rules for interest paid between two UK resident corporations. If the OECD definition of 'dividends' does exclude debt claims then none of these types of payments would be re-characterised for treaty purposes. Not surprisingly, the UK seeks to cover these types of payments within the definition of 'dividend' in its treaties.[313]

As noted at 2.1.2.3, the activity covered by the EC Parent-Subsidiary Directive (1990) is 'distributions of profits'. This phrase is not defined in the Directive and is yet to be interpreted by the ECJ.

Interest Article 11(2) of the OECD Model defines interest in terms of 'income from debt-claims of every kind, whether or not secured by

[310] For example, it is consistent with the German Corporate Tax Law (*Körperschaftsteuergesetz*) s. 8(3).

[311] This problem is remedied by the view in the previous paragraph.

[312] For the view that OECD Commentary on Art. 11 para. 19 might produce this effect, see Six (2009).

[313] For example, see UK/US Treaty (2001) Art. 10 and Australia/UK Treaty (2003) Art. 10. Both provisions change the wording of the OECD definition of 'dividends' and the definition of 'interest' in Art. 11 is expressly subject to the definition of 'dividends'.

mortgage and whether or not carrying a right to participate in the debtor's profits'. The interrelationship between this definition and Article 6 (income from land) was discussed above at 3.1.2 and, in particular, the suggestion that Article 11 rather than Article 6 governs the treatment of interest paid on a mortgage secured on land. As noted above, it appears that the definition of 'interest' has precedence over the definition of 'dividends'. So, interest paid on securities such as convertible notes, profit sharing debentures and perpetual debt will be dealt with under Article 11 rather than Article 10.[314]

This apparently formalistic approach to the definition of 'dividends' and 'interest' gives rise to tax planning opportunities using hybrid securities, further discussed below at 5.1.4. In 1992, in apparent response to this concern, the OECD amended the Commentary on Article 10 of the Model to include the following passage:

> Article 10 deals not only with dividends as such but also with interest on loans insofar as the lender effectively shares the risks run by the company, i.e. when repayment depends largely on the success or otherwise of the enterprise's business. Articles 10 and 11 do not therefore prevent the treatment of this type of interest as dividends under the national rules on thin capitalisation applied in the borrower's country.[315]

This is one of the less intuitive passages in the Commentary and it is difficult to reconcile it with the express exclusion of interest on debt claims participating in profits, which the Commentary notes in the immediately preceding paragraph is not dividends. The focus of this passage is on the risk that capital will not be repaid. It seems that interest on debt claims with a risk that the loan *capital* will not be repaid may be treated as dividends, but not interest on debt claims where the risk is that the *interest* will not be paid, i.e. profit sharing debentures. Thus, interest on perpetual debt might be reclassified (though perhaps not on a long-term loan, e.g. for 100 years) but not interest on long-term profit sharing debentures.

Not only is there an inherent inconsistency here, but also it takes a tortuous interpretation of the wording of the definitions of 'dividends' and 'interest' to reach that point. A plain reading seems to suggest that 'dividends' cannot include interest on debt claims. It must be remembered that whether a payment is one or the other is essentially a question of the appropriate rate of withholding tax. The more important point, not

[314] For example, see OECD Commentary on Art. 10 para. 24 noting, in particular, that 'interest on convertible debentures is not a dividend'.

[315] OECD Commentary on Art. 10 para. 25.

directly regulated by Articles 10 and 11 of the OECD Model, is whether the payment is deductible to the payer. This is essentially a question of Articles 9(1) and 24(4) and is further discussed below at 3.3.2.2 in the context of thin capitalisation.

The definition of 'interest' in the EU Interest and Royalties Directive (2003) is virtually identical to the definition in Article 11(2) of the OECD Model.[316] However, Article 4 of the Directive goes on to specifically deny the benefits of the Directive in the case of payments treated as a distribution under the law of the source state, payments of excessive interest, and interest paid on profit sharing debentures, convertible notes and debentures with a term in excess of 50 years. Where these exceptions apply, tax treaties (rather than EU Law) continue to be important in determining source country rights to tax such payments.

Royalties Article 12(2) of the OECD Model defines 'royalties' to mean:

> payments of any kind received as a consideration for the use of, or the right to use, any copyright of literary, artistic or scientific work including cinematograph films, any patent, trade mark, design or model, plan, secret formula or process, or for information concerning industrial, commercial or scientific experience.

This is a peculiar definition and is both narrower and broader than payment for the use of intangible property. The narrowness has caused problems with payments for the use of software. The definition is broader in the inclusion of know-how ('information concerning industrial, commercial or scientific experience').

The definition of 'royalties' in the UN Model is similar but includes some additional items. Of particular interest are payments 'for the use of, or the right to use, industrial commercial, or scientific equipment'. This peculiar addition, which was originally included in the 1963 OECD Model, means that the definition includes some types of rent for the use of tangible property. In the context of the OECD Model, this is not concerning because the addition simply reinforced that, in the absence of a PE, there was to be no source country taxation of rent for the use of anything other than immovable property. The addition has strange consequences in the context of the UN Model. Because the UN Model preserves source country taxation of royalties (at an unspecified rate), it means that a source country may tax rent from the use of this type of tangible property but not

[316] Interest and Royalties Directive (2003) Art. 2(a).

from the use of other types of tangible property. This makes the borderline between these two types of tangible property important and ripe for dispute between taxpayers and tax administrations of source countries.

Article 2 of the Interest and Royalties Directive (2003) defines 'royalties' in the same manner as the OECD Model but with the addition mentioned in the last paragraph. Because this Directive excludes source country taxation, the addition serves a similar purpose to the purpose it served in the 1963 OECD Model. This definition also includes payments for the use of software, which is not expressly covered in the OECD Model or the UN Model.

The characterisation of a payment as a royalty can give rise to substantial difficulties. Often it is not clear what is being paid for. The OECD Commentary on Article 12 of the Model discusses particular problems in distinguishing a royalty from a payment for services, for an electronic good and for the alienation of intangible property (rather than for its use). Each will be considered briefly. It is suggested that the issue is one of correctly characterising the nature of the rights acquired by the payment. Where the rights acquired have a dual nature, e.g. for services and the right to use intangible property, the OECD typically suggests an apportionment, unless the services are merely ancillary to the provision of the intangible property.[317]

In 2008, the OECD Commentary broadened its description of 'know-how' to generally cover 'undivulged information… arising from previous experience, which has practical application in the operation of an enterprise'.[318] The disclosure of know-how is essentially a transfer of information and so may be distinguished from the direct provision of services where the service provider uses know-how on their own account. The former is a royalty covered by Article 12 of the OECD Model whereas the latter is the provision of services covered by Article 7. So, payment for the provision of professional or technical advice electronically (e.g. legal, engineering, medical or accounting advice) typically does not constitute a royalty for the purposes of the Model. This seems to be one reason why some treaties extend the royalties article to cover technical service fees (see above at 3.1.4.3). Confidentiality of the information supplied is also an important feature and so the OECD suggests that payment for a confidential customer list is a payment for know-how and so a royalty.[319]

Payments for digitised products such as software, music, videos and information also cause problems in distinguishing them from royalties.

[317] For example, see OECD Commentary on Art. 12 paras. 11.6 and 17.

[318] OECD Commentary on Art. 12 para. 11.

[319] Generally, see OECD Commentary on Art. 12 paras. 11.1 to 11.5.

Some transactions, such as the electronic acquisition of a book in digital form, are merely substitutes for conventional transactions involving physical objects. A problem is that a customer purchasing a physical book usually has greater difficulty if they wish to manipulate the data in the book compared to a customer downloading a digital version, although with scanning technology this difference is decreasing. The OECD suggests that a payment for a digitised product may constitute a royalty if the payment is effectively for the right to manipulate, reproduce or display copyright material.[320] If there is only a limited right to infringe the copyright, e.g. no right to reproduce software, the payment is essentially for using the software and Article 7 of the OECD Model applies.[321]

A difficult area is distinguishing a royalty from a payment for the partial alienation of intangible property. If ownership is viewed as a right to exclusive possession, the issue becomes when has sufficient of that right been alienated (whether in a temporal or geographical sense) to constitute an alienation of the property rather than simply a payment for its use. For example, under UK law, the granting of an exclusive licence to use intellectual property is viewed as a part alienation and so payment for such a licence is taxed differently from payments for the granting of a non-exclusive licence.[322] The form of payment can also be critical, e.g. whether a lump sum or a payment varying with usage of the intellectual property. The OECD suggests that if the rights transferred 'constitute a distinct and specific property...' then payments are more likely to constitute business profits or capital gains rather than royalties.[323]

3.3.2.2 Thin capitalisation

Even where payments may be clearly characterised as falling within an OECD Model definition, they remain substitutable. *Thin capitalisation* is the problem where a subsidiary is excessively debt financed by its parent

[320] 'Payments made for the acquisition of partial rights in the copyright (without the transferor fully alienating the copyright rights) will represent a royalty where the consideration is for granting of rights to use the program in a manner that would, without such license, constitute an infringement of copyright.' OECD Commentary on Art. 12 para. 13.1.

[321] OECD Commentary on Art. 12 para. 14.

[322] For example, see *Murray* v *ICI Ltd* [1967] Ch 1038 (CA). An exclusive licence means that only the licensee may use the intellectual property, e.g. within a certain geographical location or for a certain period. A non-exclusive licence means that the licensor may grant other licences that can compete with the licensee's use. Under a sole-licence, only the licensor may compete with the licensee.

[323] OECD Commentary on Art. 12 para. 16.

corporation, which might just as easily substitute this financing with equity financing (share capital). The consequence is often substantial erosion of the tax base of the source country. From a legal perspective, the subsidiary has created a debtor/creditor relationship. If this legal form were followed for tax purposes, the interest paid by the subsidiary would be deductible for it and the recipient parent corporation might suffer only a low source country withholding tax or none at all. This can result in a flow of funds (the interest) that has not been taxed by the source country or taxed only at a low rate. By comparison, if the subsidiary had been financed with equity, the payment of dividends would not be deductible, resulting in source country taxation at its corporate tax rate of the funds out of which the dividends are paid. In addition, the source country might have the right to tax the dividends paid to the parent corporation at a low rate. Many countries have domestic tax law rules that seek to prevent the tax base erosion. These rules raise issues both under the OECD Model and EU Law.[324]

Domestic rules Source countries usually adopt one of three approaches to prevent excessive debt financing. Each involves the basic principle of disallowing interest on excessive debt, but each is different in the way in which the *excessive* amount is calculated. Some countries limit the application of their rules to the cross-border allocation of interest, raising questions of discrimination. Other countries apply their rules both domestically and internationally. Each approach results in interest paid on excessive debt being non-deductible for the payer. In addition, the rules of some countries have an effect on the recipient by re-characterising the interest paid as a dividend. This can be particularly important in a domestic scenario as it can alleviate the otherwise harsh result that the excessive interest is both non-deductible to the payer and fully taxed as interest to the recipient, i.e. economic double taxation. Re-characterisation often results in the availability of dividend relief.

The most common approach adopted by countries to the thin capitalisation problem is the safe haven approach. Under this approach, debt financing received by say a corporation from associated entities is compared to the equity financing of the corporation. If the debt, as compared to the equity, exceeds a certain ratio (the debt to equity ratio) then interest on the excessive debt is not deductible. Some countries have a simple ratio

[324] For a report drawing a link between the international tax bias for debt and the financial crisis of 2008/09, see International Monetary Fund (2009).

(e.g. 2:1) applicable to all industries but other countries adopt different ratios or formulas for particular situations. Each approach is similar in that it focuses on the volume of debt as compared to equity rather than the volume of interest paid on debt. Countries that adopt this approach often tightened the ratio when broadening their tax base and lowering corporate tax rates. Often, this approach is combined with the third approach (discussed below) to accept debt financing that exceeds the ratio if the taxpayer can show that they could borrow a similar amount from an independent third party, e.g. a bank.

A major issue under the safe haven approach is how equity capital is measured. Typically, it includes both share capital and retained profits (e.g. net assets). A further difficult issue is which debt counts, all debt or just debt financing from related parties. If the latter approach is used then the law must define related party. Further, this approach must deal with the problem of *back-to-back* arrangements. In order to avoid related party debt, a parent corporation may place a deposit with an independent bank and then the bank loans funds to the relevant subsidiary. It can be difficult to trace back-to-back arrangements, particularly in an international setting. Another issue is the time at which compliance with the ratio is measured – is it at the start of the year, the end or the highest point during the year? Corporate groups also raise issues. Is the ratio applied to the group or individual members of the group? Where this is relevant, group corporations must be defined.

An increasingly popular approach to dealing with excessive debt financing is earnings stripping rules. Broadly, this approach involves denying a deduction for interest to the extent that it exceeds a certain percentage of income net of financing costs. The US is the primary example of a country adopting earnings stripping rules where the deductibility of interest is generally limited to 50 per cent of adjusted taxable income.[325] In 2008, Germany adopted a similar approach in conjunction with a reduction in the corporate tax rate. Generally, Germany limits the deductibility of interest to 30 per cent of taxable profits before deduction of interest, taxes and depreciation.[326] It seems likely that other EU member states will follow this lead.

The third approach is to apply the arm's length standard to the *volume* of debt financing, i.e. apply transfer pricing rules. Under this approach,

[325] Internal Revenue Code (US) s. 163(j). The US rules also incorporate a safe haven based on a debt to equity ratio of 1.5:1.

[326] Income Tax Law (*Einkommensteuergesetz*) (Germany) s. 4h.

interest is deductible only to the extent that it is paid on debt that could be borrowed from an independent party. This approach is less common, though of particular relevance when applying tax treaties. It is the approach used by the UK in its domestic law.[327] Since 2004, the UK's transfer pricing rules (discussed above at 3.3.1.2) have been the primary rules regulating thin capitalisation. From the same date, those rules have applied equally to both domestic and international transactions. So these rules may simultaneously restrict the deductibility of interest based on the rate at which interest is charged as well as the amount borrowed.[328]

The transfer pricing approach also suffers problems with back-to-back arrangements. A subsidiary may be able to borrow money from an independent bank because of a guarantee provided by its parent corporation. The UK rules specifically provide that in such a case a subsidiary's borrowing capacity that is due to the guarantee is to be ignored for purposes of determining whether the bank would have loaned the funds on an independent basis.[329]

From 2010, the UK backs up its transfer pricing approach with a worldwide interest deduction cap. Interest deductions granted to UK members of a multinational corporate group are limited to the total net finance costs paid by the worldwide group (including the UK members) to external lenders.[330] The impetus for this rule is largely focused on residence/home country issues and is further discussed at 4.2.1, but it will have an impact for extreme cases in the source/host country scenario.

Generally, the UK rules do not reclassify interest paid by a subsidiary as a distribution unless the payment represents 'more than a reasonable commercial return' for the use of the funds borrowed.[331] The focus on the funds borrowed means that this re-characterisation is not generally applicable in a thin capitalisation case. As a result, the UK transfer pricing rules raise a serious risk of economic double taxation of the excessive interest.[332] Reclassification as a distribution may be useful to a non-resident

[327] As a rule of thumb, the UK tax administration is not concerned with cases where the level of debt to equity does not exceed a ratio of 1:1 and the level of interest cover (the number of times which operating profits meet interest payments) exceeds 3:1. However, the tax administration denies that this is a 'safe harbour'. See Almand and Sayers (2009).

[328] Consistent with the transfer pricing approach, the UK tax administration makes available an Advance Thin Capitalisation Agreement procedure; see Statement of Practice 04/07.

[329] TIOPA 2010 s. 153.

[330] TIOPA 2010 Part 7 (ss. 260–353).

[331] CTA 2010 s. 1000(1)E.

[332] Under TIOPA 2010 ss. 191–4 there is some scope for treating a related party guarantor as paying interest for which the borrower is denied a deduction.

lender as the UK may subject outbound interest to withholding tax but does not subject outbound distributions to withholding tax (see above at 2.1.2.2).

OECD Model The OECD Model contains no provision dedicated to the thin capitalisation issue. Rather, the OECD views thin capitalisation as a branch of the transfer pricing issue and so relies on the provisions discussed above at 3.3.1, which centre on Article 9(1). It seems clear that excessive debt financing may constitute 'conditions' in the 'financial relations' between a borrower and a lender. Accordingly, Article 9(1) authorises a source state to adjust the profits of the borrower, e.g. by denial of a deduction for interest on excessive debt. The OECD confirms that thin capitalisation rules are consistent with Article 9(1) but only 'insofar as their effect is to assimilate the profits of the borrower to an amount corresponding to the profits which would have accrued in an arm's length situation'.[333]

The limitation means that, in a tax treaty context, thin capitalisation rules based on the safe haven or earning stripping approaches should be tested against the arm's length standard. If the application of these approaches denies a deduction for interest on debt that could be borrowed at arm's length then that denial will not be authorised by Article 9(1) of the OECD Model. This issue does not arise where a country adopts the transfer pricing approach to thin capitalisation and this was a driving factor in the UK's move to that approach, i.e. consistency between treaties and domestic law.

Even where Article 9(1) of the OECD Model does not authorise them, thin capitalisation rules may be permitted in a tax treaty context. It is a fundamental of tax treaties that domestic law stands unless inconsistent with a treaty. The only provision that might deny the application of thin capitalisation rules is Article 24. As discussed above at 3.3.1.2 in the context of transfer pricing, Article 24(4) is particularly relevant. Generally, it requires that deductions be granted for payments of interest to non-residents on the same basis as that granted for the payment of interest to residents. So, if thin capitalisation rules apply to both domestic and international borrowing, they will not breach Article 24(4) and so are not limited by treaty. If, however, the rules apply only to payments of interest to non-residents, they will breach Article 24(4) unless they comply with Article 9(1). As discussed above at 3.3.1.2, Article 24(4) does not prohibit

[333] OECD Commentary on Art. 9 para. 3.

rules that comply with Article 9(1). The bottom line is that even safe haven or earnings stripping rules will not breach tax treaties provided they either (i) are disapplied where the borrowing is arm's length, or (ii) they are applied to both domestic and international transactions.

If a deduction has been denied for interest on excessive debt paid to a non-resident, a secondary issue is the level of source country taxation of that interest, i.e. the extent to which the OECD Model permits economic double taxation of such interest by both denying a deduction and taxing the interest. Assuming there is no re-characterisation of the interest, this is primarily an issue as to whether Article 11(2) or (6) applies. As discussed above at 3.3.1.2, Article 11(6) preserves domestic taxation of interest paid at an excessive rate. Therefore, the consequence of an excessive rate of interest may be full economic double taxation by both the denial of a deduction to the payer as well as taxation of the interest at full domestic rates to the recipient. An issue is whether Article 11(6) can apply to interest paid on an excessive amount of *debt*, as opposed to interest paid at an excessive *rate*. Because of the words 'having regard to the debt claim for which it is paid' in Article 11(6), the better view seems to be that it cannot and so the usual limitations in Article 11(2) would apply. The OECD recognises difficulties with Article 11(6) and suggests some less than illuminating possible alterations.[334]

A difficult issue is whether the re-characterisation of interest on excessive debt as dividends is consistent with the OECD Model. This is a separate issue from the deductibility of the interest and is primarily concerned with which Article of the Model applies to taxation of the excessive interest, i.e. whether source country taxation is limited under Article 10 or Article 11. As discussed above at 3.3.2.1, irrespective of any domestic law characterisation, the better view is that interest paid on debt claims cannot constitute 'dividends' for the purposes of Article 10. This does not necessarily prevent a domestic law re-characterisation; it prevents only the limitations in Article 10 applying to any such re-characterisation. On this basis, the limitation in Article 11 will continue to apply to the re-characterised interest, i.e. while the interest may be considered a distribution for domestic law purposes, it will continue to be interest for treaty purposes.

The OECD is less than enlightening in this area. The Commentary suggests that Article 9(1) of the Model

[334] OECD Commentary on Art. 11 para. 35.

> is relevant not only in determining whether the rate of interest provided for in a loan contract is an arm's length rate, but also whether a *PRIMA FACIE* loan can be regarded as a loan or should be regarded as some other kind of payment, in particular a contribution to equity capital.[335]

What is not clear is whether or why such a re-characterisation would be acceptable for the purposes of Article 10. Similarly, the Commentary suggests that Article 24(4) of the Model

> does not prohibit the country of the borrower from treating interest as a dividend under its domestic rules on thin capitalisation insofar as these are compatible with paragraph 1 of Article 9 or paragraph 6 of Article 11.[336]

Again, whether this can extend to the application of Article 10 over Article 11, and if so why, is not clear.

As discussed above at 3.3.1.2, the OECD extends the application of its approach to transfer pricing to dealings between a PE and the rest of its enterprise. This is further extended to prevent excessive allocation of interest expense to PEs through the concept of 'free capital'.

> The objective is... to attribute an arm's length amount of interest to the permanent establishment after attributing an appropriate amount of "free" capital in order to support the functions, assets and risks of the permanent establishment.[337]

It seems that 'free' in this sense means capital upon which a return is not mandatory, i.e. a PE equivalent of a corporation's share capital.[338] The OECD accepts that there is no single appropriate method for allocating free capital and seeks to 'authorise' various approaches. A basic premise underlying these approaches is that 'the creditworthiness of the PE is generally the same as the enterprise of which it is a part'.[339] On this basis, the capital of the enterprise should follow assets and risk. A PE should be allocated sufficient free capital to 'fund the assets and support the risks attributed to the PE'.[340] The authorised methods of allocating free capital are set out in the 2008 *Attribution of Profits* report but are beyond the scope of this study.[341] In the result, a PE may be denied a deduction for interest that is properly allocated to it under Article 7(3) of the OECD Model. Indeed,

335 OECD Commentary on Art. 9 para. 3.
336 OECD Commentary on Art. 24 para. 56.
337 OECD Commentary on Art. 7 para. 45.
338 See OECD (2008a, para. 136).
339 OECD (2008a, para. 33).
340 OECD (2008a, para. 149).
341 OECD (2008a, paras. 155–83).

it is questionable whether the concept of 'free capital' is consistent with Article 7(3), a point that is underlined by the slated deletion of Article 7(3) from the Model in 2010.

EU Law The ECJ jurisprudence with respect to the application of the fundamental freedoms to thin capitalisation rules has already been considered above at 3.3.1.4 in the context of transfer pricing.

3.3.3 *Dual characterisation: reconciliation rules*

OECD Model

Often an item of income may simultaneously fall under two or more Articles of the OECD Model. This study does not consider all articles in the Model and so the following discussion is illustrative only of some of the many overlaps that may occur. A number of Articles have specific reconciliation rules but, in other cases, there is no such express reconciliation. The general approach of the Model is that Articles appearing earlier in the Model take precedence over those appearing later, but this is not universal.

Accordingly, Article 21 of the OECD Model expressly applies only to income 'not dealt with in' earlier articles. Problems with this deceptively simple rule were discussed above at 3.1.1. At the other extreme is Article 6(4), which expressly provides that Article 6 applies to 'income from immovable property of an enterprise'. Thus, Article 6 overrides the application of Article 7 and Article 7(7) reinforces this. Consequently, the existence of a PE is irrelevant when determining the right to tax income from immovable property and, subject to the non-discrimination rule in Article 24(3), rent from immovable property might be taxed on a gross basis even if derived through a PE.

Articles 10(4), 11(4) and 12(3) of the OECD Model each contain a similar provision that effectively gives source countries the right to tax dividends, interest and royalties effectively connected with a PE as business profits rather than under those articles. In this limited sense, they give priority to Article 7. These provisions were discussed above at 3.1.4. The effect of the capital gains provision in Article 13(2) (discussed above at 3.1.5) is similar. The OECD rejection of the *force of attraction* rule was noted above at 3.1.3.3, which means that dividends, interest, royalties and capital gains received by a non-resident may not be generally attributed to a PE the recipient has in the source country. Only those that are 'effectively connected' with or derived from 'part of the business property' of the PE may be so attributed.[342] Where such payments are not effectively connected to a PE, Article 7(7) gives priority to Articles 10, 11, 12 and 13, i.e. where such payments are also business profits Article 7(7) ensures that the Article 7(1) prohibition on source country taxation does not apply.

Nevertheless, despite some express reconciliation rules, there are circumstances in which an overlap may occur between Articles in the OECD Model. A good example is when a corporation buys its own shares from a shareholder, i.e. a share buy-back. Many countries treat the gain on a share buy-back or liquidation as a dividend.[343] Such a dividend falls within the definition in Article 10(3), discussed above at 3.3.2.1. Nevertheless, the share buy-back or liquidation is still an alienation of shares within Article 13(5). How should such a case be dealt with? It might be argued that the more specific provision should apply, but it is not clear whether Article 10 or Article 13 is the more specific. Alternately, it might be argued that the provisions should be applied concurrently, but to whose benefit, the taxpayer or the tax administration? The OECD seems to be of the view that if two Articles apply concurrently, the source state can choose the Article of the Model on which to ground taxation.[344] Similar issues arise in other contexts, e.g. premiums paid on debt claims.

EU Law

Just as it is possible for two Articles of the OECD Model to apply simultaneously, it is possible for two of the fundamental freedoms of EU Law to have simultaneous application. At one time, the ECJ was not very particular about which freedom it applied in direct tax cases. However, in recent years with the increase in the number of direct tax cases, the different scope between the freedoms, particularly as regards third countries, has placed increased focus on identifying the most appropriate freedom. For present purposes, the tension is between the freedom of establishment or freedom to provide services, on the one hand, and the free movement of capital, on the other. The former are limited to inter-EU activity whereas the latter extends to movement to or from third countries (see above at 2.1.2.3).

[342] OECD Commentaries on Art. 10 para. 31, Art. 11 para. 24, Art. 12 para. 20 and Art. 13 para. 27.

[343] In the UK, this is true of share buy-backs but not liquidation distributions, CTA 2010 ss. 1000(1)B and 1030.

[344] OECD Commentary on Art. 13 para. 31.

The *Thin Cap Group Litigation* case was discussed above at 3.3.1.4.[345] That case involved the application of the UK thin capitalisation rules to UK subsidiaries of EU parent corporations as well as non-EU parent corporations (in particular, US parent corporations). The taxpayers argued breaches of each of the freedom of establishment, freedom to provide services and free movement of capital. The latter was particularly important to the subsidiaries of US parent corporations as the former freedoms do not extend to third countries. The ECJ made the following observation:

> [N]ational provisions which apply to holdings by nationals of the Member State concerned in the capital of a company established in another Member State, giving them definite influence on the company's decisions and allowing them to determine its activities, come within the substantive scope of the provisions of the [FEU] Treaty on freedom of establishment.[346]

The court proceeded to suggest that thin capitalisation rules concern situations in which there was a 'level of control' allowing one member of a corporate group to 'influence the financing decisions' of another group member.[347] Therefore, these rules must be tested by reference to the freedom of establishment and not the freedom to provide services or the free movement of capital. The ECJ continued:

> Even if it were to be accepted that such legislation might have restrictive effects on the freedom to provide services and the free movement of capital, such effects must be seen as an unavoidable consequence of any restriction on freedom of establishment and do not justify an independent examination of that legislation in the light of Articles [56 FEU] and [63 FEU].[348]

In the result, US parent corporations could not rely on the free movement of capital, as the freedom of establishment was the appropriate freedom to apply. This was the case even though a parent had no right to use the freedom of establishment as it does not extend to third countries. This

[345] Case C-524/04 *Test Claimants in the Thin Cap Group Litigation* [2007] ECR 00 (ECJ).

[346] Case C-524/04 *Test Claimants in the Thin Cap Group Litigation* [2007] ECR 00 (ECJ) at para. 27. Similar phraseology was used in a number of other cases including Case C-446/04 *Test Claimants in the FII Group Litigation* [2006] ECR I-11753 (ECJ) at para. 37.

[347] Case C-524/04 *Test Claimants in the Thin Cap Group Litigation* [2007] ECR 00 (ECJ) at para. 31.

[348] Case C-524/04 *Test Claimants in the Thin Cap Group Litigation* [2007] ECR 00 (ECJ) at para. 101 and also see para. 34.

substantial difference in approach places pressure on the test for application of when the freedom of establishment applies, i.e. 'definite influence' on a corporation's 'decisions'. No doubt this test will be of great importance in future litigation involving third countries.

The same is true with respect to the distinction between the freedom to provide services and the free movement of capital. In this regard, *Fidium Finanz* is an important case (though not a direct tax case).[349] That case involved the provision of commercial credit by a Swiss national (non-member state) to German nationals. The Swiss national argued that treatment under German law constituted a breach of the freedom to provide services and the free movement of capital. The ECJ decided that the scope of the former did not extend to Swiss nationals. Further, the granting of commercial credit was a provision of services and, therefore, the freedom to provide services was the 'predominant consideration'. Any simultaneous restriction on the free movement of capital was only an 'unavoidable consequence of the restriction on the freedom to provide services'. The situation was to be tested by reference to the freedom to provide services and not the free movement of capital. Accordingly, the claimant was denied relief.[350]

This is not to suggest that the free movement of capital is always subservient to the other fundamental freedoms. In *Holböck*, an Austrian individual exercised their freedom of establishment by holding a controlling interest in a Swiss corporation.[351] Dividends from the corporation were taxed by Austria more heavily than dividends from an Austrian corporation. The ECJ held that the rules that produced this discrimination were of general application; they applied to both controlling and non-controlling interests in foreign corporations. Therefore, the free movement of capital had potential application, though was not breached on the facts. In many cases, international tax rules designed to protect the domestic tax base are clearly targeted at controlled situations and so the free movement of capital is typically excluded.[352]

[349] Case C-452/04 *Fidium Finanz AG* v *Bundesanstalt für Finanzdienstleistungsaufsicht* [2006] ECR I-9521 (ECJ).

[350] Case C-452/04 *Fidium Finanz AG* v *Bundesanstalt für Finanzdienstleistungsaufsicht* [2006] ECR I-9521 (ECJ) at paras. 30–49.

[351] Case C-157/05 *Holböck* v *FA Salzburg-Land* [2007] ECR I-4051 (ECJ).

[352] Measures such as transfer pricing rules (discussed above at 3.3.1), thin capitalisation rules (discussed above at 3.3.2.2), controlled foreign corporation rules (discussed below at 4.1.2.2) and cross-border loss relief between group corporations (discussed below at 4.2.4).

In a reasoned order in the *KBC Bank* case, the ECJ set out guidelines for the Belgium court for reconciling the application of the freedom of establishment and the free movement of capital.[353] This involved the court looking to the purpose of the domestic legislation in issue and deciding whether it is intended to apply only to establishment situations. If the legislation is not limited to establishments, the court must look to the facts and whether, e.g. where a shareholding is involved, the shareholding enables the holder to have a definite influence on the corporation's decisions and to determine its activities. By contrast, in *Glaxo Wellcome* the ECJ followed *Holböck* and simply looked to the purpose of the legislation. It applied the free movement of capital despite the facts involving a parent corporation's holdings in subsidiaries.[354]

[353] Cases C-439/07 and 499/07 *Belgium State* v *KBC Bank NV*; *Beleggen, Risicokapitaal, Beheer NV* v *Belgium State* [2009] ECR 00 (ECJ).

[354] Case C-182/08 *Glaxo Wellcome GmbH & Co KG* v *Finanzant München II* [2009] ECR 00 (ECJ).

4

Residence country taxation

The discussion now proceeds to consider the tax treatment in the country where the income recipient is resident on the assumption that the source country has taxed in the manner discussed in Chapter 3. Accordingly, in the context of the *Base Case* (see the figure on page 5), the discussion in this chapter considers the tax treatment of Beth by Country B on the assumption that the rent from her office building in Country A has been taxed by Country A on the basis of source. This assumption is consistent with the principle of source country entitlement discussed above at 2.2.1. Consistent with the discussion in Chapter 3, there are cases in which the source country might not tax, such as where the income involved is royalties or business income in the absence of a PE. In such a case, residence country taxation is straightforward and there is no issue of that country providing foreign tax relief.

In most cases, however, the source country will tax. This is true in the context of the *Base Case*, where Country A is very likely to tax the rent because it is income from immovable property. Assuming the source country taxes, it will typically do so without reference to taxation by the residence country. By contrast, the residence country will typically take into account any tax levied by the source country. For this reason, the residence country usually has the final say as to the overall tax liability of the recipient. It also means that there is much focus on the residence country when it comes to questions of overall neutrality, such as capital import or capital export neutrality (discussed above at 2.2.1).

The following discussion is structured under two primary headings. The first heading focuses on foreign tax relief granted by the residence country. The first part of this heading considers the various methods of relief, which were outlined above at 2.2.2. The second part of the first heading focuses on particular difficulties that arise for residence countries and foreign tax relief where the foreign source income is derived through a non-resident corporation. Residence country taxation will typically be on a net basis, i.e. after the deduction of expenses. Expenses incurred in deriving foreign source income impact substantially on the nature and effectiveness of residence country taxation. They naturally affect foreign tax relief but also stand at the interface between foreign source income and domestic source income. This is particularly so when expenses cause losses. This is the subject of the second heading of this chapter.

4.1 Foreign tax relief

4.1.1 Methods

This subheading considers the methods by which a residence country may provide foreign tax relief for source country taxation. Tax relief for foreign dividends is not considered at this point (see below at 4.1.2.1). The primary methods of foreign tax relief were identified above at 2.2.2. As with other rules considered by this book, provision for foreign tax relief may have its basis in the domestic tax law of the residence country, i.e. the residence country may provide unilateral relief. Alternately or in addition, tax treaties may require the residence country to provide foreign tax relief and the OECD Model incorporates provision in this regard. Finally, EU law may influence the provision of foreign tax relief within the EU. Each of these is considered in turn.

4.1.1.1 Domestic law: unilateral relief

The domestic law of most countries imposes taxation based on residence of the person deriving the income. If the residence country taxes according to a schedular system (see above at 1.1), it will typically tax foreign source income according to the same schedules used when it taxes as a source country.[1] In other words, as a starting point, the fundamentals of the tax system will apply irrespective of the fact that what is being taxed is foreign source income. So the usual allocation, quantification (including transfer pricing), timing and characterisation rules apply, as do the rules on deductibility of expenses and tax rates.

For a taxpayer deriving cross-border income, the worst treatment by a residence country is that it imposes its taxation without any recognition

[1] The UK schedular system was an exception, which traditionally taxed some foreign source income under Cases IV and V of Schedule D, ICTA 1988 s. 18. These cases date back to 1799 and were fundamentally concerned with the timing of the tax on foreign income, see Harris (2006, pp. 413–18). The separation of foreign income under the UK schedular system is not as clear under the rewritten legislation, but see ITTOIA 2005 Part 4, Chapter 4 (ss. 402–8).

of foreign tax paid on a source basis. In this case, there is full double taxation and, if the tax rates are high enough (e.g. more than 50 per cent), it is possible for a taxpayer to be liable for more tax (on both a source and residence basis) than the income derived. Such double taxation is rare and likely to be experienced only where two countries consider the income sourced in their country, a matter that will be returned to at 5.2.1. Rather, a residence country is likely to at least consider foreign income tax as an allowable expense in deriving foreign source income, i.e. allow a deduction for foreign tax. Further, it is increasingly likely (virtually inevitable in developed countries) that a residence country will grant unilateral foreign tax relief in the form of an exemption for foreign income or a foreign tax credit for foreign tax.

Deduction The deduction method of providing foreign tax relief was not mentioned at 2.2.2 because it mitigates but does not relieve double taxation of cross-border income. Returning to the *Base Case*, the figure on page 5 assumes that Beth derives 100 rent from Country A and Country A imposes 30 in the way of tax. Further, assume that Beth is taxable at a 40 per cent rate in Country B on her worldwide income. Under the deduction method, Country B would permit Beth to deduct the Country A tax and so for Country B tax purposes she would have income of 70 (i.e. 100 less 30). Country B would impose its 40 per cent tax on that 70, giving a Country B tax liability of 28 and leaving Beth with a return of 42 net of tax. Her combined Country A and Country B tax liability is 58 (30 plus 28), which is substantially higher than either the Country A tax rate or her Country B tax rate. This is clearly a disincentive to international trade and is viewed as promoting *national neutrality*, discussed above at 2.2.1.

Relief by deduction is often used as a fallback to more comprehensive forms of foreign tax relief (unilateral or treaty based). For example, it may be used where the foreign tax is not sufficiently income tax in nature (e.g. a tax on turnover) to qualify for relief that is more comprehensive. This is particularly an issue for foreign tax credit systems, discussed below. Further, the deduction method may be more beneficial than exemption or credit where the use of foreign expenses is not as limited as the more comprehensive form of foreign tax relief. So, if foreign tax (including through the use of foreign losses) can be deducted against domestic source income, this may be more beneficial to the taxpayer than claiming ineffective foreign tax relief. This can happen where the taxpayer is in an overall loss position and so has no residence country tax liability; a deduction for foreign tax may increase the loss that can be used in future years.[2] The UK grants a deduction for foreign tax where the foreign tax credit method is ineffective, including where the taxpayer elects not to receive the credit.[3]

Exemption A deceptively simple method of providing foreign tax relief is the exemption method. In its most straightforward form, this involves excluding foreign source income from the residence country tax base. In practice, however, exemption systems often contain as many, if not more, qualifications and limitations than credit systems. So in the previous example discussed above, the residence country may simply not tax Beth with respect to the receipt of the rent from the offices in Country A, leaving the source country tax of 30 as the definitive tax burden for Beth. In this way, the exemption method is viewed as consistent with capital import neutrality (see above at 2.2.1). As Country B would have taxed Beth at 40 per cent if she had received that income domestically, the susceptibility of the exemption method to tax competition is apparent (see above at 2.2.1). Tax competition becomes particularly problematic where the source country has not taxed or has taxed at a reduced rate, i.e. not fully. Consequently, exemption is usually limited to income fully taxed by the source country such as income from land, business and employment.

Another difficulty with the exemption system is the proper allocation of expenses to the foreign source income. While this will be returned to at 4.2, at this stage it is important to point out that the exemption of income usually entails the non-deductibility of expenses. In this respect, the proper allocation of expenses between foreign and domestic source income is crucial. This has an impact on not only the type of income for which exemption might be granted but also the types of countries that might unilaterally grant an exemption.

Civil law jurisdictions often place greater emphasis on business accounts for tax purposes and so have a greater correlation between accounting profits and tax profits.[4] As a result, civil law jurisdictions are particularly likely to grant an exemption for business income attributable to a foreign PE. The accounts of the PE will be particularly important for the purposes of allocating expenses to the PE, resulting in the non-deductibility of

2 This is usually a problem where exempt foreign income reduces domestic losses or where excess foreign tax credits cannot be carried forward. These issues are further discussed below at 4.2.

3 TIOPA 2010 ss. 27, 112, 113.

4 Vann (2003, pp. 157–67).

those expenses.[5] So, not surprisingly, a number of civil law jurisdictions unilaterally exempt the profits of a foreign PE. These countries include Belgium, France, the Netherlands and Switzerland, although in recent years a number of common law jurisdictions have moved in the same direction, including Australia. Consistently, countries that exempt the profits of foreign PEs are also likely to exempt the dividends from foreign subsidiaries, discussed further below at 4.1.2.1. It is less likely that other types of foreign income will be exempt and so, in practice, exemption countries typically adopt a mix of exemption for some types of income and a foreign tax credit for other types of income.

The exemption method does not work particularly well in the face of progressive tax rates. While progression is often applied only to individual taxpayers, some countries also subject corporations to a form of progression. By contrast, source countries predominantly tax at flat rates. As a result, the exemption system tends to flatten the tax rate structure. Further, a pure exemption system can affect the taxation of domestic source income by the residence country. Consider again the example of Beth deriving 100 foreign source income where Country B exempts that income. Beth might also have Country B source income that is taxed at progressive rates. The exclusion of the source country income may mean that Beth's income does not reach higher rates that it might reach if the foreign income were taken into account. Effectively, Beth might split her income between the tax rate schedules of two different countries and pay less tax on both Country A and Country B source income.

This problem occurs if the foreign source income is effectively excluded from the tax base of the residence country. Instead of adopting exclusion, the foreign tax relief might effectively involve a reduction in the relevant tax rate of the residence country, i.e. use of the *foreign income differentiation method* (see above at 2.2.2). Few countries unilaterally adopt this approach with a positive rate on foreign source income. Belgium is a limited example. More common is where the rate is effectively reduced to zero. This can produce *exemption with progression*, which is subtly different from foreign income exclusion.

Foreign income differentiation includes foreign income in the tax base of the residence country; it just taxes that income at a rate that is lower than that applicable to domestic source income. Whether that lower rate is positive or nil, because the foreign income is included in the tax base, it

[5] This is the inverse of relying on the PE accounts for the purposes of determining source country taxation, discussed above at 3.1.3.3.

might push domestic income into higher tax brackets. Whether or not this happens will depend on the *slicing* rule adopted. Slicing rules are always required where, in the face of progression, different types of income are subject to different tax rates. If the foreign source income is considered the bottom slice, i.e. the first income derived by the taxpayer, it might mean that domestic source income is subject to higher rates. In particular, the foreign source income might exhaust a taxpayer's exemption threshold. If, however, the foreign source income is the top slice, i.e. treated as the last income derived by the taxpayer, the result is effectively the same as under the foreign income exclusion approach. An averaging rule can also be used where the foreign income and domestic source income are rateably allocated to each progressive tax bracket.

Returning to the example of Beth, presume Country B adopts exemption with progression. Country B will still not tax Beth with respect to the 100 Country A income but now that income may affect the Country B tax rate applicable to Beth's Country B income. Presume Country B taxes Beth at 20 per cent on the first 100 of income and 40 per cent thereafter and that she has 100 Country B income in addition to the Country A income. If Country B adopts a bottom slicing rule, the foreign income (despite being exempt) would exhaust Beth's 20 per cent bracket and all of the domestic source income would be taxed at 40 per cent. In this case, Beth would suffer 30 Country A tax on her Country A income and 40 Country B tax on her Country B income. If Country B adopts a rateable slicing rule, the foreign income would use up only 50 of Beth's 20 per cent tax bracket, leaving 50 of her domestic source income to be taxed at 20 per cent and 50 to be taxed at 40 per cent. In this case, Beth would suffer 30 Country A tax on her Country A income and 30 Country B tax on her Country B income (20 per cent of 50 and 40 per cent of the other 50).

Credit The credit method is often viewed as a complex method of foreign tax relief, particularly in the form of the underlying or indirect foreign tax credit, discussed below at 4.1.2.1. Returning to the example with Beth, under this method Country B would initially calculate Beth's residence tax liability without any relief for the source tax of Country A. Further, Beth's Country A income would be calculated without a deduction for the Country A tax. The inclusion of tax in calculating income is referred to as *gross-up*. So initially, Beth's Country B tax liability would be 40, i.e. 40 per cent of 100. This amount is then reduced by source country tax, i.e. 30. So Beth's Country B tax liability would be 10 (40 less 30). Her overall tax liability is 40 (30 Country A tax and 10 Country B tax), which is consistent with her residence country progressive tax rate. For this reason, the foreign tax credit method is viewed as consistent with capital export neutrality (see above at 2.2.1).

Like the exemption method, the foreign tax credit method gives rise to substantial difficulties. Its apparent purpose is to maintain consistency with the residence country's progressive tax rate system. This is consistent with the residence country being in a better position than the source country to adjust overall tax liability according to a person's ability to pay taxes, i.e. according to the principle of equity. However, whether consistency with progressive taxation is maintained (and so consistency with capital export neutrality) depends on how the residence country treats the situation in which the foreign tax exceeds the tax liability in the residence country.

Returning to the example of Beth, now presume that her Country B marginal tax rate is 20 per cent, so her Country B tax with respect to the Country A income is 20. This is less than the Country A tax of 30 and the question is what happens to the extra 10 (20 less 30). This extra amount is referred to as *excess foreign tax credits*. If Beth can use the excess against Country B tax on her Country B source income (or get a refund from Country B of the extra Country A tax), then the system is a *full* foreign tax credit. In the example, Beth has 100 Country B source income in addition to the 100 Country A source income. Under a full foreign tax credit, Country B would calculate Beth's worldwide Country B tax liability as 40, i.e. 20 per cent of 200 (100 Country A income and 100 Country B income). This amount would be reduced by the credit for the Country A tax, leaving 10 Country B tax to be paid (40 less 30).

It will be seen that the full foreign tax credit permits Country A tax to not only exhaust Beth's Country B tax liability with respect to Country A income but also reduce Beth's Country B tax liability with respect to Country B source income. It provides an inducement for foreign countries to subject residents of foreign tax credit countries to high tax rates. Such a subsidy for deriving income from high tax countries is viewed as unacceptable by virtually all foreign tax credit countries and so there are no major examples of countries that provide a full foreign tax credit. Rather, foreign tax credit countries limit the amount of foreign tax that may be credited to the amount of tax levied by the residence country with respect to foreign source income. This is referred to as an *ordinary* foreign tax credit system.

If Country B adopts an ordinary foreign tax credit, Beth will not be permitted to use her extra 10 Country A tax to offset Country B tax with respect to Country B income. In this case, Beth must calculate her Country

B tax liability with respect to her Country A source income separately from her Country B tax liability with respect to her Country B source income. Assuming Beth is taxed at 20 per cent by Country B, this means her Country B tax liability with respect to her Country A source income will be 20 and her Country B tax liability with respect to her Country B source income will also be 20. The foreign tax credit for Country A tax may reduce only the former 20 and not the latter 20. This is referred to as the *limitation on credit*, i.e. the foreign tax credit is limited to Country B tax on the Country A income. In the result, the foreign tax credit will exhaust Beth's Country B tax liability on that income but not reduce Beth's Country B tax on Country B source income. Beth pays 30 tax to Country A (on her Country A source income) and 20 tax to Country B (on her Country B source income). It will be noted that this is the same result as under the exemption system and is not consistent with Beth's Country B tax rate.

As with the exemption system, the situation becomes more complicated if Beth is subject to progressive rates in Country B. Here Country B will have to adopt a slicing rule for the same reason as a slicing rule is required where the exemption with progression method is used (see above). Assume that Country B taxes Beth at 20 per cent on her first 100 and 40 per cent thereafter. In order to work out the limitation on credit, Country B must decide whether Beth's Country A source income is the bottom slice of her income, the top slice, or should be considered pro-rata with her Country B source income. A bottom slice rule would consider the Country A income as Beth's lowest taxed income, i.e. as that taxed at 20 per cent, and so would put the greatest limit on the foreign tax credit available for Country A tax, i.e. 20. A top slice would be most favourable to Beth as it would consider the Country A source income as the highest taxed part of Beth's income and so maximise Beth's foreign tax credit, i.e. a limit of 40. A pro rata rule would produce a credit limit of 30 (for the same reasons as discussed above with respect to exemption with progression).

A limitation on credit has the potential to produce non-creditable foreign tax, however that limitation is calculated. The next question is, can the excess foreign tax be used in any other manner? It cannot be used against tax liability in the residence country on income sourced in the residence country, but can it be used on tax liability in the residence country on *other* foreign income? There are two considerations here, one in a geographical sense and one in a temporal sense. Dealing with the first, in the example Beth has income from only one source in one country, i.e. rent from Country A. But what if Beth had other Country A source income, e.g. had rent income from other countries or just had income from other countries? Could she use the excess Country A tax with respect to her rental income to reduce her Country B tax liability with respect to any of these other types of foreign income?

Assume that Beth derives not only 100 rent from Country A but 100 interest income from Country A. Country A taxes the rent at 30 per cent and the interest at 10 per cent. Country B taxes Beth at 20 per cent. Country B might require Beth to calculate her limitation on credit separately for each item of income. In this case, the limit on credit will be 20 for the rent and 20 for the interest (i.e. 20 per cent of 100 in both cases). Beth will have 10 excess foreign tax on the rent income (20 less 30) but will have 10 Country B tax liability on the interest income (20 less 10), which cannot be reduced by the excess on the rent income. This restrictive approach is referred to as a *slice-by-slice* or *item-by-item* limitation on credit.

Country B might be more flexible and permit Beth to calculate her limitation on credit for *all* Country A source income. In this case, her limitation on credit will be 40 (20 per cent of 200) and she will be permitted to credit all of the 40 Country A tax (30 plus 10). If Beth had any income from other countries, she would calculate the limitation on credit separately for each country. This is referred to as a *country-by-country* limitation on credit. It will be noted that this form of limitation permits Beth to offset lowly taxed income with highly taxed income from the *same* country. So, if Beth owned the land and was deriving the rent, such a system would provide Beth with an incentive to derive lowly taxed income from the same country in order to use the excess credits.

Country B might be more flexible and permit Beth to calculate her limitation on credit for *all* foreign income from *all* foreign countries. An example would be where the Country A interest income in the last paragraph is derived from another country, Country C. The calculations would be the same. This is referred to as a *worldwide* limitation on credit. Here, if a person has highly taxed income that produces excess credits, they have an incentive to derive lowly taxed income, not just from the country where the highly taxed income is sourced but from *any* country other than their country of residence. This is the most flexible form of ordinary foreign tax credit system and for a country with average (not very high) tax rates, can produce an effect similar to an exemption for foreign income. Therefore, such a system is susceptible to tax competition and, like the exemption system, is often viewed as encouraging the use of tax havens (further discussed at 5.2.3).

It is also possible for the limitation on credit to be calculated by reference to the type of income derived. So, for example, there might be a separate limitation on credit calculation for income from land, income from business, income from employment, income from capital, etc., *irrespective* of the country from which the income is derived. This is referred to as a *type of income* or *basket* approach to the limitation on credit. Assume that Beth derives her rent from Country A in the usual way but also derives rent from Country C, which Country C taxes at 10 per cent. If Country B applies a basket limitation and these two sources of income fall into the same basket, the calculation of the limitation on credit will be as for the country-by-country limitation. Countries that adopt a basket limitation inevitably place active income (e.g. business and employment income) in baskets separate from passive income (e.g. dividends, interest and royalties). This is viewed as making the system more robust in the face of tax competition because, as discussed above at 2.2.1, tax competition is particularly fierce with respect to passive income.

If the limitation on credit produces excess foreign tax, a further issue is whether that excess can be used in a temporal sense. In particular, can the excess be carried forward or backwards to be set against tax liability in the residence country on foreign source income of other years, subject (inevitably) to the same geographical limitation on credit? Here, as discussed below at 4.2.2, there is some sense in using the same approach as is available for losses as losses can be the reason why excess foreign tax credits arise.

The UK unilaterally adopts a foreign tax credit system. This is also the case for the US and Canada and is quite common among common law jurisdictions. The primary UK provision providing relief is s. 9 of TIOPA 2010, which provides in part:

> Credit for tax-
> (a) paid under the law of [a territory outside the United Kingdom],
> (b) calculated by reference to income arising, or any chargeable gain accruing, in the territory, and
> (c) corresponding to UK tax,
> is to be allowed against any income tax or corporation tax calculated by reference to that income or gain.

It will be noted that this is an ordinary credit, the credit being limited to UK tax on the foreign income. Further, the provision incorporates a slice-by-slice approach to calculating the credit limitation, i.e. the credit can be set against UK tax on 'that income'.[6] This can be contrasted with the US, which originally adopted a worldwide limitation and then restricted it to a basket approach.[7] In general, the UK offers no carry-forward or carry-back of excess foreign tax, so any foreign tax that cannot be used in the year that income is taxable cannot be credited. The exception is for excess foreign tax suffered by an overseas PE of a UK resident corporation. Such excess may be carried forward indefinitely and backwards up to three years.[8] Where a foreign tax credit is available, the foreign tax is not deductible, i.e. gross-up is required.[9] The limitation on credit is calculated as though the foreign income were the top slice of income for individuals, i.e. the income taxed at the highest rate. If the individual has more than one source of foreign income, the taxpayer can choose which is considered taxed at the highest rate. These rules are most favourable for the taxpayer.[10] For corporations, a pro rata limitation is used.[11]

Inevitably, foreign tax credit systems limit the *type* of foreign tax that may be credited. For example, to be creditable under the UK system, the foreign tax must correspond to UK income tax or corporation tax.[12] Further, the foreign tax must be imposed 'under the law of any territory outside the United Kingdom'. The reference to the word 'territory' is particularly flexible and enables the UK to grant unilateral relief for taxes imposed by autonomous parts of a larger nation, e.g. provincial or local income taxes. This can be particularly important, as often tax treaties do not cover such lower tier taxes. Further, foreign tax credit systems typically credit only foreign tax levied on a source basis. Section 9(1) of TIOPA 2010 refers to income 'arising' in the foreign territory.[13] Ideally, the concept of source here will be the inverse of what the country taxes based on source, e.g. in the case of the UK, the inverse of the charges discussed

[6] In the context of corporations, this is reinforced by TIOPA 2010 s. 44 and see *George Wimpey International Ltd* v *Rolfe* [1989] STC 609 (Ch).

[7] Internal Revenue Code (US) s. 904(d).

[8] TIOPA 2010 s. 73. Again, this can be contrasted with the US approach under which a taxpayer can carry excess credits back one year and forward for ten; Internal Revenue Code (US) s. 904(c).

[9] TIOPA 2010 s. 31.

[10] TIOPA 2010 s. 36.

[11] TIOPA 2010 s. 42. This is relevant only where a corporation is subject to the small companies tax rate.

[12] TIOPA 2010 s. 8. For an interesting example of a Venezuelan tax on turnover that was held to correspond sufficiently, see *Yates* v *GCA International Ltd* [1991] STC 157 (Ch).

[13] Regarding this limitation, see *Yates* v *GCA International Ltd* [1991] STC 157 (Ch).

above at 2.1.2.2. However, care must be taken because this is not always the case.[14]

As mentioned, the foreign tax credit system, even an ordinary foreign tax credit system, encourages foreign countries to tax residents from foreign tax credit countries up to their residence country rate. For this reason, it is common for capital importing countries to impose corporate tax rates as high as the major countries from which they derive their capital. It also encourages the practice of *soak-up* taxes. These are tax increases by a source state to ensure that credit is obtained in the residence state up to the limitation on credit. It is a form of adjusting source state taxation based on residence country taxation. Not surprisingly, residence countries do not take kindly to this practice and a number of countries, including the UK, have acted to deny credit for such increased taxes.[15]

Finally, as with the measure of an exemption under the exemption method, the measure of income, including the deduction of expenses, is critical in calculating the limit on credit. What is the measure or quantum of the foreign income to which the rate is applied to measure the limitation on credit? Often, this is not the same as the tax base used by the source country to impose its tax. This can cause substantial distortions in the measure of foreign tax relief. The deduction of expenses is further discussed below at 4.2.1.

4.1.1.2 OECD Model

Tax treaties require the residence country to provide foreign tax relief by either the exemption or credit method and this is reflected in Article 23 of the OECD Model. When the OECD Model was drafted, the member states could not agree as to which method was most appropriate and so they inserted alternate versions of Article 23, labelled Article 23A for the exemption method and Article 23B for the credit method. The title of Article 23A is somewhat misleading as it provides for exemption only in specified circumstances, supplementing the exemption with the credit method in other cases.

[14] In particular, Schedule D Case I (trade carried on in the UK) is broader than just income arising within the UK; ITTOIA 2005 s. 6.

[15] Under TIOPA 2010 s. 33 the credit is limited to the amount of foreign tax that would have been paid if the taxpayer had taken 'all reasonable steps ... to minimise the amount of tax payable in that territory'. In *Hill Samuel Investments Ltd* v *RCC* [2009] UKSPC SPC00738 (SC) the Special Commissioners refused to use this provision to rewrite a transaction.

It is important to determine the relationship between foreign tax relief provided by tax treaty and any unilateral relief offered by the domestic tax law. In some cases, the unilateral relief is more generous than that provided by tax treaty, in which case the taxpayer is entitled to rely on the domestic provision. Due to the broad nature of its unilateral relief, this is often the case with respect to the provision of foreign tax relief by the UK. In other cases, a tax treaty may provide relief where no unilateral relief is on offer, or the treaty relief may be more generous than any unilateral relief. For example, unilateral relief may be offered in the form of a credit where a treaty offers relief in the form of exemption. Whether replacing a credit with an exemption is beneficial to the taxpayer or not will depend on the facts of the case and, in particular, whether those facts would give rise to excess foreign tax credits and if so how such excess can be used (e.g. against tax liability on other foreign income).

A final introductory point concerns the application of the non-discrimination provisions in Article 24 of the OECD Model to residence country taxation. It seems clear that the nationality non-discrimination rule in Article 24(1) can apply to residence country taxation. The limitations on this rule were discussed above at 2.2.1. By contrast, it seems that the important provisions in Article 24(3), (4) and (5) have limited application to residence/home countries, which, considering their application to source/host countries, makes Article 24 somewhat lopsided, particularly in tax treaties between capital exporters and capital importers. In particular, these provisions may apply to discrimination of a PE or subsidiary of a non-resident when compared with another resident and so have some scope for application to the granting of foreign tax relief. As these scenarios typically involve a third connecting factor (e.g. more than two countries), they are returned to below at 5.2. What these provisions do not prevent is a residence country discriminating against deriving foreign source income, e.g. by taxing foreign source income more highly than equivalent domestic source income. An example of such discrimination is *Commission* v *Spain*,[16] discussed below at 4.1.1.3, which demonstrates the stark difference with EU Law in this regard.

Exemption Article 23A(1) of the OECD Model provides:

> Where a resident of a Contracting State derives income ... which, in accordance with the provisions of this Convention, may be taxed in the

[16] Case C-219/03 *Commission* v *Spain* [2004] ECR 0 (ECJ).

> other Contracting State, the first-mentioned State shall, subject to the provisions of paragraphs 2 and 3, exempt such income… from tax.

The residence country is required to provide exemption only where the source country has a taxing right under the treaty. Therefore, an exemption is not available with respect to all business income derived in the source country, rather only that attributable to a PE in the source country. Similarly, as the source country has no right to tax royalties, the residence country is not required to exempt these. The source country has a limited right to tax dividends and interest under Articles 10 and 11 and so an exemption by the residence country of these types of income would be inappropriate. Article 23A(2) replaces the exemption method with the credit method where these articles are involved. Article 23A(3) preserves the right of the residence country to apply exemption in the form of the exemption with progression method.

The obligation of the residence country to provide foreign tax relief under Article 23 of the OECD Model (both exemption and credit methods) is triggered only where the source country has a right to tax under the treaty. Whether the source country has a right to tax will depend on interpretation of the earlier provisions of the treaty. A source country may adopt an interpretation of a provision such that it believes it has a right to tax but the residence country may not agree with the interpretation, believing, rather, that the source country does not have a right to tax. This is particularly so in the face of Article 3(2) where, unless the context otherwise requires, undefined terms in a treaty take their meaning from the domestic law of the country applying the treaty. The question arises as to whether a residence country is obliged to provide foreign tax relief where a source country believes it has the right to tax but the residence country does not agree.

The better view seems to be that the residence country is obliged to provide relief if the source state has fairly interpreted a provision according to any special treaty meaning and residually its own domestic law. The residence country is not permitted to residually apply its own domestic law in interpreting whether the source country has a right to tax. The OECD Commentary seems to support this position but in doing so draws some fine (perhaps irreconcilable) distinctions.[17] It gives an example of a situation in which a certain gain is, in accordance with the domestic law of the source country, business profits attributable to a PE falling within Article 7. Under

[17] OECD Commentary on Art. 23 paras. 32.1–32.4. Also, see Avery Jones et al. (2006, p. 714).

its domestic law, the residence country classifies the gain as a capital gain not connected with a PE, in which case Article 13(5) prohibits source country taxation. The OECD suggests that the residence country is obliged to provide relief in this case because the difference between the source country approach and the residence country approach is a result of differences in domestic law, not differences in the direct interpretation of the treaty.

If, however, the source and residence countries adopt a 'different interpretation of facts or different interpretation of the provisions' of the treaty, the OECD suggests that the residence country can 'argue' that the source state has not taxed in accordance with the treaty and so the residence country is not obliged to grant foreign tax relief.[18] A question is whether, if the residence country believes that the source state tax is not in accordance with the treaty, it is obliged to provide foreign tax relief under any unilateral provisions. In the UK, the question may turn on whether the taxpayer has taken all 'reasonable steps' in the source state in disputing the source state charge (e.g. challenged the charge in court).[19]

A corollary to this issue is that the source state may believe a treaty prohibits it from taxing certain income when the residence country believes that it does have such a right. Without the earlier limitation to cases of 'conflicts of qualification' under domestic law, the OECD Commentary suggests that a residence country should not provide relief in such a case, e.g. in the form of an exemption, if it would produce double non-taxation. This would be inconsistent with the basic premise of Article 23 of the Model, which is to provide relief from *double* taxation.[20] For this reason, and the reason that the domestic law of a source state might not support a right to tax granted by treaty, exemption countries sometimes insert in foreign tax relief articles in their treaties a limitation that relief is required only where the income is 'liable to tax' in the source country.

Credit Article 23B(1) of the OECD Model provides:

> Where a resident of a Contracting State derives income... which, in accordance with the provisions of this Convention, may be taxed in the other Contracting State, the first-mentioned State shall allow:

[18] OECD Commentary on Art. 23 para. 32.5.

[19] TIOPA 2010 s. 33 requires taxpayers to take 'all reasonable steps' to minimise source country tax under the domestic law of the source state as well as under any 'arrangements' (treaties) of the source state.

[20] OECD Commentary on Art. 23 para. 32.6.

> a) as a deduction from the tax on the income of that resident, an amount equal to the income tax paid in that other State...
>
> Such deduction... shall not, however, exceed that part of the income tax... as computed before the deduction is given, which is attributable... to the income... which may be taxed in that other State.

A similar provision appears in Article 23A(2) with respect to dividends and interest. This provision suffers from the same difficulties with respect to different qualifications and interpretations by source and residence countries as discussed in the context of exemption under Article 23A(1). Being a credit system, however, Article 23B does not suffer from the potential for double non-taxation.

The simple credit provision in Article 23 of the OECD Model is short on details. It provides for an ordinary credit with gross-up. The type of limitation on credit specified is less clear but it seems to permit an item-by-item or at least source-by-source limitation. As the most restrictive approach to limitation on credit, this is consistent with preserving autonomy of residence countries in this respect. The Article makes no provision for the carry forward or back of excess foreign tax or for the slicing of foreign income in calculating the limit on credit (i.e. which residence country tax is 'attributable' to the foreign income, tax at the highest rate or at lower rates). In effect, Article 23B leaves the limitation on credit to be determined according to domestic law.

Tax systems are often used to encourage certain behaviour and this is true in an international environment as well. Reduced tax rates may be used by source countries in order to attract investment but the foreign tax credit method often taxes away any benefit granted by a source country. That is, under the foreign tax credit system any reduction in source country tax simply increases the amount of residence country tax collected. This is particularly concerning for developing countries, which often use tax reductions (e.g. tax holidays) in an effort to encourage development projects in their jurisdiction. As a result, some tax treaties that adopt the credit method provide for *tax sparing relief*, also known as *matching credit*. Where such relief applies, the residence country gives credit, not only for tax levied by the source country but also for the tax that would have been paid but for a tax concession. This means the benefit of any reduction in source country tax is preserved for the taxpayer and is not *clawed back* by the residence state. Often, tax sparing relief is targeted only at specific concessions and sometimes is granted by reference to specific provisions of the tax law of the source country.

The effectiveness of tax sparing relief as a development tool is debated. The US has always opposed tax sparing as a matter of policy. European countries, including the UK, have traditionally been more open to tax sparing in their treaties.[21] Considering the debate that surrounds tax sparing, it is not surprising that the OECD Model contains no provision for tax sparing relief. This is also true of the UN Model.

4.1.1.3 EU Law

As noted above at 2.2.2, Article 293 of the EC Treaty imposed on member states an obligation to negotiate with a view to eliminating double taxation within the EU. As further noted at that point, the ECJ held that this provision did not have direct effect.[22] There are no provisions in the FEU Treaty that place an obligation on member states to prevent double direct taxation. The fundamental freedoms focus on preventing particular member states discriminating or restricting cross-border activity. They do not easily deal with the situation in which the discrimination or restriction cannot be said to be the fault of a particular member state but rather is caused by the dual application of two different tax systems to the same income.

It is clear that the fundamental freedoms can apply to the foreign source income of residents. One example is useful at this point, but others will be given in the remainder of this chapter. In each of these cases, a favourable tax treatment that was available with respect to domestic source income was not granted with respect to foreign source income. In *Commission* v *Spain*,[23] certain gains on the disposal of shares in Spanish listed corporations could be reduced according to a holding period at a rate faster than gains on shares of corporations listed elsewhere. The ECJ held that this contravened the freedom to provide services and the free movement of capital provisions of the FEU Treaty. As mentioned above at 4.1.1.2, the OECD Model provides no protection against this sort of discrimination.

Despite dealing with this type of *one-sided* discrimination, the fundamental freedoms do not deal with discrimination caused by the interaction of two tax systems. *Kerckhaert and Morres*[24] concerned a Belgian couple who received dividends from a French corporation. Under the Belgium/

[21] For examples of tax sparing relief, see Bangladesh/UK Treaty (1979) Art. 22(2), Botswana/UK Treaty (2005) Art. 23(3) and India/UK Treaty (1993) Art. 24(3).

[22] Case C-336/96 *Gilly* v *Directeur des Services Fiscaux du Bas-Rhin* [1998] ECR I-2793 (ECJ).

[23] Case C-219/03 *Commission* v *Spain* [2004] ECR 0 (ECJ).

[24] Case C-513/04 *Kerckhaert and Morres* v *Belgium State* [2006] ECR I-10967 (ECJ).

France Treaty, they were entitled to a refund of dividend tax credits under the French imputation system but the dividend plus the dividend tax credit was subject to French withholding tax at the rate of 15 per cent (see above at 3.1.4.1). Belgium subjected the dividend income to a 25 per cent tax rate that applied to both domestic and foreign source income. The treaty required Belgium to grant a foreign tax credit for the French withholding tax but Belgian law denied this, having effectively engaged in treaty override. The couple argued that the refusal to grant the foreign tax credit as required by the treaty constituted a restriction on their free movement of capital.

The ECJ found no violation of the free movement of capital. The court distinguished earlier case law that had struck down provisions discriminating against foreign income. *Kerckhaert and Morres* differed from those cases because Belgium taxed foreign dividends and domestic dividends at the same rate. The court was clear that the 'adverse consequences which might arise' from Belgium's tax system were a 'result from the exercise in parallel by two Member States of their fiscal sovereignty'.[25] The decision concerned the European Commission, which quickly distanced itself from it. In particular, the Commission feels that a failure to resolve double taxation is inconsistent with the internal market.[26]

However, the ECJ has not distanced itself from *Kerckhaert and Morres*.[27] In *Columbus Container Services*,[28] a German family established a Belgium partnership and so, under German law, the family members were each considered to have a PE in Belgium. The Belgium/Germany Treaty required Germany to exempt the profits of a Belgium PE, but German domestic law overrode the treaty and replaced the exemption with a foreign tax credit. The Advocate General was of the opinion that this treatment violated both the freedom of establishment and the free movement of capital. Relying on *Kerckhaert and Morres*, the ECJ disagreed.

> Although the Member States have, within the framework of their powers referred to in paragraph 27 of this judgment, entered into numerous bilateral conventions designed to eliminate or to mitigate those negative

[25] Case C-513/04 *Kerckhaert and Morres* v *Belgium State* [2006] ECR I-10967 (ECJ) at para. 20.

[26] For example, see Gnaedinger (2006).

[27] In Case C-194/06 *Staats van Financiën* v *Orange European Smallcap Fund NV* [2008] ECR I-3747 (ECJ), an exempt Dutch investment fund was entitled to a refund of Dutch tax withheld from Dutch dividends but not foreign tax withheld from foreign dividends. Relying on *Kerckhaert and Morres*, the ECJ found this did not breach the free movement of capital.

[28] Case C-298/05 *Columbus Container Services BVBA & Co* v *Finanzamt Bielefeld-Innenstadt* [2007] ECR I-10451 (ECJ).

> effects, the fact none the less remains that the Court has no jurisdiction, under Article [267 FEU], to rule on the possible infringement of the provisions of such conventions by a contracting Member State.[29]

The taxpayer suggested that the German treatment distorted the choice between different types of establishment and, in particular, the choice as to whether to set up a Belgian presence in the form of a PE or a subsidiary. The ECJ was not persuaded:

> Member States are at liberty to determine the conditions and the level of taxation for different types of establishments chosen by national companies or partnerships operating abroad, on condition that those companies or partnerships are not treated in a manner that is discriminatory in comparison with comparable national establishments.[30]

As Germany treated German partnerships in the same way as it treated the Belgian partnership, there was no discrimination or restriction.[31]

Some suggested that Article 293 of the EC Treaty was a barrier to requiring residence states to provide relief from double taxation for purposes of promoting the internal market within the EU. As noted above at 2.2.2, this provision imposed on member states an obligation to negotiate with a view to eliminating double taxation within the EU, but the ECJ decided that it did not have direct effect. The FEU Treaty deleted Article 293, but in its current frame of mind, it is not clear that this will encourage the ECJ to seek to prevent double taxation under the fundamental freedoms. Meanwhile, the European Commission continues to argue that a failure of a residence country to provide foreign tax relief breaches the free movement of capital and in mid-2008 it commenced infringement proceedings against Belgium.[32]

4.1.2 *Problems with corporations*

As noted above at 2.1.1.1, international tax rules are premised on the basis that corporations are separate taxpayers from their owners and,

[29] Case C-298/05 *Columbus Container Services BVBA & Co* v *Finanzamt Bielefeld-Innenstadt* [2007] ECR I-10451 (ECJ) at para. 46.

[30] Case C-298/05 *Columbus Container Services BVBA & Co* v *Finanzamt Bielefeld-Innenstadt* [2007] ECR I-10451 (ECJ) at para. 53.

[31] The ECJ reached a similar conclusion in Case C-128/08 *Jacques Damseaux* v *Belgium* [2009] ECR 0 (ECJ). This was effectively a rerun of *Kerckhaert and Morres* without the complication of a refund of dividend tax credit by France, so the juridical double taxation was obvious.

[32] Case C-307/08 *Commission* v *Belgium* [2009] ECR 0 (ECJ).

in particular, that subsidiaries are separate taxpayers from their parent corporations. This causes two particular problems. First, it can result in the multiple taxation of the same economic gain in the hands of different taxpayers, i.e. economic double taxation. This results from the taxation of a corporation with respect to its profits and the taxation of the shareholder with respect to the distribution of those profits, see above at 3.1.4.1. However, such double taxation arises only if a corporation distributes dividends. If the shareholder is resident in a different jurisdiction than the corporation, taxation in the shareholder's residence country will be deferred if dividends are not distributed. This deferral is a second major problem with the use of corporations cross-border and is particularly problematic where the corporation is resident in a low tax jurisdiction.

4.1.2.1 Economic double taxation

Economic double taxation of corporate income in an international setting occurs for the same reason that it does in a domestic setting: dividends are considered a source of income separate from the corporate profits from which they are distributed. As noted above at 3.1.4.1, most countries, including the UK, address this issue of economic double taxation domestically. However, the international tax order, as represented by the OECD Model, presumes a classical system, i.e. economic double taxation, even for source countries. If a corporation is resident in a source/host country, that country will have the right to tax both the profits of the corporation (on the basis of source and residence) and the dividends of the corporation (on the basis of source). Taxation of the shareholder by their country of residence raises the potential of a third level of tax. Usually, the potential for this third level of tax is relieved by standard mechanisms of foreign tax relief, i.e. those discussed above at 4.1.1. That is, any source country taxation of the dividends will be relieved in the residence country of the shareholder, typically by means of a foreign tax credit.

That leaves the issue of whether any relief should be provided for the economic double taxation. As noted above at 3.1.4.1, there is some recognition of this problem in source country taxing rights granted under the OECD Model, particularly through the reduced 5 per cent withholding tax rate on dividends distributed to parent corporations. This is taken further in many treaties and under EU Law to exempt dividends from source country tax. The question now turns to the response of the country of the shareholder's residence and whether it is willing not only to relieve double taxation of dividends (under the methods discussed above at 4.1.1) but in addition to provide relief from economic double taxation. Such relief is often referred to as 'underlying' foreign tax relief, since it provides relief for the corporate tax that was imposed on the profits underlying (used for) the dividend distribution.

Domestic law: unilateral relief Economic double taxation of dividends can be relieved in ways that are analogous to relief from international double taxation; see above at 2.2.2. Here the corporate tax equation is analogous to the tax equation of the source country and the shareholder tax equation to the tax equation of the residence country. From the perspective of the country of the shareholder's residence, it can relieve economic double taxation (provide underlying tax relief) by exempting foreign dividends, taxing them at a reduced rate or providing a tax credit with respect to the receipt of foreign dividends by a resident shareholder. With respect to the latter approach, the credit may be related to the amount of corporate tax suffered by profits from which the dividends are distributed, i.e. an imputation system.[33]

Many countries provide unilateral relief with respect to at least some cases of international economic double taxation of dividends. This is more likely with respect to direct investors, but an increasing number of countries are also providing unilateral relief with respect to portfolio investors.[34]

Portfolio investors As mentioned, unilateral relief from international economic double taxation of dividends for portfolio shareholders is a bit *hit and miss.* Traditionally, it was most common to find relief applying only to domestic scenarios, with the classical system being the norm for foreign dividends. Relief would be given for any foreign tax levied directly on dividends (e.g. dividend withholding tax) but would not extend to corporate tax underlying a dividend. Many countries still adopt this unbalanced approach, including Australia and New Zealand.

However, the international trend is towards extending domestic dividend relief to foreign dividends. This particularly took root in Europe because of decisions of the ECJ, but has extended further afield. The UK is a good example of this trend. For a number of years, it has taxed foreign dividends at the same reduced rates as it taxes domestic dividends. It did not extend the tax credit it offers with domestic dividends to foreign dividends because it rather extended those dividend tax credits to

[33] Regarding these systems, see Harris (1996, pp. 66–72).

[34] Regarding the distinction between direct and portfolio investors, see above at 3.1.4.1.

non-residents under treaties (see above at 3.1.4.1), i.e. dealing with the issue of economic double taxation as a source country rather than as a residence country. However, ECJ decisions suggest this is a matter for residence countries and beginning in 2008 the UK extends dividend tax credits to foreign dividends received by individuals as well as domestic dividends.[35] For similar reasons, other EU countries must extend any domestic dividend relief to foreign dividends and the US adopted a similar approach in 2004.[36] For similar reasons, from 2009 the UK extends an exemption to some resident corporations in receipt of foreign dividends (see below discussion in respect of direct investors).

Direct investors With respect to direct investors (i.e. parent corporations), unilateral relief from international economic double taxation of dividends usually takes one of the two traditional forms of foreign tax relief, i.e. exemption or credit. The exemption system is straightforward, meaning that parent corporations in receipt of dividends from foreign subsidiaries are not taxed with respect thereto. In this case, the definitive tax burden is source country taxation, i.e. taxation of the underlying profits of the subsidiary plus any dividend withholding tax. Note that while the residence country has acted consistent with capital import neutrality (see above at 2.2.1), this has not been achieved, the difference being source country withholding tax.[37] Capital import neutrality would be achieved if the subsidiary retained its profits. As with exemption of PE profits, this form of foreign tax relief is often used in civil law jurisdictions. For example, it is used in France, Germany and the Netherlands.

Sometimes the exemption is available only if the recipient corporation has a substantial shareholding in the distributing foreign corporation, e.g. in the Netherlands this is 5 per cent. In this case, the method is often called a 'participation exemption'. However, in other cases, such as Germany, any shareholding by a residence corporation in a foreign corporation is sufficient to secure the exemption. Like the exemption method in general, the exemption of foreign dividends raises the issue of tax competition.

[35] The Finance Act 2008 inserted ITTOIA 2005 s. 397A, which extends the non-payable tax credit of one ninth of the distribution to UK resident individuals in receipt of dividends from non-resident companies. Until 2009, the credit was available only if the shareholding was less than 10 per cent.

[36] See US Internal Revenue Code s. 1(h)(11)(B). At present, the US dividend relief system, introduced in 2004, is set to expire.

[37] It is presumed that domestic inter-corporate dividends in the source country are exempt, which is commonly the case, e.g. with respect to the UK, CTA 2009 ss. 931B and 931D.

For this reason, a number of exemption countries switch from the exemption system to an underlying foreign tax credit system with anti-deferral mechanisms when dealing with certain lowly taxed foreign subsidiaries. This is discussed further below at 4.1.2.2.

While the UK has traditionally been a foreign tax credit country, from 2009 it has moved to a limited exemption system. The impetus for this move essentially involved EU Law issues with the non-application of its underlying foreign tax credit system to portfolio shareholders in EU corporations (see below). The exemption extends the domestic inter-corporate dividend exemption to foreign dividends received by UK resident corporations.[38] In classic UK style, while the exemption can be quite broad in that there is no minimum share capital or holding period requirement, this is not a full move to an exemption system, but rather a halfway house between exemption and credit. The exemption is available only for some (but the main types of) foreign dividends and the historic underlying foreign tax credit system continues to be available for the rest.[39] A recipient corporation may elect for the exemption not to apply, in which case the underlying foreign tax credit applies.[40]

The other common method of underlying foreign tax relief is the underlying or indirect foreign tax credit method. This method is effectively an imputation system, which is widely viewed as the most complex method of providing relief from economic double taxation.[41] When projected into an international setting, underlying foreign tax credit systems often become one of the most complex parts of a tax system. Traditionally, common law jurisdictions are more likely to adopt the foreign tax credit method than the exemption method. Countries adopting the underlying foreign tax credit method include New Zealand (in substance), the UK and the US. In recent years, there has been some movement away from this complex method in favour of exemption. Australia is a country that moved to the exemption system and, as discussed above, so did the UK from 2009, if only partially. One reason for doing so is that in the absence of anti-deferral mechanisms, the underlying foreign tax credit system behaves like an exemption system for retained profits of foreign subsidiaries. Again, this is discussed further below at 4.1.2.2.

[38] Corporation Tax Act 2009 Part 9A (ss. 931A–931W).

[39] In particular, an exemption is available for dividends paid on non-redeemable ordinary shares; Corporation Tax Act s. 931F. Any exemption is subject to anti-avoidance rules in ss. 931J–931Q.

[40] Corporation Tax Act 2009 s. 931R.

[41] Generally regarding imputation systems, see Harris (1996, pp. 135–252).

As an imputation system, the idea of an underlying foreign tax credit system is relatively simple. The recipient parent corporation should receive a foreign tax credit for source country corporate tax paid by the subsidiary with respect to the profits that are distributed to the parent, i.e. the subsidiary's corporate tax should be *imputed* to the parent corporation. Assume that a parent corporation resident in Country B has a subsidiary in Country A that derives 100 Country A source profits. Further, assume that Country A imposes corporate tax at the rate of 20 per cent. So, the subsidiary will pay 20 to Country A in corporate tax, leaving 80 available to distribute as a dividend. Further, assume that Country A imposes withholding tax on outbound dividends at the rate of 5 per cent. So, when the 80 profits net of corporate tax are distributed, Country A will impose withholding tax in the amount of 4, leaving the parent corporation in receipt of a dividend of 76 net of Country A tax.

Assume Country B has a corporate tax rate of 30 per cent. Under its direct foreign tax credit system, Country B credits the amount of Country A's dividend withholding tax of 4. Further, under its underlying foreign tax credit system, Country B grants the parent corporation a further credit for the Country A corporate tax paid by the subsidiary on the profits distributed, i.e. 20. As with the foreign tax credit system in general, the parent corporation's income for Country B purposes will be grossed-up for both the direct and underlying foreign tax, i.e. the parent corporation will have income of 100 (76 plus 4 plus 20). The Country B corporate tax on this amount is 30, which will be reduced by the direct foreign tax credit and the underlying foreign tax credit, leaving a Country B tax liability of 6 (30 less 4 less 20).

In the result, the subsidiary's profits have been taxed in total at the Country B corporate tax rate and so the underlying foreign tax credit system is viewed as consistent with capital export neutrality (see above at 2.2.1). However, this will not be achieved if the subsidiary retains its profits, rather capital import neutrality will be achieved. Further, even with respect to distributed profits, capital export neutrality will not be achieved if the combined direct and indirect tax credits exceed residence country tax, such as where the corporate tax rate in Country A is greater than that in Country B. In this case, the parent corporation will have excess foreign tax credits. As discussed above at 4.1.1, Country B will inevitably adopt an ordinary credit, meaning the excess will not be refundable and not available to set against tax on Country B source income due to the limitation on credit. Once again, it will be important to determine the nature of the limitation on credit, i.e. whether it is determined on an item-by-item, country-by-country, type of income or a worldwide basis, and whether excess credits may be carried backwards or forward.

As an imputation system, an underlying foreign tax credit system must deal with two particularly difficult issues, which increase the complexity of the system substantially. The essential problem is that the subsidiary might not distribute all of its profits and likely those profits have not all been taxed at a uniform rate. In this case, in order to work out the quantum of the credit for the parent corporation, it is necessary to identify *which* profits the subsidiary distributed so that credit is given only for foreign corporate tax imposed on *those* profits. Therefore, two important features of an underlying foreign tax credit system are first that it must require the subsidiary to keep certain records of profits and their associated foreign tax treatment, and second that it must incorporate an ordering rule that determines which of the profits recorded have been distributed. There are various methods of addressing these issues, but these are beyond the scope of this book.[42]

Recording requirements cause practical difficulties for underlying foreign tax credit systems. These must be kept with respect to the subsidiary's activities, but the subsidiary is often established and resident in a foreign jurisdiction. Unless a parent corporation has a sufficient shareholding in the subsidiary, it may not have sufficient influence to get from the subsidiary the details it needs in order to claim an underlying foreign tax credit. For this reason at the least, underlying foreign tax credit systems are limited to substantial shareholdings, typically a minimum of 10 per cent.[43] The result can be harsh for portfolio corporate shareholders, which may be subject to a full classical treatment with respect to foreign dividends whereas direct corporate shareholders receive full relief from international economic double taxation. This was particularly a problem for the UK under EU Law and is further discussed below.

It is useful to demonstrate the workings of an underlying foreign tax credit system by reference to the UK system. This system feeds into the direct foreign tax credit system discussed above at 4.1.1.1. Section 14 of TIOPA 2010 provides:

[42] Regarding recording requirements and ordering rules under imputation systems (and so underlying foreign tax credit systems), see Harris (1996, pp. 137–54 and 169–75).

[43] This is the threshold under both the UK and the US underlying foreign tax credit systems, discussed below.

(2) Credit under section 9 for overseas tax on a dividend paid by a company ('P') resident in the territory is allowed if conditions A and B are met.
(3) Condition A is that ... the recipient of the dividend is a company resident in the United Kingdom ...
(4) Condition B is that the recipient ... directly or indirectly controls ... at least 10% of the voting power in P.

It will be seen that a critical question is how to determine 'overseas tax on a dividend'. Under s. 58 of TIOPA 2010, this is calculated as 'the foreign tax borne on the relevant profits by the company paying the dividend'. Section 59 defines 'relevant profits' as-

> if the dividend ... is paid for a specified period ... the distributable profits of that period...
> if the dividend ... is not paid for a specified period ... the distributable profits of the last period for which accounts of the company were made up which ended before the dividend became payable ...

As for the ordering rule, this means the subsidiary can select the profits (of a particular period) that are considered distributed, i.e. a discretionary ordering rule. This permits a certain amount of planning to avoid or mitigate excess foreign tax credits. As for recording requirements, 'distributable profits' are essentially profits shown in accounts drawn up in accordance with the law of the subsidiary's country, i.e. accounting profits, not tax law profits.[44] Foreign tax payable with respect to particular profits is simply proportioned across the accounting profits for that period, i.e. a proportionate rule within a particular period.[45]

Further issues arise for an underlying foreign tax credit system when the foreign subsidiary distributing the dividend itself has received dividends. Assume that the Country A subsidiary holds shares in a further Country A corporation. The first subsidiary is referred to as a *first tier* subsidiary because the Country B parent corporation directly holds it. The second Country A corporation is referred to as a *second tier* subsidiary of the Country B parent corporation. Further, assume that the second tier subsidiary distributes its profits to the first tier subsidiary and that this distribution is exempt in the hands of the first tier

[44] TIOPA 2010 s. 59(8).

[45] By contrast, under the US underlying foreign tax credit, dividends paid in any taxable year are first considered paid out proportionately from post-1986 undistributed profits of the subsidiary. Dividends in excess of post-1986 profits are deemed to derive from pre-1987 profits in a last-in-first-out order by year. See US Internal Revenue Code s. 902.

subsidiary. When the profits are further distributed to the Country B parent corporation, the first tier subsidiary has paid no Country A tax with respect to the profits but the second tier subsidiary has. In order to relieve economic double taxation, Country B's underlying foreign tax credit system must *look through* the first tier subsidiary and attribute to the parent corporation the Country A corporate tax paid by the second tier subsidiary.

Of course, there could be any number of tiers of subsidiaries, particularly where more than one foreign jurisdiction is involved. The more complex the corporate structure, the more complex the process of tracking and attributing foreign tax through that structure for the purposes of an underlying foreign tax credit system that permits look through. The UK underlying foreign tax credit system contains no limit on the number of corporate tiers that can be looked through for the purposes of attributing foreign tax,[46] whereas the US system is limited to six tiers.[47]

Finally, underlying foreign tax credit systems raise important issues as to the limitation on credit, especially if they incorporate a limit narrower than a worldwide limit. If a residence country taxpayer derives income of different types from various countries subject to foreign tax at different rates, it may strike the limit on credit with respect to some income but not other income. That is, if an item-by-item or country-by-country type of income limitation is imposed, the taxpayer may suffer excess foreign tax credits that they would not suffer if a worldwide limitation were available. This was explained above at 4.1.1.1.

Instead of structuring their foreign investments in this way, the taxpayer might set up a corporation in a foreign country and derive all the different types and sources of foreign income through that corporation with the corporation sending back dividends that *mix* all this different income. A question is whether a dividend from such a *mixer* corporation is just one type of income for the purposes of the limitation on credit or whether it must be *looked through* to identify all the different types and sources of income it is funded with and apply the limitation on credit separately for each of these. Whether or not there is look through (i.e. whether mixing is permitted or not) can have a substantial impact on the amount of residence country tax levied with respect to foreign source income. The use of mixer corporations has been particularly common under the UK

[46] TIOPA 2010 s. 65.

[47] US Internal Revenue Code s. 902(b).

underlying foreign tax credit system. Typically, it involves more than one foreign jurisdiction and so is returned to at 5.2.3.3.

OECD Model Happily, after this rather complex discussion of unilateral underlying foreign tax relief, the position under the OECD Model is straightforward. It does not provide for the residence country to relieve international economic double taxation. Articles 23A(2) and 23B of the Model both suggest a foreign tax credit for dividends but only require credit for tax paid on the dividend (e.g. withholding tax) and not for any tax paid on the corporate profits underlying the dividend. If the Model were followed, the result would be full economic double taxation of corporate income, the major part by the source country but the rest by the residence country. This reinforces the presumption of a classical system underlying the OECD Model, even for inter-corporate dividends. This is surprising considering that even classical countries relieve economic double taxation for dividends distributed between resident corporations.

The Commentary notes that the Model does 'not prevent recurrent corporate taxation on the profits distributed to the parent company'.[48] If this multiple taxation occurred every time dividends were distributed across borders, it would be a disaster for international trade. So, this lack of relief in the OECD Model is not often followed in treaty practice. Treaties more commonly incorporate provision for underlying foreign tax relief, typically with different methods or thresholds applying for each of the treaty partners. Sometimes treaty relief is more generous than unilateral relief, sometimes unilateral relief remains more generous and other times treaties refer to unilateral relief offered by the contracting states.

EU Law As with source country taxation of dividends (discussed above at 3.1.4.1), whether a residence country is obliged to provide relief from international economic double taxation of dividends is affected by two primary sources of EU Law. The first is the Parent-Subsidiary Directive (1990) and the second is the fundamental freedoms.

Parent-Subsidiary Directive The scope of the Parent-Subsidiary Directive (1990) was discussed above at 3.1.4.1. In addition to elimination of source country taxation of dividends distributed between EU subsidiaries and their parent corporations, the Directive requires the state of the parent corporation to provide underlying foreign tax relief to prevent

[48] OECD Commentary on Art. 23 para. 50.

economic double taxation of the subsidiary's profits. Article 4 of the Directive provides:

> Where a parent company... receives distributed profits, the State of the parent company... shall...
>
> - refrain from taxing such profits, or
> - tax such profits while authorising the parent company... to deduct from the amount of tax due that fraction of the corporation tax related to those profits and paid by the subsidiary and any lower-tier subsidiary... up to the limit of the amount of the corresponding tax due.

Note that the Directive requires only underlying foreign tax relief; there is no need for direct foreign tax relief as the Directive prohibits withholding tax on dividends covered by it. Credit for corporate tax paid by lower-tier subsidiaries was added in 2003 and is consistent with the UK underlying foreign tax credit system, discussed above.

Article 4 of the Directive is short on specifics and seems to permit a substantial scope for residence countries to apply their own domestic rules for underlying foreign tax relief. In particular, it does not expressly incorporate a slicing rule for the purposes of exemption with progression or the limitation on credit under a foreign tax credit system (this is relevant only where the residence country applies progressive corporate tax rates). So it does not say whether the subsidiary's dividends are a top slice, bottom slice or proportionate part of the parent corporation's income. With respect to the foreign tax credit method, does Article 4 specify recording requirements or an ordering rule? Might it be argued that the reference to 'profits' must be to those as computed under International Accounting Standards, which have been generally adopted for EU corporate groups?[49] If so, this would appear consistent with the approach under the UK system. Does the reference to 'that fraction' require some sort of proportional ordering rule?[50] The UK ordering rule is rather favourable, but the validity of the last-in-first-out aspect of this rule is not without question.

[49] See International Accounting Standards Regulation (Council Regulation (EC) No. 1606/2002).

[50] It seems that the reference to 'corporation tax' can only be a reference to total corporation tax paid by the subsidiary (and lower tiers) on its distributed and retained profits. A reference to a 'fraction' of the corporation tax suffered on the distributed profits only makes no sense (it is the whole of that tax which must be credited). This approach was clearer in the pre-2003 version of Art. 4, which referred to 'that fraction of the corporation tax paid by the subsidiary which relates to those profits'. 'That fraction' of the total corporation tax could be interpreted as a proportionate amount.

Fundamental freedoms The scope of the Parent-Subsidiary Directive (1990) is quite limited and prescriptive regarding underlying foreign tax relief. The fundamental freedoms are substantially broader and more flexible in this respect. The freedom of establishment may apply to the receipt of non-portfolio dividends and the free movement of capital to portfolio dividends. Except where third countries are involved, the approach of the ECJ is similar under either freedom and, in the usual manner, is essentially a question of finding an appropriate comparator (see above at 2.2.1). Because of this similarity in approach, the following discussion takes the ECJ case law in chronological order, rather than distinguishing between portfolio and non-portfolio investors.

The landmark decision of the ECJ in *Verkooijen* involved a minimal amount of money (less than £200) but had repercussions for imputation countries running into billions.[51] A Dutch resident was employed by a Dutch subsidiary of a Belgium quoted corporation. As part of a group wide employee savings plan, Mr Verkooijen was given shares in the Belgian parent corporation. He received a dividend on these shares. Dividends from Dutch corporations entitled the shareholder to a small exemption (less than £400) with respect to the taxation of the dividends, but this was not available for Mr Verkooijen's Belgian source dividends. Mr Verkooijen argued this was contrary to the free movement of capital.

The ECJ agreed that the refusal to grant the exemption constituted an obstacle to Belgian corporations raising capital in the Netherlands. With respect to the exemption, the ECJ noted that:

> It is clear from the legislative history of that provision that the dividend exemption (and its limitation to dividends paid by companies established in the Netherlands) fulfilled a twofold objective: first, the exemption was intended to raise the level of undertakings' equity capital and to stimulate interest on the part of private individuals in Netherlands shares; second, in particular for small investors, the exemption was intended to compensate in some measure for the double taxation which would otherwise result, under the Netherlands tax system, from the levying both of corporation tax on profits accruing to companies and of tax on the income of private shareholders imposed on the dividends distributed by those companies.[52]

Neither of these objectives justified the discriminatory treatment of foreign source dividends when compared with domestic source dividends,

[51] Case C-35/98 *Secretaris van Financien* v *Verkooijen* [2000] ECR I-4071 (ECJ).

[52] Case C-35/98 *Secretaris van Financien* v *Verkooijen* [2000] ECR I-4071 (ECJ) at para. 11.

a comparison which the ECJ found appropriate. Accordingly, the Dutch rule violated the free movement of capital.

Verkooijen had broad implications for corporate tax systems that provided shareholders with greater relief from economic double taxation. In particular, it was the nail in the coffin of the standard European imputation system, which usually provided relief from economic double taxation of domestic dividends but not foreign dividends. Typically, imputation credits would be attached to domestic source dividends but not foreign dividends, for which only a direct foreign tax credit was available. The former corporate tax systems in Finland, Austria and Germany have all been held to fall foul of the fundamental freedoms based on *Verkooijen*.

In *Manninen*, a Finnish taxpayer successfully argued that the free movement of capital required that Finland grant him dividend tax credits for underlying Swedish corporate tax paid with respect to Swedish source dividends as that treatment was available with respect to Finnish dividends.[53] The ECJ's limiting interpretation of Article 65 of the FEU Treaty was noted above at 2.2.1. In *Lenz*, the ECJ held that Austrian taxation of residents at a flat 25 per cent rate on Austrian source dividends (on a gross basis) while taxing foreign source dividends at rates up to 50 per cent (on a net basis) also breached the free movement of capital.[54] In *Meilicke*, the German imputation system suffered a similar fate, the major issue being whether the *Verkooijen* decision might be limited on a prospective basis, held not.[55]

Under the old UK ACT system, resident individuals received dividend tax credits with UK source dividends but not foreign source dividends. Inevitably, this breached the *Verkooijen* principle but has not been the specific subject of an ECJ decision. Further, it was inevitable that the UK treatment of inter-corporate dividends would come under challenge. As mentioned above at 4.1.2.1, the UK exempts UK source inter-corporate dividends. When it comes to foreign dividends, however, a UK resident corporate shareholder has historically been entitled to underlying foreign tax credits, but if its shareholding is below 10 per cent in the distributing foreign corporation it is not entitled to any relief from economic double taxation. Both features of the UK corporate tax treatment of inbound dividends were in issue in the *FII* case.[56]

The ECJ assessed the underlying foreign tax credit system by reference to the freedom of establishment. The ECJ confirmed that it was not sufficient

[53] Case C-319/02 *Manninen* [2004] ECR I-7477 (ECJ).

[54] Case C-315/02 *Lenz* v *Finanzlandesdirektion für Tirol* [2004] ECR I-7063 (ECJ).

[55] Case C-292/04 *Meilicke* v *Finanzamt Bonn-Innenstadt* [2007] ECR I-1835 (ECJ).

[56] Case C-446/04 *Test Claimants in the FII Group Litigation* [2006] ECR I-11753 (ECJ).

for the UK to comply with the Parent-Subsidiary Directive (1990); it must also comply with the fundamental freedoms.[57] In that regard:

> The fact that nationally-sourced dividends are subject to an exemption system and foreign-sourced dividends are subject to an imputation system does not contravene the principle of freedom of establishment... provided that the tax rate applied to foreign-sourced dividends is not higher than the rate applied to nationally-sourced dividends and that the tax credit is at least equal to the amount paid in the Member State of the company making the distribution, up to the limit of the tax charged in the Member State of the company receiving the dividends.[58]

This restatement of the operation of an underlying foreign tax credit system provides no more specifics than are provided by the Parent-Subsidiary Directive (1990), discussed above. It does not specify a slicing rule, recording requirements or an ordering rule. As with the Directive, it may be presumed that these matters are left to the country of the parent corporation. In addition, the restatement seems limited to residence country taxation of first tier subsidiaries, but, since 2003, the Directive covers lower tier subsidiaries.

The ECJ assessed the UK taxation of portfolio corporate shareholders by reference to the free movement of capital. To the extent that the underlying foreign tax credit system was available to such shareholders (holdings of 10 per cent or more), the assessment was the same as under the freedom of establishment. The situation was different with respect to holdings below the threshold required for underlying foreign tax credits. Here, the provision of underlying relief (exemption) with respect to domestic source dividends but not foreign dividends was an unjustifiable breach of the freedom.[59] The UK had sought to justify the difference in treatment based on the substantial difficulties in determining underlying corporate tax paid on portfolio dividends. The ECJ retorted that:

> Irrespective of the fact that a Member State may, in any event, choose between a number of systems in order to prevent or mitigate the imposition of a series of charges to tax on distributed profits, the difficulties that may arise in determining the tax actually paid in another Member State

[57] Case C-446/04 *Test Claimants in the FII Group Litigation* [2006] ECR I-11753 (ECJ) at para. 45.

[58] Case C-446/04 *Test Claimants in the FII Group Litigation* [2006] ECR I-11753 (ECJ) at para. 57.

[59] Case C-446/04 *Test Claimants in the FII Group Litigation* [2006] ECR I-11753 (ECJ) at para. 65.

> cannot justify a restriction on the free movement of capital such as that which arises under the legislation at issue in the main proceedings.[60]

The case also concerned the redistribution of non-portfolio dividends by UK parent corporations. In effect, redistributions of UK source dividends produced refundable tax credits in the hands of UK shareholders whereas redistributions of foreign source dividends either did not give credit for foreign corporate taxes or, where they did, provided only non-refundable credits. Both features were also held contrary to the fundamental freedoms.

The UK acted on the latter aspects of this case in 1999 by repealing ACT and making all dividend tax credits non-refundable, see above. This is another example of a state adopting practices that are more restrictive domestically and thereby removing discrimination with respect to cross-border activities. The treatment of portfolio corporate shareholders was acted upon in 2009, by extending the inter-corporate dividend exemption system to most foreign dividends.

The UK courts have had technical difficulties in applying the ECJ judgment in the FII case.[61] The technicalities involve when the foreign tax underlying a dividend from a foreign subsidiary is the same as that underlying a dividend from a UK subsidiary. There are also problems with how to account for tax paid by second- and third-tier corporations where no tax is paid by the distributing corporation itself. The Court of Appeal's decision is the most recent, which is to refer these matters back to the ECJ. The Court of Appeal held that Article 63 of the FEU Treaty could apply to the taxation of dividends from third countries but that the discriminatory treatment was protected by the grandfather clause in Article 64 (though not in all circumstances).[62]

4.1.2.2 Controlled foreign corporations

The fundamental distinctions between establishing a foreign presence in the form of a PE or a subsidiary and between the exemption and foreign tax credit methods of providing foreign tax relief are somewhat blurred where source country tax is higher than in the residence country. In such a case, the residence country will not tax, whether the presence is in the form of a PE or a subsidiary and whether the residence country provides

[60] Case C-446/04 *Test Claimants in the FII Group Litigation* [2006] ECR I-11753 (ECJ) at para. 70.

[61] *Test Claimants in the Franked Investment Income GLO* [2008] EWHC 2893 (Ch).

[62] *Test Claimants in the Franked Investment Income GLO* [2010] EWCA Civ 103 (CA).

foreign tax relief in the form of an exemption or foreign tax credit. As discussed in Chapter 3, the form of presence may make a difference to source country taxation, but even here it won't if the source country exempts outbound dividends, as is often the case (or imposes a branch profits tax). So where source country tax is higher, capital import neutrality (see above at 2.2.1) will often be achieved, irrespective of form of presence, irrespective of whether foreign tax relief is exemption or foreign tax credit and irrespective of whether profits are retained in the source country or repatriated to the residence country.

These fundamental distinctions become particularly clear where source country tax is lower than in the residence country. For foreign tax credit countries (direct and underlying foreign tax credit), the additional tax levied by the residence country may produce capital export neutrality (see above at 2.2.1) with respect to profits derived through a foreign PE (retained or repatriated) or with respect to profits repatriated by a foreign subsidiary. However, this will not be achieved with respect to profits retained by a foreign subsidiary. As a separate tax entity, the subsidiary's profits are its own and not that of the parent corporation. Until it makes a distribution of the profits, the parent corporation has no income from the foreign presence. By contrast, as a PE is part of the residence country investor, PE profits do belong to the investor irrespective of repatriation/distribution.

This lack of residence taxation of retained profits of foreign subsidiaries is often viewed as consistent with capital import neutrality rather than capital export neutrality and so inconsistent with a foreign tax credit system. In this regard, it also makes foreign tax credit countries prone to tax competition in the same way as exemption countries. Profits derived in lowly taxed subsidiaries have a habit of never finding their way back to the jurisdiction of the parent corporation, e.g. they are invested directly from the lowly taxed subsidiary elsewhere in a multinational group. By contrast, an exemption country provides no barrier to the repatriation of profits of lowly taxed subsidiaries and so there is general consistency with capital import neutrality. Nevertheless, there is concern in exemption countries over tax competition and, in particular, *harmful* tax competition, see above at 2.2.1. These concerns are exacerbated by difficulties in applying transfer pricing rules, discussed above at 3.3.1. Multinational groups have an incentive to manipulate the pricing of inter-group transactions to enhance the profitability of lowly taxed subsidiaries.[63]

[63] More fundamentally, multinationals have an incentive to locate rights that generate firm specific benefits (additional value beyond market value transactions, i.e. residual profit)

Because of these concerns, many countries, whether exemption or foreign tax credit countries, have implemented *controlled foreign corporation* (CFC) rules. If deferral were the sole concern, CFC rules would be limited to foreign tax credit countries and they would be applied to treat foreign subsidiaries in the same manner as foreign PEs, i.e. tax them in the parent country jurisdiction on a current basis with foreign tax credits. Historically, New Zealand is an example of such an approach. However, while CFC rules attribute profits of CFCs, they do not allocate CFC losses. This somewhat unbalanced approach is not reflected in the treatment of PEs; see below at 4.2.2. CFC rules seek to do more than deal with deferral; they also seek to address tax competition, at least of the harmful variety. In this context, exemption systems need to deal with not only foreign subsidiaries but also foreign PEs. Dealing with foreign PEs is relatively simple conceptually, involving a switch from the exemption method to the foreign tax credit method of foreign tax relief. The German *switchover* provision was in issue in the *Columbus Container Services* case, discussed above at 4.1.1.3.

CFC rules are also used as a back up to other problems in the international order. Two such areas that have already been discussed are corporate residence (above at 2.1.1.2) and transfer pricing (above at 3.3.1). There are conceptual reasons for suggesting that a corporation should be treated as resident where its controlling shareholders are resident, but international tax rules do not accept this, thereby facilitating the CFC problem. CFC rules address this issue and demonstrate a strong conceptual link with the problem of corporate residence. CFC rules also help with transfer pricing issues; the shifting of profits to a foreign corporation is less problematic if the profits of that corporation will be attributed to its parent corporation in any case.[64] Further, CFC rules are often a residence country's best (perhaps sole) defence to cross-border mismatches that generate substantial amounts of tax planning, discussed further at 5.1.

CFC rules are grounded in domestic law. Residence countries have implemented them in a variety of forms, which are outlined in the following discussion, with particular focus on the UK approach. The OECD is of the view that CFC rules do not breach its Model and this is the most widely held opinion. However, it is important to consider the arguments that have been raised suggesting that CFC rules are inconsistent with

in lowly taxed subsidiaries. This is fundamental to the reason why multinationals seek to locate valuable intellectual property in such subsidiaries.

[64] *DSG Retail Ltd* v *RCC* [2009] UKFTT TC00001 (TC) is a good example of a transfer pricing dispute that arose primarily because the CFC rules failed to apply.

treaties. These arguments may be viewed as having had some influence on the manner in which CFC rules have been implemented in domestic law. Finally, the following discussion grapples with the difficult and continuing saga of whether CFC rules breach EU Law and, if so, to what extent.

Domestic law[65] CFC rules attribute the profits of a foreign corporation to resident shareholders and tax those shareholders with respect to their attribution irrespective of whether the foreign corporation distributes profits. The analogy with the treatment of foreign PEs under a foreign tax credit system is clear. However, PEs are wholly owned by the enterprise of which they are part, but foreign subsidiaries need not be wholly owned. The level of shareholding required to trigger CFC rules is a matter of debate and divergent practice among countries. At a conceptual level, the core problem is where resident shareholders control the distribution policy of the foreign corporation and so can determine when and if residence country tax is paid. This problem is essentially an extension of the corporate tax shelter problem suffered domestically when the corporate tax rate is lower than the highest individual rate. The rub is that in an international context the foreign corporate tax rate may be substantially lower than not only the highest individual tax rate in the residence country but also the residence country's corporate tax rate.

Domestically, the corporate tax shelter problem is often dealt with by having special rules applicable to closely held corporations. Sometimes, like CFC rules, these special rules attribute the profits of a closely held corporation to its shareholders.[66] The argument here is that if particular shareholders have control over a corporation's distribution policy, they have an *ability to pay* taxes out of the corporation's profits, i.e. they have income as they can call for the profits as they desire. The same approach is often the driving philosophy of CFC rules, but it suggests that such rules should be limited to foreign corporations held by a small number of resident shareholders. Other countries point out that this does not deal with the deferral and tax competition issues holistically. Here the problem is largely viewed as the lower tax rate in the foreign country, which should be addressed irrespective of whether the foreign corporation is controlled by residents. These countries tend to supplement their CFC rules, which focus on *control*, with foreign or offshore investment fund rules that apply

[65] For an overview of issues arising under CFC rules, see Arnold and McIntyre (2002, pp. 87–99).

[66] Regarding the UK rules that existed before 1988, see Harris and Oliver (2008).

in non-controlled situations. Foreign investment fund rules are generally beyond the scope of this book.

The UK CFC rules potentially apply to non-resident corporations that are 'controlled' by residents. 'Control' is not defined in terms of a certain holding but rather in terms of a person securing that 'the affairs of the company are conducted in accordance with his wishes'. Importantly, this means that both direct holdings in a foreign corporation and indirect holdings in a foreign corporation (i.e. holdings in a corporation that holds shares in the foreign corporation) count. The powers of two or more persons are amalgamated for this purpose, irrespective of whether they are related. It is possible for a single resident person with a 40 per cent interest in a foreign corporation to trigger the CFC rules if no other single person holds 55 per cent of the corporation.[67]

It will be noted that the UK CFC rules are not limited to closely held corporations. There is no *de minimus* level of shareholding that counts towards control by residents, e.g. if two residents hold 25 per cent and 24.5 per cent of a foreign corporation, respectively, another resident holding 1 per cent of the corporation will cause the CFC rules to apply. Some countries count only substantial shareholdings (aggregating the holdings of related persons). Further, in determining whether a corporate controller is resident in the UK, the tiebreaker under UK tax treaties is ignored.[68] So, a UK incorporated company that is effectively managed in a treaty country (and so resident there for the purposes of the tax treaty) is nevertheless subject to the UK CFC rules with respect to foreign subsidiaries that it controls.

The CFC rules of most countries apply only where the CFC is subject to low taxation. For example, the UK rules apply only if the tax paid by the CFC is less than three quarters of what it would have paid if it were resident in the UK.[69] Alternately, a country may be satisfied that the tax system of a particular foreign country is sufficiently robust so that it need not apply its CFC rules to corporations resident in such foreign country, i.e. a white list approach. The UK also uses this method.[70] Like other countries, the UK has learned by experience that even countries with apparently robust tax systems can be used for tax planning purposes. So, the UK white list is now couched in qualifications.[71]

[67] ICTA 1988 ss. 747 and 755D.

[68] ICTA 1988 s. 747(1B).

[69] ICTA 1988 s. 750.

[70] ICTA 1988 s. 748(1)(e).

[71] ICTA 1988 s. 748A.

Once the CFC rules apply, they attribute the profits of the CFC to persons holding interests in the CFC, whether resident or non-resident.[72] In a simple case, this might involve dividing and attributing the profits according to the level of each shareholder's shareholding.[73] The attribution process can be problematic where the CFC has different classes of shares or other rights have been issued.[74] Here, there is no certainty that the profits of the CFC will be distributed (if they ever are distributed) in accordance with the attribution. Further problems arise where the shares are sold during the tax year. In such a case, the UK apportions the attributed profits to both the seller and the buyer. Attribution usually occurs for all shareholders irrespective of whether a residence country intends to tax all those shareholders; indeed non-residents are also attributed CFC profits. This ensures that, say, a parent corporation with a 70 per cent interest in a CFC is taxed only on 70 per cent of the CFC's profits.

CFC attribution rules also deal with indirect holdings. Assume that a resident holds shares in foreign corporation A that holds shares in foreign corporation B. The holding of the resident may cause both corporations to be subject to CFC rules. Further, attribution to residents typically occurs separately for each foreign corporation. So the profits of corporation A may be directly attributed to the resident and the profits of corporation B may be attributed to the resident. With respect to corporation B, the process is direct attribution and not, for example, attribution of the profits of corporation B to corporation A and then attribution of the profits of corporation A (as increased by the corporation B attribution) to the resident.[75]

Which of the persons subject to attribution is taxed with respect to their share of the CFC's profits is often independent of who counts for the purposes of determining control of a CFC. So, even though the UK counts small shareholdings (including those of individuals) in determining whether its CFC rules apply, it taxes only *corporations* that are attributed 25 per cent of the CFC's profits. The holdings of associated persons are aggregated for purposes of calculating the 25 per cent.[76] Strangely, the UK CFC rules do not apply to tax individuals.

[72] For example, ICTA 1988 s. 747(3). In the UK, capital gains of CFCs are not subject to attribution but might be caught by a separate regime in TCGA 1992 s. 13.

[73] For example, ICTA 1988 s. 752(3).

[74] In such a case, the UK legislation prescribes only that the apportionment 'be made on a just and reasonable basis', ICTA 1988 s. 752(4).

[75] For example, see ICTA 1988 s. 752B.

[76] ICTA 1988 s. 747(5).

In addition to attributing the profits of a CFC to shareholders, CFC rules also attribute any foreign tax paid by the CFC to its shareholders.[77] This is for providing underlying foreign tax relief, which is inevitably provided in the form of underlying foreign tax credits. So, when an exemption country implements CFC rules, this means a *switchover* to the underlying foreign tax credit method, with all the complications that involves (see above at 4.1.2.1). It also means the usual limits on availability of underlying foreign tax relief, i.e. limitation to non-portfolio shareholders.[78]

If these rules are not complex enough, CFC rules are typically further complicated by limitations and exceptions. The main exception usually pertains to 'active income' (see above at 2.1.2.1), especially business income. Some countries attribute only *tainted* income to residents. This is usually passive income plus business income derived from dealings with related parties. The latter feature demonstrates clearly the connection between CFC rules and transfer pricing. The rationale for attributing only tainted income is that this tends to be more mobile than active income and so more open to tax planning and sensitive to tax competition. While this is true, treaty issues might also have influenced active business exceptions, discussed below. Other countries, including the UK, provide an exclusion from the CFC rules for foreign corporations sufficiently engaged in active business.[79] Failure to sufficiently engage in active business may result in attribution of all CFC profits, including business profits.

Other exceptions to the application of a CFC regime may apply. For example, traditionally, the UK rules did not apply if the CFC distributed sufficient of its profits, defined as 90 per cent within 18 months of the end of the relevant accounting period.[80] This exception was removed from mid-2009 as part of the foreign profits reforms (see below). There is also a *de minimus* exception where the CFC's profits do not exceed £50,000.[81] Finally, there is an exception if the transactions of the CFC achieved only a minimal reduction in UK tax or did not have a main purpose of achieving a reduction and, in either case, 'it was not the main reason... for the [CFC's] existence... to achieve a reduction in United Kingdom tax by a diversion of profits from the United Kingdom'.[82]

[77] For example, ICTA 1988 s. 747(3).

[78] In the case of the UK, this limitation is linked to the concept of 'creditable tax'; ICTA 1988 s. 751(6).

[79] ICTA 1988 s. 748(1)(b) and Sch. 25, Part II.

[80] ICTA 1988 s. 748(1)(a) and Sch. 25, Part I.

[81] ICTA 1988 s. 748(1)(d).

[82] ICTA 1988 s. 748(3).

This motive or *mud* rule was in issue before the ECJ in the context of the *Cadbury Schweppes* case, discussed below.

Despite providing for underlying relief, CFC regimes can give rise to problems of double taxation. One problem is the difference in timing between attribution and distribution. Residence country taxation at the time of attribution means exemption of dividends distributed out of attributed profits. This particularly causes problems where the source country imposes withholding tax on such dividends, as there may be no tax liability in the residence country to set the tax against. Allowing excess foreign tax credits to be carried backwards can mitigate this. The UK addresses this situation by treating tax paid on attribution as paid on account of the tax due on distribution.[83] Another problem is the simultaneous application of the CFC rules of two or more countries, e.g. where a Country C corporation holds a Country B corporation that holds a third lowly taxed corporation. Country C and Country B might both apply their CFC rules, with neither crediting tax levied under the other's rules.

Following scrutiny by the ECJ, the UK CFC regime is still under review. Some minor adjustments were made because of the introduction of the exemption for foreign dividends (discussed above at 4.1.2.1). The most recent discussion document is HMRC & HM Treasury (2010). The reform is expected for 2011.

OECD Model A number of arguments have been raised to the effect that CFC rules breach the provisions of the OECD Model. As mentioned, the official position now is:

> Thus, whilst some countries have felt it useful to expressly clarify, in their conventions, that controlled foreign companies legislation did not conflict with the Convention, such clarification is not necessary. It is recognised that controlled foreign companies legislation… is not contrary to the provisions of the Convention.[84]

Nevertheless, it is still important to explore the arguments that CFC rules do breach the OECD Model as they demonstrate the limitations of the Model and may have an impact on the manner in which CFC rules are constructed.

[83] ICTA 1988 s. 754(5) and Sch. 26 para. 4.

[84] OECD Commentary on Art. 1 para. 23.

Article 7(1) of the OECD Model was set out above at 3.1.3. As noted at that point, this provision can be divided into an exclusive right of tax and a shared right of tax. It is the exclusive right of tax in particular (i.e. that which pertains to subsidiaries) that is in issue with respect to CFC rules. As discussed above at 3.1.3.1, a subsidiary is 'an enterprise of a Contracting State', for present purposes the source/host state, and an enterprise separate from that of its parent corporation. In this context, the exclusive right to tax suggests that the 'profits' of a subsidiary 'shall be taxable only' in the source/host state. An exception would be if the parent corporation had a PE in the source/host country and the profits of the subsidiary were in some way attributable to the PE. This possibility is usually discounted based on Article 5(7) (discussed above at 3.1.3.3) and so that the mere control of a subsidiary by a parent corporation does not create a PE of the parent corporation in the country of the subsidiary.

The critical question is, how should CFC rules be characterised under the OECD Model? What do they do? Do CFC rules:

- tax the profits of the subsidiary
- tax a deemed dividend
- tax the value of the shares held in the subsidiary by the parent corporation, or
- tax something else?

If CFC rules tax the *profits of the subsidiary*, then they apparently breach the source/host country's exclusive right to tax the subsidiary in Article 7(1). The official OECD position is that tax levied under CFC rules 'does not reduce the profits of the [subsidiary] and may not, therefore, be said to have been levied on such profits'.[85] This argument is particularly weak. If accepted, it provides a simple method of avoiding obligations under a tax treaty by simply taxing someone else with respect to the income to be taxed. An interesting question is whether exclusion of business (active) profits under a CFC regime remedies any problem with Article 7(1). Article 7(1) is entitled 'Business Profits' and, as discussed above at 3.1.3.1, the concept of 'enterprise' is defined in terms of carrying on a business. So, it might be argued that the taxation of the parent corporation with respect to the subsidiary's passive income does not breach Article 7(1). A problem is that Article 7(1) clearly covers business profits from transactions with related parties and yet the business profits exception under CFC regimes often does not extend to profits from related party transactions.

[85] OECD Commentary on Art. 7 para. 13.

If CFC rules tax a deemed dividend, there might be problems with Article 10 of the OECD Model. As mentioned above at 3.1.4.1, Article 10(1), read literally, requires a dividend to be 'paid' before it can be taxed in the parent corporation jurisdiction. If Article 10(1) is not intended to restrict a country's right to tax a deemed dividend before it is paid, perhaps the reference to 'paid' should be deleted. Further, it is sometimes argued that CFC rules seek to tax a foreign subsidiary's undistributed profits and this breaches Article 10(5). Even if CFC rules are viewed as taxing a foreign subsidiary's profits, application of the wording of Article 10(5) is not without difficulty.[86] If CFC rules are viewed as fixing on the holding of the parent corporation in the subsidiary, Article 13 might be analysed in a similar manner to Article 10. Does Article 13 permit the country of the parent corporation to tax unrealised gains? If this is permitted, why does it refer to 'alienation'? In a civil law jurisdiction, where such gains might be business profits under Article 7, there is, perhaps, greater scope for interpreting 'profits' as used in that article to permit taxation of unrealised amounts.

Each of these arguments against CFC rules is sound in itself, particularly the cumulative effect of these arguments, but they do not rule out the possibility of characterising CFC rules as taxing something other than the subsidiary's profits or dividends or the parent corporation's shareholding. The UK *Bricom Holdings* case is a case in point.[87] In this case, a UK parent corporation had a 100% owned Dutch subsidiary. The subsidiary lent funds to the parent corporation and the parent corporation paid interest to the subsidiary. Under Article 11 of the Netherlands/UK Tax Treaty, the interest was exempt from UK tax, i.e. exempt from source country tax. The interest was lowly taxed in the Netherlands. The UK tax administration used the CFC rules to assess the parent corporation to UK

[86] OECD Commentary on Art. 10 para. 37 suggests Art. 10(5) 'is confined to taxation at source' and so has no impact on residence country taxation under CFC rules. Read literally, this may be true, but the general structure of Art. 10 tells against such a limited reading. Literally, Art. 10(5) actually prohibits the parent corporation jurisdiction from taxing the subsidiary's profits if the subsidiary has any (even a very small) amount of income sourced in that jurisdiction. It would be bizarre for the parent corporation jurisdiction to be prohibited from taxation when the subsidiary has some income sourced in that jurisdiction but be permitted to tax (under CFC rules) where it does not. A broader prohibition on the parent corporation jurisdiction from taxing the undistributed profits of the subsidiary is also consistent with 'paid' in Art. 10(1). Read together, there is a sound argument that Art. 10(1) and (5) prohibit CFC rules, provided CFC rules *do* tax the *profits of the subsidiary*.

[87] *Bricom Holdings Ltd* v *IRC* [1997] STC 1179 (CA).

tax on the subsidiary's profits, including the interest the parent had paid to the subsidiary. The parent corporation objected, arguing that the UK was taxing the interest paid to the subsidiary, which was expressly exempt under the tax treaty.

The Court of Appeal refused to find that application of the CFC rules with respect to the interest breached the treaty. The reasoning of the court is tortuous and smacks more than a little of form over substance. The court reasoned that what was apportioned to the parent corporation and subjected to tax under the CFC rules was not the subsidiary's actual profits (and so the interest), but a notional sum that was the product of an artificial calculation. Apparently, this meant that the interest received by the Dutch subsidiary was not included in the sum apportioned to the UK parent corporation on which tax was chargeable. The interest merely provided a measure by which an element in a conventional or notional sum was calculated. The conventional or notional sum was apportioned and taxed to the parent corporation, not the interest.

> Interest from exempt securities does not cease to be such by being included as a component element of the recipient's taxable profits... Exempt income does not change its character or lose its exemption merely because it is deemed to be the income of another person or is imputed to him... But where tax is charged on a conventional or notional sum which exists only as the product of a calculation, the fact that one of the elements in the calculation is measured by reference to the amount of exempted income does not make the exempted income the subject of the tax.
> The correct analysis is that the interest received by [the Dutch subsidiary] is not included in the sum apportioned to the taxpayer company on which tax is chargeable. It merely provides a measure by which an element in a conventional or notional sum is calculated, and it is that conventional or notional sum which is apportioned to the taxpayer company and on which tax is charged.[88]

While apparently based on (much) earlier UK case law (not decided on CFC rules), the formality of this decision does not sit easily with the fundamental nature of tax treaties and their interpretation in accordance with the Vienna Convention, particularly the obligation to interpret treaties in good faith, see above at 1.3.2. On its face, the decision appears to permit the UK to circumvent its treaty obligations and to tax income that the treaty does not permit to be taxed by the simple mechanism of deeming the income to be that of another person. Civil lawyers might shudder when faced with this style of form over substance reasoning. A cynic

[88] *Bricom Holdings Ltd* v *IRC* [1997] STC 1179 (CA) at 1196 per Millett LJ.

might suggest that the Court of Appeal had no intention of striking down the UK CFC rules in a treaty context and was willing to interpret the UK rules in whatever manner would suit that purpose. The same cynic might make the same suggestion with respect to the official OECD position.

Nevertheless, *Bricom* is widely viewed as supporting the view that CFC rules of a particular form do not breach tax treaties. For example, in 2002 the French Conseil d'Etat struck down the French CFC rules in the context of Article 7(1) of the France/Switzerland Tax Treaty.[89] These rules purported to directly tax a French parent corporation with respect to its Swiss subsidiary's profits. In a manner consistent with *Bricom*, the French authorities felt that the solution was to change the form of their CFC rules. So, in 2005, the French CFC rules were reformulated to deem certain foreign subsidiaries to distribute their retained profits as dividends. Through this mechanism, the French authorities believe that they have taken the parent corporation outside both the business profits article and the dividends article of tax treaties, i.e. Articles 7 and 10 of the OECD Model.[90]

Indeed, the French seem to believe that the profits attributed to the parent corporation now fall within the other income article (Article 21 of the OECD Model), granting them a right to tax.[91] From a UK perspective, there are two problems with this. First, the problem of whose income is being taxed continues. In pure substance, there can be little doubt that what is being taxed is the subsidiary's income. The form of CFC legislation is such that the parent is being attributed notional income and being taxed with respect thereto. So, when Article 21 says 'income of a resident… shall be taxable only in that State', the question under CFC rules remains: 'whose income is it?' In substance, it seems to be the subsidiary's income and that is 'dealt with' by Article 7, but in form, perhaps it is the parent's. If it is accepted that the income that is being taxed is that of the subsidiary, then far from permitting CFC rules, Article 21 seems to prohibit taxation in the parent corporation's jurisdiction.

The second problem with Article 21 of the OECD Model and CFC rules arises only if it is accepted that the subject of taxation is not the income of the subsidiary. In this case, the parent corporation is being taxed on notional income (i.e. an amount that has not been realised) rather than actual income, see above at 1.1. Is such a notional amount 'income' for the purposes of Article 21? If a domestic law meaning were given to that

[89] *Re Société Schneider Electric* (2002) 4 ITLR 1077 (CE).

[90] See Reeb-Blanluet (2007).

[91] Reeb-Blanluet (2007).

term, the amount would not be 'income' as generally understood under UK domestic law. The problem with interpreting the word 'income' where it appears in Articles 6 and 21 was mentioned above at 3.1.2 and 3.1.1, respectively. If it is not income and so does not fall within Article 21, does taxation under CFC rules simply fall outside of the scope of treaties? In this case, it might be suggested that the country of the parent corporation has an unrestricted taxing right.[92] As mentioned, this is problematic in that it provides a simple mechanism for countries to avoid their treaty obligations through deemed income. Further, if the OECD Model does not cover deemed income, then what is the purpose of Article 9(1)? It provides specific permission for the reallocation of income among members of a corporate group. Does the existence of this specific rule negate reallocation, e.g. under CFC rules, in other cases?

For the present, OECD member states consider that their CFC rules are compatible with tax treaties. In the UK, *Bricom* stands in the way of any challenge. CFC rules raise issues as to the fundamental nature of tax treaties. It would be foolhardy to suggest that we have heard the last of the compatibility of CFC rules with tax treaties, but for now there seems to be a standoff, at least in the UK. This is far from the case with respect to the compatibility of CFC rules with EU Law, where the battle continues.

EU Law The uneasy position of CFC rules under the OECD Model is reflected in the position of these rules under EU Law. At various points in history, a number of countries have domestically allocated the profits of a corporation to their shareholders and so taxed the shareholders with respect to undistributed profits.[93] However, CFC rules do not apply to purely domestic situations; they do not extend to attribute the undistributed profits of domestic subsidiaries to their domestic parent corporations. This unbalanced approach raises questions of discrimination and a breach of the fundamental freedoms under EU Law. Those freedoms can apply to both source/host countries and residence/home countries and this can be contrasted with the OECD Model. Article 24(5) applies to prevent some forms of discrimination of a subsidiary in the source/host country, see above at 3.1.3.4. However, there is no equivalent of Article 24(5) to prevent the residence/home country from discriminating against

[92] This argument is akin to that used by the Australian tax administration to suggest that it was entitled to tax capital gains on a source basis where a treaty did not contain a capital gains article, see above at 3.1.1.

[93] For example, with respect to the UK, see the discussion in Harris and Oliver (2008).

a parent corporation. This reflects a fundamental difference between the OECD Model and EU Law.

In the landmark decision of *Cadbury Schweppes*, the UK CFC rules came before the ECJ.[94] A UK parent corporation set up two finance subsidiaries in Ireland; it also had subsidiaries in other EU countries. Apparently, the Irish subsidiaries had no offices, employees or phones and it was accepted that they were purposely formed to take advantage of a special Irish regime that taxed them at 10% when the UK corporate tax rate was 30%. The UK tax administration sought to apply the UK CFC rules. The parent corporation argued that taxing it with respect to the Irish subsidiaries' retained profits constituted a breach of the freedom of establishment, the freedom to provide services and the free movement of capital.

The ECJ held that the UK's CFC rules constituted a restriction on the freedom of establishment because they apply to UK parent corporations with subsidiaries in low tax member states but do not apply to UK parent corporations with UK subsidiaries or subsidiaries in high tax member states. The primary issue for the ECJ was whether the UK rules could be justified.

> It follows that, in order for a restriction on the freedom of establishment to be justified on the ground of prevention of abusive practices, the specific objective of such a restriction must be to prevent conduct involving the creation of wholly artificial arrangements which do not reflect economic reality, with a view to escaping the tax normally due on the profits generated by activities carried out on national territory.[95]

The ECJ held that if 'on the basis of objective factors which are ascertainable by third parties' it is proven that a CFC 'is actually established in the host member state and carries on genuine economic activities there', the UK CFC rules could not be justified.[96] The ECJ remitted to the UK courts the issue of whether the UK CFC rules are compatible with the principles laid down by the decision. In particular, the UK courts have to decide whether the motive exception discussed above takes account of objective criteria like the existence of premises, staff and equipment in establishing whether genuine economic activities take place in the host state.

There have been two sets of developments in the UK since the decision of the ECJ in *Cadbury Schweppes*, legislative developments as well

[94] Case C-196/04 *Cadbury Schweppes* [2006] ECR I-7995 (ECJ).
[95] Case C-196/04 *Cadbury Schweppes* [2006] ECR I-7995 (ECJ) at para. 55.
[96] Case C-196/04 *Cadbury Schweppes* [2006] ECR I-7995 (ECJ) at paras. 65–70.

as progress of case law in the UK courts. With respect to the latter, in *Vodafone 2*, the Special Commissioners had referred another CFC case to the ECJ. However, with the decision in *Cadbury Schweppes*, the Commissioners withdrew the case as they felt the compatibility of the UK's CFC rules with EU Law could be decided in accordance with the principles developed by the ECJ in the *Cadbury Schweppes* case. This did not prove so easy and the Special Commissioners split on whether the motive test could be read to produce compatibility. *Vodafone 2* was then appealed to the High Court and on to the Court of Appeal.[97]

In *Vodafone* 2, the taxpayer parent corporation sought an order directing the UK tax administration to close an enquiry into its tax return. The purpose of the enquiry was to establish whether or not the taxpayer should be subject to attribution under the UK's CFC rules with respect to the profits of a wholly owned Luxembourg subsidiary. In accordance with *Cadbury Schweppes*, the primary issue was viewed as whether, due to the motive exception, application of the UK CFC rules can be limited to 'wholly artificial arrangements' intended to escape the UK tax normally payable. The judge at first instance held that it was impossible to construe the motive test in the UK CFC rules to make those rules compatible with the freedom of establishment.

The Court of Appeal took a broader approach. Despite the fact that the ECJ specifically referred to the motive test, the court suggested that interpretation of domestic legislation was a matter for the UK courts and the simple issue was whether that legislation as a whole could be read as consistent with the ECJ decision, i.e. it did not limit its consideration to interpretation of the motive test.[98] The court found that it could interpret into the UK CFC rules a new and separate exception that is consistent with the ECJ decision, i.e. an 'additional exception in respect of a controlled foreign company "if it is, in that accounting period, actually established in another member state of the EEA and carries on genuine economic activities there"'.[99] There is no further guidance on the critical question of what profits are properly attributable to an establishment and so protected by the exclusion.

The UK tax administration's view is that this attribution is properly determined according to the amendment to the CFC rules in 2007 before the *Vodafone 2* judgment. Under section 751A of ICTA 1988, a UK parent

[97] *Vodafone 2* v *RCC* [2009] EWCA Civ 446 (CA).

[98] *Vodafone 2* v *RCC* [2009] EWCA Civ 446 (CA) at paras. 33 and 34.

[99] *Vodafone 2* v *RCC* [2009] EWCA Civ 446 (CA) at para. 39.

corporation that is apportioned an amount under the CFC rules can apply to the UK tax administration for a reduction in profits of the CFC that are apportioned. The idea is to reduce the CFC's attributable profits by an amount that was derived through a European 'business establishment'. For this purpose, there must be individuals that work at the establishment. The CFC's profits are to be reduced only by the 'net economic value which… is created directly by [the] work'. In this way, the UK maintains that under its CFC rules it is still entitled to tax any passive income of a CFC with an EU establishment. It has interpreted *Cadbury Schweppes* narrowly to prevent it from taxing only the value added by actual individuals working at the EU establishment. For example, assume an Irish subsidiary of a UK parent corporation employs a financial controller at a bona fide Irish business establishment. In such a case, only the profits attributable to the value added by the financial controller are protected from the CFC rules and not all the passive income (such as interest and royalties) that the Irish subsidiary receives and the controller actively manages.

There is serious doubt as to whether the UK amendment to its CFC rules would of itself comply with the *Cadbury Schweppes* decision.[100] There are substantial inconsistencies between the UK tax administration's guidance on the amended legislation and a European Commission communication on the impact of *Cadbury Schweppes* and other decisions.[101] The fundamental question is whether, once a bona fide establishment has been created by a subsidiary in another member state, all the profits of the CFC are protected from CFC rules in the parent corporation jurisdiction or only the value added by work performed there. Of particular importance is foreign source passive income of a CFC, whether sourced in another member state or a third state. It seems inevitable that these issues will return to the ECJ. As mentioned, the UK is reconsidering its CFC rules as part of a project that generally looks at the tax treatment of foreign source income of UK corporations. In HMRC & HM Treasury (2010), the possibility of reverse thin capitalisation rules is explored; i.e. recharacterising excessive equity of a CFC as debt with interest accruing.

By comparison with this assessment of CFC rules, foreign investment fund rules, i.e. attribution in a non-controlled scenario, seem more clearly

[100] This was noted by Evans-Lombe J at first instance in *Vodafone 2* v *RCC* [2008] EWHC 1569 (HC) at para. 73. The Court of Appeal referred to ICTA 1988 s. 751A but without evaluation in this respect.

[101] Compare HMRC (2007) with European Commission (2007b).

contrary to EU Law. Following the line of cases based on *Verkooijen*, discussed above at 4.1.2.1, and *Cadbury Schweppes*, it seems likely that foreign investment fund rules are incompatible with EU Law unless they are also applied domestically. It would be an exceptional case for a non-controlling interest in a foreign corporation to constitute 'a wholly artificial arrangement'. Further, as a non-controlling interest would engage the free movement of capital, any prohibition on foreign investment fund rules might extend to third countries. Whether third country nationals can enforce the free movement of capital was discussed above at 2.1.2.3.

4.2 Expenses/losses

The discussion thus far in this chapter has been considering residence taxation of foreign source income as a concept. However, as discussed above at 1.1, income is typically a net concept involving the set off of payments received and payments made in the course of an income earning activity. As regards residence taxation, the tax system takes into account worldwide payments received less worldwide payments made. The provision of foreign tax relief, whether in the form of exemption or an ordinary foreign tax credit, means that domestic source income is taxed differently from foreign source income. So just as payments received must be allocated as being of a domestic or foreign source, payments made for which a deduction is claimed must be similarly allocated between domestic and foreign source income. In an exemption country, this is necessary to work out how much of the net worldwide profits of a taxpayer should be exempt. In a foreign tax credit country, this is necessary to work out how much residence country tax is attributable to the foreign income in order to determine the limitation on credit.

In this way, expenses stand at the interface between domestic source income and foreign source income. Expenses, whether allocated to domestic or foreign activities, may give rise to losses. Further, it is possible to have losses with respect to one activity while having profits with respect to another. Where these activities take place in different countries, an issue becomes whether and in what manner losses from one activity may offset or affect the taxation of profits on another activity. So, one issue is whether foreign losses may reduce domestic profits and so the tax charged on those profits. A second issue is whether foreign income is reduced by and soaks up (reduces) domestic losses. This issue is particularly concerned with the interaction between domestic losses and foreign tax relief.

As discussed in Chapter 3, foreign activities may be conducted indirectly through a foreign corporation. Residence/home country taxation with respect to the income or profits of foreign subsidiaries was considered above at 4.1.2. In particular, relief from economic double taxation of profits distributed by foreign corporations was considered, as was current taxation of parent corporations with respect to profits of foreign subsidiaries under CFC rules. However, the foreign corporation might make losses rather than profits. Many countries' domestic tax laws permit the netting of losses and profits of members of a corporate group. An issue is whether and if so in what circumstances may the loss of a foreign group member be used to reduce the profits of resident group members.

Each of these areas exposes substantial gaps in the OECD Model. In many cases, that Model does not regulate the situation, leaving domestic law of the residence/host country to apply. In particular, as discussed above at 4.1.2.2 in the context of CFC rules, the non-discrimination rules in Article 24 do not effectively regulate residence country taxation to any substantial extent. As a result, residence country taxation may discriminate against residents engaging in foreign activities without breaching the Model. Of course, the situation is very different under EU Law, which again assists in illustrating the limitations of the OECD Model. In the usual manner, EU Law is not without its difficulties in this area.

4.2.1 *Allocation of expenses between foreign and domestic income*

Generally

The approaches that can be adopted in allocating expenses between domestic and foreign income earning activities are best illustrated by an example. Assume that a corporation resident in Country B has domestic business activities in Country B and carries on business in Country A through a PE. Further, the corporation borrows funds, which are partly used for the Country B business and partly used for the Country A business. The amount of interest incurred on the funds borrowed that should be deductible in Country A for the purposes of calculating Country A tax was considered above at 3.1.3. In particular, Article 7(3) of the OECD Model seems to require a tracing approach and apportionment of the interest to permit a deduction of the interest to the extent it is 'incurred for the purposes' of the PE, although some countries use formulary allocation.

While Article 7(3) of the OECD Model provides only limited guidance for source countries (and is slated for deletion in 2010), there is no guidance in the Model as to how a residence country should allocate expenses between domestic and foreign income. But, like the situation of source countries, residence countries might adopt a tracing approach or a formulary allocation to apportionment.[102] Tracing can be complex as, in principle, the allocation might change depending on the use to which the funds are put at any time. It also assumes that the use to which particular funds are put can be determined with sufficient accuracy. Formulary allocation can be arbitrary and may be based, for example, on the proportion of domestic assets to foreign assets.

The reason why allocation of expenses between foreign and domestic source income is important is different depending on the type of foreign tax relief adopted. For a foreign tax credit country like the UK, worldwide income is taxable and so foreign expenses are inevitably deductible under the general rules for deduction of expenses. Here the allocation between domestic and foreign activities is important, not for the purpose of determining taxable income but for the purpose of determining the limitation on credit (see above at 4.1.1.1). Historically, the UK had little in the way of rules regulating expenses that should be attributed to foreign income for the purposes of determining the limitation of credit. The domestic law simply referred to the relevant foreign income and this was viewed as largely a reference to the domestic schedular system (see above at 2.1.2.1). As, for example, each dividend, interest or royalty was determined separately for each source (asset), this gave rise to the source-by-source approach to the limitation on credit (described at that point).

However, trading income caused a problem. In particular, a trade partly carried on in the UK could have foreign income and yet there remained a single 'source', i.e. the trade. In one case, an insurance company successfully argued that its limitation on credit was calculated by reference to the tax on this single source, i.e. its whole trading profits (including UK profits) and not just that part of the profits pertaining to the foreign income.[103] The result was a 2005 amendment, which narrowed the concept of foreign income for the purposes of calculating the limitation on credit where foreign income is received as part of a trade.[104] The limitation on credit must

[102] For example, see Arnold and McIntyre (2002, p. 48).

[103] *Legal & General Assurance Society Ltd* v *RCC* [2006] EWHC 1770 (Ch).

[104] The foreign tax credit limitation for corporation tax is determined under TIOPA 2010 s. 42.

not exceed 'the corporation tax attributable to the income arising out of the transaction, arrangement or asset in connection with which the credit arises'. That income is to be reduced by any deductible expenses directly relating to it and by a 'reasonable apportionment' of indirect expenses (e.g. general overheads) relating to the income.[105]

By contrast, the exemption method suggests that expenses incurred in deriving foreign income should not be deductible. Rather, in an ideal world, it might be expected that such expenses were deducted under source country law in calculating income liable to tax there. Unfortunately, that will not always be the case. As discussed in Chapter 3, there are a number of cases in which source countries tax on a gross basis. These include dividends, interest, royalties, some service fees and, perhaps, rent from immovable property. If the residence country adopts an exemption system with respect to such income, then the gross source country tax is final and any expenses incurred in deriving such income go unrelieved. However, as noted above at 4.1.1.1, in many of these cases an exemption country will switch to a foreign tax credit for that type of income. Even under the foreign tax credit system, source country taxation of gross amounts can cause difficulties. Despite an apparently low tax rate in the source country, expenses deducted in the residence country might reduce the credit limitation to such an extent as to give rise to excess foreign tax. For an example of this, see below at 5.2.3.1.

Even where a source country does tax on a net basis, such as in the context of profits of a PE, this does not mean that the expenses allowed in calculating source country profits are the same as those used by the residence country in determining the limitation on foreign tax credit or the denial of expenses for exemption. Any expense denied a deduction by a source country that is allocated to the foreign income by the residence country might go unrelieved. In the residence country, this misallocated expense may either trigger the limitation on foreign tax credit or reduce the exemption for foreign income below the amount of foreign income as calculated by the source country.[106]

[105] TIOPA 2010 s. 44.

[106] An early example of this is *Rolls Royce, Limited* v *Short* (1922) 10 TC 59 (CA). A UK corporation paid income tax in India on Indian branch profits and claimed a credit against UK income tax under the dominion relief rules. However, according to UK tax rules the branch made a loss. The result was that there was no Indian income (calculated according to UK rules) on which UK income tax was paid and therefore nothing to relieve Indian income tax against.

An area requiring further consideration in the allocation of expenses is with respect to the receipt of dividends, particularly where underlying foreign tax relief is available (see above at 4.1.2.1). Again, the issues are slightly different under an exemption system or an underlying foreign tax credit system. With respect to the former, a parent corporation may have incurred expenses in deriving exempt dividends from a foreign subsidiary. In particular, the parent corporation may have incurred interest on funds borrowed to finance the foreign subsidiary or incurred overhead expenses in managing its shareholding in the subsidiary (stewardship costs). How should such expenses be treated? If a residence country grants a deduction for such expenses, it will effectively reduce tax on domestic source profits. To deny a deduction results in a form of economic double taxation (presuming the expenses are paid to a recipient that is taxable).

The core of the problem is that the expenses incurred in deriving foreign dividends are, in many ways, proper expenses for the source country. Compare the position with a source/host country PE and that of a source/host country subsidiary. As discussed above at 3.1.3.3, in calculating the profits of a PE for purposes of source country taxation, a deduction should be allowed for expenses incurred for the purposes of the PE, including those incurred by the head office in the residence/home country. So, it is often the case that interest on debt borrowed by a head office in order to finance a PE is deductible in the source/host country calculation of the PE's profits. By contrast, interest on debt borrowed by a parent corporation to finance a foreign subsidiary is not deductible in the source/host country calculation of the subsidiary's profits. Here the separate tax identity of a subsidiary when compared with a PE is crucial.

The only way to reduce a subsidiary's source country profits by interest on debt incurred by its parent corporation is to *push the debt down*. That is, when the parent corporation borrows funds to finance a foreign subsidiary, it should finance that subsidiary in the form of debt (a loan) rather than equity (share capital). Alternately, the subsidiary borrows the funds and the parent corporation guarantees the borrowing. In *pushing the debt down*, a subsidiary may run headlong into thin capitalisation rules in seeking to deduct the interest paid, see above at 3.3.2.2. As noted at that point, there may be similar limitations on the deductibility of interest that is properly attributable to a PE. Some exemption countries, like Germany and the Netherlands, do permit parent corporations to deduct interest on debt used to finance share capital in foreign subsidiaries, despite the fact that dividends from such subsidiaries are exempt.

This difficulty with the financing of foreign subsidiaries appears in a slightly different form for countries such as the US (and traditionally the UK) adopting an underlying foreign tax credit. Here, the first issue is whether interest on debt used to acquire foreign shares is deductible in calculating profits. The second issue is whether that interest must be deducted in calculating the foreign profits for the purposes of the limitation on credit. If it is, the likely result is excess foreign tax credits. For example, a foreign subsidiary derives 100 profits, is subject to source country tax of 20 and distributes a dividend of 80 to a parent corporation. Assume the residence country of the parent corporation charges corporation tax at the rate of 30 per cent and the parent corporation incurs interest expense of 50 with respect to its shareholding in the subsidiary. If that interest is allocated to the foreign dividend, it will reduce the foreign income to 50 (i.e. 80 dividend plus 20 gross-up for foreign tax, less the 50 interest). In this case, the limitation on credit would be 15 (i.e. 30 per cent of 50), resulting in 5 excess foreign tax credits (15 limitation less 20 foreign tax).

If, however, the interest is deductible but not allocated to the foreign income, the limitation on credit would be 30 (i.e. 30 per cent of 100) and there would be no excess credits. There would be residual residence tax of 10 on the foreign dividends (30 limitation less 20 foreign tax) but, assuming the 50 interest is deductible against domestic source income, that would provide protection from residence country tax of 15 (30 per cent of 50) and the taxpayer is 5 better off than if the interest expense were allocated to the foreign dividends. The same is generally true of the effect of expenses on the operation of a foreign tax credit system (direct or underlying).

Added to this complexity is the problem of timing. If these expenses are deductible as incurred, they may be deducted in the home country before the profits of the foreign subsidiary are repatriated in the form of dividends. This can be particularly problematic if the subsidiary runs an active business in a low tax country, so any home country CFC rules do not apply. In such a case, the income is taxed at a low rate in the host/source country. The parent corporation gets an immediate deduction for expenses incurred in deriving that income, potentially against domestic income chargeable to tax at a much higher rate in the home country. This is an example of tax rate arbitrage.[107]

[107] The US Obama administration's proposal to defer deduction of expenses (other than research and experimentation expenditures) of a resident that are properly allocated to foreign source income until the income is subject to US tax has run into difficulty. The primary expenses are interest and US headquarters expenses.

UK parent corporations currently enjoy a broad right to deduct interest expense on borrowing to fund equity investment in foreign subsidiaries.[108] As for the limitation on credit, the UK grants the parent substantial flexibility to allocate interest expense between domestic and foreign activities.[109] The favourable system was restricted somewhat with the move to an exemption system for foreign dividends. The general deductibility of interest (even if incurred in deriving exempt foreign dividends) continues, but there is a worldwide cap on the deductibility of interest.

In addition to the thin capitalisation limitations discussed above at 3.3.2.2, interest deductions granted to UK members of a multinational corporate group are limited to the total net finance costs paid by the worldwide group (including the UK members) to external lenders, as reflected in the consolidated accounts of the worldwide group.[110] This is largely a reaction to difficulties with the UK CFC rules following *Cadbury Schweppes* (see above at 4.1.2.2). Without the full support of CFC rules, foreign subsidiaries of UK parent corporations could retain their profits but repatriate them to the UK in the form of *upstream* loans. Not only did the UK get no tax on this repatriation, but the UK parent would claim a deduction for interest paid to the foreign subsidiary. The intention is that the worldwide cap will limit such sharp practices.

EU Law

One reason why the OECD Model does not regulate deductions in calculating foreign source income for residence tax purposes is that the principles of non-discrimination in Article 24 largely do not extend to residence countries. In the usual manner, the situation is very different under EU Law. Each of the freedoms may have application if the residence country introduces a cross-border restriction through the availability of deductions in calculating foreign source income. So, in *Weidert and Paulus*, the ECJ held that a Luxembourg investment deduction available for investment into Luxembourg corporations must also be available with respect to investment in other EU corporations.[111]

Similarly, a deduction in deriving exempt domestic income must be available when deriving exempt EU source income. This was decided in

[108] This deductibility is secured by the loan relationship rules in CTA 2009 Parts 5 and 6. Regarding the loan relationship rules, see Tiley (2008, pp. 917–27). There are limitations on using losses that are created by interest deductions not incurred on trading account.

[109] TIOPA 2010 ss. 52–6 and see Tiley (2008, pp. 1222–3).

[110] TIOPA 2010 Part 7 (ss. 260–353).

[111] Case C-242/03 *Minestre des Finances* v *Weidert and Paulus* [2004] ECR I-7379 (ECJ).

2003 in the important case of *Bosal*, when the ECJ's centralist push was at a high.[112] The case concerned a Dutch parent corporation that borrowed funds to invest in the share capital of a EU subsidiary. The parent was denied a deduction for the interest on the funds because dividends from the EU subsidiaries were exempt, i.e. these were expenses in deriving foreign source income. However, if the funds had been invested in a Dutch subsidiary, the interest would have been deductible even though dividends from a Dutch subsidiary would also be exempt.[113] The Dutch pointed out that their tax treatment of the parent corporation was common in the EU and complied with Article 4(2) of the Parent-Subsidiary Directive (1990), see above at 4.1.2.1.

The ECJ made it clear that member states were required to comply with both Directives and the FEU Treaty and compliance with one would not remedy a breach of the other.[114] The restriction on the deductibility of expenses incurred by a Dutch parent with respect to its EU subsidiaries when such a deduction was available with respect to Dutch subsidiaries was a breach of the freedom of establishment. The Netherlands sought to justify its treatment on a number of grounds. In particular, it suggested that its treatment simply recognised that the expenses properly related to Dutch activities. When the income of the subsidiary was derived in another member state, it was appropriate for that member state to deduct the parent corporation's interest expense. This is the point about the different source country treatment of interest incurred in financing PEs and subsidiaries noted above. The ECJ decided not to pierce the corporate veil in this way. 'Unlike operating branches or establishments, parent companies and their subsidiaries are distinct legal persons, each being subject to a tax liability of its own'.[115] This is a good example of the ECJ's insistence that in determining compliance with EU Law, members of a corporate group must be assessed separately, see above at 2.1.1.3.

The ECJ also pointed out that, in the reverse situation, when an EU parent with a Dutch subsidiary incurred interest expense with respect to that subsidiary, the Netherlands did not permit a deduction for that interest

[112] Case C-168/01 *Bosal Holding BV* v *Staatssecretaris van Financiën* [2003] ECR I-9409 (ECJ).

[113] The situation was slightly more complex than this. A deduction was available to the extent the subsidiary (irrespective of residence) derived Dutch source income. The Dutch rule largely had the effect discussed in the text.

[114] Case C-168/01 *Bosal Holding BV* v *Staatssecretaris van Financiën* [2003] ECR I-9409 (ECJ) at paras. 25–6 and see above at 1.3.3.

[115] Case C-168/01 *Bosal Holding BV* v *Staatssecretaris van Financiën* [2003] ECR I-9409 (ECJ) at para. 32.

expense in calculating the subsidiary's taxable Dutch profits.[116] Might this point about the internal coherence or symmetry of a tax system be important generally with respect to residence country allocation of expenses between domestic and foreign income? In the *Deutsche Shell* case,[117] discussed above at 2.2.1, the ECJ decided that an expense that could not be taken into account in a source country (a currency exchange loss) must be taken into account in the residence country as a matter of freedom of establishment. With respect to source country taxation, there have been cases in which the ECJ has required a deduction for expenses incurred in 'direct connection to the activity pursued',[118] see above at 3.1.6.2.

These source country cases inevitably involved a comparison of whether in a similar situation a source country entity would be granted a deduction for the expense, but how do these cases translate in the context of a residence country? For example, assume a residence country allocates a particular expense to exempt foreign income. Allocation of the expense will reduce the foreign income and so reduce the exemption, increasing residence taxation. If the allocation is inappropriate, this may constitute a restriction prohibited by the fundamental freedoms. How would the ECJ test this? One approach would be to look to the foreign country and see whether the expense were deductible there. This seems unlikely, although the *Deutsche Shell* case might be viewed as pointing in this direction. However, in that case the ECJ was clear that the loss in question was one that by its very nature the source country could not take into account. Further, in *Kerckhaert and Morres*,[119] discussed above at 4.1.1.3, the ECJ refused to consider taxation in the source country when determining the appropriateness of residence country taxation.

Another approach would be to use the 'direct connection to the activity pursued' test from the source country cases. However, as pointed out, in those cases this test is not independent and still involves the question of whether residents could deduct the expense in question. A third approach is, perhaps, consistent both with the source country cases and with the obita in *Bosal*. It involves asking the question of whether the expense would be deductible if incurred by a non-resident in deriving

[116] Case C-168/01 *Bosal Holding BV* v *Staatssecretaris van Financiën* [2003] ECR I-9409 (ECJ) at para. 36.

[117] Case C-293/06 *Deutsche Shell* v *Finanzamt für Grossunternehmen in Hamburg* [2008] ECR I-1129 (ECJ).

[118] Case C-345/04 *Centro Equestre da Leziria Grande Lda* v *Bundesamt fur Finanzen* (*Centro Equestre*) [2007] ECR I-1425 (ECJ) at para. 23.

[119] Case C-513/04 *Kerckhaert and Morres* v *Belgium State* [2006] ECR I-10967 (ECJ).

domestic source income from the residence country. If yes, then it would be inappropriate when a resident is involved to allocate such an expense (incurred in the same circumstances) to foreign source income. If the answer is that a non-resident could not deduct the expense, then, in line with the source country cases, the ECJ might additionally require the expense to have a 'direct connection' to the foreign activity in order to be allocated to it. The coherence or symmetry of a tax system can be an important tool for identifying discrimination in the absence of comparables.[120]

While these issues have been examined in the context of an exemption country, the same issues arise for a foreign tax credit country when calculating the limitation on credit. They were before the European Free Trade Association (EFTA) Court in the *Seabrokers* case.[121] In this case, a Norwegian corporation had a PE in the UK, which was taxed on its profits in the UK. The corporation was entitled to a Norwegian foreign tax credit for the UK tax. The corporation incurred interest expense and deductible group contributions and the issue was how these should be allocated between the PE profits and Norwegian profits for the purposes of calculating the limitation on credit. The Norwegian law required the expenses to be allocated between the UK income and Norwegian income in proportion to the amount of those respective incomes. The purpose for which an expense was incurred was irrelevant.

The court found that if expenses were 'linked' to the foreign income, then they could be applied to reduce the foreign income for the purposes of the limitation on credit, irrespective of whether the source state had granted a deduction.[122] Accordingly, the court adopted a test similar to the 'direct connection' test used in ECJ source cases. If the 'expenses cannot be linked to any particular business activities', then the Norwegian proportionate rule was appropriate.[123] However:

> The attribution of debt interest expenses related solely to a taxpayer's business in the home State to the income of a branch situated in another

[120] For example, see Harris (1996, pp. 444–50) and the references cited therein.

[121] Case E-7/07 *Seabrokers AS* v *Staten v/Skattedirektoratet* (2008) 10 ITLR 805 (EFTAC). The European Free Trade Association Court applies many EU Law principles, including the freedom of establishment, and follows ECJ jurisprudence.

[122] Case E-7/07 *Seabrokers AS* v *Staten v/Skattedirektoratet* (2008) 10 ITLR 805 (EFTAC) at para. 54.

[123] Case E-7/07 *Seabrokers AS* v *Staten v/Skattedirektoratet* (2008) 10 ITLR 805 (EFTAC) at para. 55.

> EEA State when calculating the maximum credit allowance constitutes a restriction.[124]

The court did not consider possible justifications for the restriction. The group contributions were effectively loss transfers from Norwegian subsidiaries. In essence, the court decided that these could be linked only to Norwegian source income and so attribution of a portion to foreign source income was inappropriate. This is discussed below at 4.2.3. It seems inevitable that there will be further ECJ cases in this area.

4.2.2 Foreign loss/domestic income

Generally

The process by which a residence country allocates expenses to foreign activities might result in a loss from those activities. This is not to be confused with any loss calculated in the source country, which should be treated in the manner discussed in Chapter 3, including the application of any non-discrimination provision. As noted above at 4.2.1, the calculation of income under source and residence country laws is not likely to be the same and what is currently being considered is a foreign loss calculated under residence country tax law. For simplicity, the current consideration presumes a loss incurred by a foreign PE. In most countries, losses from one business activity can be set against losses from another business activity. This is the approach of the UK with respect to current year losses or those carried backwards.[125] Carried forward losses may be set only against profits of the 'same' trade as incurred the loss.[126]

A fundamental question with respect to foreign losses is whether they can be set against domestic profits. At some level, to permit such an offset would erode the domestic tax base. This is clear where the residence country adopts the exemption method of foreign tax relief. Why should it permit a foreign loss to reduce domestic profits when, if the foreign activities were profitable, it would not tax the profit? The same is generally true of a foreign tax credit country. The very purpose of the limitation on credit is to ensure that foreign tax does not reduce domestic tax on domestic profits. If foreign tax on profitable foreign activities cannot reduce domestic tax on domestic profits, why permit a loss on the foreign activities to

[124] Case E-7/07 *Seabrokers AS* v *Staten v/Skattedirektoratet* (2008) 10 ITLR 805 (EFTAC) at para. 57.

[125] CTA 2010 s. 37.

[126] CTA 2010 s. 45.

reduce domestic profits and thereby domestic tax? Arguably, these situations should be treated symmetrically. Foreign losses should be available for use only in the same way that foreign tax can be used. So, under an exemption system, foreign losses should not be usable at all.

Under a foreign tax credit system, it might be argued that because, like domestic income, foreign income is taxable, foreign losses should also be deductible generally. However, to the extent that foreign tax credits are granted, foreign income is not subject to residence tax. Does this mean that the extent to which foreign losses should be usable should depend on the rate of foreign tax? For example, if the tax rate of a residence country is 30 per cent and the tax rate of the source country is 15 per cent, the foreign losses would be deductible against domestic source income as to half. No country adopts this approach. Perhaps a stronger argument is that foreign losses should be used consistently with the method of calculating the limitation on credit, e.g. item-by-item, country-by-country, type of income or worldwide limitation, see above at 4.1.1.1.

Foreign losses are often only temporary, e.g. in the early years of starting up foreign operations, and if a residence country does grant relief against domestic profits it will recoup the benefit granted when the foreign operations turn profitable. Assume a foreign PE is set up and makes a loss of 100 in its first year and a profit of 100 in its second year. Further, assume that the source and residence countries calculate the loss and profit in the same amounts. In the source country, the PE will have a loss in year 1, which can be carried forward to reduce the profit of year 2. For source country tax purposes, there will be no tax in year 1 and no tax in year 2.

Presume that the residence country imposes tax at 30 per cent and adopts a foreign tax credit system. It permits the PE loss to reduce profits that the taxpayer has on domestic activities. In year 1, the foreign loss will reduce domestic profits and so save 30 tax on those profits. As the foreign loss has been used, there is no loss to carry forward to year 2, i.e. the opposite of the situation in the source country. In year 2, the foreign PE has profits of 100 but no source country tax to use under the foreign tax credit system of the residence country. Further, those profits are not protected by the foreign loss because it was used in the residence country in year 1. The foreign profits will be taxable in the residence country in year 2, giving rise to a tax liability of 30 that will not be reduced by foreign tax relief. This 30 tax offsets the relief given in year 1 against domestic profits, showing that permitting foreign losses to be used against domestic profits, on these facts, produces only a cash flow advantage.

This position of a foreign tax credit country does not easily translate for an exemption country. For an exemption country, in order to ensure that any foreign loss relief is temporary, such relief must be qualified by the requirement that future foreign income of the foreign PE is taxable to the extent that foreign losses have been used. This is often called a 'claw-back' of relief.

Of course, if the foreign activities produced a permanent loss, there would be a permanent reduction in residence country taxation of domestic activities. Despite the risk of permanent relief for foreign losses, residence countries are often willing to grant relief for foreign losses. This willingness recognises the importance of domestic enterprises expanding overseas and the fact that such expansion often involves losses in early years before the foreign activities turn profitable. If the residence country does not provide relief, there will be an impediment to cross-border expansion.

Many countries do not have strict rules for quarantining foreign losses. Even though the OECD Model neither requires it nor prohibits it, many countries do permit losses of a foreign PE to offset domestic source profits.[127] Belgium and the Netherlands are two examples of exemption countries that permit the use of losses of a foreign PE. This is also possible in the context of the UK, a foreign tax credit country where the general rules regarding relief for trading losses do not impose limitations on the use of foreign losses.[128]

EU Law

As noted, many European countries do permit the use of foreign losses against domestic source income. The European Commission tried to formalise this approach (and extend it to the transfer of losses within corporate groups) in 1990, at the time the Parent-Subsidiary and Mergers Directives were passed. However, the member states could not agree on the draft Losses Directive and it lay dormant. At the height of the ECJ centralist approach, there were questions as to whether what was to be prescribed by the draft Losses Directive might not be required by the fundamental freedoms in any case. As noted at 4.2.1, in the *Bosal* case,[129] the ECJ required that a parent be permitted to deduct expenses incurred in deriving exempt dividends from a foreign subsidiary. It seems a small step

[127] OECD Commentary on Art. 23 para. 44.

[128] CTA 2010 ss. 37 and 45.

[129] Case C-168/01 *Bosal Holding BV* v *Staatssecretaris van Financiën* [2003] ECR I-9409 (ECJ).

to requiring a residence country to deduct losses incurred by a foreign PE even if the profits of the PE would be exempt.

This was the issue before the ECJ in the *Lidl Belgium* case.[130] A Luxembourg PE of a German corporation incurred a loss. Profits of the PE would be exempt under the Germany/Luxembourg Tax Treaty. The German tax administration refused to permit this loss to offset German profits. The ECJ analysed the situation based on the PE as an 'autonomous fiscal entity' and decided that the German limitation did constitute a restriction on the freedom of establishment. The court noted that a German corporation with an EU PE is taxed less favourably 'than it would be if the latter were to be established in Germany'.[131]

However, following the landmark decision in *Marks & Spencer*, discussed below at 4.2.4, the ECJ accepted the German justification for this restriction. This justification involved two aspects: the need to preserve the allocation of taxing powers agreed to in the treaty and 'the need to prevent the danger that losses may be taken into account twice'.[132] The ECJ also held that the German restriction was proportionate, pointing to the fact that the loss had been relieved in Luxembourg four years later. As discussed further below at 4.2.4, it is clear that the cash flow disadvantage suffered with respect to the Luxembourg loss compared with a German loss (i.e. it took four years to get relief for the Luxembourg loss whereas a German loss would be relieved immediately) was not sufficient for the ECJ to feel that the German rule was disproportionate.

In referring to the balanced allocation of tax powers between member states, the ECJ specifically noted:

> The Member State in which the registered office of the company to which the permanent establishment belongs is situated would, in the absence of a double taxation convention, have the right to tax the profits generated by such an entity. Consequently, the objective of preserving the allocation of the power to impose taxes between the two Member States concerned, which is reflected in the provisions of the Convention, is capable of justifying the tax regime in the main proceedings, since it safeguards symmetry between the right to tax profits and the right to deduct losses.[133]

130 Case C-414/06 *Lidl Belgium GmbH & Co KG* v *Finanzamt Heilbronn* [2008] ECR I-3601 (ECJ).

131 Case C-414/06 *Lidl Belgium GmbH & Co KG* v *Finanzamt Heilbronn* [2008] ECR I-3601 (ECJ) at paras. 18–26.

132 Case C-414/06 *Lidl Belgium GmbH & Co KG* v *Finanzamt Heilbronn* [2008] ECR I-3601 (ECJ) at para. 30.

133 Case C-414/06 *Lidl Belgium GmbH & Co KG* v *Finanzamt Heilbronn* [2008] ECR I-3601 (ECJ) at para. 33.

This critical passage perhaps raises more questions than it answers. Is a member state's right to deny loss relief justified only where it is founded on an exemption for PE profits based in a tax treaty? What of the case where the treaty provides for relief by foreign tax credit? Read literally, the ECJ's reasoning would not extend to such a case. Clearly, a foreign tax credit country would be required to give loss relief, but would such a country be permitted to quarantine the foreign losses against foreign income, which serves the same purpose as a denial of foreign loss relief under an exemption system? The European Commission is of the view that quarantining is not permitted and, in 2007, sent a reasoned opinion to Germany to that effect regarding German domestic law. In 2008, Germany amended its law to remove the quarantining for EU losses.[134] This creates incongruence between the exemption and credit methods.

Can the same reasoning apply outside a tax treaty? For example, what if a treaty provides for foreign tax relief in the form of a foreign tax credit but the domestic law provides relief in the form of an exemption? Such a case could easily arise if the UK moved to an exemption system because all its treaties provide for a foreign tax credit. Might the unilateral exemption justify the denial of relief for foreign losses even if a treaty does not? What of the reverse situation where unilateral relief is in the form of a foreign tax credit and treaty relief is in the form of an exemption, e.g. the *Lidl Belgium* case? Assuming the foreign tax credit method cannot justify the denial of foreign loss relief (even if quarantining is possible), the denial of loss relief is permitted under EU Law due to the tax treaty. The result is that the treaty has created a restriction where the domestic law could not, a rather bizarre twist on the nature of tax treaties as relieving measures. Inevitably, the ECJ has not heard its last case in this area either.

As noted, despite these issues, a number of European exemption countries do permit corporations to deduct the losses of foreign PEs even though they would exempt the profits of the PEs. However, when the PE turns profitable, they tax the PE's profits (without exemption) up to the amount of loss relief previously claimed (reintegration). This would not occur if the PE were located in the country of residence of the corporation and so raises the issue of whether the reintegration itself is contrary to the freedom of establishment. This came before the ECJ in another German case, *Krankenheim Ruhesitz*.[135] While the ECJ found the reintegration a

[134] Jackson (2008b).

[135] Case C-157/07 *Finanzamt für Körperschaften III in Berlin* v *Krankenheim Ruhesitz am Wannsee-Seniorenheimstatt GmbH* [2008] ECR I-8061 (ECJ).

restriction on the freedom of establishment, it held it to be justified. In particular, the ECJ refused to 'dissociate' the reintegration with the earlier use of the losses. Therefore, the case represented one of the exceptional circumstances in which the restriction could be justified based on the 'coherence of the German tax system'.[136]

4.2.3 *Foreign income/domestic loss*

Generally

The process by which a residence country allocates expenses between domestic and foreign activities might result in a domestic loss while the foreign activities remain profitable. Again, this should not be confused with the situation of source countries, which has been discussed. At 3.1.3.3, it was noted that the OECD is firmly of the view that, for source country purposes, a PE can have a profit despite the overall enterprise suffering a loss. This is a consequence of the separate enterprise approach to calculating the profits of PEs. At 3.1.3.4, it was noted that the non-discrimination rule in Article 24(3) of the OECD Model does not require a source country to permit loss transfers from other parts of the enterprise or related enterprises to reduce source country taxation of the PE. Accordingly, there will be no relief in the source country for the residence country loss in the current scenario.

The question for the residence country is what impact the foreign profits have on the domestic loss. This is another area in which the OECD Model provides no regulation. In the absence of foreign profits, most residence countries permit a domestic loss to be carried forward and reduce domestic profits of future years, i.e. the domestic losses constitute a form of relief from taxation in future years. When foreign profits are introduced, the question is whether the foreign profits should be reduced by the domestic losses. Put another way, the question is whether the foreign profits should *eat up* (absorb) the domestic losses. Take, for example, an exemption country, i.e. a country that exempts the foreign profits. If a domestic loss is reduced by exempt foreign profits, then two forms of relief have been used to exempt the same income, i.e. foreign tax relief as well as domestic loss relief. Some would argue that this is appropriate. In the usual way, if there is no residence country tax liability then there is no need to provide foreign tax relief as there is no double taxation. Others would point to

[136] Case C-157/07 *Finanzamt für Körperschaften III in Berlin* v *Krankenheim Ruhesitz am Wannsee-Seniorenheimstatt GmbH* [2008] ECR I-8061 (ECJ) at para. 43.

the distortion this creates against deriving foreign source income and, as discussed below, this is an important issue for EU Law.

The issue materialises in a different fashion if the residence country is a foreign tax credit country. This is a difficult but important issue, as it must be remembered that even exemption countries are typically foreign tax credit countries with respect to many types of foreign income, especially passive income. As the foreign profits are included in the taxpayer's worldwide income and taxed by the residence country, it might seem instinctive that the foreign profits should be reduced by domestic losses. However, once again this results in two forms of relief being applied to the same profits. The foreign profits will effectively be protected from residence country taxation due to the domestic loss. Assuming the domestic loss is equal to or greater than the foreign profits, there is no residence country tax of those profits and so the limitation on credit is nil. This means that any source country tax levied results in excess foreign tax credits. Here the manner in which excess foreign tax credits can be used becomes critical (see above at 4.1.1.1).

Unless the residence country adopts a full credit, use of excess foreign tax credits is less favourable than the use of domestic losses. It is here that the connection between losses and foreign tax relief becomes most clear. If the taxpayer is forced to use domestic losses against foreign source income and is required to defer use of foreign tax credits, e.g. by carrying them forward, the taxpayer has used up the more flexible of the two reliefs applied to the foreign profits. Domestic losses may be carried forward to set against future foreign *or* domestic profits. Foreign tax credits, if they can be carried forward at all, may be set only against future foreign profits and often only particular types of foreign profits.

The arguments for quarantining foreign losses, so that they cannot be used against domestic profits, were discussed above at 4.2.2. Whatever the strength of those arguments, the arguments for quarantining domestic losses so that they cannot be used against foreign income at all appear weaker. Such quarantining prevents domestic loss relief being *eaten up* by foreign profits protected by foreign tax relief. However, there will be many situations where the taxpayer would like to be protected from residence country taxation of foreign income by using domestic losses. This will particularly be the case where the foreign income is subject to low source country taxation (e.g. interest and royalties). Ideally for the taxpayer, they would be permitted to use a combination of foreign tax relief and domestic loss relief to prevent dual relief. An example will demonstrate.

Presume a resident taxpayer derives 100 foreign income, subject to source country taxation of 18, and that the residence country tax rate is 30 per cent. Further, assume that the taxpayer has a domestic loss of 70. If the domestic loss were quarantined, the taxpayer would have tax liability in the residence country of 12 with respect to the foreign income (i.e. 30 less credit for the 18 source country tax). The taxpayer would like to be protected from this taxation by using some of its domestic loss. The most straightforward approach would be to permit the taxpayer to elect to use a portion of the domestic loss to reduce the amount of foreign profits subject to tax. So, the taxpayer may elect to use 40 of its domestic loss to reduce the foreign income to 60 for residence country tax purposes. The loss offset would also reduce the foreign income for purposes of the limitation on credit. Now the tax liability in the residence country is reduced to 18, i.e. 30 per cent of 60 (100 less 40), which is fully offset by the foreign tax credit for source country tax. The remaining loss of 30 (70 less the 40 used) would be carried forward in the usual manner.[137]

The UK approach is quite restrictive in this respect. Under the UK's schedular system, if the foreign income and the domestic loss relate to the same item of income, e.g. a particular trade, then the income and loss are automatically set off in the process of calculating the profit or loss from that trade generally. If, however, the foreign income and domestic loss do not fall to be taken into the same income calculation, there is a little flexibility. Assume that the domestic loss is a trading loss of a corporation. In this case, the corporation may claim to use the loss against the foreign income derived in the same year as the loss was incurred or foreign income of the previous year.[138] It seems that the claim must involve the whole of the domestic loss, i.e. partial claims are not available.[139] This appears problematic on the above facts as it means that in order to be relieved of a UK corporate tax liability of 12, the corporation would have to use the full domestic loss of 70. So, use of this mechanism can still result in the dual use of foreign tax credits and domestic losses, i.e. wasted relief.[140] The alternative for the taxpayer is to not make the claim,

[137] An alternative approach is to convert a portion of the domestic loss into a tax credit using the taxpayer's tax rate, i.e. 30 per cent of 40 gives a credit of 12. This credit, together with the foreign tax credit (i.e. 12 plus 18 gives a total of 30), exhausts residence country taxation of the foreign income. The remaining 30 of the domestic loss that is not converted would be available for carry forward in the usual manner.

[138] CTA 2010 s. 37.

[139] Tiley (2008, p. 907).

[140] If the domestic loss exceeds the foreign income, it seems that the excess could be carried forward to set against profits of the domestic trade under CTA 2010 s. 45.

in which case the whole of the domestic loss would be carried forward for use against future profits of the trade,[141] but the foreign income would be taxable in the year it is derived with credit for source country tax. The tax policy underlying the UK approach is not clear.

EU Law

In the usual way, and unlike the OECD Model, the fundamental freedoms may restrict a residence country in the way in which it sets domestic losses against foreign income. This issue arose in the *AMID* case, which the ECJ decided in 2000 at the height of its centralist approach to direct taxation.[142] A Belgian corporation conducting business in Belgium also had a PE in Luxembourg. The PE made a profit but the Belgian head office made a loss. The PE profits were exempt under the Belgium/Luxembourg Tax Treaty, but under Belgian domestic law the exempt PE profits reduced the loss of the head office, i.e. the exempt profits *ate up* the domestic loss. The corporation argued that this treatment constituted a restriction on its freedom of establishment in Luxembourg.

In a difficult and short decision that belies the complexity of the issue, the ECJ agreed that there was a breach of EU Law.

> 22 As regards the calculation of the taxable income of companies, it must be noted that, for companies incorporated under the national law of a Member State which have their seat there and have used their right of free establishment in order to create branches in other Member States, the legislation at issue in the main proceedings limits the possibility of carrying forward losses incurred in that Member State during a previous tax period where, during that same tax period, those companies made profits in another Member State through the intermediary of a permanent establishment, whereas it would be possible to set off those losses if the establishments of those companies were situated exclusively in the Member State of origin.
>
> 23 Thus, by setting off domestic losses against profits exempted by treaty, the legislation of that Member State establishes a differentiated tax treatment as between companies incorporated under national law having establishments only on national territory and those having establishments in another Member State. As the Belgian Government itself recognises, where such companies have a permanent establishment in a Member State other than that of origin and a convention to prevent double taxation binds the two States, those companies are likely to suffer a

[141] CTA 2010 s. 45.

[142] Case C-141/99 *Algemene Maatshappij voor Investering en Dienstverlening NV* v *Belgische Staat* [2000] ECR I-11619 (ECJ).

> tax disadvantage which they would not have to suffer if all their establishments were situated in the Member State of origin.

A detailed consideration of whether the ECJ will follow the *AMID* decision in the future is beyond the scope of this book, but two points are worth making. First, the essence of the problem in *AMID* is that a residence country loss could not reduce source country taxation, i.e. Luxembourg taxation. The ECJ had held earlier in the *Futura* case that a PE state was not required to reduce PE profits by a head office loss.[143] The ECJ's decision in *AMID* must be read in light of this earlier decision. So, in *AMID*, there was no possibility of the taxpayer challenging the source country tax imposed by Luxembourg, which was the primary cause of any discrimination. If Luxembourg had been required to provide loss relief, then reduction of the loss in Belgium would have been appropriate. However, as Luxembourg would not provide loss relief (and this was not required by EU Law), the Belgium treatment resulted in unrelieved Belgian losses that would not have occurred if all the activities were conducted in Belgium.

Second, the only justification put forward by Belgium in *AMID* was suggesting that Belgian corporations with EU PEs were not in the same position as Belgian corporations conducting all their activities in Belgium. Not surprisingly, the ECJ rejected this justification.[144] More sophisticated justifications have been raised in recent loss cases (in particular, the potential for avoidance and double counting of losses), discussed above at 4.2.2 and below at 4.2.4. However, in *AMID*, Belgium breached the symmetry argument discussed above at 4.2.2. As a residence country, it reduced its domestic losses by foreign profits, but if it had been the source country, it would not have reduced its source country tax by a foreign head office loss.[145]

[143] Case C-250/95 *Futura Participations SA and Singer* v *Administration des contributions* [1997] ECR I-2471 (ECJ). A problem with this case is the qualification that appears at para. 48. A PE country is entitled to ignore foreign losses only 'provided that resident taxpayers do not receive more favourable treatment'. Many countries, including Belgium, permit residents to use foreign PE losses against domestic source income. What this means in the context of the qualification is not clear.

[144] Case C-141/99 *Algemene Maatshappij voor Investering en Dienstverlening NV* v *Belgische Staat* [2000] ECR I-11619 (ECJ) at para. 32.

[145] Belgium did point to the fact that if the PE made the loss it would have granted relief against domestic profits (even though PE profits were exempt). However, this is not the symmetry argument, which requires the residence country to consider what it would do if it were the source country, not what it would do as a residence country if the foreign profit were actually a foreign loss.

It seems the same reasoning applies where what absorbs the domestic loss is exempt dividends from a foreign subsidiary. In addition to the freedom of establishment issue raised by *AMID*, there is the complication that the Parent-Subsidiary Directive (1991) governs foreign tax relief for such dividends. This issue arose in *Cobelfret*.[146] Belgium implemented the Directive by adopting the exemption method for dividends from foreign subsidiaries. However, as in *AMID*, the manner in which Belgium achieves this exemption effectively reduces domestic losses. The ECJ decided that this breached the relief required by the Directive.

As noted above, these issues manifest themselves in a different form where the residence country adopts a foreign tax credit. Here, if domestic losses are set against foreign profits, the result is likely to be excess foreign tax credits, which cannot be used as broadly as domestic losses. If *AMID* is followed, it seems that forcing a taxpayer to use domestic losses against foreign income for which foreign tax credits are available also breaches EU Law. This is consistent with the *Seabrokers* case, discussed below. The taxpayer should be entitled to reduce the foreign profits only to the extent necessary and not such as to produce excess foreign tax credits. Alternately, excess foreign tax credits arising from the use of domestic losses should be available for carry forward and use in a similar manner as domestic losses. The UK system (described above) can waste domestic losses and does not fully comply with either approach.

If this wastage occurs in the context of dividends from a foreign subsidiary (where the UK uses the underlying foreign tax credit method), there is the additional issue of whether the wastage breaches the Parent-Subsidiary Directive (1991). In *Cobelfret*, Belgium argued that its treatment under the exemption approach was at least as favourable as that which would be available under the credit method. Accordingly, Belgium presumed that use of domestic losses can cause excess foreign tax credits and still comply with the Directive. The ECJ was not persuaded and pointed out that even if this were correct, Belgium was using the exemption method, not the credit method.[147]

A related issue arises in the context of a parent corporation using the loss of a subsidiary, i.e. group relief, which is discussed in more detail below at 4.2.4. If a parent corporation is permitted to use the loss of a subsidiary

[146] Case C-138/07 *Belgium* v *NV Cobelfret* [2009] ECR 00 (ECJ).

[147] Case C-138/07 *Belgium* v *NV Cobelfret* [2009] ECR 00 (ECJ) at paras. 47–50. In particular, at para. 47 the ECJ suggested that there was 'no indication that the [exemption system] would necessarily lead to a more favourable result than [the credit system]'.

under domestic law, a question is whether part of this loss may be allocated to foreign income of the parent corporation and thereby reduce foreign tax relief of the parent corporation. This was the issue before the EFTA Court in the *Seabrokers* case discussed above at 4.2.1. The group contribution by the Norwegian corporation to its Norwegian subsidiaries was a method of transferring losses from the subsidiaries to the parent. The Norwegian domestic tax law allocated these (effectively) transferred losses proportionately between domestic income and the income from the UK PE. The amount allocated to the UK income operated to reduce the limitation on foreign tax credit and so produced excess foreign tax credits, i.e. it *ate up* the foreign tax relief. The taxpayer argued this was contrary to the freedom of establishment and that none of the transferred losses should be allocated to the foreign income.

The EFTA Court agreed. It noted that the Norwegian loss transfer system was available only with respect to Norwegian corporations. With respect to such system, a Norwegian parent corporation with a foreign PE was in the same position as a Norwegian parent corporation conducting its activities solely in Norway. This meant that both parents should receive the same reduction from Norwegian tax in respect of a group contribution.[148] Again, the court did not consider justifications.

In passing, it is noted that the UK group relief (loss transfer) system does not operate in the same manner as the Norwegian system. Where a UK parent corporation with foreign source income receives a loss transfer from a subsidiary, none of that transfer is allocated to the parent's foreign source income for purposes of calculating the parent's foreign tax credit limitation.[149]

4.2.4 *Group relief*

Generally

The domestic tax laws of many countries incorporate mechanisms to offset the losses of one member of a corporate group against the profits of another member of a corporate group. There are different methods of achieving this result. It is achieved by collapsing the identity of subsidiaries for tax

[148] Case E-7/07 *Seabrokers AS* v *Staten v/Skattedirektoratet* (2008) 10 ITLR 805 (EFTAC) at para. 67.

[149] CTA 2010 s. 137 which prescribes the transfer, reduces the recipient corporation's 'total profits' (i.e. an amount that includes the foreign income) by the amount of the transferred loss. By contrast, the limitation on credit in TIOPA 2010 s. 42 refers to 'the income'.

purposes into that of their parent corporation, i.e. consolidation, noted above at 2.1.1.1. The tax laws of other countries consider all members of a corporate group separate tax subjects but may, for example, permit the losses of one group member to be transferred to another group member. The latter is the approach of the UK, noted above at 3.1.3.4. These systems of relief for losses of group members (group relief) do not operate in cross-border scenarios. In particular, they tend to exclude at least foreign losses of foreign subsidiaries.

Source/host country aspects of cross-border group relief have been touched on. In particular, the OECD position that exclusion of PEs from group relief in the source country does not breach the non-discrimination rule in Article 24(3) of the OECD Model was noted above at 3.1.3.4. At the same point it was noted that the OECD is also of the view that exclusion of a foreign controlled subsidiary from the source/host country group relief system similarly does not breach the non-discrimination rule in Article 24(5). Whatever limits Article 24(3) and (5) impose (or do not impose) for source/host countries, the OECD non-discrimination rules do not extend to the residence/home country treatment of parent corporations with respect to losses of their subsidiaries, whether domestic or foreign.

Refusal to grant relief for foreign losses of foreign subsidiaries may be justified on the same grounds, whether the residence/home country of the parent corporation adopts the exemption or credit method of foreign tax relief. In neither case does the tax jurisdiction of the residence/home country, whether based on source or residence, extend to the foreign subsidiary. As noted above at 2.1.1.1, the international tax order (based on the OECD Model) considers a foreign subsidiary a separate person from its parent corporation. As the parent jurisdiction does not seek to tax the subsidiary's profits, it does not permit group relief with respect to the subsidiary's losses. Of course, distributions of a foreign subsidiary may be taxed, but most countries tax domestic dividends in some shape or form while not permitting shareholders to use losses of their corporation. The exception is where CFC rules apply. The incongruence of not permitting the use of CFC losses, while taxing their profits, was noted above at 4.1.2.2.

EU Law

Once again, the situation under EU Law is fundamentally different from that under the OECD Model. Not only does the concept of non-discrimination inherent in the fundamental freedoms extend to residence/home countries, but also the freedom of establishment covers the establishment of subsidiaries, not just the establishment of branches. In this narrow context, EU law associates the identity of a subsidiary with that of its parent corporation.

These issues came to a head in the context of cross-border group relief in the landmark decision of the ECJ in *Marks & Spencer*.[150] This case concerned a UK parent corporation that had established subsidiaries in Belgium, France and Germany. Each of these subsidiaries incurred losses on activities in their respective countries and the parent corporation claimed to use these losses against its UK profits under the UK group relief system. The UK tax administration rejected that claim and the parent corporation sued, claiming that this refusal was contrary to its freedom of establishment under EU Law. In particular, it pointed out that group relief would have been available if the parent corporation had established itself in Europe in the form of PEs or if it had established UK resident subsidiaries that had incurred the foreign losses.

To many, this seemed a straightforward case of unjustifiable discrimination. In the *Bosal* case (discussed above at 4.2.1), the ECJ had already rejected the argument that denial of the interest expense incurred for the purposes of EU subsidiaries was justified on the basis that the home/parent jurisdiction did not seek to tax the profits of the subsidiary. Indeed, the *Bosal* case seemed to have a striking resemblance to *Marks & Spencer*, with the difference that in *Bosal* the parent corporation actually made a payment (the interest), whereas in *Marks & Spencer* this was a notional transfer of losses (subvention payments being ignored for tax purposes). However, the *D* case had been decided in the meantime (see below at 5.2.3.2) and the ECJ had begun to restrict its centralist approach.

The ECJ began by finding that the UK group relief system was restrictive. In particular, it found that a parent corporation with resident subsidiaries was comparable to a parent corporation with EU subsidiaries.[151] The UK sought to justify this restriction through a combination of three grounds. These were outlined above at 2.2.1, but it is useful to refer to the passage from the judgment:

[150] Case C-446/03 *Marks & Spencer* v *Halsey* [2005] ECR I-10837 (ECJ).

[151] Case C-446/03 *Marks & Spencer* v *Halsey* [2005] ECR I-10837 (ECJ) at para. 34. The ECJ did not find a parent corporation with foreign subsidiaries comparable to a corporation with foreign PEs and see *X Holding* below at footnote 171.

> First, in tax matters profits and losses are two sides of the same coin and must be treated symmetrically in the same tax system in order to protect a balanced allocation of the power to impose taxes between the different Member States concerned. Second, if the losses were taken into consideration in the parent company's Member State they might well be taken into account twice. Third, and last, if the losses were not taken into account in the Member State in which the subsidiary is established there would be a risk of tax avoidance.[152]

With respect to the first of these, the ECJ noted that if a corporation had an option as to in which country its losses were taken into account, it 'would significantly jeopardise a balanced allocation of the power to impose taxes between Member States'.[153] With respect to the third, the ECJ noted that free transferability of losses 'entails the risk that within a group of companies losses will be transferred to companies established in the Member States which apply the highest rates of taxation and in which the tax value of the losses is therefore the highest'.[154] Of course, this is true, but it just reflects the existing distortion in the international order to locate deductions in high tax countries and income in low tax countries.

The ECJ concluded that these three factors did justify the restriction and moved to consider whether the UK's denial of loss relief was proportionate. The taxpayer and the European Commission argued that a proportionate response was for the UK to grant relief for the losses of foreign subsidiaries but to *claw back* the relief when the subsidiaries turned profitable. Broadly, this is what would have been required by the draft Losses Directive of 1990, mentioned above at 4.2.2. The ECJ was emphatic that such an approach required 'harmonisation rules adopted by the Community legislature'.[155] Rather, the ECJ took the following approach to proportionality:

> [T]he Court considers that the restrictive measure at issue in the main proceedings goes beyond what is necessary to attain the essential part of the objectives pursued where:
>
> – the non-resident subsidiary has exhausted the possibilities available in its State of residence of having the losses taken into account for the accounting period concerned by the claim for relief and also for previous accounting periods, if necessary by transferring those losses to a third party or by offsetting the losses against the profits made by the subsidiary in previous periods, and

[152] Case C-446/03 *Marks & Spencer* v *Halsey* [2005] ECR I-10837 (ECJ) at para. 43.
[153] Case C-446/03 *Marks & Spencer* v *Halsey* [2005] ECR I-10837 (ECJ) at para. 46.
[154] Case C-446/03 *Marks & Spencer* v *Halsey* [2005] ECR I-10837 (ECJ) at para. 49.
[155] Case C-446/03 *Marks & Spencer* v *Halsey* [2005] ECR I-10837 (ECJ) at para. 58.

- there is no possibility for the foreign subsidiary's losses to be taken into account in its State of residence for future periods either by the subsidiary itself or by a third party, in particular where the subsidiary has been sold to that third party.[156]

This passage, and in particular its second part, raise substantial questions for a domestic court. In this regard, the ECJ accepted that the burden of proof could be placed on the parent corporation.[157] So how would a parent show that a subsidiary has 'no possibility' of using its losses? Is it enough that the subsidiary ceases trading? Does the subsidiary have to be liquidated? What if the subsidiary has been sold to a third party and the third party uses the losses, cannot use the losses because of the change in ownership, or can use the losses only if the subsidiary continues to conduct the same business? Is it enough that the loss has been written off for accounting purposes? Does it make a difference if the taxpayer intentionally engages in conduct that makes it impossible to use the losses in the future?

The ECJ sent the case back to the UK courts to decide whether on the facts its test was met. In the meantime, the UK amended its legislation in a minimalist fashion.[158] This legislation does permit the transfer of losses of foreign subsidiaries that 'cannot be taken into account' in the subsidiary's country. Controversially, whether it can be taken into account must be determined at the end of the period in which the subsidiary incurred the loss. If there is a possibility that the loss can be used at that point, it is irrelevant that subsequent events show that the loss cannot be taken into account. This timing of proof issue became critical in the UK courts rehearing the *Marks & Spencer* case.

Marks & Spencer returned to the UK court that referred the matter to the ECJ. By the time the High Court reheard the matter, the French subsidiary had been sold and had used its losses under French tax law. The Belgian and German subsidiaries had ceased trading. Consistent with the amendments to the UK law following the ECJ decision, the UK tax administration argued that the time at which it should be determined whether the Belgian and German subsidiaries had exhausted all possibility of using the losses was at the end of the accounting period in which the losses were incurred. The High Court rejected this contention, as did

[156] Case C-446/03 *Marks & Spencer* v *Halsey* [2005] ECR I-10837 (ECJ) at para. 55.

[157] Case C-446/03 *Marks & Spencer* v *Halsey* [2005] ECR I-10837 (ECJ) at para. 56.

[158] CTA 2010 ss. 111–28. In October 2009 the European Commission referred the UK to the ECJ for failure to implement *Marks & Spencer*.

the Court of Appeal.[159] Rather, the appropriate time for evaluation was the point at which a claim for group relief was made. Further, the effectiveness of EU Law requires that the time for new claims be extended to within a reasonable period after the ECJ judgment.

The 'no possibility' test was to be applied to the objective facts of the subsidiary at the time of claim. The Court of Appeal refused to give the ECJ test a strict reading and suggested that it was enough if the subsidiary had no 'real' possibility of using the losses. A 'real' possibility is one that could not be dismissed as 'fanciful'. The matter was remitted to the First-Tier Tribunal to find in fact whether the Belgian and German subsidiaries satisfied this test. Meanwhile, in September 2008, the European Commission sent a reasoned opinion to the UK suggesting that the UK had not sufficiently altered its law to comply with the ECJ decision and requesting that it do so.[160] In mid-2009, the First-Tier Tribunal found that the time for assessing the 'no possibilities' test was at the time of claim for group relief. Claims that were made before the Belgian and German subsidiaries went into liquidation did not satisfy this test but those made after largely did.[161]

While *Marks & Spencer* made its tortuous journey through the UK courts, the ECJ was faced with other cross-border loss cases. The *Rewe* case is particularly peculiar and underlines the propensity of the ECJ to view the separate identity of a parent and its subsidiaries strictly.[162] During the 1990s, Germany permitted parent corporations to depreciate (write down) the value of shares held in German subsidiaries and claim a deduction. If a German subsidiary made a loss, this was likely reflected in the value of its shares and so permitting the parent corporation to write down the value of shares held in the subsidiary was an indirect form of group relief. This procedure was not available for shares held in a foreign subsidiary.

The ECJ held this was an unjustified breach of the freedom of establishment. Germany sought to justify its rules based on the balanced allocation of taxing rights argument used in the *Marks & Spencer* case, but the ECJ pointed out that in that case the UK used that ground 'in conjunction with two other grounds'.[163] The implication seems to be that justification

[159] *Marks & Spencer plc* v *Halsey* [2007] EWCA Civ 117 (CA).

[160] European Commission (2008).

[161] *Marks & Spencer plc* v *Halsey* [2009] UKFTT TC00005 (TC).

[162] Case C-347/04 *Rewe Zentralfinanz eG* v *Finanzamt Koln-Mitte* [2007] ECR I-2647 (ECJ).

[163] Case C-347/04 *Rewe Zentralfinanz eG* v *Finanzamt Koln-Mitte* [2007] ECR I-2647 (ECJ) at para. 41.

of restrictive measures cannot be based solely on the balanced allocation argument. Germany could not support this ground with the ground of taking losses into account twice. In *Marks & Spencer*, the subsidiaries' losses were being transferred to the parent corporation.[164]

> The losses at issue in the main proceedings ... related to the writing down of the book value of the shareholdings are taken into account only as regards the parent company and are subject, for tax purposes, to a different treatment from that which applies to losses incurred by the subsidiaries themselves. Such a separate treatment of, first, the losses suffered by the subsidiaries themselves and, secondly, the losses incurred by the parent company cannot, on any basis, amount to using the same losses twice.[165]

The Finnish group contribution regime was in issue in *Oy AA*.[166] If the facts of *Marks & Spencer* were close to those in *Bosal*, those in *Oy AA* were closer. In order to effect a loss transfer from a subsidiary to a parent corporation, the parent had to effect an actual financial transfer to the subsidiary, i.e. a payment. The payment was deductible for the parent but income of the subsidiary. Thus, the subsidiary's loss was cancelled and effectively transferred to the parent corporation. A group contribution was not available with respect to foreign losses incurred by foreign subsidiaries. The ECJ found this restrictive but justified. The Finnish government put forward the three grounds for justification used in *Marks & Spencer*.

Bizarrely, the ECJ found that the Finnish system 'does not concern the deductibility of losses'.[167] As in *Rewe*, this emphasises a formal approach to the interpretation of domestic tax law. So, as in *Rewe*, the Finnish government could not justify its restriction based on the risk of dual use of losses. However, the ECJ found that the Finnish restriction did protect a balanced allocation of taxing rights and prevented tax avoidance and the combination of these grounds was sufficient for purposes of justification.[168] Indeed, the court recognised that these grounds were related.

[164] Case C-347/04 *Rewe Zentralfinanz eG* v *Finanzamt Koln-Mitte* [2007] ECR I-2647 (ECJ) at para. 47.

[165] Case C-347/04 *Rewe Zentralfinanz eG* v *Finanzamt Koln-Mitte* [2007] ECR I-2647 (ECJ) at para. 48. In Case C-182/08 *Glaxo Wellcome GmbH & Co KG* v *Finanzamt München II* [2009] ECR 00 (ECJ) a German rule denied a write down for shareholdings in German corporations acquired from non-residents. The ECJ held this could be justified jointly on a balanced allocation of taxing rights and anti-avoidance. The matter was remitted to the domestic court to decide proportionality.

[166] Case C-231/05 *Oy AA* [2007] ECR I-6373 (ECJ).

[167] Case C-231/05 *Oy AA* [2007] ECR I-6373 (ECJ) at para. 57.

[168] Case C-231/05 *Oy AA* [2007] ECR I-6373 (ECJ) at para. 60.

Further, the ECJ found the restriction proportionate. There was no discussion of the potential unrelieved nature of the subsidiary's loss, as in *Marks & Spencer*. It may be presumed that this was because of the finding that the Finnish system did not concern losses.

The *Marks & Spencer* case was followed quite closely in the *Lidl* case, discussed above at 4.2.2. As in *Oy AA*, Germany was able to justify its refusal to permit the head office to deduct the losses of a foreign PE on two of the three grounds used in *Marks & Spencer*. The combination was different than in *Oy AA*, involving the balanced allocation of taxing rights and the potential dual use of losses (potential for tax avoidance was absent). While asked, the ECJ refused to be drawn on the issue of whether just one of the grounds used in *Marks & Spencer* could justify a restrictive measure. In determining whether denial of loss relief was proportionate, the ECJ followed the 'no possibility' test in *Marks & Spencer*. The court noted that Luxembourg permitted the PE to carry forward the losses and that in fact the losses were used four years after they were incurred.[169] This was sufficient to show that Germany need not grant relief.

The overall outcome of these cases is unsatisfactory and distorting. Each system targeted the same problem, use of losses within groups; they just provided relief in different forms. Each was restrictive, but could not be justified in the same fashion purely based on the formal interpretation given to them by the ECJ, despite the fact that each achieved a similar result. The German system could not be justified and under such a system the parent corporation must (indirectly) be entitled to the losses of its foreign subsidiaries. The UK system could be justified, but the parent corporation must be permitted to use the subsidiary's losses if there was 'no possibility' for the subsidiary to use them. The Finnish system could be justified and so a Finnish parent corporation could never claim use of a foreign subsidiary's foreign losses. Things cannot be left in this way. The formality of the ECJ jurisprudence will distort the form of group relief used by member states with a retarding effect on the ability of taxpayers to exercise their fundamental freedoms. Why is the Finnish system more appropriate than the German or UK system?

Further, the ECJ has refused to deal with one of the substantial problems involved in the use of cross-border losses: that of cash flow disadvantage. In *Lidl*, even though in principle loss relief might be required in the residence/home state, it was sufficient to deny that possibility where

[169] Case C-414/06 *Lidl Belgium GmbH & Co KG* v *Finanzamt Heilbronn* [2008] ECR I-3601 (ECJ) at paras. 49 and 50.

the losses were used in the source/host state within four years. So, a cross-border corporate group must wait and see when and if it can get relief, whereas a purely domestic group gets loss relief immediately. This cannot be consistent with an internal market. Further, it is at least conceptually inconsistent with cases like *Metallgesellschaft* and *Hoechst*, discussed above at 3.1.3.4.[170] In those cases, the unjustified restriction was precisely just this, a cash flow disadvantage for a cross-border group.

[Un]happily, the saga of cross-border aspects of group relief continues for the ECJ. In *X Holding*, the Netherlands refused to permit the foreign activities of foreign subsidiaries to join in their corporate group consolidation regime. The regime facilitates both the inter-group use of losses and non-recognition of gains and losses on the transfer of assets between group members. The ECJ ignored the latter aspect, applying its jurisprudence based on *Marks & Spencer* to find the Dutch regime justified and proportionate. The ECJ held that from the home state's perspective a Dutch corporation with a foreign PE is not comparable with a Dutch corporation with a foreign subsidiary, despite the Netherlands applying an exemption system to both. Importance was placed on the different treatment of PEs and subsidiaries under Articles 7 and 23 of tax treaties.[171]

At various points, the European Commission has had ambitions to coordinate cross-border loss relief, of which the draft Losses Directive of 1990 (discussed above at 4.2.2) was one attempt. However, the Commission has lacked the political support necessary to deal with the issue. Member states seem more willing to leave their fate in the hands of the ECJ than to potentially lose sovereignty in devising EU Law to regulate cross-border losses. The last Commission paper on cross-border losses was in 2006,[172] but this project seems to have stalled.[173] Recently, the Commission is more focused on its CCCTB project (see above at 3.3.1.4) as a solution to this problem. That project, in its current form, would be only a partial solution to cross-border losses as it does not encompass all EU corporate groups. The future of the CCCTB project is itself a hostage to political support.

As a final matter, the residence of group members may affect the use of domestic losses under a group relief system. There are two primary types of situation in issue. The first is where the parent of the group is non-resident and the second is where the parent of the group is resident. In

170 Cases C-397/98 and 410/98 *Metallgesellschaft Ltd* v *IRC and AG*; *Hoechst AG* v *IRC and AG* [2001] ECR I-1727 (ECJ).

171 Case C-337/08 *X Holding BV* v *Staatssecretaris van Financiën* [2009] ECR 0 (ECJ).

172 European Commission (2006).

173 See, however, European Parliament (2008b).

the first case, the issue is whether subsidiaries and PEs of group members located in the host country may use that country's group relief system. This situation was discussed above at 3.1.3.4. In particular, that discussion considered the OECD's opinion that Article 24(3) and (5) of its Model do not extend to group relief. This was contrasted with the position of the ECJ, particularly in light of its decision in *ICI*.[174]

The second case involves the situation in which the parent of the group is resident in the home country and a non-resident subsidiary holds a sub-subsidiary or PE located in the home country. This was the situation in *Société Papillon*, where a French parent corporation held French subsidiaries through a Dutch holding corporation.[175] The parent wished to consolidate with its French subsidiaries to facilitate inter-group loss relief. However, French tax law excluded a French subsidiary from a French group if it was held through a non-resident holding company but not if it was held through a French holding company.

The ECJ noted that this was not a case of cross-border losses but a question of the use of domestic losses. The French authorities argued that the loss of a French subsidiary might cause depreciation in the value of the shares held by the French parent corporation in the intermediate Dutch holding corporation. If both were recognised, this might result in double deduction of the same losses. Unlike the Advocate General, the ECJ rejected the French position, finding that it was disproportionate to the risk. The French regime provided no opportunity for the group to show that in the particular case there was no risk of double deduction of losses.[176]

[174] Case C-264/96 *ICI Plc* v *Colmer* [1998] ECR I-4695 (ECJ).

[175] Case C-418/07 *Société Papillon* v *Ministère du budget, des comptes publics et de la function publique* [2008] ECR I-8947 (ECJ). This case was applied in the UK case of *Philips Electronics UK Ltd* [2009] UK FTT 226 (TC).

[176] Case C-418/07 *Société Papillon* v *Ministère du budget, des comptes publics et de la function publique* [2008] ECR I-8947 (ECJ) at paras. 37–8 and 46–56.

5

The limited scope of treaties

Discussion in previous chapters has identified myriad limitations of tax treaties and, in particular, the OECD Model. A disconcerting feature of this is that what has been discussed are the things that treaties *do* cover. EU Law can be a useful supplement to fill the gaps and, perhaps, right wrongs, but EU Law has its limitations as well. One continual problem is the interaction between domestic law and tax treaties. A particular feature of this is trying to determine whether a term used in a treaty has a special treaty meaning or whether it derives its meaning from domestic law, i.e. the Article 3(2) issue. A classic example of this is use of the word 'income' in Articles 6 and 21, but other cases have been discussed that involve difficulties. For example, problems with the terms 'immovable property', 'alienation', 'movable property' and 'employment' have been discussed, among many others. In some cases, the difficulties arise from specific definitions inserted in tax treaties, such as the definitions of 'dividends', 'interest' and 'royalties'.

A sceptic might suggest that the more we learn about tax treaties, the more we understand how little they cover and the more we realise that what they do cover often involves distortions. A major example is the presumption of a classical system with the bias for debt over equity financing that this involves. The interaction with the taxation of returns on debt and equity financing and that of gains on sale of the underlying finance instrument is another source of distortion. Source country taxation of dividends in itself causes distortion between setting up a source country presence in the form of a PE or a subsidiary. The difference in the treatment of employment income and income from independent services causes further distortions. Other distortions are caused by the now unwavering focus on the transactional basis of allocating business profits between countries and, in particular, the fiction on fiction that is applied to PEs to fit them within this rigid framework.

Prior discussion has also identified some areas that are related to matters covered by tax treaties but which themselves are not directly covered.

Thin capitalisation and CFC rules are areas that were not considered in the historical development of tax treaties and are still commonly not specifically dealt with by them. The existence of these rules in domestic law in many ways simply reflects serious deficiencies and distortions caused by tax treaties. Considering their importance, the efforts of the OECD to deal with these matters through half-hearted attempts at amending the Commentary often make the situation less clear and underline the rigidity of the international tax treaty network against change. The allocation of expenses between domestic and foreign income and the treatment of cross-border losses are clear examples of where tax treaties are of little utility. These areas also reveal the substantial limitations of the OECD approach to non-discrimination, particularly in comparison with the approach under EU Law.

The matters noted in the previous three paragraphs underline the nature of tax treaties as short basic agreements between states that deal with only some fundamentals in a division of tax base between two countries. Unfortunately, the purpose of tax treaties is not to provide taxpayers with comprehensive answers to the taxation of their cross-border dealings, and they do not do this. These features of tax treaties underline the importance of the Vienna Convention when interpreting tax treaties and, in particular, interpreting them in good faith. Historically, the main redeeming feature of tax treaties has been that they deal with the worst cases of tax barriers to cross-border trade and investment and get countries talking about how their tax systems should integrate. In turn, this has been a factor in producing greater uniformity between the cross-border features of income tax systems, which has occurred over the last century.

It remains to be seen whether, despite the exponential increase in the number of tax treaties over the last few decades, tax treaties will prove fit for the purposes of an increasingly globalised world. If tax treaties do not deal with cross-border tax issues of increasing importance, then countries must find other ways of dealing with such issues. To the extent that tax treaties cause distortions, the rigidity of the international tax treaty network stands in the way of progress. To the extent that tax treaty rules have, in any case, been internalised into domestic law or domestic law is more generous, tax treaties are irrelevant.

Discussion in previous chapters has illustrated the limitations on tax treaties with respect to the rules contained in them, i.e. limitations with respect to what tax treaties *do* cover. This chapter is concerned with the limitations of tax treaties that arise from what they *do not* cover. The chapter will discuss these *do not* cover limitations from two perspectives. The first heading presumes a bilateral scenario, i.e. it still presumes the *Base Case*, the figure on page 5. It returns to the income tax fundamentals identified at 1.1 and asks the question, which fundamentals are not covered by tax treaties and what are the consequences if our two countries (Country A and Country B) do not agree on fundamentals not covered by tax treaties?

The second heading steps beyond a limitation inherent in tax treaties and, indeed, the *Base Case*. The international tax treaty network is *bilateral* in nature. Tax treaties seek to allocate taxing rights and resolve issues of double taxation and tax evasion between *two* countries. The real world is not that simple (if it ever was) and international transactions can involve a multitude of countries. The second heading considers tax treaty limitations arising in multilateral situations. This heading is particularly concerned with the phenomenon of regional groupings such as the EU and their interaction with the bilateral nature of tax treaties.

5.1 Mismatches between source and residence countries

Many of the substantive provisions of the OECD Model are taken up, whether directly or indirectly, with residence rules and source rules. In particular, while residence is a notion derived from domestic law, the OECD Model does contain rules for reconciling dual residence, i.e. Article 4. Further, while not expressed to be source rules, Articles 6 to 15 contain rules that specify the circumstances in which what may be considered a source country can tax. These rules are typically such that only one country is granted the right to tax based on source and so have an inherent reconciliation nature about them and sometimes there are express reconciliation rules between the rules. By contrast, what tax treaties deal with rather poorly are the basic building blocks of the income tax identified at 1.1 above, i.e. the fundamental features of a payment.

Mismatches of views taken by countries in their domestic laws on the fundamental features of a payment can produce unrelieved double taxation or double non-taxation. International tax advisers have known this for decades, but these mismatches have been exploited with increasing frequency in tax planning in the last two decades. No doubt, globalisation has played its part in this process. This exploitation is often described as 'tax arbitrage' as it involves exploiting the differences between two countries' tax laws. While initially slow to respond, and with some confusion, tax administrations have caught on and are now in a steady process of shutting down the worst cases of mismatch planning. The responses depend on information and, as will be discussed at 7.2, in recent years there has been a substantial increase in coordination between tax administrations to identify and deal with aggressive international tax planning. However, the responses are typically unilateral in nature, being based in domestic law, and so unpredictable and lacking uniformity.

The following discussion takes each of the fundamental features of a payment identified at 1.1 and considers the consequences where the source and residence countries do not take a common position on these features. It considers the tax planning opportunities and the potential pitfalls. In the usual way, the UK domestic legislation is used as a backdrop and, in particular, the manner in which the UK has sought to deal with mismatches is noted. There is no separate consideration of EU Law as the types of mismatches dealt with are usually a simple consequence of the lack of harmonisation of tax laws.

5.1.1 *Allocation of payment*

As noted at 1.1, for tax purposes, payments must be allocated as made by a person and received by another person. Even where two countries agree on the characterisation of entities as 'persons', see above at 2.1.1.1, they may disagree on which person is considered to make or receive a payment for tax purposes. To take a simple example, a subsidiary corporation borrows money from a bank but cannot afford to pay the interest. Rather than letting its subsidiary default, the parent corporation pays the interest due to the bank. Which corporation should be treated as paying the interest (and so receive a deduction), the parent corporation or the subsidiary? Or should the payment by the parent corporation be viewed as first a payment to the subsidiary and then a payment by the subsidiary to the bank? There can be disagreement on these matters.[1]

A similar problem arises with respect to the potential dual application of CFC rules, noted above at 4.1.2.2. An example was given at that point of a Country C corporation that holds a Country B corporation that holds a third lowly taxed corporation. If both Country C and Country B apply CFC rules, there is a mismatch of allocation of the subsidiary's profits. The

[1] Consider also the UK transfer pricing rule in TIOPA 2010 s. 153, mentioned above in footnote 329 of Chapter 3, which may create the reverse problem. If the parent corporation guarantees a loan made to a subsidiary, the parent corporation may be treated as paying interest to the lender even if the interest payment is in fact made by the subsidiary/borrower.

problem is that CFC rules are not typically symmetrical. At some level, they should be excluded where the parent corporation is itself a CFC of a parent in another country. This may be a matter that can be resolved only under the mutual agreement procedure, see below at 7.2.1.[2] It is often necessary for tax advisers to (legitimately) plan around this sort of problem.

By far the greater problem in international tax planning has been with *hybrid entities*. These are artificial entities, e.g. companies, partnerships and trusts, which are recognised by one country as a tax subject, and so capable of making and receiving payments (and having income), but viewed by another country as *transparent*. The domestic characterisation of entities was considered above at 2.1.1.1. In particular, one need only note the elective nature of the US check-the-box regime to recognise that taxpayers may intentionally elect to create a mismatch of entity recognition across borders, i.e. create a hybrid entity.[3] Often, however, even where an elective regime is not available, taxpayers are in a position to make an election by intentionally using a type of entity that they know is recognised as a tax subject by one country but not by another. For example, particular problems can be caused by limited partnerships.

Hybrid entities essentially raise two types of problem. The first is where the source country views a hybrid entity as transparent but the residence country views the hybrid as a tax subject, e.g. a corporation. The second is where the source country views a hybrid as a corporation but the residence country views it as transparent. Each scenario can raise issues of either double non-taxation or double taxation. However, tax advisers plan *around* the potential for double taxation (at the threat of being sued for negligence) whereas they plan *for* double non-taxation. A simple example of each scenario follows.

Presume a corporation (recognised as such by both countries) resident in Country B sets up a hybrid entity in Country A. The hybrid receives royalties sourced in Country A. Country A and Country B have concluded an OECD style tax treaty. Country A views the hybrid as transparent and so considers the corporation in Country B the recipient of the royalties. As a result, and in accordance with the OECD Model, Country A refrains from taxing the royalties. Country B, however, views the hybrid as a corporation resident in Country A, e.g. as organised under the

[2] It seems this is the French approach, see Reeb-Blanluet (2007).

[3] Before the check-the-box regime, US limited liability companies (LLCs) were treated as a partnership (transparent) for US tax purposes but a company for UK tax purposes. See Fraser (2001). As noted in Chapter 2, in mid-2009 President Obama proposed substantially tightening up the circumstances in which a foreign entity is treated as transparent.

laws of Country A or being managed there. As a result, it does not tax the hybrid, as it is neither the source nor residence country with respect to the income. The result is double non-taxation.

There are a number of factors to consider in determining whether the taxpayer will really receive this beneficial treatment. These may result in either the source or the residence country taxing. There is a risk that any general anti-abuse rule (GAAR) or doctrine in domestic law applies. While this is an important consideration, GAARs are beyond the scope of this study and many countries do not have one, or at least one that would apply to this sort of scenario. A number of countries have introduced specific legislation to deal with hybrid entities and more will be said about the UK rules shortly. CFC rules in Country B are, perhaps, the most straightforward threat (see above at 4.1.2.2). If Country B has such rules, the hybrid is likely to be a CFC of the corporation resident in Country B. It will have been subject to lower level taxation (indeed, no taxation). On the facts, there is no scope for an active income exception, though perhaps a greater issue is whether a white list country exception might apply. In any case, Country B may not have CFC rules; many countries do not.

As for Country A, its domestic law is likely to provide for the taxation of royalties sourced in its jurisdiction, typically by withholding. Here, it is the tax treaty with Country B that excludes its right to tax, or does it? Country A considers the recipient of the income to be the corporation resident in Country B. It is agreed that that corporation is a person, but in order to receive the benefits of the treaty it must also be considered resident in Country B for the purposes of the treaty. It is resident in Country B under the domestic law of Country B, but is it resident there for the purpose of Article 4 of the OECD Model? Is it 'liable to tax', and what does that phrase mean in a case like this (see above at 2.1.1.2)? It might be argued that the corporation is not and can never be 'liable to tax' with respect to the hybrid's income (CFC rules aside), but is it appropriate to interpret the phrase in such a narrow fashion? The better view is that the corporation is liable to tax and so resident in Country B for the purposes of the treaty, but this is a matter on which some disagreement is likely.

If the views of Country A and Country B are reversed, there is the potential for double taxation. Country A will view the royalties as derived by the hybrid entity and tax it with respect to them on both the basis of source and residence. By contrast, Country B will view the royalties as derived by the corporation and tax it with respect to them. An issue is whether Country A tax paid by the hybrid would qualify as a creditable tax for the purposes of the foreign tax credit system that is likely to apply in Country B with respect to the royalties. In many countries that would be problematic, as they require the tax to be paid by the 'person' seeking the credit. The UK approach seems more flexible; section 9 of TIOPA 2010 grants credit for source country tax paid and 'calculated by reference to' the relevant income. It does not specify that the person claiming the credit must be the person subject to the source country tax, rather the focus is on the income as the tax subject, i.e. an *in rem* approach (see above at 1.1).[4]

While it is generally true that tax advisers plan for hybrids to derive income where the source country views them as transparent and the residence country views them as corporations, the opposite can be true where the income derived is dividends. In *Memec*,[5] Germany attributed income of a silent partnership (in this case, dividends from Germany subsidiaries) to the general partner, a German corporation. The UK silent partner argued that under UK law it should be treated as deriving its share of this income directly. This would enable the UK silent partner to claim underlying foreign tax relief on the dividends, something that was not available if it was viewed as deriving a non-dividend return on its silent partnership interest. The Court of Appeal interpreted the situation consistently with the German approach, i.e. by considering the German general partner as deriving the dividends. This case is discussed further below at 5.1.4.

Consolidation is another example of a mismatch of allocation of income and the potential reverse distortion with respect to dividends. Under a consolidation regime, the source country may collapse the identity of group members into their source country parent corporation. Assume that A Co holds 70 per cent of the shares in A Sub. Both are resident in Country A and the domestic law of Country A consolidates the tax identity of A Sub into that of A Co so that A Co is the only Country A taxpayer. B Co, a corporation resident in Country B, holds the other 30 per cent of the shares in A Sub and receives a dividend from A Sub. Country B does not view A Co and A Sub as consolidated and so there is a risk that Country B views A Sub as not having paid any Country A tax (because all Country A tax was paid in the name of A Co). If Country B adopts an underlying

[4] A similar problem arises where membership interests (e.g. shares) in a hybrid are sold. The source country may view this as a sale of assets held by the hybrid, e.g. the land, and so grounding a source country taxing right. The residence country may view this as a sale of the shares in the hybrid, which is protected from source country tax under OECD Model Art. 13(5) (assuming Art. 13(4) is not applicable). The better view is that as the source country has taxed, under its law, in accordance with the treaty, the residence country is obliged to provide foreign tax relief. See discussion above at 4.1.1.2 and OECD Commentary on Art. 23 paras. 32.4 and 32.5.

[5] *Memec Plc* v *IRC* [1998] STC 754 (CA).

foreign tax credit, the result may be that no underlying Country A tax is available for credit. UK domestic law circumvents this problem by recognising the foreign consolidated group as 'a single company' and treating the foreign tax and the dividend as paid by that single company.[6] So the UK would grant underlying foreign tax credits with respect to the A Sub dividend for Country A tax paid by the consolidated group.

In *Bayfine*, the taxpayer planned *for* double taxation.[7] The case involved a complex UK/US set of transactions between two corporate groups. The plan was to create a loss for one corporation in each group. An offsetting gain was derived by a hybrid, recognised as a corporation for UK tax but not for US tax purposes. The US taxed the parent corporation of the hybrid on the gain whereas the UK taxed the hybrid on the gain. In the UK, the hybrid unsuccessfully argued that it was entitled to a foreign tax credit (either unilaterally or under treaty) for the tax paid by its parent corporation. Special Commissioner Avery Jones insightfully emphasised the point made earlier that:

> The problem of interpreting the Treaty arises because the UK considers the resident taxpayer to be BUK while the US treats BDE as the resident taxpayer because it disregards BUK. If the same taxpayer is a resident of both States the dual residence provisions of the Treaty will resolve residence in favour of one of them for the purpose of applying the Treaty. But the Treaty is silent about what to do when they are different persons.[8]

The second scenario involves the potential for simultaneously claiming deduction in two countries for the same expense. Presume a corporation (recognised as such by both countries) resident in Country B sets up a hybrid entity in Country A. The hybrid borrows money from a bank and uses it to buy immovable property in Country A. Country A and Country B have concluded an OECD style tax treaty. Country A views the hybrid as a corporation and so considers the hybrid the owner of the property and the payer of interest on funds borrowed. Accordingly, it can claim a deduction for depreciation of the property and the interest for Country A tax purposes. Country B, however, views the hybrid as transparent and so it views the corporation as the owner of the property and the payer of the interest. As a result, it grants the corporation a deduction for depreciation of the property and the interest for Country B tax purposes. The result is

[6] TIOPA 2010 s. 71.

[7] *Bayfine UK Products Bayfine UK* v *RCC* [2008] UKSPC SPC00719 (SC).

[8] *Bayfine UK Products Bayfine UK* v *RCC* [2008] UKSPC SPC00719 (SC) at para. 38.

a classic *double dip*, i.e. claiming the benefit of a deduction twice in more than one country.

As with the potential for double non-taxation of income, there are limitations on an ability to achieve a double dip for deductions. In particular, in a simple scenario, there is really no abuse and the double deduction of expenses is appropriate and necessary. If the hybrid is profitable, then Country A will tax the profits (net of the expenses). Country B may view the hybrid as a PE in Country A and will apply the exemption method or foreign tax credit method of foreign tax relief. If the former, then Country B will not tax and the expenses will be denied, so there is no double taxation and no double dip. If a foreign tax credit is available, then as Country B is taxing on a worldwide basis, it should grant a deduction for appropriate foreign expenses, which will reduce the limitation on credit. Indeed, if the hybrid is profitable, the risk is still against the taxpayer in that the corporation may not get a foreign tax credit for the Country A tax paid by the hybrid.

The risk for tax administrations is where the deductions in Country A cause a loss. Country A will say this is a loss of the hybrid whereas Country B will say it is a loss of the corporation. Again, this is not of itself beneficial to the taxpayer (after all, they have suffered a loss), but might be if current loss relief can be obtained simultaneously in both Country A and Country B. So, for example, if the hybrid entity is part of a corporate group in Country A, perhaps the hybrid's loss can be used against profits of another group member and so provide a real tax saving. This will depend on the domestic rules of Country A. This sort of relief might be available, particularly where Country A is actually the home country for a corporate group, i.e. where its parent corporation is resident, and Country B is the country of residence of a foreign subsidiary of the group (but the subsidiary holds the hybrid).

Further, perhaps the corporation's foreign loss can be used for Country B tax purposes. This potential was discussed above at 4.2. Often the Country A loss (presumed to be a PE loss) will be available to reduce Country B source income whether Country B adopts the exemption or credit method of foreign tax relief. If Country B uses the credit method, even if it quarantines foreign losses, perhaps the Country A loss can be used against lowly taxed foreign income of the Country B corporation, e.g. passive income from a tax haven. Note that if Country B relief is secured, the taxpayer has effectively secured a form of cross-border loss relief that is typically not available if the Country A entity had been set up as a subsidiary corporation rather than as a hybrid.

Accordingly, it is not obtaining current relief for the Country A loss that is the problem, the problem is when such current relief is obtained twice. The domestic loss relief systems of *some* countries deal with *some* of these possibilities. So, for example, if the UK were Country A, it seems the hybrid's loss would be available for transfer to another UK group member.[9] If the UK were Country B, then generally the loss of the Country A PE would be available for use against UK source income unless the loss were from an overseas property business.[10] However, the corporation could not surrender the loss of the Country A PE to another UK group member under the UK's group relief system if that loss had been used under a group relief system in Country A.[11] In the usual way, the UK's policy choices in this area are not particularly coherent.

In 2005, the UK acted to shut down schemes involving international tax arbitrage, i.e. schemes involving cross-border mismatches including the use of hybrid entities. An impetus for this shutdown was information secured under the US style regime for disclosure of tax avoidance schemes introduced in 2004.[12] Under section 232 of TIOPA 2010, the UK tax administration has power to serve a corporation a notice with respect to a 'deduction scheme' under which the corporation claims a deduction for UK tax purposes. '[O]ne of the main purposes' of the scheme must be to achieve a UK tax advantage. 'Deduction scheme' is defined by reference to sections 236 to 242, which are broken into three parts; the first part deals with schemes involving hybrid entities.

The effect of the notice is that the UK tax administration can deny the corporation a deduction.[13] The power is a broad discretion to shut down double dips using hybrid entities that involve UK tax and is qualified only by the purpose of the scheme. There is no attempt to determine in which of two countries a deduction is more appropriate. If two countries simultaneously adopt this style of rule, the risk is that the expense will not be relieved at all. The 2005 anti-arbitrage rules do not expressly cover the double non-taxation of income using hybrid entities. This leaves the UK somewhat exposed as a source country (although the deduction rules may

[9] CTA 2010 s. 99.

[10] Compare CTA 2010 s. 37 with CTA 2010 s. 66. Under the latter provision, the losses of a corporation from an overseas property business may be carried forward and set against future profits of that business only. This is a particularly restrictive quarantining rule.

[11] CTA 2010 s. 106.

[12] This disclosure regime was introduced in Finance Act 2004 ss. 306–19.

[13] TIOPA 2010 s. 243.

be of some assistance) and seems to presume that the UK CFC rules are sufficiently robust to cover any problems where the UK is the residence country.

Finally, tax arbitrage of the hybrid variety can also involve the use of PEs because, as discussed above at 3.1.3.3, PEs may be allocated payments in a similar manner to persons. So, for example, a source country may consider that income is not derived through a PE and so not tax the income as business profits (e.g. apply a low or no withholding tax). By contrast, the residence country may consider that the income is derived through a source country PE and so exempt the foreign income as a form of (unnecessary) foreign tax relief. The result can be double non-taxation. Similarly, the source country may recognise a PE and so grant a deduction for an expense whereas the residence country does not and so recognises the expense as well, i.e. a double dip. Commissionaire arrangements, where civil law countries do not recognise an undisclosed agent as an agent and so do not recognise an agency PE, cause particular problems of these types.[14] The UK anti-arbitrage rules do not expressly apply to hybrid PEs, only hybrid 'persons'.

5.1.2 *Quantification*

Each of the source and residence countries must quantify a cross-border payment, and it does not necessarily follow that they will quantify the payment in the same amount. For a start, they are likely to quantify the payment in different currencies, which raises issues of the appropriate exchange rate. Further, in non-arm's length scenarios, the consideration for a cash payment may in real terms be more or less than the payment. This is the transfer pricing issue discussed above at 3.3.1, through which related parties may try to manipulate the source of income. Transfer pricing adjustments in some non-arm's length scenarios are authorised by Article 9(1) of the OECD Model. Transfer pricing was discussed as essentially a question of source country taxation and, in particular, quantifying income sourced in a particular country. This is fundamentally true, but the scope of Article 9(1) is rather peculiar and requires further investigation.

Source countries primarily use Article 9(1) of the OECD Model to increase the tax base subject to source country taxation. However, the scope of Article 9(1) is broader. For example, it can be used by residence countries

[14] See Vann (2006, p. 363).

and, in that context, may have implications for foreign tax relief. In particular, a residence country might use Article 9(1) to increase the foreign income of a resident. This is most likely to happen where the residence country is applying the foreign tax credit method but, conceptually, it could happen for an exemption country where it uses exemption with progression. Increasing the amount of foreign income will increase the tax base of the residence country, but should also increase the limitation on credit under a foreign tax credit system. Decreasing the foreign income will have the opposite effect. Under Article 23, the residence country will nevertheless be required to provide relief for source country tax levied 'in accordance with' the tax treaty and this will be as determined under the source country tax law, not the residence country tax law, see above at 4.1.1.2.

Whether a source country or a residence country has an incentive to make a transfer pricing adjustment depends on the type of cross-border transaction in question. Most transactions recognised for income tax purposes actually involve at least two payments, one in kind payment, being the activity or asset that represents wealth created, and a cash payment in return. It is the in kind payment that is important for tax purposes and that needs to be focused on. In most scenarios, from where and to where a cash payment is made does not affect the tax consequences of a transaction.[15] In arm's length scenarios, the in kind payment is quantified by reference to the cash payment (subject to currency exchange issues). In non-arm's length scenarios, the cash payment does not serve this purpose and the fundamental issue is seeking an appropriate quantification of the in kind payment.

In-kind payments may involve international factors in two scenarios:

1. The payment represents wealth created in the country of the recipient but the payer is resident elsewhere.
2. The payment represents wealth created in the country of the payer but the recipient is resident elsewhere.

Both cases involve a person resident in a country that is not the country of the source of income (wealth created). In one case, that person is the maker of the in kind payment and in the other, that person is the recipient of the payment. First case scenarios typically involve the use of an asset or provision of services in one country where the owner of the asset or the provider of the services is resident in another country. They can also involve the transfer of an asset situated in one country where the owner of

[15] This is because the payment of cash usually represents the transfer of an asset (cash) that has no built in gain or loss. The exception is where cash is in a foreign currency.

the asset is resident in another country. By contrast, second case scenarios typically involve the transfer of an asset situated in the country in which its owner is resident to another country. Each case has the potential to raise a conflict between the countries concerned as to quantification of the payment if the transaction is not at arm's length.

The first case is the *Base Case* scenario, Figure 1 on page 5. The in kind payment is the use of Beth's premises in Country A (which is value transferred from Beth to Allan) and the cash payment is the rent paid by Allan. This book has studied their transaction from three perspectives. The first was Country A taxation of Beth with respect to the rent, above at 3.1. The second was the deductibility of the payment for Allan, above at 3.2. The third was the Country B taxation of Beth with respect to the rent including allocation of expenses, above at 4.1 and 4.2. The payment/transaction needs to be quantified for each of these three purposes. Both Country A and Country B need to quantify the payment for the purposes of calculating Beth's income. Country A also needs to quantify the payment for the purposes of calculating Allan's income, i.e. the size of the deduction granted will affect the quantum of Allan's income for Country A purposes.

If Allan and Beth are related, then Article 9(1) of the OECD Model may apply. The limits on the application of Article 9(1) of the OECD Model were noted above at 3.3.1.1. In particular, it applies only in the context of businesses and seems focused on artificial entities, i.e. has limited application to individuals. But assume Article 9(1) does apply to Allan and Beth, i.e. assume their activities are both sufficient to constitute an 'enterprise' and that they are related corporations. In this scenario, a source country (Country A) has little incentive to make a transfer pricing adjustment to increase the amount of rent paid. It may be presumed that any increase in rent for Beth will increase the deduction available to Allan, with no net benefit for the source country.[16]

Indeed, there may be cases of this first variety in which the source country has an incentive to lower the amount of income. For example, if the income is interest or royalties, the source country has a limited taxing right, but Article 24(4) of the OECD Model will require that it give the recipient of the in kind payment (Allan) a deduction for the cost, i.e. the cash payment (to Beth). The lower the deduction the higher Allan's income and the tax paid to Country A. Increasing Allan's income will produce

[16] However, care must be taken in analysing domestic tax law. For example, if the source country applies a withholding tax to a cash payment, this may not be reduced just because the payer is denied a deduction for part of the cash paid.

more Country A tax revenue than increasing Beth's income. The interests of a residence country will typically be diametrically opposed. The lower the source country tax, the less foreign tax credit relief as a proportion of residence country tax and so the greater the incentive to increase the amount of foreign income. This is precisely the type of scenario in which a residence country might seek to make an adjustment under Article 9(1).

The second case does not classically involve a clash of source and residence, at least in the simple fashion that this book has presented the matter so far. That is because the income is sourced in the same country as the residence of its owner. In the second scenario, it is the recipient of the in kind payment, not its maker, that is not resident in the source country. An example will illustrate this second scenario and the issues that arise. Assume a subsidiary resident in Country A manufactures chairs there and sells them to its parent corporation resident in Country B. The parent corporation attaches a brand name and resells the chairs in Country B. In determining the amount of the subsidiary's Country A profits, Country A has a legitimate interest as a source country in the price that the subsidiary receives for the chairs. CFC rules aside, Country B's interest is not about calculating the profits of the subsidiary, which it will not tax, but about calculating the profits of the parent corporation from reselling the chairs, the cost of the chairs being deductible in calculating those profits.

So, in this second scenario, quantifying the in kind payment is typically an issue of allocating source between two countries, i.e. Country A and Country B.[17] It is important for Country A in terms of a direct increase in income sourced in Country A. It is important to Country B in terms of an indirect increase in income sourced in Country B by decreasing a deductible expense. Unlike the first scenario, where Country A may have an incentive to decrease the quantum of the in kind payment, in the second scenario Country A has an incentive to increase it. Further, in the first scenario Country B may have an incentive to increase the in kind payment but in the second case has an incentive to decrease it. It will be noted that the dominant factor is typically whether a country is the country of the recipient of the in kind payment, and so the country obliged to give a deduction for the cost of that payment.

A fundamental condition to the application of Article 9(1) of the OECD Model is that the scenario involves a person resident in one country that

[17] This second scenario could also involve Country B taxation purely on a residence basis, such as where the parent corporation receives the in kind payment (and incurs its cost) in the context of a foreign PE.

carries on a business and a related person resident in another country that carries on a business. Both scenarios outlined above can meet this condition and so Article 9(1) has potential application in either scenario. Note that for the purposes of Article 9(1), it is not important whether a country increases the in kind payment (to increase the income of one party to the transaction) or decreases the in kind payment (to reduce a deduction of the other party). Further, it is irrelevant whether a country seeks to make an adjustment as a source country or as a residence country, although for reasons discussed above, it is most common to make the adjustment (increase or decrease) as a source/host country.

If a country uses Article 9(1) to increase the profits of an enterprise, this will cause economic double taxation if the other country does not adjust the profits of the other enterprise in the opposite direction. For example, assume a first scenario case involving the payment of 100 in interest by a person resident in the source country to a person resident in another. The payer has 150 gross receipts and wishes to deduct the interest, leaving a profit of 50. However, the source country adjusts the interest to 70, leaving profits of 80 to be taxed. If the residence country of the recipient taxes the full 100 interest, there is economic double taxation (even if it grants foreign tax relief). In particular, the source country will have indirectly taxed 30 of the interest as an increase in profits of the payer and directly taxed the remaining 70 as the source country. The residence country will grant foreign tax relief only for the amount directly taxed and the remaining 30 may be subject to full residence country taxation despite the fact that it was indirectly subject to source country tax in the hands of the payer.

Similarly, economic double taxation can arise in a second scenario case. Assume the subsidiary (above) sells the chairs to the parent corporation for 50 but the source country (Country A) increases this to 80. Assume the parent corporation resells the chairs for 150, making a profit of 100, which is taxable in its country of source/residence (Country B). Economic double taxation will result, unless Country B reduces the profits of the parent corporation by the same amount as Country A increased the profits of the subsidiary, i.e. 30.

To alleviate this form of economic double taxation, which arises from a mismatch of quantification, Article 9(2) of the OECD Model provides for the making of a corresponding adjustment:

> Where a Contracting State includes in the profits of an enterprise of that State – and taxes accordingly – profits on which an enterprise of the other

> Contracting State has been charged to tax in that other State and the profits so included are profits which would have accrued to the enterprise of the first-mentioned State if the conditions made between the two enterprises had been those which would have been made between independent enterprises, then that other State shall make an appropriate adjustment to the amount of the tax charged therein on those profits.

Despite the inelegant wording, the idea is that if one country makes an appropriate transfer pricing adjustment to the profits of one party to a transaction, then the other country should make the opposite adjustment to the profits of the related other party. It will be noted that this provision applies only where an enterprise of a state is taxed by *that* state and the other enterprise is taxed by *its* state. In other words, the scope of Article 9(2) is limited. The scenario must involve two associated enterprises resident in two different countries. The increase of taxation must be by the residence country of one of the enterprises. The other country is obliged to make an adjustment in the taxation of the other enterprise only if it is resident in that other country. The provision cannot apply to source taxation of a non-resident and so cannot apply to PEs.[18]

Because of the divergent interests of countries discussed above, Article 9(2) of the OECD Model can be a source of disagreement between countries. In particular, countries often disagree as to whether a primary transfer pricing adjustment is appropriate, i.e. whether it meets the requirements of Article 9(2) for requiring the other country to make a corresponding adjustment. In essence, these are disputes between countries as to what is an arm's length price. Transfer pricing disputes between countries are to be resolved through the mutual agreement procedure of Article 25 (which governs the procedure whereby tax authorities of different countries resolve matters of double taxation). The procedure is slow and countries are not obliged to resolve the double taxation. The mutual agreement procedure is discussed further below at 7.2.1.

5.1.3 *Timing of payment*

As explained above at 1.1, an income tax is periodic in that it is assessed according to income derived during specified periods, typically a tax year. As building blocks of the income tax base, payments (whether made or

[18] OECD Model Art. 7 does not address this problem. Since November 2009, Draft OECD Model Art. 7(3), slated for introduction in 2010, contains a provision based on OECD Model Art. 9(2) that would address this incongruence.

received) must be allocated to particular periods. With respect to cross-border payments, there is the substantial risk that a payment will be recognised for tax purposes by one country at a different time or for a different period to when it is recognised by another country. This might happen in a number of manners, especially where the countries adopt different tax years or where one country uses the accrual basis and the other the cash basis for determining taxable income.[19] The timing issues are particularly problematic for foreign tax credit countries.

Assume that a corporation resident in Country B has a PE in Country A. The PE manufactures watches in Country A and purchases a factory in Country A for this purpose. Typically, the cost of the factory will not be immediately deductible. Conceptually, the cost should be deducted over the useful life of the factory, i.e. the cash payment made for the factory should be spread out and recognised over a number of years. However, Country A and Country B do not grant depreciation at the same rate. Country A depreciates the factory at 20 per cent per year whereas Country B depreciates the factory at 5 per cent per year. So, if the factory cost 1,000,000, Country A will grant a deduction of 200,000 for five years but Country B will grant a deduction of 50,000 over twenty years.

In Country A, the depreciation deduction may produce a loss for the PE in the first five years, i.e. where its profits before depreciation are 200,000 or less. However, if those profits are above 50,000, the corporation will have profits from the PE in each of those five years for Country B tax purposes. If Country B adopts a foreign tax credit system, it will fully tax those profits, but there will be no Country A tax to credit if the profits before depreciation do not exceed 200,000. After five years, the situation may reverse. There will be no depreciation deduction for the PE in Country A, meaning that it is more likely to make profits. But the deduction will continue in Country B for another fifteen years, making it likely that the PE profits will be more in Country A after year 5 than in Country B. This will have an impact on the calculation of the limitation on credit in Country B.

For example, suppose that in year 6 the PE makes a profit for Country A purposes of 100,000, which Country A taxes at 30 per cent, i.e. 30,000 tax.

[19] Under a cash basis, cash payments made and received are recognised only when actually paid, i.e. when the transfer takes place. Under an accrual basis, payments made and received are recognised when all events entitling a person to receive have occurred or all events required to impose the obligation to pay have occurred. Countries typically use the accrual basis for business income, but sometimes the cash basis can be used by small business.

However, due to the continued depreciation, Country B calculates the PE profits as 50,000 (i.e. 100,000 less 50,000 depreciation). It also taxes at 30 per cent but as its tax base is smaller, the Country B tax on the PE profits is 15,000 (i.e. 30 per cent of 50,000), and this is the limitation on credit (see above at 4.1.1.1). So the corporation will have excess foreign tax credits of 15,000 and a major issue is how these excess credits can be used.

Looking at the big picture, with equal tax rates it might be expected that Country B will levy no tax on the PE profits due to foreign tax credit relief. However, due to the depreciation differences, Country B has taxed in the years in which its depreciation rate was slower than Country A but there are excess foreign tax credits in years in which the Country B depreciation rate is greater than that in Country A. The result can be double taxation and a lot depends on the use of excess foreign tax credits in Country B. Carrying them forward will not resolve the problem if the corporation has no residence tax liability on foreign profits in the future. Carry back does resolve the problem, but carry back is rare and almost never available for a period as substantial as five years.

Similar mismatches between a source country and a residence country can arise from the basis of tax accounting, i.e. cash or accrual, or the timing of the tax year and whether it is on a current or a preceding year basis. For most countries, the tax year is the calendar year, but there are variations. In the UK, it is 1 April to 31 March for corporations and 6 April to 5 April for individuals. In Australia, the tax year is 1 July to 30 June. Further, a (decreasing) number of countries still operate on a preceding year basis. This means that taxable income for, say, 2010 is determined by reference to profits made in 2009. These mismatches can cause timing problems.

For example, assume that a person resident in Country B owns land in Country A. The land is sold on 1 January in year 2 and the person makes a gain of 100. Country A adopts the calendar year but uses a preceding year basis. Therefore, as the gain is made in year 2, it is not taxable in Country A until the end of year 3. By contrast, Country B has a tax year of 1 April to 30 March and uses a current year basis. So it taxes the gain at the end of its tax year ending 30 March in year 2, i.e. 21 months before Country A. How should a foreign tax credit system work in such a scenario? In principle, the UK unilateral foreign tax credit system is sufficiently flexible to cover this because what can be credited is foreign tax calculated 'by reference' to the gain, irrespective of the timing of that taxation.[20] However,

[20] TIOPA 2010 s. 9 and see above at 4.1.1.1.

the administrative matter of paying the tax and later claiming a credit, including reopening an assessment, is another matter.

A further example demonstrates the impact of accrual versus cash accounting. Assume that a corporation resident in Country A borrows funds from an individual resident in Country B. The funds are borrowed for three years, but interest is not paid until the end of the three years, i.e. a deferred interest security. Country A taxes the corporation on a current year basis, granting a deduction for the interest as it accrues. So, one third of the interest is deductible in year 1, one third in year 2 and one third in year 3. By contrast, Country B taxes the individual on a cash basis and so does not tax until year 3. The timing advantage between deduction in Country A and taxation in Country B can be substantial. This sort of problem is not just with respect to interest; it can result from deferred royalties, service fees, rent, insurance premiums, etc.

Even just in Country A there can be a timing mismatch, e.g. between deduction for the corporation and the imposition of any withholding tax, which may be on a cash basis. Here Country A has granted a tax advantage, i.e. the deduction, without the security of taxing the interest. Problems can also arise in the reverse, where Country A imposes withholding tax on the interest on payment but Country B taxes the interest on an accrual basis. Again, this raises issues of the timing of any foreign tax credit in Country B for the withholding tax levied in a subsequent year.

The domestic laws of many countries address the problems of deferred interest securities (though countries commonly struggle in dealing with other forms of deferred income).[21] Others may deny a deduction for interest to non-residents until it is paid, i.e. a cash basis.[22] Indeed, often the problem for tax advisers is the reverse, i.e. not planning for deferral but planning to avoid temporary double taxation. Selectively applying such rules to international transactions can raise issues of discrimination. Under the OECD Model, this will not usually be an issue for residence countries, e.g. with respect to accrual taxation of deferred

[21] See Ault and Arnold (2010, pp. 309–16). In the UK, corporations will typically deduct interest as it accrues under the loan relationship rules. Interest accruing in favour of a corporation will be treated similarly. However, interest accruing in favour of an individual is still largely dealt with on a cash basis, with special rules dealing with the income/capital divide; see Tiley (2008, pp. 575–86).

[22] For example, the UK tax law incorporates such a restriction with respect to certain interest paid to a resident of a non-qualifying territory; see Corporation Tax Act 2009 s. 373. All EU member states are qualifying.

interest.[23] However, for the source country, Article 24(4) requires that payments of interest to non-residents 'be deductible under the same conditions as if they had been paid to a resident'. The timing of a deduction is a relevant 'condition', but as noted above at 3.2, question whether the provision has any application to interest that has accrued but not been paid. Under EU Law, a difference in treatment of such an international transaction compared to a purely domestic one, whether by the source or residence country, is likely to breach the fundamental freedoms.

5.1.4 Characterisation of payment

The final fundamental feature of a payment is its character. Just as countries may disagree about allocation (including entity characterisation), quantification and timing, they may disagree about the nature of an international transaction and so the character of payments made under the transaction. The problem is that the tax treatment of a payment will often depend on its character. If source and residence countries characterise a payment differently, the result may be permanent double taxation or double non-taxation. As with the allocation issue, in the past couple of decades, with the increase in globalisation, tax advisers have increasingly sought to plan for double non-taxation. Some countries, including the UK, are now in the process of reacting against this planning.

Most often, what is being characterised is the cash payment made in return for the in kind payment, see above at 5.1.2, but, in the usual manner, the cash payment will take its character from the in kind payment, i.e. the consideration. As with the other mismatches, there can be a mismatch between source and residence countries as to characterisation of the cash payment in the hands of the recipient. Usually, this sort of mismatch does not cause serious issues and is often only a question of appropriate rate of tax by the source country. If the source country taxes in accordance with a tax treaty (determined under its law, see above at 4.1.1.2), then the residence country will be obliged to grant foreign tax relief for source country tax even if it disagrees with the source country classification. Where unilateral foreign tax relief is offered, the issue is typically only one of whether the income in question is sourced in the source country. If it is, foreign tax relief will be granted irrespective of any mismatch of characterisation.

[23] Although question whether the reference to 'paid' in OECD Model Art. 11(1) means that a residence country cannot tax until interest is paid, i.e. a cash basis. A similar point was discussed in the context of dividends above at 3.1.4.1.

Underlying foreign tax relief can cause problems in this area and is further discussed below.

Most tax planning with respect to cross-border mismatches of characterisation has been with respect to a mismatch between characterisation of a cash payment in the hands of the payer in one country and that in the hands of the recipient in another. The classic problem here has been with the debt/equity divide (or lack thereof) and so the classification of a payment as interest or dividends, see above at 3.3.2. For example, assume that a subsidiary resident in Country A issues a hybrid instrument, say redeemable preference shares, to its parent corporation resident in Country B. The subsidiary pays the parent corporation a dividend of 100 in accordance with the terms of the instrument. Presume the tax law of Country A characterises the instrument as debt and so the payment as interest,[24] whereas Country B characterises the instrument as equity and so the payment as dividends.[25] Assume the corporate tax rates are 30 per cent in both Country A and Country B.

Country A will grant the subsidiary a deduction of 100 for the payment. This means that the subsidiary can protect an equal amount of profits from Country A tax, a potential saving of 30 (30 per cent of the payment). An exception is where the payment triggers a thin capitalisation regime in Country A, see above at 3.3.2.2. Country A may impose a withholding tax on the outbound payment and the appropriate domestic withholding tax rate (that for interest or that for dividends) may depend on whether the re-characterisation as interest is also effective for withholding tax purposes. If an OECD Model style tax treaty applies to the payment, that domestic withholding tax rate will be limited by Article 10 and not Article 11 because the relevant definitions of 'dividends' and 'interest' in those articles adopt a relatively formal approach, see above at 3.3.2.1.

By contrast, Country B views the payment as a non-portfolio dividend and may grant underlying tax relief. So, if Country B exempts non-portfolio dividends, the payment has secured double relief, i.e. a deduction in Country A and an exemption in Country B. The double non-taxation arises more subtly for underlying foreign tax credit countries like the UK. If, due to the deduction, the subsidiary has no Country A income and so pays no Country A tax, Country B will tax the parent corporation with respect to receipt of the dividend without any credit. But assume that the

[24] Australia is an example of a country that, in certain circumstances, might effectively do this; see Income Tax Assessment Act 1997 (Australia) s. 25–85(3).

[25] The UK is an example of a country that has traditionally accepted the character of redeemable preference shares as shares, though this has been complicated by Corporation Tax Act 2009 Part 6 Chapter 7 (ss. 522–35).

subsidiary otherwise has taxable income and pays Country A tax, e.g. it has 300 profits before the deduction and so after the deduction pays 60 in Country A tax (i.e. 30 per cent of 200, being 300 less 100). In such a case, there is underlying tax and the Country B underlying foreign tax credit system may operate to grant credit for at least some of the Country A tax. While not as obviously abusive as where an exemption system is involved, this still involves the provision of dual relief, i.e. deduction in Country A and a (potentially reduced) credit in Country B.

A similar result can be achieved in other contexts. The UK and the US had a particular problem with long-term debentures (loans) issued by US corporations to UK residents. The UK respected form, characterising the return as interest, whereas the US re-characterised the debentures as equity. When the payer exhausted their profits, any additional interest was effectively characterised as a repayment of capital that might not be taxed in the US. The UK addressed this problem by amending the domestic definition of 'distribution' to cover this sort of long-term debenture.[26]

A similar problem can arise with respect to sale and repurchase agreements, sometimes referred to as 'stock lending' agreements or 'repos'. Under such an agreement, shares in a corporation (e.g. a subsidiary) might be transferred to a bank for a price but subject to a right of repurchase, i.e. a legal mortgage. In substance, this is a loan secured on the shares but, in form, it is a transfer and the bank receives dividends. Some countries respect the form and, if the dividends have a foreign source, grant the bank underlying foreign tax relief. Some countries respect the substance of the transaction, treating the parent corporation as receiving the dividends (subject to inter-corporate dividend relief) and then repaid as interest to the bank. The result is a deduction for the parent corporation, and so potentially double relief. This sort of tax planning can be complex and risky. The UK has introduced rules in its domestic law in an effort to close potential abuses.[27]

A similar style of mismatch can arise in the context of finance leasing.[28] Like a legal mortgage of shares, this involves the financier, often a bank, obtaining legal title to an asset that in substance (and in terms of risk)

[26] CTA 2010 ss. 1000(1)F and 1015.

[27] Repurchase agreements and manufactured dividends are regulated by CTA 2010 ss. 780–814 and ITA 2007 Part 11 (ss. 565–614), and see Tiley (2008, pp. 1074–5).

[28] A finance lease is one where, for example, the asset is leased to the same lessee over the entire period of its life, perhaps with a primary and secondary leasing period, and with a rebate of rental at the end of the period up to the amount of any sale proceeds accruing to the lessee.

belongs to another party (the borrower). If a country respects the legal form, the bank is the owner, may claim depreciation of the asset and receives rent from the user of the asset. If a country respects the substance, the bank is a lender and the user of the asset is the owner. Here the user claims depreciation and what the bank receives is not rent but interest and a return of capital. So, if the country of use respects the substance, the user gets a deduction for depreciation and the notional interest. If the country of the bank accepts the form, the bank gets depreciation and is taxed on the rent. This *double dip* for depreciation can be favourable because many (most) countries offer depreciation under their tax laws at a faster rate than economic depreciation, e.g. the depreciation received in the country of the bank is more than the difference between the notional interest in the country of the user and the rent received. Again, tax planning in this area is not for the faint hearted.[29]

A slightly different mismatch can arise with respect to the capital/revenue distinction. One country may characterise a distribution in the course of the liquidation of a corporation as a capital distribution,[30] while another country characterises it as a dividend to the extent that the corporation has profits.[31] This type of mismatch does not so clearly give rise to cases of double non-taxation, but tax planning may seek to exploit differences in tax rates on income and capital gains. It might also affect whether underlying foreign tax relief is available.

A final but important example of mismatch of characterisation involves the situation where a country makes a primary transfer pricing adjustment and then makes a secondary adjustment. Primary and secondary adjustments were discussed above at 3.3.1.1. In particular, a secondary adjustment may recognise for tax purposes a value transfer with respect to the provision of goods or services between related parties. Where the value is transferred from a subsidiary to a parent corporation, it may be treated as a dividend and, in other cases, as a loan on which interest should be received. Problems can arise where one country makes a secondary adjustment with respect to a cross-border transaction but the other country does not recognise the adjustment, i.e. one country positively characterises the value transfer as something but the other country does not recognise it at all.

[29] The form of finance leasing was respected in the famous UK avoidance case of *Barclays Mercantile Business Finance Ltd* v *Mawson* [2004] UKHL 51 (HL). The decision of the House of Lords was addressed legislatively by Capital Allowances Act 2001 ss. 70A–70E and see Tiley (2008, pp. 525–6).

[30] This is the position of the UK, see *IRC* v *Burrell* [1924] 2 KB 52 (CA).

[31] For example, see Income Tax Assessment Act 1936 (Australia) s. 47.

For example, assume a subsidiary resident in Country A transfers goods for 200 to a parent corporation resident in Country B when the arm's length value of the goods is 300. Assume that Country A makes a primary transfer pricing adjustment and so increases the subsidiary's profits by 100 (300 less 200). Further, assume that Country A makes a secondary adjustment, treating the 100 value transferred to the parent corporation as a dividend. This means that the value transferred is not deductible to the subsidiary and Country A may impose a withholding tax. The value transferred has been subjected to two levels of tax by Country A, as profits of the subsidiary and as a dividend, i.e. a classical system.

Presume Country B accepts Country A's primary adjustment and so decreases the profits of the parent corporation by 100 (e.g. through an equivalent increase in the cost of goods). However, if Country B does not recognise Country A's secondary adjustment, there will be no relief for the dividend withholding tax. On the upside, the lack of recognition means that Country B will not tax the value transfer, i.e. the equivalent of underlying foreign tax relief in the form of an exemption. Where the source country denies a deduction for interest under its thin capitalisation rules (see above at 3.3.2.2), the situation is similar. Assuming Country A makes the primary adjustment to the subsidiary's profits under the equivalent of Article 9(1) of the OECD Model, Country B will be required to reduce the parent corporation's profits by a similar amount. Problems arise where Country A re-characterises the excessive interest as a dividend and subjects it to withholding tax and Country B does not accept the secondary adjustment.[32]

Now presume the situation is reversed, and the value transfer is from the parent corporation to the subsidiary and Country B makes a primary adjustment that is accepted by Country A. Country B might make a secondary adjustment to treat the 100 value transferred as a loan on which the subsidiary should pay interest. Assume the market interest rate is 10 per cent, Country B might treat the parent corporation as having additional interest of 10 (10 per cent of 100) and tax it. If Country A does not accept Country B's secondary adjustment, it will not grant the subsidiary

[32] Contrast OECD Commentary on Art. 23 paras. 67–9. The Commentary assumes that the excessive interest may be properly re-characterised as a dividend for the purposes of OECD Model Art. 10. That position has some difficulties, see above at 3.3.2.1. A surprising feature of this Commentary is the suggestion that the residence country might be obliged to provide 'relief for any… economic double taxation of the interest as if the payment was in fact a dividend' when the OECD Model does not provide for such relief. A corresponding adjustment under Art. 9(2) is only residually referred to.

a deduction for the deemed interest. It will also not subject the deemed interest to withholding tax, but any benefit of that will be taxed away by Country B's foreign tax credit system. The result is effective double taxation, i.e. the deemed interest of 10 represents value added that is taxed to the subsidiary by Country A and that Country B also taxes without foreign tax relief. The only possible resolution of this sort of problem under tax treaties is through the mutual agreement procedure, i.e. Article 25 of the OECD Model, see further below at 7.2.1.

The UK anti-arbitrage rules introduced in 2005 were discussed above at 5.1.1 in the context of mismatches of entity characterisation. In addition to dealing with this scenario, they extend to hybrid instruments and give the UK tax administration power to shut down double dip deductions. In particular, 'qualifying scheme' covers instruments under which a person can elect to alter a relevant characteristic of the instrument, largely an issue of income or capital. It also expressly covers convertible shares, convertible securities and debt treated as equity under accounting principles. There are special extensions for instruments issued between connected persons.[33] These rules are targeted at the situation where the UK grants a deduction and so, in a simple scenario, where the UK is the source of a payment.

The UK rules were also extended separately to situations where a UK resident is effectively in receipt of a payment that was deductible in the country of the payer. In particular, s. 57(3) of TIOPA 2010 provides:

> No underlying tax is to be taken into account ... if, under the law of any territory outside the United Kingdom, a deduction is allowed to a resident of the territory in respect of an amount determined by reference to the dividend.

A similar limitation was incorporated in the inter-corporate dividend exemption in 2009.[34] This is a good example of the way the world is changing. A decade ago, it would have been nearly unthinkable that a country's right to tax would depend in this way on the manner in which another country had taxed.

There are other ways in which to achieve double non-taxation where a payment is deductible in the country of the payer but is not taxable in the country of the recipient. Non-taxation in the country of the recipient might be because the receipt is viewed as a capital receipt rather than as a dividend. The UK had particular problems with deferred subscription

[33] TIOPA 2010 ss. 237–42.

[34] CTA 2009 ss. 931B(c) and 931D(c).

agreements involving a contribution of capital by a US parent corporation to a UK subsidiary (deductible in the US, not taxable in the UK). This was the subject of a special rule introduced in 2005.[35] Surprisingly, the provision covered this scenario only and not generally the problem of deduction in a foreign country and exemption in the UK.

Finally, a mismatch in entity characterisation (discussed above at 5.1.1) might cause a mismatch of characterisation of a payment. The OECD Commentary gives the example of a situation in which the source/host country characterises an entity as a corporation and the residence/home country characterises it as a transparent partnership. The source/host country will characterise payments to the shareholder/partner as dividends and so may impose a withholding tax. The residence/home country will characterise the partner as receiving business profits, effectively ignoring any repatriation of funds. The OECD confirms that in such a case the residence/home country is not obliged to provide any foreign tax credit for dividend withholding tax imposed by the source/host country.[36]

This was also part of the issue at stake in the *Memec* case, discussed above at 5.1.1.[37] The case further involved the issue of whether the UK parent corporation's return on the investment in the German silent partnership, deductible to the general partner in Germany, was a dividend on which the UK corporation could claim underlying foreign tax relief in the UK. The Court of Appeal held this was not a dividend and so was fully taxable in the UK. Such an argument would now be resolved by section 57(3) of TIOPA 2010 (above).

5.2 Beyond the bilateral

This chapter concerns the limited scope of tax treaties. In that context, the last heading discussed limitations that arise as between two countries that have concluded a tax treaty. These limitations arise from the nature of what tax treaties cover. In particular, it was suggested that many of the substantive provisions of the OECD Model are taken up with residence and source rules. Many of these have an inherent reconciliation nature about them that prevents mismatches of source or residence between two

[35] TIOPA 2010 s. 250. Where this provision applies, the UK subsidiary might have to treat the capital contribution as income. For background to the problem, see Sheppard (2005).

[36] OECD Commentary on Art. 23 paras. 69.1–3.

[37] *Memec Plc* v *IRC* [1998] STC 754 (CA).

treaty countries. For that reason, the focus under the first heading was on issues that the OECD Model does not deal with to a substantial extent, i.e. the fundamental features of a payment. In particular, it considered mismatches that can occur in a purely bilateral setting and these tend not to include mismatches of source or residence.

As discussed above at 1.2.2, tax treaties are almost always bilateral in nature. This heading steps beyond the bilateral scope of previous discussion to consider the limitations of tax treaties arising in a multilateral scenario. Whatever difficulties tax treaties resolve as between two countries, they do not necessarily resolve these where three or more countries are involved (triangular situations). Each of the mismatches that may occur with respect to the fundamental features of a payment as between two countries (discussed under the first heading) may equally feature in the context of triangular situations. So, for example, with respect to the royalty example discussed above at 5.1.1, the payer of the royalty or the hybrid could be resident in a third country with the same potential for double non-taxation. However, these are not the subject matter of this heading because the limitations they reveal about tax treaties are not inherently multilateral in nature. They are just matters that tax treaties do not deal with.

Triangular situations reveal limitations even in the matters quite well covered by the OECD Model, i.e. allocation of source and residence. In particular, the resolution of the source of income as between two countries to a tax treaty will not bind third countries or either country to the treaty with respect to third countries. Similarly, the resolution of residence of a person as between two countries to a tax treaty will not bind third countries or either country to the treaty with respect to third countries. The first two subheadings consider mismatches of source and residence in triangular situations.

At the start of Chapter 3, it was noted that a person seeking to invest in a foreign country (the target country) usually makes an initial decision whether to invest directly in that country or to do so indirectly through an intermediary (e.g. a subsidiary) resident there. In practice, the decision is more likely to additionally involve (especially where tax advisers get involved) whether any intermediary is established in the target country or, as a first step, in some third country. Intermediaries raise substantial issues for international taxation and highlight the bilateral nature of tax treaties. By using intermediaries and back-to-back payments, the source and character of a particular payment can be manipulated. Where a tax haven is used in conjunction with an intermediary, this can result in similar problems to those arising from the mismatches discussed above at 5.1, i.e. effective non-taxation. The third subheading considers the difficult issue of re-sourcing and re-characterising arising from the use of third country intermediaries.

5.2.1 *Mismatch of source: PEs and third countries*

A mismatch of source of income involves the simultaneous sourcing of income in two or more countries or considering income as not sourced in any country. In a bilateral situation, income may be sourced in neither country, in which case the other income article of any tax treaty may apply to give the residence country sole taxing rights. The reference to income 'wherever arising' in Article 21 of the OECD Model makes its application to income from third countries clear, see above at 3.1.1. It is possible, however, that a tax treaty gives a country a right to tax on a source basis but that country does not tax because the source rule in its domestic law is different. For example, the domestic law of one country may consider interest sourced where the funds borrowed are used whereas another country may, consistent with the OECD Model, consider interest sourced where the payer is resident. If the payer of interest is resident in the first country but the funds are not used there, it is possible that no country claims to be the source country. The OECD Model does not resolve such a mismatch, accepting that tax treaties do not create a charge to tax, see above at 1.2.2.

What the OECD Model does better is to resolve source country taxing rights where both countries to a tax treaty claim to be the source state. In most cases, the Model will resolve which of the two countries has the right to tax based on source.[38] However, it will do this only within the confines of the treaty. In particular, because of Article 1, the Model applies only to residents of either contracting state. So, a qualification on any reconciliation of source under the OECD Model is that the person deriving the income is a resident of one of the two contracting states. The OECD Model does not resolve disputes as to source between two countries where the person deriving the income is resident in a third country. Further, while there are instances in which the OECD Model seems to permit income to have a dual source and so potentially grants two contracting states taxing

[38] In *Bayfine UK Products Bayfine UK* v *RCC* [2008] UKSPC SPC00719 (SC) (discussed above at 5.1.1) an issue was whether the effect of the UK/US Tax Treaty was that each country considered the income sourced in the other country. This involved a peculiar provision found in many US treaties and its interaction with the use of hybrid entities.

rights based on source, this issue is resolved by requiring the residence country to provide foreign tax relief irrespective of whether the residence country purports to tax based on source or residence.

Beyond the bilateral, where two countries claim the right to tax based on source but the person deriving the income is resident in a third country, the OECD Model cannot resolve the potential for double taxation based on source. Outside a mismatch of allocation (see above at 5.1.1), the main (it seems all) examples of this involve PEs. The problem here is the schizophrenic nature of the PE concept. There has been some debate as to whether the PE concept is essentially a source based concept or a residence based concept.[39]

On the one hand, PEs are often treated in a manner consistent with residents. So, the source of interest and royalties is typically the residence of the payer but equally a PE country if the PE bears the interest or royalties, see above at 3.1.4.2 and 3.1.4.3. Under Article 13(2), the source country also preserves taxing rights with respect to capital gains on movable property attributable to a PE, something which is otherwise reserved for the residence country, see above at 3.1.5. Similarly, Article 15(2) may preserve source country taxing rights for employment income based on residence of the payer or that the income is borne by a PE, see above at 3.1.6.1. Article 7 empowers a PE country to tax foreign source income of a PE, see above at 3.1.3.3. Similar non-discrimination rules apply to both PEs and subsidiaries, i.e. Article 24(3) and 24(5) and see above at 3.1.3.4. Often, residence countries exempt profits attributable to a foreign PE, which is consistent with the treatment of the profits of a foreign subsidiary (a non-resident person), see above at 4.1.1 and 4.1.2.1.

On the other hand, often a PE, as a place of business, is the location of economic activity giving rise to income, and this seems to have been the original logic underlying the PE concept. Distributions of a PE are not recognised as income.[40] PEs are not separate legal persons, cannot be 'resident' persons and so are not entitled to the benefits of tax treaties. In particular, the OECD Model contains reconciliation rules for dual residence, see above at 2.1.1.2, but these rules do not apply to PEs, i.e. the OECD Model does not treat a person as partly resident in a PE country. Consequently, a PE country is not obliged to give foreign tax relief because of Article 23 alone. Indeed, in a modern integrated world, there is reason

[39] For example, see Vann (2003, pp. 142–6).

[40] Contrast the use of branch profits taxes, see above at 3.1.4.1.

for suggesting that the predominant importance of the PE concept is to support defects in determining the residence of artificial legal persons.[41]

Multiplicity of source can result from both the source like and the residence like features of a PE. In particular, when a PE receives payments, the source features seem to predominate. When a PE makes payments, the residence features seem to predominate. Each of these scenarios is analysed in turn.

5.2.1.1 Payments received by PEs

Generally As mentioned, the OECD Model permits a PE country to tax the foreign source income of a PE. Assume, for example, that a corporation resident in Country B has a PE in Country A2 that receives interest from a resident of Country A1. Under any Country B/Country A2 tax treaty, Country A2 will be permitted to tax the payment from Country A1 as part of the business profits of the PE. In itself, this suggests residence features of a PE, but that may be deceptive for at least two reasons. First, while a PE is not the source of payments received contributing to its profits, there can be little doubt that business conducted through a PE *is* the source of the net profits (i.e. after expenses) of the PE. In this context, dual sourcing of income is not quite the mismatch that it seems.

Country A1's rules are focusing on the source of a particular payment, i.e. the interest, and, as discussed above at 1.1, payments are the building blocks of taxable profits. Country A2 is focusing on the net profits of the PE. Unless a look through rule is adopted, it seems appropriate to suggest that the source of the business profits is where the business is carried on. Under a look through rule, business profits would be sourced where the payments that they are made up of are sourced. Allocation of expenses in such a scenario can be problematic. The OECD Model does not adopt look through rules and this is not just the case with business profits of a PE, but with the dividends of a corporation as well. Dividends are sourced where the distributing corporation is resident and not where the profits from which the dividend is distributed are sourced, see above at 3.1.4.1.

Similarly, the OECD Model does not consider a subsidiary resident where its parent is resident. Further, the Model does not consider

41 'Hence the PE concept is central to the operation of the OECD model convention, even between countries where income flows are in balance. It overcomes problems of defining corporate residence by ensuring that taxing rights follow substantive activities. In other words, in the developed world the PE concept is mainly a residence-based or at least a supporting concept for entities', Vann (2003, p. 147).

payments like interest and royalties to be sourced where the funds from which they are paid are sourced. This nature of a PE as the source of business profits is reinforced by the fact that, under the OECD Model, while a PE can have foreign source income, a PE cannot hold a PE. That is, a PE located in Country A2 cannot hold a PE located in Country A1. The Country A1 PE can be held only by the corporation resident in Country B. By contrast, a subsidiary located in Country A2 can hold a subsidiary or a PE located in Country A1.

The second reason for suggesting that in the current scenario the PE concept behaves predominantly like a source concept is that the PE country is not expressly obliged to provide any foreign tax relief under the OECD Model. So, in the above example, under the Country A1/Country B tax treaty, Country B is obliged by Article 23 to provide foreign tax relief for any Country A1 tax levied on the interest. Indeed, in determining any limitation on Country A1's right to tax the interest, the rate under Article 11 of this treaty applies and not, for example, the one under any Country A1/Country A2 tax treaty. Further, under the Country A2/Country B treaty, Country B is obliged to provide foreign tax relief for any Country A2 tax levied on the profits of the PE. By contrast, Country A2 is not obliged to provide foreign tax relief for Country A1 tax. Any Country A1/Country A2 tax treaty is not applicable because the corporation (being the only relevant person) is not resident in either country, i.e. the requirements of Article 1 of that treaty are not met.

In the scenario in question, there *may* be double taxation based on source, even if the countries in question have all concluded OECD Model style tax treaties between them. However, the domestic charge to tax of some countries does not extend to cover the foreign source income of non-residents and so the foreign source income of a PE situated there. The UK is not an example of such a country and, in particular, UK PEs of non-residents may be subject to tax with respect to their foreign source income under Schedule D Case I.[42] By contrast, Australia's domestic jurisdictional rules do not extend to tax foreign source income of non-residents.[43] Peculiarly, however, Australia's tax treaties contain a provision stating that any income that may be taxed in Australia under a tax treaty 'shall for the purposes of the laws of Australia relating to its tax be deemed to arise from sources in Australia'.[44] As Australia is a dualist state and

[42] CTA 2009 s. 5(3).

[43] Income Tax Assessment Act 1997 s. 6–5(3).

[44] For example, Australia/UK (2003) Art. 21.

treaties are enacted into law,[45] this is a strange example of taxing rights under treaty having the potential to tax a situation where tax would not be levied under general domestic law.

Assuming domestic law charges a PE to tax with respect to foreign source income, a PE may claim foreign tax relief on two potential grounds. The first is unilateral relief, which in the usual way depends on domestic law (see above at 4.1.1.1). Despite earlier limitations (discussed below), the UK now extends foreign tax relief to UK PEs of non-residents. A unilateral foreign tax credit is available for:

> tax ... paid under the law of [a territory outside the UK] in respect of the income or chargeable gains ... of a permanent establishment in the United Kingdom of a non-UK resident company.[46]

Second, the PE may claim an entitlement to foreign tax relief under the non-discrimination provision in a tax treaty between the PE country and the country of the head office, i.e. under Article 24(3) of the Country A2/ Country B tax treaty. Article 23 of this treaty does not apply to the PE because it is not a resident person. Article 24(3) may require the PE country to grant foreign tax relief to a PE if the same is available to resident enterprises (see above at 3.1.3.4).

An enterprise resident in the PE country might have two forms of foreign tax relief available to it, i.e. unilateral relief or tax treaty relief. The OECD Commentary begins on this topic by suggesting that 'it is right… to grant to the permanent establishment credit for foreign tax… when such credit is granted to resident enterprises under domestic laws'.[47] So, if the PE state grants unilateral foreign tax relief to residents, Article 24(3) of the OECD Model requires that relief be granted to PEs with respect to their foreign source income. If unilateral relief is not available, difficult questions arise as to whether Article 24(3) requires a PE to be extended the benefits of any source country/PE country tax treaty (Country A1/ Country A2 treaty). The OECD does not adopt a firm position on this issue, simply noting that some member states are willing to provide relief and some are not and suggesting a provision that may be inserted in a tax treaty to clarify the matter.[48]

[45] Treaties are given effect in Australian domestic law by the International Tax Agreements Act 1953.

[46] TIOPA 2010 s. 30(3).

[47] OECD Commentary on Art. 24 para. 67. See also Commentary on Art. 23 para. 10.

[48] OECD Commentary on Art. 24 para. 70.

Returning to the facts of the above example, presume that the domestic law of Country A1 imposes an interest withholding tax of 20 per cent. Further, assume that under the Country A1/Country B tax treaty the rate is limited to 15 per cent, but under the Country A1/Country A2 tax treaty it is limited to 10 per cent. As mentioned above, in determining its right to tax, Country A1 is limited by its tax treaty with Country B, not that with Country A2. So Country A1 will impose interest withholding tax of 15 per cent. However, if the PE were a resident enterprise of Country A2, it would have the benefit of the Country A1/Country A2 tax treaty and so the withholding tax would have been only 10 per cent.

This leads the OECD to suggest that in order to remove any discrimination of the PE, Country A2 should credit only the withholding tax that a resident enterprise would have suffered, i.e. 10 per cent. The result is that not all the Country A1 tax will be credited and so the discrimination of the PE is not fully relieved. Whether Country A1 causes this residual discrimination such that Country A2 should not be obliged to relieve it is a matter for debate. In the reverse scenario, where the Country A1 tax treaty with Country B provides for a lower rate of withholding tax than the Country A2 treaty, the OECD suggests that only the tax actually levied should be credited.[49]

These issues were raised in the UK case of *Sun Life Assurance Co of Canada* v *Pearson*, which involved a Canadian Insurance Company with a UK PE through which it derived foreign investment income.[50] At that time, UK unilateral foreign tax relief did not extend to UK PEs of non-residents. The Canadian company argued that the equivalent of Article 24(3) in the Canada/UK Tax Treaty required the UK to extend foreign tax credits to the UK branch. Vinelott J quoted the (former) OECD Commentary without express approval. He simply noted that domestic law implementation of the treaty was subject to domestic law provisions, including the requirement that credit was available only to residents. This treaty override (see above at 1.2.2) meant that the Canadian company could not rely on the equivalent of Article 24(3).[51] The problems caused by this case have been resolved by the granting of unilateral relief to UK PEs (see above).

Finally, it is noted that as far as the residence country is concerned (Country B), two tax treaties apply, the Country A1/Country B treaty and the Country A2/Country B treaty. Country A1 has a right to tax and

[49] OECD Commentary on Art. 24 para. 70.

[50] (1984) 59 TC 250 (CA).

[51] (1984) 59 TC 250 (CA) at 315–17.

Country B must grant a foreign tax credit for tax levied by it. Similarly, Country B must grant foreign tax relief for tax levied by Country A2. If Country B grants foreign tax credits with respect to taxes paid by foreign PEs, then Country B will grant the resident corporation credit for both Country A1 tax and Country A2 tax. This will relieve double taxation unless the combined effect of the two source country taxes produces excess foreign tax credits. If Country B grants an exemption for the profits of foreign PEs, it will not be obliged to grant foreign tax credits for Country A1 tax as it did not tax the interest and so the foreign tax credit limitation is nil.

EU Law This position under Article 24(3) of the OECD Model can be compared with the position under EU Law. In *Saint-Gobain*,[52] a German PE of a French corporation held shares in a US subsidiary and, indirectly through German subsidiaries, shares in Swiss, Austrian and Italian subsidiaries. Germany denied underlying foreign tax relief, unilateral or under tax treaty, with respect to dividends received by the German PE. In particular, German domestic law adopted an underlying foreign tax credit system for resident parent corporations and, under many tax treaties (including those in issue), extended this to an exemption. The French corporation argued that this was contrary to its freedom of establishment. Germany sought to justify its treatment on the basis that PEs were not comparable to resident corporations. In particular, it pointed out that repatriation from a PE was not subject to German tax but a dividend of a resident corporation to a non-resident was.[53] Further, it argued that tax treaties with third countries, e.g. the US, were beyond EU Law.

The ECJ rejected these arguments. In the usual way, it found PEs and subsidiaries comparable. The ECJ noted that despite the taxation of non-residents being 'theoretically limited to "national" income', German PEs were subject to tax in respect of foreign dividends, just like German resident corporations.[54] Both were subject to German tax with respect to the receipt of foreign or domestic dividends. Denial of underlying foreign tax relief to the PE, which was available to a German corporation holding similar shares, was a disincentive to establishment as a PE. This restriction

[52] Case C-307/97 *Compagnie de Saint-Gobain, Zweigniederlassung Deutschland* v *Finanzamt Aachen-Innenstadt* [1999] ECR I-6161 (ECJ). For a case note on this decision, see Oliver (2000).

[53] The events occurred before introduction of the Parent-Subsidiary Directive (1990).

[54] Case C-307/97 *Compagnie de Saint-Gobain, Zweigniederlassung Deutschland* v *Finanzamt Aachen-Innenstadt* [1999] ECR I-6161 (ECJ) at para. 48.

was not justified by the lack of German taxation of repatriations of PEs. Accordingly, Germany was required to extend unilateral underlying foreign tax credits to German PEs.

In the context of tax treaties, the ECJ noted that member states are free to allocate taxing rights by treaty but, in exercising the rights so allocated, member states must comply with EU Law. This also applied to treaties concluded with third countries:

> In the case of a double-taxation treaty concluded between a Member State and a non-member country, the national treatment principle requires the Member State which is a party to the treaty to grant to permanent establishments of non-resident companies the advantages provided for by that treaty on the same conditions as those which applied to resident companies.[55]

Note that the ECJ required Germany to extend to the PE not just unilateral underlying foreign tax credits but an exemption under tax treaty where that would be available to a resident corporation.

The UK's response to this case in 2000 was noted above, i.e. the extension of unilateral foreign tax relief to PEs. It has not been necessary to extend tax treaty relief to UK PEs because all of the UK's treaties are consistent with the unilateral relief in that they provide for foreign tax credits. As required by the *Saint-Gobain* case, this UK extension covers not just direct foreign tax credits but also indirect foreign tax credits.

Saint-Gobain makes it clear that, under EU Law, tax treaty foreign tax relief must be extended to PEs. What it does not make clear is the issue noted above, i.e. whether source country withholding tax to be credited is limited to that which would have been imposed under the source country/PE country tax treaty (the Country A1/Country A2 tax treaty in the above example). Consistent with the OECD position on this issue, there is reason for suggesting that such a limit does not contravene EU Law even if it results in some double taxation (the difference between the 15 per cent and 10 per cent withholding tax in the above example). This additional tax is levied due to the source country of the interest not granting relief under the rate applicable under its treaty with the PE country (rather it uses the rate under its treaty with the residence country). Consistent with the *Kerckhaert and Morres* case, discussed above at 4.1.1.3, a PE country is not obliged by EU Law to provide foreign tax relief if it otherwise behaves in a non-discriminating manner.

[55] Case C-307/97 *Compagnie de Saint-Gobain, Zweigniederlassung Deutschland* v *Finanzamt Aachen-Innenstadt* [1999] ECR I-6161 (ECJ) at para. 58.

5.2.1.2 Payments made by PEs

Generally As noted, PEs are often used as an apparent exception to a rule based on residence, e.g. that payments are sourced where the payer is resident or a general exclusion to source country tax. In itself, this suggests residence features of a PE, or does it? The OECD Model seems to draft these rules as an afterthought and so residence is the dominant rule, but on another view, this is not the case. For example, surely the real source rule is that a payment or gain is sourced in the economic activity that generated it and not the residence of the payer. On this view, the primary and appropriate source rule is that payments made through a place of business (a PE) are sourced there, and using the PE concept as the source of a payment, far from being the exception, is the dominant rule. If this is accepted, what is the purpose of the back-up rule based on the residence of the payer?

The residence of a payer as a source rule is, perhaps, not such a large exception to the rule that payments made through a place of business are sourced there. By definition (Article 5 of the OECD Model), a person can have a PE in their country of residence, i.e. the PE concept is not limited to a place of business outside the country of residence of the person carrying on a business. Consider this in the context of the definition of source of interest in Article 11(5) (or that of royalties in Article 12(5) of the UN Model). Massive amounts of cross-border interest (perhaps the majority) are incurred in the context of a business. Most businesses are conducted at a 'fixed place' and so the PE as the source of interest rule is essentially the sole source rule for interest incurred in the context of a business, applying irrespective of whether the person paying the interest is resident in the country in which the PE is located.

A similar analysis is available with respect to capital gains in the context of Article 13(2) of the OECD Model. Unlike the source rule in Article 11(5), Article 13(2) is essentially a residual rule for movable property (though, considering the order of Article 13, not drafted that way). Unlike Article 11(5), which gives dominance to a PE irrespective of residence of the payer, Article 13(2) applies to the movable property of a PE only if the PE is located outside the country of residence of its owner. For movable property, this gives dominance to the residual residence rule in Article 13(5), but, at some level, this is just a matter of form. The substance rule is very similar to the source rule in Article 11(5); gains from the alienation of movable property of a business are sourced where the business is located, irrespective of the residence of the business owner.

Similar analysis can be used with respect to Article 15(2) of the OECD Model. It is drafted as an exception to the primary source rule in Article 15(1) (place of exercising the employment). Whether place of exercise is an appropriate source rule can be questioned (see discussion above at 3.1.6.1). Equally cogent arguments can be made in favour of a source rule based on the place of business of the employer, i.e. the business activity in which the employee participates (irrespective of presence) and generating the funds from which the employee is paid. In this light, despite a messy form, the source rule in Article 15 involves two features. First, if an employee is present in a country for a sufficiently long period, i.e. 183 days, presence dominates. Second, where this is not the case, if presence within a country is coupled with allocation of the employment to a business in that country, that is sufficient to source employment income in that country. Like the source rule in Article 11(5), the PE requirement in Article 15(2)(c) does not require that the PE be situated outside the country of residence of the employer. In this context, Article 15(2)(b) is the residual rule that, where the employee is employed through, say, a foreign PE, nevertheless presence of the employee and residence of the employer is sufficient to ground source country taxing rights.

This focus on the place of business as predominantly a source rule is backed up by the structure of the OECD Model. At 3.1.3, it was noted how the structure of Article 7 is such that it applies to both subsidiaries and PEs. A substantial amount of what subsidiaries do is conducting business. In the context of the history of the Model, this is likely to have been predominantly true. In form, Article 7 applies only to PEs located outside the country of residence of their owner. But if the form is looked through, the substance of Articles 7, 9 and 21 is a rule that profits, determined on an arm's length basis, derived through a place of business may be taxed in the country of location. This rule is supported by Article 24(3) and (5), which, despite their form, result in a simple rule that a country in which a business is situated must not discriminate in the taxation of that business due to control or ownership by a non-resident.

In all of these matters, rather than the PE concept supporting or mimicking the residence concept, residence is used to support the dominance of the place of business as the primary source rule. Indeed, even where residence appears to be residually important, e.g. in the context of corporations, this may be misleading. There are strong arguments for suggesting that the taxation of a corporation based on residence is really no more than source based taxation of the stakeholders in the corporation.[56] The peculiar exception to all of this is source taxation of dividends under Article 10 of the OECD Model. Dividends are always sourced where the corporation paying the dividends is resident. There is no exception to source dividends in a PE country, e.g. when the activities of a PE generate the profits distributed.

While the OECD Model may incorporate the place of business as its predominant source rule in a bilateral context, in a multilateral context this logic breaks down. As noted, in a multilateral setting, tax treaties concluded based on the OECD Model can result in income being simultaneously sourced in two countries. Interest paid by a PE is a good example of this. Presume a PE in Country A1 owned by a person resident in Country A2 pays interest to a person resident in Country B. Under Article 11(5) of the Country A1/Country B tax treaty, the interest is sourced in Country A1 and it is entitled to tax. Under Article 11(5) of the Country A2/Country B tax treaty, the interest is sourced in Country A2 and it is entitled to tax. Any Country A1/Country A2 tax treaty does not resolve this dual taxation based on source because the person deriving the interest is not resident in either country. As with the situation discussed above at 5.2.1.1, under its tax treaties, Country B will be obliged to give foreign tax relief for both source country taxes, but its tax liability may be insufficient to absorb both taxes.

As a practical matter, the UK tax administration accepts that interest paid by a UK resident can be sourced outside the UK if a foreign PE of a UK resident borrows money and pays the interest thereon. Likewise, it is possible for a UK PE of a non-resident to pay UK source interest.[57]

Similar problems can arise with respect to royalties, where these are subject to source taxation in a similar fashion to interest, e.g. under the UN Model. It cannot happen with respect to dividends, as residence of the payer is the exclusive source rule. Further, it cannot happen with respect to employment income because presence of the employee is required in any case, and that can be in only one jurisdiction.

Finally, dual sourcing of income can arise in other circumstances. For example, in the context of hybrid entities (see above at 5.1.1), two countries may identify the payer differently and, as a result, each view a payment as sourced in their jurisdiction. As noted at that point, similar issues can arise with respect to PEs, e.g. where two countries simultaneously

[56] See Harris (1996, pp. 474 and 502–3).

[57] Savings and Investment Manual SAIM9090 & 9095; www.hmrc.gov.uk/manuals, accessed 14 March 2010. The analysis relies on *Westminster Bank Executor and Trustee Company (Channel Islands) Limited* v *National Bank of Greece SA* [1961] AC 255 (HL).

allocate the same payment to a PE situated in their jurisdiction. Even where two countries agree on the identity of a payer, they may both view the payer as resident in their jurisdiction. This can also result in dual source. Dual residence of a person in a multilateral setting is considered below at 5.2.2.

EU Law As noted above at 3.1.4.2, the dual sourcing of interest that can arise under the OECD Model (or royalties under the UN Model) does not arise in the context of the EU Interest and Royalties Directive (2003). In particular, source is determined by reference to the location of the payer and under Article 1(6), where a PE is considered the payer of interest, 'no other part of the company shall be treated as the payer'. At first blush, this may appear to be a sensible resolution to dual sourcing in a multilateral setting such as that applicable to the Directive, but is it? Article 1(1) requires only the source state (effectively the country of the payer) to exempt the interest from withholding tax. So, if a PE in Country A1 owned by a corporation resident in Country A2 pays interest or royalties to a corporation resident in Country B and all countries are EU member states, the Directive does not expressly prevent Country A2 taxing the interest. Country A2 will be entitled to do so under tax treaties concluded by it based on the OECD Model. It is a question for the ECJ whether such taxation is inconsistent with the spirit of the Directive.

Outside the scope of the Directive, dual taxation based on source of interest or royalties remains. Would this breach the fundamental freedoms? The issue at stake is whether the source of a single payment may simultaneously be allocated to and taxed by the country of a PE (Country A1) and the country of the residence of the payer (Country A2). Analogies are a risky thing when dealing with the ECJ. However, there are two arguments that a second source based tax by the country of residence of the payer is contrary to the fundamental freedoms. First, when the country of the PE already taxes, the second tax might be viewed as an indirect restriction on residents of Country A2 establishing a PE in Country A1, e.g. the dual source tax might make it more difficult for the Country A1 PE to borrow funds. Alternately, the second source tax might constitute a restriction on the free movement of capital between Country A1 and Country B or the freedom to provide services between those two countries. The strange feature about the latter argument is that it involves a restriction by neither a country that is the home nor the host country. Nevertheless, the fundamental freedoms may apply. They simply prohibit restrictions, without specifying which country imposes them. Question whether any such restriction would be cured where Country B is in a position to credit both source country taxes.[58]

5.2.2 *Mismatch of residence*

The OECD Model tiebreaker rules for dual residence were discussed above at 2.1.1.2. However, these rules in Article 4 have a limited scope; they apply only for the purposes of the tax treaty in question. This causes particular problems in a multilateral setting, which is the focus of the following discussion. These problems are of two types, the first dealing with taxation of the dual resident person and the second with the potential dual sourcing of payments by reason of the dual residence of the payer. The discussion is limited to dual resident corporations.

5.2.2.1 Taxation of the person

Generally The OECD Model may resolve issues of double taxation of profits derived by a dual resident corporation even in a multilateral setting. For example, presume that a corporation is managed in Country B1, incorporated in Country B2 and derives income from Country A. Presume that under domestic law the corporation is resident in both Country B1 and Country B2. The corporation is resident in Country B1 for the purposes of the Country A/Country B1 tax treaty and so that country will have a right to tax the profits of the corporation subject to foreign tax relief. Similarly, the corporation is resident in Country B2 for the purposes of the Country A/Country B2 tax treaty and so that country will have a right to tax the profits of the corporation subject to foreign tax relief. In particular, the residence tiebreaker in the Country B1/Country B2 tax treaty has no direct application for the purposes of the treaties with Country A (though may have the indirect effect described below).

However, the Country B1/Country B2 tax treaty will resolve any double taxation based on residence. That treaty will consider the corporation resident in Country B1, assuming its effective management is there. On that basis, because income from Country A is not 'dealt with' by the preceding articles of the treaty, Article 21 of that treaty, applying to income 'wherever arising' (see above at 3.1.1), will allocate the right to tax income from Country A exclusively to Country B1.

[58] This is essentially an extension of the issues mentioned above at 3.1.4.2.

As noted above at 2.1.1.2, the position of Country A is not so clear. Assume the income is interest. Which limitation on its right to tax interest applies, that in its tax treaty with Country B1, that with Country B2 or both? If the limit in Country B2 applies and the rate at which Country A can tax is lower than in the tax treaty with Country B1, this might provide a way for corporations to plan to reduce source country taxation. In 2008, the OECD added to the Commentary on Article 4 in an effort to deal with this issue.[59] In particular, the OECD argues that the corporation, while resident in Country B2 for domestic purposes, is not a resident under the Country A/Country B2 treaty as it falls within the second sentence in Article 4(1). Because of the Country B1/Country B2 tax treaty, the corporation is subject to tax in Country B2 only with respect to 'income from sources' in Country B2.

Less clear is the situation where the dual resident corporation has losses. Here the OECD Model is of little use because, as noted above at 4.2, it does not cover losses, at least not expressly. Presume the facts outlined above but now the corporation has a PE in Country A that makes a loss. As noted above at 4.2.2, many countries permit the use of foreign losses of resident corporations against domestic source profits, including by way of set off against the profits of group members, i.e. group relief. The UK is such a country. So, in the current context, there is a risk that the PE losses will be taken into account in each of the three countries (including by way of group relief).[60]

As noted above at 2.1.1.2, the UK has sought to address this problem with a special domestic law rule. Where a UK resident corporation is treated as resident in a foreign country because of a tiebreaker for the purposes of a tax treaty, the corporation is treated as not resident in the UK for domestic law purposes as well.[61] So, where the UK is Country B2, the corporation is non-resident for UK tax purposes and group relief is not available with respect to foreign losses, see above at 4.2.4.

[59] OECD Commentary on Art. 4 para. 8.2.

[60] Indeed, because the OECD Model does not cover losses, this problem of dual resident corporations using losses multiple times can arise in a purely bilateral setting. Assume the PE and its loss are located in Country B1. Despite the tiebreaker in the Country B1/Country B2 tax treaty, the corporation may still be resident in Country B2 for purposes of its domestic corporate group relief system. This could be particularly problematic because if the PE subsequently turns profitable in the future, the treaty will prevent any claw back taxation by Country B2. It is possible that in monist countries, see above at 1.2.2, the direct application of the treaty would cause the corporation to be resident in Country B1 for the purposes of Country B2's domestic law and so group relief.

[61] CTA 2009 s. 18.

EU Law Dual resident corporations raise issues under EU Law in the context of both the fundamental freedoms and the direct tax directives. As noted above at 2.1.1.3, EU Law is premised on nationality rather than residence. While not without doubt, it is presumed that corporations have an EU nationality if they are incorporated or have their statutory seat in a member state. Accordingly, prima facie, such corporations are entitled to benefit from the fundamental freedoms. As noted above at 2.1.2.3 and 3.3.3, this concept of nationality limits the scope of most of the freedoms, but does not limit the free movement of capital. ECJ case law has decided that where two or more freedoms can apply, the predominant freedom applies irrespective of whether the taxpayer can benefit only from the subsidiary freedom. In particular, where the freedom of establishment properly applies, the taxpayer cannot argue the free movement of capital. An issue is whether using a dual resident corporation may circumvent this limit. An example will illustrate the issue.

The *Thin Cap* case was discussed above at 3.3.2.2 and 3.3.3. It was noted how the ECJ refused to apply the free movement of capital to the US parent corporations as the freedom of establishment was the appropriate freedom to analyse the situation.[62] This meant UK subsidiaries of these parents could not argue the invalidity of the UK thin capitalisation rules. However, what if the parent corporation was incorporated in the EU but resident outside the EU by virtue of a tax treaty? This could happen with, say, an Irish incorporated company that is effectively managed from Australia with a UK subsidiary.[63] For tax purposes, the corporation is resident in Australia and that is the dominant connecting factor, but it is nevertheless incorporated in Ireland. Prima facie, the establishment of the UK subsidiary by this corporation meets the requirements of Article 49 of the FEU Treaty, i.e. a national of a member state establishing itself in another member state.

Even if there are doubts about corporations where nationality is generally referred to in the fundamental freedoms, this issue is raised especially in the context of the freedom of establishment by Article 54 of the FEU Treaty (discussed above at 2.1.2.3). Assuming the Irish corporation has its registered office in Ireland, then Article 54 prescribes that it 'shall… be treated in the same way as natural persons who are nationals of Member

[62] The ECJ took a similar approach in Case C-492/04 *Lasertec Gesellschaft für Stanzformen mbH* v *Finanzamt Emmendingen* [2007] ECR I-3775 (ECJ).

[63] It could not happen with respect to the US as the US uses incorporation only as a test of corporate residence.

States'. In a contrived case, there may be abuse of law issues,[64] but in commercially justified circumstances there seems little standing in the way of application of the freedom of establishment in such a case.

The reverse could also raise issues, where an Australian incorporated company that is resident in Ireland establishes a UK subsidiary. On general principles, the corporation is not an Irish national and Article 54 does not treat it like one. The corporation may have its 'central administration or principal place of business within the Community', but it is not 'formed in accordance with the law of a Member State'. These situations demonstrate fundamental differences between connecting factors under EU Law and those under international tax law based on the OECD Model. The differences are emphasised by the ECJ giving dominance to one freedom where more than one may apply.

What of the Parent-Subsidiary Directive (1990) and the Interest and Royalties Directive (2003)? For example, take an Irish incorporated company resident in Australia with a German subsidiary. May such a corporation claim the benefits of a German exemption from withholding tax under these Directives, despite the fact that Germany would have a right to withhold tax under the Australia/Germany Tax Treaty? The answer is 'no'. This is dealt with in Article 2(1)(b) of the Parent-Subsidiary Directive and Article 3(a)(ii) of the Interest and Royalties Directive by providing that a corporation is not a 'company of a Member State', if under a tax treaty concluded with a third state it is considered resident outside the EU. However, the situation is not dealt with symmetrically. The Australian incorporated company resident in Ireland is not entitled to the benefits of the Directives because it does not fall within the forms of entity listed in the Annexes to these Directives. Those forms are limited to entities formed within the EU.

These provisions may not resolve all issues. What if there is no tax treaty between the EU state of incorporation and the foreign state of management, do the Directives then apply? Both incorporate the additional requirement that the corporation be 'subject to' an EU corporate tax 'without being exempt'.[65] Imagine a scenario in which the corporation, resident in a non-treaty third country by reason of management, is incorporated in an EU country that exempts the dividends, interest or royalties under its domestic law, e.g. because they are connected with a foreign PE.

[64] Regarding abuse of law in the context of EU tax law, see Schön (2008).

[65] Parent-Subsidiary Directive (1990) Art. 2(1)(c) and Interest and Royalties Directive (2003) Art. 3(a)(iii).

The Directives do not require the dividend, interest or royalties be subject to tax, just the corporation, which it is on any income not effectively connected with a foreign PE. The Interest and Royalties Directive (2003) deals with this issue, though not the Parent-Subsidiary Directive (1990). The former does not apply 'where interest or royalties are paid… to a permanent establishment situated in a third State'.[66]

Even where the Directives are precluded, it has been argued that a dual resident company incorporated in the EU might be entitled to the fundamental freedoms. If this is so, could the freedoms result in an exemption from dividend, interest or royalty withholding tax? *Denkavit*,[67] discussed above at 3.1.4.1, demonstrates that the fundamental freedoms may require an exemption from dividend withholding tax even where the Parent-Subsidiary Directive (1990) does not apply. Further, *Bosal* (noted above at 1.3.3 and 4.2.1) demonstrates that the tax law of a member state must comply with the fundamental freedoms as well as Directives.[68] The argument is stronger in the case of dividends, where, *if* the freedom of establishment applies, the comparator is likely to be dividends distributed between domestic corporations, which are typically exempt. The case seems quite weak with respect to interest and royalties, where domestic law is unlikely to provide an exemption and where the ECJ is unlikely to make a comparison between the Australian resident/Irish incorporated parent and an EU resident parent corporation entitled to the benefits of the Interest and Royalties Directive (2003) (see below at 5.2.3.1). However, question whether such a corporation might claim to deduct expenses and be taxed at the domestic corporate rate where this is more favourable than the withholding tax on the gross amount, see above at 3.1.4.2.

5.2.2.2 Payments made by the person: dual source

Generally Just as a PE and its head office may result in dual sourcing of certain payments made by them, so can the dual residence of a person making a payment. With respect to interest (and royalties) paid by PEs, this was discussed above at 5.2.1.2. While conceptually the issues are similar with respect to dual resident corporations making payments, the legal analysis is different. For example, presume that a corporation managed in Country A1 and incorporated in Country A2 pays interest (or

[66] Interest and Royalties Directive (2003) Art. 1(8).

[67] Case C-170/05 *Denkavit International BV, Denkavit France SARL* v *Ministre de l'Economie, des Finances et de l'Industrie* [2006] ECR I-11949 (ECJ).

[68] Case C-168/01 *Bosal Holding BV* v *Staatssecretaris van Financiën* [2003] ECR I-9409 (ECJ).

royalties) to a resident of Country B. Here the OECD position noted above at 5.2.2.1 appears to resolve the dual source problem. The Country A1/ Country B tax treaty will apply to give Country A1 a right to tax the interest (or royalties) under the equivalent of Article 11 of the OECD Model (Article 12 of the UN Model).

The Country A2/Country B tax treaty also applies but Country A2 is not given a right to tax under that treaty because of the residence of the payer. This is because, as discussed above at 5.2.2.1, the paying corporation is not resident in Country A2 because of the equivalent of the second sentence of Article 4(1) of the OECD Model. Article 21 would then prescribe taxation in Country B only. Bizarrely, this depends on there being a tax treaty between Country A1 and Country A2 with a tiebreaker clause. If that is not the case, the corporation is still subject to tax in Country A2 because of its residence (incorporation there). Therefore, it would be resident under the Country A2/Country B tax treaty, the interest (or royalties) would be sourced there and Country A2 entitled to tax. If both Country A1 and Country A2 have a right to tax under their treaties with Country B, Country B would be obliged to provide relief for both source taxes.

Similar issues can arise where there is no tax treaty with Country B, but here there would be reliance on unilateral relief offered in Country B. Country B domestic law is likely to source the interest in only one of Country A1 or Country A2, likely Country A1. Therefore, only this tax is likely to qualify for unilateral relief. There is no potential for requiring Country B to give dual relief unless it has a tax treaty with Country A2 that gives that country a right to tax. In this case, Country B may give unilateral relief for Country A1 tax and tax treaty relief for Country A2 tax.

As noted, the dual sourcing problem cannot arise in the context of dividends and PEs, but it can arise in the context of dual resident corporations. In the case of dividends and dual resident corporations, the analysis is the same as with respect to interest and royalties. However, here there may be a mismatch between the form of underlying foreign tax relief granted by Country B for dividends from Country A1 compared with dividends from Country A2. For example, Country B may offer no unilateral relief or unilateral relief by underlying foreign tax credit when it uses the exemption method under its tax treaties. Similarly, some countries use different methods in different tax treaties. Traditionally, the UK has been consistent as between tax treaties and between tax treaties and unilateral relief, all incorporating the foreign tax credit method. This consistency broke down in 2009 with the introduction of a unilateral exemption for inter-corporate dividends.

EU Law The issue for consideration is how EU Law might apply to a payment made by a corporation that is incorporated in the EU but managed in a third country. The Parent-Subsidiary Directive (1990) and the Interest and Royalties Directive (2003) can apply to such a case only where the recipient is an EU corporation. In such a case, assuming the holding requirement is met (see above at 3.1.4.2), the issue under the Interest and Royalties Directive is where the payment 'arises'. As with the situation discussed above at 5.2.2.1, the requirement that the payment not be made or received by a PE in a third country means that the Directive is unlikely to apply in the current scenario, even if the corporation is 'of a Member State'.

By contrast, in the case of dividends, if the distributing corporation is 'of a Member State', it seems the Parent-Subsidiary Directive (1990) could apply to prohibit the EU state of incorporation from imposing withholding tax. More interesting is whether the state of the recipient is obliged to provide underlying foreign tax relief. This could be particularly important where, for example, the country of the recipient does not provide unilateral relief or have a tax treaty with the third country (country of management of the payer). On the face of the Directive, it seems the country of the recipient would be so obliged; again assuming the dual resident distributing corporation is 'of a Member State'. However, Article 1(2) specifically preserves the right of member states to apply anti-fraud or abuse provisions.

As far as the fundamental freedoms are concerned, it is noted that the mere incorporation of a company in a member state may not amount to an 'establishment' there. Further, if the corporation is inactive, the freedom to provide services and the free movement of capital may not apply. This apparent focus on substance can be contrasted with the potential formalism of the Directives and the OECD Model.

5.2.3 Intermediaries: re-sourcing and other re-characterisation

Many of the effects and planning discussed in the chapter so far may be replicated by using a third country intermediary. In such a case, the investment into a source/host country (Country A) by the resident/home country (Country B) investor is not made directly but indirectly through an intermediary established in a third country (Country I). As far as deriving income from the Country A investment is concerned, the important feature of using an intermediary is that it replaces one relationship (source/investor) for two (source/intermediary and intermediary/

investor).[69] This also means that a single payment of cross-border income, involving source and residence, might be replaced with two payments involving different sources and different residences.

From the perspective of both Country A and Country B, the use of an intermediary typically results in a change of both the location of source and the residence of the person deriving the income. However, the consequences will be deeper. For Country A, there is a change in who receives the payment, though probably not the quantity, timing or character of the payment. For Country B, there is a change in who makes the payment and potentially the timing of the payment and its character, though perhaps not its quantity.

This subheading begins by looking at the establishment of an intermediary in Country I. It considers the factors that might be important in determining the form of intermediary and the functions it performs. This consideration points out the benefits a taxpayer might seek with respect to source country and residence country taxation through using an intermediary. The subheading then considers the response of source and residence countries to the use of third country intermediaries.

5.2.3.1 Intermediate country

Tax advisers spend much time and energy mulling over the most appropriate holding location in a given setting, i.e. the country in which to set up an intermediary. This book does not seek to evaluate holding company locations or even to produce a list of desirable features of such a location. Rather, the approach is to analyse the use of intermediaries and their countries within the conceptual framework offered by this book. It does so by considering the factors that might be important in selecting the form of an intermediary and then considering the factors that might be important in determining the functions of the intermediary. In each case, these factors include the expected response of source/host and residence/home countries.

The establishment of an intermediary in a third country involves the creation of a taxable presence there. Chapter 3 considered the two main forms in which a tax presence may be established in a source country, i.e. a PE or subsidiary. These are also the main forms of intermediary that are used when setting up in an intermediate country. Typically, the point of

[69] This is a standard issue wherever an intermediary is used. Using a family corporation as an example, Harris and Oliver (2008) discuss the generic tax issues that arise through use of an intermediary.

setting up an intermediary is to intercept income that would otherwise be derived by the residence/home country investor and so the following discussion presumes the intermediary derives income. Before an intermediary can derive income, it must be funded and this is typically done by a capital injection by the residence/home country investor. The investor usually has a choice as to the form of capital injection, e.g. whether debt or equity (loan capital or share capital). An intermediary might also be funded with external capital, e.g. funds borrowed from a bank secured by the residence/home country investor with a mortgage or guarantee. The form of financing affects the type of income that the investor derives from the intermediary, if any.

PE Classic holding locations typically tax an intermediary owned by a non-resident in a similar fashion whether the intermediary is a PE or a subsidiary, though this need not be the case and any difference might affect the form selected. The form of intermediary selected is more likely to affect taxation by the source/host country and the residence/home country. If a PE intermediary is used, it will not constitute a person resident in the intermediate country and so the PE is not entitled to the benefits of tax treaties concluded between that country and other countries (but see above at 5.2.1.1). From the source country's perspective, this means the recipient is resident in the residence country and so any tax treaty with that country applies.

If the residence country adopts a foreign tax credit system, then the current taxation of the PE (and the direct application of the tax treaty with the source country) will mean that there is little tax benefit to be gained through using an intermediate PE. This changes dramatically if the residence country exempts the profits of foreign PEs. Here, the taxpayer has the choice of continuing to use the residence country's tax treaty network but being taxed at the rate applicable in the intermediate country. In an extreme case, the residence country will be a high tax country and the intermediary country a tax haven, which typically have few, if any tax treaties. The source country will nevertheless be obliged to provide source tax relief in accordance with the tax treaty with the residence country.

For example, assume a bank resident in Country B sets up a branch (PE) in a low tax country, Country I, and then derives interest income through the branch from a resident of Country A. Country A will limit its interest withholding tax by reference to its tax treaty with Country B. If Country B applies an exemption system to profits of a foreign PE, the benefit for the bank can be substantial. Indeed, if Country B applies the exemption unilaterally, e.g. a country like the Netherlands, it is not even important whether there is a tax treaty between Country I and Country B. The same might apply to the deriving of other income subject to low source country tax such as royalties or business profits not connected with a Country A PE (but connected with the Country I PE).

Subsidiary The potential tax benefits of setting up a subsidiary in the intermediate country are different and somewhat broader than those from setting up a PE. As noted, the PE route does not really work where the residence country adopts a foreign tax credit system. The potential tax benefits of setting up a subsidiary apply irrespective of whether the residence country is an exemption or credit country. These benefits tend to be of two main types: access to the tax treaty network of the intermediate country and access to a lower corporate tax rate.

Access to treaty network: treaty shopping Unlike a PE, a subsidiary is a person resident in the intermediate country and so an enterprise of that country (see above at 3.1.3.1). It is, therefore, entitled to the benefits of tax treaties concluded by the intermediate country. If the intermediate country has a better tax treaty network than the residence country, under which source country taxing rights are limited, a resident of the residence country has an incentive to set up a subsidiary in the intermediate country in an effort to access that country's tax treaty network. This is the problem of *treaty* or *forum shopping*, which is an important feature of use of intermediaries. Even where the intermediate country's tax rate is higher than that in the source or residence country, using an intermediate country's tax treaty network can save taxes. This largely results from a reduction in source country tax under treaty. An example will illustrate.

A corporation resident in Country B sets up a subsidiary in Country I, which derives 100 royalties from Country A. The respective corporate tax rates are 20 per cent, 35 per cent and 25 per cent. Country A imposes a domestic withholding tax of 25 per cent on outbound royalties. There is no tax treaty between Country A and Country B, but there is one between Country A and Country I, which, like the OECD Model, exempts royalties from source country taxation. Assume the corporation incurs 50 interest expense in deriving the royalties, e.g. on funds borrowed to acquire or develop the intellectual property on which the royalties are paid. If the corporation derived the 100 royalties directly from Country A, it would suffer 25 in withholding tax. Assuming Country B provides a unilateral foreign tax credit, it would calculate the limitation on credit as 10 (100 royalties less 50 interest gives net foreign income of 50, 20 per cent of which is 10). This would give rise to an effective source country tax of 50 per cent and excess foreign tax credits of 15 (10 less 25 source country tax).

By contrast, by using the Country A/Country I tax treaty, the situation can be vastly improved. Presume the Country B corporation licenses the intellectual property to the Country I subsidiary and that subsidiary pays 90 in royalties for the licence. If the Country A/Country I tax treaty is applied, instead of levying 25 in tax, Country A will levy no tax. Country I taxes the subsidiary with respect to the 100 royalties received but will grant a deduction for the 90 royalties paid under the licence from the Country B corporation. So, the subsidiary's taxable income in Country I is 10 (100 less 90) and its tax liability to Country I is 3.5. Country I does not subject the outbound royalties to source country tax. Country B will tax these royalties to the Country B corporation, which may deduct the interest it pays in calculating its Country B tax liability. Its net foreign profits are 40 (90 less 50 interest) and its Country B tax is 8 (20 per cent of 40).

Further, presume the Country I subsidiary distributes its net profits of 6.5 (10 less 3.5) as a dividend to the Country B corporation. If Country B applies the exemption system to dividends from foreign subsidiaries, there is no further tax to pay. The total tax paid is 3.5 to Country I and 8 to Country B. By using the intermediary subsidiary, the Country B corporation could save 13.5 (25 less 3.5, less 8), i.e. more than half the total tax. If Country B adopts an underlying foreign tax credit system with a country-by-country or worldwide limit (see above at 4.1.1.1), it could save more. Here the dividend will be grossed up to 10 (6.5 plus Country I tax of 3.5). The Country B corporation's total net income is now 50 (40, as before, plus the 10 grossed-up dividend). Its limitation on credit will be 10 (20 per cent of the 50 net foreign income) and so the 10 Country B tax liability will be reduced by all of the Country I tax of 3.5, leaving a net Country B tax liability of 6.5. Now the total tax levied is 10 (3.5 Country I plus 6.5 Country B), which is consistent with the Country B tax rate, and the tax saving by using the subsidiary is 15 (25 less 10). This example also demonstrates that there are cases in which a foreign tax credit system is more beneficial to the taxpayer than an exemption system.

There are many variations on this theme, but they all seek to achieve the same thing: a reduction in source country taxation as well as full relief in the residence country for expenses and any foreign tax imposed. Benefits can also be achieved where there is a tax treaty between Country A and Country B, but the Country A/Country I tax treaty reduces source country taxation by a greater amount. The core of the problem is inconsistencies in the international tax treaty network, whether holes in that network or differences between tax treaties. The distortions that this creates are obvious. A comparative high tax country like the Netherlands has nevertheless been a favoured location for holding corporations precisely for these reasons. It has liberal expensing rules, exemption of profits of foreign PEs and dividends from foreign subsidiaries, lack of withholding tax on outbound interest, royalties and, under its tax treaties, non-portfolio dividends and a substantial tax treaty network under which treaty partners have agreed to substantial reductions in source country tax. In the context of the EU, the full removal of source country taxation under the Parent-Subsidiary Directive (1990) and the Interest and Royalties Directive (2003) make the potential benefits from forum shopping more acute.

Access to lower corporate tax Where an intermediary is not used for treaty shopping purposes, it may still be used as a device to reduce taxation. This will usually be possible only where the tax rate in the intermediate country is less than that in the residence country. This can happen in the same manner using a subsidiary as when using a PE (described above). One difference is that source country taxing rights will be determined under the Country A/Country I tax treaty and not the Country A/Country B tax treaty. Second, if the profits of the Country I subsidiary are to be repatriated to Country B, using such an intermediary will produce benefits only if Country B exempts dividends from foreign subsidiaries, i.e. like the exemption in the case of using a PE.

In the case of the PE, it was pointed out that no benefit is produced if the residence country adopts a foreign tax credit system. That need not be the case if a subsidiary is used. Here, as noted above at 4.1.2.2, the underlying foreign tax credit system behaves like an exemption system until the subsidiary repatriates the profits in the form of a dividend. So, foreign subsidiaries are often used as *dividend traps*, meaning that they retain their profits and rarely distribute dividends to their parents. They may use their retained profits to finance other activities of an international group by way of share capital or loan capital, in which case they essentially perform a financing or treasury function. Of course, a subsidiary can be used as a dividend trap in a bilateral scenario, but often it will not be as effective as it can be in a multilateral scenario. An example will illustrate.

Presume that a corporation resident in Country B wishes to establish business operations in Country A and does so by establishing a subsidiary there. However, the Country B corporation does not finance the Country A subsidiary directly but through a holding corporation resident in Country I. The tax rate in each of Country A and Country B is 30%, but Country I is specifically selected because its tax rate is 5%. The Country B corporation finances the Country I holding corporation with share capital, either in cash or an in kind contribution such as in the form of transfer of intellectual property. The Country I holding corporation then funds the Country A subsidiary, again either in the form of loan capital or use of the intellectual property. Assume the Country A subsidiary makes 100 profits net of financing expenses but pays 80 in deductible expenses to the Country I holding corporation.

Country A will levy 6 in tax (30 per cent of 100 less 80). It may also levy some withholding tax on the interest or royalties but presume this is small or reduced under tax treaty so that it can all be credited in Country I. Country I provides foreign tax relief for any Country A tax imposed on the income of the holding corporation. The tax liability of the holding corporation will be, therefore, a maximum of 5 per cent, i.e. 4 (5 per cent of 80). If no dividend is distributed to the Country B corporation, the overall tax liability would be 10, which is potentially 20 less than the 30 (30 per cent of 100) that might have been levied if the investment had been made directly into Country A.

Capital exporting and capital importing countries are not particularly pleased with the use of intermediary corporations in third countries. They may seek to use a number of mechanisms to address the situation, which are discussed below, from the perspective of both the source country (5.2.3.2) and the residence country (5.2.3.3). Some of the mechanisms, like thin capitalisation, transfer pricing and CFC rules, have been discussed but need to be considered further in the current context. Other mechanisms, such as limitations on tax treaty entitlement, have not been discussed. Whether and to what extent these mechanisms address the issues depends on some of the factors discussed above. These include the form of the intermediary, the functions it performs, especially whether it is used to derive active or passive income, whether the intermediary distributes or retains its profits and whether the intermediary is seeking to use a tax treaty concluded by the intermediary country.

5.2.3.2 Source country taxation

Source countries' primary concern with the use of intermediaries is the treaty shopping issue. The erosion of the source country tax base through tax deductible payments, such as interest and royalties, is a problem in a purely bilateral setting and has given rise to responses such as thin capitalisation rules, see above at 3.3.2.2. Source countries can also respond through high withholding taxes in a non-treaty scenario. However, as discussed above at 3.1.4, tax treaties tend to reduce withholding taxes. Rightly or wrongly, tax treaties represent the outcome of negotiations between *two* particular countries. In those negotiations, countries believe they give up certain rights. Typically, what they give up is taxing rights as a source country and the extent to which they give up such rights may depend on the extent to which the other country reciprocates. This is clearest in the context of source country withholding taxes.

In such an environment, it is not surprising that source countries are concerned with *free riding* on their *sacrifices* using intermediaries established by third country residents in the treaty partner state. Tax treaties based on the OECD Model do not incorporate the concept of *most favoured nation* treatment, which is common in trade agreements. A country entering into a tax treaty does not promise to treat residents of the other contracting state as beneficially as the residents of any other country. This means, for example, that Country A may reduce its withholding tax on interest payments to residents of Country X to 10 per cent but reduce it to nil on payments to residents of Country Y. Such an imbalanced treatment (especially with such a highly mobile type of income) is just asking for persons resident outside Country Y to seek to obtain the benefits of the Country A/Country Y tax treaty. If treaty shopping were accepted, it could result, indirectly, in most favoured nation treatment.

US Model: limitation of benefits An extreme example of this is the US, where the domestic withholding tax on gross dividends, interest and royalties is 30 per cent,[70] but these are often reduced to nil under its tax treaties. These rates can make certain activities in the US prohibitive unless tax treaty protection is available. With such a distortion, it is not surprising that the US, in particular, has sought to protect itself from treaty shopping. It does so by incorporating 'limitation of benefits' clauses in its tax treaties. It is the policy of the US to conclude tax treaties only if they have such a clause in them. Limitation of benefits clauses are notoriously the longest and most complicated provisions in US tax treaties and tax treaties in general. The content of these clauses differs from tax treaty to tax treaty, but Article 22 of the 2006 US Model Tax Treaty illustrates their general thrust.[71]

Article 1(1) of the US Model makes the application of the Model to resident persons subject to the rest of the Model. In particular, this is an

[70] Internal Revenue Code (United States) s. 881.

[71] United States (2006).

indirect reference to Article 22. This provision begins by limiting the benefits of the Model to residents of the contracting states who are 'qualified persons'. The definition of this term has a number of qualifying categories and begins by accepting that individuals resident in a contracting state are entitled to the benefits of the Model. Accordingly, the provision is targeted at artificial persons and, in particular, corporations. Corporations are entitled to the benefits of the Model if their shares are listed and 'regularly traded' on a recognised stock exchange in the contracting state of which the corporation is resident. Alternately, at least 50 per cent of voting and value of its shares must be owned, directly or indirectly, by no more than five corporations that meet the listing test.

The test is different for corporations that are neither listed nor closely owned by listed corporations. Here the corporation must be 50 per cent owned, by voting and value, by persons entitled to the benefits of the Model on at least half the days in the tax year in question. In addition, deductions claimed by the corporation that are paid or accrue, directly or indirectly, to persons who are not entitled to the benefits of the Model must be less than 50 per cent of the corporation's gross income. A resident corporation can nevertheless be granted the benefits of the Model with respect to income derived in connection with or that is incidental to a trade or business conducted in its residence country. Residually, the competent authority (typically the tax administration) of a contracting state may grant the benefits of the Model to a corporation resident in the other contracting state if satisfied that the corporation is not established, acquired or maintained for the purposes of securing tax treaty benefits.

The US limitation of benefits clause is a useful illustration of what is wrong with the concept of corporate residence as generally applied (see above at 2.1.1.2). Using the place of incorporation or place of central, effective or principal management are imperfect (to say the least) supplements to the residence of individuals. Corporations *do not exist* and to speak of them as having a residence is, in a literal sense, nonsense. Corporations constitute an amalgam of income producing activities combined with the interests of various stakeholders. It is only sensible to speak of corporations having a residence by reference to these activities or stakeholders. Indirectly, this is what the US limitation of benefits clause does.

However, the US approach is isolationist from at least two perspectives. First, it means that a corporation that has many shareholders resident in different countries cannot get the benefit of US tax treaties. With increasing globalisation of markets and corporate ownership, this bilateral view of the world is outdated. Second, if a corporation resident in

Country I is owned by residents of Country B, while the US may deny the benefits of the Country I tax treaty, there is no attempt to grant the corporation the benefits of the Country B tax treaty. These difficulties are left to the discretion of the US tax administration. Many countries would not accept granting their tax administration such broad discretion in applying tax law.

OECD Model: beneficial owner and conduit companies The OECD adopts a softer approach to treaty shopping than the US limitation of benefits approach. In the usual OECD manner, this has involved minimal adjustment to the Model and substantial and sometimes questionable adjustments to the Commentaries. At the forefront of the OECD approach is the concept of 'beneficial owner', which is used in the context of Articles 10, 11 and 12 (dividends, interest and royalties). The 1977 version of the OECD Model incorporated a limitation (dating from 1974) that qualified the source country reduction in taxes on dividends, interest and royalties to the situation in which the beneficial owner of the income is a resident of the other contracting state.

The OECD Commentary suggests that the beneficial owner concept is targeted at the argument that simple payment to a resident, such as a resident agent, is sufficient to secure tax treaty benefits. However, the Commentary adds:

> The term "beneficial owner" is not used in a narrow technical sense, rather, it should be understood in its context and in light of the object and purposes of the Convention, including avoiding double taxation and the prevention of fiscal evasion and avoidance.
>
> It would be equally inconsistent with the object and purpose of the Convention for the State of source to grant relief or exemption where a resident of a Contracting State, otherwise than through an agency or nominee relationship, simply acts as a conduit for another person who in fact receives the benefit of the income concerned... [A] conduit company cannot normally be regarded as the beneficial owner if, though the formal owner, it has, as a practical matter, very narrow powers which render it, in relation to the income concerned, a mere fiduciary or administrator acting on account of the interested parties.[72]

The Commentary suggests that the Model should also be applied the other way round, i.e. a beneficial owner is entitled to a source country reduction even if the income is not received directly.[73]

[72] OECD Commentary on Art. 10 paras. 12 and 12.1.

[73] OECD Commentary on Art. 10 para. 12.2.

In the context of the law of equity, common law jurisdictions are familiar with the concept of beneficial ownership, although it is usually used in the context of ownership of property and not ownership of income. This raises the sensitive issue of whether the concept of beneficial ownership where used in a tax treaty has a special treaty meaning or derives its meaning from domestic law under the equivalent of Article 3(2) of the OECD Model. It seems clear that the OECD is of the view that the term should be interpreted according to a special treaty meaning as outlined in the Commentary. Civil law jurisdictions are likely to accept this position, as their domestic law is typically unfamiliar with the concept of beneficial ownership.

But what about common law jurisdictions? The concept of beneficial ownership was first used in a tax treaty between two common law jurisdictions in 1966 and found its way from there into the OECD Model.[74] In its original context, it seems likely that the contracting states intended to use the domestic law meaning. The domestic law meaning of beneficial owner in common law countries appears narrower than that suggested by the OECD. In particular, a shareholder is not the beneficial owner of a corporation's property or income, only the shares held in the corporation. Only in rare circumstances would a common law court consider that a corporation did not beneficially own property or income that had been allocated to the corporation. The exceptions revolve around the corporation acting as a trustee or where the corporate identity is pierced (lifting the corporate veil). The first is typically a formal matter and the second is rare.

The meaning of 'beneficial owner' in tax treaties is increasingly important and controversial, as a couple of cases will demonstrate. *Indofood* is a somewhat strange case, involving a UK court in a civil action being asked to interpret the Indonesia/Netherlands Tax Treaty with respect to a hypothetical corporation.[75] An Indonesian parent corporation incorporated a Mauritian subsidiary for the purposes of issuing loan notes to investors resident in various jurisdictions, which the parent corporation guaranteed. The Mauritian subsidiary on-loaned the proceeds of the notes to the parent corporation, which paid interest to the subsidiary, which paid interest to the note-holders. The arrangement was designed to take advantage

[74] See 1966 protocol to the 1945 UK/US Tax Treaty, which was followed in the 1966 Canada/UK Tax Treaty.

[75] *Indofood International Finance Ltd* v *P Morgan Chase Bank Na* [2006] EWCA Civ 158 (CA).

of a reduction in Indonesian interest withholding tax to 10 per cent under the Indonesia/Mauritius Tax Treaty. When that treaty was terminated, the issue arose as to whether the Indonesian parent had a right to terminate the loan notes due to a material tax change. This was possible provided restructuring was unreasonable, an issue that was to be determined according to UK law.

The trustee representing the note-holders argued that it was reasonable to restructure using a new Dutch subsidiary and taking advantage of the Indonesia/Netherlands Tax Treaty, which also incorporated a 10 per cent interest withholding tax. The parent corporation countered that any such subsidiary would not be the beneficial owner of the interest, so not entitled to the 10 per cent rate under that treaty and, therefore, restructuring was not reasonable. Indirectly, the UK court had to rule (on the balance of probabilities) on how an Indonesian court would interpret the concept of 'beneficial owner' in the Indonesia/Netherlands Tax Treaty. Similarly, it could have been argued that the actual Mauritian subsidiary was not entitled to the benefits of the terminated Indonesia/Mauritius Tax Treaty because it was not the beneficial owner of the interest.

The UK Court of Appeal noted a circular from the Indonesian tax administration in which it interpreted the concept of 'beneficial owner'. Citing from the circular, Morritt C in the leading judgment held that:

> The term 'beneficial owner' is to be given an international fiscal meaning not derived from the domestic laws of contracting states. As shown by those commentaries and observations, the concept of beneficial ownership is incompatible with that of the formal owner who does not have 'the full privilege to directly benefit from the income'.[76]

Morritt C continued to note the terms under which any new subsidiary would have to pass on to the note-holders the interest paid to it by its parent corporation. In particular, the subsidiary would be precluded from finding any other source of funds with which to pay the note-holders.

> In both commercial and practical terms the issuer [subsidiary] is, and Newco would be, bound to pay on to the principal paying agent that which it receives from the parent guarantor... In practical terms it is impossible to conceive of any circumstances in which either the issuer or Newco could derive any 'direct benefit' from the interest payable by the parent guarantor except by funding its liability to the principal paying agent or issuer respectively. Such an exception can hardly be described

[76] *Indofood International Finance Ltd* v *P Morgan Chase Bank Na* [2006] EWCA Civ 158 (CA) at para. 42.

> as the 'full privilege' needed to qualify as the beneficial owner, rather the position of the issuer and Newco equates to that of an 'administrator of the income'.[77]

The UK tax administration quickly accepted the Court of Appeal decision as authorising a special treaty meaning for 'beneficial owner' generally and not limited to the context of the case, i.e. Indonesian interpretation of an Indonesian treaty.[78] There must be some doubt as to giving the case such a broad authorisation, particularly considering the way in which Morritt C cited from the Indonesian tax administration circular.[79]

Further doubt in this regard has been cast from two sources. The first is the 10 July 2008 Technical Explanation to the Fifth Protocol of the 1980 Canada/US tax treaty issued by the US Senate but with the agreement of the Canadian authorities. That Explanation states that '[i]n general, the term "beneficial owner" refers to the person to which the income is attributable under the laws of the source country'. In footnote 74 it continues:

> Because the term "beneficial owner" is not specifically defined under the treaty, it has the meaning which it has under the law of the treaty country imposing the relevant tax, i.e., the source country, pursuant to Article III, paragraph 2 of the treaty.

The important point is the rejection of an international fiscal meaning for 'beneficial ownership'. Even if this is accepted, using the source country meaning is also controversial. Only by looking to the rules in the residence country can tax treaties ensure that source country and residence country taxation of income is matched under a tax treaty.

The importance of the treatment in the residence country is emphasised by the second source that casts doubt on 'beneficial ownership' having an

[77] *Indofood International Finance Ltd* v *P Morgan Chase Bank Na* [2006] EWCA Civ 158 (CA) at para. 44. It had also been argued that any new Dutch subsidiary would not be resident in the Netherlands for the purposes of the Indonesia/Netherlands Tax Treaty. This emphasises the importance of the beneficial ownership concept as a back up to defects in the tests of corporate residence. Members of the Court of Appeal could not agree on the residence issue.

[78] See paragraph INTM332050 of International Tax Manual at www.hmrc.gov.uk/manuals/intmanual/INTM332050.htm, accessed 14 March 2010. For a critical analysis of the UK tax administration's adoption of this decision for UK tax purposes, see Fraser and Oliver (2007).

[79] At the time of the *Indofood* case, there was no Indonesian case law on the concept of beneficial ownership in tax treaties. However, it is now clear that there was an important case going through the Indonesian courts at the time of the *Indofood* case. In 2007, the Supreme Court of Indonesia struck down a loan note issue, with devastating effect, based on tax evasion through treaty shopping. See Karyadi (2007).

international fiscal meaning. *Prévost Car* involved a Canadian resident corporation manufacturing buses that was used as a joint venture vehicle for a Swedish corporation and a UK corporation.[80] The joint venture partners held the Canadian corporation through a Dutch holding corporation. The question was whether the Dutch holding corporation was the beneficial owner of dividends received from the Canadian corporation and so entitled to the reduced dividend withholding tax rate under the Canada/Netherlands Tax Treaty. The shareholders agreement between the Swedish and UK joint venture partners provided that the Dutch holding corporation was to distribute not less than 80 per cent of its profits. The Dutch holding corporation was not a party to this agreement, had no employees in the Netherlands and no assets, other than its shareholding in the Canadian corporation. It was accepted that the holding corporation was not an agent, trustee or nominee for the joint venture partners.

Evidence was led that under Dutch law, the holding corporation would be regarded as the beneficial owner of the dividend unless it were legally obligated to pass on the dividends to its shareholders. Further, under Dutch law the shareholders agreement did not limit the discretion of the directors in deciding whether and if so what dividends to declare. Associate Chief Justice Rip in the Canadian Tax Court discussed the *Indofood* case, noting that the reasoning of the UK Court of Appeal had regard to the substance over form principle required by Indonesian law. He also noted that there was some inconsistency with the Dutch approach to beneficial ownership.[81] This view adds to the doubt over whether *Indofood* has general application. Associate Chief Justice Rip also dealt with the argument that, in domestic law, beneficial ownership is used in the context of ownership of assets and not income. He noted that dividends 'are in and by themselves also property and are owned by someone'.[82]

> [T]he 'beneficial owner' of dividends is the person who receives the dividends for his or her own use and enjoyment and assumes the risk and control of the dividend he or she received....When corporate entities are concerned, one does not pierce the corporate veil unless the corporation is a conduit for another person and has absolutely no discretion as to the use or application of funds put through it as conduit, or has agreed to act on someone else's behalf pursuant to that person's instructions without any right to do other than what that person instructs it, for example,

[80] *Prévost Car Inc* v *The Queen* [2009] FCA 57 (FCA).

[81] *Prévost Car Inc* v *The Queen* [2008] TCC 231 (TC) at para. 93.

[82] 'The words "beneficial owner" in plain ordinary language used in conjunction with dividends is not something alien.' *Prévost Car Inc* v *The Queen* [2008] TCC 231 (TC) at para. 99.

> a stockbroker who is the registered owner of the shares it holds for clients.[83]

Associate Chief Justice Rip held that there was no evidence that the Dutch holding corporation was a mere conduit for the joint venture partners. In particular, the joint venture partners would have no cause of action against the holding corporation if it failed to distribute dividends, they would only have an action against each other under the shareholders agreement. Until the holding corporation declared a dividend, the dividends received from the Canadian subsidiary were its property and its property alone. The Canadian Federal Court of Appeal upheld Justice Rip's judgment.[84]

Prévost Car casts some doubt on the scope of the *Indofood* case and whether the concept of 'beneficial ownership' will always have a treaty meaning. The Canadian court was willing to find a holding corporation to be a beneficial owner of dividends despite having no employees or assets other than its shareholding. However, the case is distinguishable from *Indofood* in that, as a matter of Dutch corporate law, the directors of the holding corporation were not bound to pass on the dividends received to the joint venture partners. This is different from the finding of the UK Court of Appeal in *Indofood* that the new holding corporation would be bound to pass on the interest received and had no discretion as to the source of funds to be used to pay the note-holders. So, there may be a substantial difference between back-to-back dividends and other back-to-back payments like interest and royalties where there is no discretion in the holding corporation.

If the OECD concept of beneficial ownership does deal with the treaty shopping issue, it does not do so comprehensively. It is contained only in Articles 10, 11 and 12 of the OECD Model and not in other provisions that might be used for purposes of treaty shopping.[85] In particular, it is not part of the capital gains article and yet a holding corporation will both hold assets and receive a return on those assets. Just as a source country's

[83] *Prévost Car Inc* v *The Queen* [2008] TCC 231 (TC) at para. 100. There is some consistency here with the finding on the facts of the *Indofood* case.

[84] *Prévost Car Inc* v *The Queen* [2009] FCA 57 (FCA). In particular, at paras. 13 and 14 the court reproduced most of the passage quoted above and suggested that it 'captures the essence of the concepts of "beneficial owner"'. At para. 15 the court rejected the tax administration's suggestion that the beneficial owner is 'the person who can, in fact, ultimately benefit from the dividend'.

[85] Conceptually, there seems to be a connection between 'beneficial ownership' and the 'effectively connected' requirement for PEs contained in OECD Model Arts 10(4), 11(5), 12(3) and 21(2).

taxing right over dividends, interest and royalties may vary from tax treaty to tax treaty, so may a source country's right to tax gains on alienation of the underlying asset. This problem has already been discussed in the context of land holding corporations and substantial shareholdings (see above at 3.1.5). Is it conceivable that a holding corporation might be entitled to the benefits of a particular tax treaty with respect to the alienation of shares, bonds or intellectual property but not with respect to the dividends, interest or royalties paid on those assets?[86]

EU Law: most favoured nation and limitation of benefits As noted, a fundamental feature of the international tax treaty network is that it does not incorporate most favoured nation treatment. In the context of the EU, it seems natural to think that an internal market requires most favoured nation treatment, i.e. that investors receive the same treatment from a source country irrespective of in which EU country the investor is based. In other words, it seems that imposing different taxes, especially withholding taxes, depending on which tax treaty is applicable is inconsistent with the very nature of the EU as seeking to create an internal market. This would amount to a revolution against tax treaties and, in 2005, was a step too far for the ECJ. The *D* case as a turning point in ECJ direct tax jurisprudence was mentioned above at 2.2.1. It followed two important events. One was a change in the make-up of the judges of the ECJ following the addition of ten new members to the EU in 2004. The second was the rejection in referendum of the EU constitution in two of the founding states, France and the Netherlands.

The *D* case involved the Dutch wealth tax eliminated in 2000.[87] Dutch law restricted the wealth tax personal allowance to non-residents whose wealth was at least 90 per cent in the Netherlands. The main issue was whether the free movement of capital required the granting of this allowance to non-residents (in this case a German) regardless of the 90 per cent rule. Of relevance to the present discussion was the second argument. The German taxpayer also argued that because the Belgium/Netherlands Tax Treaty allowed Belgian residents to claim the same personal allowance as residents of the Netherlands, the same advantage should be granted to the

[86] OECD Commentary on Art. 4 para. 8.2 was adjusted in 2008 to open the possibility that conduit corporations might be denied the benefits of tax treaties if 'exempted from tax on their foreign income by privileges tailored to attract conduit companies'. The suggestion is that they might be excluded from the definition of 'resident' due to the second sentence of OECD Model Art. 4(1).

[87] Case C-376/03 *D* v *Inspecteur van de Belastingdient* [2005] ECR I-5821 (ECJ).

German taxpayer. The Germany/Netherlands Tax Treaty did not grant such allowance and so this amounted to a most favoured nation argument.[88] Though understanding the revolution this would cause in EU tax treaties, in October 2004 and before the events mentioned above, AG Colomer accepted this argument, finding that a German investor in the Netherlands was comparable to a Belgian investor in the Netherlands.

In mid-2005, the ECJ bluntly rejected the AG's opinion, a rare occurrence (although it seems to have been happening with increasing frequency in direct tax cases).

> 60. It is to be remembered that, in order to avoid the same income and assets being taxed in both the Netherlands and Belgium, Article 24 of the Belgium–Netherlands Convention allocates powers of taxation between those two Member States and Article 25(3) lays down a rule under which natural persons resident in one of those two States is entitled in the other to the personal allowances which are granted by it to its own residents.
> 61. The fact that those reciprocal rights and obligations apply only to persons resident in one of the two Contracting Member States is an inherent consequence of bilateral double taxation conventions. It follows that a taxable person resident in Belgium is not in the same situation as a taxable person resident outside Belgium so far as concerns wealth tax on real property situated in the Netherlands.
> 62. A rule such as that laid down in Article 25(3) of the Belgium–Netherlands Convention cannot be regarded as a benefit separable from the remainder of the Convention, but is an integral part thereof and contributes to its overall balance.

It is difficult to reconcile this decision with the requirements of the internal market other than to suggest that the ECJ was of the opinion that the EU was not quite ready for the full-blown effects of an internal market. How can it be that for the purposes of the fundamental freedoms a non-resident is often comparable with a resident but not comparable with another non-resident? For the purposes of EU Law, it is not clear how this consequence 'follows' from the existence of a tax treaty. Surely, non-residents are more comparable than a non-resident and a resident, irrespective of the existence of a tax treaty? The implication seems to be that non-residents can be comparable, but not when a tax treaty is concluded. The indirect consequence of the *D* case is that a source state may discriminate between EU member state investors through tax treaties. The potential for tax treaties

[88] There was no wealth tax in either Belgium or Germany at this time.

to act as barriers to further EU integration was also noted above at 4.2.2 in the context of the *Lidl* case.

There is a fundamental connection between the most favoured nation issue and treaty shopping. As noted above, treaty shopping using artificial entities such as corporations is a consequence of the lack of uniformity in the treatment of non-residents, i.e. the lack of most favoured nation treatment. Treaty shopping is an effort by taxpayers to engage in *self-help* most favoured nation treatment. Reaction against treaty shopping by using limitation of benefits clauses and, in the context of passive income payments, the beneficial ownership requirement was noted above. The most favoured nation issue reappeared before the ECJ in the *ACT* case.[89] This case also dealt with the related issue of the compatibility of limitation of benefits clauses with EU Law.

The *ACT* case was discussed above at 3.1.4.1. In that case, the ECJ reasoned that if the UK did not tax dividends received by non-resident shareholders from UK corporations, the non-resident shareholders were not comparable with resident UK shareholders. This meant that denying dividend tax credits to non-resident shareholders while granting them to resident shareholders did not breach the fundamental freedoms. The ECJ dealt with two other important issues in this case. The UK granted dividend tax credits to non-resident shareholders under some of its tax treaties but not others. So, for example, Dutch parent corporations were granted refundable dividend tax credits with dividends from UK subsidiaries but German parent corporations were not.[90] The ECJ simply followed the *D* case on this issue, finding that because of the differences in the tax treaties, a Dutch parent corporation and a German parent corporation were not comparable.[91]

The limitation of benefits issue was also raised in the *ACT* case. In some of the tax treaties granting dividend tax credits to non-resident corporations, the credit was not available if persons resident outside the treaty partner controlled the recipient corporation. For example, under the UK/Netherlands Tax Treaty, if a recipient Dutch resident corporation was not listed, it was entitled to a dividend tax credit only if it could show that:

[89] Case C-374/04 *Test Claimants in Class IV of the ACT Group Litigation* v *CIR* [2006] ECR I-11673 (ECJ).

[90] Regarding the treatment of such Dutch parent corporations under the Parent-Subsidiary Directive (1990) see Case C-58/01 *Oce Van der Grinten NV* v *IRC* [2003] ECR I-9809 (ECJ), discussed above at 3.1.4.1.

[91] Case C-374/04 *Test Claimants in Class IV of the ACT Group Litigation* v *CIR* [2006] ECR I-11673 (ECJ) at paras. 88–91.

> it is not controlled by a person or two or more associated or connected persons together, who or any of whom would not have been entitled to a tax credit if he had been the beneficial owner of the dividends.[92]

So, if a Dutch corporation was controlled by a German corporation it would not be entitled to dividend tax credits but if it were controlled by a Dutch or Italian corporation it would be.[93]

The importance of this argument cannot be understated. Most EU member states have concluded tax treaties with the US containing a limitation of benefits clause. Pre-2005 case law with respect to aviation agreements (the *Open Skies* litigation) suggested that entering into a treaty with a third country (the US) containing a limitation of benefits clause may *of itself* breach the fundamental freedoms even if the US was the one doing the discriminating.[94] The member state facilitated this discrimination by entering into the treaty. In the *ACT* case, the ECJ swept away the arguments by extending the scope of the *D* case:

> 89 The same applies to the provisions of the [Double Tax Conventions] which make the grant of such a tax credit subject to the condition that the non-resident company is not owned, directly or indirectly, by a company resident in a Member State or a non-member country with which the United Kingdom has concluded a DTC which does not provide for such a tax credit.
>
> 90 Even where such provisions extend to the situation of a company which is not resident in one of the contracting Member States, they apply only to persons resident in one of those Member States and, by contributing to the overall balance of the DTCs in question, are an integral part of them.

How can this be? Where a tax treaty applies, not only is a person resident outside the treaty countries not comparable to one within, but the treaty can discriminate between corporations resident in the same country depending on their ownership. And this result is suggested without a whisper of the earlier *Open Skies* litigation, which relied heavily on Article 54 of the FEU Treaty. As noted above at 2.1.2.3, Article 54 expressly requires that corporations:

> formed in accordance with the law of a Member State and having their registered office, central administration or principal place of business within the Union shall, for the purposes of [freedom of establishment], be

[92] Netherlands/UK Tax Treaty (1980) Art. 10(3)(d)(i).

[93] Dividend tax credits were also granted under the Italy/UK Tax Treaty (1988) Art. 10(3).

[94] Cases C-466, 467, 468, 469, 471, 472, 475, 476/98 *Commission of the European Communities v UK, Denmark, Sweden, Finland, Belgium, Luxembourg, Austria, Germany* [2002] ECR I-9427 (ECJ).

treated in the same way as natural persons who are nationals of Member States.

As noted at a number of points in this book, the ECJ has consistently viewed members of a corporate group separately in applying the fundamental freedoms. This is clear in the *Bosal* case (see above at 4.2.1) and, perhaps, the clearest example is in the formalistic approach to the concept of withholding tax in the Parent-Subsidiary Directive (1990) as evidenced by the *Burda* case (see above at 3.1.4.1).[95] These cases are consistent with Article 54, but why is the situation different in the context of tax treaties?[96] Despite continually suggesting that tax treaties are subject to EU Law, the ECJ is increasingly permitting tax treaties to distort the internal market. How far may tax treaties go in creating distortions? The ECJ has not heard its last case on this important issue.

5.2.3.3 Residence country taxation

Foreign tax relief: mixers The effect of using a third country intermediary on foreign tax relief granted by the residence/home country depends on the manner in which the intermediary is used. If a PE intermediary is used, the situation is much as described above at 5.2.3.1. The Country A/Country B tax treaty will apply to income derived from Country A by the PE, including any foreign tax relief. However, the Country B/Country I tax treaty will also apply (if there is one) and this may be more important, especially where it requires Country B to grant foreign tax relief in the form of

[95] Case C-168/01 *Bosal Holding BV* v *Staatssecretaris van Financiën* [2003] ECR I-9409 (ECJ) and Case C-284/06 *Finanzamt Hamburg-Am Tierpark* v *Burda GmbH* [2008] ECR I-4571 (ECJ).

[96] Might a difference be that the freedom of establishment was evident in these other cases? It seems unlikely that this, of itself, should make a difference. In Case C-194/06 *Staats van Financiën* v *Orange European Smallcap Fund NV* [2008] ECR I-3747 (ECJ) the ECJ found that a unilateral concession granted by the Netherlands to investment funds (effectively foreign tax credits granted to a fund were passed to shareholders in the fund) which was reduced by the proportion of non-resident shareholders in a fund was contrary to the free movement of capital. At paras. 72–4, the ECJ reasoned that the denial of the concession affected not only the non-resident shareholders in the fund but also resident shareholders. This meant that potential investors might be less willing to invest in a fund that had non-resident shareholders than one with resident investors. Further at para. 79, relying on Case C-170/05 *Denkavit International BV, Denkavit France SARL* v *Ministre de l'Economie, des Finances et de l'Industrie* [2006] ECR I-11949 (ECJ) (discussed above at 3.1.4.1), the ECJ noted that as the Netherlands taxed both resident and non-resident shareholders in a fund, they were comparable and both should be entitled to the benefit of passing through foreign tax credits.

exemption. If Country B has a foreign tax credit system, it will typically grant credit for taxes imposed by both Country A and Country I.

If a Country I subsidiary is used, the treatment by Country B will depend on whether the subsidiary makes repatriations to the Country B corporation in the form of deductible payments, dividends or not at all (i.e. retention).[97] Problems can arise for foreign tax relief in the residence country in the first scenario. Assume the subsidiary resident in Country I derives interest income from Country A, which Country A subjects to a 10 per cent withholding tax. The subsidiary pays the interest on to its Country B parent corporation as interest. The result is likely to be no Country I tax. Country I is likely to tax only the difference between the interest received and the interest paid, and foreign tax relief for the Country A tax is likely to exhaust this. Assuming Country I does not tax the outbound interest, the parent corporation will not receive any foreign tax relief in Country B with respect to the receipt of the interest from the subsidiary. In particular, and unlike the situation of a PE, Country B will not grant foreign tax relief for the Country A withholding tax. The result can be a form of economic double taxation.

The issues are different where dividends are repatriated. Here, the issue becomes one of underlying foreign tax relief, discussed above at 4.1.2.1. Assuming Country B does provide such relief, either unilaterally or under a tax treaty with Country I, it will adopt either the exemption or credit method. The exemption method is straightforward and produces results similar to those where the exemption method is used for a PE intermediary. The credit method, however, raises fundamental questions as to the type of foreign tax credit system adopted and, in particular, calculation of the limitation on credit.

The various methods of calculating the limitation on credit were discussed above at 4.1.1.1. In particular, it was noted that a worldwide limitation is most beneficial to the taxpayer and an item-by-item limitation is least favourable. By their nature, intermediaries re-characterise and re-source income. The interest that was originally derived from Country A (above) has been re-characterised and re-sourced into dividends from Country I. If Country B accepts this re-characterisation and re-sourcing for the purposes of its underlying foreign tax credit system, taxpayers may convert a country-by-country, type of income or item-by-item limitation into a worldwide limitation. The intermediary would derive income from

[97] A discussion of the first two scenarios follows. The third scenario is considered under the next subheading.

different countries or of different types or items and *mix* these into a single dividend from Country I. An intermediary used in this way is often called a *mixer* corporation.

Take, for example, a corporation resident in Country B that sets up a subsidiary in Country I. The subsidiary derives interest income of 100 from Country A1, which Country A1 taxes at 10 per cent. The subsidiary also derives business income of 100 from a PE in Country A2, which Country A2 taxes at 40 per cent. Country I imposes no additional tax on the subsidiary's income. The subsidiary distributes a dividend of 150 to its parent corporation, i.e. 90 net profits from Country A1 plus 60 net profits from Country A2. Assume Country B imposes tax at the rate of 30 per cent and adopts an item-by-item foreign tax credit system. If the parent corporation derived the income directly, it would calculate the limitation on credit separately for the Country A1 and Country A2 income. The limitation would be 30 for each (30 per cent of 100), resulting in 20 Country B tax for the Country A1 income (30 less 10) and 10 excess credits for the Country A2 income (30 less 40). A country-by-country or type of income limitation would produce the same results.

However, if Country B respects the character of the dividends from the subsidiary and that they are sourced in Country I, the situation is very different if it grants underlying foreign tax credits. Gross-up for the underlying Country A1 and Country A2 tax makes taxable income of 200 (150 dividend plus 10 Country A tax and 40 Country B tax) and a limitation on credit of 60 (30 per cent of 200). The result is a Country B tax liability of 10 (60 less 10 less 40) and no excess credits. The parent corporation is 10 better off because by using a mixer corporation it has turned an item-by-item limitation into a worldwide limitation.

If the residence country wants to maintain the integrity of its limitation on credit, it must adopt *look through* rules. It must look through the dividend and the mixer corporation and treat dividends as deriving their character and source from the profits from which they are distributed.[98] In the context of modern corporate groups that involve myriad corporations with myriad relationships and transactions, the complexity of an underlying foreign tax credit system that seeks to adopt a look through approach should not be underestimated. The US underlying foreign tax credit system is notoriously complex for precisely this reason. Historically, the UK tolerated mixer corporations, and many were located in the Netherlands. An attempt at reform in 2000 resulted in a confused

[98] Generally, see Harris (1999).

system that adopts only partial look through.[99] Mixer corporations can still be effective, within limits.

Intermediary retention: CFC rules CFC rules were discussed above at 4.1.2.2. As noted at that point, they are relevant for residence countries irrespective of whether they provide foreign tax relief by way of exemption or credit. Further, CFC type rules may be extended to the profits of lowly taxed PEs where a country otherwise adopts the exemption method in the form of a switchover to the credit method. For exemption countries, the issues arise irrespective of distribution. For foreign tax credit countries, the issues typically arise only where a foreign subsidiary retains its profits. Here, the issues are really the same as those that arise in a purely bilateral scenario and so the discussion above at 4.1.2.2 is relevant.

However, in a multilateral setting, some features of a CFC regime become particularly important. The very nature of an intermediate corporation is that it will be dealing with third countries and often with related corporations. These features place particular emphasis on some exceptions to CFC rules. If a CFC is established in a white listed country, a question is whether the exemption from the CFC rules extends to foreign source income derived by the CFC. Any active business exemption raises issues as to whether the type of activities conducted in the intermediate corporation qualifies for the exemption.

An example is captive insurance. Some corporate groups find that they cannot obtain reasonable arm's length insurance cover for some of the risks that they face. In such an environment, the group may seek to self-insure by setting up its own corporation that insures the rest of the group. That corporation will then take premiums and meet claims of group members in conducting an insurance business. The same can be true of treasury or financing functions.[100] Usually, it will not be difficult to prove that such a corporation is conducting active business, but equally there is a risk that the premiums or fees charged are excessive in an effort to inflate the profits of the corporation and protect them from higher level tax. As mentioned at 4.1.2.2, many countries, including the UK, exclude dealings with related parties when assessing whether the active income exemption applies.

[99] TIOPA ss. 67–9. The system was amended again in 2009.

[100] For a UK CFC case involving a captive insurance company used to insure risks of travel agents, see *Association of British Travel Agents Ltd* v *IRC* [2003] STC (SC) 194 (SC).

Intermediary corporations may also be used actively in coordinating dealings with independent third parties where the activities do not belong particularly to any one country. These activities can include coordinating sales where, for example, the intermediate corporation deals with internet orders from numerous countries and determines which supply depot will meet an order. Purchasing can be conducted in the same way. Outsourcing of services, e.g. contract manufacturing, is another function that can be performed by an intermediate corporation. Each of these activities involves business that is conducted with independent parties and so have the maximum chance of falling within any active business exception to CFC rules. Nevertheless, just as with passive income or related party income, use of an intermediate corporation in this way has the potential of trapping profits in a low tax country. For tax advisers, CFC rules do not stop the game of trapping profits in low tax countries; they just make achieving it that more complex.

EU Law EU Law once again raises difficult issues with respect to each of the scenarios discussed above. The first scenario involved an intermediary receiving lowly taxed income from a source country and passing it on in a deductible form to its controlling corporation. The issue is whether there are any circumstances in which EU Law might require the country of the parent corporation (Country B) to grant foreign tax relief for source country tax (in the example, Country A tax paid on the interest). While there are other factors at work, Country B has caused a distortion in cross-border investment, it grants underlying foreign tax relief where a foreign establishment is financed with equity but not where it is financed with debt. This is particularly acute in the current scenario where the Country I tax liability is not sufficient to provide relief for the Country A tax.

Nevertheless, it is unlikely that EU Law would require Country B to grant foreign tax relief to resolve this. For a start, it seems that as the intermediary is controlled by the Country B corporation, only the freedom of establishment will be considered. Unless Country I is in the EU, that freedom has no application, see discussion of the *Thin Cap* case, above at 3.3.3.[101] Even if Country I is an EU member state, *Kerckhaert and Morres* (discussed above at 4.1.1.3) suggests that Country B is not obliged to provide any foreign tax relief, even if dividends were received from

[101] Case C-524/04 *Test Claimants in the Thin Cap Group Litigation* [2007] ECR 00 (ECJ).

the Country I intermediary.[102] The Parent-Subsidiary Directive (1990) cannot apply because it is very unlikely that the interest received by the Country B corporation from the intermediary could be considered a 'distribution of profits', though the term is undefined in the Directive. Further, Country B is likely to provide the same treatment, with the same problem if the intermediary were established in Country B, so there is no discrimination. Finally, the problem lies in the source country taxation of the interest and, if that country is an EU member state, there is a chance that it would be required to make allowance for directly associated expenses, see above at 3.1.4.2. So, perhaps the problem lies there.

In the second scenario, the intermediary pays dividends to the Country B corporation and the issue is the nature of foreign tax relief provided by Country B. No particular issues seem to arise if Country B adopts an exemption system.[103] If Country B adopts an underlying foreign tax credit system, EU Law issues might arise if Country I is an EU member state. In this case, the Parent-Subsidiary Directive (1990) and the freedom of establishment will apply. The general position was discussed above at 4.1.2.1. In particular, it was noted that neither the Directive nor case law based on the *FII* case prescribe a particular method of calculating the limitation on credit and an item-by-item approach, such as the UK's, seems permissible.[104] However, mixing is a different issue because it is not necessarily inconsistent with an item-by-item approach and that is the least required by EU Law.

Read literally, the wording of Article 4 of the Parent-Subsidiary Directive (1990) seems to permit mixing. It is the 'corresponding tax due' on the distributed profits received that is the limitation on credit. The country of the parent corporation must allow as a deduction against this limit 'corporation tax… paid by the subsidiary and any lower-tier subsidiary'. The reference to lower-tier subsidiaries makes it clear that the tax that must be credited may come from a mixture of sources. There is no permission to divide a dividend and calculate the corresponding tax due separately for each part.

The position under the freedom of establishment is less clear. The *FII* case, discussed above at 4.1.2.1, refers only to crediting of tax 'paid in

[102] Case C-513/04 *Kerckhaert and Morres* v *Belgium State* [2006] ECR I-10967 (ECJ).

[103] Issues might arise if Country B applies exemption with progression, but these are not explored in this book.

[104] Case C-446/04 *Test Claimants in the FII Group Litigation* [2006] ECR I-11753 (ECJ).

the Member State of the company making the distribution'.[105] Of itself, this seems to require mixing of tax paid on different sources of income by the subsidiary in its country of residence. In *FII*, the ECJ followed the wording of the Parent-Subsidiary Directive before its extension to lower-tier subsidiaries in 2003. Assuming the ECJ would extend its reasoning consistently with the 2003 amendments, the better view seems to be that the freedom of establishment also permits mixing. The subsidiary as a whole is the parent corporation's establishment and, if the freedom requires the crediting of underlying tax, it seems inconsistent with the freedom to divide the establishment or its dividends into pieces and calculate multiple foreign tax credit limitations. A single establishment seems to suggest a single credit limitation, at least for each dividend.

The final scenario discussed above concerned retention by the intermediary and, in particular, CFC rules in the parent corporation's country of residence (Country B). The compatibility of CFC rules with EU Law was considered above at 4.1.2.2. As discussed above, setting up an intermediary involves an exercise of establishment by the parent corporation, and so only the freedom of establishment is relevant. This freedom has no application where the intermediary is established outside the EU. If it is established within the EU, then *Cadbury Schweppes* suggests that the residence country (Country B) may apply its CFC rules only if that establishment is a 'wholly artificial arrangement'.[106] It seems inevitable that this limitation on the application of CFC rules applies even if the CFC derives income from other member states. Outside of this scenario, the matter is less clear.

Consider the situation in which the intermediary, established in the EU, derives income from third countries. May the country of the parent corporation tax this income of the subsidiary under its CFC rules before any distribution? If the intermediary country taxes the foreign income to the intermediary, e.g. with a foreign tax credit, there seems little justification for treating the foreign income differently from other income derived by the intermediary. The intermediary is a bona fide exercise of the parent corporation's freedom of establishment and the foreign income is part of that establishment.[107] But what if the intermediary country does not tax the foreign income, i.e. provides foreign tax relief in the form of

[105] Case C-446/04 *Test Claimants in the FII Group Litigation* [2006] ECR I-11753 (ECJ) at para. 57.

[106] Case C-196/04 *Cadbury Schweppes* [2006] ECR I-7995 (ECJ).

[107] However, note the restrictive manner in which the UK tax administration interpreted *Cadbury Schweppes*, discussed above at 4.1.2.2.

an exemption? This would not necessarily constitute the intermediary a wholly artificial arrangement, but might it be suggested that the foreign income is not properly within the jurisdiction of establishment because it is not within that country's tax system? The matter is unclear.

Similarly unclear is the situation where the subsidiary in Country I itself establishes a subsidiary in another country, i.e. a second-tier subsidiary of the parent corporation. As explained at 4.1.2.2, CFC rules apply directly to each tier of subsidiary. So the CFC rules may apply to attribute the profits of the second-tier subsidiary directly to the parent corporation and not to the first-tier subsidiary and then to the parent corporation. Might this *leapfrog* effect of CFC rules with the second-tier subsidiary be contrary to the freedom of establishment with respect to the first-tier subsidiary? Again, there are two scenarios here: where the second-tier subsidiary is established in the EU and where it is not.

If the second-tier subsidiary is established within the EU, it seems inescapable that the CFC rules cannot be applied unless it is a wholly artificial arrangement. While not without doubt, if the second-tier subsidiary is a wholly artificial arrangement, it seems unlikely that the parent corporation would be protected from its country's CFC rules on the basis that the activities of the second-tier subsidiary constitute part of the parent's freedom of establishment of the first-tier subsidiary, assuming the latter is not a wholly artificial arrangement. If the country of the first-tier subsidiary applied its own CFC rules, would that make a difference and would the ECJ give priority to one set of CFC rules over another (i.e. Country B's or Country I's CFC rules)? This is not clear.

If the second-tier subsidiary is established outside the EU and is a wholly artificial arrangement, the argument seems stronger for applying the CFC rules of the parent corporation's country. This may be viewed as an attempt to avoid Country B's taxation. Once again, if the country of the first-tier subsidiary (Country I) applies CFC rules as well, the situation becomes less clear. But what if the second-tier subsidiary is not a wholly artificial arrangement? Is it an establishment of the first-tier subsidiary, the parent corporation or both? In any case, the freedom of establishment of the second-tier subsidiary will not provide protection from CFC rules because it is established outside the EU. But if it is a bona fide establishment might it be argued that it constitutes part of the freedom of establishment of the first-tier subsidiary?

To adapt the facts of the *Cadbury Schweppes* case, assume the Irish subsidiary was a bona fide establishment and it had a second-tier subsidiary in Mauritius conducting the bona fide business of captive insurance.

Could the UK CFC rules *leapfrog* the Irish subsidiary and apply to the profits of the Mauritian subsidiary without breaching the freedom of establishment of the Irish subsidiary? Would it make a difference if the Mauritian subsidiary distributed all its profits to the Irish subsidiary, or whether Ireland provides foreign tax relief in the form of exemption or credit, or whether Ireland applied CFC rules?[108] It seems likely that CFC cases brought before the ECJ will become ever more sophisticated.

[108] Evans-Lombe J touched on these issues in *Vodafone 2* v *Revenue & Customs Commissioners* [2008] EWHC 1569 (HC) at para. 73. 'The new [ITCA 1988] s. 751A underlines this point. In order to be effective it requires that s. 748(3) be construed so as to include the "artificial arrangements" condition, but seeks to deal with the potential loophole where profits earned outside the EU are channelled through a CFC resident in a member state which is "established" there within the criteria of the *Cadbury* case. There is a further loophole not yet apparently addressed. What happens if a UK-resident parent, wishing to avoid tax, purchases an "established" company resident in another member state, but uses it as a "letter box" for investment transactions, unassociated with its existing business, using no additional staff or premises, but which contributes substantially to that company's profits? HMRC contends correctly that the CFC legislation was enacted as an anti-avoidance measure. There are a number of ways of doing this.'

6

Changes of source and residence

Previous chapters have largely presumed a scenario of an existing and continuing cross-border investment or income flow. In that context, Chapter 2 considered the competing jurisdictions to tax of source and residence countries. The purpose of this chapter is to consider the tax consequences of creating, transferring, terminating or varying those jurisdictions. As a result, this chapter is largely concerned with the effect on the *tax attributes* of a taxpayer of a change in jurisdiction. *Tax attributes* are features of a tax system attributable to a taxpayer that are carried forward to future periods. The most common example of a tax attribute is the tax value of assets. The value of an asset for tax purposes in one period may have an impact on the taxability of the holder of the asset in future periods, e.g. where the asset is sold or otherwise disposed of. The same can be true of liabilities. There are other types of tax attributes, such as the carry forward of losses and tax credits.

One matter that is not considered a tax attribute is human capital. While humans are clearly assets in that they have the capacity to produce income, as do other assets, humans are not recognised as assets for tax purposes and have no *tax value*. So, while many countries complain of 'brain drain' when residents with earning capacity leave their jurisdiction, no country seeks to tax exiting individuals on the basis of their potential earnings (or give humans a tax value when they arrive in a jurisdiction). Countries may make it difficult to shake off residence but that is about the limit of their efforts. The issue is not mute, especially for countries that provide state funded education that may be viewed as an investment in the human capital that later takes flight.

This chapter is structured under two primary headings. The first considers changes in the source/host country jurisdiction and the second changes in residence/home country jurisdiction. The issues covered by this chapter are at the fringes of what can usefully be achieved in a book of this nature. They tend to be largely technical matters of domestic law and little regulated by international tax norms such as those in the OECD

Model. The exception is within the EU, where EU Law has important implications.

In practice, globalisation means that the issues covered by this chapter are of particular significance. Globalisation has caused particular impetus for changes in the manner in which multinationals structure their business activities. With respect to source countries, multinationals seek efficiency gains by centralising control and management of manufacturing, research and distribution functions.[1] This 'business restructuring' typically involves the 'redeployment of functions, assets and/or risks between associated enterprises, with consequent effects on the profit and loss potential in each country'.

Since the mid-1990s, business restructurings have typically consisted of:

- Conversion of full-fledged distributors into limited-risk distributors or commissionnaires for a related party that may operate as a principal,
- Conversion of full-fledged manufacturers into contract-manufacturers or toll-manufacturers for a related party that may operate as a principal,
- Rationalisation and/or specialization of operations (manufacturing sites and/or processes, research and development activities, sales, services),
- Transfers of intangible property rights to a central entity (e.g. a so-called 'IP company') within the group.[2]

Similarly, globalisation has caused increased source/host country activity in cross-border takeovers, including by way of mergers and divisions. However, the pressure is not purely on source countries. Residence countries find it increasingly difficult to found their jurisdiction to tax based on corporate residence. There have been high-profile examples in recent years of multinationals 'jumping ship' by moving the residence of their parent corporation offshore. This problem is becoming acute in the UK and some link it to an increasingly aggressive approach to the taxation of foreign profits, particularly the UK tax administration's responses to ECJ decisions in *Marks & Spencer* and *Cadbury Schweppes*.[3] The ongoing review of the taxation of foreign profits intends to soften this approach.

Any tax advice that involves planning (as opposed to the effects of an existing arrangement) needs to consider the types of issues covered by

[1] OECD (2008c, para. 53).

[2] OECD (2008c, para. 3).

[3] Case C-446/03 *Marks & Spencer* v *Halsey* [2005] ECR I-10837 (ECJ) and Case C-196/04 *Cadbury Schweppes* [2006] ECR I-7995 (ECJ). Regarding a number of high profile cases of corporations moving their residence from the UK for tax reasons, see Jackson (2008c).

this chapter. Because the rules that govern these issues are highly technical and context and country specific, this chapter covers the issues in outline only.

6.1 Changes of source jurisdiction

There are only so many ways in which a jurisdiction to tax based on source may change. The source of income may be created, the source may be terminated, ownership of the source may be transferred or the form of the source activity may be varied. Each of these possibilities is considered in turn. The discussion briefly outlines the issues for both the source/host country and the country of the owner's residence. This is followed by an outline of additional issues arising under EU Law.

6.1.1 Creation of source

As noted at 2.1.2.1, income and wealth may be created by the provision of labour, the use of assets or a combination of both. So to create a source of income within a particular jurisdiction typically involves locating assets or labour there. For reasons discussed above, it is only pre-existing assets that carry with them tax attributes and so assets not labour is the subject of the present discussion. Of particular relevance is the expansion of an existing foreign business into a source country. As noted in Chapter 3, business activity will typically give rise to a source country jurisdiction to tax only when a PE or subsidiary is created. The present discussion focuses on the transfer of existing assets from one country (for present purposes considered to be the residence/home country) to a PE or subsidiary in another country (the source country).

Transfer of assets to PE

The current situation involves the transfer of an existing business asset from a head office in one country (the residence country) to a PE in another (the source country). Typically, this will involve tangible movable assets, although the OECD recognises that it is possible to attribute intangible property to a PE.[4] The primary issue for the countries concerned is whether the transfer is recognised as a disposal (realisation) by the head

[4] OECD (2008a, paras. 105–28).

office to the PE. As there is no actual change of ownership (as the PE is part of the head office entity), this could only be due to a deemed disposal. Supported with the application of transfer pricing rules, such a disposal may give rise to the crystallisation of any unrealised gain (or loss) with respect to the asset, and so tax consequences in the residence country. It will also affect the cost base of the asset for the PE for both the residence and source countries.

The OECD Model does not restrict the right of residence countries to tax any gain on transfer of an asset to a foreign PE. This is a matter for domestic law. A residence country has an interest in taxing such a gain because after the transfer it will lose its jurisdiction to tax the gain as a source country. This is particularly acute if the residence country uses the exemption method of foreign tax relief for foreign PEs. The right to tax a gain accruing with respect to an asset will be lost if it is transferred to a foreign PE. However, this will also be an issue if the residence country adopts the foreign tax credit method as the PE state will secure the primary taxing right with respect to any subsequent disposal of the asset to a third party via Article 13 of the OECD Model. If the PE country does tax the gain, the residence country will be required to credit that tax under Article 23B.

While assets used in a business may incorporate unrealised gains, they may also incorporate unrealised losses. If transfers to a foreign PE are recognised at market value, the residence country might find that loss assets are transferred to a foreign PE and not gain assets. This would be an example of *cherry picking*, whereby related parties may transfer assets between themselves in order to crystallise losses. It is for this reason that many countries, including the UK, have a book value rule for transfers between related parties.[5] Recognising gains but not losses on transfers to foreign PEs involves a clear inconsistency.

For the PE country, the issue is the cost base of the asset in the hands of the PE. The two options here are taking the historic cost base of the head office or granting a step up (or down) in cost base to market value. On a subsequent disposal of the asset by the PE, the former may result in taxation by the PE country of gains accruing before the asset fell within its jurisdiction. Historically, many countries have not viewed such taxation as inconsistent with the OECD Model. However, with the broader adoption of the separate enterprise approach to PEs in Article 7 of the OECD

[5] For example, TCGA 1992 s. 171.

Model and its Commentary, there is a strong argument that a PE must take the transferred asset at its market value.[6]

Consistent with the matters discussed in Chapter 5, the source and residence countries may take differing views of this matter. This can result in double taxation or non-taxation of some gains. Double taxation can arise where the residence country taxes at the time of transfer but the PE country requires the PE to take up the asset at its historic cost. In such a case, the PE country may tax the gain already taxed by the residence country when the PE disposes of the asset to a third party. Question whether such an approach would be inconsistent with Article 24(3) of the OECD Model. It is not clear how the cost base (tax value) of assets transferred to a PE might be affected by this provision, the point of comparison with an independent enterprise being unclear. However, as noted, it is arguable that the new approach to Article 7 requires a market value cost base.

Non-taxation can arise in the reverse case where the residence country does not tax the outbound transfer but the PE country gives the PE a market value cost base. On a subsequent disposal by the PE, the PE state will not tax the gain accruing before the asset was transferred to the PE. The residence country may still tax such a gain if it uses the foreign tax credit method of foreign tax relief but not if it uses the exemption method.

A particular country may now take inconsistent views depending on whether it is the residence or PE country. For example, historically the UK has not recognised the transfer of an asset into or out of its jurisdiction as a realisation event unless it involves a transfer of ownership. As discussed above, the new approach to Article 7 of the OECD Model may require the UK to give a market value cost base to an asset transferred into the jurisdiction, at least where the asset is transferred to a UK PE. By contrast, there is no regulation where the asset is transferred out of the jurisdiction to a foreign PE and here the UK's traditional approach continues to apply.

EU Law issues arising from such a transfer are largely unexplored by the ECJ.[7] From the residence country's perspective, it is arguable that a transfer to a PE in another member state is comparable to a transfer between places of business within the residence country. This might suggest that taxation by the residence country of the unrealised gain at the time of transfer to the PE is contrary to the freedom of establishment or free movement of capital, although deferral of that taxation until the

[6] OECD (2008a, e.g. at para. 231).

[7] The Mergers Directive (1990) does not cover this sort of transfer.

time of disposal to a third party is likely to be acceptable.[8] Such a position seems at odds with the new approach to Article 7 of the OECD Model.

By contrast, as far as the PE country is concerned, it may be argued that taxation of any gain attributable to the period before transfer to the PE (e.g. on disposal to a third party) is a restriction on the creation of a PE if the residence country also taxes that gain. However, foreign tax relief provided by the residence country seems capable of curing any such restriction.[9]

Transfer of assets to subsidiary

The considerations are different where the outbound transfer is to a subsidiary established in the source country rather than a PE. Here there is a transfer of ownership and a realisation as the subsidiary is a separate legal entity from the parent corporation in the residence country. The residence/home country would have the right to tax any gain on the disposal including by reason of applying transfer pricing rules, and Article 9 of the OECD Model supports this.

Considerations in the source/host country are more difficult. Here the issue is the same as with respect to the PE scenario: does the subsidiary take a market value cost base or is the cost base the historic cost of the asset in the hands of the foreign parent? It is doubtful that Article 9 of the OECD Model can have any impact in such a scenario so as to require the source/host country to give the subsidiary a market value cost base. This can be contrasted with the possible application of Article 7 in the PE scenario discussed above. As with Article 24(3) in the case of a PE, using Article 24(5) to argue that the subsidiary must be given a market value cost base is problematic.

The reason why the source/host country might impose the parent corporation's historic cost on the subsidiary is analogous to the PE situation discussed above. At that point, it was noted that transfers of assets between places of business of a single entity within the same country are not a taxing event because there is no change of ownership. As part of their corporate

[8] This scenario falls within the European Commission's study of exit taxes. Presently, the European Council prefers to deal with this matter through a suggested coordination between member states in the form of guiding principles. In particular, these guidelines recognise the right of the home country (where the head office is situated) to tax the transfer. See European Union (2008).

[9] The European Council guidelines suggest that where the home country (where the head office is situated) reserves its right to tax the transfer (whether currently or on a deferred basis), the PE country should take 'the market value on the transfer date when calculating the subsequent added value in the event of disposal'. See European Union (2008).

group taxation system, many countries provide an analogous treatment for transfers between two corporations within a corporate group. So, for example, a transfer of a capital asset between two resident members of a 75 per cent corporate group in the UK is considered to take place for an amount that gives rise to neither gain nor loss (book value transfer).[10]

If the residence/home country extends this group relief to outbound transfers, then a step up in cost base to market value by the source/host country in the hands of the subsidiary might result in some non-taxation. When the asset is disposed of to a third party, neither country will tax any gain attributable to the period before transfer to the subsidiary. As with the case of a PE, if the residence/home country taxes any gain on the transfer to the subsidiary, but the source/host country transfers the parent corporation's cost base to the subsidiary, any subsequent transfer to a third party may produce some double taxation. Again, these problems of non-taxation or double taxation arise from mismatch, i.e. countries taking different approaches to the same issue. They are more extensive in the case of a subsidiary than a PE because (absent the application of controlled foreign corporation rules) there is no scope for the foreign tax credit method to provide any reconciliation.

The UK does not generally extend the book value transfer rule to international transfers between parent corporations and their subsidiaries.[11] Where the UK is the source/host country of the subsidiary, this results in a cost base of market value. Where the UK is the residence/home country of the parent corporation, the result is a potential immediate charge to UK corporation tax of any gain on the transfer.[12] This is inconsistent with the UK treatment of the PE scenario discussed above. Further, the potential immediate charge to tax where the UK is the residence/home country raises issues of incompatibility with EU Law, which, in the present situation, are generally similar to those discussed in the context of a PE.

6.1.2 Termination of source

The present situation involves the termination by a person resident in one country of a source of income located in another country, i.e. the reverse of

[10] TCGA 1992 s. 171. This provision applies automatically, i.e. it is not elective.

[11] In particular, see TCGA 1992 s. 171(1A), which requires the transfer to involve resident corporations or UK PEs of non-resident corporations.

[12] This also means that any loss will be recognised. However, as the parent corporation and the subsidiary will be 'connected persons', the loss will be quarantined and available only to reduce gains on transfers between those two parties; TCGA 1992 s. 18.

the creation scenario considered at 6.1.1. To the extent that this situation involves the sale of assets to a third party, the considerations discussed below at 6.1.3 will be relevant. Otherwise, the termination of a source investment will typically involve moving tangible movable property. It may be possible to move intangible property, but equally the termination of an intangible investment may involve abandoning the intangible. The present situation will again be considered by looking first at the liquidation of a PE and then the liquidation of a subsidiary.

Transfer of assets from a PE

The liquidation of a PE will typically involve the sale of property, including immovables, and residually the repatriation of any remaining property (typically tangibles) to head office. As mentioned, the liquidation may involve the abandonment of some property such as intangibles. Sale and abandonment will typically involve a disposal with any resulting tax consequences for the PE. Repatriation is different as, because the PE is not a separate legal entity, there is no loss of ownership. An issue is whether the source country will nevertheless recognise a disposal for tax purposes.

Article 7 of the OECD Model seems to permit treating repatriation of assets on the liquidation of a PE as a notional disposal subject to tax.[13] An additional issue is whether this notional disposal falls within a domestic charge to tax in the source country. For example, in the UK it is generally accepted that a 'disposal' for capital gains purposes requires a transfer of ownership.[14] On this basis, the repatriation of an asset from a UK PE to a foreign head office is unlikely to constitute a disposal and so fall within charge to UK tax. Any unused carry-forward losses of the PE in the source country are likely to represent an intangible benefit that disappears with the liquidation of the PE. In the case of the UK, it may be possible to carry forward any such loss to set against the profits of another UK PE if that PE is part of the same trade as the liquidated PE (see below at 6.1.3).

In the residence country, the issue is whether the repatriation of an asset from a foreign PE affects the cost base of the asset for the head office, i.e. whether the head office gets a step up in cost to market value. A tax treaty based on the OECD Model seems to have no impact on this issue. A step up seems likely in a country that adopts the exemption method with respect to profits of foreign PEs. However, in the UK, a foreign tax credit country in this respect, the repatriation is not recognised as a disposal and so there

[13] OECD Commentary to Article 7 paras. 21 and 22.

[14] See Tiley (2008, p. 709).

will be no step up to market value. Any carried-forward loss of the liquidated PE recognised by the residence country is likely to be treated in the same manner as where the PE is sold, as to which, see below at 6.1.3.

EU Law issues reflect those discussed at 6.1.1, with a twist. The liquidation of a PE involves no obvious exercise of the freedom of establishment. Even if the establishment of the head office were recognised for this purpose, this establishment is not of a national of another contracting state (but rather a national of the head office state). Perhaps the free movement of capital might have some residual application in this regard. If the comparator is the transfer of an asset by a PE to another place of business within the source country then there is at least an argument that the source country may not impose a charge to tax when a PE repatriates an asset to head office. Again, there is a possible inconsistency between the OECD approach and EU Law.

The failure of a country like the UK to give a step up in cost base on repatriation may raise EU Law issues when the head office finally sells the asset. If the source country has legitimately taxed the part of the gain accruing while the PE held the asset (whether at the point of repatriation or disposal to the third party), there may be some double taxation and no obvious method to relieve it.[15] There is some argument that the residence country should provide a step up in cost base. Equally, however, the ECJ may find that the double taxation is just a consequence of the joint exercise of the jurisdiction to tax, as in *Kerckhaert and Morres* (see above at 4.1.1.3).[16]

Transfer of assets from a subsidiary

The liquidation of a source/host country subsidiary is likely to yield very different results to the liquidation of a PE. In this case, there will be two consequences of the liquidation. First, all the assets of the subsidiary will be disposed of. This may result in the subsidiary realising gain or loss on disposal. The UK adopts such an approach, including a market value rule where the assets are distributed/disposed of to the foreign parent corporation.[17] For reasons discussed above at 6.1.1, the UK book value rule

[15] One possibility under an OECD Model style tax treaty is use of Art. 25(3) to residually relieve double taxation by mutual agreement.

[16] Case C-513/04 *Kerckhaert and Morres* v *Belgium State* [2006] ECR I-10967 (ECJ). The European Council guidelines discussed above at 6.1.1 also apply in the context of transfers from a PE to a head office, European Union (2008). However, these guidelines do not directly bind member states.

[17] TCGA 1992 ss. 17 and 18. As noted in footnote 12, any loss on disposal is quarantined and may only be set against gains on disposal to the parent corporation.

for transfers between group corporations would not be available. Further, any unused losses of the subsidiary would be lost with its liquidation.

The second consequence of liquidating the subsidiary is that remaining assets of the subsidiary will be distributed to the parent corporation. As noted at 3.3.3, some countries, including the UK, treat liquidation distributions as solely in exchange for the disposal of shares in the liquidated corporation. Where the source/host country adopts such an approach, it may have limited taxing rights over any gain on the disposal due to Article 13(5) of the OECD Model. Other countries, including for example Australia and Germany, view profits distributed in liquidation as a dividend and subject that part to any dividend withholding tax, subject to limits in Article 10 and EU Law. With respect to the latter, question whether a liquidation distribution is a 'distribution of profits' for the purposes of the Parent-Subsidiary Directive (1990).[18]

The residence/home country of the parent corporation may not agree on the classification of such a distribution by the source/host country. Nevertheless, for reasons discussed above at 4.1.1.2, the residence/home country is obliged to provide foreign tax relief with respect to any dividend withholding tax, even if, as in the case of the UK, it classifies a liquidation distribution as solely in exchange for the disposal of shares.

The situation is typically different with respect to any tax imposed by the source/host country on the subsidiary due to the disposal of assets occurring because of the liquidation. Here, underlying foreign tax relief is likely to be available only if the residence/home country classifies part of the liquidation distribution as a dividend. The UK, for example, will not classify the liquidation distribution of a foreign subsidiary as a dividend and this means that an underlying foreign tax credit or exemption is not available.[19] However, in many cases this will not be relevant, as the UK will not tax the gain on disposal of an active subsidiary's shares by the UK parent corporation due to the substantial shareholder exemption.[20] Many

[18] As noted below at footnote 21, the Parent-Subsidiary Directive (1990) Art. 4(1) specifically excludes liquidation distributions from the requirement that the country of the parent corporation provides underlying foreign tax relief. There is no such requirement in Arts. 5 and 6, which exempt the distributions of subsidiaries from source country taxation. The implication seems to be that a source country cannot tax distributions of profits in the liquidation of a subsidiary to a parent corporation.

[19] TIOPA 2010 s. 14 simply refers to a 'dividend', as do the relief from double taxation articles in UK tax treaties. CTA 2009 s. 931A excludes the inter-corporate dividend exemption for capital distributions.

[20] TCGA 1992 Sch. 7AC.

European countries that also adopt a participation exemption would adopt a similar approach.[21]

The parent corporation acquires the assets disposed of by the subsidiary (other than those assets that are lost or expire). This raises the issue of the cost base of these assets in the hands of the parent corporation for purposes of the residence/home country tax system. Again, the choice is between using the book value of the assets in the hands of the subsidiary or using market value (step up in cost base). Unlike in the situation of the liquidation of a PE, in this case a UK parent corporation would receive a step up in cost base. As discussed above at 6.1.1, this is because the UK book value rule does not apply where international factors are involved.

6.1.3 *Transfer of ownership of source*

The present situation involves the sale by a person resident in one country of a source of income located in another country. Generally, this is a realisation event and gives rise to possible taxation of gain on the disposal both in the source country and the residence country. For the source country, this is generally governed by Articles 7 and 13 of the OECD Model and was discussed above at 3.1.5. For the residence country, this will be an issue of foreign tax relief for any source country tax and was discussed above at 4.1.1.

As for the carry-forward of tax attributes with respect to the source country investment, there are two matters worthy of further discussion. The first relates to the non-chargeability of the transfer if it is between related parties. This is viewed as a variation of the source country investment and is discussed below at 6.1.4. The second is the consequences of the change of ownership for any losses that may have been incurred from the source before the transfer and that are being carried forward. The discussion of this second issue is limited to the consequences on the sale of a PE and the sale of a subsidiary. Each of these is considered in turn. There are no further EU Law issues in the present situation in addition to those discussed above at 3.1.5 and 4.1.1.

Transfer of a PE

Because a PE is not a separate legal entity, the sale of a PE to a third party is a sale of the assets of the PE rather than the sale of an ownership interest

[21] The Parent-Subsidiary Directive (1990) Art. 4(1) specifically excludes liquidation distributions from the requirement that the country of the parent corporation provides underlying foreign tax relief.

in the PE. So under many countries' tax laws, different assets of the PE (e.g. trading stock, depreciable assets and non-depreciable assets) must be considered separately to determine any gain or loss on the disposal. This gain or loss will be attributable to the PE and so the source country will have a right to tax under Article 7 or 13 of the OECD Model. The residence country must provide foreign tax relief for any source country taxation under Article 23. This will be by way of either exemption or foreign tax credit.

If the PE has incurred a loss, most countries will view this as a loss attributable to the owner of the PE rather than the assets that constitute the PE. Consequently, if there are carry-forward losses attributable to the PE, these will stay with the transferor rather than move to the acquirer of the PE. It is irrelevant whether the PE activities are carried on in the same manner as before the acquisition. The situation on the sale of a subsidiary, discussed below, is very different.

Post sale, use of the losses by the former owner of the PE may be problematic and must be considered from the perspective of both the source country and the residence country. The problem in the source country may be the lack of available source country profits to set the losses against. For example, in the UK the PE losses of a non-resident corporation can be used against any other profits of the corporation subject to UK corporation tax in the year the loss was incurred or in the previous year.[22] As non-PE UK source income of a non-resident corporation is subject to UK income tax rather than corporation tax, this means that any such losses can only be set against profits of that PE or another UK PE. The result is that the PE losses cannot be set against income subject to UK withholding tax, such as passive rents, royalties and interest. Many other countries adopt a similar approach of not permitting PE losses to offset income subject to final withholding tax.

Losses of a UK PE that cannot be used in the way discussed in the previous paragraph can be carried forward, but only for set off against profits of the trade of which the PE is a part.[23] With the sale of the PE, these losses are likely to be unusable. The exception is the rare situation where the non-resident continues (overseas) the trade of which the PE is a part and then creates a further PE in the UK as part of that continuing trade. It seems arguable that in such a case the losses of the previous PE may offset

[22] CTA 2010 s. 37. If the whole trade of which the PE is a part (including any part of the trade outside the PE country) is discontinued on the sale, the carry-back period is extended to three years.

[23] CTA 2010 s. 45.

any profits of the new PE subject to UK corporation tax. This sort of treatment is not common in other countries.

So far as the residence country is concerned, the use in the residence country of losses of a foreign PE was discussed above at 4.2.2. As noted at that point, often the losses of a foreign PE may be used against domestic source income. In the UK, the rules discussed above also govern the use by the head office of losses incurred by a foreign PE provided the PE is part of a trade that is partly carried on in the UK. In such a case, the foreign PE losses may be set against any taxable profits of the UK corporation of the current or previous year (three year carry-back if the whole trade is ceased). Unused losses belong to the whole trade (and not just the foreign PE) and so may continue to be carried forward to reduce the profits of the trade despite the sale of the PE that gave rise to the losses. Again, this treatment is quite peculiar to the UK. If the foreign PE is not part of a trade carried on in the UK (e.g. part of a trade carried on wholly outside the UK), then any loss may be carried forward only to set against chargeable profits of that trade, i.e. cannot be set against any other chargeable profits of the UK corporation.[24]

Transfer of a subsidiary

The situation is very different with respect to the sale of a subsidiary. The subsidiary is a separate legal entity and the sale will be a sale of the shares in the subsidiary rather than a sale of the assets of the subsidiary. Typically, this means that Article 7 of the OECD Model is inapplicable and the source/host country is granted only limited, if any, taxing rights under Article 13. This difference with the treatment of the sale of a PE is a major distortion that was touched on at 3.1.5 and in practice is the subject of substantial amounts of tax planning.

A further consequence of the separate legal identity of the subsidiary is that any losses incurred from the activities of the subsidiary belong (subject to any consolidation regime) to the subsidiary and stay with the subsidiary despite the owner selling the subsidiary. This also makes for a major difference in the treatment of the sale of subsidiaries when compared with the sale of PEs. Again, the situation requires investigation from the perspective of both the source/host country and the residence/home country.

Assuming the subsidiary remains a resident of the source/host country, the subsidiary will be able to carry forward its losses despite the change of ownership unless the country has anti-abuse rules to prevent this. Most

[24] CTA 2010 s. 37(5).

countries have rules that prevent a corporation carrying forward losses after a change of control of the corporation. These rules are highly technical and vary from country to country. Assuming more than 50 per cent of the shares in the subsidiary are sold, most countries, including the UK, prohibit the future use of losses incurred before the takeover. Typically, the issue of whether the new or old owner of the corporation is resident or non-resident is irrelevant under these rules and so no obvious issues of discrimination arise.

Many countries have a saving rule that permits future use of the losses despite a takeover if the corporation continues to conduct substantially the same business activity as before the change in control. In the UK, this is expressed in terms of denying the use of the losses if there is both a change in control and a 'major change in the nature or conduct' of the trade that gave rise to the loss.[25] Where these saving rules apply, the new owner indirectly becomes the owner of the losses incurred before the acquisition. This is very different from the situation discussed with respect to the sale of a PE.

As for the residence/home country, as noted above at 4.2.4, generally no relief for the losses of foreign subsidiaries is available to set against profits of a domestic parent corporation or other group members. So there is no possibility of using the actual losses of the subsidiary in that country. However, losses of the subsidiary may cause the owner of the subsidiary to make a loss on the sale of the shares in the subsidiary. This possibility of a reflective duplication of the losses of a subsidiary is a fundamental feature of the artificial nature of corporations.[26]

If a parent corporation is selling shares in a foreign subsidiary, many countries exempt any gain and refuse to recognise any loss on the sale. The UK adopts this approach if the subsidiary is a trading subsidiary and certain other conditions are met.[27] There is some inconsistency here with the UK treatment of the sale of a PE where the UK would exercise jurisdiction to tax based on residence (subject to foreign tax credit relief). If the shares do not meet the trading subsidiary test, the UK quarantines the use of any loss on sale of the shares so that it may only reduce capital gains on the disposal of assets.[28] However, the loss is not otherwise quarantined and so can be used against gains on UK assets.

[25] CTA 2010 ss. 673 and 674.

[26] Use of a reflective loss was in issue in Case C-347/04 *Rewe Zentralfinanz eG* v *Finanzamt Koln-Mitte* [2007] ECR I-2647 (ECJ), discussed above at 4.2.4.

[27] TCGA 1992 Sch. 7AC.

[28] TCGA 1992 s. 8.

6.1.4 Variation of form of source

The form of a source of income may be varied. The point in this case is that there is some formal event involving the creation, transfer or termination of a source, or a combination of these, but the quantum of interest of the source holder both before and after the event may be viewed as similar. That is, in the variation case the original source may be viewed as in some way identifiable with the source after the event. The present situation involves variation of the form of a source and not its geographical location, i.e. the source country both before and after the event is presumed to be the same.

The ways in which a source may be varied are limited. One form of source may be substituted for another form, a case of conversion. Second, one source may be merged with another source, whether the holder of the other source is related in some way with the holder of the first-mentioned source or not. Third, a source of income may be split, divided or demerged into two or more smaller or fragmented sources. Each of these variations will be considered in turn.

These scenarios essentially involve cross-border amalgamations and reconstructions, possibly the most complex part of international tax. Consistent with the nature of this chapter, the following discussion is relatively high level and avoids technical details. In particular, triangular situations and those involving hybrid entities are not considered. Further, the discussion focuses on the treatment of corporations as the most common, i.e. the treatment of individuals is not dealt with. In the context of EU Law, the Mergers Directive (1990) is particularly relevant in each of these scenarios and will be cited frequently, but a detailed consideration of this Directive must be sought elsewhere. The fundamental freedoms are referred to less frequently, but the potential for their application in particular cases should not be discounted.

6.1.4.1 Conversions

The present situation involves converting the form of a source of income. Except in extreme cases, this involves the incorporation or de-incorporation of the source of income, i.e. the inserting or removal of a corporation between the source of income and its owner. It is rare for one type of asset to actually be converted into another type of asset, but this can happen, e.g. with the conversion of securities. Consistently, the present discussion focuses on the two main examples of the conversion case, the conversion of a source country PE into a subsidiary and the conversion of a subsidiary into a source country PE.

PE into subsidiary In an international setting, it is common to expand a business into a new country through a PE and then, when the business is profitable and established, to convert it into a subsidiary. In this way, early year losses, a common feature of new expansion overseas, may be granted relief in the residence/home country, see above at 4.2.2. When the new overseas presence becomes profitable, conversion into a subsidiary may ensure that the profits are not taxable in the residence/home country, at least not before repatriation. This makes the availability of incorporation relief when a PE is converted into a subsidiary important. Some residence/home countries seek to recapture the use of foreign PE losses on incorporation of that PE.[29] The UK does not seek such a recapture.

The present situation presumes that a corporation resident in Country B has a PE in Country A. The corporation forms a new subsidiary and transfers the PE to it, usually in exchange for shares in the subsidiary. If the assets forming the PE incorporate any unrealised gains (their market value is higher than their tax value), the transfer to the subsidiary may result in recognition and taxation of such gains to the parent corporation. Many countries, including the UK, provide for deferral of charge to tax on incorporation.[30] Often the relief is available only if the whole business or an identifiable segment of a business is transferred, but in other cases the relief is available on an asset-by-asset basis.[31] A further issue is, where a business is transferred, whether any carried-forward losses from that business may also be transferred to the subsidiary. Most often the answer is 'no', but in the UK this is possible where a parent corporation transfers a trade to a 75 per cent subsidiary.[32]

These issues are replicated for both source/host and residence/home countries. Assuming the new subsidiary is resident in the source/host country, that country has the right to tax any gain on the transfer of the PE's assets. An issue is whether it will grant incorporation deferral to the

[29] This is recognised by the Mergers Directive (1990) Art. 10(1)[2].

[30] In the UK, the precise form of relief depends on whether the incorporator is an individual or a parent corporation. For individuals, relief may be provided by ITTOIA 2005 s. 178 (trading stock), Capital Allowances Act 2001 s. 267 (depreciation of plant and machinery) and TCGA 1992 ss. 162 and 165 (capital assets). For parent corporations, relief may be provided by CTA 2010 s. 948 (depreciation of plant and machinery) and TCGA 1992 s. 171 (capital assets). No relief for trading stock is provided for corporations.

[31] The UK adopts a mixed approach, the most flexible rules being TCGA 1992 ss. 165 and 171, which can be applied on an asset-by-asset basis. Generally regarding incorporation relief, see Tiley (2008, pp. 854–6).

[32] CTA 2010 s. 944.

non-resident owner of the PE. Often this will be the case, as it is in the UK under the provisions cited in the last paragraph.

The residence/home country will also have the right to tax any gain on the transfer, subject to an obligation to provide foreign tax relief for any source/host country tax either unilaterally or under the equivalent of Article 23 of the OECD Model. Again, the residence/home country may grant incorporation deferral. The problem with granting this deferral is that the residence/home country will lose its right to tax disposals of the assets by the new subsidiary, as the subsidiary is resident in the source/host country. For this reason, the UK does not grant incorporation deferral as a residence/home country in this situation.[33] The residence/home country will have the right to tax any gain on the disposal of the shares in the new corporation held by the incorporator, but this will be subject to any prior right of the source/host country to tax.

The new subsidiary may be resident in the same country as the owner of the PE rather than in the PE country. In this situation, the PE of the owner will become a PE of the new subsidiary. This situation is unlikely to make much difference to treatment in the source/host country. For example, the UK would still grant incorporation deferral as the assets remain within the charge to corporation tax. The change in situation is more likely to mean a different treatment in the residence/host country, as that country will no longer lose its taxing rights over the PE assets. So, for example, where the new subsidiary is resident in the UK and the parent corporation is also resident there, incorporation deferral will be available despite the transferred assets being situated in another country. If the new subsidiary is resident in some third country, the UK will not grant incorporation deferral.

Within the EU, the Mergers Directive (1990) affects the conversion of a PE into a subsidiary. The Directive formally applies to certain 'operations' involving companies from two or more member states.[34] It does not apply to operations involving only one company, e.g. the incorporation of a PE held by an individual. In particular, it applies to a 'transfer of assets', which covers the typical conversion of a PE into a subsidiary. The transfer must be of a 'branch of activity', defined as assets and liabilities, that,

[33] An exception is TCGA 1992 s. 162, which applies irrespective of whether the business remains within the charge to UK tax. This is because when this provision applies, the new corporation, in any case, receives the capital assets at market value for tax purposes, i.e. a step up in cost base.

[34] Mergers Directive (1990) Art. 1(a).

in principle, constitutes an 'independent business, that is to say an entity capable of functioning by its own means'.[35] So, it is not possible to transfer individual assets in this situation under the protection of the Directive. Further, the transfer must be in return for 'securities' in the receiving company, although no quantum of holding is specified.

Article 10 of the Directive is particularly relevant to the present situation. Through a convoluted process, it requires the source/host country to exempt capital gains on the disposal of the PE's assets,[36] although it seems that this is conditional on the new corporation not receiving a step up in tax value of these assets (as would typically happen where the transfer is taxed).[37] Unused losses of the PE must also be available for transfer to the new corporation, but only if the transfer would be available between two resident corporations. The UK loss transfer rules permit a UK PE of a non-resident corporation to transfer current year losses to a similar UK PE or a resident corporation provided all the corporations are within a 75 per cent held group.[38]

Article 10 of the Directive also requires the residence/home country to refrain from taxing the transfer of the PE. The exception to this exemption is where that country taxes the parent corporation on a worldwide basis. In this case, the residence/home country is required to give a deemed foreign tax credit for tax that the source/host country would have levied if it had not exempted the transfer. The UK, as a worldwide country, has implemented this requirement.[39]

Subsidiary into PE Less common is the conversion of a subsidiary into a PE. This may be achieved in a number of manners. The subsidiary may continue but transfer its source/host country business to its parent corporation. There are two primary issues here: recognition of any gain on the transfer and, where the transfer is not at market value, a possible dividend distribution to the parent corporation. Again, both the source/host and residence/home countries face these issues.

The source/host country may provide deferral from tax on the transfer as it retains taxing rights over the assets in the form of the PE of the parent

35 Mergers Directive (1990) Art. 2(j).

36 The process is convoluted because the substantive provisions are in Mergers Directive (1990) Arts. 4, 5 and 6, which are applied via Art. 9 with a particularly important deeming rule in Art. 10(1)[3]. The rule seems to be intended to cover the recapture of depreciation (balancing charges) but this is not entirely clear.

37 Mergers Directive (1990) Art. 4(4).

38 CTA 2010 ss. 99 and 107.

39 TIOPA 2010 s. 122 and TCGA 1992 s. 140C, discussed further below.

corporation. Deferral is possible in the UK.[40] If the transfer is not at market value, the source/host country may view the transfer as a dividend and subject it to dividend withholding tax. While the UK may recognise a distribution, it does not tax non-resident corporations in receipt of distributions from UK corporations, see above at 3.1.4.1.[41]

An additional issue for the source/host country is the treatment of any unused losses of the subsidiary on transfer of its business to the PE. Group relief may be available between the subsidiary and the PE if the subsidiary continues, although some countries, like the UK, permit group relief only in the year in which the loss is incurred.[42] However, if the subsidiary goes into liquidation, it will no longer qualify for group relief in the UK because the parent corporation will no longer be considered to have the requisite holding for the purposes of that relief. Alternately, it is possible to transfer losses (even carried-forward losses) from the subsidiary's trade to the PE with the transfer of the trade itself.[43] Again, as a 75 per cent beneficial holding is required, this option is available only for transfers before any liquidation.

As for the residence/home country, it will be gaining a direct right to tax the transferred assets (subject to an obligation to provide foreign tax relief), as subsequently a resident corporation will hold them. The issue for it is whether to recognise the transfer at the subsidiary's book value or to give a market value cost (step up). The UK approach with respect to this issue seems somewhat confused.[44] If the transaction is at less than market value, the residence/home country must also determine whether to recognise a distribution to the parent corporation or not. If it does, underlying foreign tax relief will be an issue. In the UK, the undervalue might

[40] CTA 2010 s. 944 (depreciation of plant and machinery) and TCGA 1992 s. 171 (capital assets). No relief for trading stock is provided.

[41] CTA 2010 s. 1020. This rule is excluded for transactions between UK resident group corporations. The exemption of distributions to non-resident corporations seems to remedy any issue of discrimination under EU Law and, in any case, the Parent-Subsidiary Directive (1990) likely covers the distribution.

[42] CTA 2010 s. 99.

[43] CTA 2010 s. 944.

[44] For trading stock, a market value cost may be granted under the equivalent of OECD Model Art. 9(2) (corresponding adjustment) of any applicable tax treaty, but this seems to be excluded if deferral relief is provided in the source/host country. (TIOPA 2010 ss. 147 and 155 (trading stock) seems inapplicable because typically there will be no UK tax advantage.) CTA 2010 s. 948 seems to mandate (without election) a book value transfer for assets subject to capital allowances. For capital assets, TCGA 1992 ss. 17 and 18 (s. 171 is inapplicable) seem to require a market value cost.

be taxed with underlying relief if it constitutes a 'dividend' and 'income' in the hands of the UK parent corporation.[45]

The issues are broadly the same if the subsidiary does not continue. It may be liquidated or, under reorganisation rules, dissolved without liquidation. Availability of the latter option depends on the corporate law of the country in question. Often, it is not available in common law countries like the UK. Dissolution of the subsidiary may make a difference to classification of the transfer of assets to the parent corporation. The assets will still be disposed of and this will raise issues of taxation of the subsidiary in the source/host country and the tax value of the assets in the hands of the parent corporation under both the tax law of that country and the residence/home country. These issues broadly follow those discussed above.

In addition, there will be a clear distribution by the subsidiary to the parent corporation, particularly if it is liquidated. As noted above at 3.3.3, some countries classify this for tax purposes as a dividend to the extent of the subsidiary's residual profits, which the source/host country may subject to dividend withholding tax. Other countries, like the UK, classify liquidation distributions as an affair of capital. There is also a disposal of the shares in the subsidiary, which in a typical case will be taxable only in the residence/home country, see above at 3.1.5. The UK may exempt such a disposal from taxation under the substantial shareholder exemption.[46]

As for the treatment of losses in the residence/home country, it is very unlikely that the loss of a foreign subsidiary carrying on business overseas can be transferred to a foreign PE of the resident parent corporation. Such relief would not be available in the UK, although, within the EU, there may be some argument for the extension of the section 944 procedure (mentioned above) based on the *Marks & Spencer* decision, discussed above at 4.2.4.[47] In particular, it seems that this procedure would

[45] TIOPA 2010 s. 57 provides an underlying foreign tax credit against corporation tax in respect of a 'dividend'. A 'dividend and other distribution' may be subject to corporation tax if it is not 'capital in nature'; Corporation Tax Act 2009 s. 931A (contrast individuals who are only subject to income tax on 'dividends' of non-resident corporations; ITTOIA 2005 s. 402). Importantly, the definition of 'distribution' in CTA 2010 s. 1000 does not apply in determining whether a distribution of a non-resident corporation is a 'dividend'. If the amount is 'capital in nature', it is likely a 'capital distribution' for the purposes of TCGA 1992 s. 122. In this regard, the substantial shareholder exemption may be relevant, TCGA 1992 Sch. 7AC.

[46] TCGA 1992 Sch. 7AC.

[47] Case C-446/03 *Marks & Spencer* v *Halsey* [2005] ECR I-10837 (ECJ).

be available where a UK resident subsidiary with a foreign PE transferred the trade incorporating the PE to its UK resident parent corporation.

It remains to consider the other issues where the subsidiary is not resident in the source/host country. Rather, the subsidiary is resident elsewhere but has a PE in the source/host country that is transferred to its parent corporation. For many source/host countries, including the UK, this is unlikely to make a difference. In the UK, both the subsidiary's PE and the subsequent parent corporation's PE are within the charge to corporation tax and transfers between them will be treated largely in the same fashion as transfers between two resident corporations. If a source/host country recognises a dividend on the transfer, it is unlikely to seek to tax, as from its perspective this will be a dividend distributed between two non-resident corporations.

Similarly, in the residence/home country, the treatment is likely to be the same where the subsidiary is resident elsewhere than in the source/host country. The exception may be where the subsidiary is resident in the residence/home country (with a PE in the source/host country). Here, the subsidiary will already be within the charge to residence/home country taxation with respect to its foreign activities. So, in the UK, this will make a difference to the treatment of the transfer of assets between the subsidiary and the parent corporation.[48] It will also make a difference as to whether there is any distribution between the subsidiary and the parent corporation.[49] Further, any distribution will now be between two resident corporations and so will likely be exempt (no foreign tax credit).[50] Group relief is likely to be available for current year losses, and carried-forward losses of the subsidiary should be available for transfer with its trade to the parent corporation, before the subsidiary goes into any liquidation.[51]

Within the EU, the Mergers Directive (1990) is again relevant for the conversion of a subsidiary into a PE. This conversion may constitute a 'merger' if the parent corporation holds all the securities in the subsidiary, i.e. it is a wholly owned subsidiary, and the subsidiary is dissolved without going into liquidation.[52] This is difficult and uncommon in the UK and

[48] For trading stock, the transfer should be at market value; TIOPA 2010 s. 147. Capital assets, including those subject to capital allowances, will be transferred at book value; CTA 2010 s. 948 and TCGA 1992 s. 171.

[49] CTA 2010 s. 1000 will apply.

[50] CTA 2009 ss. 931B and 931D.

[51] CTA 2010 ss. 99 and 944, respectively.

[52] Mergers Directive (1990) Art. 2(a)(iii). In exceptional cases, there might also be a 'transfer of assets' under Art. 2(c), but this would involve the subsidiary continuing and the

at least requires approval by a court. The Directive generally requires the two corporations to be from different member states and so relief provided by the Directive is not available where the subsidiary and parent corporation are resident in the same country.[53]

Where the Directive does apply, the substantive provisions of the Directive apply, including non-taxation of capital gains and the possible transfer of losses. These were discussed above in the context of the conversion of a PE into a subsidiary. In addition, Article 7 of the Directive is relevant in the present scenario. It excludes from taxation any gain on the disposal of the shares held by the parent corporation in the subsidiary. This is commonly covered by a participation exemption under domestic law.[54] It must be remembered that the Directive applies only where the subsidiary is dissolved without liquidation.

6.1.4.2 Mergers

The issues discussed above at 6.1.4.1 are matters that an average tax adviser might face. The matters discussed under this subheading are more technical, country specific and specialist. They are covered in outline only in this book for purposes of completeness. They concern the merging of sources of income where multiple parties are involved in a cross-border setting. The rules that govern these scenarios are typically an extension of the rules that apply to purely domestic situations. Within the EU, these are overlaid with the Mergers Directive (1990). As with the last subheading, the focus is on PEs and corporations, rather than other particular sources of income.

The mergers considered by this subheading are fundamentally of two types. The first involves one corporation acquiring a business from another corporation in return for the first corporation issuing shares to the other corporation or its shareholders. For present purposes, this is referred to as an 'assets merger'. The second involves one corporation acquiring the shares of another corporation in return for the first corporation issuing shares to the existing shareholders of the other corporation. For present purposes, this is referred to as a 'corporate merger'. Commonly, in either case, the acquisition is made through a special purpose vehicle, i.e. a holding corporation. This can be important for a number of tax reasons,

parent corporation issuing shares to the subsidiary, something that the corporate law of many countries, including the UK, would resist.

[53] Mergers Directive (1990) Art. 1.

[54] The UK's rather narrow participation exemption for capital gains is in TCGA 1992 Sch. 7AC.

including the form of financing the acquisition and future strategies for exit from the acquisition. However, the use of holding corporations in the context of a merger is beyond the scope of this book.

Assets mergers The present scenario involves a corporation (the acquirer) resident in one country (the home country) acquiring from another corporation (the transferor) a business (the target business) located in another country (the host country) in return for the acquirer issuing shares to the transferor or the transferor's shareholders. The transferor may be resident in the host country or not. If not, the business is presumed to constitute a host country PE.

The issues raised by an assets merger are similar to those discussed above at 6.1.4.1 in the context of converting a PE into a subsidiary. There will be a disposal of the business and issues arise as to the recognition of any gain on that disposal and the treatment of other tax attributes of the business such as carried-forward losses. In addition, there is the issue of the cost base (tax value) of the issued shares in the hands of the transferor or transferor's shareholders. Many countries have rules that deal with assets mergers in a purely domestic scenario. Most often, the present situation requires a consideration of how those basic rules apply when international factors intervene.

For example, in the UK relief is available from any capital gains arising on an assets merger provided that 'substantially the whole' of the transferor's 'business' is transferred to the acquirer in return for the acquirer issuing shares to the transferor's shareholders (not the transferor itself).[55] Post merger, the shareholders in the transferor spread the cost base (tax value) of their existing shares in the transferor over any shares they continue to hold in the transferor and the shares they receive in the acquirer, according to their respective market values. No gain is recognised on the disposal of any shares in the transferor.[56] There is greater flexibility within 75 per cent corporate groups.[57]

[55] TCGA 1992 s. 139 and Sch. 5AA. It seems no relief is available for any balancing charge for excess capital allowances as Capital Allowances Act 2001 s. 266 requires the acquirer and transferor to be under common control. There is also no relief for a gain on the transfer of trading stock.

[56] TCGA 1992 s. 136.

[57] This is due to TCGA 1992 s. 171. In addition, relief from balancing charges under Capital Allowances Act 2001 s. 266 may be available and any carried-forward losses attributable to a transferred trade may be transferred under CTA 2010 ss. 944 and 948.

In an international scenario, these UK rules continue to apply provided the business is and remains within the charge to corporation tax. So, where the business is located in the UK, i.e. the UK is the host country, there will be relief from tax on the transfer of assets.[58] Relief for shareholders on disposal of any shares in the transferor is not subject to any international qualification, but the UK does not tax capital gains of non-residents unless the assets are held through a UK PE, see above at 3.1.5.

The position is generally the same where the UK is the home country and so tax relief will be available only on the transfer of the foreign business where both the transferor and the acquirer are resident in the UK. However, relief is unilaterally extended to the situation where a foreign PE of a UK corporation is transferred to a non-resident corporation in return for more than 25 per cent of the ordinary share capital of the non-resident corporation.[59]

Within the EU, the Mergers Directive (1990) will apply provided the acquirer and the transferor are from different member states.[60] The present scenario is a 'transfer of assets'.[61] The meaning of this phrase was discussed above at 6.1.4.1. It is not clear that the scope of its meaning coincides with 'substantially the whole' of a business as used in UK domestic law, but this law is extended in an EU setting to cover the transfer of 'part of a trade' situated in the UK.[62] In any case, the Directive has direct effect (see above at 1.2.3 and 1.3.3). The operative provisions of the Directive triggered by a 'transfer of assets' were also considered above at 6.1.4.1, including the transfer of assets at book (tax) value and the possibility for the transfer of losses.[63] There is no provision in the Directive dealing with the treatment of shareholders in the transferor (who will be receiving shares in the acquirer) in the case of a 'transfer of assets'.

The Directive does not specify any particular quantum of shares to be issued by the acquirer in the case of a transfer of assets. Where the UK is the home country, the UK requirement that the acquirer issue 25 per cent of its ordinary shares is in apparent conflict with the Directive. Accordingly, relief is provided with respect to any gain on transfer by a UK corporation of an EU PE to another EU corporation in exchange for

58 TCGA 1992 s. 139(1A).
59 TCGA 1992 s. 140.
60 Mergers Directive (1990) Art. 1.
61 Mergers Directive (1990) Art. 2(d).
62 TCGA 1992 s. 140A (transfer of UK business) and Capital Allowances Act 2001 s. 561.
63 Mergers Directive (1990) Arts. 4, 5 and 6 applied by Art. 9.

securities issued by the acquirer. Rather than exempt the foreign transfer from UK corporation tax, the UK seeks to implement Article 10(2) of the Directive. In this case, any net gain on the transfer is taxable, but a foreign tax credit is available for the tax that would have been collected in the country of the PE but for the Mergers Directive.[64] It seems that allowances and charges may arise in this case under the Capital Allowances Act 2001.

An assets merger may also involve a 'partial division' under the Directive.[65] This requires that the transferor retain at least 'one branch of activity'. There seems to be scope for conflict here with the UK requirement of transfer of 'substantially the whole' of the transferor's business, but again relief has been especially extended in an EU context.[66] In the case of a partial division, the same operative provisions apply as in the case of a 'transfer of assets'. In addition, taxation of the shareholders in the transferor may be excluded, e.g. where part of the holding in the transferor is disposed of or where the issue of shares to the shareholders by the acquirer might otherwise be considered a distribution by the transferor.[67]

Corporate mergers The present scenario involves a corporation (the acquirer) resident in one country (the home country) acquiring shares in another corporation (the target) that has a business located in another country (the host country) in return for the acquirer issuing shares to the target's shareholders. The target may be resident in the host country or not. If not, the business is presumed to constitute a host country PE. Where the target is not dissolved, the merger is a simple share exchange involving the question of taxation of gains on the disposal of shares in the target and the cost base (tax value) of the shares received in the acquirer. An additional issue is the cost base of the shares in the target received by the acquirer. Further, if there is a change in control of the target there may

[64] TCGA 1992 s. 140C and TIOPA 2010 s. 122. This relief does not apply where relief is available under TCGA 1992 s. 140, i.e. where the transferor is issued with more than 25 per cent of the ordinary shares in the transferee.

[65] Mergers Directive (1990) Art. 2(c).

[66] In particular, TCGA 1992 ss. 140A and 140C. The UK rules in TCGA 1992 Sch. 5AA para. 4 seem to assume that the whole undertaking of a corporation is a single business, i.e. a corporation with multiple businesses is not envisaged.

[67] Mergers Directive (1990) Art. 8(2). Again, this exemption might be lost if the shareholder is granted a step up in cost base with respect to holdings in the transferor and acquirer post merger; Art. 8(5).

be limitations on the target's ability to use certain tax attributes in the future, such as the use of carried-forward losses and excess credits.

Where the target is dissolved, there is the additional issue of the disposal of assets by the target and the possible classification of this disposal as a distribution. Further, as the target disappears, there is no possibility for it to continue to use tax attributes such as carried-forward losses or credits. So, an additional issue is whether such tax attributes may be transferred to and used in the future by the acquirer. In the UK, the dissolution is most likely to be by way of liquidation as the UK (like a number of common law jurisdictions) does not have a simple corporate procedure for legal mergers (fusions), as do many other countries.[68] Again, countries' tax laws often have basic rules governing mergers in domestic scenarios. The question is whether and in what manner these might be extended in an international scenario.

In the UK, most mergers are done by way of share exchange. The UK has very liberal rules for deferring any shareholder gain on a disposal of shares in a target.[69] In particular, the acquirer need have or acquire only 25 per cent of the target or make a general offer for the shares in the target irrespective of the level of shares it actually acquires. As for the acquirer, typically it is considered to acquire the shares in the target at market value, i.e. a step up in cost base.[70] Most other countries transfer the cost base of the former shareholders in the target to the acquirer. The share exchange may result in a change in control of the target. The target will lose its ability to carry forward trading losses only if it also suffers a major change in its trade.[71]

If, in addition, the target is to be dissolved, the UK has no general rules for the transfer of tax attributes in such a situation. Rather, the issues and treatment will be similar to those discussed above at 6.1.4.1 with respect

[68] In particular, a fusion in the UK usually requires court approval; Companies Act 2006 Parts 26 and 27 (ss. 895–941). These rules are supplemented for cross-border fusions by the Companies (Cross-Border Mergers) Regulations 2007 (SI 2007/2974), but still require court approval.

[69] TCGA 1992 s. 135. It is also possible to do this by way of 'reconstruction' under TCGA 1992 s. 136 (discussed above in the context of assets mergers). This involves a cancellation of existing shares in the target and a reissue of target shares to the acquirer in return for the acquirer issuing shares to the target's former shareholders, see Cooklin (2008, p. 618).

[70] TCGA 1992 s. 17 (although interpreting this rule to apply is not without technical difficulty).

[71] CTA 2010 s. 673. The rules for the future use of capital losses (including unrealised losses) are very different and complex; see TCGA 1992 ss. 16A, 177A, 179, 179A, 184A-F and Sch. 7A and Tiley (2008, pp. 680–4, 967–73).

to the conversion of a subsidiary into a PE. In particular, it is likely to be advantageous to transfer the target's business to the acquirer before the liquidation process begins. Any relief for the transfer may be complicated by the existence of built-in or carried-forward capital losses in the target or carried-forward capital losses in the acquirer, but these matters are beyond the scope of this book.

Projecting these issues into an international setting, relief for shareholders on disposal of shares in the target is not subject to any international qualification, i.e. similar to the situation in an assets merger. The international features for a transfer of a trade from the target to the acquirer (if the target is to be liquidated) were outlined above at 6.1.4.1 in the context of the conversion of a subsidiary into a PE.

Within the EU, again the Mergers Directive (1990) will apply provided the acquirer and the target are from different member states.[72] The present scenario is an 'exchange of shares' or a 'merger', the latter requiring a dissolution without liquidation, which is unlikely in the UK.[73] In particular, a 'merger' requires 'all the assets and liabilities' of the target to be transferred to the acquirer. An 'exchange of shares' requires the acquirer to have or obtain 'a majority of the voting rights' in the target. As noted above, the UK rules on share exchanges are more generous than this.

The operative provisions of the Directive triggered by a 'merger' are the same as those considered above at 6.1.4.1, including the transfer of assets at book (tax) value and the possibility for the transfer of losses.[74] There are no analogous provisions for share exchanges. In particular, there is no provision preventing the loss of tax attributes such as losses of the target if it suffers a change in control. In the case of either a merger or a share exchange, shareholders are not to be taxed in respect of the disposal of their shares in the target.[75] In the usual way, this non-taxation may be lost if the shareholder receives a step up in cost base, but it seems that the step up must be at the election of the shareholder and not determined by the cost base at which the acquirer takes up the target's shares.[76]

[72] Mergers Directive (1990) Art. 1.

[73] Mergers Directive (1990) Art. 2(e) and (a), respectively.

[74] Mergers Directive (1990) Arts. 4, 5 and 6. In the case of a merger/fusion involving the UK, TCGA 1992 ss. 140E and 140G may also be relevant to prevent tax being charged on the disposal of assets of the target and shares in the target.

[75] Mergers Directive (1990) Art. 8.

[76] In Case C-285/07 *AT* v *Finanzamt Stuttgart-Körperschaften* [2008] ECR 00 (ECJ), a French corporation acquired a German corporation by way of share exchange. The

In recent years, the UK has seen, as host state, a number of high profile 'inversions' or 'migrations'. This involves inserting a foreign parent corporation between an existing UK resident parent corporation and its shareholders. This is usually done by having the foreign parent corporation issue shares to the UK corporation's shareholders in exchange for their shares in that UK corporation, i.e. a share exchange. Post merger, subsidiaries under the UK corporation can be restructured to be held directly by the new foreign parent corporation. This can be particularly useful for extracting foreign passive income from the scope of the UK's CFC regime, but other accusations have been made against the UK corporate tax system in recent years to warrant this sort of inversion. These include an increasingly strict approach to tax planning (as tax avoidance) including a disclosure regime, increasing compliance costs (including with respect to transfer pricing documentation), increasingly complex tax law, uncompetitive corporate tax rates and uncertainty regarding international tax reforms.[77]

6.1.4.3 Divisions

The issues discussed under this subheading are analogous to those discussed above at 6.1.4.2 in that they are technical, country specific and specialist. They concern the demerging, division or splitting of a source of income where multiple parties are involved in a cross-border setting. In the usual way, these rules are an extension of the rules that apply to purely domestic situations and, within the EU, are overlaid with the Mergers Directive (1990). Again, the focus is on PEs and corporations.

As with the mergers considered above at 6.1.4.2, the divisions considered by this subheading are fundamentally of two types. The first involves the situation where a corporation wishes to transfer ownership of a business that it holds to its own shareholders, here referred to as an 'assets division'. This may involve a simple distribution in kind giving rise to

French corporation recorded the shares of the German corporation in its books at their market value. German law required the German shareholders to treat the exchange as taking place at the same value, i.e. market value. This resulted in a step up in cost base for the German shareholders of the shares acquired in the French corporation but also resulted in the taxation of the disposal of their shares in the German corporation. The ECJ held this additional restriction (based on the book value at which the French corporation took up the shares in the target) and the resulting taxation were contrary to the Mergers Directive (1990).

77 See Cooklin (2008).

the type of issues discussed above at 6.1.3. The situation considered here involves the transfer of that business to a new holding corporation, which in return issues shares to the shareholders of the transferor. The second type is the simple and common division involving a corporation that holds shares in a subsidiary distributing those shares to its own shareholders, here referred to as a 'corporate division'.

Assets divisions The present scenario involves a corporation (the transferor) resident in one country (the home country) with a PE located in another country (the host country) transferring that PE to a corporation (the receiving corporation) in return for the receiving corporation issuing shares to the shareholders in the transferor. The receiving corporation may be resident in the host country or not.

One issue in the assets division case is whether any gain may be realised on the transfer of the PE by the transferor to the receiving corporation. If the PE has carried forward tax attributes such as losses, a further question is whether these can be transferred to the receiving corporation with the PE. Finally, there is the additional issue of the cost base of the shares in the receiving corporation received by the shareholders of the transferor and the disposal of shares in the transferor (if any). An underlying issue is whether the nature of the division gives rise to recognition of a distribution by the transferor corporation or not. Again, countries' tax laws often have basic rules governing divisions in domestic scenarios. The question is whether and in what manner these might be extended in an international scenario.

In the usual way, the UK uses a number of uncoordinated rules to deal with assets divisions. Relief from recognition of any gain on the transfer of at least 'substantially the whole' of a business to the receiving corporation is available.[78] Under separate rules, if the transferor ceases to carry on a trade and the receiving corporation begins to carry it on, carried-forward losses attributable to that trade may be transferred to the receiving corporation with the trade.[79] This is because the same persons own the transferor and the receiving corporation.[80] The same rule provides relief from the recapture of any excess depreciation granted to the transferor

[78] TCGA 1992 s. 139. The definition of 'reconstruction' in Sch. 5AA was extended in 2002 to specifically include divisions.

[79] CTA 2010 s. 944.

[80] CTA 2010 s. 941.

with respect to transferred assets. There is no analogous relief for any gain on the transfer of trading stock.

The UK excludes assets divisions from distribution treatment provided certain conditions are met.[81] In particular, the transferor may retain at most a minor interest in the trade of which the PE is a part. As for changes in the shares held by the transferor's shareholders, this constitutes a 'reconstruction' for the purposes of UK tax on capital gains.[82] The result is no recognition of any gain on disposal (if any) of shares in the transferor. The cost base of the shares held by the shareholders in the transferor before the division is spread over shares held in the transferor and receiving corporation post division, according to their respective market values.

In an international scenario, these UK rules continue to apply provided the business of which the PE is a part is and remains within the charge to corporation tax. So, where the business is located in the UK, i.e. the UK is the host country, there will be relief from tax on the transfer of the PE.[83] The capital gains treatment of shareholders on acquisition of shares in the receiving corporation and disposal (if any) of shares in the transferor is not subject to any international qualification. The position is the same where the UK is the home country and so tax relief will be available only on the transfer of the PE where both the transferor and receiving corporation are resident in the UK. The exemption of any distribution arising from an assets division was qualified by the requirement that both the transferor and receiving corporation be resident in the UK, but in late 2009 this was amended to refer to other member states.[84]

Within the EU, again the Mergers Directive (1990) will apply provided the transferor and receiving corporation are from different member states.[85] The Directive envisages two types of assets division. The situation currently under consideration is a 'partial division', commonly referred to as a 'split-off'.[86] The requirements of a partial division were outlined above at 6.1.4.2 in the context of assets mergers.

[81] CTA 2010 ss. 1073–99.

[82] TCGA 1992 s. 136 and Sch. 5AA.

[83] TCGA 1992 s. 139(1A). Relief from balancing charges and transfer of losses are subject to a similar qualification; CTA 2010 ss. 944 and 948.

[84] CTA 2010 s. 1081.

[85] Mergers Directive (1990) Art. 1.

[86] Mergers Directive (1990) Art. 2(c).

The consequences of such a division were also mentioned at that point, including the transfer of assets at book (tax) value and the possibility for the transfer of losses and non-recognition of any gain to the shareholders of the transferor corporation.[87] Also discussed at that point were the special UK rules implementing the Directive, which are extended to cover asset divisions.

The second type of assets division envisaged by the Directive is a full 'division', commonly referred to as a 'split-up'.[88] This requires the assets and liabilities of the transferor be split and transferred to at least two separate receiving corporations in exchange for the issue of shares by those corporations to shareholders of the transferor. In order to qualify, however, the transferor must be dissolved without going into liquidation. As previously mentioned, UK corporate law does not facilitate this type of reorganisation without a court approval and so this option is discounted from the present discussion.[89]

Corporate divisions The present scenario involves a parent corporation resident in one country (the home country) with a subsidiary that has a business located in another country (the host country) transferring the shares that it holds in the subsidiary to its own shareholders. The subsidiary may be resident in the host country or not. If not, the business is presumed to constitute a host country PE. This form of division is commonly referred to as a 'spin-off'. A corporate division may have tax consequences for each of the parties involved. The shareholders may be considered to have received a distribution and there is the question of the cost base of the shares they acquire in the subsidiary. The parent corporation has disposed of its shares in the subsidiary, raising the issue of recognition of any gain on the disposal. The subsidiary has suffered a direct change in ownership, raising the question of the carry forward of tax attributes such as losses.

The UK rules excluding assets divisions from the definition of 'distribution' also apply to corporate divisions.[90] The requirement is that the subsidiary whose shares are distributed is at least a 75 per cent subsidiary of the parent corporation. This type of distribution is expressly

[87] Mergers Directive (1990) Arts. 4, 5, 6 and 8(2).

[88] Mergers Directive (1990) Art. 2(b).

[89] Special rules for European companies are not considered.

[90] CTA 2010 s. 1076.

excluded from being a capital distribution for purposes of capital gains and the reorganisation rules are applied.[91] These provisions do not deal with the treatment of the parent corporation on disposal of the shares in the subsidiary. Often this will be covered by the substantial shareholder exemption.[92] Where this is not available, another possibility is to transfer the shares in the subsidiary to a new holding corporation in return for that corporation issuing shares to the parent corporation's shareholders.[93] If, because of the division, the subsidiary moves out of the 75 per cent corporate group of which it was formerly a part, it can continue to use carried-forward losses only if it suffers no major change in the conduct of its trade.[94]

Projecting these issues into an international setting, the distribution is an exempt distribution only if both the parent corporation and the subsidiary are resident in the EU. The discussion above in the context of assets divisions is relevant in this regard. In the present case, the risk that a resident might be taxed due to receiving the shares where the subsidiary is not resident in the UK seems greater. This may well be a 'distribution' of the parent corporation and, if not, it is likely to be a capital distribution with respect to the shares held in the parent corporation and so may give rise to a capital gain.[95] As far as the disposal by the parent corporation of the shares in the subsidiary is concerned, the UK substantial shareholder exemption applies to both shares in resident subsidiaries and shares in non-resident subsidiaries.

Within the EU, the present form of corporate division does not easily fall within the Mergers Directive (1990). If the shares in the subsidiary are transferred to a new holding corporation, and the holding corporation issues shares to the parent corporation's shareholders, the operation may constitute a 'partial division' or 'transfer of assets'.[96] The parent corporation and the holding corporation would have to be from

[91] TCGA 1992 s. 192.

[92] TCGA 1992 Sch. 7AC.

[93] This may also be an exempt distribution under CTA 2010 s. 1077, but may also make use of the rules discussed above with respect to assets divisions, i.e. TCGA 1992 ss. 136 and 139.

[94] CTA 2010 ss. 673 and 724. That is, the subsidiary suffers a change of ownership despite its underlying or indirect ownership not having changed. The rules for the future use of capital losses (including unrealised losses) are very different and complex; see footnote 71 above.

[95] CTA 2010 s. 1000(1)B and TCGA 1992 s. 122.

[96] Mergers Directive (1990) Art. 2(c) and (d).

different member states.[97] However, in order to qualify, the shares held by the parent corporation must fall within the definition of a 'branch of activity'.[98] It is not clear that the simple holding of shares in a subsidiary can qualify as such. If it can, then the only relevant operative provision appears to be the transfer of the shares to the new holding corporation at book (tax) value.[99]

6.2 Changes of residence jurisdiction

Assets are sources of income the ownership of which can be transferred. By contrast, residence is a matter particular to a person and cannot be transferred. Further, save in exceptional circumstances, it is not possible to vary residence. Accordingly, there are only two sets of issues pertaining to changes of residence: those on the creation of residence and those on termination. Each will be considered in turn.

6.2.1 Commencing residence

Tax attributes that may be affected by commencing to be resident in a particular country typically involve the cost base (tax value) of assets that are thereby brought within the charge to tax in that country. Usually, these are assets located outside the country. The choice here is between historic cost, e.g. the price for which the foreign asset was originally acquired, and market value at the time residence is commenced, i.e. a step up in cost base. The UK does not grant a step up in cost base when residence is commenced. The consequence is that when the person subsequently disposes of an asset that was brought within the UK tax jurisdiction by the acquisition of UK residence, the UK may tax gains attributable to the time before the person became resident.

Other types of carried-forward tax attributes are unlikely to be recognised by the residence country when a person commences residence. For example, if the person has a carried-forward loss in their previous country of residence, this will not be recognised by their new country of residence.

Complications can occur in the year in which a person obtains residence. An issue is whether a person can be resident for full years only or whether they can also be resident for a part of a year. If a person

[97] Mergers Directive (1990) Art. 1.
[98] Mergers Directive (1990) Art. 2(j).
[99] Mergers Directive (1990) Art. 4.

is considered resident for full years only, the country may tax foreign source income derived before residence is commenced if it is derived in the same year as the residence commences.[100] If a person can be resident for part of a year, complications may occur with respect to exemption, credit and rate thresholds. Often, these are applicable only to residents and an issue is whether those thresholds are apportioned where a person is resident for part of a year only. The UK tax administration does accept that a person can be resident for part of a tax year, but the UK does not generally seek to apportion exemptions, credits and rate thresholds.[101]

A change in residence can often cause a change in the source of payments made by the person and so cause a change in the taxation of the recipient of such payments. In the context of the OECD Model, this is particularly relevant in the case of interest. The country where the payer becomes resident may thereby gain a right to tax the interest, see above at 3.1.4.2. The same is true of dividends where a distributing corporation moves residence. In some cases, this may improve the tax situation of the recipient. Foreign subsidiaries of UK corporations with low taxed profits (not subject to the CFC regime) have been known to move their residence to the UK before distributing those profits. Once resident in the UK, their distributions were covered by the UK inter-corporate dividend exemption rather than, at least historically, the underlying foreign tax credit regime, thus avoiding UK corporation tax on the distribution.[102]

6.2.2 *Cessation of residence*

The cessation of residence gives rise to a similar set of issues. Here, there is typically a loss of tax jurisdiction over assets located outside the country. The question is whether these assets are treated as disposed of at market

[100] This may result in a person being considered resident in two countries for a particular year. Regarding the application of the tiebreaker in OECD Model Art. 4(2) in such a case, see Commentary to Art. 4 para. 10.

[101] *Smallwood* v *RCC* [2009] EWHC 777 (Ch) especially at para. 44 and generally, see Tiley (2008, p. 1102). Of particular relevance for present purposes, the threshold for the small companies rate of tax is calculated by reference to profits on which corporation tax is borne; CTA 2010 s. 32. As noted above at 2.1.1.2, the *Smallwood* case also suggests that a person can be resident for part of a year for tax treaty purposes.

[102] The inconsistency has been removed by the introduction of the general exemption for inter-corporate dividends introduced in 2009, CTA 2009 ss. 931B and 931D.

value when residence is lost. Taxation arising on such a deemed disposal is commonly referred to as an 'exit charge'. The UK does not impose an exit charge on migrating individuals, but there is a potential charge if a former resident disposes of assets whilst non-resident and then reacquires UK residence.[103]

The situation for corporations that lose their UK residence is different.[104] They are treated as disposing of all their assets for market value just before residence ceases.[105] The exception is for assets that are subsequently held through a UK PE. The purpose of this provision is to crystallise a UK charge to corporation tax on chargeable gains before jurisdiction over those gains is lost. The tax charge may be postponed if the emigrating corporation is a 75 per cent subsidiary of another UK corporation, in which case the charge will be triggered by certain future events including the sale of the emigrated subsidiary.[106] There is no equivalent charge for income gains, e.g. disposal of trading stock or recapture of excess capital allowances.

Where residence is moved to another EU member state, there is a serious question as to whether any exit charge is consistent with free movement of individuals or, in the case of corporations, the freedom of establishment. Case law applicable to individuals confirms the inappropriateness of exit charges, but it seems some proportionate measures may be acceptable.[107] What may be acceptable in the context of corporate exit charges is currently unclear. In particular, under prior UK tax law, a corporation needed Treasury consent to move its residence from the UK. In an early direct tax case, the ECJ refused to find that this was contrary to the freedom of establishment.[108]

As noted above at 6.1.1, the European Council has issued guidelines with respect to exit charges, including on a change of corporate residence.[109] These guidelines recognise a right to impose exit taxes, whether on a current or deferred basis, and, where that right is exercised, require

[103] TCGA 1992 s. 10A.

[104] Simply moving the effective management of the corporation to another country may cause residence to be lost, even for corporations incorporated in the UK. This assumes an OECD Model style treaty applies; see above at 2.1.1.2.

[105] TCGA 1992 s. 185.

[106] TCGA 1992 s. 187.

[107] Case C-9/02 *Hughes de Lasteyrie du Saillant* [2004] ECR I-2409 (ECJ) and Case C-470/04 *N* v *Inspecteur van de Belastingdienst Oost/kantoor Almelo* [2006] ECR I-7409 (ECJ).

[108] Case 81/87 *R* v *HM Treasury & CIR (ex parte Daily Mail and General Trust plc)* [1988] ECR 5483 (ECJ).

[109] European Union (2008).

the country to which the corporation is moved to give a market value cost to assets for tax purposes. The guidelines do not bind member states or the ECJ in applying the fundamental freedoms. It is noteworthy that member states could not even agree to prevent exit charges where a European company transfers its registered office from one member state to another.[110]

[110] Mergers Directive (1990) Arts. 12, 13 and 14 prevent exit charges for European Companies, but only with respect to assets connected with a PE in the state from which the corporation is emigrating. The Directive may be viewed as recognising a right to impose exit taxes.

7

Bilateral administrative issues

After dealing with source country and residence country taxing rights, the OECD Model is rounded out with a number of provisions targeted at bilateral tax administration issues. There are four core areas of tax administration, collection of information, assessment, dispute resolution and collection of tax. A tax administration needs access to information for purposes of making or checking tax assessments. This access may be either voluntary (e.g. by the taxpayer submitting a return) or forced (e.g. audit powers). Based on the information collected, an assessment or tax decision will be made. These are of two types, either self-assessment by the taxpayer or an administrative assessment, including an amendment of a self-assessment.

Once an assessment or tax decision is set or accepted by the tax administration, there is scope for dispute with the taxpayer regarding, among other things, the quantum of the assessment. Accordingly, tax laws typically provide two mechanisms for resolving disputes. The first is a review procedure internal to the tax administration, commonly called an 'objection' procedure. If the taxpayer and the tax administration fail to reach agreement, there is usually a subsequent independent review. Commonly, this will be to a specialist tax tribunal with the potential for further appeal to the general courts, although in some countries the appeal is directly to the general courts.

Finally, at least when the assessment or tax decision is not disputed (or not capable of dispute), there is the issue of collecting tax or enforcing the decision. Here again there are usually two mechanisms. There is collection directly from the taxpayer and the taxpayer's assets but the tax laws of most countries also provide for situations in which recovery may be from a third party, e.g. a person owing money to the taxpayer such as a bank.

The OECD Model devotes three provisions to core tax administration issues in a bilateral setting. Each of these involves the 'competent authorities' of the contracting states. Provision for definition of this phrase appears in Article 3(1)(f) of the Model. It is usually the tax administration, a representative (e.g. the Commissioner) or the Minister of Finance. Article 26 deals with the exchange of information between tax administrations of the contracting states. Article 25 provides a peculiar mechanism for the resolution of disputes, not between the taxpayer and the contracting states but between the contracting states themselves, although the taxpayer may get involved. Article 27 is devoted to assistance in the collection of taxes.

Each of these provisions is considered in turn and the discussion expands to cover certain multilateral agreements including those between EU member states. While the issues covered by this chapter are important, this is not a book focused on tax administration. Accordingly, and in a similar vein to the last chapter, the following discussion provides a brief overview only.

7.1 Exchange of information

A tax administration's power to require the provision of information is critical in any tax system, but this is particularly so in an income tax. The information needed to calculate income tax liability is often exclusively in the possession of the taxpayer. Most countries' tax administrations fought and won the battle over access to taxpayer information many years ago but this is more problematic in a cross-border setting. The powers of a tax administration will not extend into another country without that country's agreement or questionable behaviour, such as acting without agreement. The OECD Model has always contained a provision for the cooperation of tax administrations in exchanging information.

As noted above at 2.2.1, exchange of information became the central aspect of the OECD's harmful tax competition project in the late 1990s. As part of the outcome of that project, in 2002 the OECD produced an agreement on Exchange of Information in tax matters. Unlike the OECD Model, this is a multilateral treaty. The OECD's exchange of information project was given a particular boost because of events beginning in 2008. Bank secrecy has been a perennial problem in exchange of information. Wealthy individuals hide their untaxed wealth in secret foreign bank accounts that their country of residence cannot access. Jurisdictions such as Switzerland, Belgium, Liechtenstein, Luxembourg and the Cayman Islands built their banking industry on the back of such secrecy and have strongly resisted moves for greater exchange of information. This was one of the reasons why a number of them dissented from the OECD Harmful Tax Competition Report.

In 2008, a Liechtenstein bank employee, reported to have received a large sum, provided information to the German tax administration on bank accounts held by high-profile German residents. The fall-out was enormous, exposing high-wealth residents of many other western countries. In the lead-up to the G-20 Summit of April 2009, the OECD threatened to expose a number of countries, not on their uncooperative tax haven list, as not complying with their standards for information exchange. The summit itself called for an end to bank secrecy and threatened sanctions against uncooperative jurisdictions identified by the OECD. The result was a spat of bilateral information exchange agreements between western countries and the countries concerned.[1]

This heading first considers Article 26 of the OECD Model. It then briefly considers OECD inspired information exchange agreements. Finally, it considers the EU context. There are two measures directed to information exchange in tax matters between EU member states. The first is a multilateral treaty concluded between member states, which treaty is not part of EU Law. The second is the Savings Directive (2003). All of the measures considered under this heading (but to a more limited extent in the case of the Savings Directive) incorporate similar provisions and concepts and no doubt affected the development of each other.

7.1.1 OECD Model

Article 26(1) of the OECD Model permits the competent authorities of the treaty partners to exchange information 'as is foreseeably relevant for carrying out the provisions' of the treaty. More controversial, it also permits exchange for the 'administration or enforcement of domestic laws concerning taxes of every kind and description', whether imposed by the treaty partners, their political subdivisions or local authorities. This seems a peculiarly broad provision to find in a treaty devoted to direct taxation and so may extend to the tax liability of persons that are a resident of neither contracting state. In this respect, the provision has similarities with Article 24 on non-discrimination. This seems to be one reason for specific treaties devoted to exchange of information, considered below at 7.1.2.

[1] Regarding the acquisition of the Liechtenstein bank details, with particular reference to the UK, see Jackson (2008a).

Exchange of information typically takes one of three different forms. It may be provided to comply with a request of the competent authority of the treaty partner. Some information is provided automatically and this is particularly the case with computer-generated records. Thirdly, the competent authority may provide information of its own initiative, i.e. spontaneously, such as where it feels that the competent authority of the treaty partner may view the information as relevant.

A providing competent authority may use its usual information gathering powers for the purposes of collecting the information to be supplied but is not obliged to do anything that the receiving competent authority could not do itself under its own laws. It is also not obliged to disclose commercial secrets or processes or provide disclosure where to do so would be contrary to public policy. Paragraph (5) of Article 26 of the OECD Model specifically states that information cannot be withheld solely by reason that it is held by a bank or financial institution.[2] By contrast, a receiving competent authority must keep information received as secret in accordance with its usual tax secrecy measures.

Article 26 of the OECD Model concerns the exchange of information by competent authorities. The taxpayer has no right in the Model to be notified that information has been or will be exchanged, although this might be a requirement of domestic law.

7.1.2 Information exchange agreements

As mentioned, a number of specialist treaties provide for assistance in tax administration and, in particular, exchange of information. The main treaty in this regard is the 1988 Convention on Mutual Administrative Assistance in Tax Matters developed by the Council of Europe and the OECD. There are currently 16 signatories to this convention, the UK having signed in 2007.[3] An Explanatory Report accompanies the Convention.

As with Article 26 of the OECD Model, the Convention applies irrespective of the residence or nationality of any person affected and with respect to a wide range of taxes, including taxes on income, profits and

[2] Bank secrecy countries including Austria, Luxembourg and Belgium traditionally reserved their right to not include Article 26 in their tax treaties. These countries have now withdrawn their reservations and so all OECD countries now accept Article 26.

[3] The delay of the UK in signing this convention seems to have been based on its historic resistance to providing assistance in the collection of foreign taxes, see below at 7.3. This legal obstacle was overcome by the Finance Act 2006 Part 9 (ss. 173–6).

capital gains. Section I of Chapter III of the Convention covers exchange of information. Like the OECD Model, it provides for on request, automatic and spontaneous exchange, but unlike that Model, it does so expressly. In addition, it provides for tax administrations of contracting parties to conduct simultaneous tax examinations and for the tax administration of one party to conduct examinations in the territory of other contracting parties.

The general inclusion of Article 26 of the OECD Model in the enormous bilateral tax treaty network means that in a vast number of cross-border circumstances tax administrations have provision for exchange of information. In many ways, the most likely countries to be excluded from such provision are the type of countries that the OECD harmful tax competition project was targeted at. As mentioned above, as an outcome of that project the OECD released in 2002 a Model Agreement on Exchange of Information on Tax Matters. The Model is targeted at countries that typically find it difficult (or do not wish) to conclude standard tax treaties due to their low tax/tax haven status.

The 2002 Model has many similarities with Article 26 of the OECD Model and the 1988 Convention on Mutual Administrative Assistance in Tax Matters. In the usual way, it is accompanied by a Commentary. The 2002 Model provides for exchange of information on request and particularly for exchange of information held by banks and regarding the ownership of various entities such as trusts and foundations. It also provides for the tax administration of a contracting state to conduct tax examinations in the other contracting state. There is the usual confidentiality/secrecy clause.

Around the time of the G-20 Summit in April 2009 numerous exchange of information agreements were concluded between members and low tax/tax haven jurisdictions and these were based on the 2002 Model (more than 25 agreements were concluded between January and April 2009). The treaty network based on the 2002 Model now numbers in excess of 100 and includes such financial centres as Andorra, Bahrain, Bermuda, the British Virgin Islands, the Cayman Islands, Guernsey, the Isle of Man, Jersey, Liechtenstein, Monaco and the Netherlands Antilles. The success of this network in the fight against tax evasion remains to be seen.

7.1.3 EU Law

As long ago as the mid-1970s, the European Communities (which became the EU) approved a Directive on Mutual Assistance for the Exchange of

Information in order to combat tax avoidance and evasion.[4] The range of taxes covered by the Directive is not as broad as Article 26 of the OECD Model or the 1988 Convention on Mutual Administrative Assistance in Tax Matters. Like the latter Convention, it expressly provides for on request, automatic and spontaneous exchange. It also provides for the collaboration of tax administrations and so simultaneous tax examinations and tax examinations in other member states are possible. As noted above at 2.2.1, the application of this Directive (or its non-application) may be important in determining available justifications to restrictions on the fundamental freedoms.

In February 2009, the European Commission released a draft directive to replace the 1977 Directive.[5] In particular, the draft would cover all taxes with a greater focus on cooperation between tax authorities. Like the 2002 OECD Model Agreement on Exchange of Information on Tax Matters, the draft would suppress the right to restrict exchange of information solely on the grounds of bank secrecy. Further, member states would be obliged to provide the same level of cooperation to their EU partners as they have agreed to with any third country. As a draft directive, this proposal requires the consent of every member state.

As also noted above at 2.2.1 and 3.1.4.2, the Savings Directive (2003) is essentially another instrument for exchange of information. It requires interest paid by a 'paying agent' (commonly a bank) in one member state to a beneficial owner resident in another to be disclosed to the residence state. For this purpose, paying agents are required to identify the beneficial owners of the payments they make and their residence. The paying agent passes this and other information regarding the payment on to the tax administration of the agent's state of establishment. This tax administration then engages in an automatic exchange of the information with the tax administration of the state of the beneficial owner. The Savings Directive expressly applies the provisions of the Exchange of Information Directive.

7.2 Dispute resolution

As mentioned, there are primarily two forms of review of tax decisions, internal review by the tax administration and independent review through the tribunal/court structure. In an international setting, these are

[4] Council Directive 77/779/EEC.

[5] European Commission (2009b).

affected by the tripartite relationship discussed above at 2.2.1. There are two tax administrations and two court systems that may engage in review of an international tax decision. These are the primary and most common forms of review of international tax decisions, but as their features are not particular to an international setting, they are not the focus of the present discussion. Rather, the focus is on special rules that provide for unified or coordinated internal or independent review in an international setting. The primary benefit of such a review is that, as it involves the authorities of both countries concerned, the taxpayer may be provided with a holistic solution to double taxation, the primary reason for review in an international setting.

The discussion below considers two review mechanisms. Both incorporate a procedure for mutual agreement between competent authorities, but both are now supported with potential arbitration to reinforce the procedure. The first mechanism is found in Article 25 of the OECD Model. The second is the EU Arbitration Convention. Both mechanisms facilitate internal rather than independent review of cross-border tax decisions and so in principle neither mechanism binds the taxpayer. By contrast, no independent court or tribunal hears and binds parties in international disputes based on tax treaties. The ECJ fulfils this role in the context of international tax disputes governed by EU Law, as does the World Trade Organisation Appellate Body in the context of the law of the GATT.

7.2.1 OECD mutual agreement procedure

Article 25 of the OECD Model provides for coordinated review by the competent authorities of taxation covered by a tax treaty, known as the 'mutual agreement procedure'. While at first blush this seems a rather peculiar procedure, on another view it is a logical extension in a bilateral setting of the typical internal review (objection) procedure adopted by most tax administrations domestically. The taxpayer generally instigates the mutual agreement procedure. This does not exclude the taxpayer's right to proceed with a dispute in the court system of either contracting state, but a tax administration may be reluctant to take up a taxpayer's case if the matter is being pursued through the courts.

Where the taxpayer considers that the actions of either contracting state will or may result in taxation contrary to the tax treaty, the taxpayer may instigate the mutual agreement procedure by presenting a case to the competent authority of their residence country. There is a three-year time limitation for presenting a case.[6] Article 25(2) of the OECD Model then obliges the competent authority of the residence country, if it cannot resolve the case itself, to approach the competent authority of the other state with a view to resolving the issue bilaterally. The authorities communicate directly, i.e. without going through diplomatic channels.[7] The residence country competent authority is required only to 'endeavour' to resolve the case with the other competent authority and so the authorities are not bound to agree a solution. Again, this is consistent with the internal review procedures of most countries.

The main legal difficulty with any mutual agreement between the competent authorities is whether there is an internal law bar to the effectiveness of the agreement. For example, domestic law time limits may prevent a tax assessment being amended in favour of the taxpayer. Article 25(2) of the OECD Model seeks to overcome this difficulty by prescribing that any agreement reached is to be implemented despite any domestic law time limits. However, a substantial number of countries, including the UK, do not include this prescription in their treaties.[8] Nevertheless, the UK does override domestic time limits for implementing mutual agreements in its domestic law.[9] It seems that one of the reasons why this provision is necessary is the absence of a formal internal review procedure in the UK.

Another difficulty is the interrelationship between any mutual agreement and court decisions. Some countries have an internal law provision that gives effect to a mutual agreement even if it is contrary to a court decision, but in others, the internal law does not permit the mutual agreement to override a court decision. The normal procedure would be for the mutual agreement to bind the tax administration, but not the taxpayer, much in the same manner as a tax rulings system. This would leave the taxpayer open to challenge the agreement in the courts. This is the position taken in the OECD Commentary. While it is likely that the UK rule mentioned in the last paragraph should be interpreted in this manner, the matter is not without doubt. To prevent any potential inconsistency, it is common for implementation of a mutual agreement to be subject to acceptance of the agreement by the taxpayer and settling of any court proceedings.[10]

6 OECD Model Art. 25(1).

7 OECD Model Art. 25(4).

8 See OECD Commentary on Art. 25 paras. 53, 54 and 97. Further, regarding this prescription, see OECD (1995–2000) paras. 4.43–4.51.

9 TIOPA 2010 ss. 124 and 125.

10 See OECD Commentary on Art. 25 paras. 31, 45 and 76. Generally, regarding the relationship between mutual agreements and interpretation of tax treaties by courts, see Avery Jones (1999).

The most frequent cases referred for mutual agreement are transfer pricing adjustments, although commonly there are also issues of which article of a treaty is applicable in a particular case.[11] The mutual agreement procedure can also be used by tax administrations to agree a tax treatment in advance, such as in the case of advance pricing agreements. The UK's use of this procedure in the case of advance pricing agreements was noted above at 3.3.1.2. The implementing legislation requires the pricing in a particular case to be determined according to the agreement rather than the law that would otherwise be relevant.[12]

The major problem with the mutual agreement procedure has not been agreements reached by competent authorities but rather their failure to reach agreements. In 2008, Article 25(1) and (2) of the OECD Model were supplemented with an arbitration procedure by introduction of a new paragraph (5).[13] This is triggered where the competent authorities fail to reach an agreement under Article 25(2) within two years after the presentation of the case by one competent authority to the other. This is not an independent review of the taxpayer's issues, but merely an extension of the mutual agreement procedure. The taxpayer has no express right to participate in this arbitration, other than to request that it occur. Further, it is not a requirement that the arbitrators be independent, they may well be tax officials of the competent authorities. Consequently, the OECD recognises that the taxpayer should not be bound by an arbitrator's decision.[14]

In addition to the specific case mutual agreement procedure instigated by the taxpayer, Article 25(3) of the OECD Model provides for what is commonly referred to as interpretative mutual agreement.[15] This provision obliges the competent authorities to 'endeavour' to resolve 'any difficulties or doubts arising as to the interpretation or application' of the tax treaty. The intention is that any agreement under Article 25(3) applies generally and is not limited to any specific case. A difficult issue is whether any interpretative agreement binds or should in any way influence interpretation of a tax treaty by the courts. This is similar to the issue discussed above with respect to specific case mutual agreement.

[11] See OECD Commentary on Art. 25 para. 9.

[12] TIOPA 2010 s. 220.

[13] Regarding OECD Model Art. 25(5), see Ault and Sasseville (2009).

[14] OECD Commentary on Art. 25 para. 76.

[15] The arbitration procedure in OECD Model Art. 25(5) does not apply to agreement under Art. 25(3).

Article 31 of the Vienna Convention on the Law of Treaties dealing with interpretation of treaties raises particular difficulties in this regard. Paragraph 3 of that Article provides:

> There shall be taken into account, together with the context:
>
> a. any subsequent agreement between the parties regarding the interpretation of the treaty or the application of its provisions.

If this provision covers a mutual agreement between competent authorities, it seems that domestic courts would be influenced by it (though perhaps not bound). This would be a somewhat bizarre reversal of the respective roles of courts and tax administrations. The usual rule is that tax administrations are to follow court decisions, not vice versa.

There are a number of difficulties in applying Article 31 to persuade courts to follow mutual agreements. First, question whether a mutual agreement is 'between the parties' for this purpose. Typically, the Executive concludes tax treaties, not the tax administration. In some countries, the fact that the tax administration is an entity separate from the government may be relevant in this regard. Even where it is not a separate entity, question whether Article 25 of the OECD Model is an effective delegation of power to the tax administration for this purpose.

Second, regard should be had to the nature of the mutual agreement procedure and its context in a tax treaty. It is an agreement between tax administrations and there seems no reason to imply in the provision an effect on persons that are not parties to the contract. Again, the approach in Article 25 of the OECD Model is consistent with a typical tax rulings system, involving case specific (private) rulings and interpretive (public) rulings. (Although, unlike public rulings, there is no requirement that mutual agreements be published.) The usual approach is that tax rulings are binding on the tax administration but not taxpayers. This is consistent with the separation of rule making powers and the administration of those rules.

There is some UK case law consistent with the position that mutual agreements between competent authorities are not binding on courts. In *Commerzbank*, Mummery J was considering a joint statement issued by the UK and US tax administrations under the 1945 tax treaty:

> [T]his joint statement has no authority in the English courts. It expresses the official view of the revenue authorities of the two countries. That view may be right or wrong. Although Article XX A authorises the competent authorities to communicate with each other directly to implement the

> provisions of the convention and 'to assure its consistent interpretation and application' it does not confer any binding or authoritative effect on the views or statements of the competent authorities in the English courts.[16]

However, this does not remove all doubts about the legal status of mutual agreements under UK law. The wording of the treaty in question merely allowed 'communication' between the competent authorities, rather than 'resolution' of difficulties or doubts as provided in Article 25(3) of the OECD Model.

Finally, the second sentence of Article 25(3) of the OECD Model empowers the competent authorities to 'consult together for the elimination of double taxation in cases not provided for in the Convention'. If this provision is interpreted to empower tax administrations to make positive rules contrary to the law otherwise governing a case, it raises constitutional issues.[17] Again, this type of argument is little different from that which arises under a general binding tax rulings system. The usual response is that a tax administration can use this sort of power only in a way that reasonably interprets the wording of the rule in question or in a case where the tax administration is given some form of discretion. Historically, the UK refrains from including the second sentence of Article 25(3) in its tax treaties but it has crept into recent treaty practice.

In 2007, the OECD published a Manual on Effective Mutual Agreement Procedures. Its purpose is to provide basic information on the operation of Article 25 of the OECD Model and to identify best practices for the mutual agreement procedure. The Manual does not impose any binding rules on member countries.[18]

7.2.2 EU Arbitration Convention

In the EU context, the Arbitration Convention is relevant.[19] This instrument was originally proposed as a directive but was finally concluded as a separate treaty. One of the main reasons for this was to remove interpretation issues from the jurisdiction of the ECJ. All members of the EU are a party to this Convention. The Arbitration Convention has similarities

[16] *IRC* v *Commerzbank* (1990) 63 TC 218 (Ch) at 241. The relevant article was added to the US/UK treaty (1945) in 1966.

[17] These are recognised by OECD Commentary on Article 25 para. 55.

[18] The Manual can be accessed on the OECD website at www.oecd.org, accessed 15 March 2010.

[19] Convention 90/436/EEC.

with Article 25 of the OECD Model, and parts of it are based on that OECD provision. In particular, it provides for mutual agreement between member states, although within strict time limits. Further, it is clear that the arbitration provisions of this Convention had a direct impact on the drafting of the OECD arbitration provision in Article 25(5) of the OECD Model. The Convention is supplemented with a Code of Conduct adopted by way of resolution of the EU Council.[20] This Code is a political agreement only, i.e. not part of the Convention.

Given a comprehensive bilateral tax treaty network between EU members states, it may be wondered why the Arbitration Convention was considered necessary. The OECD mutual agreement procedure was considered to have certain shortcomings. In particular, contracting states are not required to reach an agreement, at least before the introduction of an arbitration clause. The taxpayer has no right to be represented in mutual agreement proceedings. A PE has no right to instigate mutual agreement proceedings under the OECD Model. Each of these matters is addressed in the Arbitration Convention.

The Arbitration Convention is also narrower than Article 25 of the OECD Model (and substantially so). It applies only to disputes concerning transfer pricing and the allocation of profits between head office and PE or between PEs.[21] Indeed, Article 4 of the Convention reflects verbatim the wording in Articles 9(1) and 7(2) of the OECD Model.[22] Consequently, the Convention applies to an 'enterprise' of a member state, a term that will take its meaning from the relevant double tax treaty.[23] Where an enterprise of a member state has a PE situated in another member state, the PE itself is deemed an enterprise of the other state.[24] This is a major shift from the position under the OECD Model where PEs are not entitled to the benefits of a treaty (see above at 5.2.3.1).

The Arbitration Convention provides for taxpayers to be informed by member states proposing to make transfer pricing adjustments. In terms similar to Article 25(1) and (2) of the OECD Model, the Convention then provides a mutual agreement procedure.[25] Under Article 7 of the Convention, an advisory commission is to be set up if the competent

20 European Union (2005).

21 Arbitration Convention Arts. 1 and 4.

22 There is no possibility of formulary apportionment as in OECD Model Art. 7(4), as to which, see above at 3.3.1.3.

23 Arbitration Convention Art. 3(2).

24 Arbitration Convention Art. 1(2).

25 Arbitration Convention Arts. 5 and 6.

authorities fail to reach an agreement within two years of the date on which the case was first submitted. The enterprises in question expressly retain their domestic law remedies, i.e. the potential for court proceedings, despite the referral to a commission.

As with arbitration under Article 25(5) of the OECD Model, the membership of an advisory commission is not independent. It consists of a Chairman and two representatives of each competent authority together with an even number of independent persons appointed by mutual agreement from a list of independent persons nominated by member states. Importantly, the associated enterprises concerned may provide information and submissions to the commission. The commission must deliver its opinion no more than six months from the date on which the matter is referred to it. The decision is by a simple majority. The competent authorities must then decide to eliminate the double taxation within six months of the opinion. The decision may vary from the commission's opinion but if the competent authorities do not agree, they are obliged to follow the opinion.[26] It will be seen that the nature of the Arbitration Convention is to encourage states to resolve issues by mutual agreement.

7.3 Assistance in collection of tax

The final matter for brief consideration is mutual assistance by tax administrations in collecting each other's taxes. It is one thing for a tax administration to raise a tax assessment with respect to persons and events outside its territorial jurisdiction, it is quite another to enforce such an assessment through the collection of tax. The relevance of enforcement difficulties in determining economic allegiance and connecting factors was noted above at 2.1. Physical enforcement would breach the territorial sovereignty of the other country, making the only realistic possibilities enforcement by order of a court in the other country or with the assistance of the tax administration of the other country. Often tax authorities are empowered with collection mechanisms akin to those used by bailiffs in the execution of court orders.

The general law position in the UK and many other common law countries is that the courts will not enforce, either directly or indirectly, foreign tax laws.[27] Some countries, historically including the UK, take the

[26] Arbitration Convention Arts. 9–13.

[27] *Government of India* v *Taylor* [1955] AC 491 (HL). Generally, regarding enforcement of foreign tax laws in the UK, see Tiley (2008, pp. 1119–25). See also the footnote to OECD Model Art 27 and OECD Model Commentary on Art. 27 para. 1.

additional position that non-enforcement by the courts similarly means non-enforcement by the tax administration, although it is not clear why this must necessarily be so. This strict position began to change with the push against harmful tax competition in the late 1990s, see above at 2.2.1. As noted at that point, this push involved parallel projects of the OECD (Harmful Tax Competition Report) and the EU (Code of Conduct). In due course, each of these organisations piloted projects for mutual assistance in the collection of taxes. Each will be considered in turn.

7.3.1 OECD Model

In 2003, the OECD inserted a new Article 27 into the Model dedicated to assistance in the collection of taxes. This Article sits peculiarly with others in the Model as it is prefaced with a statement that it should be included in a tax treaty only where providing assistance is possible under domestic law. The consequence is that there is no need for formal reservations to the Article (and there are none). The Article begins by providing that contracting states must lend assistance in the collection of 'revenue claims'. This phrase is defined in paragraph (2); the point is that, like Articles 24 and 26, the provision is not limited to taxes covered by a particular treaty. The competent authorities are to settle by mutual agreement the mode of application of the Article.

Article 27(3) of the OECD Model provides for a competent authority to request of the other competent authority assistance in the collection of a revenue claim. A request may be made only if the taxpayer cannot 'prevent' the collection of the claim under the laws of the requesting country. The other competent authority is then to collect the claim 'in accordance with the provisions of its laws applicable to enforcement and collection of its own taxes'. Paragraph (4) makes similar provision for assistance in pre-emptive measures in the collection of revenue claims, referred to as 'measures of conservancy'. Under paragraph (8), a contracting state is not required to assist unless the requesting state has 'pursued all reasonable measures of collection... under its laws or administrative practice' or where the 'administrative burden... is clearly disproportionate' to the taxes to be collected.

As in the case of the mutual agreement procedure, in 2007 the OECD published a Manual on Implementation of Assistance in Tax Collection. Its purpose is to provide basic information on the operation of Article 27 of the OECD Model and to identify best practices in this regard.[28]

[28] The Manual can be accessed on the OECD website at www.oecd.org, accessed 15 March 2010.

As mentioned, the traditional approach of the UK is that it would not provide assistance in the collection of foreign taxes. This changed (beginning with the EU Directive discussed at 7.3.3) and the Finance Act 2006 made specific provision for international tax enforcement arrangements.[29] In particular, this provision covers arrangements for the exchange of information, recovery of foreign tax and service of documents relating to foreign tax.

7.3.2 Assistance in collection agreements

The OECD/Council of Europe-sponsored 1988 Convention on Mutual Administrative Assistance in Tax Matters was discussed above at 7.1.2 in the context of its exchange of information provisions. Not surprisingly, the provisions of the Convention that pertain to assistance in recovery of taxes (Articles 11 to 16) were influential in the drafting of Article 27 of the OECD Model. For present purposes, they are similar to (though not the same as) the Model provision.

7.3.3 EU Law

Within the EU, mutual assistance in the collection of taxes is governed by the Directive on Mutual Assistance for the Recovery of Claims.[30] This Directive began as a limited mechanism for recovery of certain levies and customs duties. It was extended in 1979 to include the recovery of value added tax.[31] For present purposes, the important amendment came in 2001 when the Directive was extended to include assistance in recovery of taxes on income and capital.[32] The UK implemented this Directive, as amended, by enactment in 2002.[33] The Directive provides more detailed rules than Article 27 of the OECD Model or the 1988 Convention on Mutual Administrative Assistance in Tax Matters, but the ground covered is of a similar nature. In February 2009, the European Commission released a draft directive to improve and replace the 1976 Directive.[34] In particular, this draft would cover all taxes of member states and provide greater scope for cooperation. It was approved by the Council of Ministers in early 2010.

[29] Finance Act 2006 Part 9 (ss. 173–6).
[30] 76/308/EEC.
[31] 79/1071/EEC.
[32] 2001/44/EEC.
[33] Finance Act 2002 s. 134 and Sch. 39.
[34] European Commission (2009a).

Conclusion

This book has set about identifying, explaining, categorising and analysing, at a basic level, the rules that govern income taxation of international commercial transactions. The lasting impression is one of various sets of overlaying, largely uncoordinated and complex measures that deal with some matters (not necessarily the most important) better than others. The messy structure, if it can be called that, appears to be crumbling under the pressures of globalisation. Of course, none of the independent measures that form the basis of the international tax 'system' was designed to deal with a world as highly integrated as the one in which they are currently being used.

While interested parties, such as the OECD, have valiantly strived to adapt the existing system to a modern environment, they are trying to use a system designed for gas valve technology to regulate twenty-first century computer generated transactions. As noted at the start of Chapter 5, it seems inevitable that the old system of bilateral tax treaties will be abandoned at some point this century. The question and major challenge is whether that system will be abandoned in favour of an intentionally structured system designed to best deal with modern situations or whether the new system will develop as a set of ad hoc rules with a loose attempt at coordination.

At present, we are set on the latter course. Countries are crumbling under the weight of their ever-expanding tax laws. In developed countries, many (if not most) people who deal with these laws day to day feel the situation is out of control, with very little hope for substantial structural reform. The situation is worse in an international setting, which involves the multiple interactions of these laws. This manifests itself in the layer upon layer of sets of rules governing international taxation. This basic book has faced statutes, regulations, tax administration rulings, bilateral treaties, multilateral treaties, model treaties, protocols, exchange of notes, commentaries, directives, codes of conduct, manuals and guidelines. The gaps appearing in the old system, due to changes in the way business is done, are being filled in an ad hoc fashion, patches on an outdated structure.[1]

Perhaps the major structural defect in the existing system is its inflexibility, which causes chronic problems when there is as much change as there has been in the last twenty years. The source of this inflexibility is a network of more than 3,600 bilateral tax treaties. This figure is jaw dropping. Anyone who thinks about it, even briefly, will ask: 'Why?' The consequence is that tax treaties are becoming increasingly irrelevant per se. The network is too inflexible to deal with new issues as they arise and so these are being dealt with through other mechanisms. Further, countries are slowly adapting their domestic laws to standards based on the OECD Model. For example, many countries, including the UK, have introduced the OECD PE concept and transfer pricing rules into domestic law. Similarly, withholding taxes are increasingly being limited under domestic law to OECD type rates. Unilateral foreign tax relief is now the norm.

Some of the problems with the OECD Model based tax treaty network are not as evident in the context of EU Law, but it has its own difficulties. The multilateral basis of the treaty with a central court is a great help in terms of uniformity and consistency. Unfortunately, the cases that come before the ECJ are ad hoc and the taxpayer does not currently receive a multilateral solution to cross-border restrictions, as the *Kerckhaert and Morres* case graphically illustrates.[2] The EU has power to address new issues in a dynamic way, but this power is effectively stymied by the unanimity requirement for directives, leaving undue power in the hands of the ECJ, a non-representative and non-accountable entity. It has become clear, at least since 2005 in tax matters (the *D* case),[3] that the ECJ *is* a political entity. Perhaps that is to be expected of what is essentially a constitutional court.

What is the way forward? A basic book of this nature cannot seriously seek to address such a question, but perhaps a few comments are in order. The first is essentially a plea for a greater role for lawyers and accountants in tax policy. Perhaps the role of economists in the development of tax policy has become disproportionate to their utility. Everything might

[1] The best example of this is the tendency of the OECD to try to fill gaps through the Commentary rather than amendment of the Model. Major examples of this are the approach to PEs, intellectual property, thin capitalisation, CFCs, losses, dual residence, third country situations and treaty abuse (including beneficial ownership) rules.

[2] Case C-513/04 *Kerckhaert and Morres* v *Belgium State* [2006] ECR I-10967 (ECJ).

[3] Case C-376/03 *D* v *Inspecteur van de Belastingdient* [2005] ECR I-5821 (ECJ).

be economics, but economics is not everything. The people who *use* and *abuse* tax systems in the face of globalisation are lawyers and accountants, not economists, so why should we expect economists to have answers as to what international tax reform requires? Fundamentally, such reform involves taking a fine balance between respecting the autonomy of countries and the need for international coordination. That, of course, is a difficult balance to make, but complicated economics and political point scoring do not necessarily help.

If the fate of the OECD Model is to become a set of standards, then perhaps that is what it should be. One possibility is a movement towards a set of non-binding internationally agreed standards for the tax treatment of international transactions. An independent international body could periodically assess countries' tax systems by reference to these standards and a report made public. This information might be particularly useful to multinationals considering investing (or disinvesting) in a country. Is this really a radical idea? Effectively, the OECD already operates such a system for the purposes of information exchange and a similar system operates for purposes of budget transparency.[4] Perhaps such a system could be coordinated with an international tribunal, set up to hear disputes regarding compliance with the standards. This is just one thought; no doubt there are many other possibilities.

Whatever the fate of the international tax order, the primary goal of this book has been more modest. Its aim has been to demonstrate that the current morass of international tax rules can be considered and analysed in a holistic and structural fashion. Typically, even the most mind-blowing technical rules can be boiled down to comparatively simple structural issues that even people who do not have a technical tax background can grapple with. Indeed, those with a more general tax expertise are better positioned to assess the way forward than the technicians who draft the current jungle of rules. Those rules are commonly targeted at specific situations, with little consideration of the bigger structural picture and related issues. If fundamental international tax reform is ever to occur, there must first be a consensus on a sound structure for that reform, a blueprint for better basics.

[4] The International Monetary Fund monitors the budget transparency system based on periodic 'Reports on the Observance of Standards and Codes'. See www.imf.org/external/np/fad/trans/index.htm, accessed 15 March 2010.

REFERENCES

Almand, K . and D. Sayers (2009), 'Hot Topics in Thin Capitalisation', *Tax Journal*, **968**, pp. 5–6

Arginelli, P . and C. Innamorato (2008), 'Italy: The Interaction between Tax Treaties and Domestic Law: An Issue of Constitutional Legitimacy', *European Taxation*, June, pp. 299–304

Arnold, B . (2004), 'Tax Treaties and Tax Avoidance: The 2003 Revisions to the Commentary to the OECD Model', *International Tax Bulletin*, **58**, 6, pp. 244–60

(2006), 'At Sixes and Sevens: The Relationship between the Taxation of Business Profits and Income from Immovable Property under Tax Treaties', *International Tax Bulletin*, **60**, 1, pp. 5–18

(2008), 'New Services PE Rule in the Canada–U.S. Treaty Protocol', *Worldwide Tax Daily*, 15 July, 2008 WTD 136–8

Arnold, B. and M. McIntyre (2002), *International Tax Primer*, 2nd edn (The Hague: Kluwer Law International)

Ault, H. and B. Arnold (eds.) (2010), *Comparative Income Taxation: A Structural Analysis*, 3rd edn (The Netherlands: Kluwer Law International)

Ault, H. and J. Sasseville (2009), '2008 OECD Model: The New Arbitration Provision', *Bulletin for International Taxation*, **63**, 5/6, pp. 208–15

Avery Jones, J . (1991), 'Bodies of Persons', *British Tax Review*, pp. 453–65

(1999), 'The Relationship between the Mutual Agreement Procedure and Internal Law', *EC Tax Review*, **8**, 1, pp. 4–7

(2005), 'Place of Effective Management as a Residence Tie-Breaker', *Bulletin for International Fiscal Documentation*, **59**, 1, pp. 20–4

(2009), '2008: OECD Model: Place of Effective Management – What One Can Learn from the History', *Bulletin for International Taxation*, **63**, 5/6, pp. 183–6

Avery Jones, J., P. Baker, L. De Broe et al. (2009), 'The Definitions of Dividends and Interest in the OECD Model: Something Lost in Translation?', *British Tax Review*, pp. 406–52

Avery Jones, J., H . Depret, M . van de Wiele et al. (1991), 'The Non-Discrimination Article in Tax Treaties', *British Tax Review*, Part I pp. 359–85, Part II pp. 421–52

Avery Jones, J., L . De Broe, M. Ellis et al. (2006), 'The Origins of Concepts and Expressions Used in the OECD Model and Their Adoption by States', *British Tax Review*, pp. 695–765

Avery Jones, J., P. Harris and D. Oliver (eds.) (2008), *Comparative Perspectives on Revenue Law: Essays in Honour of John Tiley* (Cambridge, UK: Cambridge University Press)

Avi-Yonah, R . (2007), 'What Can the U.S. Supreme Court and the European Court of Justice Learn from Each Other's Tax Jurisprudence?', 3 December, available at SSRN http://ssrn.com/abstract=1048821 accessed 17 March 2010

(2009), 'Xilinx and the Arm's-Length Standard', *Worldwide Tax Daily*, 9 June, 2009 WTD 108-1

Avi-Yonah, R. and K. Clausing (2007), 'A Proposal to Adopt Formulary Apportionment for Corporate Income Taxation: The Hamilton Project', University of Michigan Law & Economics, Olin Working Paper No. 07–009, available at SSRN http://ssrn.com/abstract=995202 accessed 17 March 2010

Baker, P. (2000), 'Taxation and the European Convention on Human Rights', *British Tax Review*, pp. 211–377

(2001–), *Double Taxation Conventions: A Manual on the OECD Model Tax Convention on Income and on Capital* (London: Sweet & Maxwell)

(2008), 'Taxation, Human Rights and the Family', in Avery Jones, Harris and Oliver (eds.), pp. 232–43

Barnard, C. (2007), *The Substantive Law of the EU: The Four Freedoms,* 2nd edn (Oxford: Oxford University Press)

Brooks, K. (2008), Inter-Nation Equity: The Development of an Important but Underappreciated International Tax Value', in R. Krever and J. Head, *Tax Reform in the 21st Century* (London: Kluwer Law International), available at SSRN http://ssrn.com/abstract=1292370 accessed 17 March 2010

Burns, L. and R. Krever (1998), 'Individual Income Tax', in V. Thuronyi (ed.), *Tax Law Design and Drafting*, Vol. 2 (Washington DC: IMF), Chapter 14, pp. 495–563

Cooklin, J. (2008), 'Corporate Exodus: When Irish Eyes are Smiling', *British Tax Review*, pp. 613–23

Daunton, M. (2008), 'Land Taxation, Economy and Society in Britain and its Colonies', in Avery Jones, Harris and Oliver (eds.), pp. 197–218

Desai, M . and J. Hines (2003), 'Economic Foundations of International Tax Rules', a paper prepared for the American Tax Policy Institute, Washington DC, December, available at www.americantaxpolicyinstitute.org/pdf/economic_foundation_internal.pdf accessed 17 March 2010

(2004), 'Old Rules and New Realities: Corporate Tax Policy in a Global Setting', Ross School of Business Paper No. 920, October, available at SSRN http://ssrn.com/abstract=606222 accessed 17 March 2010

Drevet, S.A . and V. Thuronyi (2009), 'The Tax Treaty Network of the U.N. Member States', *Worldwide Tax Daily*, 3 June, 2009 WTD 104-12

European Commission (2001), 'Company Taxation in the Internal Market', COM(2001)582 final

(2004), 'European Tax Survey', Commission Staff Working Paper, SEC(2004)1128

(2006), 'Communication on the Tax Treatment of Losses in Cross-Border Situations', COM(2006)824 final

(2007a), 'Communication on the work of the EU Joint Transfer Pricing Forum in the Field of Dispute Avoidance and Resolution Procedures and on Guidelines for Advance Pricing Agreements within the EU', COM(2007)71

(2007b), 'Communication on the Application of Anti-Abuse Measures in the Area of Direct Taxation – within the EU and in Relation to Third Countries', COM(2007)785

(2008), 'Corporate Taxation: Commission Requests the United Kingdom to Properly Implement an ECJ Ruling on Cross-Border Loss Compensation', Press Release IP/08/1365

(2009a), 'Proposal for a Council Directive Concerning Mutual Assistance for the Recovery of Claims Relating to Taxes, Duties and Other Measures', COM(2009)28

(2009b), 'Proposal for a Council Directive on Administrative Cooperation in the Field of Taxation', COM(2009)29

European Parliament (2008a), 'Report on the Impact of the Rulings of the European Court of Justice in the Area of Direct Taxation', Press Release IP/A/ECON/ST/2007–27

(2008b), 'EU Action Needed on Tax Treatment of Cross-border Corporate Losses', Press Release 20080111IPR18259

(2009), 'Resolution of 10 March 2009 with Recommendations to the Commission on the Cross-border Transfer of the Registered Office of a Company', 2008/2196(INI)

European Union (1997), 'Resolution of the Council and the Representatives of the Governments of the Member States, Meeting within the Council of 1 December 1997 on a Code of Conduct for Business Taxation', in van Raad (ed.) (2009), pp. 2346–53

(1999), 'Report on the Code of Conduct (Business Taxation)/Primarolo Group', in van Raad (ed.) (2009), pp. 2354–62

(2005), 'Code of Conduct for the Effective Implementation of the Arbitration Convention', 2695/2/04 REV 2, in van Raad (ed.) (2009), pp. 2280–85

(2008), 'Council Resolution on Coordinating Exit Taxation', 2911th Economic and Financial Affairs, Brussels, 2 December

Finance Ministers (2009), 'Finance Ministers Issue Statement on International Tax Fraud and Evasion', *Worldwide Tax Daily*, 23 June, 2009 WTD 119–21

Fraser, R . (2001), 'Respectez les animaux étrangers! The Inland Revenue List on Entity Classification', *British Tax Review*, pp. 158–61 and J.D. Oliver (2007), 'Beneficial Ownership: HMRC's Draft Guidance on Interpretation of the *Indofood* Decision', *British Tax Review*, pp. 39–57

Fuller, J. (2008), 'U.S. Tax Review', *Worldwide Tax Daily*, 30 July, 2008 WTD 147–10

Gnaedinger, C. (2003), 'EU Critiques Accession States' Company Tax Rules', *Worldwide Tax Daily*, 23 July, 2003 WTD 141-1

(2006), 'European Commission Disagrees with ECJ on Double Taxation', *Worldwide Tax Daily*, 16 November, 2006 WTD 221-3

Gordon, K. (2004), 'Interpreting Statutes', *Taxation*, **152**, 3946, 26 February, pp. 506–8

Gutmann, D., S. Austry and P. Le Roux (2009), 'Tax Treatment of Foreign Pension Funds', *European Taxation*, **49**, 1, pp. 21–8

Harris, P. (1996), *Corporate/Shareholder Income Taxation and Allocating Taxing Rights Between Countries: A Comparison of Imputation Systems* (Amsterdam: IBFD)

(1999), 'An Historic View of the Principle and Options for Double Tax Relief', *British Tax Review*, pp. 469–89

(2000), 'Origins of the 1963 OECD Model Series: Working Party 12 and Article 10', *Australian Tax Forum*, **15**, pp. 3–223

(2006), *Income Tax in Common Law Jurisdictions: From the Origins to 1820* (Cambridge, UK: Cambridge University Press)

(forthcoming), *Income Tax in Common Law Jurisdictions:* 1820 *to Present*

Harris, P. and J.D. Oliver (2008), 'Family Connections and the Corporate Entity: Income Splitting through the Family Company', in Avery Jones, Harris and Oliver (eds.), pp. 244–87

HMRC (2007), 'Changes to Controlled Foreign Companies Rules', Draft Guidance, 17 December

HMRC and HM Treasury (2010), 'Proposals for Controlled Foreign Companies (CFC) Reform: Discussion Document', January 2010

International Monetary Fund (2009), 'IMF Report Analyzes Effects of Debt Bias in Tax Policy', *Worldwide Tax Daily*, 12 June, 2009 WTD 114-16

Jackson, R. (2008a), 'More Tax Cheats in Doghouse Over Liechtenstein Tax Evasion', *Worldwide Tax Daily*, 31 March, 2008 WTD 62-2

(2008b), 'Germany Eases Rule for Deducting Cross-Border Losses', *Worldwide Tax Daily*, 6 August, 2008 WTD 152-01

(2008c), 'Henderson Global Investors to Leave U.K. for Ireland', *Worldwide Tax Daily*, 29 August, 2008 WTD 169-4

Kandev, M.N. and B. Wiener (2009), 'Some Thoughts on the Use of Later OECD Commentaries after Prévost Car', *Worldwide Tax Daily*, 1 June, 2009 WTD 102-15

Karyadi, F. (2007), 'Indonesian Supreme Court Nullifies Treaty Shopping Practice', *Worldwide Tax Daily*, 26 February, 2007 WTD 38-4

Kent, R. (1999), 'Entity Classification – *Oxnard Financing SA v Rahn and Others*', *British Tax Review*, pp. 125–8

Kingston, S. (2007), 'A Light in the Darkness: Recent Developments in the ECJ's Direct Tax Jurisprudence', *Common Market Law Review*, **44**, 5, pp. 1321–59

Klauson, I. (2008), 'ECJ Sides with Estonia in Burda Case', *Worldwide Tax Daily*, 9 July, 2008 WTD 132-6

Lang, M. (2004), *Double Non-taxation, International Fiscal Association, Cahiers de droit*, Vol. 89a (Amersfoort: Sdu Fiscale & Financiële Uitgevers)

Lang, M., J. Herdin and I. Hofbauer (eds.) (2005), *WTO and Direct Taxation, Eucotax Series on European Taxation*, vol. 10 (The Hague: Kluwer Law International)

McDaniel, P.R. (2004), 'The David R. Tillinghast Lecture: Trade Agreements and Income Taxation: Interactions, Conflicts, and Resolutions', *Tax Law Review*, **57**, 2, pp. 275–300

Mason, R . (2008), 'Made in America for European Tax: The Internal Consistency Test', *Boston College Law Review*, **49**, 5, pp. 1277–326

Malgari, D. (2008), 'Denmark Terminates Tax Treaties with France, Spain', *Worldwide Tax Daily*, 13 June, 2008 WTD 115-3

Monti, M. (2003), 'EU Commissioner Monti Discusses State Tax Aid', *Worldwide Tax Daily*, 26 May, 2003 WTD 103-12

O' Brien, M. (2008), 'Taxation and the Third Country Dimension of Free Movement of Capital in EU Law: The ECJ's Rulings and Unresolved Issues', *British Tax Review*, pp. 628–66

OECD (1992–), *Model Tax Convention on Income and on Capital, Committee on Fiscal Affairs* (Paris: OECD)

(1995–2000), *Transfer Pricing Guidelines for Multinational Enterprises and Tax Administrations* (Paris: OECD)

(1998), *Harmful Tax Competition: An Emerging Global Issue* (Paris: OECD)

(2003), 'Are the Current Treaty Rules for Taxing Business Profits Appropriate for e-Commerce?', discussion draft of 26 November 2003, in van Raad (ed.) (2005), pp. 798–857

(2007), 'Application and Interpretation of Article 24 (Non-discrimination)', discussion draft of 3 May 2007, in van Raad (ed.) (2009), pp. 850–73

(2008a), *Report on the Attribution of Profits to Permanent Establishments* (Paris: OECD)

(2008b), 'Draft Alternative Article 7 of the OECD Model Tax Convention and Related Commentary', discussion draft of 7 July 2008, in van Raad (ed.) (2009), pp. 753–79

(2008c), '*Transfer Pricing Aspects of Business Restructurings*', discussion draft of 19 September 2008 (Paris: OECD)

(2008d), *OECD in Figures: 2008* (Paris: OECD)

(2009), 'OECD Issues Brief on International Tax Evasion', *Worldwide Tax Daily, 21 April*, 2009 WTD 82-21

Oliver, J.D . (1998), 'Ship-Money', *British Tax Review*, pp. 1–3

(2000), 'Entitlement of a Permanent Establishment to Third State Treaty Benefits: *Saint-Gobain*', *British Tax Review*, pp. 174–81

(2001), 'Effective Management', *British Tax Review*, pp. 289–95

O' Shea, T. (2007), 'ECJ and Taxation of Residents and Nonresidents – Deduction of Expenses', *Worldwide Tax Daily*, 10 May, 2007 WTD 91-9

Owen, P. (2003), 'Can Effective Management be Distinguished from Central Management and Control?', *British Tax Review*, pp. 296–305

Parillo, K. (2009), 'CCCTB Proposal Postponed Until at Least End of 2009', *Worldwide Tax Daily*, 2 February, 2009 WTD 19-1

van Raad, K. (ed.) (2005), *2005/06 Materials on International and EC Tax Law* (Leiden: International Tax Center)

(ed.), (2009), *2009/10 Materials on International and EC Tax Law* (Leiden: International Tax Center)

Reeb-Blanluet, S. (2007), 'France Releases Guidance on New CFC Tax Regime', Worldwide Tax Daily, 2 February, 2007 WTD 23-1

Sasseville, J. (2008), 'Treaty Recognition of Groups of Companies', in G. Maisto (ed.), *International and EC Tax Aspects of Groups of Companies,* EC and International Tax Law Series, Vol. 4 (Amsterdam: International Bureau of Fiscal Documentation), pp. 129–36

Schön, W. (2004), 'World Trade Organization Law and Tax Law', *Bulletin for International Fiscal Documentation*, **58**, 7, pp. 283–96

(2008), 'Abuse of Rights and European Tax Law', in Avery Jones, Harris and Oliver (eds.), pp. 75–98

Scott, C. (2004), 'OECD Targets Additional Financial Centers in Expanded Tax Haven Crackdown', *Worldwide Tax Daily*, 7 June, 2004 WTD 109-1

Sheppard, L. (2005), 'U.K. Goes After Deferred Subscription Arrangements', *Worldwide Tax Daily*, 4 April, 2005 WTD 63-4

(2006), 'European Union: Year in Review', *Worldwide Tax Daily*, 10 January, 2006 WTD 6-6

Six, M. (2009), 'Hybrid Finance and Double Taxation Treaties', *Bulletin for International Taxation*, **63**, 1, pp. 22–5

Smith, A.S. (1776), *An Inquiry into the Nature and Causes of the Wealth of Nations*, Vol. 36 of Adler, M.J. (ed.) (1990), *Great Books of the Western World*, 2nd edn. (Chicago: Encyclopedia Britannica Inc.)

Terra, B. and P. Wattel (2008), *European Tax Law,* 5th edn (London: Kluwer Law International)

van Thiel, S. (2008), 'European Union: Justifications in Community Law for Income Tax Restrictions on Free Movement: Acte Clair Rules That Can Be Readily Applied by National Courts', *European Taxation*, **48**, 6 and 7, pp. 279–90 and 339–50

Tiley, J. (2008), *Revenue Law,* 6th edn (London: Hart Publishing)

(2010), 'United Kingdom', in Ault and Arnold (eds.), pp. 145–72

United Nations (2001), *United Nations Model Double Taxation Convention between the Developed and Developing Countries* (New York: United Nations)

United States (2006), *United States Model Income Tax Convention* (15 November 2006)

United States Internal Revenue Service (2009), 'U.S. Regs' Treatment of Interest Does Not Violate Treaty', *Worldwide Tax Daily*, 24 April, 2009 WTD 33-28

Vann, R. (2003), 'Reflections on Business Profits and the Arm's-Length Principle', in B. Arnold, J. Sasseville and E. Zolt (eds.), *The Taxation of Business Profits under Tax Treaties* (Toronto: Canadian Tax Foundation), pp. 133–69

(2006), 'Tax Treaties: The Secret Agent's Secrets', *British Tax Review*, pp. 345–82

(2008), 'The History of Royalties in Tax Treaties 1921–61: Why?', in Avery Jones, Harris and Oliver (eds.), pp. 166–96

Vogel, K. (1997), *Klaus Vogel on Double Taxation Conventions*, 3rd edn (Boston: Kluwer Law International)

Weiner, J. (2008), 'OECD Updates Model Tax Convention', *Worldwide Tax Daily*, 1 July, 2008 WTD 127-1

INDEX